The
Jean Bowring
Cookbook

By the same author
CAKE ICING AND DECORATING
JEAN BOWRING'S NEW CAKE DECORATING BOOK

The Jean Bowring Cookbook

ANGUS AND ROBERTSON

First published in 1970 by
ANGUS AND ROBERTSON (PUBLISHERS) PTY LIMITED

102 Glover Street, Cremorne, Sydney
2 Fisher Street, London
107 Elizabeth Street, Melbourne
167 Queen Street, Brisbane
89 Anson Road, Singapore

Reprinted 1971, 1972

© Jean Bowring 1970

National Library of Australia
card number and ISBN 0 207 12062 5

PRINTED IN HONG KONG

ACKNOWLEDGMENT

I wish to thank the Herald and Weekly Times Ltd
for permission to use the black and white photographs
and the colour illustrations from *Australian Home Beautiful.*

CONTENTS

INTRODUCTION

BEFORE YOU START . . .

COOKING can be fun for the cook when everything goes right, but just sheer hard work when something goes wrong.

Modern appliances and labour-saving ideas have taken the drudgery out of cooking, but they have their limits, and in the end it is the human touch that will enable you to cook intelligently and always be sure of good results.

To be successful you must first understand what you are doing, so before you take even a bowl out of the cupboard, read through the recipe—not only the ingredients but the method as well. You'd be wise to put your ingredients out on the kitchen table or work-bench in the order of mixing: this is a good way of making sure you have them all. Weigh or measure exactly—never try to guess quantities—and do follow the method faithfully. Finally, don't forget to check that you have the right size and type of cooking utensil for the dish you are going to make.

OVEN TEMPERATURES

The oven temperature is a most important part of baking. It is no use spending time, energy and good ingredients in making up a recipe only to ruin the dish by undercooking or overcooking.

Don't make a guess at the temperature: follow the one given in the recipe, and if you have an instruction book supplied by the manufacturer of your cooker, study it carefully. Preheating temperatures can vary according to the type of cooker you are using, but actual baking temperatures are the same regardless of the type of fuel used.

Baking temperatures for the recipes in this book are based on the following scale:

250° to 325°F. Slow oven.
325° to 400°F. Moderate oven.
400° to 450°F. Hot oven.
450° to 500°F. Very hot oven.

MEASURING

The spoon measurements given in the recipes refer to the standard teaspoon, dessertspoon and tablespoon and are level unless otherwise stated. To measure a dry ingredient take a spoonful of it and level off the top with the blade of a knife. Lumps in ingredients such as bicarbonate of soda, salt or cream of tartar should be either sieved or crushed before measuring.

Cup measurements for both liquid and dry ingredients are based on the standard 8-ounce measuring cup. When measuring, place the cup on a flat surface and measure at eye-level.

When spooning or pouring a dry ingredient into the measuring cup, do not pack it down or tap the cup on the table, otherwise you will have more of the ingredient than you should have. (This does not apply to brown sugar, which should be firmly packed into the measuring cup.)

Should the recipe call for sifted flour or icing sugar, sift before measuring.

Treacle, golden syrup or honey should be warmed before being measured. Never dip the measuring spoon or cup into it: instead, pour the treacle, honey or golden syrup from the tin or jar into the measure first, then into the main mixture (use a rubber scraper to make sure all of it is included).

SPOON AND CUP MEASUREMENTS

1 level tablespoon of	butter golden syrup honey lard margarine fat	equals 1 ounce
1½ level tablespoons of	barley gelatine rice sugar	equals 1 ounce
2 level tablespoons of	cocoa cornflour currants custard powder flour icing sugar sago sultanas	equals 1 ounce
1 measuring cup of	breadcrumbs (soft white) coconut suet (finely grated)	equals 2–3 ounces equals 3 ounces equals 3½ ounces
1 measuring cup of	flour icing sugar ground nuts currants cocoa	equals 4 ounces
1 measuring cup of	peel (chopped) rice (ground) sugar (brown, loosely packed) sultanas	equals 5 ounces
1 measuring cup of	dates (chopped) sago sugar (brown, firmly packed) tapioca	equals 6 ounces
1 measuring cup of	rice	equals 7 ounces
1 measuring cup of	butter lard margarine	equals 8 ounces
1 measuring cup of	honey or golden syrup	equals 12 ounces
2 measuring cups of	liquid	equals 16 ounces
2½ measuring cups of	liquid	equals 1 pint

METRIC CONVERSIONS

SOLIDS   1 kilogramme (kg.) = 1,000 grammes (gm.) = 2 lb. 3¼ oz. (approx.)

Grammes into ounces (approx.)

gm.	oz.	gm.	oz.
50	1¾	300	10½
100	3½	350	12½
150	5¼	400	14
200	7	450	16
250	9	500	17½

Ounces into grammes (approx.)

oz.	gm.	oz.	gm.
1	28	9	255
2	57	10	283
3	85	11	312
4 (¼ lb.)	113	12 (¾ lb.)	340
5	141	13	368
6	170	14	397
7	198	15	426
8 (½ lb.)	227	16 (1 lb.)	454

LIQUIDS   1 litre = 1,000 millilitres (ml.) = 1¾ pints (approx.)

Millilitres into fluid ounces (approx.)

ml.	fl. oz.	ml.	fl. oz.
25	1	300	10½
50	1¾	350	12¼
100	3½	400	14
150	5¼	450	15¾
200	7	500 (½ litre)	17½
250 (¼ litre)	8¾		

Fluid ounces into millilitres (approx.)

fl. oz.	ml.	fl. oz.	ml.
1	28	11	312
2	57	12	341
3	85	13	369
4	114	14	398
5 (¼ pint)	142	15 (¾ pint)	426
6	170	16	454
7	199	17	483
8	228	18	511
9	256	19	540
10 (½ pint)	284	20 (1 pint)	568

LINEAR MEASUREMENTS   1 metre = 100 centimetres (cm.) = $39\frac{1}{2}$ inches (approx.)
(for pots, pans, cake tins, etc.)

Centimetres into inches (approx.)

cm.	in.	cm.	in.
10	4	22	$8\frac{3}{4}$
12	$4\frac{3}{4}$	24	$9\frac{1}{2}$
14	$5\frac{1}{2}$	26	$10\frac{1}{4}$
16	$6\frac{1}{4}$	28	11
18	7	30	$11\frac{3}{4}$
20	$7\frac{3}{4}$	32	$12\frac{1}{2}$

Inches into centimetres (approx.)

in.	cm.	in.	cm.
5	13	9	23
6	15	10	25
7	18	11	28
8	20	12	30

TEMPERATURES   100 degrees Centigrade (boiling point) = 212 degrees Fahrenheit

Centigrade (C.) into Fahrenheit (F.)

deg. C.	deg. F.	deg. C.	deg. F.
120	248	200	392
130	266	210	410
140	284	220	428
150	302	230	446
160	320	240	464
170	338	250	482
180	356	260	500
190	374		

Fahrenheit into Centigrade

deg. F.	deg. C.	deg. F.	deg. C.
250	121	400	205
275	135	425	219
300	149	450	233
325	163	475	246
350	177	500	260
375	191		

COOKING TERMS AND PROCESSES

A la King: Food served in a rich cream sauce sometimes flavoured with sherry.

A la carte: According to the menu.

Appetizers: Small tasty portions of food served before dinner or as the first course of a meal; or finger savouries for party menus.

Au lait: Served with milk.

Au gratin: Mixed or masked with a white sauce then covered with grated cheese and breadcrumbs and baked or grilled until the cheese melts and the topping browns.

Aspic: A savoury jelly. Originally made from meat stock but now often made from fish or vegetable stock or tomato juice and thickened with gelatine.

Bake: To cook by dry heat.

Barbecue: To roast foods over coals or on a spit. While cooking, the food is basted frequently with a highly seasoned sauce.

Baste: To moisten meat or other foods while baking with dripping or juices from the pan or an additional liquid.

Batter: A blended mixture of flour and a liquid.

Blanch: To remove strong odours; to whiten; to remove the skin from nuts.

Blend: To mix two or more ingredients, usually one a liquid, to a smooth paste.

Boiling point: When the surface of the water is bubbling briskly. The temperature of the water will be 212°F.

Bouquet-garni: A bunch of sweet herbs.

Braise: To cook meat by browning, then simmering in a small amount of liquid in a covered dish in the oven or over direct heat.

Broil: To grill.

Canapé: A small shape of fried or toasted bread or pastry spread with well-seasoned food.

Caramel: A preparation of sugar and water cooked to near burning point and used as a colouring. Also a confection.

Caramelize: To heat sugar in a small saucepan or pan until it melts and browns; or to heat foods containing sugar until a light brown colour and of a caramel flavour.

Chantilly: A dish containing whipped cream.

Charlotte: A sweet or savoury mixture in a dish lined and topped with thin slices of buttered bread; or a gelatine dessert moulded in a dish lined with sponge fingers.

Cocktail: An alcoholic or non-alcoholic drink served before a meal; fruit or fish with a tart sauce served as the first course of a meal.

Compote: Whole or large pieces of fruit gently cooked in a syrup. The whole pieces of fruit should retain their shape.

Condiments: Food seasonings such as salt, pepper, vinegar, herbs and spices. Relishes are frequently called condiments as are nuts, sultanas, coconut and other accompaniments of curry.

5

Consommé: A clear soup, usually highly seasoned.

Cream: To beat or work ingredients such as butter and sugar together until the mixture is the consistency of thick cream.

Croissants: Rich French crescent-shaped rolls.

Croquettes: A mixture of chopped or minced cooked food bound together with egg or a thick white sauce, shaped, then coated with egg and breadcrumbs before being deep fried.

Croutons: Cubes of toasted or fried bread.

Dariole: A small mould.

Demi-tasse: A small cup of after-dinner coffee.

Deep, wet or French frying: Cooking in a deep pan in sufficient oil or fat to cover the food being cooked.

Devilled: Highly seasoned.

Dice: To cut into small cubes.

Dredge: To sprinkle food with a dry ingredient, usually flour or sugar.

Dripping: Fat containing meat juices.

Dry or shallow frying: Foods fried in just enough fat or oil to cover the bottom of the frying pan.

Entrée: The course which immediately precedes the main course of a formal dinner; or the main dish of an informal meal.

Fat: Shortening such as butter, margarine, lard or suet.

Fillet: A piece of flesh with skin and bone removed.

Flake: To break into small pieces, usually done with a fork.

Fold in: To add one ingredient to another without loss of air. The lighter ingredient (such as egg white) is always heaped onto the heavier ingredient and combined with a down-up-and-over movement.

Fondue: A prepared dish of melted cheese; or a mixture heated in a chafing dish into which small portions of food are dipped before eating.

Forcemeat: Stuffing.

Frappé: Sweetened fruit juices frozen to a mushy consistency.

Fricassee: A white stew.

Fritters: Food such as fruit, meat, vegetables or fish covered or mixed with batter and fried.

Frosting: A type of icing.

Flan: An open tart.

Garnish: To decorate one food with another.

Gateau: A richly decorated cake often served as a dessert.

Glaze: A liquid brushed over food to improve the appearance or flavour.

Goulash: A thick meat stew of Hungarian origin.

Haricot: A brown stew.

Hollandaise: A sauce made with eggs and butter.

Hors-d'oeuvres: Small piquant titbits served before the soup course at a formal dinner.

Julienne: Food (usually vegetables) cut into fine strips.

Kebabs: Small pieces of food (usually meat and vegetables) threaded on a skewer and grilled.

Kirsch: A cherry-flavoured liqueur.

Kedgeree: A dish consisting of rice and fish of Indian origin.

Knead: To work a flour dough by hand using a pressing action until smooth and elastic to the touch.

Lard: The fat obtained from pig meat. Also a method of treating meat by placing strips of salt pork or bacon on top of lean meat, or by drawing narrow strips of salt pork or bacon through lean meat. The latter is done with a special larding needle.

Legumes: Vegetables such as peas, beans and lentils.

Macedoine: A combination of fruits or vegetables cut into small dice.

Marinade: A mixture of oil and an acid such as vinegar or lemon juice or French dressing in which food is soaked before cooking to develop flavour and make more tender.

Mayonnaise: A dressing for salad consisting of oil, vinegar, egg yolks and flavourings.

Mask: To cover food with a sauce.

Meringue: A mixture of stiffly beaten egg white and sugar used as a topping for pies and other desserts; also a type of biscuit.

Mince: Similar to chopping, but a finer cut.

Mocha: A coffee flavour or a mixture of coffee and chocolate.

Minestrone: A thick Italian vegetable soup.

Mousse: A frozen dessert made with whipped cream and fruit; or a gelatine-set dish of meat, fish or vegetables.

Parboil: To boil foods until partly cooked.

Pare: To cut off the skin or peel of fruits or vegetables.

Pectin: The setting agent in fruits.

Parfait: A frozen dessert consisting of egg whites and yolks cooked with a hot syrup and combined with whipped cream. Or a dessert consisting of layers of ice cream, fruit, and cream or jelly served in special tall glasses.

Pasteurize: To kill bacteria by heating.

Pâté de foie gras: Goose liver paste.

Petits-fours: Small iced cakes.

Pizza: A large flat tart of Italian origin.

Poach: To cook food slowly in water or liquid just below boiling point.

Pot roast: To roast meat in a saucepan. This is done by browning the meat in a little fat in the saucepan and then adding a little liquid. The saucepan is tightly lidded during cooking.

Purée: Food which has been cooked and then pressed through a sieve. Also a type of soup in which the vegetables and cereal (if used) are sieved.

Ragout: A thick well-seasoned stew.

Ramekins: Small individual ovenproof dishes in which food is cooked and served.

Roe: The eggs of fish.

Roux: Equal proportions of shortening and flour mixed together and used as a thickening for soups and sauces.

Sauté: To toss food gently in butter or other shortening over gentle heat.

Scald: To heat food in liquid to a temperature just below boiling point; or to immerse food in boiling liquid for a short time.

Scallop: To bake food in an ovenproof dish in layers with sauce and breadcrumbs.

Score: To make light cuts in the surface of the food.

Sear: To brown the surface of meat by intense heat. This may be done in a pan or in the oven.

Shred: To cut with a knife or a coarse grater into fine, narrow pieces.

Shortening: Any kind of fat suitable for cooking.

Sift: To remove the lumps from dry ingredients by passing through a sieve, or to mix them evenly by putting them through a strainer.

Simmer: To cook at a temperature just below boiling point.

Sliver: To cut or shred into lengths.

Steep or soak: To immerse in liquid for a period of time.

Soufflé: A light sweet or savoury mixture generally puffed up with stiffly beaten egg whites. It may be hot or cold. The latter is usually set with gelatine.

Sterilize: To kill bacteria by a high degree of heat.

Stew: To cook gently for a long period with the temperature at simmering point.

Stock: The liquid obtained by simmering meat, bones, vegetables and flavourings in water for several hours. Fish bones and heads may be used in place of meat. For a quick stock dissolve a soup cube in water.

Truss: To tie a fowl or other meat so that it will hold its shape during cooking.

Torte: Very rich layers of cake, often made with crumbs, eggs, ground nuts and topped with whipped cream, also applied to very rich dessert cakes.

Truffles: A fungus that grows underground and is used for garnishing and flavouring; also a type of confection.

Tutti-frutti: A mixture of fruits.

Velouté: A rich white sauce made with ham, chicken or veal stock and seasoned with a bouquet garni.

Vinaigrette: A sauce of oil, vinegar and seasonings.

APPETIZERS

Dips and Spreads

AVOCADO AND TUNA DIP

1 medium-sized avocado
4 ounces drained tuna
1 tablespoon chopped parsley
1 teaspoon chopped chives
a few drops of Worcester sauce
a little mustard
1 teaspoon mayonnaise
salt and pepper to taste

Halve the avocado and scoop out the flesh. Place it in a bowl with the other ingredients and beat to a smooth consistency. Use as a dip or make a little firmer and spread on cracker biscuits.

AVOCADO BUTTER

1 medium-sized avocado
6 ounces soft butter
1½ teaspoons gelatine
1 tablespoon boiling water
1 tablespoon cream
1 tablespoon lemon juice
a dash of garlic salt (optional)

Peel and mash the avocado, add the softened butter and beat until thoroughly blended.

Soften the gelatine in the boiling water and stir until it dissolves. Cool slightly and add the cream. Add this mixture to the avocado together with the lemon juice, and the garlic salt if liked. Turn into a small dish and spread, smoothing the top. Cover and chill thoroughly. (It will keep in the refrigerator for about a week, or it can be frozen and kept longer.)

BLUE-CHEESE DIP

6 ounces cream cheese
3 tablespoons milk
4 ounces crumbled blue cheese
1 tablespoon finely chopped
  spring onions
¼ cup chopped olives
salt and pepper

Beat the cream cheese until light. Gradually beat in the milk, then add the blue cheese, spring onion and olives, with salt and pepper to taste. Blend well. Chill before using.

CHICKEN AND ALMOND DIP

¼ cup very finely chopped
  cooked chicken
1 tablespoon chopped celery
1 tablespoon chopped browned
  almonds
1 tablespoon chopped parsley
a little mayonnaise

Combine the chicken, celery, almonds and parsley. Mix well, then add enough mayonnaise to make a dip or spread consistency.

9

Savoury dips with cracker biscuits, pretzels, potato chips, nuts and olives

CHICKEN LIVER AND MUSHROOM DIP

½ pound chicken livers
4 level tablespoons butter
1 small can of mushrooms
2 tablespoons very finely
  chopped onion
¼ cup finely chopped parsley
salt and pepper to taste
about ½ cup mayonnaise

Sauté the chicken livers in the butter until brown. Place on the chopping board and chop, or put through the mincer. Place in a bowl with the remaining ingredients, adding enough mayonnaise to make a dip consistency.

CHOPPED ALMOND SPREAD

3 dessertspoons finely chopped
  toasted almonds
4 ounces cream cheese
1 dessertspoon chopped chutney
a pinch of salt
cream

Blend the almonds with the cream cheese, chutney, salt and enough cream to make the mixture spread easily.

Spread generously on cracker biscuits or Melba toast.

CREAM DIP

4-ounce packet of cream cheese
1 tablespoon icing sugar
a pinch of salt
1 cup cream

Blend the cream cheese in a small bowl with the icing sugar and salt. Stir in 1 tablespoon of the cream and beat until fluffy.

Beat the remainder of the cream in another bowl until thick, then fold into the cream cheese mixture. Serve with fresh strawberries.

CREAMY CHIVE DIP

4-ounce packet cream cheese
1 tablespoon mayonnaise
1 or 2 tablespoons milk
1 teaspoon chopped parsley
½ teaspoon Worcester sauce
1 tablespoon chopped chives
1 teaspoon mixed mustard
1 or 2 hard-boiled eggs

Allow the cream cheese to soften to room temperature. Beat until soft and fluffy, then mix in the mayonnaise, 1 tablespoon milk, the parsley, Worcester sauce, chives and mustard. Add the chopped eggs and enough milk to make a dip consistency.

CRUNCHY HAM DIP

1 cup sour or fresh cream
1 cup chopped cooked ham
½ cup chopped blanched
  almonds or peanuts
1 dessertspoon Worcester sauce
1 dessertspoon prepared mustard
a pinch of cayenne pepper

If using fresh cream, whip until it begins to thicken. Combine the cream with the other ingredients and beat until well mixed. Chill for 2 to 3 hours.

DEVILLED EGG AND TUNA DIP

3 hard-boiled eggs, mashed
1 teaspoon anchovy paste
½ a small can of tuna, drained
  and flaked
1 teaspoon finely minced onion
garlic salt to taste
a dash of cayenne pepper
a dash of Tabasco
a little mayonnaise

Combine all the ingredients, using just enough mayonnaise to make a dip consistency.

EGG AND PARSLEY DIP

4 ounces cream cheese
a dash each of salt and pepper
a pinch of herbs
1 tablespoon lemon juice
1 dessertspoon finely chopped
  onion
½ teaspoon Worcester sauce
½ teaspoon mixed mustard
a little mayonnaise or cream
3 hard-boiled eggs
1 dessertspoon finely chopped
  parsley

Beat the cream cheese until smooth. Add the salt, pepper, herbs, lemon juice, onion, Worcester sauce and mustard, blending thoroughly. Add enough mayonnaise or cream to make a dip consistency. Fold in the chopped eggs and the parsley.

11

OYSTER CHEESE DIP

1 can of smoked oysters
4-ounce packet of cream cheese
1 spring onion
1 tablespoon very finely
   chopped celery
$\frac{1}{4}$ teaspoon Worcester sauce
1 teaspoon lemon juice
pepper and salt to taste
a pinch of paprika
$\frac{1}{2}$ level teaspoon mustard
a little milk

Drain the oysters and chop them finely. Combine all the ingredients except the milk in a bowl and beat until well blended. Add enough milk to make a smooth consistency (it should take only about a tablespoonful).

PINEAPPLE DIP

4 ounces cream cheese
1 tablespoon canned
   unsweetened milk or cream
salt and pepper
2 tablespoons crushed pineapple
1 or 2 tablespoons finely diced
   cooked bacon

Place the cream cheese and the milk in a bowl and cream well. Add the remaining ingredients and blend well. Chill before using.

PRAWN DIP

5 ounces shelled prawns
$\frac{1}{2}$ pound cream cheese
1 dessertspoon Worcester sauce
$\frac{1}{2}$ teaspoon onion salt
a pinch of cayenne pepper
a little milk

Cut the prawns into small pieces and combine with the cream cheese and the seasonings, adding enough milk to make a dip consistency.

SMOKED OYSTER DIP

4 ounces cream cheese
1 tablespoon mayonnaise
$\frac{1}{2}$ teaspoon Worcester sauce
$\frac{1}{2}$ teaspoon prepared mustard
a few drops of lemon juice
1 dessertspoon chopped chives
salt and pepper
a little cream or top milk
$\frac{1}{2}$ a can of smoked oysters

Soften the cream cheese to room temperature and cream it until smooth. Add the mayonnaise, Worcester sauce, mustard, lemon juice and chives, seasoning to taste with salt and pepper. Blend thoroughly, adding a little cream on top of the milk to make a good dip consistency.

   Chop the well-drained oysters and fold into the mixture. Chill well before using.

SMOKED OYSTER SPREAD

4 ounces cream cheese
1 small can of smoked oysters
2 teaspoons lemon juice
$\frac{1}{8}$ teaspoon chilli sauce

Soften the cream cheese and blend in the drained and finely chopped oysters. Season with the lemon juice and chilli sauce. Spread on small rounds of brown, rye or pumpernickel bread or on cracker biscuits.

THREE CREAM-CHEESE DIPS

1. Blend one 4-ounce packet of cream cheese with a little milk. Stir in about ⅛ teaspoon of curry powder, ¼ teaspoon of finely chopped onion, ½ a cup of chopped olives and a dash of paprika.

2. To one 4-ounce packet of cream cheese add 1 tablespoon of cream, 1 teaspoon of sherry and 2 dessertspoons of chopped spring onions.

3. Take one 4-ounce packet of cream cheese and add 2 teaspoons of anchovy paste, some grated or finely minced onion and a few drops of lemon juice.

Cold Finger Savouries

ASPARAGUS HAM ROLLS

Toss 1-inch pieces of well-drained asparagus in French dressing. Roll a strip of ham slightly narrower than the asparagus around each piece, securing with cocktail picks. Serve cold.

CAVIARE CANAPÉS

12 rounds of bread about 2
    inches in diameter
hot oil for frying
2 hard-boiled eggs
salt and pepper
paprika
1 teaspoon finely chopped
    parsley
1 teaspoon finely minced onion
2-ounce can of caviare
1 lemon
small sprigs of parsley

Fry the bread rounds in the hot oil until golden brown on both sides. Drain on paper.

Remove the yolks from the hard-boiled eggs and press through a fine sieve, then season with salt, pepper and paprika. Finely chop the whites and season in the same way, adding the chopped parsley.

Spread each round of fried bread with egg-white mixture, then make a border with sieved egg yolk. Place some of the minced onion in the centre of each round, top with a little caviare and sprinkle the whole with lemon juice.

Decorate each canapé with a sprig of parsley. Serve cold.

CELERY STUFFED WITH SARDINES

1 can of sardines
1 cup mashed potato
1 teaspoon lemon juice
½ teaspoon Worcester sauce
1 teaspoon prepared mustard
1 teaspoon mayonnaise
½ teaspoon garlic salt
a pinch of sugar
celery stalks cut into 3½-inch
    pieces
chopped chives or parsley for
    garnishing

Drain the oil from the sardines and mash them with a fork. Add the mashed potato, lemon juice, Worcester sauce, mustard, mayonnaise, garlic salt and sugar.

Crisp the pieces of celery by soaking them in iced water. Before serving, wipe them dry and fill with the sardine mixture. Sprinkle with the chopped chives or parsley.

CHEESE BALLS

Combine a 4-ounce packet of cream cheese with enough chopped chive or shallot to flavour. Take teaspoonfuls of the mixture and roll into small balls.

Have ready either grated carrot, chopped parsley or finely chopped nuts in which to roll the balls until covered. Chill until required.

CHEESE BUTTERFLIES

1 cup plain flour
a good pinch of salt
a pinch of cayenne pepper
$\frac{1}{2}$ level teaspoon dry mustard
2 ounces butter or margarine
1 ounce grated cheese
1 egg yolk
2 tablespoons milk
a squeeze of lemon juice

For the filling

2 tablespoons grated cheese
1 hard-boiled egg, finely
   chopped
a dash each of salt, cayenne
   pepper and mustard
1 tablespoon mayonnaise
strips of gherkin for garnishing

Sift the flour, salt, cayenne and mustard. Rub in the butter and margarine and add the grated cheese. Beat the egg yolk with the milk and lemon juice and stir into the mixture, making a fairly firm dough. Turn onto a lightly floured board and knead only until smooth on the outside. Roll thinly and cut into rounds with a 1½-inch cutter. Place on a greased shallow oven tray and bake in a hot oven, 425°F., for about 10 minutes or until lightly browned. Allow to cool.

Combine the four ingredients for the filling, mixing well. Spread half the baked cheese rounds with this mixture. Cut the remaining rounds in halves and arrange them on top of the filling to resemble the wings of a butterfly. Place a strip of gherkin down the centre of each to represent the body, and attach two small narrow pieces of gherkin for the feelers. Serve cold.

CHEESE STRAWS

1¼ cups plain flour
a pinch of cayenne pepper
1 level teaspoon dry mustard
$\frac{1}{2}$ level teaspoon salt
4 ounces butter
1½ cups grated cheese
1 egg yolk
2 tablespoons cold water
a good squeeze of lemon juice

Sift the flour, cayenne, mustard and salt. Rub in the butter and add the grated cheese. Beat the egg yolk with the water and lemon juice and add to the dry ingredients, making a rather firm dough.

Turn onto a lightly floured board and knead only until smooth. Roll $\frac{1}{8}$ inch thick and cut into strips 4 inches long and $\frac{1}{4}$ inch wide. Place on a greased slide and bake in a moderate oven, 350°F., for about 12 minutes, or until a pale straw colour.

Re-roll the scraps of pastry and cut a number of rings. To make them use a round cutter about 1½ inches in diameter and a smaller one $\frac{3}{4}$ inch in diameter. Bake as for the straws. Allow to cool on the tray.

To serve, arrange bundles of the straws in the cheese rings. Garnish with parsley.

CHEESIES

¾ cup self-raising flour
⅛ teaspoon cayenne pepper
¼ teaspoon salt
¾ cup grated cheese
3 tablespoons melted butter
coconut

Sift the flour into a bowl with the cayenne and salt and add the cheese. Pour in the melted butter, making a rather dry dough.

Take teaspoonfuls and roll into balls, then roll each ball in coconut. Place on a greased shallow tray and press flat with the back of a fork. Bake in a slow oven, 325°F., for about 15 minutes or until the cheesies are a golden brown.

CHICKEN CANAPÉS

1 cup finely chopped cooked
    chicken
2 teaspoons mayonnaise
½ cup chopped salted almonds
2 tablespoons chopped sweet
    pickle
cracker biscuits
sliced stuffed olives for
    garnishing

Blend the chicken with the mayonnaise. Stir in the almonds and pickle. Spread on small cracker biscuits and garnish with slices of stuffed olives.

CHICKEN CROUTES

12 small rounds of fried bread or
    12 small cracker biscuits
4 ounces chicken or ham
1 tablespoon mayonnaise
small tomatoes
salt and pepper
12 stuffed olives

Drain the rounds of fried bread, or butter the biscuits. Mix finely chopped chicken or ham with the mayonnaise. Cut the tomatoes into 12 thin slices.

Place a slice of tomato on each croute or biscuit and season with salt and pepper. Add a little of the chicken mixture to each, and top with a stuffed olive.

CHICKEN LIVER PÂTÉ

a little butter
1 pound chicken livers
1½ tablespoons mayonnaise
1 tablespoon lemon juice
1 tablespoon softened butter
1 dessertspoon finely minced
    onion
a few drops of hot pepper sauce
½ teaspoon salt
½ teaspoon dry mustard
a dash of pepper

Melt a little butter in a heavy-base pan. Add the chicken livers. Cover and cook until they change colour. Cool, then put through a mincer. Blend thoroughly with the mayonnaise, lemon juice, softened butter, onion, pepper sauce, salt, mustard and pepper.

Place the mixture in a greased mould and chill for a few hours before unmoulding onto a serving platter. Surround with cracker biscuits, dishes of chopped hard-boiled egg, chopped spring onion and finely chopped parsley.

CHILLED CHICKEN ROLLS

brown bread
softened butter
1 cup chopped chicken
a little mayonnaise
salt and pepper
small sprigs of parsley

Trim the crusts from thin slices of brown bread. Flatten each slice by rolling it with a rolling-pin on a damp cloth. Spread with softened butter.

Mix the chicken with about 1 tablespoon mayonnaise, and season to taste with salt and pepper. Spread on the bread. Tuck a sprig of parsley in at each end and roll up. Wrap in waxed paper and then in a damp cloth, and chill until serving time.

Brush walnuts or almonds with garlic-flavoured dressing and bake in a moderate oven, 350°F., for 10 minutes

CURRIED CHICKEN BOATS

Blend the meat paste with the chutney, curry powder, almonds and cheese spread. Chill until just before serving. Spoon a little into each pastry boat and garnish with stuffed olives or gherkins.

1 small can of chicken and
    veal paste
2 teaspoons chutney
1 teaspoon curry powder
⅓ cup chopped toasted almonds
4-ounce jar of cream cheese
    spread
3 dozen pastry boats
stuffed olives or gherkins for
    garnishing

DEVILLED ALMONDS

Place the almonds in a saucepan, cover with cold water and bring to the boil. Remove from the heat, drain, remove the brown skins and dry the almonds.

Heat the butter or oil in a frying pan and, when very hot, add the almonds. Stir occasionally until they are lightly browned all over.

Lift out and drain on paper. Sprinkle with salt and cayenne, shaking the paper to make sure the seasonings cover the almonds.

4 ounces almonds
1½ ounces butter or 3 tablespoons
    olive oil
salt
cayenne pepper

16

DEVILLED HAM CHIPS

2 cups plain flour
a good pinch of cayenne pepper
4 ounces butter
1 can of devilled ham paste
melted butter
poppy seeds

Sift the flour with the cayenne and rub in the 4 ounces of butter until the mixture is crumbly. Stir in the ham paste, forming the mixture into a dough. Chill for about 30 minutes.

Roll out on a lightly floured board to about ¼ inch thick and cut into 2-inch rounds with a fluted cutter. Place on greased shallow oven trays. Brush the top of each round with melted butter and sprinkle with poppy seeds. Bake at 400°F. for 10 to 12 minutes. Remove from the oven and allow to cool on the trays.

HAM AND CHEESE BALLS

4 ounces cream cheese
6 ounces finely chopped ham or
  corned beef
½ teaspoon Worcester sauce
1 dessertspoon chopped pickle
a squeeze of lemon juice
a pinch of cayenne pepper
salt
minced chives
finely chopped parsley

These may be prepared the day before they are required.

Soften the cream cheese and blend in thoroughly the very finely chopped ham and the Worcester sauce, pickle, lemon juice, cayenne and salt (add salt sparingly). Take portions and form into balls about the size of a marble.

Just before serving, roll the balls in equal quantities of chives and parsley mixed together.

DEVILLED HAM CORNUCOPIAS

For the filling
1 dessertspoon mayonnaise
1 small jar of devilled ham
2 hard-boiled eggs, finely
  chopped
1 dessertspoon prepared mustard
paprika or finely chopped parsley

Take 20 thin slices of bread and cut into rounds with a 2-inch cutter. Flatten each round with a rolling-pin and spread both sides with melted butter. Roll up to form cornucopias and secure with cocktail picks. Place on a shallow oven tray and bake at 350°F. for 15 minutes or until lightly browned. Remove the picks.

Combine all filling ingredients except the last item. Chill the mixture, then fill each bread cornucopia with a generous teaspoonful. Sprinkle with paprika or finely chopped parsley.

HAM AND CHEESE ROLLS

straight bread rolls
2 tablespoons soft butter
4 ounces grated tasty cheese
3 anchovies, chopped
6 ounces ham, chopped or
  minced
1 hard-boiled egg
a little mayonnaise

Cut the ends off each straight bread roll and scoop out the bread, leaving a crust shell. Mix the butter, cheese, anchovies, ham, chopped hard-boiled egg and mayonnaise to make a stiff paste. Blend thoroughly and pack firmly into the bread-roll crusts. Wrap in foil and chill for several hours. Cut each roll into ¼-inch to ½-inch slices before serving.

17

HAZELNUT CHEESE BITES

4 ounces blue-vein cheese
¾ cup chopped toasted hazelnuts
a pinch of salt
1 small can of pineapple pieces

Cream the cheese and stir in the nuts. Add the salt. Take portions and roll into small balls. Chill until firm.

You will need a packet of cocktail picks. Drain the pineapple pieces and place a hazelnut cheese-ball and a piece of pineapple on each pick. Spear them into an apple or an orange and serve on a platter.

LIVERWURST CANAPÉS

6 ounces liverwurst
1 teaspoon tomato sauce
¼ teaspoon prepared horseradish
1 teaspoon prepared mustard
1 teaspoon Worcester sauce
10 slices pumpernickel
butter
sliced stuffed olives for
    garnishing

Remove the liverwurst from its casing and let it stand at room temperature to soften before mixing with the tomato sauce, horseradish, mustard and Worcester sauce. Stir until smooth. Spread on buttered rounds of pumpernickel and garnish with slices of stuffed olive.

MINTED PINEAPPLE

Roll chunky pieces of canned or fresh pineapple in softened cream cheese, then toss in very finely chopped mint. Serve on cocktail picks.

OYSTER MORNAY

1 ounce butter
1 dessertspoon chopped shallot
2 level tablespoons plain flour
½ teaspoon salt
½ teaspoon dry mustard
a pinch of cayenne pepper
1 cup milk
lemon juice
1 dessertspoon mayonnaise
2 dozen oysters
2 tablespoons soft white
    breadcrumbs
2 tablespoons grated cheese
lemon wedges and parsley sprigs
    for garnishing

Melt the butter in a saucepan and sauté the shallot until soft but not brown. Add the flour, salt, mustard and cayenne pepper and stir until smooth. Cook for 1 minute without browning. Add the milk and stir until the sauce boils and thickens. Simmer for 2 minutes, then add I teaspoon of lemon juice and the mayonnaise.

Place a spoonful of this sauce in each of six lightly greased ramekin dishes or scallop shells. Top each with 4 well-drained oysters, then spoon over the remainder of the sauce. Sprinkle the top with breadcrumbs and grated cheese and bake in a moderate oven, 350°F., until the top browns and the sauce bubbles. Serve with lemon wedges and parsley sprigs.

OYSTERS KILPATRICK

salt and pepper
12 oysters
Worcester sauce
4 tablespoons tomato sauce
4 tablespoons grated cheese
3 ounces butter
lemon quarters for serving

Season the oysters on half shells and add a few drops of Worcester sauce to each. Now add a sprinkling of tomato sauce and top with grated cheese. Place a small piece of butter on each oyster and bake in their own shells in a moderate oven for 5 minutes. Serve with quartered lemons.

PARTY SANDWICH LOAF

3 four-ounce packets cream
    cheese
½ cup cream or top milk
1 sandwich loaf of fresh or day-
    old bread
4 types of savoury filling (see
    below)
radish roses, celery curls and
    cucumber slices for garnishing
finely chopped parsley for
    topping

The fillings used are a matter of personal taste. Our loaf contains cheese and gherkin, chicken salad, ham salad and egg salad fillings.

Cheese and gherkin filling. Mix 6 ounces of grated sharp-flavoured cheese to a paste with about 3 dessertspoons of warm milk and add 1 tablespoon chopped gherkin.

Chicken salad filling. Combine and chill ½ a cup of minced cooked chicken, ½ a cup of finely chopped celery, 2 dessertspoons of pickle or chutney, ½ a teaspoon of salt, a dash of pepper and 2 dessertspoons of mayonnaise.

Ham salad filling. Combine and chill 2 cups of minced cooked ham or luncheon meat, 2 dessertspoons of minced green pepper, ½ a teaspoon of prepared mustard, 1 dessertspoon of chopped shallot or onion and 2 dessertspoons of mayonnaise.

Egg salad filling. Combine and chill 2 chopped hard-boiled eggs, 2 dessertspoons of finely chopped olives or gherkins, ½ a teaspoon of salt, a dash of pepper, ½ a teaspoon of prepared mustard and 2 dessertspoons of mayonnaise.

To assemble the loaf

Blend the cream cheese with the cream to a good spreading consistency. Trim all the crusts from the bread and cut it lengthwise into five slices of even thickness.

Place one slice of bread on a board and cover evenly with the cheese and gherkin filling. Cover with the second slice of bread and add the chicken salad filling, spreading it evenly. Add the third slice of bread and top with the egg salad filling, then the fourth slice and the ham salad filling. Top with the remaining slice of bread. Press lightly but firmly together.

Spread the top, sides and ends evenly with cream cheese, then roughen it slightly to give a frosted appearance. Place on a serving dish, surround with the radish roses, celery curls and cucumber slices and sprinkle the top with the finely chopped parsley.

PEANUT COCKTAIL BISCUITS

1 cup plain flour
½ level teaspoon salt
1 level teaspoon mustard
a pinch of cayenne pepper
2 ounces butter
4 ounces grated cheese
1 egg yolk
1 egg white
1 cup chopped salted peanuts

Sift the flour with the salt, mustard and cayenne. Rub in the butter and add the grated cheese. Mix to a rather dry dough with the egg yolk, adding a little water if necessary.

Turn onto a floured board and knead until smooth on the outside. Roll thinly and cut into rounds, using a 2-inch cutter. Brush the tops with egg white and sprinkle with the chopped peanuts. Place on a shallow tray and bake in a hot oven, 400°F., for about 12 minutes.

19

SALAMI CUBES

Spread softened cream cheese on ½-inch cubes of salami or other prepared or canned meat. Roll each cube in finely chopped parsley and serve on cocktail picks.

SALMON PATÉ

two 4-ounce packets of cream
   cheese
1 dessertspoon chilli sauce
2 dessertspoons chopped parsley
1 rounded dessertspoon chopped
   spring onions
½ teaspoon Tabasco
1-pound can of salmon
½ teaspoon salt
a good pinch of pepper
1 teaspoon lemon juice
sliced stuffed olives for
   garnishing

Blend the cream cheese in a bowl until smooth and add the chilli sauce, parsley, spring onion, and Tabasco. Stir in drained and flaked salmon. Flavour with the salt, pepper and lemon juice and beat the mixture until it is thoroughly blended. Pack into a 3-cup mould, cover and chill for at least 3 hours.

At serving time unmould onto a serving dish and garnish with slices of stuffed olives. Serve with assorted cracker biscuits.

SALMON SAVOURIES

4-ounce can of salmon
3 dessertspoons mayonnaise
2 dessertspoons finely minced
   celery
a dash of Worcester sauce
a dash of chilli sauce
1 teaspoon lemon juice
thin slices of peeled cucumber
   butter
thin slices of white bread
celery and parsley for garnishing

Drain and flake the salmon and mix with the mayonnaise, celery, sauces and lemon juice.

Butter the bread and cover half the slices with the thinly sliced cucumber. Spread with the salmon mixture. Cover with the remaining buttered bread to make sandwiches. Press firmly and cut off the crusts. Wrap in greaseproof paper and chill for several hours.

To prepare for serving, cut each sandwich into three, then into two. Serve with a celery and parsley garnish.

SAUSAGE WEDGIES

2 cups mashed potato
1 tablespoon mayonnaise or
   prepared horseradish
¼ cup grated cheese
a pinch of cayenne pepper
1 tablespoon chopped gherkin
salt
8 slices Continental sausage about
   5 inches in diameter and less
   than ¼ inch thick

Combine the potato, mayonnaise, cheese, cayenne and gherkin, adding salt to taste. Spread one slice of the sausage with a thick coating of the mixture and top with another slice of sausage. Repeat these layers twice, finishing with sausage: you will have four layers of sausage and three of filling. Press firmly together and wrap in waxed paper. Repeat with the remaining sausage and filling. Store in a cold part of the refrigerator but do not freeze.

Before serving, cut into slender pie-shaped wedges, using a sharp, thin-bladed knife (wipe the blade with a damp cloth each time you cut a slice). Arrange the wedges on a platter, laying them on their sides.

SAVOURY BOATS

2 cups plain flour
½ level teaspoon baking powder
a pinch of salt
4 ounces butter or margarine
2 tablespoons water with a
   squeeze of lemon juice

Sift the flour with the baking powder and salt. Rub in the butter and mix to a firm dough with the water and lemon juice. Turn onto a lightly floured board and knead only until smooth on the outside. Roll thinly and cut into shapes to line patty tins or boat-shaped tins. Prick the bottom of each to prevent the centre rising. Bake in a hot oven, 400°F., for 12 to 15 minutes or until lightly browned. Remove from the tins and allow to cool.

CURRIED CHICKEN FILLING

½ cup diced peeled apple
¼ cup chopped onion
1 clove of garlic, crushed
1 tablespoon butter
2 dessertspoons plain flour
salt and pepper
1 teaspoon curry powder
1 cup chicken stock
1½ cups diced cooked chicken
1 teaspoon chopped parsley

Sauté the apple, onion and garlic in the butter for 5 minutes without browning. Stir in the flour with salt and pepper to taste and the curry powder. Stir until smooth, then cook for 1 minute. Add the chicken stock and cook, stirring well, until the mixture boils and thickens. Add the diced chicken and cook until thoroughly heated. Use to fill the cooked pastry shells. Sprinkle with chopped parsley. This quantity will fill about 2 dozen boats.

BRAIN AND WALNUT FILLING

1 set cooked brains
½ pint white sauce
1 rounded tablespoon chopped
   walnuts
1 teaspoon chopped parsley
salt
cayenne pepper
parsley sprigs or stuffed olives

Cut the brains into small pieces and mix into the sauce with the walnuts and parsley. Season with salt and cayenne pepper. Place a spoonful in each pastry boat and reheat before serving. Garnish with sprigs of parsley or stuffed olives.

Brain and Walnut Boats
Oyster Patties

21

CRAB FILLING

½ pint white sauce
1 small can of crabmeat, drained
  and well minced
1 teaspoon chopped parsley
a dash of cayenne pepper
a squeeze of lemon juice

Combine all the ingredients and use to fill the boats. Reheat before serving.

HAM AND GHERKIN FILLING

½ pint white sauce
2 ounces chopped cooked ham
1 or 2 chopped gherkins
1 hard-boiled egg, chopped
½ level teaspoon mustard

Combine all the ingredients and use to fill the boats. Reheat before serving.

PRAWN FILLING

½ pint white sauce
4 ounces shelled and chopped (or
  frozen) prawns
1 teaspoon lemon juice
a pinch of cayenne pepper

Combine all the ingredients. Spoon into the cooked pastry boats and reheat. Garnish with tiny parsley sprigs, and, if liked, top each with a prawn.

OYSTER FILLING

½ pint white sauce
1½ dozen oysters
lemon juice
a pinch of cayenne pepper
a pinch of mustard
1 teaspoon anchovy sauce
  (optional)

Combine all the ingredients and use to fill the boats. Reheat before serving.

SESAME BITES

5 tablespoons plain flour
½ teaspoon salt
a pinch of cayenne pepper
¼ teaspoon dry mustard
2 ounces butter or margarine
2 ounces grated cheese
sesame seeds
1 egg yolk
½ teaspoon lemon juice
milk for glazing

Sift the flour, salt, cayenne and mustard. Rub in the butter, then add the grated cheese and 1 tablespoon of sesame seeds.

Beat the egg yolk and the lemon juice together and add to the dry ingredients, making into a firm dough.

Knead lightly on a floured board and roll ¼ inch thick. Cut into shapes with a small floured biscuit cutter. Brush the tops with a little milk and sprinkle with sesame seeds. Place on an ungreased shallow oven tray and bake in a moderate oven, 350°F., until a pale golden colour—about 12 to 15 minutes. Cool on the tray.

STUFFED EGGS

6 hard-boiled eggs
½ level teaspoon salt
a good pinch of cayenne pepper
½ level teaspoon dry mustard
½ teaspoon Worcester sauce
3 dessertspoons mayonnaise or
    salad dressing

Shell the eggs and cut in halves lengthwise. Remove the yolks and place in a bowl, keeping the whites intact. Mash the yolks or press them through a fine sieve. Mix in the salt, pepper, mustard, Worcester sauce and mayonnaise. Pipe or pile back into the egg whites.

ZIPPY STUFFED EGGS

6 hard-boiled eggs
1 teaspoon gherkin spread
½ teaspoon Worcester sauce
1 teaspoon mustard sauce
cream
sliced gherkin or olive for
    garnishing

Shell the eggs and cut each in halves lengthwise. Scoop out the yolks without breaking the whites. Mash the yolks and mix them with the gherkin spread, Worcester sauce, mustard sauce and enough cream to make a spreading consistence.

    Spoon the mixture into the egg-white cases and garnish each with a slice of gherkin or olive.

Hot Finger Savouries

APPETIZER MEATBALLS WITH FLAVOURED SAUCES

For the meatballs

1½ pounds finely minced steak
½ cup soft white breadcrumbs
2 tablespoons milk
1½ teaspoons salt
1 egg
1 clove of garlic

Combine the minced steak, breadcrumbs, milk, salt, egg and crushed garlic, blending lightly. Shape into balls about the size of a large marble. Arrange on shallow trays and bake in a hot oven, 500°F., for about 5 minutes or until lightly browned. (Alternatively, fry them in a little oil or butter until brown all over.) Remove and add to the prepared sauce (recipes follow), including any pan drippings. Reheat the meatballs and serve with sauce.

STROGANOFF SAUCE

¼ cup butter or margarine
1 small onion
2 tablespoons plain flour
1½ cups beef broth
½ cup commercial sour cream
½ teaspoon dill
salt and pepper
4-ounce can of buttered
    mushrooms

Heat the butter in a pan and add chopped onion. Sauté until tender but not brown. Stir in the flour, cook until blended and bubbly. Slowly stir in the broth. Cook, stirring until thickened. Add the sour cream, dill, salt and pepper to taste, and the mushrooms. Reheat until boiling.

two 15-ounce cans of pineapple
    pieces
1¼ cups chicken stock
¼ cup brown sugar
¾ cup vinegar
1 dessertspoon soy sauce
1 dessertspoon tomato sauce
3 rounded tablespoons cornflour
a little cold stock or water
1 cup chopped spring onions
3 small green peppers, seeded and
    cut into cubes

4 rashers of bacon
1 medium-sized onion
1 clove of garlic
1 large can (1 pound 15 ounces)
    of tomatoes
1 teaspoon basil
1 teaspoon oregano
1 bayleaf
½ cup beef stock
1 tablespoon cornflour
¼ cup red wine or stock
1 teaspoon sugar
½ teaspoon salt
¼ teaspoon pepper

¼ cup butter
1 large onion
1 clove of garlic
1 level tablespoon curry powder
2 tablespoons plain flour
2 teaspoons sugar
½ teaspoon salt
a dash of cayenne pepper
1½ cups chicken stock or water
    with 1 chicken-soup cube
½ cup cream

SWEET AND SOUR SAUCE

Drain the syrup from the pineapple and combine it with the chicken stock, brown sugar, vinegar, and soy and tomato sauces. Blend the cornflour with a little cold stock or water and stir into the mixture. Cook, stirring well over medium heat until the sauce boils and thickens. Add the chopped onions and the cubed green peppers. Simmer for 5 minutes. Add the pineapple pieces. Reheat before serving.

ITALIAN TOMATO SAUCE

Dice the bacon and sauté until crisp. Drain from the pan (and discard) all but 1 tablespoon of the fat. Add finely chopped onion, crushed garlic and the tomatoes, basil, oregano, bayleaf and stock.

Bring to the boil and simmer for 30 minutes. Blend together the cornflour, red wine, sugar, salt and pepper. Stir into the tomato mixture and cook, stirring well, until the mixture boils and thickens. Reheat the meatballs and serve with the sauce.

CURRY SAUCE

Heat the butter in a large saucepan. Chop the onion finely and sauté it until soft but not brown. Add crushed garlic, then curry powder, and cook for 1 minute. Add the flour, sugar, salt and cayenne and cook until smooth. Stir in the stock and the cream. Cook, stirring well until the mixture boils and thickens. Simmer for 3 minutes. Reheat the meatballs and serve with the sauce.

BACON SNACKS

Remove the rind from rashers of bacon. Spread the rashers with prepared mustard, roll them up and thread on skewers. Grill or bake until the bacon fat is clear. Serve hot on cocktail picks.

24

CANAPÉS MONTE CRISTO

Toast small rounds of bread on one side and spread the untoasted side with butter. Top with minced ham flavoured with mustard, cayenne pepper, nutmeg and salt, and mixed to a spreading consistency with mayonnaise. Add a slice of cheddar cheese (cut to the shape of the bread) and place on a baking tray. Dust the tops with paprika. Cook under a heated griller or in the top of a hot oven until the cheese melts and browns. Serve hot.

CHEESE MATCHSTICKS

white bread, preferably several
    days old
melted butter
grated cheese
cayenne pepper
mustard

Slice the bread about $\frac{1}{4}$ inch thick and remove the crusts. Cut the slices into sticks about 3 inches long (or the width of the sandwich loaf) and $\frac{1}{4}$ inch wide and dip into melted butter.

Mix some grated cheese with a little cayenne and mustard and toss the bread in the mixture, making sure each piece is thoroughly coated.

Place on a baking tray and bake in a moderate oven, 350°F., until the sticks become crisp and lightly brown. They may be served hot or cold, but are best when hot.

Curried Chicken Boats and Cheese Puffs. In the background, Devilled Ham Chips

25

CHEESE PUFFS

1 cup self-raising flour
½ teaspoon salt
a pinch of cayenne pepper
1 ounce butter
¾ cup grated Cheddar cheese
1 egg, beaten
2 to 3 tablespoons milk
hot oil or lard for frying

Sift the flour, salt and cayenne. Rub in the butter and add all but 2 tablespoons of the grated cheese. Mix into a scone dough with the combined beaten egg and milk. Turn onto a lightly floured board and knead until smooth.

Form the dough into a long roll about 1 inch in diameter. Cut off pieces about ½ inch thick and roll into balls. Drop them into deep hot oil or lard and fry for 3 to 4 minutes. Drain on paper. Toss them in the reserved cheese. Serve hot.

CRABMEAT BACON ROLLS

6-ounce can of crabmeat
1 tablespoon tomato juice
a little beaten egg
1 cup soft white breadcrumbs
a dash each of salt and pepper
1 teaspoon chopped parsley
1 teaspoon chopped celery leaves
12 bacon slices

Drain and flake the crabmeat if necessary. Mix the tomato juice with the egg and add the breadcrumbs, seasonings, parsley, celery leaves and crabmeat. Mix thoroughly. Take small spoonfuls and make into rolls about 2 inches long.

Remove the rind from the bacon slices and cut them into pieces to wrap round the crabmeat rolls. Secure each with a cocktail pick. Place on a shallow oven tray and bake in a moderate oven for about 12 minutes, or until the bacon is cooked.

DEVILLED HAM CANAPÉS

1 can of devilled ham
1 dessertspoon mayonnaise
2 hard-boiled eggs
1 dessertspoon prepared mustard
20 rounds of fried bread, each about 2 inches in diameter
finely chopped parsley or some paprika

Combine the devilled ham with the mayonnaise, chopped eggs and mustard, blending well. Spread thickly on the rounds of fried bread. Sprinkle with parsley or paprika and serve hot or cold.

FISH BALLS

2 cups dry mashed potato
1 large can of herrings in tomato sauce
1 teaspoon tarragon vinegar
1 egg
2 tablespoons milk
1 cup breadcrumbs
oil or fat for frying

Place the mashed potato in a bowl. Mash the herrings and mix them with the potato. Flavour with the tarragon vinegar and bind with a little beaten egg. Beat the remaining egg into the milk.

Take teaspoonfuls of the fish mixture and shape into small balls, using a little seasoned flour if necessary. Dip each ball in the egg glazing and then cover with breadcrumbs. Deep-fry in hot fat until a golden brown. Drain on paper and serve as appetizers.

½ cup chopped ham
2 tablespoons chutney
rounds or fingers of toasted
    bread
a little cream
1 or 2 tablespoons grated cheese

HAM AND CHEESE TOASTIES

Blend the chopped ham and chutney and spread on the toasted bread. Moisten the surface of each with a little cream and sprinkle with the grated cheese. Heat in the oven until the cheese melts.

OYSTER AND BACON CANAPÉS

Lightly toast some rounds of white bread, then butter them. Place a fresh or canned oyster on each, then top the oyster with a small piece of bacon. Arrange the canapés on a flat oven tray and grill or bake until the bacon fat is clear. Serve hot.

OYSTER PATTIES

½ pound puff pastry
1 ounce butter
2 level tablespoons plain flour
salt
a pinch of cayenne pepper
¼ teaspoon mustard (optional)
½ cup milk
3 tablespoons oyster liquid
1½ dozen oysters
1 tablespoon cream
1 teaspoon anchovy sauce
    (optional)
lemon and parsley for garnishing

Roll the pastry ¼ inch thick. Using a 1½-inch round cutter, cut into rounds. With a ½-inch cutter mark the centre of each round and cut halfway through. (If the cutters are dipped in almost boiling water each time they are used, the cut will be cleaner and the pastry will rise better.) Place on a shallow oven tray and bake in a hot oven, 450°F. for about 10 to 12 minutes.

To make the filling, melt the butter in a small saucepan and add the flour, salt, cayenne and mustard. Stir until smooth and cook for 1 minute without browning. Add the milk and oyster liquid and stir until the sauce boils and thickens. Cook for 2 minutes. Add the bearded oysters, cream and anchovy sauce (if you have included the mustard omit anchovy sauce).

Remove the tops from the baked cases, add a teaspoonful of the cream oyster mixture to each, and replace its top. Reheat if necessary. Serve hot, garnished with lemon and parsley.

PARTY PIES

1 cup plain flour
1 level teaspoon baking powder
a good pinch of salt
2 ounces butter
1½ cups dry mashed potato
1 egg

Sift the flour, baking powder and salt into a bowl and rub in the butter. Add the mashed potato and mix to a smooth dough with the well-beaten egg. Cover and chill for about 1 hour.

Place the pastry on a lightly floured board and roll to about ⅛ inch thick. Cut into rounds with a floured pastry cutter and use to line greased patty tins. Add a teaspoonful of the desired filling, then top with another round of potato pastry. Brush the tops with beaten egg and milk. Bake at 450°F. for 10 to 15 minutes. Serve hot.

Mushroom filling. Melt 1 dessertspoon of butter in a pan and sauté a finely chopped small onion until soft but not brown. Add an 8-ounce can of sliced mushrooms, salt and pepper to taste, and 1½ teaspoons of cream or top milk. Mix well and allow to cool before using.

Curry filling. Sauté a finely chopped small onion in 1 dessert-spoon of butter until soft but not brown. Add ½ a cup of chopped cooked ham or beef, ½ a small tomato (chopped), 1 cup of cold cooked rice, a pinch of salt and 1 teaspoon of curry powder.

Savoury Pinwheels

SAVOURY PINWHEELS

2 ounces butter
½ cup grated sharp cheese
2 teaspoons chopped parsley
1 teaspoon prepared mustard
1 dessertspoon tomato sauce
1 teaspoon Worcester sauce
6 slices of fresh bread about
⅛ inch thick
Stuffed olives

Cream the butter and cheese, then blend in the next four ingredients.

Remove the crusts from the slices of bread and spread the bread generously with the cheese mixture. Place a row of stuffed olives at one end. Roll each slice up like a jelly roll and fasten with cocktail picks. Wrap in greased paper and chill thoroughly.

Just before serving, cut each roll in two and toast until brown. Serve hot.

To serve cold, cut into slices ¼ inch thick.

SMOKED HAM CANAPÉS

1 ounce butter
¼ cup boiling water
¼ cup sifted plain flour
a dash of salt
1 egg
¼ cup Swiss grated cheese

For the filling

4 ounces smoked ham sausage
⅓ cup finely chopped celery
2 dessertspoons chopped green
  pepper
½ teaspoon prepared horseradish
⅓ cup mayonnaise or salad
  dressing

Melt the butter in the boiling water, then stir in the flour and the salt. Cook, stirring well over medium heat, until the mixture forms a ball which does not separate. Remove from the heat and cool slightly. Add the egg and beat vigorously until smooth. Stir in the cheese.

Take level teaspoonfuls of the dough and drop onto a greased oven tray. Bake at 400°F. for 20 minutes. Remove from the tray and allow to cool.

To make the filling combine the chopped ham sausage with the remaining ingredients and chill. Just before serving split the puffs and fill them. Heat before serving.

28

Swedish Meatballs

SWEDISH MEATBALLS

¾ pound finely minced steak
¾ cup dry breadcrumbs
¾ teaspoon cornflour
1 small onion, peeled and minced
a pinch of allspice
1 egg, beaten
½ cup cream
½ teaspoon salt
1 clove of garlic, crushed

Combine all the ingredients in a bowl and mix well. Shape into small balls in a little seasoned flour.

Heat about 2 tablespoons of fat or oil in a frying pan and cook the meatballs until they are golden on all sides and cooked through. This will take about 12 minutes. Drain well.

For a party savoury these meatballs may be made the day before they are required, then covered with foil and reheated in a moderate oven. Stick a cocktail pick into each meatball and serve as a savoury.

SWISS ONION CAKE

1½ cups plain flour
1 teaspoon sugar
½ teaspoon salt
4 ounces butter or margarine
3 tablespoons milk

For the filling

4 slices bacon
2 medium-sized onions
2 eggs, beaten
1 egg yolk, beaten
¾ cup sour or fresh cream
1 tablespoon plain flour
½ teaspoon salt
a dash of pepper

Sift the flour, sugar and salt into a bowl. Rub in the butter and mix to a light dough with the milk. Pat two-thirds of the dough into the bottom of a greased 8-inch sandwich tin. Bake at 425°F. for about 10 minutes or until lightly browned. Cool. Reduce the oven temperature to 325°F.

Cut the bacon into ¼-inch strips and fry until crisp. Drain, remove from the pan. Chop the onions and cook in the bacon fat until tender. Combine the remaining ingredients with the bacon and onion. Pat the left-over one-third of the dough round the edge of the cooled, cooked pastry mixture, pour in the filling and bake until set, about 20 minutes. Cut into wedges and serve as an appetizer.

TITBITS

Take small strips of bacon and roll them round small pieces of cheese, chunks of pineapple, slices of cooked sausage or pieces of gherkin. Secure each with a cocktail pick. Place on a shallow baking tray. Bake or grill until the bacon is cooked. Serve hot.

For a cold savoury, use ham instead of bacon and do not cook.

Another way with bacon rolls is to remove the rind from streaky bacon rashers, cut each rasher into 2 or 3 pieces, and spread lightly with mustard or chutney, then roll the bacon round a chunky piece of banana, a stuffed olive, a cooked and peeled prawn or a sweet gherkin. Secure each with a cocktail pick and bake or grill until the bacon is cooked. Serve hot.

TONGUE AND CHUTNEY CANAPÉS

½ cup finely chopped cooked tongue
½ cup chopped chutney
¼ teaspoon cayenne pepper
½ teaspoon curry powder
about 20 rounds white bread, 1½ inches in diameter
mayonnaise
grated cheese

Mix together the tongue, chutney, cayenne and curry powder. Place the rounds of bread on a baking tray and cover them generously with the meat mixture. Dot with mayonnaise and sprinkle with grated cheese. Place in a hot oven, about 500°F., and bake for 5 minutes.

First Course Appetiser Cocktails

AVOCADO AND SEAFOOD COCKTAIL

3 firm ripe avocado pears
lemon juice
3 tablespoons whipped cream or mayonnaise
salt
cayenne pepper
1 cup flaked salmon, crabmeat, cooked prawns or chopped cooked lobster
finely chopped parsley
lemon slices for garnishing

Cut each avocado in half lengthwise, remove the seed and scoop out most of the flesh with a teaspoon (leaving a firm margin round the skin). Brush the inside of each half with lemon juice to prevent discolouring.

Mash the flesh with a fork and add to the whipped cream or mayonnaise. Season to taste with salt and cayenne pepper. The mixture should be the consistency of whipped cream.

Fold the salmon in lightly and use to fill the avocado shells. Sprinkle the edge of each with some finely chopped parsley and garnish with slices of lemon. Serve well chilled.

FRUIT MEDLEY

3 oranges
2 bananas
2 slices canned or fresh pineapple, diced
lemon juice
sugar

Peel and section the oranges and combine them with the peeled and sliced bananas and the diced pineapple. Sprinkle with lemon juice and sweeten to taste with sugar. Chill. Serve in chilled cocktail glasses or in hollowed-out halves of orange shells.

GOLD COASTER

1 ripe banana
lemon juice
2 cups canned fruit cocktail, chilled and drained
1 cup ripe strawberries, washed, hulled, halved and chilled
1 cup cantaloup balls, well chilled
1 small bottle ginger ale

Peel the banana, cut into slices and dip in lemon juice to prevent discolouring. Combine with the remaining fruit, cover and chill for several hours. Just before serving pour a little ginger ale over the fruit, and if liked, a dash of aromatic bitters. Spoon into chilled cocktail glasses.

MELON AND PINEAPPLE COCKTAIL

1 cup watermelon balls
1 cup cantaloup balls
15-ounce can of pineapple pieces
$\frac{1}{2}$ cup syrup drained from the pineapple
$\frac{1}{2}$ cup orange juice
1 tablespoon lemon juice
maraschino cherries and mint sprigs for garnishing

Combine the three fruits in a bowl, cover and chill for several hours. In another container mix the fruit syrup with the fruit juices. At serving time place the fruit in individual serving glasses and spoon over some of the fruit-flavoured syrup. Serve well chilled. Garnish if liked with a maraschino cherry and a mint sprig.

MELON BALL COCKTAILS

Melon balls either alone or in combination with other fruits make an ideal first course. They can be scooped out with a melon baller or a teaspoon. Here are four ideas:

1. Watermelon, cantaloup or honey-dew balls, well chilled and sprinkled with dry ginger ale or dry sherry. Garnish each with a glacé cherry and a mint sprig.

2. Combine $\frac{1}{2}$ a cup of water with $\frac{1}{2}$ a cup of sugar, stir until boiling, then cook for 5 minutes. Cool and add 1 tablespoon of lemon juice and 2 tablespoons of orange juice. Spoon over a combination or any one of the melon balls and garnish with a glacé cherry and a mint sprig.

3. Use papaw instead of melons. Mix with equal quantities of berries (any type). Place in cocktail glasses and sprinkle with lemon juice. Garnish with a glacé cherry and a sprig of mint.

4. Boil $\frac{1}{2}$ a cup of sugar with $\frac{1}{2}$ a cup of water for 5 minutes and pour it over 3 tablespoons of chopped mint. Add 3 tablespoons of lemon juice and 1 tablespoon of orange juice. Cover and let stand for 1 hour. Strain, chill and pour it over cubes or balls of papaw.

31

PAPAW AND BERRY COCKTAIL

1½ cups small cubes or balls of
    papaw
1½ cups quartered strawberries
    or other berries
lemon juice
pineapple juice
strawberry halves or berries for
    garnishing

Combine the papaw cubes or balls with the quartered strawberries. Divide evenly between six cocktail glasses. Sprinkle
each with a little lemon juice. Pour about 1 dessertspoon of
pineapple juice over each serving before garnishing with the
berries. Serve well chilled.

PINEAPPLE MINT COCKTAIL

1 fresh pineapple
½ cup sugar
½ cup water
1 cup fresh mint leaves
sherry to taste
glacé cherries and mint sprigs for
    garnishing

Peel and core the pineapple and cut into cubes. Combine the
sugar and water in a saucepan, and stir over medium heat until
the sugar dissolves and the mixture boils. Boil for 5 minutes.
Pour this syrup over the crushed or chopped mint leaves, then
cover and let stand until cold. Strain, and add 1 tablespoon of
sherry.

Place the pineapple cubes in individual serving dishes and
spoon over the liquid, adding a little more sherry if liked. Top
each with a glacé cherry and a mint sprig.

SEAFOOD COCKTAILS

For the cocktail sauce

¼ cup sweet mayonnaise
½ cup undiluted tomato soup
¼ level teaspoon curry powder
1 teaspoon Worcester sauce
1 teaspoon lemon juice
salt and pepper
¼ cup cream, semi-whipped

Combine the mayonnaise with the tomato soup. Add the next
4 ingredients (these can be adjusted to suit your taste). Just
before using fold in the semi-whipped cream.

PRAWN COCKTAIL

Line small cocktail glasses with small well-washed and drained
lettuce leaves. Arrange shelled prawns in the centre and spoon
over the cocktail sauce, using about 2 tablespoonfuls for each
glass. Garnish with tiny sprigs of parsley and triangles of
thinly sliced lemon. Serve well chilled.

WHITEBAIT COCKTAIL

Use freshly cooked or drained, canned whitebait. (To cook
fresh whitebait toss it in melted butter in a pan until the tiny
fish have lost their transparent appearance; season with salt and
pepper; cool.) Place 1 to 2 tablespoons of the whitebait in each
cocktail glass, add about 2 tablespoons of cocktail sauce to
each, and garnish with tiny parsley sprigs and thinly sliced
lemon triangles.

LOBSTER COCKTAIL

As for whitebait, using chopped cooked lobster.

This may be a combination of any fish, either cooked or canned, and fresh oysters. For each seafood cocktail allow 2 oysters and either 1 prawn or 2 to 3 small shrimps, with 1 tablespoon of salmon and 1 tablespoon of chopped cooked lobster. Spoon over 2 tablespoons of the cocktail sauce and garnish with tiny parsley sprigs and triangles of thinly sliced lemon. Serve well chilled.

CELERY AND SALMON COCKTAIL

Drain and flake 1 pound of canned salmon. Mix with 1 cup of chopped celery. Divide evenly between six cocktail glasses and top each with about 1 tablespoon of cocktail sauce. Garnish with tiny lemon triangles and parsley sprigs.

STRAWBERRY AND PINEAPPLE COCKTAIL

15-ounce can of cubed pineapple
3 cups fresh strawberries
$\frac{1}{4}$ cup mint leaves
crystallized cherries and mint sprigs for garnishing

Drain the pineapple. Hull and wash the strawberries. Place the pineapple syrup in a saucepan and bring it to the boil. Pour it over the mint leaves, cover and let stand until cool. Chill the pineapple cubes, the strawberries and the mint syrup.

At serving time, spoon the fruit into cocktail glasses and add some of the minted syrup. Garnish each with a cherry and a sprig of mint.

TOMATO JUICE COCKTAIL

1 large can of tomato juice
1 teaspoon Worcester sauce
1 teaspoon lemon juice
whipped cream (optional)
lemon wedges and parsley sprigs for garnishing

Combine the tomato juice, Worcester sauce and lemon juice, mixing well. Refrigerate for at least 1 hour. Pour into serving glasses. Top each with a small spoonful of whipped cream if liked. Garnish with lemon wedges and parsley sprigs.

BEVERAGES

BANANA NOG

2 medium-sized fully ripe
    bananas
1 cup vanilla ice cream
1⅓ cups chilled evaporated milk
2 eggs
2 teaspoons vanilla essence

Combine the ingredients in an electric blender and mix for 30 seconds. Pour into chilled glasses and top each with a scoop of vanilla ice cream sprinkled with ground nutmeg.

BANQUET PUNCH

⅔ cup boiling water
2 teaspoons tea leaves
12-ounce can of unsweetened
    pineapple juice
1 cup unsweetened grapefruit
    juice
1 cup orange juice
½ cup lemon juice
1 cup sugar
2 cups iced water
aromatic bitters (optional)
crushed ice
2 pints chilled ginger ale.

Pour the boiling water over the tea. Cover and let stand for 5 minutes. Strain. Combine the fruit juices and tea and add the sugar. Stir until dissolved. Chill, then add the iced water. If liked, add aromatic bitters to taste. Have some crushed ice ready in a punch bowl and pour the mixture over it. Now add the ginger ale by pouring it slowly down the sides of the bowl.

CAFÉ AU LAIT

1 level tablespoon instant coffee
4 teaspoons sugar
2 cups cold milk
vanilla- or coffee-flavoured ice
    cream

Combine the coffee, sugar and milk in a shaker, glass jar or blender. Shake or blend well. Pour into tall glasses and top each with a scoop of ice cream.

COFFEE MALTED

Reduce the sugar by 2 teaspoons and add 2 tablespoons malted milk powder. Blend or shake, then serve in tall glasses, topping with a scoop of ice cream.

CHERRY BRANDY

Take 2 pounds of dark cherries. Wash them and cut the stalks to within about a quarter of an inch of the fruit: it is most important that a little of the stem is left on.

    You will need equal quantities of cherries, sugar and brandy so mark the jar in which you will be storing the cherry brandy into three equal portions.

Now measure out into separate containers the sugar, then the brandy, then the cherries. Place the cherries in an earthenware bowl, add the sugar, and then the brandy. Leave in a convenient warm place for a couple of days, and once or twice a day swirl the cherries in the brandy syrup, but do not stir the mixture. When the sugar has completely dissolved, pour into the jar, cork and seal and put away for 6 months. At the end of the storing period the fruit will have dissolved or shrivelled into the mixture, and all that has to be done is to strain out the little bits of stalk and seeds.

CHOCOLATE SYRUP

2 level tablespoons cocoa
1¼ cups hot water
1 cup sugar
a pinch of salt
½ teaspoon vanilla essence

Blend the cocoa with a little of the hot water, add the remainder of the water and cook, stirring well, until the mixture is well blended. Add the sugar and salt and bring to the boil. Boil for 2 minutes, stirring constantly. Remove from the stove and add the vanilla. Cool, then place in tightly lidded jars and store in the refrigerator.

To make chocolate milk shakes add 1 or 2 tablespoonfuls to a glass of hot or cold milk.

CLARET CUP

1 lemon
¼ pint water
4 ounces sugar
2 oranges
1 quart bottle of claret
a sprig of borage if available
a few thin slices of cucumber
1 quart soda water

Thinly peel the rind from the lemon and place it in a saucepan with the water and sugar. Stir until the sugar has dissolved, then simmer gently for 10 minutes. Allow to cool. Strain into a jug. Squeeze the juice from the oranges and lemon and add, together with the claret, the borage and cucumber. Chill. Add the soda water just before serving.

CREAMY MOCHA

2 cups cold coffee
2 cups cold cocoa made with milk
2 tablespoons cream
¾ cup milk
2 level tablespoons sugar
8 ice cubes, crushed

Combine all the ingredients and shake or blend until foamy.

CUMQUAT LIQUEUR

1 pound cumquats
2 pounds sugar
1 large bottle of brandy

Wash the cumquats and prick each one all over with a darning needle or a fine skewer. Place in a large jar in alternate layers with sugar to the same depth. Pour on the brandy.

Allow to stand for a week, shaking or lightly stirring occasionally to dissolve the sugar. Be careful not to break the fruit. By the end of a week all the sugar should have dissolved, but it may take a few days longer in cold weather.

Seal the tops of the jars, preferably by dipping the lid in melted paraffin wax after screwing it on. Put away in a cool dark place for six months. Strain off the liquid and use as a liqueur. (The well-drained cumquats may be served with coffee, but they are very strong.)

FIFTY-FIFTY

2 oranges
2 lemons
3 pounds sugar
1 ounce tartaric acid
2 quarts boiling water

Wash the oranges and lemons and grate the rind from them. Squeeze the juice, strain out any seeds, and place it in a heat-proof bowl with the sugar. Add the tartaric acid. Pour the boiling water over and stir until the sugar and the acid have dissolved. Bottle and seal.

To serve, use about 2 tablespoonfuls in a glass filled with either iced water or ginger ale. For party use, pour into a punch bowl and float slices of orange and lemon on top.

Frosted Coffee Cup

FROSTED COFFEE CUP

2 level tablespoons instant coffee
1 quart boiling water
1 large can of unsweetened
    evaporated milk
1 cup fresh milk
6 ounces sugar
6 or 8 tablespoons vanilla ice
    cream

Dissolve the instant coffee in the boiling water and place in a saucepan with both milks and the sugar. Bring slowly to the boil, then remove from the heat and allow to cool. Chill well.

Serve in 6 or 8 tall glasses, topping each with a tablespoonful of ice cream.

FRUIT PUNCH 1

2 cups boiling water
3 dessertspoons tea
1 cup lemon juice
1½ cups fresh orange juice
1 cup pineapple juice
1 cup sugar
6 cups iced water or chilled
    ginger ale

Pour the boiling water over the tea and stand for 5 minutes. Strain and cool.

Combine the fruit juices with the sugar and stir until the sugar is dissolved. Combine with the tea. Chill thoroughly.

Just before serving, mix with the iced water or chilled ginger ale and pour onto ice cubes in a punch bowl.

FRUIT PUNCH 2

1 cup sugar
1 cup cold water
juice of 6 lemons
juice of 6 oranges
2 pints dry ginger ale
pulp of 6 passionfruit

Combine the sugar and water in a saucepan. Stir over the heat until the sugar dissolves, then simmer for 5 minutes. Cool. Add the strained juice of the lemons and oranges. Chill until serving time, then add dry ginger ale and the passionfruit pulp.

If the lemons and oranges are a little on the sour side it may be necessary to add a little more sugar.

FRUIT PUNCH FOR 35

2½ cups water
3 cups sugar
1 quart ginger ale or champagne
2½ cups pineapple juice
5 cups orange juice
2 cups lemon juice
1 cup ripe strawberries
3 cups iced water
lemon and orange slices
mint sprigs

Make the syrup for the punch the day before the party: measure the water into a saucepan, add the sugar and stir over medium heat until it dissolves. Boil for 5 minutes. Cool. Pour into a jug, cover and leave overnight. Chill the ginger ale or champagne and the pineapple juice ready for the following day.

On the day of the party squeeze the juice from the oranges and lemons and chill it. Wash the strawberries and cut each into three lengthwise. Just before serving the punch pour the syrup, fruit juices and iced water into the punch bowl, spoon the strawberries in, and garnish with slices of lemon and orange and sprigs of mint. At the last moment pour in the chilled ginger ale or champagne.

GALA GARNISHES

FROSTY RIMS

To frost the rims of drinking glasses dip each rim lightly in lemon juice and then in sugar. Chill till just before needed.

Half fill the refrigerator freezing-trays with water and freeze till firm. Place on top of each ice cube any one (or a combination) of the following: red or green maraschino cherries, halved or sliced; canned pineapple titbits; fresh mint sprigs; fresh unhulled strawberries; fresh stoned cherries. Now cover with water to fill each section, and freeze until firm.

FLAVOURED ICE CUBES

Instead of using water for ice cubes substitute fruit juices, sherry, whisky or wine, then freeze in the usual way and empty into the punch bowl just before serving. Or float one of the cubes in the top of each glass of fruit punch.

GINGER BEER PLANT

Put 8 sultanas, the juice of 2 lemons, 1 teaspoon of lemon pulp, 4 teaspoons of sugar, 2 teaspoons of ground ginger and 2 cups of cold water into a screw-topped jar. Leave for 2 or 3 days or until the mixture begins to ferment.

Now each day for 1 week add to the plant 2 teaspoons of ground ginger and 4 teaspoons of sugar. At the end of the week it should be ready to make into ginger beer, for which you will need 4 cups of boiling water, 4 cups of sugar, and the juice of 4 lemons.

Place the sugar and the boiling water in a large bowl and add the lemon juice. Strain the plant into this through fine muslin and squeeze dry. Add 28 cups of cold water. Bottle in air-tight bottles. The ginger beer should be kept for about 3 days before using.

To keep the plant alive, divide into half the mixture that was squeezed in the muslin. Discard one half and put the other half in a screw-topped jar with 2 cups cold water. Keep feeding each day for 1 week by adding 4 teaspoons of sugar and 2 teaspoons of ginger.

Sufficient to fill 11 bottles.

GOLDEN MINT RECEPTION PUNCH

sprigs of mint
2 cups sugar
4 pints boiling water
4 pints orange juice
2⅓ cups lemon juice
2½ cups pineapple juice
2 pints ginger ale
2 pints soda water
12 ounces brandy (optional)

Early in the day wash the mint and place in a saucepan with the sugar and boiling water. Simmer, uncovered, for 10 minutes. Cool, then refrigerate for several hours. Meanwhile chill the fruit juices.

Just before serving strain the mint syrup and add the fruit juices, the well chilled ginger ale, and the soda water. Add the brandy if liked. Serve in glasses or pour into a punch bowl and float ice cubes and thin slices of fruit on top.

Served in 5-ounce glasses this is sufficient for 50 people.

ICED TEA

Make the tea twice as strong as usual, using 4 teaspoons of tea to 2 cups of boiling water. Infuse for 3 minutes, no longer. Strain into glasses one-third full of cracked ice. Sweeten to taste and put a thin slice of lemon into each glass of tea. The infusion should be chilled quickly to retain the flavour.

A sprig of mint in each glass gives a refreshing and new flavour to the iced tea.

JUNKET MILK TREAT

1 fruit-flavoured junket tablet
1 tablespoon cold water
1 glass cold milk
2 teaspoons sugar

Crush the junket tablet and dissolve it in the tablespoon of cold water. Add the chilled milk and the sugar and stir until the sugar has dissolved. Use at once.

If using plain junket tablets, flavour with vanilla essence and dust the top with a little nutmeg or cinnamon.

LEMON CHAMPAGNE

3 or 4 lemons
4 breakfast cups sugar
½ cup seeded raisins
1 pint boiling water
2 gallons cold water

Slice the lemons and place them in a bowl with the sugar and the raisins. Add the boiling water, stirring well, then add the cold water. Throw a cover over the bowl and let the mixture stand for 3 or 4 days (during hot humid weather 3 days is usually enough, but it should stand a full 4 days if made during the winter). Strain the drink and place in clean bottles. Tie the corks down and keep for about 2 weeks before using. This is a very active drink.

LEMON CORDIAL

1 quart boiling water
1½ pounds sugar
½ teaspoon essence of lemon
1 ounce citric or tartaric acid

Combine the water and sugar in a saucepan and stir over low heat until the sugar has dissolved and the mixture comes to the boil. Boil for 10 minutes. Dissolve the citric acid in the syrup and strain into a bowl. Add the lemon essence. Allow to cool. Bottle and cork securely.

To serve, place about 2 tablespoons of the syrup in a glass and fill with ice cold water.

LEMON SYRUP

8 pints lemon juice
6 pounds white sugar
1 ounce lemon essence
1 ounce citric acid
1 gramme sodium benzoate

Strain the lemon juice and mix with the sugar, lemon essence, citric acid and sodium benzoate. Stir well until all the sugar has dissolved. Pour into clean, dry bottles and cork down well. Allow to stand for several days before using. This quantity should fill about 8 soft drink bottles.

To serve, place a little in a glass and fill with cold water.

LEMONADE

1 cup water
1 cup sugar
rind of 2 lemons cut into pieces
1 cup lemon juice
4 cups iced water

Combine the water, sugar and cut-up rind in a saucepan. Stir over low heat until the sugar has dissolved. Boil for 7 minutes. Cool, then strain. Add the lemon juice and the iced water. Pour over ice cubes in glasses.

MAKE-BELIEVE CHAMPAGNE

1 cup sugar
1 cup water
1 cup grapefruit juice
½ cup orange juice
1 quart chilled ginger ale

Combine the sugar and water in a saucepan, bring to the boil and boil for 5 minutes. Cool. Add the fruit juices. Chill. At serving time lightly stir in the ginger ale.

MOCK CHAMPAGNE

1 cup sugar
1 cup water
¼ cup orange juice
1 cup grape juice
¼ cup lemon juice
2 pints ginger ale

Combine the sugar and water in a saucepan and stir over medium heat until the sugar dissolves and the mixture boils. Boil for 3 minutes. Cool. Add the fruit juices. Chill for several hours.

Just before serving add the chilled ginger ale. Serve in tall glasses or in a punch bowl with ice cubes.

In place of the 2 pints of ginger ale, 1 pint of sparkling white wine and 1 pint of ginger ale may be used.

PARTY PUNCH 1

3 cups unsweetened pineapple
  juice
juice of 5 oranges
juice of 5 lemons
1 cup sugar
3 pints ginger ale
3 pints soda water
1 cup strawberries, quartered
cucumber slices, orange slices
  and mint sprigs for garnishing

Combine the pineapple, orange and lemon juice with the sugar. Chill thoroughly. Just before serving add the ginger ale, soda water and quartered strawberries. Pour over a pile of ice cubes in a punch bowl.

Float thin slices of cucumber and orange and some mint sprigs on top.

PARTY PUNCH 2

Boil 6 cups of cold water with 2 cups of sugar and 3 cups of grated pineapple and juice for 30 minutes. Add 2 cups of strained orange juice and ½ a cup of strained lemon juice. Chill. Just before serving add 2 pints of soda or iced water.

If liked, the lemon juice and the soda or iced water may be omitted and 2 or 3 bottles of lemonade added instead.

PASSIONFRUIT CORDIAL

1 pint water
5 cups sugar
5 level teaspoons citric acid
1 pint orange or lemon juice
18 passionfruit

Combine the water, sugar and citric acid in a saucepan and bring to the boil. Cool, then add the orange or lemon juice. Stir in the passionfruit pulp and mix well. Bottle and seal securely. Use as a cordial, diluting the syrup with iced water, lemonade or soda water.

PINEAPPLE PUNCH 1

1 medium-sized pineapple
1 pint water
mint sprigs
1 cup sugar
juice of 6 lemons
juice of 6 oranges
1 pint soda water, well chilled
3 passionfruit
3 bananas

Wash and peel the pineapple. Cut the flesh into pieces (reserve it for use in a dessert; it is not needed for the punch). Place the skin and core of the pineapple in a saucepan with the water and bring to the boil. Boil for 20 minutes. Add the mint sprigs and allow to cool.

Strain the pineapple syrup and add the sugar. Stir until dissolved, heating if necessary. Cool, then add the lemon and orange juice. Chill well. Just before serving add the soda water, passionfruit and sliced bananas.

PINEAPPLE PUNCH 2

2 cups strong tea
$\frac{3}{4}$ cup lemon juice
1$\frac{3}{4}$ cups orange juice
1 tablespoon lime juice
1 cup sugar
about 12 sprigs of mint
4 slices canned pineapple and the syrup from the can
4 pints ginger ale
4 pints soda water
crushed ice

Place the tea, lemon juice, orange juice, lime juice and sugar in a large bowl. Stir well until the sugar has dissolved, then add the mint. Place in the refrigerator for 2 hours.

Shortly before serving, strain the punch and add the chopped pineapple pieces and the syrup from the can. Place in a punch bowl and pour the ginger ale and soda water down the side of the bowl. Add some crushed ice.

SUMMER CUP

4 pounds sugar
3 pints water
6 oranges
4 lemons
1 ounce tartaric acid
1 ounce citric acid
1 packet Epsom salts

Combine the sugar and water in a saucepan. Bring to the boil and allow to boil for 5 minutes. Cool. Grate the rind from the oranges and lemons, squeeze the juice, and put both in a bowl.

Combine the tartaric acid with the citric acid and the Epsom salts. Add to the fruit juices and grated rinds, pour in the cooled syrup and stir until dissolved. Bottle and seal securely.

To serve, pour about 2 tablespoons of the syrup into a glass and fill with iced water.

TEA PUNCH

1 pint hot strong tea, freshly made
2 tablespoons castor sugar
juice of 3 lemons
$\frac{1}{2}$ pint chilled ginger ale or soda water
a few thin slices of unpeeled cucumber
sprigs of mint
strips of lemon peel

Pour the hot tea over the sugar. Cool and add the lemon juice. Strain into a large jug. Chill.

Just before serving add the chilled ginger ale or soda water, cucumber slices, mint sprigs and strips of lemon peel. Strain into ice-cold glasses with a thin slice of lemon in each glass.

BISCUITS

ABERNETHY BISCUITS

1½ cups plain flour
½ level teaspoon baking powder
4 ounces butter
½ cup sugar
½ teaspoon grated lemon rind
1 teaspoon caraway seeds
1 egg yolk
1 dessertspoon lemon juice

Sift the flour and baking powder into a bowl, rub in the butter and add the sugar, lemon rind and caraway seeds.

Beat the egg yolk with the lemon juice and add to the dry ingredients, making into a firm biscuit dough. Chill well.

Roll the dough on a lightly floured board to about ⅛ inch thick and cut into 2-inch circles. Place on a greased biscuit tray and prick the surface with a fork. Bake in a moderate oven, 350°F., for 10 to 15 minutes.

ALMOND CREAMS

For the biscuit base

4 ounces butter
½ cup castor sugar
1 egg yolk
1 tablespoon water
a few drops of almond essence
2 cups plain flour
1 level teaspoon baking powder
a pinch of salt
2 level tablespoons ground
  almonds
almond paste (recipe follows)
apricot jam
lemon- or almond-flavoured
  glacé icing

For the almond paste

4 ounces ground almonds
8 ounces sifted icing sugar
1 egg yolk
1 tablespoon sherry
a squeeze of lemon juice

First make the biscuit base. Cream the butter with the sugar, then add the egg yolk, water and almond essence. Sift the flour with the baking powder and salt and stir into the creamed mixture together with the ground almonds. Turn onto a lightly floured board and knead until smooth. Roll thinly and cut into rounds with a fluted or fancy-shaped cutter. Place on a greased biscuit tray and bake in a moderate oven, 350°F., for 12 to 15 minutes. Cool.

To make the almond paste mix the ground almonds with the icing sugar, then beat the egg yolk with the sherry and lemon juice and add, making rather a dry dough. Turn onto a board dusted with sifted icing sugar, roll thinly and cut into rounds the same size as the biscuits. Brush the underside of each biscuit with a little thinned and sieved apricot jam, place a round of almond paste over this and cover with another biscuit round. Top each with a thin lemon- or almond-flavoured glacé icing.

ALMOND DATE COOKIES

½ pound dates
2 tablespoons water
1 teaspoon grated orange rind
4 ounces butter
⅓ cup sugar
1 egg yolk
½ teaspoon vanilla essence
1 cup plain flour
a pinch of salt
almonds for topping

Chop the dates and place in a saucepan with the water and grated orange rind. Simmer gently for about 5 minutes or until the dates are soft, stirring well. Beat to a pulp and place in a bowl to cool.

Cream the butter with the sugar, add the egg yolk and the vanilla and beat well. Stir in the sifted flour and salt. Chill for about 1 hour. If you find the mixture a little soft to handle, add a little more flour: it should not require more than 1 extra tablespoonful.

Take pieces of the dough and shape into balls about 1 inch in diameter. Place them 2 inches apart on a greased biscuit tray. Make a deep indentation in the centre of each ball with the thumb. Bake in a slow oven, 300°F., for 25 to 30 minutes. Remove to a wire cooler and, while still warm, fill the centre of each cookie with a little of the cooled date mixture. Top each with a split almond.

ALMOND MACAROONS

a pinch of salt
2 egg whites
¾ cup sugar
½ cup ground almonds

Add the salt to the egg whites and beat until stiff. Gradually add the sugar, continuing to beat. Place the bowl over a saucepan of almost boiling water and beat for 10 minutes. Fold in the ground almonds. Drop teaspoonfuls of the mixture onto a greased biscuit tray and bake in a slow oven, 300°F., for about 45 minutes. Remove from the tray and allow to cool.

Apricot Almond Cookies

APRICOT ALMOND COOKIES

½ cup dried apricots
¼ cup sugar for apricots
4 ounces butter
⅓ cup sugar for cookies
1 egg yolk
¼ teaspoon almond essence
1 cup plain flour
a pinch of salt
halves of blanched almonds for
   topping

Soak the apricots overnight in enough cold water to cover them. Drain, then mash or put through a sieve. Add the ¼ cup of sugar and cook over medium heat until thick, stirring constantly.

For the cookies, cream the butter with ⅓ cup of sugar and add the egg yolk and almond essence, beating well. Stir in the sifted flour and salt, mixing well. Take pieces of the dough and shape into balls about 1 inch in diameter. Place 2 inches apart on a greased biscuit tray. Make a deep indentation with the thumb in the centre of each uncooked ball of dough and bake in a slow oven, 300°F., for 20 to 25 minutes. Remove the cookies to a cake cooler and, while still warm, fill the centres with cooled apricot. Decorate each cookie with half a blanched almond.

BISCUIT BON-BONS

For the pastry

4 ounces butter
¾ cup icing sugar
1 teaspoon vanilla essence
1½ cups plain flour
a pinch of salt

For the icing

1 pound icing sugar
4 tablespoons water
1 teaspoon vanilla essence
colouring

For the filling

use either whole candied cherries,
   chopped dates mixed with
   chopped nuts, chopped candied peel and raisins, or
   chopped mixed fruit with
   chopped nuts, and flavour
   with brandy or liqueur

For the topping

cherries, cachous or nuts

Cream the butter with the sifted icing sugar and vanilla. Sift the flour with the salt and work it into the creamed mixture. Turn onto a lightly floured board and knead until smooth on the outside. Divide the dough into portions of about 1 dessert-spoonful each, and wrap each round 1 level teaspoon of filling.

Place the filled biscuits on a greased biscuit tray, leaving a little room for them to spread. Bake in a moderate oven, 350°F., for about 15 minutes or until the biscuits are set and golden in colour.

While still slightly warm dip in icing made by mixing the sifted icing sugar with the water and vanilla and colouring as desired. Decorate the top of each with a piece of cherry, a cachou or a piece of nut.

BROWN SUGAR SHORTBREAD COOKIES

8 ounces soft butter
½ cup (firmly packed) light
   brown sugar
2½ cups sifted plain flour

Beat the butter and sugar in a large bowl until light and fluffy. Blend in the sifted flour until smooth and well combined. The dough will be firm. Chill for several hours.

Divide the chilled dough in half. Working one piece at a

time, roll to about ⅓ inch thick and cut into rounds with a 1½-inch diameter cutter. Place about 1 inch apart on ungreased shallow oven trays and bake at 300°F. for about 20 minutes or until a light golden colour. Lift onto a wire cooler immediately.

BURNT BUTTER BISCUITS

4 ounces butter
½ cup sugar
1 egg yolk
½ teaspoon vanilla essence
1 cup plain flour
1 level teaspoon baking powder
a pinch of salt
halved blanched almonds for
    topping

Place the butter in a saucepan and melt over medium heat. Continue cooking until it turns a light brown colour. Allow to cool.

Add the sugar and beat until light and fluffy. Add the egg yolk, beat again, then add the vanilla.

Sift the flour with the baking powder and salt and stir into the mixture, mixing well. Take spoonfuls of the dough and roll into small balls in the palms of the hands.

Space them evenly on a greased biscuit tray. Top each biscuit with a halved blanched almond. Bake in a moderate oven, 375°F., for 10 to 15 minutes. Cool on the tray.

BUTTERSCOTCH BISCUITS

6 ounces butter
1 cup (firmly packed) brown
    sugar
2 eggs
1 teaspoon vanilla essence
1 tablespoon vinegar
1 cup unsweetened canned milk
2½ cups plain flour
1 level teaspoon bicarbonate of
    soda
½ level teaspoon baking powder
½ level teaspoon salt
1 cup chopped walnuts

For the frosting

4 ounces butter or margarine
1 pound sifted icing sugar
¼ cup boiling water

Cream the 6 ounces of butter with the brown sugar until light and fluffy. Add the beaten eggs and mix well. Flavour with vanilla and stir in the vinegar and milk.

Sift the flour, soda, baking powder and salt and add to the creamed mixture. Mix well and add the nuts.

Drop by rounded dessertspoons onto a greased shallow oven tray, leaving a little room for the biscuits to spread. Bake in a moderate oven, 350°F., for about 15 minutes or until browned and firm to the touch. Cool.

For the frosting, place the butter or margarine in a small saucepan and cook over medium heat until it turns a golden colour. Gradually add the sifted icing sugar and enough boiling water to make a good consistency: the frosting should hold its shape. Spread a little on the top of each biscuit and, if liked, decorate with a piece of walnut.

4 ounces soft butter
¾ cup sugar
1 egg
1 dessertspoon milk
1 teaspoon vanilla essence
1¼ cups plain flour
¼ teaspoon baking powder
¼ teaspoon salt
1 ounce semi-sweet chocolate,
    melted

CARNIVAL COOKIES

Cream the butter with the sugar until light, then beat in the egg. Add the milk and vanilla. Sift the flour with the baking powder and salt and stir into the mixture, making a firm dough. Divide the dough in two and add the melted chocolate to one portion. Knead each mixture separately, make into rolls and chill until required. From this mixture make the following:

Burnt Butter Biscuits
Dutch Butter Biscuits

HALF AND HALFS

Make one portion of plain dough and one of chocolate dough into rolls about 1 inch in diameter. Wrap separately and chill. Now cut lengthwise through the centre of each roll. Brush the cut surface with a little hot milk and press one white and one chocolate piece together. Wrap and re-chill. Cut into slices and bake on a greased biscuit tray in a moderate oven, 350°F., for about 12 minutes.

RIBBONS

Roll both the chocolate and the plain mixture into rectangles measuring 7 inches by 8 inches. Cut each in half. Brush with hot milk and stack in layers, alternating the chocolate with the white. Wrap and chill, cut into strips and bake as for Half and Halfs.

BULL'S EYES

Make the chocolate dough into a roll 1 inch in diameter and about 6 inches long. Roll the plain dough into a rectangle measuring 6 inches by 4 inches and about $\frac{1}{2}$ inch thick. Brush the plain dough with hot milk, then roll it round the chocolate roll. Wrap and chill, then cut into slices and bake in a moderate oven.

PINWHEELS

Roll the chocolate dough into a rectangle of 5 inches by 6 inches. Roll the plain dough into a rectangle measuring $5\frac{1}{2}$

46

Carnival Cookies

inches by 6 inches. Brush with hot milk and place the chocolate on top of the plain dough. Roll up as for a jelly roll, commencing where you have the extra half inch of dough. Wrap and chill, then slice before baking.

WAGGON WHEELS

Join the two layers as for the Half and Half cookies, but this time slice through again and join again alternating the plain with the chocolate pieces. Wrap and chill, then slice before baking.

CHERRY COCONUT COOKIES

4 ounces butter
1½ tablespoons icing sugar
¼ teaspoon vanilla essence
½ an egg or 1 egg yolk
1 cup plain flour
a pinch of salt
2 tablespoons coconut
1 ounce chopped cherries

Beat the butter and icing sugar to a soft cream and add the vanilla, then the half egg or the egg yolk. Sift the flour and the salt and stir into the creamed mixture, then add the coconut and cherries.

Turn onto a lightly floured board and knead slightly to make smooth on the outside. Mould into one long roll about 1½ inches in diameter. Wrap in greaseproof paper and place in the refrigerator to chill.

Cut into ¼-inch slices and place on a greased biscuit tray and bake for 12 to 15 minutes in a moderate oven, 350°F.

The uncooked dough for these cookies may be left in the refrigerator for several weeks.

47

CHOCMALLOWS

For the chocolate portion
3 ounces butter
3 ounces castor sugar
2 eggs
2 teaspoons cinnamon
1 tablespoon cocoa
1½ cups self-raising flour
a pinch of salt
2 tablespoons milk

For the chocolate icing
3 dessertspoons cocoa
3 cups icing sugar
½ teaspoon vanilla essence
3 teaspoons melted butter
a pinch of cream of tartar
4 tablespoons milk
apricot jam

For the mallow portion
1 cup sugar
1 cup water
2 dessertspoons gelatine
¼ level teaspoon cream of tartar
2 dessertspoons lemon juice
1 dessertspoon rose-water
coconut

To make the chocolate portion, cream the butter with the sugar until light and fluffy, add the unbeaten eggs one at a time, beating well, then fold in the sifted dry ingredients alternately with the milk. Spoon into greased gem irons and bake at 400°F. for 15 minutes. Turn out, cool, then level the tops (if necessary) and coat the rounded side with icing.

To make the icing, sift the cocoa and icing sugar and add the vanilla, melted butter and cream of tartar. Mix to a smooth, thick cream with the milk. Warm until thin enough to coat the cakes. When set, brush the uniced side with apricot jam and press lightly into the mallow portion.

To make the mallow, place the sugar, water, gelatine and cream of tartar in a saucepan. Stir until boiling, then boil steadily for 10 minutes. Cool, add the lemon juice and rose-water and beat until light, fluffy and white. Spoon into gem irons which have been greased and lightly dusted with icing sugar. Allow to set. Unmould and toss in coconut (keeping the flat side uncoated) before joining to the chocolate cakes.

6 ounces butter
¼ cup sugar
1 egg
⅓ cup ground almonds
¼ teaspoon almond essence
10 ounces plain flour

For the icing

4 ounces dark chocolate
slivered almonds

For the filling

1 level dessertspoon gelatine
2 tablespoons cold water
½ cup cream
¼ teaspoon vanilla essence
1½ teaspoons cocoa
1 egg white
3 level dessertspoons sugar

CHOCOLATE ALMOND CREAMS

Beat the butter and sugar to a cream. Add the beaten egg, ground almonds and almond essence and then the sifted flour. Turn the dough onto a lightly floured board and knead only until smooth on the outside. Roll thinly and cut into rounds with a 2½-inch cutter. Place on a greased biscuit tray and bake in a moderate oven, 350°F., for about 10 or 12 minutes. Remove from the tray and allow to cool.

Break the chocolate into small pieces and place it in a bowl. Stand the bowl in a saucepan containing hot water and stir until it has melted. Cover half the biscuit rounds with chocolate and sprinkle with the slivered almonds.

Meanwhile, make the filling. Combine the gelatine with the cold water and stir over boiling water until it has dissolved. Cool. Combine the cream with the vanilla, cocoa and cooled gelatine. Beat until the mixture forms peaks that will just hold their shape. In another bowl beat the egg white until stiff and gradually add the sugar. Continue beating until stiff, then fold into the chocolate mixture. Refrigerate until needed.

Just before serving place or pipe a dab of the chocolate cream filling on the plain biscuit and cover with a chocolate-topped biscuit.

CHOCOLATE ALMOND ROYALS

4 ounces butter
¼ cup icing sugar
1 egg yolk
1½ cups plain flour
a pinch of salt
¾ cup ground almonds

Soften the butter but do not allow it to melt. Beat until creamy, then add the icing·sugar and beat again. Add the egg yolk, then the sifted flour and salt and the ground almonds, mixing well. Turn onto a floured board and knead only until smooth on the outside. Roll out ⅛ inch thick and cut into rounds with a 1¼-inch cutter. Place on a greased biscuit tray and bake in a moderate oven, 350°F., for 12 to 15 minutes. Cool.

Join the biscuits in pairs with chocolate almond butter cream (recipe follows), ice the tops with chocolate glacé icing and decorate each biscuit with a split blanched almond.

CHOCOLATE ALMOND BUTTER CREAM

2 ounces butter
¼ cup ground almonds
1 cup sifted icing sugar
1 level tablespoon cocoa

Soften the butter and add the ground almonds, then stir in the icing sugar and cocoa and beat until well blended. A little almond essence may be added to enhance the almond flavour.

CHOCOLATE ALMOND SLICES

2 ounces semi-sweet chocolate
  pieces
1 tablespoon milk
6 ounces butter
½ cup sugar
½ teaspoon vanilla essence
2 level cups plain flour
a pinch of salt
½ cup chopped blanched
  almonds

Melt the chocolate in the milk over hot water. Cool. Cream the butter with the sugar until light and fluffy, then stir in the vanilla and the cooled chocolate mixture.

Sift the flour with the salt and add to the mixture together with the almonds, blending well. Shape into two rolls about 1½ inches in diameter, wrap in waxed or greaseproof paper and chill. When required, cut into ¼-inch slices and bake on a greased biscuit tray in a moderate oven, 350°F., for 12 to 15 minutes.

CHOCOLATE BISCUIT CAKE

½ pound icing sugar
2 level dessertspoons cocoa
1 egg
1 teaspoon vanilla essence
5 ounces Copha or other white
  vegetable shortening
½ pound milk-coffee or other
  sweet plain biscuits

Line a 6-inch square pan with greaseproof paper. Sift the icing sugar and cocoa into a bowl and add the lightly beaten egg and the vanilla.

Melt the Copha over low heat: it should be warm, not hot. Pour it onto the other ingredients and mix until smooth and beginning to thicken.

Arrange alternate layers of chocolate mixture and biscuits in the prepared tin, starting and finishing with chocolate mixture. Leave in a cool place to set. Remove from the tin and slice as required.

COFFEE BISCUIT CAKE

A coffee biscuit cake may be made by varying the above ingredients a little: use 12 ounces icing sugar, omit the cocoa and add 1 tablespoon of coffee essence.

49

CHOCOLATE BUBBLES

6 ounces butter
¾ cup sugar
1 egg
1½ cups plain flour
1 level teaspoon cream of tartar
½ level teaspoon bicarbonate of
 soda
2 dessertspoons cocoa
1 tablespoon coconut
1 cup rice bubbles
vanilla essence

For the icing

4 ounces icing sugar
1 rounded tablespoon cocoa
1 dessertspoon butter
1 tablespoon water

Cream the butter with the sugar, then add the egg, beating well. Sift the flour, cream of tartar, soda and cocoa and add to the creamed mixture. Fold in the coconut, rice bubbles and vanilla. Place spoonfuls on a greased biscuit tray and bake in a moderate oven, 350°F., for about 15 minutes. When cold, ice the tops with chocolate icing and top each biscuit with half a walnut or an almond.

To make the icing, sift the icing sugar and cocoa together, add the softened butter and mix to a thick consistency with about 1 tablespoon of water. Heat gently for about 1 minute, then ice the biscuits.

CHOCOLATE CHIP CHEWS

½ cup sweetened condensed milk
½ level teaspoon baking powder
1½ cups coconut
¾ cup coarsely chopped chocolate (or 1 packet chocolate
 pieces)
¼ cup chopped cherries
¼ cup chopped walnuts

Grease a biscuit tray. Combine all the ingredients in a bowl, mixing well. Take teaspoonfuls of the mixture and drop onto the tray, leaving a little room for spreading. Bake in a slow oven, 300°F., for about 30 minutes or until golden. Transfer from the tray to a wire cooler. Allow to become quite cold before storing in airtight tins.

CHOCOLATE TORTINAS

4 ounces butter
1 egg yolk
1 tablespoon water
1¼ cups sifted plain flour
1 teaspoon baking powder
1 teaspoon sugar
2 cups chocolate pieces
2 eggs
¾ cup sugar
3 tablespoons melted butter
1 teaspoon vanilla essence
2 cups finely chopped nuts

Beat the butter until creamy, then add the egg yolk and the water. Sift the flour with the baking powder and add with the sugar to the creamed mixture. Press into a well-greased 11-inch by 7-inch shallow tray and bake at 350°F. for 10 minutes.

Remove from the oven, quickly sprinkle with the chocolate pieces and return to the oven for 1 minute. Remove again from the oven and spread the chocolate evenly over the slice.

Beat the 2 eggs until thick, then beat in the ¾ cup sugar and stir in the melted butter, the vanilla and the nuts. Spread this over the chocolate layer and replace in a moderate oven. Bake for 25 minutes. Cut into squares.

4 ounces butter
¾ cup sugar
1 teaspoon vanilla essence
1 egg
2 ounces chocolate, melted and
  cooled
2 cups plain flour
2 level teaspoons baking powder
½ level teaspoon salt
1½ level teaspoons cinnamon
1 tablespoon strong black coffee
1 cup finely chopped walnuts

a pinch of salt
1 egg white
¼ cup sugar
¾ cup coconut
½ teaspoon vanilla essence

4 ounces butter
¼ cup icing sugar
1 egg yolk or ½ an egg
1½ cups plain flour
a pinch of salt
3 level tablespoons finely
  chopped walnuts

For the filling
¼ cup cream
2 ounces cream cheese
1 level tablespoon sugar
a pinch of salt
a few drops of vanilla essence
1 dessertspoon each of chopped
  candied pineapple and dates
1 dessertspoon each of chopped
  nuts and cherries
1 teaspoon grated orange rind

For the icing
4 tablespoons icing sugar
lemon juice to blend
walnut halves for topping

CINNAMON CHOCOLATE THINS

Cream the butter with the sugar and vanilla essence, then beat in the egg and continue beating until the mixture is light coloured. Blend in the cooled melted chocolate. Sift the flour, baking powder, salt and cinnamon and add to the mixture alternately with the cold black coffee. Mix in the finely chopped nuts.

Shape into two rolls, each about 1½ inches in diameter. Wrap in waxed paper and refrigerate until required. Using a sharp knife, cut into ¼-inch slices and arrange on lightly greased biscuit trays. Bake in a moderate oven, 350°F., for 12 to 15 minutes. Cool on a wire cooler.

COCONUT MACAROONS

Add the salt to the egg white and beat until stiff. Add the sugar a dessertspoonful at a time, beating well after each addition. The mixture should be thick enough to stand in stiff peaks. Fold in the coconut and flavour with vanilla.

Grease a biscuit tray and place a sheet of greased or wet paper on it. Drop teaspoonfuls of the mixture at evenly spaced intervals, leaving a little room for the meringues to spread. Bake in a slow oven, 300°F., for 30 to 40 minutes.

CONTINENTAL WALNUT CREAMS

Cream the butter with the sifted icing sugar, add the egg yolk and beat until smooth. Sift the flour and salt and add to the mixture together with the walnuts. Turn onto a well-floured board and knead only until smooth on the outside.

Roll out ⅛ inch thick, cut into rounds or ovals and place on a lightly greased biscuit tray. Bake in a moderate oven, 350°F., for about 15 minutes. Cool.

To make the filling, whip the cream until thick, then blend in the remaining ingredients. Join in pairs with filling between. Ice the top with the lemon icing and decorate with half a walnut.

CORNFLAKE CRISPS

2 egg whites
a pinch of salt
½ cup sugar
4 cups cornflakes
¾ cup chopped nuts
¾ cup coconut
2 tablespoons melted butter

Beat the egg whites in a clean dry bowl with the salt until stiff. Stir in the dry ingredients, then add the melted butter, mixing well. Place by dessertspoonfuls on a greased biscuit tray and bake in a moderate oven, 350°F., for 10 to 15 minutes.

CRISPY FILLED COOKIES

For the filling

½ cup raisins, chopped
¼ cup water
1½ tablespoons sugar
1 dessertspoon cornflour
a pinch of salt
1 dessertspoon lemon juice

For the cookies

1¾ cups plain flour
1 level teaspoon baking powder
a pinch of salt
4 ounces butter
3 ounces brown sugar
¼ cup water
1 teaspoon vanilla essence
1 cup crushed cornflakes

Combine all the ingredients for the filling in a saucepan and stir over gentle heat until thick. Turn into a bowl and allow to cool.

To make the cookies first sift the flour, baking powder and salt together. Now beat the butter and brown sugar to a soft cream and add the water and vanilla alternately with the sifted flour. Mix well, then stir in the cornflakes and chill and dough until firm. Knead only until smooth on the outside. Roll out ⅛ inch thick and cut into 2-inch rounds with a fluted cutter. Place half the number of rounds on a greased biscuit tray and place a teaspoonful of the cooled filling on each. Top with rounds of biscuit dough, pressing them lightly on. Bake at 400°F. for about 15 minutes. Cool, then ice with lemon-flavoured glacé icing.

CRUNCHY DATE ROUNDS

4 ounces butter
¼ cup white sugar
¼ cup brown sugar
1 egg
1 teaspoon vanilla essence
1¼ cups plain flour
½ level teaspoon bicarbonate of
   soda
½ level teaspoon salt
½ cup chopped dates
½ cup broken walnuts
1½ cups coarsely crushed cereal
   flakes

Cream the butter with the white and brown sugar until light. Add the beaten egg and vanilla, mixing in well. Sift the dry ingredients and add to the creamed mixture, blending well. Stir in the dates and nuts.

Have the crushed cereal on a piece of paper. Drop the biscuit mixture by teaspoonfuls onto the cereal, toss to cover, then place on a greased biscuit tray. Top each with a walnut half if liked. Bake in a moderate oven, 350°F., for 12 to 15 minutes. Allow to cool on the tray.

DANISH BRANDY CREAMS

1½ cups plain flour
4 ounces butter
¼ cup sugar
1 egg yolk
1 tablespoon cream
1 tablespoon brandy

For the filling

1 egg
1 tablespoon sugar
1 tablespoon cornflour
1 cup milk
¼ pint cream
½ teaspoon vanilla essence
1 dessertspoon brandy

Sift the flour into a bowl, rub in the butter and add the sugar. Blend the egg yolk with the cream and brandy, stir into the flour mixture and mix to a firm dough. Turn onto a lightly floured board, knead only until smooth on the outside, then roll out about ⅛ inch thick.

Cut into rounds with a floured 2-inch cutter and place on a greased biscuit tray. Bake in a moderately hot oven, 400°F., for about 5 minutes. When cold, ice half the biscuit rounds with chocolate glacé icing and top with a blanched almond half or a piece of crystallized cherry. Just before serving, place 2 teaspoons of filling on each plain biscuit round and top with a chocolate-coated biscuit.

To make the filling, combine the egg, sugar and cornflour in a bowl and blend with a little of the cold milk. Heat the remainder of the milk and, when almost boiling, pour onto the blended mixture and stir until smooth. Return the mixture to the saucepan and cook, stirring over medium heat until it boils and thickens. Cool thoroughly. Fold in the whipped cream and flavour with the vanilla and brandy. Chill for 30 minutes before using.

DANISH SUGAR COOKIES

4 ounces butter
¾ cup sifted icing sugar
½ cup ground almonds
1 teaspoon vanilla essence
1½ cups plain flour
a little castor sugar

Cream the butter until soft. Gradually add the sifted icing sugar and beat until creamy. Stir in the ground almonds and the vanilla. Blend in the sifted flour, using the hand if necessary. Shape the dough into a roll about 1½ inches in diameter. Sprinkle a little castor sugar on a piece of waxed paper and use to wrap the dough. Chill until required.

Using a sharp knife, cut the dough into thin slices about ¼ inch thick. Place on a lightly greased biscuit tray and bake in a moderate oven, 375°F., for 8 to 10 minutes.

DATE AND NUT KISSES

3 egg whites
a pinch of salt
1 cup sugar
4 ounces chopped walnuts
8 ounces chopped dates

Place the egg whites in a warm, dry bowl with the salt. Beat until stiff. Gradually beat in the sugar, adding it a dessert-spoonful at a time. The mixture should be thick and glossy. Fold in the chopped nuts and dates.

Drop the mixture from a dessertspoon onto a lightly greased biscuit tray, allowing a little room for the kisses to spread. Bake in a slow oven, 300°F., for about 30 minutes or until they just begin to colour. Reduce the heat to 250°F. and bake for a further 10 minutes.

DATE PINWHEELS

4 ounces butter
½ cup brown sugar
½ cup white sugar
1 egg
½ teaspoon vanilla essence
2 cups plain flour
½ level teaspoon bicarbonate of
soda
½ level teaspoon salt

For the filling

1 pound dates
½ cup sugar
½ cup water or orange juice
½ cup finely chopped walnuts

Cream the butter with the brown and white sugar until fluffy. Beat in the egg, then add the vanilla. Sift the flour, soda and salt and stir into the creamed mixture. Chill, then divide the dough in half.

Lightly flour the pastry board and roll one part of the dough into a rectangle ¼ inch thick measuring 12 by 8 inches. Carefully spread half the date filling evenly over the dough. Beginning at the long edge, roll up like a jelly roll. Repeat with the remaining dough and filling. Wrap each roll in waxed paper and refrigerate until needed. Cut into slices ¼ inch thick, using a sharp knife, and place on lightly greased biscuit trays. Bake at 375°F. for about 8 to 10 minutes.

To make the filling place the finely chopped dates in a saucepan with the sugar and water or the orange juice. Cook, stirring well, until the mixture is thick and reasonably smooth. Cool. Just before using, add the finely chopped walnuts.

DATE TRUFFLES

Take about 4 ounces of dates and chop them finely. Soak in either rum or brandy for about 20 minutes, long enough to absorb the flavour. Now beat 2 egg whites until stiff and fold in 2 ounces of ground almonds, ⅓ cup of sugar and the dates.

Have ready one quantity of biscuit pastry (recipe on page 55). Roll the pastry thinly and cut into rounds with a 2½-inch fluted cutter. Place a small spoonful of the filling on each round of pastry, moisten the edges with water and fold the pastry over so as to enclose the filling. Bake in a moderate oven, 350°F., for 12 to 15 minutes. Cool. Dust with icing sugar before serving.

DUTCH BUTTER BISCUITS

8 ounces butter
¾ cup sugar
1 egg yolk
2½ cups plain flour
1 rounded teaspoon mixed spice
1 rounded teaspoon grated
chocolate
a pinch of salt
1 egg white
1 tablespoon chopped almonds
1 tablespoon sugar

Cream the butter with the ¾ cup of sugar and beat in the egg yolk. Sift the flour with the spice and add to the creamed mixture, then stir in the grated chocolate. Press into a well-greased 11-inch by 7-inch shallow tray to about ⅓ inch thick.

Add a pinch of salt to the egg white and beat until stiff. Spread this on the uncooked slice and sprinkle with a mixture of chopped almonds and sugar. Bake in a moderate oven, 350°F., for 25 to 30 minutes. Cut into finger lengths while hot and leave in the tin to cool.

DUTCH CHEESE COOKIES

4 ounces cream cheese
4 ounces butter
½ cup sugar
¼ teaspoon almond essence
1½ cups plain flour
1 level teaspoon baking powder
a pinch of salt
1½ cups cornflakes
glacé cherries

Beat the cream cheese with the butter, sugar and almond essence until fluffy. Sift the flour, baking powder and salt and add to the creamed mixture, mixing thoroughly. Cover and refrigerate the dough until required.

Coarsely crush the cornflakes and cut the whole glacé cherries into quarters. Shape the dough into small balls and roll them in crushed cornflakes. Place on ungreased biscuit trays, flatten slightly, and top each cookie with a piece of cherry. Bake at 350°F. for about 20 minutes. Remove from the trays and allow to cool on a wire cooler.

FLORENTINA BISCUITS

3 ounces peel
4 ounces almonds
3 ounces sugar
1 ounce plain flour
¼ pint cream
4 ounces dark chocolate for
   coating

Chop the peel and the almonds and combine with the sugar. Stir in the plain flour, then the cream. Place in teaspoonfuls on a greased biscuit tray, leaving room for spreading. Bake in a slow oven, 300°F., for about 25 minutes. Remove from the tray and allow to cool.

Break up the chocolate and melt it over hot, not boiling water. Spoon a little onto each biscuit, then spread roughly over the surface. Leave until the chocolate has set.

FORCER BISCUITS

7 ounces butter or margarine
3 rounded tablespoons icing
   sugar
1 egg yolk
½ teaspoon vanilla essence
2½ cups plain flour

Cream the butter with the sifted icing sugar until light and fluffy. Add the egg yolk and the vanilla, then stir in the sifted flour, blending well. Place in a biscuit forcer and pipe into shapes on a greased biscuit tray. Bake in a moderate oven, 350°F., for about 12 minutes. Remove from the tray and allow to cool. Join in pairs with butter icing.

FOUNDATION BISCUIT MIXTURE

4 ounces butter or margarine
¼ cup castor sugar
2 egg yolks
½ teaspoon vanilla essence
2 cups plain flour
½ level teaspoon baking powder
a pinch of salt

Cream the butter with the sugar until light and fluffy. Add the egg yolks and the vanilla and beat well. Sift the flour with the baking powder and salt and add to the creamed mixture, making a firm dough. Turn onto a lightly floured board and knead only until smooth on the outside. Roll out ⅛ inch thick, cut into the desired shapes and bake on a greased biscuit tray in a moderate oven, 350°F., for about 10 minutes.

FRUIT AND NUT CRISPS

6 ounces butter
1 cup brown sugar
1 egg
1 teaspoon vanilla essence
2½ cups plain flour
¼ level teaspoon baking powder
½ level teaspoon bicarbonate of
   soda
a pinch of salt
¾ cup rolled oats
½ cup chopped nuts
½ cup sultanas
1 cup cornflakes

Cream the butter with the sugar until light and fluffy. Add the egg and beat well. Flavour with the vanilla. Sift the flour with the baking powder, soda and salt and stir into the mixture, blending thoroughly. Stir in the rolled oats, chopped nuts and sultanas, then the cornflakes. Drop in teaspoonfuls onto a greased biscuit tray and bake in a moderate oven, 350°F., for about 15 minutes. Remove from the tray to cool.

GINGERBREAD MEN

3 ounces butter or margarine
½ cup brown sugar
1 egg
1 tablespoon golden syrup
¼ teaspoon soda dissolved in 1
   teaspoon milk
2 cups plain flour
½ teaspoon ground ginger
½ teaspoon cinnamon
a little royal icing
crystallized cherries, or currants
orange peel

Cream the butter with the sugar, then add beaten egg and the golden syrup. Add soda and milk. Sift the flour and spices and stir into the mixture, making rather a dry dough. Turn onto a lightly floured board and knead only until smooth on the outside.

Roll the dough thinly and cut out with a special gingerbread-man cutter. Place on a greased biscuit tray and bake in a moderate oven, 350°F., for about 15 minutes. Cool.

Using small dabs of royal icing, attach cherries or currants to represent eyes on each gingerbread man, also for buttons down his front, and a piece of orange peel for his mouth. Outline his collar, cuffs, hair-line and belt with royal icing, pressing it through a fine icing tube or a paper cone.

HAZELNUT CRESCENTS

½ pound softened butter,
   preferably unsalted
1 cup castor sugar
1 cup ground hazelnuts
2 cups plain flour
¼ teaspoon salt
2 teaspoons vanilla essence
icing sugar

Cream the butter with the sugar, then add the hazelnuts. Sift the flour with the salt and add to the mixture with the vanilla. Work the dough with the hands until it will hold together (the consistency will depend on the softness of the butter). If too firm add about a dessertspoon of iced water.

Take teaspoonfuls of the mixture and shape in the hands into crescents. Place on a greased biscuit tray and bake in a slow oven, 300°F., for about 20 minutes or until cooked and only faintly coloured on the outside.

Remove from the oven and dust heavily with sifted icing sugar. Set aside to cool thoroughly before storing in airtight tins.

Though best made with unsalted butter, these biscuits may be made with salted butter.

LEMON BUTTER DAISIES

8 ounces butter
½ cup sugar
2 egg yolks
1 slightly rounded teaspoon
  grated lemon rind
2½ cups plain flour
½ level teaspoon baking powder
a pinch of salt
1 dessertspoon lemon juice

For the decoration

1 egg white
coloured sugar
split blanched almonds

Cream the butter and gradually add the sugar. Beat until light and fluffy, then add the slightly beaten egg yolks and the lemon rind. Stir in the flour which has been sifted with the baking powder and salt. Add the lemon juice, mixing well. Chill for several hours.

Turn out and knead lightly, then roll out ⅛ thick thick. Cut into rounds with a scalloped-edge cutter about 2½ inches in diameter. Place on a greased biscuit tray and bake in a moderate oven, 350°F., for 10 to 15 minutes.

To decorate, brush each cookie with egg white and sprinkle with coloured sugar. Decorate with split almond halves to represent daisy petals.

MERINGUES

2 egg whites
¼ level teaspoon cream of tartar
a pinch of salt
4 slightly rounded tablespoons
  sugar
¼ teaspoon vanilla essence
cream

Place the egg whites in a clean, dry, preferably warm bowl, add the cream of tartar and salt and beat until stiff. Gradually add the sugar (about a dessertspoonful at a time) and continue beating until thick and glossy. Flavour with vanilla. Place in spoonfuls on a greased biscuit tray (or pipe through a cream tube) and bake in a slow oven, 300°F., for about 1 hour.

Before serving join together with whipped and flavoured cream. If liked a little chocolate may be melted and spooned on top of each double meringue.

MINCEMEAT COOKIES

6 ounces butter
1 cup sugar
¼ teaspoon vanilla essence
1 teaspoon grated lemon rind
1 egg
2½ cups plain flour
¼ level teaspoon salt
¼ level teaspoon bicarbonate of
  soda
1 teaspoon cinnamon
½ cup prepared fruit mince
½ cup chopped nuts

Cream the butter with the sugar, then add the vanilla and the grated lemon rind.

Beat the egg and add it to the creamed mixture, blending in well. Add the sifted dry ingredients alternately with the fruit mince, then stir in the nuts. Shape into rolls about 1½ inches in diameter, wrap in greased paper and chill until firm or until required. Cut into slices ¼-inch thick and place on a greased biscuit tray. Bake in a moderate oven, 350°F., for about 15 minutes.

ORANGE BATONS

4 ounces butter
1 cup sugar
1 egg
grated rind of 1 orange
3 cups plain flour
1½ level teaspoons baking
    powder
a pinch of salt
⅓ cup orange juice
2 ounces dark chocolate

For the orange cream

1 ounce butter
3 rounded tablespoons icing
    sugar
grated rind of 1 orange
orange juice

Cream the butter with the sugar until light and fluffy. Beat the egg and add it to the creamed mixture with the grated orange rind. Beat well, then stir in the combined sifted flour, baking powder and salt alternately with the orange juice. Mix well and chill for several hours.

Put the dough into a biscuit forcer and press out on a greased biscuit tray in strips about 3 inches long and 1 inch wide. Bake in a moderate oven, 350°F., for 10 to 12 minutes. Cool. Join the batons in pairs with orange-flavoured butter cream made by beating the 1 ounce of butter to a cream and gradually adding the icing sugar, grated orange rind and enough orange juice to make a good consistency.

Melt the chocolate over hot water. Dip one end of each baton in it and place on greaseproof paper until the chocolate sets.

ORANGE COCONUT DROPS

4 ounces butter or margarine
½ cup sugar
1 teaspoon grated orange rind
2 eggs
1 cup self-raising flour
1 cup cornflour
a pinch of salt
4 ounces coconut

Beat the butter and sugar to a soft cream and add the grated orange rind. Beat the eggs and gradually add to the creamed mixture.

Sift the flour with the cornflour and salt and stir into the mixture together with the coconut. Place in teaspoonfuls on a greased biscuit tray and bake in a moderate oven, 350°F., for 12 to 15 minutes. Cool slightly before removing from the tray.

ORANGE DROP COOKIES

4 ounces butter
¾ cup sugar
1 teaspoon grated orange rind
½ teaspoon vanilla essence
1 egg
2 cups sifted plain flour
¼ teaspoon salt
½ level teaspoon bicarbonate of
    soda
½ cup orange juice
½ cup chopped nuts
½ cup chopped dates

For icing and decoration

fruit-flavoured glacé icing
crystallized cherries, or nuts

Cream the butter with the sugar, then add the grated orange rind and vanilla. Add the egg, beating well. Sift the flour with the salt and soda and add to the mixture alternately with the orange juice. Fold in the nuts and dates and blend thoroughly. Drop in teaspoonfuls on a greased biscuit tray, leaving a little room for spreading. Bake in a hot oven, 400°F., for 10 to 12 minutes.

When the cookies are cold, top each one with a dab of fruit-flavoured glacé icing and a piece of cherry or nut.

Party Sandwich Loaf
Sweet and Sour Beefballs, Chicken Tetrazzini,
Apricot Gateau, Chocolate Charlotte Russe,
Apple Parfaits, Asparagus and Egg Salad, Cocktail Spirals

ORANGE RAISIN SHORTBREAD

4 tablespoons orange juice
4 ounces seeded raisins
1½ cups plain flour
4 ounces butter
¼ cup castor sugar

Place the orange juice and raisins in a small saucepan and bring slowly to the boil. Turn into a bowl and allow to cool, preferably overnight.

Sift the flour into a bowl and rub in the butter. Add the sugar and form into a dough (if the butter is soft there should not be any necessity to use water). Knead it lightly on a board and divide in half.

Roll both pieces of dough into equal-sized rounds. Place one round on a well-greased biscuit tray, spread with the raisins, then top with the remaining shortbread dough. Press the edges down firmly and pinch a frill round the edge. Prick the surface with a fork. Bake at 325°F. for about 45 minutes. Mark into wedges, and when cool remove from the tray. Dust with sifted icing sugar before serving.

PEANUT BISCUITS

4 ounces butter
½ cup sugar
1 egg
½ teaspoon vanilla essence
3 ounces shelled peanuts
2 rounded teaspoons cocoa
1¾ cups self-raising flour
a pinch of salt

Cream the butter with the sugar until light and fluffy. Add the egg and vanilla and beat well. Stir in the peanuts. Sift the cocoa with the flour and salt and add to the creamed mixture, mixing well. Place in teaspoonfuls on a greased biscuit tray, allowing a little room for each to spread. Bake in a moderate oven, 350°F., for about 20 minutes. Remove to a wire cooler and cool thoroughly before storing in an airtight tin.

POLKA DOT COOKIES

2 ounces butter or margarine
1 rounded dessertspoon brown sugar
1 rounded dessertspoon white sugar
½ teaspoon vanilla essence
1 egg
½ cup self-raising flour
a pinch of salt
2 level tablespoons chopped walnuts
4 ounces chopped dark chocolate or chocolate pieces

Combine the butter in a bowl with the brown and white sugar. Beat until creamy, then stir in the vanilla and the beaten egg.

Sift the flour with the salt and stir into the creamed mixture. Add the nuts and chocolate. Place in teaspoonfuls on a greased biscuit tray and bake in a moderate oven, 350°F., for 10 to 12 minutes. Allow the cookies to cool on the tray.

Spritz Biscuits and assorted iced biscuits

RASPBERRY CRUNCHIES

3 ounces butter
$\frac{1}{4}$ cup sugar
$\frac{1}{2}$ teaspoon vanilla essence
2 egg yolks
1 cup plain flour
$\frac{1}{2}$ cup self-raising flour
a pinch of salt

For the filling

2 egg whites
$\frac{3}{4}$ cup sugar
$1\frac{1}{2}$ cups coconut
$\frac{1}{4}$ teaspoon almond essence
raspberry jam

Beat the butter with the sugar until creamy. Flavour with the vanilla and beat in the egg yolks. Sift the flours and the salt and stir into the mixture, making a medium dough. Knead lightly on a floured board and roll thinly. Cut into rounds with a fluted cutter and use to line greased patty tins. Place a small spoonful of raspberry jam in the centre of each.

To make the filling beat the egg whites until stiff and gradually add the sugar, beating well after each addition, then fold in the coconut and flavour with the almond essence. Place a teaspoonful in each pastry case. Bake at 350°F. for 15 to 20 minutes.

SHORTBREAD ALMOND DROPS

$\frac{3}{4}$ cup butter
$\frac{3}{4}$ cup icing sugar
$1\frac{1}{4}$ cups sifted self-raising flour
1 cup ground rice
1 teaspoon vanilla essence
blanched almonds for topping

Cream the butter until soft, then add the sifted icing sugar and beat until fluffy. Add the sifted self-raising flour and the ground rice. Flavour with the vanilla.

Take spoonfuls of the dough and roll into small balls in the palms of the hands. Place on a greased biscuit tray and press down with the back of a fork. Top each with a blanched almond. Bake in a moderate oven, 350°F., for about 15 minutes. Cool.

SHORTBREAD FINGERS

7 ounces butter
3 rounded tablespoons castor sugar
$\frac{1}{2}$ teaspoon vanilla essence
$2\frac{1}{4}$ cups plain flour
$\frac{1}{2}$ cup rice flour

Beat the butter to a cream, add the sugar and beat again. Flavour with the vanilla. Sift the plain and the rice flour together and stir into the mixture.

Turn onto a lightly floured board and knead only until smooth on the outside. Roll out about $\frac{1}{8}$ inch thick and cut into finger lengths about $\frac{3}{4}$ inch wide. Pinch the ends of each finger and prick the surface with a fork. Place on a shallow biscuit tray and bake in a moderate oven, 325°F., for about 20 to 30 minutes. Cool on the tray.

SNITTENS

6 ounces butter
$\frac{1}{2}$ cup brown sugar
$\frac{1}{2}$ cup white sugar
1 egg and 1 egg yolk
2 cups plain flour
$\frac{1}{2}$ teaspoon salt
$\frac{1}{2}$ teaspoon cinnamon
$\frac{1}{2}$ teaspoon bicarbonate of soda
$\frac{1}{4}$ pound dates
$\frac{1}{4}$ pound preserved or dried figs
$\frac{1}{2}$ cup chopped walnuts

Cream the butter with the white and brown sugar until light and soft. Add the egg and egg yolk and beat again. Sift the flour with the salt, cinnamon and soda and stir into the mixture. Add chopped dates, figs and walnuts.

Blend all ingredients thoroughly, then form into a roll about 1 inch in diameter and wrap in waxed paper. Chill for 1 hour or until required for use.

Cut the chilled roll into slices about $\frac{1}{4}$ inch thick and place them on greased biscuit trays, allowing each a little room for spreading. Bake in a hot oven, 400°F., for 10 to 12 minutes or until lightly browned.

SPICED CHERRY BELLS

4 ounces butter
3 ounces brown sugar
1 tablespoon golden syrup
1 small egg
1½ cups plain flour
¼ level teaspoon bicarbonate of
    soda
a pinch of salt
½ teaspoon ground ginger
½ teaspoon instant coffee

For the filling

2 tablespoons brown sugar
1 dessertspoon butter
¾ cup chopped walnuts
2 dessertspoons sherry or fruit
    juice
glacé cherries

Cream the butter with the brown sugar. Add the golden syrup then the unbeaten egg, blending thoroughly. Add the sifted dry ingredients. Mix well and turn onto a lightly floured board. Knead lightly. Chill for about 30 minutes.

Roll out ⅛ inch thick and cut into rounds with a 2-inch cutter. Place on a greased biscuit tray. Put about ½ teaspoon of filling on each biscuit and shape into bells by folding the sides of the dough to meet over the filling. Place a piece of glacé cherry at the open end of each bell to represent the clapper.

Bake in a moderate oven, 350°F., for 12 to 15 minutes.

To make the filling, combine all the ingredients in the order given.

SPRINGERLES

4 eggs
1 pound icing sugar
a few drops of almond essence
grated rind of 1½ lemons
4½ cups sifted self-raising flour
1 teaspoon baking powder
a pinch of salt

Beat the eggs until light. Add the sugar gradually. Flavour with the almond essence and grated lemon rind. Beat with a wooden spoon until thoroughly blended. Measure the flour, baking powder and salt into a sifter and sift it over the mixture, adding a quarter at a time and blending well after each addition. The dough will be very stiff.

Cover and chill the mixture for 3 or 4 hours. Roll out a small amount at a time ¼ inch thick. Cut into squares, cover and allow to stand overnight to dry the tops. Bake on a greased biscuit tray in a moderate oven, 350 F., for about 20 minutes. Cool before serving. These biscuits will keep for 3 to 4 weeks.

SPRITZ BISCUITS

4 ounces butter
¼ cup fine sugar
1 egg yolk
1 tablespoon lemon juice
1½ cups plain flour
1 tablespoon ground almonds
candied cherries

Beat the butter and sugar to a soft cream, then beat in the egg yolk and the lemon juice. Fold in the sifted flour and the ground almonds. The mixture should be soft enough to force through a biscuit forcer or a cream rose tube.

Make small swirls on a lightly greased biscuit tray, allowing a little room for the biscuits to spread. Top each with a small piece of cherry. Bake in a moderate oven, 350°F., for 8 to 10 minutes.

SULTANA OATMEAL WAFERS

8 ounces butter
1 cup sugar
1 teaspoon vanilla essence
2 eggs
1¾ cups plain flour
1 level teaspoon baking powder
1 level teaspoon cinnamon
¾ level teaspoon bicarbonate of
   soda
½ level teaspoon salt
2 cups quick cooking oats
8 ounces sultanas
1 cup finely chopped walnuts

Cream the butter with the sugar and vanilla until fluffy. Beat in the eggs one at a time. Sift the flour, baking powder, cinnamon, soda and salt, blend into the creamed mixture, then stir in the oats, sultanas and finely chopped walnuts, mixing thoroughly.

Divide the mixture into three equal parts and form each portion into a roll about 1½ inches in diameter. Wrap separately in waxed paper and refrigerate until needed.

Using a sharp knife cut into slices about ¼ inch thick. Bake on ungreased biscuit trays in a moderate oven, 350°F., for about 10 to 12 minutes or until lightly browned.

SWISS BISCUITS

4 ounces butter
4 ounces icing sugar
2 egg yolks
1 teaspoon finely grated lemon
   or orange rind
3 dessertspoons sherry
2 cups plain flour
1 level teaspoon baking powder
cherries for topping

Beat the butter to a soft cream and gradually add the sifted icing sugar. Beat until well mixed, then add the egg yolks, grated fruit rind and sherry. Sift the flour with the baking powder and stir into the mixture.

Force through a biscuit forcer onto a greased biscuit tray and top each with a piece of cherry. Bake in a moderate oven, 350°F., for 15 minutes or until the biscuits are a light fawn colour.

VIENNESE SHORTBREADS

4 ounces butter
¾ cup sugar
2 eggs
¾ cup plain flour

For the topping

2 ounces butter
¼ cup sugar
2 tablespoons cream (or canned
   milk)
1 tablespoon chopped almonds
1 tablespoon plain flour
2 tablespoons slivered almonds

Beat the 4 ounces of butter and ¾ cup of sugar to a soft cream. Add the eggs one at a time, beating well after each addition. Fold in the sifted plain flour. Place in a well-greased 8-inch shallow pan. Bake in a moderate oven, 350°F., for about 25 minutes.

While the shortcake is cooking, make the topping: combine the butter and sugar in a saucepan with the cream and 1 table-spoon of chopped almonds. Cook over medium heat until warm and creamy, stirring well. Blend in the flour and simmer for about half a minute. Remove from the heat.

As soon as the shortcake has been removed from the oven, spread the nut mixture on top. Sprinkle with the slivered almonds, then bake for a further 20 minutes. Cool slightly before removing from the tin.

VIENNESE STARS

4 ounces butter
½ cup sugar
1 egg
¼ teaspoon vanilla essence
¼ teaspoon almond essence
2 cups plain flour
¼ level teaspoon bicarbonate of
    soda
½ level teaspoon cream of tartar
2 rounded tablespoons cornflour
a pinch of salt
jam
sifted icing sugar for topping

Cream the butter well with the sugar, then add beaten egg. Flavour with the vanilla and almond essences. Sift the flour with the soda, cream of tartar, cornflour and salt, and stir into the creamed mixture, making a firm dough.

Turn onto a lightly floured board, knead only until smooth on the outside, then divide in half. Roll one piece of dough thinly and cut into rounds with a 2-inch fluted cutter. Place on a greased biscuit tray and brush the tops lightly with water.

Roll the remainder of the dough thinly and cut into rounds with the same cutter. Using a small star-shaped cutter, cut the centre from each of these rounds. Place a circle on each of the rounds on the baking tray. Fill the centres with a little jam.

Bake in a moderate oven, 350°F., for 15 to 20 minutes. Cool on the tray and dust with sifted icing sugar before serving.

WALNUT BRANDY CRISPS

2 dessertspoons brandy
1 cup finely chopped walnuts
5 ounces butter
3 ounces sugar
3 dessertspoons golden syrup
1¼ cups plain flour
a pinch of salt
½ level teaspoon bicarbonate of
    soda dissolved in 3 dessert-
    spoons milk

Pour the brandy over the nuts and let them soak. Meanwhile, cream the butter with the sugar, then add the golden syrup. Now add the nuts and brandy.

Sift the flour and salt and stir into the creamed mixture, then stir in the soda and milk.

Place in teaspoonfuls on a greased biscuit tray and bake in a slow oven, 300°F., for 25 minutes.

WALNUT FROSTIES

4 ounces butter
1 cup white sugar
2 eggs
½ teaspoon vanilla essence
1½ cups plain flour
1 level teaspoon baking powder
½ level teaspoon salt

For the topping

1 egg white
1 cup light brown sugar
½ teaspoon vanilla essence
¾ cup finely chopped walnuts

Cream the butter with the sugar and add beaten eggs. Flavour with the vanilla. Sift the flour with the baking powder and salt and add to the mixture, blending thoroughly.

Drop in teaspoonfuls onto a greased biscuit tray and, using a knife, spread each spoonful into a round (this is easier if the knife is first dipped into hot water). The biscuit should be about ¼ inch thick.

For the topping beat the egg white until stiff, gradually beat in the brown sugar, and flavour with the vanilla. Smooth a little on each cookie and sprinkle with nuts. Bake in a moderate oven, 350°F., for about 7 minutes. Cool slightly before removing from the tray.

YO-YOS

6 ounces butter or margarine
3 ounces icing sugar
6 ounces plain flour
2 ounces custard powder
½ teaspoon vanilla essence

For the filling

1 cup icing sugar
1½ level tablespoons cocoa
1 tablespoon boiling water
1 rounded teaspoon butter
½ teaspoon vanilla essence

Cream the butter with the icing sugar. Sift the plain flour with the custard powder. Work the flour into the creamed butter and flavour with vanilla.

Take spoonfuls of the mixture and roll into balls in the hands. Place on a greased biscuit tray and press each biscuit lightly with the back of a fork. Bake in a moderate oven, 350°F., for about 20 minutes, but do not allow the biscuits to brown. When cold, join together in pairs with the chocolate filling.

To make the filling sift the icing sugar and cocoa into a bowl and add the boiling water and the butter. Beat until smooth, then flavour with the vanilla.

Biscuit Slices

APRICOT BARS

⅔ cup dried apricots
1½ cups cold water
1 cup plain flour
3 ounces butter
¼ cup white sugar
2 eggs
1 cup light brown sugar
⅓ cup plain flour
½ level teaspoon baking powder
¼ teaspoon salt
1 teaspoon vanilla essence
½ cup chopped walnuts
icing sugar

Place the apricots in a saucepan and add the cold water. Bring slowly to the boil, then cook for 10 minutes. Drain and cool. Chop finely.

Sift the cup of flour into a bowl and rub in the butter. Stir in the white sugar, then press into the bottom of a well-greased 8-inch-square tin. Bake in a moderate oven, 350°F., for 25 minutes.

Beat the eggs with the brown sugar until light and creamy. Sift the ⅓ cup flour with the baking powder and salt and add to the creamed mixture, beating until combined. Stir in the vanilla and walnuts and the chopped cooked apricots. Spread this mixture evenly over the baked layer, replace in the moderate oven and bake for a further 30 minutes or until the top is dry.

Cool in the tin. Dust the top with sifted icing sugar and cut into fingers or squares to serve.

BRANDIED FRUIT SLICES

For the filling

3 ounces sultanas
3 ounces currants
3 ounces raisins
1 ounce butter, melted
1 tablespoon sugar
grated rind of ½ lemon
1 teaspoon cinnamon
1 tablespoon brandy

For the pastry

2 cups plain flour
4 ounces butter
1 tablespoon sugar
1 egg yolk
1 tablespoon cold water

For the topping

¼ cup brown sugar
1 tablespoon plain flour
1 tablespoon butter
a few chopped nuts

Prepare the fruit filling the day before you need it if possible. To make it, put the fruits through a mincer and add the melted butter, sugar, grated lemon rind, cinnamon and brandy.

Sift the 2 cups of flour for the pastry and rub in the butter. Add the sugar. Beat the egg yolk with the water and mix into the dry ingredients to make a rather firm dough. Roll out the dough to line a well-greased 11- by 7-inch shallow oven tray. Fill with the fruit mixture.

Combine all the ingredients for the topping in a bowl, then sprinkle them over the fruit filling. Bake at 375°F. for about 25 minutes. Take care not to overbrown the topping. Cut into finger lengths while still warm.

BROWNIE SQUARES

4 ounces semi-sweet chocolate
½ pound butter
3 eggs
1½ cups sugar
1 teaspoon vanilla essence
1½ cups plain flour
¼ teaspoon salt
4 ounces chopped walnuts

Melt the chocolate and butter in a small saucepan. Beat the eggs well and gradually beat in the sugar. When the mixture is thick and creamy, stir in the vanilla and the chocolate mixture, then add the sifted flour and salt and lastly the chopped walnuts. Pour into a well-greased 9-inch square tin and smooth the mixture well into the corners. Bake in a moderate oven, 350°F., for 40 minutes. Do not overbake, since the centre of this mixture should be fudge-like and not hard.

Cool completely before cutting into squares.

BUTTERSCOTCH SLICES

4 ounces butter
½ cup light brown sugar
1 egg
1 dessertspoon golden syrup
1½ cups self-raising flour
a pinch of salt
1 cup sultanas
½ cup chopped walnuts
4 ounces lemon glacé icing

Cream the butter with the sugar until light, then add the egg and the golden syrup and beat well. Stir in the sifted flour and salt and then add the sultanas and walnuts, blending thoroughly.

Spread evenly in a well-greased 11-inch by 7-inch shallow tray and bake in a moderate oven, 350°F., for about 20 minutes. When cold, ice with the lemon-flavoured glacé icing and allow to set. Cut into finger lengths to serve.

BUTTERSCOTCH SQUARES

4 ounces butter
3 rounded tablespoons sugar
1 egg
¾ cup chopped dates
½ teaspoon vanilla essence
1½ cups self-raising flour
a pinch of salt

For the icing

1 cup (firmly packed) brown
  sugar
1 heaped tablespoon butter
¼ cup milk
½ teaspoon vanilla essence

Melt the butter in a saucepan and add the sugar. Stir until the sugar has dissolved. Remove from the heat and transfer the mixture to a bowl. Add the beaten egg, mixing well, then the dates and vanilla.

Sift the flour with the salt and stir into the mixture. Spread evenly in an 11-inch by 7-inch shallow tray which has been lined on the bottom with greased paper. Bake in a moderate oven, 350°F., for about 30 minutes.

To make the icing combine all the ingredients except the vanilla in a saucepan and stir over medium heat until the mixture boils. Boil for 5 minutes without stirring. Remove from the heat, flavour with the vanilla, then beat until the mixture begins to thicken. Spread quickly over the slice. When cold, cut into squares or finger lengths.

The success of this icing depends on the boiling: if it does not thicken when beaten, return the mixture to the saucepan and boil for several more minutes. Beat again. It should have a fudge-like consistency.

CANADIAN COCONUT SLICES

1 cup coconut
1 cup crushed cornflakes
1 cup self-raising flour
½ cup sugar
1 dessertspoon cocoa
4 ounces butter

For the icing

1 cup icing sugar
1 tablespoon cocoa
½ teaspoon vanilla essence
1 tablespoon hot water

Combine the coconut, cornflakes, flour, sugar and cocoa in a bowl. Melt the butter and stir into the dry ingredients, mixing well. Press into a well-greased 11-inch by 7-inch shallow tray and bake in a moderate oven, 350°F., for 20 to 25 minutes. Cool.

To make the icing sift the icing sugar and cocoa into a saucepan and add the vanilla and hot water. Stir until smooth, then place briefly over medium heat. Spread over the cooled slice and allow to set. Cut into finger lengths to serve.

CANADIAN DATE SLICES

1 cup chopped dates
¾ cup water
1 teaspoon bicarbonate of soda
4 ounces butter
¾ cup sugar
2 eggs
1 dessertspoon golden syrup
1¾ cups plain flour
2 teaspoons cocoa
½ cup chopped walnuts

Mix the dates with the water and soda and let stand while you prepare the other ingredients.

Cream the butter with the sugar, then gradually add the well-beaten eggs and the slightly warmed golden syrup. Sift the flour with the cocoa and stir into the mixture. Add the date mixture and the walnuts, blending well.

Spread evenly in a well-greased 9-inch square lamington tin and bake in a moderate oven, 350°F., for 35 to 40 minutes. Cut into slices when cold.

CARAMEL FRUIT FINGERS

4 ounces butter
½ cup brown sugar
1 egg
½ teaspoon vanilla essence
1 cup self-raising flour
a pinch of salt
¾ cup chopped dates
¾ cup chopped nuts
icing sugar

Melt the butter in a saucepan and add the sugar. Stir until the mixture boils. Cool, then add the well-beaten egg and the vanilla.

Sift the flour with the salt and stir into the mixture together with the dates and nuts.

Spread in a well-greased 11-inch by 7-inch shallow tray and bake in a moderate oven, 350°F., for 20 to 30 minutes. Cut into finger lengths while hot and leave in the tin to cool. Dust with sifted icing sugar before serving.

CHERRY MALLOW BARS

For the biscuit base

4 ounces butter
½ cup sugar
½ teaspoon vanilla essence
1 egg yolk
2 tablespoons cold water
2 cups plain flour
1 teaspoon baking powder
a pinch of salt

For the cherry mallow

1 heaped dessertspoon gelatine
¼ cup cold water
½ cup boiling water
1 cup sugar
1 tablespoon glucose
pink colouring
1 teaspoon lemon juice
½ cup chopped maraschino
    cherries

For the topping

4 ounces dark eating chocolate

Cream the butter and sugar for the biscuit base. Add the vanilla, then the egg yolk and the water, blending well. Sift the flour with the baking powder and salt and stir into the mixture, making a firm dough. The consistency will vary according to the firmness of the butter—if it is too soft to handle add an extra tablespoon of plain flour.

Roll the dough out and use it to line the bottom of a well-greased 9-inch by 12-inch shallow tray. Prick the surface with a fork to prevent rising in the centre, and bake in a moderate oven, 350°F., for about 20 minutes. Cool.

To make the cherry mallow, soak the gelatine in the cold water then dissolve it over boiling water. Add the ½ cup of the boiling water to the sugar and glucose, place in a saucepan and stir over medium heat until both the sugar and glucose have dissolved. Add the dissolved gelatine and cool slightly. Add a few drops of pink colouring and the lemon juice and beat until thick. (The mixture should be thick enough to show the trails of the beater.) Add the chopped cherries. Spread over the cooled biscuit base and chill until firm.

Melt the chocolate over hot, not boiling water, and spread over the cherry mallow. Chill until set. Cut into finger lengths to serve, using a hot wet knife.

CHERRY-RIPE SLICES

1 pound malt biscuits
3 ounces white vegetable
    shortening
2 ounces chopped glacé cherries
½ pound coconut
½ teaspoon cochineal
¾ cup evaporated milk
1 tablespoon castor sugar
½ teaspoon almond or vanilla
    essence

Grease an 11-inch by 7-inch shallow baking tray and place a layer of biscuits in the bottom. Melt the shortening and stir into the remaining ingredients, blending thoroughly. Spread over the biscuits. Top with another layer of biscuits, pressing them firmly into the mixture.

Ice with chocolate icing (see chocolate bubble squares, page 70). When set cut into small pieces for serving.

67

Peanut Biscuits
Caramel Fruit Fingers
Cherry Mallow Bars

6 ounces short or biscuit pastry
jam
2 ounces butter
¼ cup sugar
1 egg
1 tablespoon milk
3 ounces stale cake crumbs
¾ cup plain flour
a good pinch of mixed spice
1½ cups mixed fruit

CHESTER SQUARES

Divide the pastry into two pieces, having one slightly larger than the other. Roll the larger piece to line a greased 11-inch by 7-inch shallow tray. Spread the surface of the uncooked pastry with jam.

Cream the butter with the sugar and add the beaten egg and milk. Stir in the cake crumbs and then the sifted flour and spice and the fruit. Spread this mixture over the jam in the partly prepared slice, and when quite smooth spread with a little more jam.

Roll the remainder of the pastry to fit the top of the slice. Brush the edges with water, place the top pastry on and trim the edges. Brush with water or egg white and sprinkle with a little sugar. Bake in a moderate oven, 350°F., for about 25 minutes. Remove from the oven, and while still hot cut into squares. Cool, then sift some icing sugar over the top.

½ cup self-raising flour
1 cup plain flour
a pinch of salt
1 cup chopped dates
½ cup chopped walnuts
1 cup sugar
2 eggs
1 tablespoon milk
½ teaspoon vanilla essence
4 ounces butter, melted.

CHINESE CHEWS

Sift the flours and salt into a bowl and add the dates, walnuts and sugar. Beat the eggs, add the milk and vanilla, and stir in the melted butter. Add this to the flour mixture. Spread in a well-greased 11-inch by 7-inch shallow tray and bake in a moderate oven, 350°F., for 40 minutes. While still hot, cut into finger lengths and leave to cool on the tray.

Choco Cheese Slices

CHOCO CHEESE SLICES

For the biscuit base

1 cup plain flour
¼ teaspoon salt
4 ounces butter
½ teaspoon grated orange rind
3 dessertspoons cold water
¾ cup chocolate pieces

For the topping

1 dessertspoon gelatine
¼ cup cold water
8 ounces cream cheese
¾ cup sugar
¼ cup milk
¼ cup cream
1 teaspoon grated orange rind
1 teaspoon vanilla essence
chocolate pieces for decorating

Sift the flour and salt, rub in the butter and add the orange rind, then mix with the cold water to form a firm dough. Turn onto a lightly floured board, knead only until smooth on the outside and roll to a rectangle measuring 8 inches by 10 inches.

Place this pastry on a greased shallow oven tray and pinch a frill round the edge. Prick the surface with a fork. Bake at 400°F. for 12 to 15 minutes. Sprinkle the ¾ cup chocolate pieces over the top, let stand for a minute or two, then spread evenly over the cooked pastry. Allow to become cold and set.

Soften the gelatine in the cold water and dissolve it over hot water. Mix the cream cheese with the sugar and gradually add the milk and cream. Flavour with the grated orange rind and the vanilla and gradually add the cooled gelatine, beating well. Chill this mixture until it begins to thicken slightly, but is not set. Spread it evenly over the chocolate layer and garnish the top with more chocolate pieces. Cut into finger lengths to serve.

CHOCOLATE BANANA BARS

3 ounces butter
½ cup light brown sugar
1 egg, slightly beaten
1 ripe banana, mashed
1¾ cups plain flour
1½ level teaspoons baking
   powder
a pinch of salt
½ teaspoon vanilla essence
½ cup chopped walnuts
3 ounces chocolate pieces

Cream the butter with the brown sugar until light and fluffy. Add the egg, blending well, then beat in the mashed banana.

Sift the flour with the baking powder and salt and blend into the creamed mixture. Add the vanilla, walnuts and chocolate pieces. Mix well.

Spread in a well-greased 11-inch by 7-inch shallow tray and bake at 350°F. for about 30 minutes. While still warm cut the mixture into bars and allow to cool in the tin.

CHOCOLATE BUBBLE SQUARES

1 cup coconut
1 cup rice bubbles
1 cup icing sugar
1 cup powdered milk
5 ounces copha
1 teaspoon vanilla essence

For the chocolate icing

1½ cups icing sugar
2 tablespoons cocoa
2 tablespoons water and ½ teaspoon vanilla essence (or 2
   tablespoons fruit juice)

Combine the four dry ingredients for the slice in a bowl, blending well. Melt the copha without allowing it to become too hot, add the vanilla and pour onto the dry ingredients, mixing well. Press into a well-greased 11-inch by 7-inch shallow tray and chill until set.

For the icing, sift the icing sugar and cocoa and add the liquid. Stir over medium heat for about 1 minute or until it reaches a good consistency. Spread over the slice and allow to set before cutting into squares.

CHOCOLATE CRUNCH BARS

4 ounces butter
½ cup sugar
1 cup cornflakes
½ cup coconut
1 cup sifted self-raising flour
a pinch of salt

For the chocolate icing

1 cup sifted icing sugar
1 tablespoon cocoa
1 teaspoon melted butter
1 tablespoon milk
a few drops vanilla essence
coconut, chopped nuts or grated
   chocolate for topping

Melt the butter in a saucepan, then stir in the remaining ingredients. Press evenly into a greased 9-inch square shallow baking tin. Bake in a moderate oven, 350°F., for 12 to 15 minutes. Cut into finger lengths while still hot and allow to cool before icing.

For the icing, sift the icing sugar and cocoa into a saucepan, add the melted butter and milk and stir until smooth. Heat briefly, flavour with vanilla and spread over the cooled bars. They may be topped while still soft with coconut, chopped nuts or grated chocolate.

CHOCOLATE DELIGHT BARS

4 ounces butter
1 egg yolk
1 tablespoon water
1¼ cups sifted plain flour
1 teaspoon baking powder
1 teaspoon sugar
2 cups chocolate pieces
2 eggs
¾ cup sugar
3 tablespoons melted butter
1 teaspoon vanilla essence
2 cups finely chopped walnuts

Cream the 4 ounces of butter and add the egg yolk and the water. Sift the flour with the baking powder and add to the creamed mixture together with the teaspoonful of sugar.

Press into a well-greased 11-inch by 7-inch shallow tray and bake in a moderate oven, 350°F., for 10 minutes. Sprinkle at once with the chocolate pieces and return the tray to the oven for 1 minute. Remove, then spread the melted chocolate over the surface of the pastry, using a large knife or spatula.

Beat the 2 eggs until thick and lemon-coloured, then beat in the ¾ cup sugar. Stir in the melted butter and add the vanilla and nuts. Spread this over the chocolate layer in the oven tray and replace in a moderate oven, 350°F., for about 35 minutes. Cut into fingers.

CHOCOLATE MARSHMALLOW SLICES

For the biscuit base
4 ounces butter
½ cup sugar
1 egg
1 cup lightly crushed cornflakes
1 cup coconut
2 level dessertspoons cocoa
1 cup self-raising flour
a pinch of salt

For the marshmallow
2 cups sugar
2 tablespoons liquid glucose
¾ cup boiling water
1 heaped tablespoon gelatine
¾ cup boiling water
1 teaspoon vanilla essence

*For the chocolate peppermint
   topping*
3 ounces copha
½ cup drinking chocolate
a few drops of peppermint
   essence

Cream the butter and sugar for the base, add beaten egg, then stir in the cornflakes and coconut and the sifted cocoa, flour and salt.

Press into a well-greased 11-inch by 7-inch shallow tray and bake in a moderate oven, 350°F., for 20 to 30 minutes. Allow to cool before adding the marshmallow layer.

To make the marshmallow, first dissolve the sugar and glucose in half the boiling water, then dissolve the gelatine in the other half. Mix together, beating until the mixture thickens (about 20 or 25 minutes). Add the vanilla essence. Pour over the cooled base.

To make the chocolate peppermint topping, melt the copha over a low heat, stir in the drinking chocolate and flavour with the peppermint essence. Spread over the marshmallow. Mark into squares or fingers before the chocolate icing sets.

CHOCOLATE RUM STICKS

12 ounces semi-sweet chocolate
   pieces
1 cup sweetened condensed milk
a dash of salt
2 teaspoons rum
1½ cups chopped walnuts

Melt the chocolate in a double saucepan over hot, not boiling, water. Stir in the condensed milk and salt. Remove from the stove, then beat with a mixer until smooth. Stir in the rum and walnuts. Have ready a wax-paper-lined loaf tin measuring 7 by 3 by 2 inches. Pour the mixture in and chill for 24 hours.

Cut into ½-inch slices, then cut each slice lengthwise into three. Store in an airtight container.

4 ounces butter
½ cup sugar
1 teaspoon golden syrup
1 cup self-raising flour
¾ cup coconut

For the topping
½ cup sweetened condensed
  milk
2 ounces butter
1 cup icing sugar
1 tablespoon cocoa
1 cup coconut

For the pastry base
4 ounces butter
½ cup sugar
1 dessertspoon water
2 egg yolks
½ teaspoon vanilla essence
1½ cups plain flour
2 level dessertspoons cocoa
2 level tablespoons powdered
  milk
1½ level teaspoons baking
  powder
¼ level teaspoon salt

For the filling
2 egg whites
¼ cup sugar
1 teaspoon almond essence
½ teaspoon vanilla essence
7 ounces coconut
1 dessertspoon water

For the biscuit base
4 ounces butter
½ cup sugar
1 egg
½ teaspoon vanilla essence
1 cup self-raising flour
1 tablespoon cocoa

For the filling
1 rounded cup coconut
1 tablespoon icing or castor
  sugar
½ cup milk

CHOCOLATE SLICES

Cream the butter with the sugar until light and fluffy, then add the golden syrup. Add the sifted flour, then stir in the coconut, blending well. Spread in a well-greased 11-inch by 7-inch shallow tray and bake in a moderate oven, 350°F., for about 20 minutes.

To make the topping, combine the condensed milk and butter in a saucepan and stir over medium heat until melted and thoroughly blended. Remove from the heat and beat in the icing sugar, cocoa and coconut. Spread over the slice while it is still hot. When cold, cut into squares or finger lengths.

CHOCOROONS

Cream the butter with the sugar until light and fluffy. Add the water, egg yolks and vanilla, mixing well. Blend in the sifted flour, cocoa, powdered milk, baking powder and salt, making a firm dough. Chill for 1 hour.

Beat the egg whites for the filling until stiff and gradually add the sugar. Flavour with almond and vanilla essence and fold in the coconut and water. Mix well.

Divide the dough into three for easier handling. Take one portion and roll to a rectangle about 10½ by 5 inches, and ⅛ inch thick; cut in half and spread one half with one-third of the coconut filling. Top with the other piece of rolled dough, pressing lightly together. Cut into pieces ¾ inch wide and about 2½ inches long and place on a lightly greased tray. Bake at 325°F. for about 15 minutes. Cool.

Repeat the above procedure with the remaining two pieces of dough.

Frost the tops and ends of each chocoroon with melted chocolate or chocolate glacé icing.

CHURCHILL SQUARES

Cream the butter with the sugar, then add the well-beaten egg and the vanilla. Sift the flour with the cocoa and add to the creamed mixture, blending thoroughly.

Spread half the mixture in an 11-inch by 7-inch shallow tray. Cover with the filling, made by mixing the three ingredients together in the order given. Top with the remaining chocolate mixture and bake in a moderate oven, 350°F., for about 20 minutes.

When cold, cover the top with chocolate glacé icing. Allow the icing to set, then cut the cake into squares.

Chocoroons

COCONUT SLICES

Cream the butter and sugar for the biscuit base, add the egg yolk, then the milk. Stir in the sifted flour and salt. Spread evenly on the bottom of a well-greased 11-inch by 7-inch shallow tray. Spread with the jam.

For the meringue beat the egg white until stiff, then gradually beat in the sugar. Add the vanilla and stir in the coconut. Spread over the jam layer and bake in a moderate oven, 350°F., for 30 minutes. While still hot cut into finger lengths and leave to cool in the tin.

For the biscuit base

4 ounces butter
½ cup sugar
1 egg yolk
2 tablespoons milk
1½ cups self-raising flour
a pinch of salt
3 tablespoons raspberry or
   apricot jam

For the coconut meringue

1 egg white
½ cup sugar
¼ teaspoon vanilla essence
½ cup coconut

73

DANISH SLICES

6 ounces shortcrust or biscuit
  pastry
2 tablespoons tart jam
3 ounces butter
3 slightly rounded tablespoons
  sugar
½ teaspoon vanilla essence
2 eggs
2 tablespoons sultanas
1½ cups self-raising flour
a pinch of salt
1 level teaspoon mixed spice
3 tablespoons milk
4 ounces lemon-flavoured or
  chocolate glacé icing (use 1
  cup icing sugar)
chopped nuts

Line a greased 11-inch by 7-inch shallow tray with the pastry. Spread with the jam.

Beat the butter and sugar to a soft cream and add the vanilla. Beat the eggs and add gradually to the creamed mixture. Stir in the sultanas.

Sift the flour with the salt and spice and add to the mixture alternately with the milk. Spread evenly over the jam layer, place in a moderate oven, 350°F., and bake for about 30 minutes. Cool, then cover with lemon or chocolate glacé icing and sprinkle with nuts.

DATE SLICES

For the filling

½ pound dates
¼ cup cold water with a squeeze
  of lemon juice (or ¼ cup fruit
  juice)
a pinch of nutmeg

For the biscuit

4 ounces butter or margarine
3 rounded tablespoons sugar
1 egg (or 1 egg yolk and 2
  tablespoons cold water)
½ teaspoon vanilla essence
2 cups plain flour
1 level teaspoon baking powder
a pinch of salt

Chop the dates and place them in a saucepan with the water and lemon juice (or the fruit juice). Stir over low heat until the dates are soft. Allow to cool and add the nutmeg.

To make the biscuit base, cream the butter with the sugar, add the egg (or egg yolk and water) and the vanilla. Sift the flour, baking powder and salt and stir in, making a firm dough. Turn onto a lightly floured board and knead only until smooth on the outside.

Take a little more than half the dough and roll to line a greased 11-inch by 7-inch shallow baking tray. Spread the cooled date mixture over the uncooked pastry. Glaze the edges. Roll the remainder of the pastry to cover the top. Trim, then pinch the edges together and glaze the top with water or egg white and sprinkle with sugar. Bake in a moderate oven, 350°F., for 30 to 40 minutes. Cut into fingers while still hot and leave to cool in the tray.

DATE WAFERS

2 ounces butter
8 ounces chopped dates
¾ cup sugar
½ teaspoon vanilla essence
4 cups rice bubbles
½ cup coconut

Combine the butter, dates and sugar in a saucepan and stir over gentle heat until the dates are soft. Add the vanilla and pour onto the rice bubbles. Mix well.

Have ready a greased shallow tray which has been sprinkled with half the coconut. Spread the mixture evenly in the tin, pressing it down firmly with the back of a wooden spoon. Cover the top with the remaining coconut. Place in the refrigerator and chill until firm. Turn out of the tin, cut into squares and store in airtight tins.

DUTCH SLICES

For the biscuit base

4 ounces butter
¼ cup sugar
1 egg
1½ cups self-raising flour
a pinch of salt

For the topping

raspberry jam
4 ounces butter
3 rounded tablespoons sugar
2 eggs
¼ cup milk
1½ cups self-raising flour
a pinch of salt
1 teaspoon cocoa
1 level teaspoon cinnamon
chopped nuts

Cream the butter and sugar for the biscuit base. Add the beaten egg, then stir in the sifted flour and salt. Turn onto a floured board and knead only until smooth on the outside. Roll to line a greased 11-inch by 7-inch shallow tray. Spread with raspberry jam.

Cream the butter and sugar for the topping, add the beaten eggs, then the milk. Sift the flour with the salt, cocoa and cinnamon and stir lightly and evenly into the mixture. Spread this cake batter over the jam-covered pastry and sprinkle the top with nuts. Bake in a moderate oven, 350°F., for 30 to 35 minutes.

FRUITY BARS

For the filling

1 cup dates
1 cup raisins
2 tablespoons orange or lemon
   juice
¼ cup apricot jam
1 teaspoon grated orange or
   lemon rind

For the pastry

4 ounces butter
½ cup sugar
2 eggs
1 teaspoon vanilla essence
3 cups self-raising flour
a pinch of salt

For the topping

4 ounces orange or lemon glacé
   icing

Place chopped dates and chopped raisins in a saucepan with the orange or lemon juice. Stir over gentle heat until soft. Add the jam and the grated rind and allow to cool.

Cream the butter and sugar for the biscuit pastry and add the well-beaten eggs and the vanilla. Sift the flour with the salt and stir into the mixture, making a soft dough. Chill for about 1 hour.

Take a little more than half the biscuit pastry and roll to line the bottom and sides of a greased 11-inch by 8½-inch scone tray. Cover with the cooled fruit mixture, then with the remainder of the pastry, rolled to fit the top. Bake in a hot oven, 400°F., for 10 minutes, then reduce the heat to 350°F. and bake for a further 30 minutes. Let it cool in the scone tray for 10 minutes, then turn out onto a wire cooler and allow to cool completely. Cut into finger lengths and drizzle some of the soft glacé icing over them through a paper icing cone with a medium-sized opening.

FRUITY CARAMEL BARS

For the biscuit base

2 ounces butter
¼ cup brown sugar
1 cup self-raising flour
a pinch of salt

For the topping

2 eggs
1¼ cups brown sugar
½ cup chopped raisins
¼ cup chopped cherries
¼ cup chopped walnuts
1 cup coconut
4 tablespoons plain flour
1 level teaspoon baking powder

Cream the butter with the ¼ cup of brown sugar, then stir in the sifted flour and salt. Press into a well-greased 7-inch by 11-inch shallow tray and bake at 350°F. for about 10 minutes.

Beat the eggs and brown sugar for the topping, blend in the remaining ingredients, and spread evenly over the baked biscuit base. Return to the oven and bake for a further 35 to 40 minutes. Allow to cool before removing from the tray.

Before cutting into finger lengths for serving, either dust with sifted icing sugar or cover with a fruit-flavoured glacé icing.

FUDGE FINGERS

4 ounces butter or margarine
½ cup sugar
1 cup sultanas
1 teaspoon vanilla essence
1 egg
½ pound crushed plain sweet
   biscuits

For the chocolate icing

½ cup brown sugar
1 tablespoon butter
1 tablespoon water
1 tablespoon liquid glucose
2 ounces chocolate pieces
chopped nuts for topping

Place the butter, sugar and sultanas in a saucepan and stir until the butter and sugar have dissolved and the mixture is bubbling. Remove from the heat and add the vanilla and beaten egg, beating well. Stir in the finely crushed biscuits, blending thoroughly. Press into a well-greased 9-inch-square tin, and while still warm cover with the chocolate icing and sprinkle with the chopped nuts. Allow to set before cutting into finger lengths.

To make the icing, combine the brown sugar, butter, water and glucose in a saucepan. Stir over low heat until the sugar and glucose have dissolved, then bring to the boil. Remove from the heat and add the chocolate pieces, stirring until they have dissolved. Cool for about 5 minutes or until the chocolate has a good spreading consistency.

HEDGEHOG SLICES

4 ounces butter
½ cup sugar
2 level tablespoons coconut
2 level tablespoons cocoa
1 beaten egg
¾ cup chopped walnuts
½ pound crushed sweet biscuits

Place the butter, sugar, coconut and cocoa in a saucepan and stir until the butter has dissolved. Cook for 2 minutes. Cool slightly, then add the egg and walnuts and enough of the crushed biscuits to make a good consistency. Press firmly into an 11-inch by 7-inch greased shallow tin. When cold, ice with chocolate icing. Cut into small finger lengths.

LEMON BISCUIT SLICES

¼ pound butter or margarine
½ tin sweetened condensed milk
½ pound Marie biscuits
1 cup coconut
grated rind of 1 lemon

For the icing

1½ cups icing sugar
2 tablespoons lemon juice

Melt the butter, add the condensed milk and stir until thoroughly blended. Crush the biscuits with a rolling-pin and place them in a bowl with the coconut and grated lemon rind. Mix well. Pour in the melted butter mixture, blending well. Press evenly into a well-greased 11-inch by 7-inch shallow tray. Chill until set.

To make the icing, sift the icing sugar into a saucepan, add the lemon juice, and stir over low heat for about 1 minute or until it has a good spreading consistency. Cover the biscuit with the icing and chill until it sets. Cut into finger lengths to serve.

LEMON COCONUT BARS

For the biscuit base

3 ounces butter
¼ cup sugar
1 egg
½ teaspoon vanilla essence
1½ cups plain flour
½ level teaspoon baking powder
a pinch of salt
4 tablespoons lemon butter

For the topping

2 ounces softened butter
4 ounces castor sugar
1 egg
4 ounces desiccated coconut
3 tablespoons cream or canned
   unsweetened milk

Cream the butter and sugar for the base, then add the egg and vanilla, beating well. Add the sifted dry ingredients, mixing to a medium dough, turn onto a floured board and knead only until smooth on the outside. Roll to line the base of a greased 11-inch by 7-inch shallow tray. Spread with the lemon butter (when passionfruit are in season, the pulp of 2 or 3 passionfruit may be added to the lemon butter).

Beat together the softened butter and the castor sugar for the topping and stir in the well-beaten egg. Mix in the coconut, then the cream or the canned milk. Spread this carefully and evenly over the lemon-butter layer. Bake in a moderate oven, 350°F., for about 30 minutes. If the coconut tends to become overbrowned during the cooking, cover it with a piece of paper. Cut into finger lengths while still warm and leave to cool in the tray.

LEMON GINGER BISCUIT SLICES

4 ounces butter
½ cup sugar
2 tablespoons coconut
1 tablespoon lemon juice
grated rind of 1 lemon
1 egg
¼ cup chopped crystallized
   ginger
up to ½ pound crushed plain
   sweet biscuits
4 ounces lemon glacé icing
extra coconut for topping

Place the butter, sugar, coconut and lemon juice in a saucepan and stir until well mixed. Cook for 2 minutes. Remove from the heat, cool slightly and add the grated lemon rind, the beaten egg and chopped ginger, with enough crushed biscuits to make a good consistency.

Press firmly into a well-greased 7-inch square sandwich tin and chill until firm. Cover the top with lemon-flavoured glacé icing and sprinkle with coconut. Cut into finger-sized pieces to serve.

LEMON HEDGEHOG SLICES

4 ounces butter
½ cup sugar
2 level tablespoons coconut
1 tablespoon lemon juice
1 egg
½ cup chopped almonds
1 dessertspoon grated lemon rind
up to ½ pound crushed plain sweet biscuits
6 ounces lemon glacé icing
½ cup coconut for topping

Place the butter, sugar, coconut and lemon juice in a saucepan and stir until the sugar and butter have dissolved, then cook for 2 minutes. Cool slightly, add beaten egg, then the almonds, lemon rind and enough of the crushed biscuits to make a good consistency.

Press firmly into a greased 11-inch by 7-inch shallow tray. Chill until firm, then cover with lemon glacé icing and sprinkle with coconut. When the icing has set, cut the slab into finger lengths.

LEMON MARSHMALLOW SLICES

For the shortcake base
3 ounces butter
3 rounded tablespoons sugar
1½ cups plain flour
1 teaspoon baking powder
a pinch of salt
a little milk if necessary

For the filling
3 dessertspoons cornflour
1 cup water
½ cup sugar
1 teaspoon butter
2 teaspoons gelatine
juice and rind of 1 lemon

For the marshmallow
1 cup sugar
1 cup water
½ teaspoon vanilla essence
2 teaspoons lemon juice
1 tablespoon gelatine

To make the shortcake base, beat the butter and sugar to a soft cream and stir in the sifted flour, baking powder and salt, adding a little milk if the mixture seems too dry. Roll to fit a greased 11-inch by 7-inch shallow tray and bake in a moderate oven, 350°F., until golden brown—about 10 to 15 minutes.

Make the filling by blending the cornflour with a little of the water, then adding the remaining ingredients and stirring over medium heat until the mixture boils and thickens. Cook for 2 minutes, cool until lukewarm and spread over the biscuit base.

Combine the ingredients for the marshmallow in a saucepan and stir over medium heat until the mixture boils. Continue boiling for 5 minutes. Allow to become cool, then beat until white and thick. Pour over the lemon slice and, if liked, sprinkle with coconut. Cut into fingers to serve.

½ cup dried apricots
4 ounces butter
¼ cup white sugar
1⅓ cups plain flour
½ teaspoon baking powder
¼ teaspoon salt
1 cup brown sugar
2 eggs
½ teaspoon vanilla essence
½ cup chopped almonds

LUSCIOUS APRICOT BARS

Wash the apricots, cover with cold water and bring to the boil. Simmer for 10 minutes. Cool and chop. Mix the butter with the white sugar and 1 cup of the flour until crumbly. Press into a greased 11-inch by 7-inch shallow tray. Bake in a moderate oven, 350°F., for about 20 minutes.

Sift the remaining ⅓ cup of flour with the baking powder and salt. Beat the eggs well, then with the mixer at low speed gradually beat the brown sugar into them. Mix in the sifted flour and the vanilla, then the almonds and the cooled apricots. Spread this mixture over the baked layer, return the tray to the oven and bake for a further 20 to 25 minutes. Cut into bars and roll each bar in sifted icing sugar.

For the biscuit base
3 ounces butter or margarine
¼ cup sugar
½ teaspoon vanilla essence
1 egg
1½ cups plain flour
¼ level teaspoon baking powder
a pinch of salt

For the topping
4 tablespoons lemon cheese
2 ounces softened butter
¼ cup castor sugar
1 egg
4 ounces desiccated coconut
3 tablespoons cream or
    evaporated milk

For the crunchy base
1 cup coconut
½ cup sugar
1 cup self-raising flour
1 cup cornflakes
2 tablespoons cocoa
4 ounces butter

For the marshmallow
1 cup sugar
½ cup cold water
1 tablespoon lemon juice
1 tablespoon gelatine dissolved
    in ¼ cup boiling water

For the icing
3 ounces copha or other white
    vegetable shortening
½ cup drinking chocolate

4 ounces butter or margarine
⅔ cup brown sugar
¾ cup chopped dates
½ cup chopped walnuts
1 cup self-raising flour
1 egg
½ teaspoon vanilla essence

LUSCIOUS LEMON SLICES

Cream the butter and sugar for the pastry and add the vanilla, then the egg. Mix well. Sift the flour with the baking powder and salt and stir into the mixture, making a firm dough. Turn onto a floured board and knead only until the pastry is smooth on the outside. Roll to line a greased 11-inch by 7-inch shallow tray. Spread with the lemon cheese.

Beat the butter and sugar together for the topping, then add the well-beaten egg. Mix the coconut with the cream or evaporated milk and stir in. The mixture should be soft enough to spread. Place spoonfuls of it here and there on the lemon cheese, then with a spatula or a rubber scraper spread it evenly over the surface.

Bake the slice in a moderate oven, 350°F., for about 20 minutes. Should the coconut darken as the slice cooks, cover it with a sheet of brown paper. Cut into finger lengths while still hot. Allow to cool in the tin.

MARSHMALLOW SQUARES

Mix the coconut, sugar, sifted flour, cornflakes and cocoa for the crunchy base. Melt the butter and pour onto the dry ingredients. Mix well, then press into a 9-inch square tin and bake in a moderate oven, 350°F., for about 25 minutes. Cool.

For the marshmallow mix the sugar, cold water and lemon juice, then add the dissolved gelatine. Beat until thick, spread over the cooled biscuit base and allow to set.

Combine the ingredients for the icing and spread evenly over the marshmallow. When set cut into squares with a knife which has been dipped in hot water.

MELT 'N' MIX DATE SLICES

Melt the butter in a saucepan and add the brown sugar. Stir over low heat until syrupy (all the sugar crystals do not dissolve, but this does not matter).

Combine the chopped dates and walnuts with the sifted self-raising flour in a bowl. Pour on the warm but not hot butter mixture, then stir in the beaten egg and the vanilla.

Pour into a well-greased 11-inch by 7-inch shallow tray and bake in a moderate oven, 350°F., for about 20 minutes or until golden brown. Allow to cool, then cover with a lemon or chocolate glacé icing, using one cup of sifted icing sugar. Cool, then cut into fingers.

Old-fashioned Raisin Squares

OLD-FASHIONED RAISIN SQUARES

1 cup chopped raisins
1 cup water
4 ounces butter
1 cup sugar
1 egg
1¾ cups plain flour
1 level teaspoon bicarbonate of
   soda
1 level teaspoon nutmeg
½ level teaspoon ground cloves
1 level teaspoon allspice
a pinch of salt
½ cup chopped nuts

Place the chopped raisins in a saucepan with the water and bring to the boil. Remove from the stove and add the butter. Stir until it has dissolved, then cool the mixture to lukewarm. Stir in the sugar and the egg.

Sift the remaining ingredients except the nuts, and add to the mixture. Now stir in the nuts. Spread evenly in a well-greased 11-inch by 7-inch shallow baking tray and bake in a moderate oven, 350°F., for about 20 minutes. Cut into squares while still warm and serve dusted with icing sugar.

ORANGE SPICE BARS

6 ounces butter
1½ cups brown sugar
2 eggs
1 teaspoon grated orange rind
3 dessertspoons orange juice
2 cups plain flour
1 level teaspoon bicarbonate of
   soda
1 teaspoon cinnamon

Cream the butter with the sugar until light and fluffy. Add the beaten eggs, then the orange rind and juice. Mix well.

Sift the flour with the soda, cinnamon, nutmeg, salt and cloves and stir into the creamed mixture. Add the chopped nuts.

Spread evenly in a well-greased 9-inch by 12-inch shallow tray and bake in a moderate oven, 350°F., for 35 to 40 minutes or until the top is brown and firm to the touch. Cool in the tin for about 15 minutes, then spread with orange glaze.

½ teaspoon nutmeg
¼ teaspoon salt
¼ teaspoon ground cloves
1 cup chopped walnuts

For the orange glaze

2 teaspoons grated orange rind
3 tablespoons orange juice
2 cups sifted icing sugar
2 tablespoons flaked coconut

For the biscuit base

3 ounces butter
1½ cups self-raising flour
a pinch of salt
1 egg yolk
½ teaspoon lemon juice
cold water

For the topping

raspberry jam
2 egg whites
3 ounces castor sugar
4 ounces fine cake crumbs
2 ounces coconut
a little lemon juice
2 dessertspoons raspberry jam
cochineal or other red colouring

½ cup soft butter
¼ cup light brown sugar
1 egg
½ teaspoon vanilla essence
2 dessertspoons milk
port wine
4 ounces ground almonds
6 level dessertspoons plain flour
½ level teaspoon baking powder

For the glaze

1 cup sifted icing sugar
a dash of salt
1 dessertspoon soft butter
1 dessertspoon port wine
2 tablespoons chopped almonds

To make the glaze, add the orange rind and juice to the sifted icing sugar. Heat briefly. Sprinkle with coconut before the glaze has set. Cut into finger lengths.

PARISIENNE SLICES

Rub the butter into the sifted flour and salt and then stir in the egg yolk and lemon juice with enough cold water to make a rather firm dough. Turn onto a floured board and knead lightly, then roll to line an 11-inch by 7-inch shallow tray.

Spread the uncooked dough with raspberry jam, then with the egg white and cake-crumb topping. To make it, beat the egg whites until stiff, then gradually add the sugar and continue beating until thick and glossy. Stir in the cake crumbs, coconut, lemon juice and raspberry jam. Colour with cochineal or other red colouring.

Bake in a moderate oven, 350°F., for about 25 minutes or until firm to the touch. Cool. Ice the top with coffee-flavoured glacé icing and sprinkle with chopped walnuts and chopped cherries. Cut into finger lengths.

PORTUGUESE ALMOND SQUARES

Cream the butter with the sugar, then add the egg. Flavour with the vanilla, then add the milk, about 2 dessertspoons of port wine, and the ground almonds. Sift the flour with the baking powder and stir in. Spoon into a lightly greased 9-inch square slab tin and bake in a moderate oven, 350°F., for about 15 or 20 minutes. As soon as the slice is removed from the oven, brush it with more port wine. Cool to room temperature, then cover with the glaze. Sprinkle with nuts.

To make the glaze mix the icing sugar, salt, soft butter and port wine and heat briefly to a soft spreading consistency. Tint a light pink with food colouring.

RASPBERRY SLICES

3 ounces butter
¼ cup sugar
1 egg yolk
1 dessertspoon water
½ teaspoon vanilla essence
3 rounded tablespoons plain
   flour
3 rounded tablespoons
   self-raising flour
a pinch of salt

For the filling

1 egg white
a pinch of salt
½ cup sugar
1 cup coconut
2 tablespoons raspberry jam
½ teaspoon grated lemon rind
1 tablespoon lemon juice
1 tablespoon melted butter

Cream the butter and sugar for the pastry base and add the egg yolk, water and vanilla. Sift the flours with the salt and stir into the mixture, making a medium dough. Turn onto a lightly floured board and knead only until smooth on the outside. Roll to line a greased 11-inch by 7-inch shallow tray.

Place the egg white for the filling in a warm, dry bowl, add the salt and beat until stiff. Gradually beat in the sugar, then stir in the coconut, jam, lemon rind and juice and melted butter. Spread this mixture over the uncooked pastry and bake in a moderate oven, 350°F., for about 30 minutes. Cut into slices while warm and leave to cool in the tin.

TOFFEE BARS

½ cup brown sugar
½ cup white sugar
8 ounces butter
2 teaspoons vanilla essence
½ teaspoon salt
2 eggs
1 cup sifted plain flour
1 cup rolled oats
6 ounces semi-sweet chocolate
   pieces
⅓ cup chopped walnuts
⅓ cup coconut

Heat the oven to 350°F. Combine the sugars, soft butter, vanilla, salt and eggs and beat with a wooden spoon until thoroughly mixed. Sift the flour and measure it, then add 1 cup to the mixture together with the rolled oats. Mix well.

Spread evenly in a well-greased 11-inch by 7-inch shallow tray and bake for about 1 hour. Remove from the oven and allow to cool in the pan.

Melt the chocolate over hot water and spread over the slice. Sprinkle half the slice with shredded coconut and the other half with chopped nuts.

When cold, with the chocolate set, cut into bars for serving.

CAKES

AMERICAN FRUIT CAKE

6 ounces mixed peel
8 ounces dates
8 ounces seeded raisins
4 ounces almonds
4 ounces walnuts
8 ounces glacé cherries
4 ounces candied pineapple
1¾ cups plain flour
½ pound butter
3 slightly rounded tablespoons
    sugar
½ cup honey
5 eggs
1 level teaspoon allspice
½ level teaspoon ground cloves
½ level teaspoon nutmeg
1 level teaspoon baking powder
1 level teaspoon salt
¼ cup orange juice

Chop the peel and the dates, raisins and nuts, quarter the cherries and cut the pineapple into bite-sized pieces. Mix all together, then sift ¼ cup of the flour over the mixture.

Beat the butter and sugar to a cream and add the honey. Add the eggs one at a time, beating well after each addition.

Sift the remainder of the flour with the spices, baking powder and salt and add to the creamed mixture alternately with the orange juice. Mix well, then add the fruit and mix again.

Place in an 8-inch cake tin which has been lined with two thicknesses of white and two of brown paper (with the paper about 1 inch above the rim of the tin). Bake in a slow oven, 275°F., for about 4 hours.

APPLE COFFEE CAKE

1½ cups plain flour
2 level teaspoons baking powder
½ cup sugar
2 eggs
½ cup milk
½ teaspoon vanilla essence
¼ cup melted butter
3 medium-sized tart apples
⅓ cup brown sugar
1 level teaspoon cinnamon

Sift the flour and baking powder into a bowl and add the sugar. Combine the beaten eggs with the milk, vanilla and melted butter and stir into the flour, mixing into a soft batter. Pour into a well-greased 9-inch-square cake tin.

Peel and slice the apples and overlap them on the top of the batter. Mix the brown sugar and cinnamon and sprinkle over the top.

Bake at 400°F. for about 25 minutes. Serve as a dessert cake with whipped cream.

APPLESAUCE CAKE

4 ounces butter
¾ cup sugar
2 eggs
1¾ cups sifted plain flour
1 level teaspoon baking powder
½ level teaspoon bicarbonate of
    soda

Grease an orange-loaf tin and line the bottom with greased paper.

Cream the butter and sugar and gradually beat in the well-whisked eggs. Beat until light and fluffy.

Sift the dry ingredients together and add to the creamed mixture alternately with the apple purée, beating well after each addition. Stir in the nuts.

½ teaspoon cinnamon
½ teaspoon nutmeg
1 cup sweetened apple purée
½ cup chopped walnuts

For the glaze

½ cup icing sugar
1 dessertspoon water

3 eggs, separated
a pinch of salt
¾ cup sugar
3 level tablespoons plain flour
1 rounded teaspoon baking
    powder
3 level tablespoons arrowroot
vanilla essence

6 ounces butter
¾ cup sugar
3 eggs
½ teaspoon vanilla essence
¾ cup milk
3 cups self-raising flour
a pinch of salt
pink colouring
about 3 tablespoons raspberry
    jam
chocolate glacé icing

2½ cups plain flour
a pinch of salt
1 level teaspoon baking powder
¾ level teaspoon bicarbonate of
    soda
6 ounces butter
1 cup sugar
2 eggs
2 ounces semi-sweet chocolate
1 teaspoon vanilla essence
1 cup mashed bananas

Place in the prepared tin and bake in a moderate oven, 350°F., for about 1 hour. Cool in the tin for about 10 minutes, then turn onto a wire cooler.

While the loaf is still warm, spread the top with a glaze made by combining ½ cup of sifted icing sugar with 1 dessert-spoon of water.

ARROWROOT SPONGE

Beat the egg whites with a pinch of salt until stiff. Gradually add the sugar and continue beating until thick and glossy. Add the yolks one at a time, beating well after each addition.

Sift the flour, baking powder and arrowroot three times. Fold into the egg mixture and flavour with vanilla.

Divide evenly between two well-greased 7-inch sandwich tins and bake in a moderate oven, 350°F., for 20 to 25 minutes. Cool.

Join the cake with whipped and sweetened cream or your favourite filling, and dust the top with sifted icing sugar.

AUSTRALIA CAKE

Cream the butter and sugar. Beat the eggs and add them gradually. Mix the vanilla with the milk and sift the flour with the salt. Add the milk to the creamed mixture alternately with the flour.

Divide into two equal portions. Colour one half a pale pink. Place alternate spoonfuls of the pink and the white mixtures in a well-greased 9-inch square slab tin. Dot with the jam, then smooth the surface with the back of the spoon.

Bake in a moderate oven, 350°F., for 45 to 50 minutes. When cold, cover the top with 6 ounces of chocolate glacé icing (page 140).

BANANA CHOCOLATE CAKE

Sift the flour with the salt, baking powder and soda. Prepare two 8-inch sandwich tins by greasing and lining the bottom with paper.

Cream the butter and sugar until light and fluffy. Add the eggs one at a time, beating well after each addition. Melt the chocolate over hot water and add to the creamed mixture, then add the vanilla. Mix in the sifted dry ingredients alternately with the milk and the mashed bananas.

Divide evenly between the sandwich tins and bake in a moderate oven, 350°F., for 30 to 35 minutes. Turn onto a wire cooler.

6 ounces milk
½ pint cream with sugar and
    vanilla for flavouring
sliced banana and chocolate curls
    for decorating

When the cake is quite cold, split each layer in two and then rejoin the four layers with whipped and sweetened cream, reserving a little for the top. Decorate with whipped cream, shaved chocolate and banana slices which have been dipped in lemon juice to prevent them from discolouring.

BOILED FRUIT CAKE

1 pound mixed fruit
5 ounces butter
1 cup sugar
1 rounded teaspoon spice
1 cup water (or ½ cup water and
    ½ cup sherry)
½ level teaspoon bicarbonate of
    soda
2 eggs
1¼ cups self-raising flour
1 cup plain flour

Place the fruit, butter, sugar, spice and water in a saucepan and bring to the boil. Boil for 3 minutes. Allow to become almost cold. Mix the soda with the well-beaten eggs and add to the boiled mixture. Sift the flours together and stir in.

Place in an 8-inch cake tin which has been lined with greased paper. Bake in a moderate oven, 325°F., for about 1¼ hours.

This cake is best left for one or two days before being cut.

BOILED SULTANA CAKE

1 pound sultanas
¾ cup water
½ pound butter
1 cup sugar
1 teaspoon vanilla essence
3 eggs
3 cups plain flour
1 level teaspoon baking powder
a pinch of salt
1 rounded teaspoon mixed spice
2 tablespoons hot water

Place the sultanas and ¾ cup of water in a saucepan and bring slowly to the boil, then boil for 5 minutes. Drain well and allow the sultanas to cool thoroughly.

Cream the butter, sugar and vanilla essence until light and fluffy. Beat in the eggs one at a time, beating well after each addition. Fold in the cooled sultanas.

Sift the flour with the baking powder, salt and mixed spice and add to the creamed mixture. Add the hot water and mix thoroughly.

Turn into an 8-inch cake tin which has been greased and its base lined with greased paper. Bake in a moderate oven, 325°F., for 1½ hours. Cool on a wire cooler.

BRANDY FRUIT CAKE

6 ounces butter
1 cup castor sugar
3 whole eggs
1 egg yolk
2½ cups plain flour
1 level teaspoon baking powder
a pinch of salt
½ cup brandy
3 tablespoons orange juice
1 cup seeded raisins, chopped
1 cup chopped mixed peel
1 cup chopped walnuts
1 cup shredded coconut
¼ cup chopped candied
    pineapple

Cream the butter and sugar until light and fluffy. Beat the whole eggs and the egg yolk slightly, then add gradually to the creamed mixture, beating well.

Sift the flour with the baking powder and salt and add to the creamed mixture alternately with the brandy and orange juice. Stir in the chopped raisins, peel and walnuts and then the coconut and chopped pineapple.

Turn the mixture into an 8-inch cake tin which has been lined with two thicknesses of white and two of brown paper. Bake in a slow oven, 275°F., for 2½ hours.

CANADIAN DATE CAKE

½ pound butter
1 cup sugar
3 eggs
1 teaspoon vanilla essence or grated orange rind
2 cups self-raising flour
1 cup plain flour
a pinch of salt
¾ cup milk
½ pound stoned and chopped dates
orange or lemon glacé icing for topping

Line an 8-inch round or square cake tin with greased paper.

Beat the butter and sugar to a soft cream and gradually add the well-beaten eggs. Flavour with the vanilla or the grated orange rind. Sift the flours with the salt and add to the creamed mixture alternately with the milk. Stir in the dates.

Place in the prepared tin and bake in a moderate oven, 350°F., for 1¼ hours. When cold cover the top with the fruit-flavoured icing (page 142) and decorate with a few whole dates.

CANDIED FRUIT CAKE

1 cup plain flour
1 level teaspoon baking powder
a good pinch of salt
½ pound candied pineapple, chopped
½ pound whole glacé cherries, with a few extra for decorating
¾ pound chopped dates
2 eggs
½ cup sugar
½ pound whole unblanched almonds
¼ pound whole Brazil nuts
¼ pound walnut halves

Sift the flour with the baking powder and salt into a bowl. Add the pineapple, cherries and dates, mixing well. Line two 9-inch by 3-inch log tins with aluminium foil and grease the inside lightly.

Beat the eggs until frothy, then gradually beat in the sugar. Add the fruit, mixing well. Blend in the nuts.

Divide the mixture between the two tins and press down firmly. Decorate the top with whole cherries and, if liked, a few more nuts.

Bake in a slow oven, 275°F., for about 1¾ hours. Allow the cake to stand in the tin for 5 minutes, then remove it and take off the foil. When quite cold, wrap in greaseproof paper and foil and store in the refrigerator. Allow to come to room temperature before serving.

CARAMEL CAKE

4 ounces butter or margarine
½ cup sugar
2 eggs, separated
2 ounces loaf sugar
1 dessertspoon water
¼ pint hot milk
2 cups plain flour
1 rounded teaspoon baking powder
a pinch of salt
apricot jam
sifted icing sugar, or 4 ounces orange glacé icing

Cream the butter with the ½ cup sugar. Blend in the egg yolks.

Place the loaf sugar in a saucepan with the water and cook over medium heat to a light brown colour. Cool till it is lukewarm, then add the milk and stir until the caramel has dissolved.

Sift the flour with the baking powder and salt and add to the creamed mixture alternately with the caramel-flavoured milk. Fold in the stiffly beaten egg whites.

Divide evenly between two well-greased 7-inch sandwich tins and bake in a moderate oven, 350°F., for 20 to 25 minutes. Turn onto a cake cooler.

When the cake is cold, join with apricot jam and sift some icing sugar over the top, or ice with orange glacé icing.

CHERRY AND NUT CAKE

½ pound almonds
¼ pound mixed peel
¼ pound sultanas
½ pound cherries
¾ pound butter
1 cup sugar
4 eggs
3 cups plain flour
1 level teaspoon baking powder
a pinch of salt
½ teaspoon mixed spice
grated rind of ½ orange
grated rind of ½ lemon
3 or 4 tablespoons milk or
    brandy

Blanch and chop the almonds, chop the mixed peel, sultanas and cherries and mix thoroughly.

Cream the butter and sugar until light and fluffy. Add the eggs one at a time, beating well after each addition. Sift the flour with the baking powder, salt and spice, then stir into the creamed mixture. Add the prepared fruits together with the grated orange and lemon rind and the milk or brandy.

Mix thoroughly, then place in an 8-inch cake tin which has been lined with two thicknesses of white and two of brown paper. Bake in a slow oven, 275°F., for about 3½ hours.

CHIFFON CAKE

Sift into a bowl 1 cup of plain flour, ¾ cup of sugar, 1½ level teaspoons of baking powder and ½ level teaspoon of salt. Make a well in the centre and add ½ cup of good salad oil, 4 unbeaten egg yolks, ¾ cup of water, 1 teaspoon of vanilla essence and the grated rind of 1 lemon. Beat with a spoon until smooth.

In a second bowl place 4 egg whites and ½ level teaspoon of cream of tartar and beat until very stiff. Pour the egg-yolk mixture gently into the egg-white mixture, folding in lightly. Pour immediately into an ungreased 10-inch tube tin. Bake at 325°F. for 55 minutes, then increase the heat to 350°F. for a further 10 or 15 minutes, or until the top springs back when lightly touched.

When you take the cake out of the oven turn the tin upside down, placing the centre tube over a bottle so that the cake hangs free of the table until it is cold. Then loosen the sides of the cake with a spatula, turn the tin over and tap the edges sharply to release the cake.

When it is quite cold, cut the cake through the centre to make two layers. Spread one layer with whipped cream, place the other layer on it and cover top and sides with more cream. Now cover the sides with chopped and lightly browned almonds or browned coconut.

CHOCOLATE CAKE

4 ounces butter or margarine
1 cup castor sugar
½ teaspoon vanilla essence
2 eggs, separated
1½ cups self-raising flour
a pinch of salt
3 level tablespoons cocoa
½ cup milk

For the filling and topping

2 ounces butter
1 cup icing sugar
1 level tablespoon cocoa
1 dessertspoon coffee essence
1 tablespoon boiling water
½ teaspoon vanilla essence
2 tablespoons chopped nuts

Cream the butter and sugar and add the vanilla. Beat the egg yolks into the creamed mixture. Sift the flour, salt and cocoa twice and fold into the creamed mixture alternately with the milk. Beat the egg whites stiffly and fold in.

Divide evenly between two well-greased sandwich tins which have been lined on the bottom with a round of greased paper. Bake in a moderate oven for about 20 to 25 minutes. Cool.

Make the filling and topping by creaming the butter with the icing sugar and cocoa then adding the coffee essence, boiling water and vanilla. It may be necessary to add a little more sifted icing sugar to make a good spreading consistency. Use half to join the two layers together and spread the remainder on top. Sprinkle with the chopped walnuts before serving.

CHOCOLATE CHERRY CAKES

4 ounces butter or margarine
¾ cup sugar
1 egg
2 ounces semi-sweet chocolate
¼ cup chopped cherries
½ cup chopped nuts
1½ cups plain flour
1 level teaspoon bicarbonate of
    soda
a pinch of salt
5 ounces milk

For the icing

2 ounces semi-sweet chocolate
3 dessertspoons milk
1 cup icing sugar
1 teaspoon vanilla essence
3 level dessertspoons butter
1 egg

Cream the butter and sugar, add the egg and beat well. Melt the chocolate over hot water and beat into the creamed mixture. Stir in the chopped cherries and nuts. Sift the flour with the soda and salt and stir in alternately with the milk, mixing lightly and evenly (do not beat).

Line the bottom of an 8-inch square tin with greased paper and grease the sides. Spread the mixture evenly in the tin and bake in a moderate oven, 350°F., for 45 minutes. Allow to cool.

Melt the chocolate for the icing over hot water. Stir in the milk, icing sugar and vanilla, then the softened butter and egg. Chill by placing the bowl containing the mixture over ice cubes for about 10 minutes. Now beat until fluffy and spread over the cake. Mark into squares before the icing has set and place a piece of walnut or cherry in the centre of each square.

CHOCOLATE FLUFF SANDWICH

3 eggs, separated
½ cup sugar
1 dessertspoon plain flour
¾ cup arrowroot
½ level teaspoon bicarbonate of
    soda

Prepare two 7-inch sandwich tins by greasing and lining the bottom of each with a round of greased paper.

Add a pinch of salt to the egg whites and beat until soft peaks form. Gradually add the sugar and continue beating until thick and glossy. Add the egg yolks one at a time, beating well after each addition.

1 teaspoon cocoa
½ level teaspoon cream of tartar
1 teaspoon golden syrup,
    warmed
whipped cream for filling
chocolate glacé icing and nuts
    for topping

Sift the flour, arrowroot, soda, cocoa and cream of tartar three times. Fold into the egg mixture and then add the warmed golden syrup.

Divide evenly between the prepared tins and bake in a moderate oven, 350°F., for 22 to 25 minutes.

When the cakes are cold split each layer in two, then rejoin the four layers with whipped and sweetened cream. Ice the top with chocolate glacé icing (page 140) and sprinkle the edge of the icing with chopped nuts.

CHOCOLATE FRUIT CAKE

8 ounces glacé cherries
8 ounces sultanas
4 ounces mixed peel, chopped
1 pound raisins
8 ounces coarsely chopped
    walnuts
8 ounces slivered, blanched
    almonds
4 ounces coarsely chopped dried
    apricots
8 ounces plain flour
1 level teaspoon salt
¼ level teaspoon bicarbonate of
    soda
8 ounces butter
8 ounces sugar
5 eggs
2 teaspoons vanilla essence
4 ounces semi-sweet chocolate,
    melted
⅓ cup rum for wrapping the cake
    to store

Line a greased 9-inch tube pan with greased paper. Quarter the cherries and place in a bowl with the sultanas, peel, raisins, nuts and apricots. Set aside.

Sift the flour with the salt and soda. Heat the oven to 275°F.

Beat the butter and sugar until light and fluffy and add the unbeaten eggs one at a time, beating well after each addition. Add the vanilla and the melted chocolate, mixing well. Fold in the flour and the fruit.

Place in the prepared tin and bake for about 3 hours. Cool in the tin for 1 hour, then remove and cool completely. Wrap in a rum-soaked cloth and store for at least 2 weeks before cutting.

Chocolate Fruit Cake

89

CHOCOLATE KUGLOAF

5½ ounces butter
1 cup sugar
4 eggs, unbeaten
2 cups plain flour
3 level teaspoons baking powder
a pinch of salt
½ cup milk
1 teaspoon vanilla essence
2 level tablespoons cocoa
1 tablespoon hot water
chocolate glacé icing

Have ready a well-greased fluted ring mould. Cream the butter and sugar until light and fluffy. Add the eggs one at a time, beating well after each addition. Sift the flour with the baking powder and salt and stir alternately with the combined milk and vanilla.

Blend the cocoa with the hot water. Take one-third of the cake mixture and stir this chocolate mixture into it.

Place one-third of the plain cake mixture in the bottom of the mould and cover with half the chocolate mixture. Add another third of the plain, then the remainder of the chocolate and top off with the remainder of the plain mixture. With a knife, lightly swirl through the cake mixture in the tin to give a marbled effect.

Bake in a moderate oven, 350°F., for 50 to 60 minutes. Cool slightly, then turn out and sprinkle the surface with sifted icing sugar or cover with chocolate glacé icing (page 140).

CHOCOLATE ORANGE MARBLE CAKE

4 ounces butter
1½ cups sugar
2 teaspoons grated orange rind
2 eggs, separated
2½ cups plain flour
4 level teaspoons baking powder
a pinch of salt
1 cup milk
1½ ounces dark chocolate, melted

For the frosting

¼ cup butter
2 teaspoons grated orange rind
2 tablespoons orange juice
1 pound sifted icing sugar
2 or 3 ounces dark chocolate, melted
coconut or chopped walnuts (optional)

Grease three 7-inch sandwich tins and line the bottom of each with greased paper.

Cream the butter and sugar for the cake and add the grated orange rind. Beat until fluffy. Add the egg yolks, beating well.

Sift the flour with the baking powder and salt and add to the creamed mixture alternately with the milk. Beat the egg whites until stiff and fold in.

Divide the mixture in two and add the melted chocolate to one half, mixing well. Alternating the white and chocolate mixtures, spoon the cake batter into the three prepared tins. Lightly swirl a knife through each to give a marbled effect when cooked. Bake in a moderate oven, 350°F., for 25 to 30 minutes. Turn out onto a wire cooler and allow to become quite cold.

Make the frosting by beating the butter with the orange rind and juice and gradually adding the sifted icing sugar. Set aside three-quarters of this and add the melted chocolate to the remaining quarter.

Use some of the white frosting to join the cake layers together. Cover the top and sides of the cake with the remainder.

With a rose or star icing tube, pipe the chocolate frosting in a pattern on the top of the cake. The sides may be covered with coconut or finely chopped walnuts.

90

Citrus Chiffon Pie, Charlotte Russe, and a
strawberry-decorated Orange Sponge Cake

Chocolate Kugloaf

3 level tablespoons cocoa
½ cup milk
4 ounces butter
¾ cup castor sugar
3 eggs
2 cups self-raising flour
1 tablespoon rum
rum-flavoured butter cream for
   filling and topping
chocolate-dipped almonds for
   decorating

For the butter cream

3 ounces butter
2 cups sifted icing sugar
2 teaspoons rum

3 or 4 eggs, separated
a pinch of salt
½ cup sugar
1 cup plain flour
1 rounded teaspoon baking
   powder
1 rounded dessertspoon cocoa
1 level teaspoon cinnamon
1 teaspoon butter melted in 2
   tablespoons boiling water
chocolate glacé icing

CHOCOLATE RUM CAKE

Blend the cocoa with a little of the cold milk. Heat the remaining milk and pour onto the blended cocoa. Return to the saucepan and stir until boiling. Allow to cool.

Cream the butter with the castor sugar. Beat the eggs well and gradually add to the creamed mixture. Sift the flour and add alternately with the cocoa-flavoured milk. Lastly add the rum.

Divide evenly between two well-greased sandwich tins which have been lined on the bottom with greased paper. Bake in a moderate oven, 350°F., for about 30 minutes. Turn out and allow to cool.

Join the layers with rum-flavoured butter cream and ice the top with the same mixture. Decorate with blanched almonds which have been dipped in melted chocolate.

To make the butter cream, beat the butter to a soft cream, gradually beat in the sifted icing sugar, and flavour with the rum.

CHOCOLATE SPONGE

Beat the egg whites with a pinch of salt until stiff. Gradually add the sugar and continue beating until thick and glossy. Add the egg yolks one at a time, mixing thoroughly.

Sift the flour with the baking powder, cocoa, and cinnamon. Stir lightly into the egg and sugar mixture, then lightly stir in the mixture of water and melted butter.

Divide evenly between two well-greased 7-inch sandwich tins and bake in a moderate oven, 350°F., for 20 to 25 minutes.

When cool join together with whipped or mock cream and ice the top with chocolate glacé icing (page 140).

91

Toffee Almonds, Marshmallows, Whisky Balls,
Rum Balls, French Jellies, Ribbon Nut Fondant

CHOCOLATE SWISS ROLL 1

3 eggs, separated
a pinch of salt
3½ rounded tablespoons castor
    sugar
½ teaspoon vanilla essence
1 cup self-raising flour
2 level tablespoons cocoa
2 tablespoons cold water
whipped and sweetened cream
sifted icing sugar for topping

Beat the egg whites with the salt until peaks form. Gradually add the sugar and continue beating until thick and glossy. Beat in the egg yolks one at a time. Flavour with the vanilla.

Sift the flour and cocoa together three times, then fold into the egg mixture. Add the cold water.

Spread evenly in a 9-inch by 12-inch Swiss roll tin which has been well greased and lined on the bottom with greased paper. Bake in a moderate oven, 350°F., for 12 to 15 minutes.

Turn out onto a paper which has been sprinkled with sugar, quickly cut the crusts from the sides and roll up. Lift onto a wire cake cooler.

When the cake is quite cold unroll and fill with whipped and sweetened cream or with orange or lemon filling. Re-roll, then dust the top with sifted icing sugar.

CHOCOLATE SWISS ROLL 2

4 eggs, separated
a pinch of salt
½ cup fine sugar
1 cup plain flour
2 level teaspoons baking powder
2 level tablespoons cocoa
2 tablespoons hot water
mock or whipped cream
sifted icing sugar for topping

Beat the egg whites with a pinch of salt until stiff. Gradually add the sugar and beat until the mixture will stand in thick, glossy peaks. Add the egg yolks one at a time, beating in thoroughly.

Sift the flour with the baking powder and cocoa three times. Fold into the egg and sugar mixture, then lightly stir in the hot water.

Place in a paper-lined and greased 9-inch by 12-inch Swiss roll tin and bake in a moderate oven, 375°F., for 12 to 15 minutes.

Turn out onto a paper dusted with icing sugar, quickly cut off the side crusts and roll up. Place on a cake cooler.

When the cake has become quite cold unroll and spread with either whipped cream or mock cream. Re-roll, then dust the top with sifted icing sugar.

CHOCOLATE WALNUT CAKE

½ pound butter
1 cup castor sugar
4 eggs
2 cups plain flour
2 rounded tablespoons rice flour
1 rounded teaspoon baking
    powder
a pinch of salt
3 tablespoons sherry
1 ounce grated chocolate
½ pound shelled walnuts
½ teaspoon vanilla essence
6 ounces chocolate glacé icing
    and some halved walnuts to
    decorate

Line an 8-inch round cake tin with greased paper. Beat the butter and sugar to a soft cream and gradually add the well-beaten eggs.

Sift the flour with the rice flour, baking powder and salt and add to the creamed mixture alternately with the sherry, chocolate, broken or chopped walnuts and the vanilla.

Place in the prepared tin and bake in a moderate oven, 350°F., for about 1½ hours. When cold, ice the top with chocolate glacé icing (page 140) and decorate with walnut halves.

CHRISTMAS CAKE

¼ pound sultanas
¼ pound mixed peel
¼ pound seeded raisins
¼ pound currants
2 ounces cherries
¼ pound chopped blanched
  almonds
4 tablespoons brandy, whisky or
  sherry
¼ pound butter
¼ pound white sugar
¼ pound brown sugar
4 eggs
10 ounces plain flour
a good pinch of salt
½ level teaspoon baking powder
½ level teaspoon mixed spice
½ level teaspoon nutmeg

Line an 8-inch cake tin with two thicknesses of brown and two of white paper. Prepare the fruit the day before the cake is to be made. Blanch and chop the almonds, remove the sugar from the cherries and chop them. Chop the mixed peel and if the raisins are large cut them into pieces no larger than the sultanas. Sprinkle with half the brandy, whisky or sherry and leave to stand overnight.

Beat the butter and sugar to a soft cream and add the eggs one at a time, beating well after each addition. Add half the fruit and nuts, then the remainder of the brandy.

Sift the flour with the salt, baking powder and spices and add half to the creamed mixture. When well blended add the remainder of the fruit, then the remainder of the flour. Place in the prepared tin.

With an electric stove, pre-heat the oven to 325°F., place the cake in the centre of the oven and immediately reduce the heat to 275°F. Bake for 3 to 3½ hours.

If using a gas oven, pre-heat the oven to 275°F., place the cake in the centre of the lower half of the oven (or in such a position that the top of the cake will not be higher than the centre of the oven). Bake at 275°F. for 3 to 3½ hours.

CHRISTMAS CONFECTION CAKE

1½ cups shelled whole Brazil
  nuts
1½ cups walnut halves
½ pound stoned dates
⅔ cup chopped candied peel
¼ cup red maraschino cherries
¼ cup green maraschino cherries
¼ cup seeded raisins
¾ cup plain flour
½ teaspoon baking powder
½ teaspoon salt
¾ cup sugar
1 teaspoon vanilla essence
3 eggs

Grease the bottom and sides of an 8-inch by 5-inch orange-loaf tin and line with one layer of greased paper.

Combine the whole Brazil nuts in a large bowl with the walnut halves, dates, chopped peel, well-drained cherries and seeded raisins.

Sift the flour with the baking powder and salt and mix with the sugar. Add to the nuts and fruit, mixing thoroughly. Add the vanilla to the beaten eggs and stir in. It will be fairly stiff.

Spoon the mixture into the prepared tin, levelling it with the back of a wooden spoon. Bake in a slow oven, 300°F., for 2 to 2½ hours.

Leave in the tin to cool for about 10 minutes, then loosen round the edge and turn out onto a cake cooler. When cold wrap in plastic and store in the refrigerator. Do not decorate this cake.

CINNAMON SPONGE

4 eggs, separated
a pinch of salt
½ cup castor sugar
1 cup self-raising flour
a good pinch of salt
1 teaspoon cinnamon

Beat the egg whites with the salt until soft peaks form. Gradually add the sugar, beating well after each addition until the mixture is thick and glossy. Add the egg yolks one at a time.

Sift the flour, salt, cinnamon and cocoa three times and fold into the egg mixture. Heat the water and butter until the butter has dissolved, then stir in evenly.

93

1 slightly rounded teaspoon
    cocoa
1 tablespoon water
1 slightly rounded teaspoon
    butter
whipped cream, or lemon filling
    or lemon cheese
lemon glacé icing

Divide the mixture between two well-greased 7-inch sandwich tins and bake in a moderate oven, 350°F., for 20 to 25 minutes. Turn onto a wire cooler.

When the cake is quite cold join the layers with whipped and sweetened cream or with lemon filling (see page 145) or lemon cheese.

Cover the top with lemon-flavoured glacé icing (page 142).

COCOA RIPPLE CAKE

4 ounces butter
4 ounces sugar
2 eggs
1¾ cups plain flour
2 level teaspoons baking powder
a pinch of salt
⅔ cup milk
¼ cup cocoa
⅓ cup sugar
⅓ cup broken walnut pieces
3 dessertspoons butter
4 ounces chocolate glacé icing
walnut halves to decorate

Cream the 4 ounces of butter and 4 ounces of sugar until light and fluffy. Add well-beaten eggs, beating well after each addition.

Sift the flour with the baking powder and salt and add to the creamed mixture alternately with the milk. Spoon half into a well-greased 8-inch ring mould.

Mix the cocoa, sugar and walnut pieces and sprinkle over the cake mixture in the tin. Dot with butter, then cover with the remainder of the cake mixture.

Bake in a moderate oven, 375°F., for about 35 minutes. Turn onto a wire rack to cool.

Cover with chocolate glacé icing (page 140) and decorate with walnut halves.

COCONUT CAKE

6 ounces butter
¾ cup sugar
2 teaspoons grated orange rind
3 eggs
1 cup plain flour
1 cup self-raising flour
a pinch of salt
1 cup coconut
2 tablespoons milk
2 tablespoons orange juice
4 ounces orange glacé icing
2 tablespoons coconut for
    topping

Grease a 6-inch cake tin and line the bottom with a round of greased paper.

Beat the butter and sugar to a soft cream and add the grated orange rind. Gradually beat in the well-whisked eggs.

Sift the flours with the salt and add to the creamed mixture alternately with the coconut and the combined milk and orange juice.

Place in the prepared tin and bake in a moderate oven, 325°F., for about 1¼ to 1½ hours.

When the cake is cold cover the top with orange-flavoured glacé icing and sprinkle with coconut.

6 ounces butter
¾ cup sugar
3 eggs
2 tablespoons chopped walnuts
2 rounded tablespoons coconut
2 cups self-raising flour
3 level dessertspoons cocoa
a pinch of salt
¾ cup milk
chocolate icing

COCONUT FUDGE CAKE

Cream the butter and sugar until light and fluffy. Gradually add well-beaten eggs, then stir in the nuts and coconut.

Sift the flour with the cocoa and salt and add to the creamed mixture alternately with the milk.

Divide evenly between two 10-inch by 3-inch bar tins and bake in a moderate oven, 350°F., for 30 minutes, or place in one 7-inch square tin and bake for 50 to 60 minutes.

When the cake is cold cover with chocolate icing.

For the batter

1½ cups plain flour
1½ level teaspoons baking
   powder
¼ teaspoon salt
2 eggs
1 cup sugar
¼ cup melted butter
½ cup milk

For the filling and topping

1½ cups light brown sugar
2 dessertspoons plain flour
2 dessertspoons cinnamon
3 dessertspoons melted butter
a pinch of salt
1 cup chopped nuts

COFFEE CAKE

Make the filling by combining the brown sugar, flour, cinnamon, melted butter, salt and nuts. Mix and set aside.

Sift the flour with the baking powder and salt. Beat the eggs until light and foamy, then add the sugar a spoonful at a time, beating well after each addition. Stir in the melted butter. Add the sifted dry ingredients alternately with the milk and beat until smooth.

Spread a layer of this batter in the bottom of a greased 8-inch round sandwich tin. Sprinkle with half the filling and cover with the remainder of the batter. Top with the remainder of the spiced sugar mixture.

Bake at 350°F. for 50 to 60 minutes. Serve warm.

½ cup butter
1 cup castor sugar
2 eggs, separated
1 tablespoon coffee essence
½ cup milk
1½ cups self-raising flour
a pinch of salt

For the filling

whipped cream, sweetened and
   flavoured
coffee-flavoured glacé icing
chopped nuts (optional)

COFFEE CREAM CAKE

Beat the butter and sugar to a soft cream, then add the egg yolks and beat again.

Mix the coffee essence with the milk. Sift the flour with the salt and add to the mixture alternately with the coffee-flavoured milk. Lastly fold in the stiffly beaten egg whites.

Place in a well-greased 7-inch cake tin which has been lined on the bottom with greased paper. Bake in a moderate oven, 350°F., for about 40 minutes.

When the cake has cooled, split it through the centre and fill with whipped and sweetened cream. Ice the top with coffee-flavoured glacé icing and, if liked, decorate with chopped walnuts.

4 ounces butter
½ cup castor sugar
1 egg
1 cup plain flour
a pinch of salt
1 level teaspoon baking powder
2 medium-sized apples
1 teaspoon cinnamon
1 teaspoon ginger
1 tablespoon brown sugar
1 dessertspoon lemon juice
2 tablespoons sultanas
1 tablespoon chopped walnuts
whipped cream (if to be served
    as a dessert cake)

1 cup currants
3 cups raisins
1 cup chopped peel
2 cups sultanas
1 cup halved cherries
1 cup diced candied pineapple
1 cup blanched almonds
2½ cups plain flour
1 level teaspoon nutmeg
1½ level teaspoons cinnamon
½ level teaspoon ground cloves
½ level teaspoon baking powder
½ pound butter
1⅓ cups firmly packed brown
    sugar
6 eggs
1 ounce semi-sweet chocolate,
    melted
¼ cup brandy
¼ cup orange juice

4 ounces butter
½ cup sugar
2 eggs
3 ounces chopped dates
1 mashed banana
2 teaspoons lemon juice
1½ cups self-raising flour
2 tablespoons milk

DANISH APPLE CAKE

Cream the butter and sugar until light and fluffy, then add the well-beaten egg. Sift the flour with the salt and baking powder and stir in, mixing well.

Spread half this mixture in the bottom of a greased and lined 8-inch sandwich tin.

Peel and core the apples and slice them thinly. Place half on top of the cake mixture in the tin and sprinkle with the cinnamon, ginger, brown sugar and lemon juice. Top with the sultanas, then add the remainder of the sliced apple. Sprinkle with the chopped walnuts. Cover with the remainder of the cake mixture. Bake in a moderate oven, 350°F., for 45 to 50 minutes.

Serve warm cut into wedges with whipped cream as a dessert cake, or cold as a cake.

DARK CHRISTMAS FRUIT CAKE

Combine the currants, raisins, peel, sultanas, cherries, pineapple and halved almonds in a large bowl with 1 cup of the flour until the fruit is well coated. Sift the remaining flour with the nutmeg, cinnamon, cloves and baking powder.

Beat the butter with the sugar until creamy, then add the eggs one at a time, beating well after each addition. Add the melted chocolate. Stir in the flour alternately with the brandy and fruit juice, mix until smooth, then stir in the fruit mixture.

Turn into a 10-inch cake tin which has been lined with two thicknesses of brown and two of white paper and bake in a slow oven, 275°F., for 3½ to 4 hours.

DATE AND BANANA CAKE

Beat the butter and sugar to a soft cream. Add the eggs one at a time, beating well after each addition. Stir in the dates, banana and lemon juice.

Sift the flour and add to the creamed mixture alternately with the milk.

Place in an orange-loaf tin or a 6-inch round or square cake tin which has been greased and lined on the bottom with greased paper. Bake in a moderate oven, 350°F., for about 30 to 40 minutes.

If liked the cake may be iced with a lemon-flavoured glacé icing.

4 ounces butter
¾ cup brown sugar
2 eggs
1½ cups self-raising flour
1 teaspoon cinnamon
1 teaspoon nutmeg
a pinch of salt
½ cup milk
½ pound chopped dates
1 tablespoon rum

For the icing
1¼ cups icing sugar
1 dessertspoon butter
1 dessertspoon rum
a squeeze of lemon juice

4 ounces butter
1 cup sugar
2 eggs
1 teaspoon vanilla essence
½ pint sour or fresh cream
2 cups plain flour
1½ level teaspoons baking
   powder
1 level teaspoon bicarbonate of
   soda
a pinch of salt
1 cup chopped raisins

For the topping
½ cup sugar
1 cup coarsely chopped walnuts
1 level teaspoon cinnamon

½ pound butter
1 cup sugar
5 eggs
⅓ cup ground almonds
2½ cups plain flour
1 level teaspoon baking powder
½ teaspoon salt
1 cup raisins
1 cup currants
½ cup chopped peel
1 dessertspoon grated orange rind
1 tablespoon orange juice
almond halves and strips of
   lemon peel for decorating

DATE AND RUM CAKE

Line the bottom of an orange-loaf tin with greased paper and thoroughly grease the sides. Beat the butter and sugar to a soft cream, then add the eggs one at a time, beating well after each addition.

Sift the flour with the spices and salt and add to the mixture alternately with the milk. Stir in the chopped dates and the rum.

Place in the prepared tin and bake in a moderate oven, 350°F., for about 1 hour and 10 minutes.

While the cake cools, make the icing. Sift the icing sugar. Melt the butter in a saucepan, add the rum and lemon juice, and stir into the icing sugar. Beat to a good spreading consistency and cover the top of the cooled cake with it. If liked, decorate with some dates.

DE LUXE COFFEE CAKE

Cream the butter and sugar until light and fluffy. Add the eggs one at a time, beating well after each addition. Flavour with the vanilla, then blend in the cream. Sift the flour with the baking powder, salt and soda and stir into the creamed mixture.

Spread half the mixture in a well-greased 8-inch-square cake tin. Combine the ingredients for the topping and sprinkle half of it over the layer of cake mixture in the tin. And the chopped raisins. Cover with the remainder of the cake mixture, then with the rest of the topping.

Bake in a moderate oven, 350°F., for about 50 minutes. To serve, cut into squares.

DUNDEE CAKE

Beat the butter and sugar until light and creamy. Beat the eggs and add them gradually, then fold in the ground almonds.

Sift the flour with the baking powder and salt. Chop the raisins, combine them with the currants and peel, then add to the creamed mixture. Stir in the flour, then the grated orange rind and juice.

Place in an 8-inch cake tin which has been lined with two thicknesses of paper. Decorate the top with the almond halves and strips of peel. Bake in a slow oven, 275°F., for 2 hours or until cooked.

DUTCH FRUIT CAKE

¼ pound butter
1 cup sugar
1 cup cold water
¼ pound currants
¾ pound sultanas
½ pound raisins
2 ounces mixed peel
1 teaspoon nutmeg
1 teaspoon mixed spice
1 tablespoon lemon juice
2 eggs
1 cup self-raising flour
1½ cups plain flour
1 dessertspoon golden syrup
½ level teaspoon bicarbonate of
    soda
1 tablespoon boiling water

Prepare an 8-inch cake tin by lining it with greased paper.

Combine the butter, sugar, cold water, fruit, spices and lemon juice in a saucepan. Bring to the boil, stirring well, then boil for 3 minutes. Cool.

Beat the eggs until light and lemon coloured and add them to the cooled mixture. Add the sifted flours, then the golden syrup. Lastly add the soda which has been dissolved in the boiling water.

Place in the prepared tin and bake in a moderate oven, 325°F., for about 2 hours.

This cake improves with keeping. Wrap and store for at least three days before cutting.

DUTCH RING CAKE

4 ounces flaky pastry
1 cup ground almonds
5 ounces sugar
1 small egg
grated rind of 1 lemon
apricot jam
2 tablespoons icing sugar
1 teaspoon lemon juice
cherries and angelica for
    decorating

Roll the pastry into a strip 16 inches long and 4 inches wide.

Make the filling by mixing the ground almonds with the sugar and adding the egg and lemon rind. Knead this well together and shape into a roll about 15 inches long. Place on the rolled pastry.

Brush the edges of the pastry with water and roll up loosely, making sure the seam comes underneath the roll. Shape the roll to form a ring, joining the ends together. Place on a greased shallow oven tray. Brush the top with egg or milk and prick with a fork.

Bake in a hot oven, 425°F., for 25 to 30 minutes. When the cake is cooked, but still hot, brush the surface with apricot jam.

Mix the icing sugar with the lemon juice, and a little water if required, to make a thin lemon glaze. Pour over the roll. Allow to cool, then decorate the top with sliced cherries and pieces of angelica.

ENGLISH PLUM CAKE

¾ pound butter
1 cup sugar
4 eggs

Line an 8-inch cake tin with two thicknesses of paper. Beat the butter and sugar to a soft cream, then add the eggs one at a time, beating well after each addition.

3 cups plain flour
1 level teaspoon baking powder
a pinch of salt
1 level teaspoon mixed spice
4 ounces raisins
4 ounces cherries, chopped
4 ounces sultanas
4 ounces mixed peel, chopped
4 ounces almonds, blanched and
  chopped
grated rind of $\frac{1}{2}$ orange
grated rind of $\frac{1}{2}$ lemon
4 tablespoons brandy or milk

2 ounces butter
$\frac{1}{3}$ cup sugar
$\frac{1}{2}$ teaspoon vanilla essence
1 egg, separated
1 cup self-raising flour
a pinch of salt
$\frac{1}{4}$ cup milk

For the filling
$\frac{1}{4}$ cup brown sugar
1 teaspoon cinnamon
1 tablespoon melted butter
$\frac{1}{4}$ cup chopped walnuts
1 tablespoon plain flour
1 tablespoon coconut

4 cups peeled and sliced tart
  apples
$\frac{1}{2}$ cup raisins
$\frac{1}{2}$ cup sugar
$\frac{1}{4}$ cup water
1 dessertspoon lemon juice
$\frac{1}{2}$ teaspoon cinnamon
$\frac{1}{4}$ teaspoon nutmeg
4 ounces butter
1 cup sugar
1 egg
$2\frac{1}{2}$ cups plain flour
$\frac{1}{2}$ teaspoon salt
2 level teaspoons baking powder
$\frac{1}{2}$ cup milk
$\frac{1}{2}$ teaspoon vanilla essence
1 tablespoon icing sugar

Sift the flour with the baking powder, salt and spice and add, then mix in the fruit, nuts and grated rind, and finally the brandy or milk.

Place in the prepared tin and bake in a slow oven, 300°F., for $2\frac{1}{2}$ to 3 hours.

FRENCH COFFEE CAKE
Cream the butter with the sugar and add the vanilla. Add the egg yolk and beat well.

Sift the flour with the salt and add to the creamed mixture alternately with the milk. Beat the egg white until stiff and fold in.

Place half the mixture in a well-greased 7-inch sandwich tin which has been lined on the bottom with greased paper. Combine the ingredients for the filling, mixing well. Sprinkle half over the cake mixture. Spread with the remainder of the cake mixture, then sprinkle with the rest of the filling.

Bake in a moderate oven, 375°F., for about 40 minutes. Cool in the tin for 5 minutes before turning out onto a wire cooler.

GERMAN APPLE CAKE
Combine the apples, raisins, sugar, water, lemon juice, cinnamon and nutmeg in a saucepan, bring to the boil and simmer until the apples are soft but will still hold their shape—about 10 minutes.

Lift out the fruit and continue to boil the liquid until it has reduced to 1 tablespoonful. Pour this over the apples and allow to cool.

Cream the butter and sugar and add the well-beaten egg. Sift the flour with the salt and baking powder and add to the creamed mixture alternately with the milk and vanilla. Mix well.

Spread a little more than half the batter in the bottom of a greased 9-inch spring-form pan. Bring the batter to a depth of about half an inch up the sides of the pan. Spoon the cooled apple into the centre, spreading it evenly, then carefully cover with the remaining batter.

Bake in a moderate oven, 350°F., for about 1 hour or until the cake begins to shrink away from the sides of the pan. While still warm dust the top with sifted icing sugar. The cake may be served warm or cold.

GERMAN PLUM CAKE

12 ounces raisins
8 ounces sultanas
3 tablespoons rum
8 ounces butter
8 ounces sugar
grated rind of 1 lemon
6 eggs
2 cups plain flour
¼ level teaspoon baking powder
a pinch of salt
½ teaspoon nutmeg
½ teaspoon ground cloves

The day before the cake is to be made, chop the raisins and combine with the sultanas. Sprinkle with the rum and allow to stand overnight.

Line an 8-inch cake tin with two thicknesses of white and two of brown paper.

Beat the butter and sugar to a soft cream, add the lemon rind and beat again. Add the eggs one at a time, beating well after each addition.

Sift the flour with the baking powder, salt, nutmeg and cloves. Add to the creamed mixture alternately with the soaked fruit. Mix thoroughly.

Place in the prepared tin and bake in a slow oven, 300°F., for 1 hour. Reduce the heat to 275°F. and cook for a further 1¼ hours or until cooked. Allow to cool.

Sprinkle the top with a little more rum, then wrap and store for at least two or three days before cutting.

GINGER FLUFF SPONGE

4 eggs, separated
a pinch of salt
½ cup sugar
½ cup arrowroot
2 rounded dessertspoons plain
flour
1 level teaspoon cinnamon
1 rounded dessertspoon cocoa
2 level teaspoons ground ginger
1 level teaspoon cream of tartar
½ level teaspoon bicarbonate of
soda
1 dessertspoon golden syrup
(warmed)
chocolate or lemon icing

Beat the egg whites with the salt until stiff. Gradually add the sugar, beating well, then add the egg yolks and beat again. Sift the dry ingredients together three times, fold them lightly into the egg mixture, then add the slightly warmed golden syrup.

Divide evenly between two well-greased 8-inch sandwich tins which have been lined on the bottom with greased paper. Bake in a moderate oven, 350°F., for 20 to 25 minutes.

When cold join together with either mock or whipped cream or with lemon cheese. Cover the top with a chocolate or a lemon-flavoured icing.

GINGERBREAD

3 level cups plain flour
1 level teaspoon bicarbonate of
soda
3 level teaspoons ginger
a pinch of salt
2 rounded tablespoons butter
2 rounded tablespoons brown
sugar
1 egg
¾ cup golden syrup
1 cup milk

Sift the flour with the soda, ginger and salt. Rub in the butter and add the sugar.

Beat the egg and mix with the slightly warmed golden syrup and the milk. Pour into the flour mixture and stir until smooth.

Place in two well-greased bar tins or in a 7-inch round tin which has been lined with paper. Bake in a moderate oven, 350°F., for 30 to 35 minutes if cooked in the bar tins, 40 to 45 minutes if cooked in the round tin.

Ginger Fluff Sponge

2 cups self-raising flour
a pinch of salt
4 ounces butter
¾ cup sugar
1 teaspoon grated orange rind
2 eggs, separated
½ cup chopped walnuts
¾ cup milk

For the filling

½ cup sugar
3 level dessertspoons cornflour
a good pinch of salt
1½ cups undrained canned
   crushed pineapple
1 dessertspoon butter
1½ teaspoons lemon juice
½ cup chopped walnuts

For the chocolate icing

2 ounces butter
4 ounces sifted icing sugar
1 level tablespoon cocoa
orange juice
walnuts (optional) to decorate

GOLD COAST PINEAPPLE CAKE

Sift the flour and salt twice. Beat the butter and sugar to a cream, add the grated orange rind, then beat in the egg yolks one at a time. Stir in the chopped walnuts, then add the sifted flour alternately with the milk. Beat the egg whites stiffly and fold in lightly and thoroughly.

Divide the mixture evenly between two well-greased 7-inch sandwich tins and bake in a moderate oven, 350°F., for about 20 to 25 minutes. Cool.

To make the filling combine the first four ingredients in a saucepan, stir until boiling and cook for 2 minutes, then add the remaining ingredients. Allow to become quite cold. Reserving a couple of tablespoons of this filling for the top, join the layers with the filling.

Beat the butter and icing sugar for the chocolate icing then add the cocoa and enough orange juice to make a good spreading consistency. Ice the sides of the cake and the outer part of the top, leaving the centre uncovered. Fill the centre with the reserved pineapple filling. Decorate with walnuts if liked.

GOLDEN DATE CAKE

4 ounces butter
¾ cup sugar
2 eggs
1 teaspoon vanilla essence
2 cups plain flour
2 slightly rounded teaspoons
    baking powder
a pinch of salt
¾ cup milk
1 cup chopped dates
½ cup chopped nuts
orange butter cream
dates and walnut halves to
    decorate

Cream the butter and sugar until light and fluffy. Gradually add the well-beaten eggs and flavour with the vanilla.

Sift the flour with the baking powder and salt and add to the creamed mixture alternately with the milk. Stir in the chopped dates and nuts.

Divide evenly between two well-greased 8-inch sandwich tins which have been lined on the bottom with a round of greased paper. Bake in a moderate oven, 350°F., for 30 to 35 minutes. Remove from the tins and allow to cool.

Join the two layers with orange-flavoured butter cream, frost the top with the same cream, and decorate with dates and walnut halves, or with orange segments.

GOLDEN FRUIT CAKE

1 tablespoon butter
¼ cup golden syrup
¼ cup brandy
½ pound glacé pineapple
¼ pound glacé apricots
½ pound sultanas
¼ pound mixed peel
¼ pound glacé cherries
½ pound butter
1⅓ cups (firmly packed) light
    brown sugar
grated rind of 1 orange and 1
    lemon
4 eggs
¼ pound ground almonds
2½ cups plain flour
½ level teaspoon baking powder
a good pinch of salt
1 level teaspoon cinnamon
1 level teaspoon ginger

Combine the tablespoon of butter with the golden syrup and brandy in a saucepan and stir over medium heat until the butter has melted and the syrup softened. Bring to the boil and simmer for 3 minutes. Cool.

Cut the fruit into uniform-sized pieces. Line an 8-inch cake tin with two thicknesses of brown and two of white paper.

Beat the half pound of butter and the brown sugar to a soft cream and add the orange and lemon rind. Add the eggs one at a time, beating well after each addition. Stir in the ground almonds. Add half the fruit and half the brandy syrup to the mixture.

Sift the flour with the baking powder, salt, cinnamon and ginger and add half to the mixture. Add the remaining fruit and syrup, then the remainder of the flour. Blend thoroughly.

Place in the prepared tin and bake in a slow oven, 275°F., for 3 to 3½ hours.

GOLDEN PINEAPPLE CAKE

2 cups self-raising flour
a pinch of salt
1¼ cups castor sugar
3 ounces butter
3 egg yolks
¼ pint plus 2 tablespoons milk
¼ teaspoon lemon essence

Grease two 8-inch sandwich tins and line the bottom of each with greased paper. Sift the flour with the salt and sugar.

Slightly soften the butter and add the egg yolks, half the milk and the lemon essence. Fold in the sifted dry ingredients, beat to a smooth batter, then add the remainder of the milk and beat for 2 minutes.

Divide the mixture evenly between the two tins and bake

For the filling

2 ounces butter
1 cup icing sugar
grated rind of 1 orange
1 teaspoon orange juice

For the topping

½ pint cream
a little sugar
vanilla essence
2 tablespoons lemon cheese
3 rings of preserved pineapple
cherries
4 tablespoons chopped walnuts

4 ounces butter
1 cup brown sugar
2 eggs, separated
2 tablespoons golden syrup
¼ cup chopped walnuts
2 cups self-raising flour
1 level teaspoon cinnamon
½ level teaspoon ground nutmeg
¼ teaspoon ground cloves
a pinch of salt
½ cup milk

For the frosting and decoration

1 tablespoon butter
4 tablespoons icing sugar
1 dessertspoon milk
1 teaspoon coffee essence
1 teaspoon cocoa
3 tablespoons powdered milk
walnut halves for decorating

4 ounces butter
1 cup castor sugar
2 eggs, separated
¼ teaspoon vanilla essence
1½ cups self-raising flour
a pinch of salt
1 teaspoon cinnamon

at 375°F., for 20 minutes, then reduce the temperature to 325°F. and bake for a further 15 minutes. Allow to stand for a few minutes before turning out of the tins.

Make the filling by creaming the butter and sifted icing sugar and adding the orange rind and juice. Use some of this to join the two layers. Spread the remainder round the sides of the cake and coat with the chopped nuts.

Whip the cream, flavouring with a little sugar and vanilla, and spread it over the top of the cake. Place the lemon cheese in the centre and decorate with the drained pineapple pieces, the remainder of the cream piped through a cream tube, and a few cherries.

GOLDEN SPICE CAKE 1

Cream the butter with the brown sugar until light and fluffy. Beat in the egg yolks one at a time. Add the golden syrup, then the chopped walnuts.

Sift the flour with the spices and salt and fold into the creamed mixture alternately with the milk.

Beat the egg whites in a warm, dry bowl until soft peaks form. Fold them into the cake batter.

Place the mixture in a well-greased 7-inch cake tin which has been lined on the bottom with greased paper. Bake in a moderate oven, 350°F., for 50 to 60 minutes. Turn out and allow to cool.

Cover the top with frosting and decorate with walnut halves. To make the frosting beat the butter until creamy, gradually beat in the sifted icing sugar and half the milk, then add the coffee essence and the cocoa, mixing well. Beat in the powdered milk and the remainder of the milk and continue beating until the mixture is very smooth.

GOLDEN SPICE CAKE 2

Beat the butter and sugar to a light and fluffy cream, then beat in the egg yolks. Flavour with the vanilla. Sift the flour with the salt, spices and cocoa and add to the butter mixture alternately with the milk. Beat the egg whites stiffly and fold in.

Divide the mixture evenly between two well-greased 7-inch sandwich tins and bake in a moderate oven, 350°F., for 20 to 25 minutes. Turn out and allow to cool.

103

1 teaspoon ground ginger
1 teaspoon allspice
½ teaspoon nutmeg
1 dessertspoon cocoa
½ cup milk
1 cup cream
1 tablespoon sugar (for cream)
1 cup finely chopped nuts
cherries and angelica for
    garnishing

Add the tablespoon of sugar and a little spice to the cream and beat until stiff. Make four layers by splitting each of the two cake layers in halves, then join them with some of the whipped cream. Now coat the top and sides of the cake with the remaining cream and gently press some of the chopped nuts round the sides (this will take about three-quarters of the chopped nuts). Use the remaining chopped nuts to cover a circle about 3 inches in diameter in the centre. Garnish the edge of this centre with halves of crystallized cherries and pieces of angelica.

HARVEST LOAF CAKE

Cream the butter and sugar and gradually add the well-beaten eggs.

Sift the flour with the soda, spices and salt and stir into the creamed mixture alternately with the mashed pumpkin. Stir in the chocolate pieces and the ½ cup of chopped walnuts.

Place in a 9-inch by 5-inch loaf tin which has been well greased and lined on the bottom with greased paper. Sprinkle the top with the remainder of the nuts. Bake in a moderate oven, 350°F., for 1¼ hours.

While the cake is still warm pour the glaze over it. To make, mix all the ingredients in a saucepan and stir until the sugar melts.

4 ounces butter
1 cup sugar
2 eggs
1¾ cups self-raising flour
½ level teaspoon bicarbonate of
    soda
1 teaspoon cinnamon
½ teaspoon ground nutmeg
¼ teaspoon ground ginger
¼ teaspoon ground cloves
½ teaspoon salt
¾ cup mashed pumpkin
4 ounces chocolate pieces
½ cup chopped walnuts

For the glaze and topping
½ cup castor sugar
¼ teaspoon cinnamon
¼ teaspoon nutmeg
1 or 2 tablespoons top milk or
    cream
¼ cup chopped walnuts for top-
    ping

HAWAIIAN TEA CAKE

Cream the butter and sugar and gradually add the well-beaten egg. Sift the flour with the salt and add to the creamed mixture alternately with the milk.

Spread half the cake mixture in a well-greased 7-inch sandwich tin and cover with the well-drained pineapple. Top with the remainder of the cake mixture.

Bake in a moderate oven, 350°F., for 25 to 30 minutes. Turn out carefully onto a wire cooler and while still hot brush with the melted butter and sprinkle with a mixture of sugar and cinnamon.

2 ounces butter
¼ cup sugar
1 egg
1 cup self-raising flour
a pinch of salt
2 tablespoons milk
½ cup well-drained canned
    shredded pineapple

For the topping
1 teaspoon butter, melted
¼ teaspoon cinnamon
1 teaspoon sugar

Hazelnut Torte

HAZELNUT TORTE

3 eggs, separated
a pinch of salt
½ cup sugar
1 cup plain flour
2 level tablespoons cocoa
1 level teaspoon cream of tartar
½ level teaspoon bicarbonate of
  soda
½ teaspoon vanilla essence
1 dessertspoon butter melted in
  2 tablespoons hot water

For the nut cream filling

¼ pint cream
3 slightly rounded tablespoons
  castor sugar
1½ cups finely ground hazelnuts
2 ounces butter
½ teaspoon vanilla essence

For the chocolate glaze

1 cup icing sugar
1 tablespoon cocoa
about 1 tablespoon milk
1 teaspoon butter

Beat the egg whites with the salt until soft peaks form. Gradually add the sugar and continue beating until the mixture is thick and glossy. Add the egg yolks one at a time, beating well.

Sift the flour with the cocoa, cream of tartar and soda and fold into the sugar and egg mixture. Flavour with the vanilla and add the mixture of water and butter.

Pour into a well-greased 11-inch by 7-inch shallow tray which has been lined on the bottom with greased paper. Bake at 375°F. for 10 to 15 minutes. Turn onto a wire cooler.

When cold, cut in half down the centre, then split each piece horizontally into two, making four layers altogether.

Make the nut cream by combining the cream, sugar and ground hazelnuts in the top of a double saucepan and cooking over boiling water, beating until thick. Remove from the heat and cool. Chill the mixture for about 30 minutes, then add the softened butter and vanilla and beat until light and creamy. Use some of this filling to join the four cake layers together, and frost the top and sides with the remainder. Chill.

Meanwhile, make the glaze: Sift the icing sugar and cocoa into a saucepan and add the milk and butter, then heat briefly over low heat. Spread over the top of the torte, then place the cake in the refrigerator for about 30 minutes or until set. Cut into slices to serve.

105

HONEY SPONGE ROLL

3 eggs, separated
a pinch of salt
½ cup sugar
¾ cup plain flour
1 slightly rounded teaspoon
   baking powder
1 tablespoon honey
2 tablespoons water
1 teaspoon caramel or burnt
   sugar for colouring
   (optional)
whipped cream for filling
icing sugar or castor sugar for
   topping

Prepare a 9-inch by 12-inch Swiss roll tin by greasing it first and then lining the bottom with greased paper.

Beat the egg whites with the salt until stiff, then gradually add the sugar and continue beating until thick and glossy. Add the egg yolks one at a time, beating well after each addition.

Sift the flour and baking powder three times. Mix the honey with the water and add the caramel if used. Fold the flour into the sugar and egg mixture, then stir in the honey mixture.

Spread evenly in the prepared tin and bake in a moderate oven, 350°F., for about 20 minutes. Turn out onto a damp cloth, roll up, then place on a paper sprinkled with sugar and unroll. Now cut off the side crusts and re-roll. Cool on a wire cooler. Unroll and spread with whipped and flavoured cream, then re-roll and sprinkle with castor sugar or sifted icing sugar.

HUNGARIAN APPLE CAKE

2 dessertspoons butter
½ cup brown sugar
2 teaspoons cinnamon
½ cup chopped walnuts
6 ounces butter
¾ cup sugar
3 eggs, separated
3 cups plain flour
a pinch of salt
4 level teaspoons baking powder
1¼ cups sour cream
2 small apples, peeled, cored and
   finely chopped

Mix the 2 dessertspoons of butter with the brown sugar, cinnamon and chopped nuts until crumbly. Set aside.

Beat the 6 ounces of butter and the ¾ cup of sugar to a soft cream, then beat in the egg yolks one at a time. Sift the flour with the salt and baking powder and add to the creamed mixture alternately with the sour cream. Fold in the stiffly beaten egg whites.

Place half the mixture in a greased and lined 9-inch tube pan. Sprinkle with the crumbly butter, sugar and walnut mixture, then add the chopped apples. Cover with the remainder of the cake batter.

Bake in a moderate oven, 350°F., for about 1¼ hours. Cool in the tin for 15 minutes, then turn out onto a wire cooler. Cut into wedges to serve.

HUNGARIAN COFFEE CAKE

8 ounces butter
¾ cup sugar
4 eggs, separated
3 cups plain flour
3 level teaspoons baking powder
¼ teaspoon salt
1 cup milk

For the topping

½ teaspoon cinnamon
1 teaspoon mixed spice
½ cup sugar
1 level tablespoon cocoa

Grease a 9-inch tube tin. Beat the butter to a cream, add the sugar and beat until light and fluffy. Add the egg yolks one at a time, beating well after each addition.

Sift the flour with the baking powder and salt and stir into the creamed mixture alternately with the milk. Beat the egg whites in a clean dry bowl until stiff, then fold into the cake mixture.

Combine the ingredients for the topping.

Spread one-third of the cake mixture in the bottom of the prepared tin, sprinkle with one-third of the spicy topping, add another third of the cake mixture, then another third of the topping. Add the remainder of the cake mixture, then the rest of the topping.

Bake in a moderate oven, 350°F., for about 1 hour or until a skewer inserted in the middle comes out clean. Cool in the tin.

HUSSAR CAKE

2½ cups sifted plain flour
1½ level teaspoons baking
  powder
½ level teaspoon bicarbonate of
  soda
6 ounces butter
1 cup sugar
½ cup redcurrant jelly
3 eggs
½ level teaspoon cinnamon
½ level teaspoon nutmeg
⅛ teaspoon ground cloves
1 ounce dark chocolate, finely
  grated
¾ cup sour cream
crème de cacao or cherry
  brandy
whipped and sweetened cream

Grease a 9-inch tube pan. Sift the flour with the baking powder and soda.

Beat the butter and sugar to a soft cream and beat in the redcurrant jelly. Add the eggs one at a time, beating well after each addition. Add the cinnamon, nutmeg, cloves and grated chocolate. Stir in the sour cream alternately with the sifted flour.

Place in the prepared tin and bake in a moderate oven, 350°F., for 50 to 60 minutes or until a skewer inserted in the middle of the cake comes out clean. Cool for 10 minutes before removing from the tin.

Leave until the following day. Split the cake into two layers and sprinkle one layer with the cherry brandy. Whip the cream and spread between the layers, reserving some to decorate the top.

½ pound unpeeled almonds
2 small whole eggs and 6 small
  separated eggs
1 cup sugar
grated rind of 1 lemon
1 dessertspoon lemon juice
fine white breadcrumbs

For the icing and decoration

2 ounces grated chocolate
4 tablespoons milk
1 tablespoon butter
¼ teaspoon vanilla essence
about 2 cups icing sugar
whole blanched almonds for
  decorating

JAGERTORTE (HUNTER'S CAKE)

This cake must be made in a spring-form pan because it is too delicate to be turned out of an ordinary cake tin.

Finely mince the unpeeled almonds. Combine 2 whole eggs with 6 of the egg yolks and beat for about 5 minutes. Stir in the almonds, sugar, lemon rind and juice, then fold in the 6 stiffly beaten egg whites.

Sprinkle some fine white breadcrumbs on the bottom and sides of a well-greased 9-inch spring-form pan. Pour in the cake mixture. Bake in a moderate oven, 375°F., for 1 hour. Let the cake cool before gently removing it from the tin.

Ice the top and sides with chocolate icing and decorate with whole blanched almonds.

To make the icing, first melt the chocolate with the milk and butter. Cool, add the vanilla, and work in 2 cups of sifted icing sugar or enough to make a soft, spreading consistency, warming it gently over hot water before pouring over the cake.

For the pastry

1½ cups plain flour
a pinch of salt
6 ounces butter
about 2 tablespoons cold water

KERST KRANS

Sift the flour with the salt, cut or rub in the butter and add enough water to mix to a dough, using a knife. Turn onto a floured board, knead only until smooth on the outside, then roll into a strip 4 inches wide, 12 inches long and about ⅛ inch thick.

To make the filling combine the almonds and sugar and add the beaten egg and lemon rind. Make into a strip about 1 inch

For the filling

1 cup ground almonds
½ cup sugar
1 egg
grated rind of 1 lemon

For the topping

glacé lemon icing
pieces of crystallized cherry

4 ounces butter
½ cup sugar
3 eggs
¼ teaspoon vanilla essence
2 cups self-raising flour
a pinch of salt
3 tablespoons milk

For the filling and topping

3 ounces unsweetened chocolate,
   grated
3 ounces sweetened chocolate,
   grated
¾ cup coconut

4 ounces butter
3 slightly rounded tablespoons
   sugar
2 eggs
2 cups self-raising flour
1 level teaspoon ground ginger
½ level teaspoon mixed spice
⅓ cup milk
1 tablespoon golden syrup
3 ounces chopped crystallized
   ginger
½ cup lemon butter

For the icing

2 ounces butter
1 cup icing sugar
a little grated lemon rind

thick. Dampen the edges of the pastry and place the strip of filling in the centre, then roll the pastry round the filling. Place on a greased baking tray and twist into a round shape (i.e. have the seam of the pastry underneath). Brush with a little beaten egg and water.

Bake in a hot oven at 400°F. for 20 minutes. Cool.

Ice the top with lemon glacé icing and decorate with pieces of cherry.

LAZY DAY CHOCOLATE CAKE

Grease a 7-inch cake tin and line the bottom with greased paper. Beat the butter and sugar to a soft cream, then gradually beat in the well-whisked eggs. Flavour with the vanilla.

Sift the flour with the salt and add to the creamed mixture alternately with the milk.

Combine both chocolates and melt them over hot water. Stir in the coconut.

Place half the cake mixture in the prepared tin and cover with half the chocolate mixture. Add the remainder of the cake mixture, then spread over it evenly the remainder of the chocolate mixture.

Bake in a moderate oven, 350°F., for 50 to 60 minutes. Turn out and allow to cool.

LEMON AND GINGER CAKE

Cream the butter and sugar until light and fluffy. Gradually add the beaten eggs, beating well after each addition. Sift the flour with the ginger and spice and mix the golden syrup with the milk. Add the flour and the syrup and milk mixture alternately to the creamed mixture and stir in the chopped ginger.

Grease a 7-inch round cake tin well and line the bottom with greased paper. Spoon half the cake mixture into the tin, then add the lemon butter, spreading it evenly but keeping it from the sides of the cake tin. Top with the remainder of the cake mixture.

Bake in a moderate oven, 350°F., for about 50 or 55 minutes. Allow the cake to remain in the tin for a few minutes after removing it from the oven. Cool on a wire rack.

Top with an icing made by beating the butter with the icing sugar and flavouring with the lemon rind. Thin slices of crystallized ginger may be used to decorate the top.

LEMON CAKE

4 ounces butter or margarine
3 slightly rounded tablespoons
   sugar
grated rind of 1 lemon
2 eggs
1¼ cups self-raising flour
1 dessertspoon lemon juice
1 tablespoon milk

For the filling
rind and juice of ½ lemon
1 egg
½ cup sugar
1 ounce butter

For the topping
¼ pint fresh cream
1 teaspoon sugar
½ teaspoon vanilla essence
pieces of cherry and angelica
   (optional)

Beat the butter and sugar to a soft cream, add the grated lemon rind, then well-beaten eggs.

Sift the flour and add to the creamed mixture alternately with the lemon juice and milk.

Place in a well-greased 8-inch recess tin and bake in a moderate oven, 350°F., for 30 to 40 minutes. Cool.

To make the filling, beat the lemon rind and juice in a bowl with the egg and sugar, then add the butter. Stand the bowl over a saucepan containing enough boiling water to reach halfway up the sides of the bowl. Cook, stirring well, until the mixture is smooth and thick. Cool. Fill the recess with this lemon mixture.

Whip the cream, adding the sugar and vanilla, and pipe or spread it over the lemon filling. If liked, decorate with pieces of cherry and angelica.

LEMON COFFEE CAKE

1½ cups self-raising flour
¼ teaspoon salt
3 ounces butter
½ cup sugar
grated rind and juice of 1 lemon
2 eggs
2 tablespoons milk

For the topping
2 tablespoons self-raising flour
2 tablespoons brown sugar
¼ cup chopped nuts
1 dessertspoon butter

Sift the flour with the salt. Cream the butter and sugar with the lemon rind until light and fluffy, add the beaten eggs, beating well after each addition, then add the lemon juice. Fold in the sifted flour and salt, then add the milk.

Spread the mixture in a 7-inch cake tin which has been greased and lined on the bottom with greased paper. Sprinkle over the topping, made by combining the flour, brown sugar and nuts with the slightly softened butter.

Bake in a moderate oven, 350°F., for about 45 minutes. Cool before serving.

LEMON LOAF CAKE

4 ounces butter
½ cup sugar
1 teaspoon grated lemon rind
2 eggs
1¼ cups self-raising flour
¼ cup plain flour
a pinch of salt
½ cup milk

For the lemon glaze
3 teaspoons sugar
3 tablespoons lemon juice

Grease a 9-inch by 5-inch loaf tin and line the bottom with greased paper. Beat the butter, sugar and lemon rind to a soft cream, then gradually beat in the well-whisked eggs.

Sift the plain flour with the self-raising flour and salt and add to the creamed mixture alternately with the milk. Place in the prepared tin and bake in a moderate oven, 350°F., for 40 to 45 minutes.

Make the glaze by mixing the sugar with the lemon juice. As soon as the cake comes from the oven pour over the glaze and allow the cake to remain in the tin for 10 minutes before turning out to cool.

LIGHT FRUIT CAKE 1

1 cup sultanas
1 cup seeded raisins
¼ cup chopped cherries
¼ cup blanched and chopped
  almonds
¼ cup mixed peel
½ pound butter
1 cup sugar
4 eggs
3 cups plain flour
3 level teaspoons baking powder
1 level teaspoon nutmeg
1 level teaspoon mixed spice
a pinch of salt
2 tablespoons milk
2 tablespoons brandy

Prepare the fruit and nuts. Line an 8-inch cake tin with two thicknesses of brown and two of white paper. Beat the butter with the sugar until creamy. Add the eggs one at a time, beating well after each addition. Stir in the fruit and nuts.

Sift the flour with the baking powder, salt and spices and add to the creamed mixture alternately with the milk and brandy. Place in the prepared tin and bake at 325°F. for about 2 hours.

LIGHT FRUIT CAKE 2

4 ounces ground almonds
4 ounces glacé cherries
4 ounces chopped mixed peel
1 pound chopped raisins
8 ounces chopped candied
  pineapple
½ cup plain flour
8 ounces butter
8 ounces sugar
4 eggs
1 teaspoon almond essence
⅓ cup brandy
¼ cup milk
10 ounces plain flour
1 level teaspoon baking powder

Line an 8-inch deep-sided cake tin with two thicknesses of white and two of brown paper. Heat the oven to 275°F. Combine the almonds, cherries, mixed peel, raisins, pineapple and the ½ cup of plain flour.

Beat the butter and gradually add the sugar, beating until creamy. Add the eggs one at a time, beating well after each addition. Flavour with the almond essence.

Combine the brandy with the milk and add to the creamed mixture alternately with the sifted flour and baking powder. Blend well, then fold in the fruit mixture.

Spoon into the prepared tin and bake for 3 to 3½ hours. Test with a skewer. Turn out of the tin, and when the cake has cooled slightly, remove the paper. Wrap well and store for at least 2 weeks to mature.

LINCOLN LOG

5 eggs, separated
¼ teaspoon cream of tartar
5 ounces sugar
1 teaspoon grated orange rind
½ teaspoon vanilla essence
1½ tablespoons dry sherry
1 cup self-raising flour
a pinch of salt
1 teaspoon gelatine
1 tablespoon cold water
½ pint cream
sugar and vanilla essence for
  cream

Place the egg whites in a bowl and beat until soft peaks form. Add the cream of tartar and continue beating until stiff. Gradually beat in 3 ounces of the sugar, adding it to the mixture a tablespoonful at a time.

In another bowl beat the egg yolks until light and lemon coloured, then beat in the remaining 2 ounces of sugar and the orange rind, vanilla and sherry.

Fold the egg-white mixture into the egg-yolk mixture, then stir in lightly and evenly the sifted flour and salt. Pour into a greased and lined 12-inch by 9-inch Swiss roll tin and bake in a moderate oven, 375°F., for about 20 minutes.

Turn onto a damp cloth and roll up. Let it stand for 2 minutes. Remove the cloth and re-roll, then leave until cold.

For the chocolate frosting

2 ounces dark eating chocolate
1 tablespoon butter
about 2½ cups sifted icing sugar
a pinch of salt
2 tablespoons milk
1 teaspoon vanilla essence

Mix the gelatine with 1 tablespoon cold water and dissolve it over hot water. Add it to the sweetened whipped vanilla-flavoured cream. Unroll the cake and carefully spread with this cream then re-roll and spread with the chocolate frosting, running the tines of a fork lengthwise down the roll. Chill until the frosting has set.

To make the chocolate frosting combine the ingredients and beat till smooth.

MADEIRA CAKE

½ pound butter
grated rind of ½ a lemon
a pinch of ground cinnamon
1¼ cups castor sugar
5 eggs
3¼ cups plain flour
1 rounded teaspoon baking
   powder
a pinch of salt
½ cup milk
chopped peel

Grease an 8-inch round cake tin and line the bottom with greased paper. Beat the butter to a soft cream, adding the grated lemon rind and the cinnamon. Add the sugar and continue beating until light and fluffy. Add the eggs one at a time, beating well after each addition. Should the mixture show any sign of separating or curdling, add a teaspoon of the measured quantity of flour.

Sift the flour, baking powder and salt three times, then add to the creamed mixture alternately with the milk. Turn into the prepared tin and bake at 325°F. for about 1¾ hours. After the first half-hour's baking sprinkle the top with the chopped peel.

MOCHA CREAM ROLL

3 eggs, separated
4 slightly rounded tablespoons
   sugar
4 slightly rounded tablespoons
   plain flour
2 level tablespoons cocoa
1 level teaspoon cream of tartar
½ level teaspoon bicarbonate of
   soda
2 tablespoons hot water
½ teaspoon vanilla essence

For the filling

2 dessertspoons sifted icing sugar
1 rounded teaspoon instant
   coffee
½ teaspoon vanilla or rum
½ pint cream

Grease a Swiss roll tin and line the bottom with greased paper. Add a pinch of salt to the egg whites and beat until soft peaks form. Gradually add the sugar and continue beating until thick and glossy. Add the egg yolks one at a time, beating well after each addition.

Sift the flour with the cocoa and cream of tartar. Dissolve the soda in the hot water. Add the vanilla to the egg mixture, then fold in the sifted flour mixture. Lastly add the soda and water.

Spread evenly in the prepared tin and bake in a moderate oven, 375°F., for 12 to 15 minutes. Turn out onto a damp cloth and cut off the side crusts. Roll up quickly and place on a wire cooler.

When quite cold, unroll and spread with the cream filling. Re-roll and dust the top with sifted icing sugar.

To make the filling, combine the icing sugar, instant coffee and vanilla with the cream and beat until stiff.

MOCHA LAYER CAKE

½ cup butter
1 cup castor sugar
1 teaspoon vanilla essence
2 eggs, separated
1½ cups self-raising flour
3 level tablespoons cocoa
a pinch of salt
½ cup milk

For the filling and topping

1 rounded teaspoon sugar
½ teaspoon vanilla essence
½ pint cream
1 rounded teaspoon instant
   coffee
1 teaspoon gelatine dissolved in
   1 tablespoon water
½ cup chopped nuts
candied cherries (optional)

Beat the butter to a soft cream, add the sugar and continue beating until fluffy. Flavour with the vanilla and add the egg yolks. Beat well. Sift the flour with the cocoa and salt and stir in alternately with the milk.

Beat the egg whites stiffly and fold into the cake mixture. Divide evenly between two well-greased sandwich tins which have been lined on the bottom with greased paper. Bake in a moderate oven, 350°F., for about 20 minutes. Cool.

To make the filling and topping add the sugar and vanilla to the cream and whip until thick, then add the coffee and dissolved gelatine, stirring until evenly mixed.

Spread some of the coffee cream between the cake layers, and use the remainder to cover the top and sides. Decorate the sides with chopped nuts and the top with candied cherries.

ORANGE CAKE

6 ounces butter or margarine
¾ cup sugar
2 teaspoons grated orange rind
3 eggs
1 cup plain flour
1 cup self-raising flour
2 tablespoons milk or strained
   orange juice

Cream the butter with the sugar and orange rind until light and fluffy. Beat the eggs well and gradually add to the creamed mixture, beating well after each addition.

Sift the plain and self-raising flours together and stir in alternately with the milk or orange juice.

Place in a well-greased loaf tin or a 6-inch round cake tin. Bake at 325°F. for about 1 or 1¼ hours.

When cold cover the top with orange-flavoured glacé icing and decorate with small sections of orange.

ORANGE COFFEE CAKE

2½ cups self-raising flour
a pinch of salt
3 dessertspoons butter
3 dessertspoons sugar
1 egg
¾ cup milk

Sift the flour with the salt, rub in the butter, and add the sugar. Combine the beaten egg with the milk and stir into the flour mixture, making a soft dough.

Turn onto a floured board and knead lightly. Divide in two, one piece slightly larger than the other. Roll this larger piece to fit an 8-inch tart plate which has been well greased. Sprinkle

For the orange filling
⅓ cup brown sugar
⅓ cup chopped walnuts
2 dessertspoons plain flour
1 dessertspoon grated orange
   rind
a pinch of salt
2 dessertspoons melted butter

For the topping
1 to 1½ tablespoons orange juice
4 ounces sifted icing sugar
chopped walnuts

4 ounces butter
½ cup sugar
grated rind of 1 orange
2 eggs
1½ cups plain flour
2 level teaspoons baking powder
a pinch of salt
¼ cup milk

For the date filling
4 ounces chopped dates
½ cup boiling water
1 teaspoon grated orange rind
1 dessertspoon honey

For the orange frosting
1½ ounces butter
1 teaspoon grated orange rind
1 cup icing sugar

5 ounces butter
½ cup plus 1 tablespoon sugar
1 dessertspoon grated orange
   rind
3 eggs
2¼ cups plain flour
2 slightly rounded teaspoons
   baking powder
a pinch of salt
⅓ cup milk
¼ cup orange juice
orange Vienna icing (see recipe
   page 146) and grated chocolate
   for filling and topping

with the orange filling (made by combining all the ingredients in a bowl). Roll the remainder of the paste to fit the top of the tart plate. Slash the edges of the top layer with scissors.

Bake in a hot oven, 425°F., for 20 minutes. Drizzle with orange glaze while still warm. To make the glaze mix the orange juice with the sifted icing sugar, beat briefly and pour over the cake. Top with the chopped walnuts.

ORANGE DATE CAKE

Cream the butter and sugar with the grated orange rind for the cake, then add the eggs one at a time, beating well after each addition. Sift the flour with the baking powder and salt and add to the creamed mixture alternately with the milk.

Place half the cake mixture in a greased ring tin, cover with the cooled date filling and top with the remainder of the cake mixture. Bake in a moderate oven, 350°F., for about 40 or 45 minutes. When cold cover with orange frosting.

To make the filling place the chopped dates in a saucepan, add the boiling water and stir until soft. Remove from the heat, add the orange rind and the honey and allow to become quite cold before using in the cake.

To make the frosting beat the butter and orange rind to a cream, then gradually beat in the sifted icing sugar. Add a little orange juice if the mixture is too stiff.

ORANGE DREAM CAKE

Cream the butter with the sugar, then add the grated orange rind.

Beat the eggs in a separate bowl until doubled in volume, then gradually add to the creamed mixture, beating well. Sift the flour with the baking powder and salt and stir in alternately with the milk and orange juice.

Divide evenly between two well-greased 8-inch sandwich tins which have been lined on the bottom with greased paper. Bake in a moderate oven, 350°F., for about 30 minutes.

When cold join the layers with half the Vienna icing, spread the remainder on top and decorate with shaved chocolate.

113

ORANGE GINGER CAKE

4 ounces butter
½ cup sugar
1 egg
½ cup golden syrup
1⅓ cups plain flour
1 level teaspoon ground ginger
1 level teaspoon bicarbonate of
    soda
¼ teaspoon salt
⅓ cup cold tea
2 teaspoons grated orange rind

Beat the butter and sugar until creamy, then add the egg, beating until light and fluffy. Beat in the golden syrup.

Sift the flour with the ginger, soda and salt and add to the creamed mixture alternately with the cold tea. Add the grated orange rind.

Place in an 8-inch square cake tin and bake in a moderate oven, 350°F., for about 35 minutes.

Serve warm or cold. To serve warm as a shortcake, split through the centre and fill generously with peaches and whipped cream, then pile more peaches and cream on top.

ORANGE LAYER CAKE

4 ounces butter
½ cup sugar
1 teaspoon grated orange rind
3 eggs, separated
1½ cups self-raising flour
1 rounded tablespoon cornflour
¼ cup milk
¼ cup orange juice

For the filling

2 ounces butter
1 cup icing sugar
grated rind of 1 orange
1 tablespoon orange juice

For the icing

4 ounces icing sugar
1 tablespoon orange juice

Grease two 7-inch sandwich tins and line the bottom of each with a round of greased paper. Beat the butter and sugar to a cream and add the grated orange rind. Add the egg yolks, beating well.

Sift the flour with the cornflour and mix the milk with the orange juice. Add these alternately to the creamed mixture. Beat the egg whites stiffly and fold in.

Divide the cake mixture evenly between the prepared tins and bake in a moderate oven, 350°F., for 20 to 25 minutes. Turn out and allow to cool.

For the filling beat the butter until soft and gradually work in the sifted icing sugar, orange rind and juice. Use to join the two cake layers.

To make the icing sift the icing sugar into a saucepan and add the orange juice. Stir with a wooden spoon until smooth, then heat briefly over medium heat. Pour over the cake and allow to set.

If liked, the top of the cake may be decorated with fresh orange sections, grated orange rind or coconut.

ORANGE OR LEMON MACAROON CAKE

2 ounces butter
½ cup sugar
grated rind of 1 orange or
    1 lemon
2 egg yolks
5 tablespoons milk
1 cup self-raising flour
a pinch of salt

For the topping
2 egg whites
½ cup sugar
½ cup coconut
½ teaspoon vanilla essence

Grease a 7-inch cake tin and line the bottom with a round of greased paper. Beat the butter, sugar and orange rind to a soft cream. Add the egg yolks and beat again. Stir in the milk alternately with the sifted flour and salt. Place in the prepared tin.

Beat the egg whites in a warm dry bowl with a pinch of salt until stiff peaks form. Gradually beat in the sugar, then fold in the coconut and vanilla. Spread on top of the uncooked cake mixture and bake in a moderate oven, 350°F., for 45 minutes.

ORANGE SPONGE

3 or 4 eggs, separated
½ cup sugar
1 tablespoon hot water
1 dessertspoon butter
1 cup self-raising flour
½ teaspoon grated orange rind
1 tablespoon orange juice
½ pint cream
1 tablespoon icing sugar
½ teaspoon grated orange rind
(for cream)
chopped nuts

Beat the egg whites with a pinch of salt until stiff. Gradually add the sugar, beating until the mixture stands in glossy peaks. Beat in the egg yolks one at a time, then add ½ teaspoon of grated orange rind.

Heat the water and butter in a saucepan and stir until the butter has dissolved, then add the orange juice.

Sift the flour three times and lightly fold it into the eggs, then add the mixture of water, butter and orange juice.

Divide evenly between two well-greased sandwich tins and bake in a moderate oven, 350°F., for 20 to 25 minutes. Turn out onto a wire cooler to become quite cold.

Whip the cream with the icing sugar and ½ teaspoon of grated orange rind and use half to sandwich the two layers together. Cover the top with the remaining whipped cream and sprinkle the chopped nuts round the edge.

ORANGE TEA CAKE

1 egg, separated
a pinch of salt
½ cup sugar
1 teaspoon grated orange or
    lemon rind
⅓ cup milk
1 tablespoon orange juice
1 cup self-raising flour
1 tablespoon butter, melted

For the icing

1 cup icing sugar
1 tablespoon orange juice
coconut

Beat the egg white with the salt until stiff, then gradually add the sugar, beating until glossy peaks form. Stir in the egg yolk and the grated orange or lemon rind.

Combine the milk and orange juice and add to the egg and sugar mixture, then stir in the sifted flour. Lastly add the melted butter.

Place in a well-greased 7-inch sandwich tin and bake in a moderate oven, 350°F., for 20 to 25 minutes. Turn out onto a wire cooler to become quite cold.

Cover the top with warm icing, made by blending the sifted icing sugar with the orange juice and heating briefly over low heat. Sprinkle with coconut and allow the icing to set before cutting the tea cake into slices.

ORANGE TUTTI FRUTTI CAKE

6 ounces butter
1 cup castor sugar
½ teaspoon lemon essence
3 eggs
2¼ cups plain flour
1¼ level teaspoons baking
    powder
a pinch of salt
⅓ cup orange juice
⅓ cup milk

Cream the butter with the castor sugar and flavour with the lemon essence. Add the well-beaten eggs a little at a time.

Sift the flour with the baking powder and salt and add to the creamed mixture alternately with the combined orange juice and milk.

Divide between two well-greased 8-inch sandwich tins which have been lined on the bottom with greased paper. Bake in a moderate oven, 350°F., for 30 to 35 minutes. Turn out and allow to cool while you make the filling.

Combine the sugar and cornflour in a bowl and blend to a

115

For the filling

⅔ cup sugar
2½ level tablespoons cornflour
¾ cup water
1 tablespoon lemon juice
2 tablespoons orange juice
1 egg
2 tablespoons chopped and well-
  drained pineapple pieces
2 tablespoons passionfruit pulp
1 dessertspoon grated orange
  rind
2 ounces butter

smooth paste with the water, lemon juice and orange juice. Stir in the beaten egg. Cook over boiling water until the mixture thickens. Add the pineapple pieces, passionfruit pulp, orange rind and butter. Chill thoroughly before using in the cake.

Split the two layers of cake through their centres to make four layers, then join them with the fruit filling, reserving enough to spread over the top.

PLAIN CAKE

6 ounces butter
½ cup sugar
2 eggs
½ teaspoon vanilla essence
½ cup milk
2 cups self-raising flour
a pinch of salt

Beat the butter and sugar until light and creamy. Gradually add the well-beaten eggs, beating well after each addition.

Combine the vanilla with the milk and add to the mixture alternately with the sifted flour and salt.

Place in a well-greased orange-cake tin which has been lined on the bottom with greased paper. Bake in a moderate oven, 350°F., for about 45 minutes. Cool.

If liked this cake may be topped with lemon, orange or chocolate glacé icing.

POUND CAKE

8 ounces butter
1 cup sugar
4 eggs
8 ounces sultanas
2 ounces cherries, chopped
4 ounces mixed peel
2 ounces blanched almonds,
  chopped
2½ cups plain flour
a pinch of salt
1 level teaspoon nutmeg
1 level teaspoon mixed spice
3 level teaspoons baking powder
2 tablespoons milk
2 tablespoons sherry

Line an 8-inch cake tin with a piece of greased paper. Beat the butter and sugar to a soft cream. Gradually add the well-beaten eggs, beating well after each addition. Stir in the sultanas, cherries, peel and almonds.

Sift the flour with the salt, spices and baking powder and add to the creamed mixture alternately with the milk and sherry.

Place in the prepared tin and bake at 325°F. for about 1¾ to 2 hours.

PUMPKIN FRUIT CAKE

½ pound mixed fruit
¼ pound butter
1 cup brown sugar
1 cup water
1 level teaspoon bicarbonate of
    soda
¾ cup cold mashed pumpkin
1 cup self-raising flour
1 cup plain flour
a pinch of salt
1 teaspoon mixed spice
½ teaspoon nutmeg
1 dessertspoon golden syrup

Line a 9-inch by 5-inch loaf tin with two thicknesses of greased paper. Combine the fruit, butter, brown sugar and water in a saucepan and bring to the boil. Simmer for 10 minutes. Cool slightly and add the soda.

When almost cold, add the mashed pumpkin, the sifted dry ingredients and the golden syrup. Mix well.

Bake at 325°F. for 1¼ to 1½ hours.

RICH BOILED FRUIT CAKE

1 pound sultanas
¾ pound raisins
¼ pound mixed peel
¼ pound cherries, chopped
2 ounces dates, chopped
2 ounces apricots or prunes,
    chopped
2 level tablespoons golden syrup
3 tablespoons rum or sherry
¾ cup water
½ pound butter
½ pound light brown sugar
5 eggs
1 teaspoon Parisian essence
10 ounces plain flour
2 ounces self-raising flour
¼ teaspoon salt
¼ teaspoon cinnamon
2 level teaspoons mixed spice
¼ level teaspoon nutmeg
2 ounces blanched almonds

If preferred, use 2½ pounds of mixed fruit instead of the first 6 ingredients above.

Place all the fruit, the golden syrup, the rum and the water in a saucepan and bring to the boil. Simmer for 2 minutes, stirring occasionally. Pour into a bowl, cover and allow to stand overnight.

Cream the butter and sugar, then add the eggs one at a time, beating well after each addition. Stir in the Parisian essence.

Sift the flours with the salt and spices and stir half into the fruit mixture, mixing lightly, then blend into the creamed mixture. Stir in the remainder of the flour.

Place in a 9-inch tin which has been lined with two thicknesses of brown and two of white paper. Arrange the almonds on top. Bake in a slow oven, 275°F., for about 3½ hours.

RUSSIAN WALNUT CAKE

2¼ cups broken walnut pieces
⅓ cup fine arrowroot-biscuit
    crumbs
1¼ tablespoons plain flour
1 level teaspoon baking powder
7 eggs, separated
1 dessertspoon lemon juice
1 cup sugar

Grease three 9-inch sandwich tins and line the bottom of each with greased paper. Lightly dust with flour.

Whirl the broken walnut pieces a few at a time in a blender (you should have about 2½ cups of lightly packed nuts). Reserve 1½ cups of the nuts. Mix the remaining cupful with the biscuit crumbs, baking powder and flour.

Beat the egg whites in a large bowl until frothy. Add the lemon juice and continue beating until the mixture holds soft,

117

1 teaspoon grated lemon rind
1 dessertspoon rum
rum cream filling
   (recipe follows)
mocha butter cream
   (recipe follows)
¼ cup cherry or other berry jam
12 walnut halves

1 teaspoon gelatine
1½ dessertspoons cold water
½ pint cream
¼ cup sifted icing sugar
1 tablespoon rum

1 teaspoon vanilla essence
1 teaspoon instant coffee powder
3 ounces soft butter
1 cup sifted icing sugar
1 dessertspoon cream

4 ounces butter
½ cup sugar
3 eggs
2 level cups plain flour
2 level teaspoons baking powder
¼ level teaspoon ground nutmeg
a pinch of salt
2 teaspoons caraway seeds
½ cup chopped mixed peel
¼ cup chopped blanched
   almonds
⅓ pint milk

distinct peaks. Gradually beat in ½ cup of the sugar and beat until stiff. Fold in 1 cup of reserved nuts.

In another bowl beat the egg yolks lightly, then gradually beat in the remaining ½ cup of sugar. Beat until thick and lemon coloured, then blend in the nut and biscuit mixture, the grated lemon rind and the rum. Blend about a quarter of the egg-white mixture into the egg-yolk mixture, then gently fold in the remaining egg whites.

Divide evenly between the prepared tins. Bake in a moderate oven, 350°F., for about 25 minutes or until the cake begins to leave the sides of the pan.

Cool for 3 minutes, run a knife round the sides to loosen the cakes and invert them on a wire cooler. Remove the paper from the bottom and allow to cool.

Use the rum cream filling to join the three layers together. Spread mocha butter round the sides and make a band about 1 inch wide round the outside edge of the top of the cake. Coat the sides of the cake with the remaining ⅓ cup of nuts.

Spread the jam on the unfrosted centre of the cake. Decorate with butter cream through a star tube to make a border, and decorate with the walnut halves. Chill for at least 1 hour before serving.

RUM CREAM FILLING
Soften the gelatine in the cold water, then dissolve it over boiling water. Whip the cream in a chilled bowl until it begins to thicken, then beat in the icing sugar. Continue beating while adding the rum and dissolved gelatine.

MOCHA BUTTER
Blend the vanilla into the coffee powder. Beat the butter until smooth and add the vanilla and coffee mixture. Gradually beat in the sifted icing sugar and the cream. Beat until light and smooth.

SCOTTISH SEED CAKE

Grease an orange-loaf tin and line the bottom with greased paper. Cream the butter and sugar and gradually beat in the well-whisked eggs.

Sift the flour with the baking powder, nutmeg and salt. Stir in the caraway seeds.

Add the chopped peel and nuts to the creamed mixture, then add the flour mixture alternately with the milk.

Place in the prepared tin and bake at 325°F. for about 1½ hours.

Russian Walnut Cake

SPICED BANANA CAKE

4 ounces butter
¾ cup firmly packed brown
   sugar
2 eggs
½ teaspoon vanilla essence
2 tablespoons golden syrup
2 ripe bananas, mashed
1¾ cups self-raising flour
2 level tablespoons cornflour
½ level teaspoon ground nutmeg
2 level teaspoons cinnamon
¼ cup warm strong black coffee
3 tablespoons lemon-flavoured
   Vienna icing
4 ounces lemon or
   coffee-flavoured glacé icing
chopped or halved walnuts to
   decorate

Cream the butter and sugar until light and fluffy. Add the eggs one at a time, beating well after each addition. Flavour with the vanilla. Beat in the golden syrup and stir in the mashed bananas.

Sift the flour with the cornflour and spices and add to the creamed mixture alternately with the coffee.

Divide equally between two well-greased 7-inch sandwich tins which have been lined on the bottom with greased paper and bake in a moderate oven, 350°F., for 20 to 30 minutes. Turn out onto a wire cooler.

When the cake is quite cold join the two layers with the Vienna icing (page 146) and ice the top with lemon- or coffee-flavoured glacé icing (page 142). Decorate with chopped or halved walnuts.

SPEEDY MARBLE CAKE

6 ounces butter or margarine
1 cup sugar
4 eggs
1 teaspoon vanilla essence
2 cups plain flour
3 level teaspoons baking powder
½ cup milk
a pinch of salt
⅓ cup chocolate pieces

Grease an 8-inch cake tin with butter and line the bottom with a piece of greased paper. Cream the butter and sugar and, when fluffy, gradually add the well-beaten eggs. Flavour with the vanilla.

Sift the flour with the baking powder and salt and add to the creamed mixture alternately with the milk.

Take out one-third of the cake mixture and flavour with the chocolate which has been melted by stirring over hot water. The remainder is left plain: place half of it in the bottom of the

119

For the icing

1 cup sifted icing sugar
1 slightly rounded tablespoon
  cocoa
1 teaspoon vanilla essence
1 tablespoon water
walnuts (for topping)

prepared tin, cover with the chocolate mixture, then add the rest of the plain mixture, spreading it evenly. Draw the blade of a large knife through the two mixtures to give a marbled effect. Bake in a moderate oven, 350°F., for 50 to 60 minutes. Turn out on a wire cake cooler.

Place the ingredients for the icing in a saucepan and stir over low heat for a few minutes, until the icing reaches a good spreading consistency—do not allow it to overheat or it will discolour on cooling. Pour over the top of the cake and decorate with walnut halves.

SPONGE SANDWICH

3 or 4 eggs, separated
a pinch of salt
½ cup sugar
1 cup plain flour
1 level teaspoon cream of tartar
1½ tablespoons hot water
1 dessertspoon butter
½ level teaspoon bicarbonate of
  soda
½ teaspoon vanilla essence

Beat the egg whites and salt until stiff. Gradually add the sugar, sprinkling it over the egg whites about a dessertspoonful at a time. Beat until the mixture is thick and glossy, then beat in the egg yolks one at a time.

Sift the flour and the cream of tartar three times. Heat the water, butter and soda. Fold the flour into the egg mixture, then quickly add the soda mixture. Flavour with the vanilla.

Divide evenly between two well-greased 7-inch sandwich tins and bake in a moderate oven, 350°F., for 20 to 25 minutes. Turn out onto a wire cooler.

When the cake is quite cold, join the layers with your favourite filling or with jam and whipped cream. Cover the top with a glacé icing or simply dust it with sifted icing sugar.

In place of the plain flour, cream of tartar, and bicarbonate of soda you could use self-raising flour (or, in place of the cream of tartar and bicarbonate of soda, you could use 2 level teaspoonfuls of baking powder with the plain flour).

STRAWBERRY DESSERT CAKE

4 eggs, separated
½ cup sugar
1¼ cups self-raising flour
a good pinch of salt
2 tablespoons water
1 rounded teaspoon butter
¼ teaspoon vanilla essence
1 box strawberries
½ pint cream
1 dessertspoon sugar (for cream)
cherry brandy, sherry or fruit
  juice

Add a pinch of salt to the egg whites and beat until stiff. Gradually add the sugar and continue beating until the meringue stands in glossy peaks. Add the egg yolks one at a time, beating well after each addition.

Sift the flour and salt three times and fold into the egg and sugar mixture, then heat the water and butter and stir in lightly with the vanilla. Place in a well-greased ring tin and bake in a moderate oven, 350°F., for about 40 minutes. Cool.

Wash and hull the strawberries. Take a little more than half of them and crush with a fork. Add the sugar to the cream, whip until thick, then fold in the crushed strawberries.

Sprinkle the cooled sponge with the cherry brandy or sherry or fruit juice, then coat it all over with the strawberry cream. Fill the centre with the whole strawberries. Serve as a dessert cake for afternoon tea, or as a dinner dessert accompanied by an egg custard.

120

STREUSEL COFFEE CAKE

4 ounces butter
¾ cup sugar
2 eggs
½ teaspoon vanilla essence
1 cup milk
3 cups self-raising flour
½ teaspoon salt

For the topping

2 level tablespoons plain flour
2 level teaspoons cinnamon
2 level tablespoons butter or
    margarine
½ cup brown sugar
½ cup chopped nuts

Beat the butter and sugar for the cake to a soft cream and add the well-beaten eggs. Mix the vanilla into the milk, then add half to the butter, sugar and cream mixture.

Sift the flour with the salt and add to the creamed mixture alternately with the remainder of the milk. Turn into a well-greased orange-loaf tin which has been lined on the bottom with greased paper.

To make the topping sift the flour with the cinnamon, rub in the butter or margarine and add the brown sugar and nuts. Sprinkle on top of the uncooked cake.

Bake in a moderate oven, 350°F., for 1 hour and 10 minutes. Serve cold, sliced and buttered.

STUFFED DATE CAKE

8 ounces dates
2 ounces walnuts
5 ounces butter or margarine
¾ cup firmly packed brown
    sugar
½ teaspoon vanilla essence
3 eggs, separated
2½ cups self-raising flour
½ level teaspoon nutmeg
½ level teaspoon cinnamon
a pinch of salt
½ cup milk

Stuff the dates with the nuts. Cream the butter and sugar and flavour with the vanilla, then add the egg yolks one at a time, beating well.

Sift the flour with the nutmeg, cinnamon and salt and add to the creamed mixture alternately with the milk.

Beat the egg whites in a separate bowl until stiff. Fold into the cake mixture. Spread half in a greased and lined 7-inch by 11-inch shallow tray and cover with the stuffed dates. Spread the remaining cake mixture over the dates.

Bake in a moderate oven, 350°F., for 30 to 40 minutes. When cool cut into squares.

SULTANA CAKE

½ pound butter
1 cup sugar
4 eggs
2 cups sultanas
¼ cup peel
3 cups plain flour
1 level teaspoon allspice
1 level teaspoon nutmeg
a pinch of salt
3 level teaspoons baking powder
2 tablespoons milk
2 tablespoons sherry

Line an 8-inch cake tin with greased paper. Cream the butter and sugar and gradually add the well-beaten eggs. Stir in the sultanas and peel.

Sift the flour with the spices, salt and baking powder and add to the creamed mixture alternately with the milk and sherry.

Place in the prepared tin and bake at 325°F. for about 2 hours.

SUMMER FRUIT CAKE

¼ pound crystallized pineapple
¼ pound candied cherries
¼ pound chopped mixed peel
1½ tablespoons orange juice
1 teaspoon grated orange rind
¼ pound butter
½ cup firmly packed brown
   sugar
2 eggs
¼ cup plain flour
1¼ cups self-raising flour
1 level teaspoon nutmeg
a pinch of salt
3 tablespoons milk
1 tablespoon brandy
1 tablespoon orange juice
½ cup sultanas
¼ pound blanched and chopped
   almonds

Remove the sugar from the candied fruits and chop them into small pieces. Mix with the peel, the 1½ tablespoons of orange juice and the orange rind. Allow to stand overnight.

Line a 7-inch cake tin with two thicknesses of white and two of brown paper.

Cream the butter and brown sugar and gradually add the well-beaten eggs. Sift the plain and self-raising flour with the nutmeg and salt and add to the creamed mixture alternately with the combined milk, brandy and orange juice.

Stir in the sultanas and chopped almonds before adding the soaked fruits. Mix thoroughly.

Turn into the prepared tin and bake at 325°F. for 2 hours.

SWISS APPLE CAKE

5 ounces butter
¾ cup sugar
3 eggs
1¾ cups plain flour
2 level teaspoons baking powder
¼ teaspoon salt
1 teaspoon grated lemon rind
2 medium-sized apples
2 dessertspoons sugar for apples
2 tablespoons apricot jam
   thinned with a little water

Beat the butter and the ¾ cup sugar to a soft cream. Add the eggs one at a time, beating well after each addition.

Sift the flour with the baking powder and salt and add with the grated lemon rind to the creamed mixture. Place in a well-greased 8-inch cake tin.

Peel and core each apple and cut each into five wedges, then cut each wedge, on the rounded side, half-way through into slices. Fan these out and arrange evenly on top of the cake mixture. Sprinkle with the 2 dessertspoons of sugar.

Bake in a moderate oven, 350°F., for 1 hour. As soon as the cake comes from the oven brush it with the hot thinned apricot jam.

Serve cold as a cake, or warm with custard or cream as a dessert.

TIGER CAKE

4 ounces butter
½ cup sugar
2 eggs
½ teaspoon vanilla essence
1 cup self-raising flour
½ cup plain flour
⅓ cup milk
2 level dessertspoons cocoa
1 tablespoon water

Cream the butter and sugar until light and fluffy, then gradually add the well-beaten eggs. Flavour with the vanilla.

Sift the flours and add to the creamed mixture alternately with the milk. Divide in half, and to one portion add the blended cocoa and water.

Place each mixture in one of two 7-inch sandwich tins which have been greased and lined on the bottom with greased paper. Bake in a moderate oven, 350°F., for about 30 minutes. Turn out onto a wire cooler and allow to get cold.

122

Tiger Cake

orange-flavoured butter cream
dates and orange rind to decorate

Cut each cake into two layers. Join with whipped and sweetened cream or butter icing, alternating the white and chocolate layers to make a four-layer cake.

Frost the outside of the cake with orange-flavoured butter icing (page 146) and decorate with dates and orange rind.

TRIPLE CHOCOLATE CAKE

4 ounces butter
¾ cup castor sugar
1 egg
2 ounces semi-sweet chocolate
  pieces
¼ cup chopped cherries
½ cup chopped nuts
1½ cups plain flour
1 level teaspoon bicarbonate of
  soda
a pinch of salt
5 ounces milk

For the icing

2 cups sifted icing sugar
2 level tablespoons cocoa
rum or vanilla essence
4 level tablespoons butter

Cream the butter and sugar. Beat the egg well and add gradually to the mixture, beating thoroughly after each addition. Soften the chocolate over hot water and stir into the creamed mixture, then add the chopped cherries and nuts.

Sift the flour, soda and salt twice and add to the butter mixture alternately with the milk. Stir lightly but thoroughly.

Line the bottom of an 8-inch round cake tin with greased paper and grease the sides with butter. Turn the mixture into the tin and bake in a moderate oven, 350°F., for about 45 minutes. Turn out and allow to cool.

To make the icing sift the icing sugar with the cocoa, beat the butter to a cream and gradually add the sifted icing sugar. Flavour with vanilla or rum.

When the cake is quite cold, spread this frosting over the top and sides of the cake and decorate with chocolate leaves.

CHOCOLATE LEAVES

Real rose leaves are the basis of the chocolate leaves. When picking them, be sure to leave a little of the stem—this will make the handling much easier.

123

First rinse the leaves and dry the rose leaves thoroughly.

Break up a block of dark eating chocolate and melt it over hot, not boiling, water. Remove from the heat and beat until smooth.

Using a new watercolour paint-brush, thickly paint the underside of each rose leaf with a smooth layer of chocolate, spreading it just to the edges. Refrigerate until the chocolate is quite firm.

To remove the chocolate shape, hold the leaf by the small stem, insert the point of a knife at the tip of the leaf and peel the rose leaf from the chocolate. You'll find that every vein of the leaf has been moulded into the chocolate, giving it a true-to-life appearance.

Place the chocolate leaves on waxed paper as you detach them from the rose leaves. Handle them gently and don't subject them to heat of any kind or they will melt or lose their shape. Keep in the refrigerator until required.

Small ivy leaves may be used in place of rose leaves.

VELVET SPICE CAKE

6 ounces butter
½ cup white sugar
½ cup firmly packed brown sugar
3 eggs, separated
2½ cups self-raising flour
½ teaspoon mixed spice
a pinch of salt
½ cup coffee
¼ cup milk

For the filling and frosting

4 ounces butter
2 cups sifted icing sugar
1 teaspoon coffee essence
a little rum
2 ounces chocolate
1 cup chopped walnuts

Cream the butter with the white sugar and the brown sugar until light and fluffy. Gradually add the egg yolks, beating well.

Sift the flour with the spice and salt and add to the creamed mixture alternately with the combined coffee and milk.

Beat the egg whites in a separate bowl until stiff, then fold them lightly and evenly into the cake mixture. Divide evenly between two well-greased 8-inch sandwich tins and bake in a moderate oven, 350°F., for 30 to 35 minutes.

Beat the butter for the frosting and gradually work in the sifted icing sugar and the coffee essence. Flavour with the rum. Use some of this mixture to join the two layers of cake together, then spread the remainder over the top and sides.

Melt the chocolate and run it over the top of the cake, allowing it to drip down the sides. Sprinkle with walnuts. Allow to set before serving.

VIENNESE SWISS ROLL

4 eggs, separated
a pinch of salt
3 slightly rounded tablespoons
    castor sugar
a squeeze lemon juice
1½ ounces of plain flour
1 level teaspoon baking powder

Beat the egg whites with the salt until soft peaks form. Gradually add the sugar, continuing to beat until the mixture is thick and glossy. Add the egg yolks one at a time, beating well after each addition. Add the lemon juice.

Sift the flour with the baking powder and cinnamon and add the ground walnuts or almonds. Fold into the egg and sugar mixture lightly but thoroughly.

Viennese Swiss Roll

½ level teaspoon cinnamon
2½ ounces ground walnuts or
  almonds
jam
whipped cream for filling
3 ounces grated chocolate or 4
  ounces chocolate glacé icing
  (page 142)

¼ pound blanched almonds
2 ounces cherries
½ pound seeded raisins
½ pound sultanas
¼ pound currants
¼ pound mixed peel
5 tablespoons whisky
2 rounded tablespoons sugar and
  1 teaspoon water (for caramel)
½ pound butter
½ cup firmly packed brown sugar
½ cup white sugar
1 tablespoon marmalade or fig
  jam
4 eggs
2½ cups plain flour
½ level teaspoon baking powder
½ level teaspoon nutmeg
a good pinch of salt
½ level teaspoon mixed spice

Turn into a greased 9-inch by 12-inch Swiss roll tin which has been lined on the bottom with greased paper. Bake in a moderate oven, 350°F., for 20 to 25 minutes. Turn out onto a paper dusted with castor sugar and roll up.

When the cake is cold, unroll it and spread with a thin layer of jam, then cover with the whipped cream. Re-roll, then sprinkle the top with either sifted icing sugar or grated chocolate, or cover the entire surface of the roll with chocolate glacé icing.

WHISKY FRUIT CAKE

Prepare the fruit and nuts the day before the cake is to be made: chop the almonds, remove any sugar from the cherries, and chop the fruit and the peel into uniform-sized pieces. Mix these all together, sprinkle with 1 tablespoon of the whisky and allow to stand overnight.

Place the sugar and water for the caramel in a saucepan and stir over medium heat until the sugar has dissolved. Cook until it is a honey colour, then remove from the heat and pour in the remainder of the whisky. At this stage the caramel will harden, so return the saucepan to the stove and stir over low heat until it has melted and combined with the whisky. Set aside to cool.

Cream the butter and sugars well, add the marmalade or jam, then the eggs one at a time, beating well between each addition. Add half the caramel and whisky mixture, then stir in half the fruit and finally the remainder of the caramel and whisky.

Sift the flour with the baking powder, nutmeg, salt and spice and stir half into the creamed mixture, then add the remainder of the fruit and the other half of the flour mixture.

If liked the mixture may be darkened with a little Parisian essence.

Place in an 8-inch cake tin which has been lined with two thicknesses of brown and two of white paper. Bake in a slow oven, 300°F., for about 3 hours.

125

WHITE FRUIT CAKE

1 pound sultanas
4 ounces crystallized pineapple
4 ounces glacé cherries
½ cup chopped dates
½ cup chopped dried apricots
½ cup chopped dried figs
8 ounces seeded raisins
4 ounces mixed peel, chopped
8 ounces blanched and slivered
  almonds
2 cups desiccated coconut
2 cups sifted plain flour
1½ level teaspoons baking
  powder
1 teaspoon salt
½ pound butter
1 cup sugar
5 eggs
1 teaspoon rum
½ cup unsweetened pineapple
  juice

Combine the fruits with the peel, nuts and coconut. Sift the flour with the baking powder and salt and sprinkle ½ cup of it over the mixed fruits, mixing well.

Cream the butter and sugar until light and fluffy. Add the eggs one at a time, beating well after each addition. Add the rum. Stir in the sifted flour mixture alternately with the pineapple juice, mixing well. Add the fruit and stir until mixed.

Line an orange-cake tin and an 8-inch ring tin with white paper and divide the mixture evenly between the two tins. Bake in a slow oven, 275°F., for 2½ hours. Or bake in a 9-inch or 10-inch tin which has been lined with paper, allowing 4 to 4½ hours at 275°F.

Small Cakes and Tartlets

ALMOND CHEESECAKES

½ pound good shortcrust pastry
a little raspberry jam, lemon
  cheese or passionfruit butter
1 whole egg
1 tablespoon sugar
2 tablespoons ground almonds
  or coconut
2 tablespoons cake crumbs
2 drops almond essence
1 egg white
whole blanched almonds

Line greased patty tins with rounds of the thinly rolled pastry. Place a little jam in the bottom of each. Beat the whole egg with the sugar and add the ground almonds, or coconut, the cake crumbs and the almond essence. Fold in the stiffly beaten egg white.

Place a dessertspoonful of the mixture in each patty case and top with a whole blanched almond. Bake in a moderate oven, 350°F., for 15 minutes, reducing the heat to 300°F. after the first 5 minutes.

ALMOND SHORTBREAD

8 ounces butter
¾ cup castor sugar
3 cups plain flour
1 cup ground almonds
1 whole egg or 2 egg yolks
vanilla essence or 1 teaspoon grated lemon rind
sugar and cinnamon mixed

Beat the butter and sugar to a light cream, then work in the next four ingredients to make a firm dough. Wrap in grease-proof paper and chill for about 1 hour.

Roll out on a lightly floured board and cut into shapes. Coat with the sugar and cinnamon mixture and bake at 325°F. for about 25 minutes.

APPLE CAKES

4 ounces butter or margarine
½ cup sugar
½ teaspoon vanilla essence
2 eggs
2 cups self-raising flour
¼ level teaspoon salt
4 tablespoons milk
1 cup well-drained cold stewed apple
4 ounces lemon glacé icing

Cream the butter with the sugar, and flavour with the vanilla. Gradually add the beaten eggs, then stir in the sifted flour and salt alternately with the milk.

Place 1 teaspoon of the cake mixture in each greased patty tin, and 1 teaspoon of stewed apple and cover with another spoonful of the cake mixture.

Bake in a moderate to hot oven, 375° to 400°F., for about 15 minutes.

When cold, ice the tops with lemon-flavoured glacé icing.

CHEESECAKE MINCE TARTS

6 ounces short or biscuit pastry
1¾ cups prepared fruit mince (page 199)
8 ounces cream cheese
2 well-beaten eggs
1 cup cream
½ level teaspoon grated lemon rind
1 teaspoon rum
½ cup sugar
1 level dessertspoon plain flour
icing sugar

Roll the pastry thinly and use to line small greased patty tins. Reserve half the prepared fruit mince and spoon the remainder into the uncooked pastry shells.

Soften the cream cheese at room temperature, then beat until smooth. Add the eggs, beating well, then stir in the cream, grated lemon rind and rum or other flavouring.

Mix the sugar with the flour and stir into the cream mixture. Spoon some of this into each pastry case.

Bake at 275°F. for 30 minutes or until the cheesecake mixture has set and the pastry is lightly browned. Top each tart with more fruit mince and dust with sifted icing sugar before serving.

CHEESECAKES

6 ounces short or biscuit pastry
jam or lemon chees
3 ounces butter or margarine
3 slightly rounded tablespoons sugar
½ teaspoon vanilla essence
1 egg
1½ cups self-raising flour
4 tablespoons milk

Roll the pastry thinly and cut into rounds with a floured cutter. Use the rounds to line greased patty tins.

Place half a teaspoonful of jam or lemon cheese in the bottom of each uncooked pastry case.

Beat the butter and sugar to a soft cream, flavour with the vanilla, and gradually add the beaten egg.

Sift the flour with a pinch of salt and add to the creamed mixture alternately with the milk.

Place a spoonful of the cake mixture in each pastry case. Decorate the tops with strips of the left-over pastry.

Bake in a moderate oven, 350°F., for 15 minutes. Remove from the tins while hot and dust the tops with sifted icing sugar before serving.

CHOCOLATE CHERRY CAKES

4 ounces butter
¾ cup sugar
1 egg
2 ounces semi-sweet chocolate
¼ cup chopped cherries
½ cup chopped nuts
1½ cups plain flour
1 level teaspoon bicarbonate of
    soda
a pinch of salt
5 ounces milk

For the icing

2 ounces semi-sweet chocolate
3 dessertspoons milk
1 cup icing sugar
1 teaspoon vanilla essence
1 egg
3 level dessertspoons softened
    butter

Cream the butter with the sugar, then add well-beaten egg. Melt the chocolate over hot water and add to the creamed mixture, then stir in the cherries and nuts.

Sift the flour with the soda and salt and stir in lightly and evenly alternately with the milk (do not beat).

Line the bottom of an 8-inch square cake tin with paper and grease the sides. Pour the cake mixture in and smooth the top to make it even. Bake in a moderate oven, 350°F., for 45 minutes. Allow to cool.

Melt the chocolate for the icing over hot water. Stir in the milk, icing sugar, vanilla, egg and softened butter. Chill by placing over ice cubes for about 10 minutes, then beat well until fluffy. Spread over the cake, mark into squres before the icing has set and place either a piece of walnut or a cherry in the centre of each square. Cut before serving.

CHOCOLATE CHIP MERINGUES WITH COFFEE CREAM

4 egg whites
a pinch of salt
1 cup sugar
1 teaspoon lemon juice
¾ cup chopped dark eating
    chocolate

For the coffee cream

1½ cups milk
4 egg yolks
½ cup sugar
⅓ cup cornflour
½ teaspoon vanilla essence
1 dessertspoon instant coffee

Beat the egg whites with the pinch of salt until very stiff but not dry. Gradually add the sugar, beating until the meringue is thick and glossy and will hold its shape. Fold in the lemon juice and the chopped chocolate.

Pipe or spoon onto a lightly greased oven tray, allowing a little space between the meringues—they will spread slightly. Bake in a slow oven, 300°F., for about 1 hour (the meringues should be firm to the touch but not hard in the centre). While they are still warm press the base of each to form a shell. Let them get cold, then join in pairs with the coffee cream.

To make the coffee cream, first scald the milk and allow it to cool. Mix the egg yolks with the sugar and beat until light and fluffy, then blend the cornflour with a little of the cooled milk and stir into the egg and sugar mixture. Gradually add the remaining milk. Return the mixture to the saucepan and cook, stirring well, until it almost reaches boiling point. Continue cooking and stirring at this temperature for about 10 minutes, then remove from the heat and flavour with the vanilla and instant coffee. Cool before using.

CHOCOLATE ÉCLAIRS

For the pastry

½ pint water
2 ounces butter
1 cup plain flour
a pinch of salt
3 eggs
¼ teaspoon vanilla essence

For the filling

½ pint cream
1 tablespoon icing sugar
1 teaspoon vanilla essence

For the icing

4 ounces icing sugar
1 dessertspoon cocoa
1 to 2 tablespoons water
½ teaspoon vanilla essence

Place the water and butter in a saucepan and stir until boiling. Add the sifted flour and salt and stir until smooth. Cook, stirring all the time until the mixture leaves the sides of the saucepan. Cool.

Beat the eggs until light and fluffy and at least doubled in volume. Add gradually to the pastry mixture and flavour with the vanilla.

Using a forcing bag, squeeze the mixture out in 3-inch lengths on a shallow greased tray. Bake in a hot oven, 450°F., for 10 minutes, then reduce to 350°F. and bake for a further 20 or 30 minutes. Cool on a tray away from draughts.

Whip the cream with the icing sugar and vanilla. Slit the side of each éclair, remove any soft centre and fill with the whipped cream.

Make the chocolate icing by combining all the ingredients and heating briefly over low heat. Or melt 4 ounces of dark chocolate over hot water and spread a little on top of each éclair.

CHOCOLATE KISS CAKES

2 ounces butter
2 slightly rounded tablespoons
   brown sugar
1 egg
¼ teaspoon vanilla essence
½ cup self-raising flour
1 rounded tablespoon cocoa
4 tablespoons cornflour
a pinch of salt
some jam and icing sugar

Beat the butter and sugar to a soft cream and beat in the well-whisked egg. Flavour with the vanilla. Sift together the flour, cocoa, cornflour and salt and stir into the mixture.

Place in small teaspoonfuls on a greased shallow oven tray and bake in a moderate oven, 350°F., for about 8 minutes.

Turn out onto a wire cooler. When quite cold join in pairs with jam and sift icing sugar over the top.

COFFEE KISSES

4 ounces butter
3 slightly rounded tablespoons
   sugar
1 egg
1 tablespoon coffee essence
1¾ cups self-raising flour

For the filling

1 tablespoon butter
1½ cups sifted icing sugar
1 tablespoon coffee essence

Beat the butter and sugar to a cream. Add the well-beaten egg and the coffee essence. Sift the flour and stir into the mixture. Place in teaspoonfuls on a greased shallow oven tray and bake in a moderate oven, 350°F., for 8 to 12 minutes. When quite cold join in pairs with the coffee filling.

To make the filling, beat the butter to a cream. Gradually beat in the sifted icing sugar, and add the coffee essence.

129

CREAM PUFFS

2 ounces butter
½ pint water
a pinch of salt
1 cup plain flour
3 eggs
whipped and sweetened cream
sifted icing sugar for topping

Combine the butter, water and salt in a saucepan and bring to the boil. Remove from the heat, stir in the sifted flour and continue stirring until smooth. Return the saucepan to the stove and cook, stirring well with a wooden spoon, until the mixture leaves the sides of the saucepan. Cool slightly.

Beat the eggs in a separate bowl until they have doubled in volume, then slowly add them to the slightly cooled flour mixture, beating until smooth and shiny.

Place dessertspoonfuls of the mixture on greased shallow oven trays and bake in a hot oven, 450°F., for 10 minutes. Reduce the heat to moderate, 350°F., and continue baking for a further 20 minutes or until the puffs are thoroughly dry. Allow to cool.

To serve, split each puff, remove any soft centre, and fill with the whipped cream. Dust the tops with sifted icing sugar.

FAIRY CAKES

3 ounces butter
3 slightly rounded tablespoons
  sugar
1 egg
1¼ cups plain flour
2 level teaspoons baking powder
a pinch of salt
2 ounces cornflour
4 tablespoons milk
½ teaspoon vanilla essence
jam
sifted icing sugar for topping

Beat the butter and sugar to a soft cream, then add the beaten egg. Sift together the flour, baking powder, salt and cornflour and add to the creamed mixture alternately with the combined milk and vanilla.

Place small teaspoonfuls of the mixture in greased patty tins. Add ½ teaspoon of jam to each, then cover with more cake mixture.

Bake in a moderate oven, 375°F., for 15 to 20 minutes. Dust with sifted icing sugar before serving.

FRANGIPANI TARTS

For the pastry

3 ounces butter
2 slightly rounded tablespoons
  sugar
½ teaspoon vanilla essence
1 egg
¾ cup plain flour
¾ cup self-raising flour
a pinch of salt

For the filling

3 slightly rounded tablespoons
  sugar
1 rounded dessertspoon plain
  flour

Cream the butter and sugar until fluffy, then add the vanilla. Stir in the lightly beaten egg, then add the sifted flours and salt, mixing to a rather firm dough.

Turn onto a lightly floured board and knead only until smooth on the outside. Roll thinly and cut into rounds to line small patty tins. Prick the bottom of each to prevent rising in the centre. Bake in a moderate oven, 350°F., for 12 to 15 minutes. Cool.

To make the filling combine the sugar, flour, salt and egg yolks in a saucepan, stir until smooth, add the milk and stir over medium heat until the mixture boils and thickens. Simmer for 5 minutes, stirring occasionally. Remove from the heat and add the butter and coconut. Cool.

Place a small spoonful of the filling in each cooked pastry case, add a teaspoon of the pineapple and cover with another spoonful of the filling.

130

a pinch of salt
2 egg yolks
1 cup milk
1 ounce butter
1 rounded tablespoon coconut
1 small can of crushed pineapple,
  well-drained

For the topping

2 egg whites
4 tablespoons sugar

For the meringue topping beat the egg whites in a warm, dry bowl until stiff, then gradually beat in the 4 tablespoons of sugar. Continue to beat until the meringue stands in stiff, glossy peaks, then pile or pipe some on top of each tart. Place in a slow oven to lightly set and tint the meringue. Cool before serving.

FRENCH PASTRY CREAMS

1 pound prepared puff pastry
1 egg white
castor sugar
1 punnet strawberries
$\frac{1}{2}$ pint cream whipped with sugar
  and vanilla essence
icing sugar for topping

Divide the pastry in half. Roll one piece on a lightly floured board into a 6-inch by 9-inch rectangle. Mark the centre of the 9-inch length, then brush the surface of the pastry with egg white and sprinkle lightly with castor sugar.

Fold over the two 6-inch edges of the pastry to meet at the mark in the centre. Press the layers lightly together, brush with egg white and sprinkle with more sugar.

Fold in the outer edges of either side of the pastry to meet in the centre and again press lightly. Now fold the pastry in half lengthwise and once more press lightly.

Using a broad-bladed knife cut the pastry into slices $\frac{1}{4}$ inch thick. Place on a lightly floured board and flatten each slice with a rolling-pin. Bake on a greased shallow oven tray in a hot oven, 450°F., for about 10 minutes or until the slices are golden. Lift off and allow to cool.

Take the remaining half of the pastry and prepare and bake in the same way.

Wash and hull the strawberries. Flavour and whip the cream. Place a teaspoonful of cream on one pastry shape, add a few sliced strawberries and top with another piece of pastry. Dust the top of each with sifted icing sugar and, if liked, another spoonful of cream and a whole strawberry.

HORNS OF PLENTY

2 whole eggs plus 1 egg yolk
5 level tablespoons castor sugar
2$\frac{1}{2}$ level tablespoons plain flour
whipped and sweetened cream

Place the eggs, sugar and flour in a bowl and beat with a rotary beater until the mixture is lemon-coloured.

Grease and warm a shallow baking tray and drop the mixture by teaspoonfuls onto it. Spread each with a large knife or spatula until about 3 inches in diameter.

Bake in a hot oven, 400°F., for 4 or 5 minutes or until the rounds are golden round the edges. Remove from the tray while hot, and immediately roll into horn shapes.

Cool, then fill with whipped and sweetened cream.

131

LAMINGTONS

8 ounces butter
1 cup sugar
3 eggs
1 teaspoon vanilla essence
2 cups self-raising flour
1 cup plain flour
a pinch of salt
$\frac{3}{4}$ cup milk

For the boiled icing

2 cups brown or white sugar
$\frac{1}{2}$ cup milk or water
1 heaped tablespoon cocoa

Cream the butter with the sugar, then gradually add the well-beaten eggs. Flavour with the vanilla. Sift the flours and salt and add to the creamed mixture alternately with the milk.

Place in a well-greased 9-inch square slab tin which has been lined on the bottom with greased paper. Bake in a moderate oven, 350°F., for about 50 minutes. Turn out and allow to cool. Leave until the following day before icing.

To make the boiled icing, place the ingredients in a saucepan, stir until boiling, then cook for 2 or 3 minutes or until the icing drips from the spoon like a hair. If too thick, add a little more milk.

To shape and ice the lamingtons, cut the cake into about 40 pieces and coat each, one at a time, with the chocolate icing and roll in coconut. Place each lamington on a wire cake cooler as soon as it is coated with icing and coconut, to allow the icing to set.

LEMON CAKE SQUARES

3 ounces butter
1 cup sugar
2 eggs
$1\frac{1}{2}$ cups plain flour
$1\frac{1}{2}$ level teaspoons baking powder
$\frac{1}{4}$ level teaspoon salt
$\frac{1}{2}$ cup milk
grated rind of 1 lemon

For the topping
$\frac{2}{3}$ cup sugar
juice of 1 lemon

Beat the butter and sugar to a soft cream. Gradually add the well-beaten eggs. Sift the flour, baking powder and salt and stir into the creamed mixture alternately with the combined milk and grated lemon rind.

Place in a well-greased 9-inch square cake tin and bake in a moderate oven, 350°F., for 25 minutes.

While the cake is baking mix the sugar with the lemon juice for the topping. Carefully spoon this over the cake after it has been baking for 25 minutes. Bake for a further 5 or 10 minutes. Cut into squares while still warm.

LITTLE GREEN FROGS

4 ounces butter
$\frac{1}{2}$ cup sugar
$\frac{1}{2}$ teaspoon vanilla essence
2 eggs
2 cups self-raising flour
a pinch of salt
4 tablespoons milk
pink colouring

For the icing and decoration
1 cup icing sugar
1 tablespoon hot milk or fruit juice
green colouring
$\frac{1}{2}$ cup whipped cream
silver cachous

Beat the butter and sugar to a soft cream. Flavour with the vanilla and gradually beat in the well-beaten eggs. Sift the flour and salt and add to the creamed mixture alternately with the milk. Colour pink with cochineal or pink vegetable colouring.

Heat and grease some gem irons, place a spoonful of the mixture in each recess and bake in a hot oven, 400°F., for about 12 minutes. Turn out and allow to cool.

Sift the icing sugar into a small saucepan and add the milk or fruit juice to make into a thick icing. Colour a pale green with vegetable colouring. Heat the icing briefly and spoon it over the cakes. Allow to become firm and set.

To decorate the little frogs take a small sharp-pointed knife and cut a wide strip for the frog's mouth, then add a dab of cream for each eye, topping each dab with a silver cachou. If liked, the mouth may be filled with whipped cream.

Mocha Halo Cakes

MOCHA HALO CAKES

3 ounces butter
3 rounded tablespoons castor
   sugar
2 eggs
1½ cups self-raising flour
1 level teaspoon cinnamon
1 level tablespoon cocoa
1 teaspoon instant coffee
2 tablespoons milk

For the topping and decoration

2 ounces butter
1 cup sifted icing sugar
1 teaspoon vanilla essence
2 ounces chocolate, chopped or
   grated
walnut halves

Cream the butter and sugar until light and fluffy, then gradually add well-beaten eggs. Sift the flour with the cinnamon and cocoa and mix the coffee with the milk. Add the sifted dry ingredients to the creamed mixture alternately with the combined milk and coffee.

Place spoonfuls in small greased patty tins and bake in a moderate oven, 350°F., for about 15 minutes. Cool.

Beat the butter and icing sugar to a soft cream for the icing and flavour with the vanilla. Spread the top of each cooled cake with some of this butter cream.

Soften the chocolate over hot water and add to the remainder of the butter cream. Using a star icing tube, pipe a ring of chocolate icing round the edge of each cake and decorate the centre with a walnut half.

133

NEENISH TARTS

2 tablespoons plain flour
a pinch of salt
1 cup ground almonds
6 tablespoons sifted icing sugar
1 egg white

For the filling

2 ounces butter
1¾ cups icing sugar
1 tablespoon rum

For the topping

4 ounces glacé icing
1 tablespoon cocoa

Sift the flour and salt into a bowl and add the ground almonds and icing sugar. Beat the egg white lightly and stir into the dry ingredients, making a stiff paste.

Turn onto a pastry board, roll out thinly and cut into rounds with a fluted cutter large enough to line small greased patty tins. Prick the bottom well and bake in a moderate oven, 375°F., for 12 minutes. Cool.

Make the filling by creaming the butter well and gradually beating in the icing sugar. Flavour with the rum and beat until very light. Spread some of this filling in the bottom of each tart case and chill until firm.

Make up the glacé icing (page 142) and divide in half. Add the sifted cocoa to one half. Ice each tart, making one half chocolate and the other plain. Allow to set before serving.

ONE EGG-WHITE MERINGUES

1 egg white
1 cup sugar
1 teaspoon vinegar
2 tablespoons boiling water
1 level teaspoon baking powder
1 teaspoon vanilla essence

Place the egg white, sugar, vinegar and boiling water in the large bowl of an electric mixer and beat at high speed until very thick. Fold in the baking powder and the vanilla lightly, using a wooden spoon.

Pipe or spoon the mixture onto oven trays which have been covered with greased paper. Bake in a slow oven, 250°F., for 1 hour.

ORANGE CHEESE CAKES

4 ounces short or biscuit pastry
orange marmalade
2 ounces butter
2 slightly rounded tablespoons
    sugar
grated rind of 1 orange
1 egg
1 cup self-raising flour
a pinch of salt
1 tablespoon orange juice
1 tablespoon milk

Roll the pastry thinly and cut into rounds to line small greased patty tins. Place half a teaspoon of orange marmalade in the bottom of each.

Beat the butter and sugar to a soft cream and add in the grated orange rind and the well-beaten egg. Sift the flour with the salt and add to the creamed mixture alternately with the combined orange juice and milk.

Place a teaspoonful of the mixture in each tart case. Re-roll any scraps of pastry and cut into thin strips. Twist a strip and place on top of each cake. Bake in a moderately hot oven, 375°F., for about 15 minutes.

ORANGE DOUGHNUTS

2 cups self-raising flour
a good pinch each of salt, nut-
    meg and cinnamon
½ cup sugar
2 level teaspoons grated orange
    rind

Sift the flour, salt and spices into a bowl. Add the sugar and the orange rind. Mix to a scone-dough consistency with the combined beaten egg, melted butter and milk.

Turn onto a lightly floured board and knead slightly into a round shape. Roll out ½ inch thick and cut into rings with a floured doughnut cutter or two scone cutters.

1 egg
1 tablespoon melted butter
½ cup milk
sugar and lemon juice (or marmalade jam) for serving

4 ounces butter
½ cup sugar
2 eggs
2 ounces chocolate pieces
½ cup chopped walnuts
grated rind of 1 orange
2 level cups self-raising flour
a pinch of salt
⅓ cup milk
orange glacé icing
chopped walnuts or grated
    chocolate for topping

1 cup plain flour
1 level teaspoon cream of tartar
½ level teaspoon bicarbonate of
    soda
2 ounces butter
½ cup castor sugar
1 egg
⅓ cup milk
some well-drained crushed pine-
    apple
lemon glacé icing
thin slices of crystallized ginger
    for topping

3 cups self-raising flour
a pinch of salt
4 ounces butter
½ cup sugar
1 egg
¼ pint milk
¼ teaspoon vanilla essence
jam
icing sugar for topping

Have ready some fuming fat. Drop the doughnuts a few at a time into the hot fat and as they become brown turn and cook them on the other side.

Drain on white paper, sprinkle with sugar and serve with lemon juice or marmalade jam.

ORANGE SURPRISE CAKES

Beat the butter and sugar to a soft cream, and gradually add the well-beaten eggs. Stir in the chocolate, walnuts and orange rind.

Sift the flour with the salt and add to the creamed mixture alternately with the milk. Mix well.

Place spoonfuls in greased patty tins or in paper patty cases and bake at 375°F. for about 20 minutes.

When cold ice with orange glacé icing (page 142) and top with either chopped walnuts or grated chocolate.

PINEAPPLE SURPRISES

Sift the flour, cream of tartar and bicarbonate of soda twice. Beat the butter and sugar to a soft cream, then add to the beaten egg, beating well. Mix in the sifted dry ingredients alternately with the milk.

Grease a dozen small patty tins and place a small spoonful of the mixture in the bottom of each, making a slight depression in the centre. Top with a teaspoonful of the drained pineapple, then with a little more cake mixture so that each patty tin is two-thirds full.

Bake in a moderate oven, 350°F., for 12 to 15 minutes. When cold, ice with lemon-flavoured glacé icing (page 142) and top each cake with a thin slice of crystallized pineapple.

RASPBERRY BUNS

Sift the flour and salt into a bowl, rub in the butter and add the sugar.

Beat the egg and add the milk and vanilla. Stir into the dry ingredients, making a soft dough. Turn onto a floured board and knead lightly.

Cut into 12 even-sized pieces. Knead each piece into a round, make a hollow in the centre and add a little jam. Glaze the edges with egg and milk (it could be a little saved from mixing), then pinch them together to enclose the jam.

Glaze the tops with egg and milk and place on a greased shallow oven tray. Bake in a moderate oven, 375°F., for about 15 minutes.

Dust with icing sugar before serving.

SHORTBREAD

7 ounces butter
3 slightly rounded tablespoons
  castor sugar
$\frac{1}{2}$ teaspoon vanilla essence
$2\frac{1}{4}$ cups plain flour
6 level tablespoons rice flour

Beat the butter to a cream, add the sugar and beat until well mixed, then add the vanilla. Sift the plain flour with the rice flour and stir into the creamed mixture, making a dry dough.

Press evenly into a well-greased 8-inch sandwich tin. Pinch a frill round the edge and prick the surface with a fork. Mark into eight wedges with the back of a knife.

Bake at 325°F. for 35 to 40 minutes. Leave to cool in the tin for a few minutes before turning out.

SHORTBREAD FINGERS

Roll the dough to about $\frac{1}{4}$ inch thick and cut into fingers about 1 inch wide and 3 inches long. Prick with a fork, place on a greased slide and bake for about 15 minutes.

SHORTBREAD BUTTONS

Take teaspoonsfuls of the mixture, roll into balls and space evenly on a shallow oven tray. Bake in a moderate oven for about 10 or 12 minutes. Cool, then dot each with some fruit-flavoured glacé icing and decorate with a nut or a piece of cherry.

SNOW CAKES

3 ounces butter
3 slightly rounded tablespoons
  sugar
$\frac{1}{2}$ teaspoon vanilla essence
2 eggs
$1\frac{1}{4}$ cups self-raising flour
a pinch of salt
2 tablespoons milk

For the frosting and covering

1 tablespoon cornflour
1 cup milk
1 tablespoon butter
2 tablespoons castor sugar
$\frac{1}{2}$ teaspoon vanilla essence
coconut to cover

Beat the butter and sugar to a soft cream, flavour with the vanilla, then gradually add the well-beaten eggs. Sift the flour with the salt and add to the creamed mixture alternately with the milk.

Place spoonfuls of the mixture in greased patty tins and bake in a moderate oven, 350°F., for 15 minutes. Cool.

Blend the cornflour for the frosting with a little of the milk. Heat the remainder of the milk and when almost boiling pour onto the blended mixture, stirring until smooth, then return the mixture to the saucepan. Cook, stirring constantly until it boils and thickens. Beat the butter and castor sugar to a cream, flavour with the vanilla and whip the thickened milk into this creamed mixture. Spread the tops and sides of the cooled cakes with this frosting, then toss in coconut.

SPONGE BUTTERFLIES

3 eggs, separated
4 slightly rounded tablespoons
  sugar
$\frac{1}{2}$ teaspoon vanilla essence or 1
  teaspoon grated orange or
  lemon rind

Beat the egg whites with a pinch of salt until stiff. Gradually add the sugar and continue beating until thick and glossy. Add the egg yolks one at a time, beating in well.

Sift the flour and salt three times. Melt the butter in the milk or water.

Add the vanilla essence or grated fruit rind to the eggs, then

136

4 rounded tablespoons
    self-raising flour
a pinch of salt
1 tablespoon milk or water
1 rounded teaspoon butter

For the filling and topping

whipped cream
jam or lemon cheese
sifted icing sugar

lightly stir in the sifted flour. Add the milk or water and the butter.

Place spoonfuls of the mixture in well-greased patty tins and bake in a hot oven, 400°F., for 10 or 12 minutes. Turn out and allow to cool.

Using a small sharp-pointed knife, cut the centres from the cakes. Add a dab of either jam or lemon cheese and then fill with whipped cream.

Cut the piece removed from each cake in half, and place on top of the cream to represent the wings of a butterfly. Dust with sifted icing sugar.

SPONGE KISSES

2 eggs, separated
¼ cup sugar
½ teaspoon vanilla essence
½ cup self-raising flour
a pinch of salt

For the filling and topping

jam
whipped and sweetened cream
sifted icing sugar

Beat the egg whites with a pinch of salt until soft peaks form. Gradually add the sugar and continue beating until thick and glossy. Add the egg yolks one at a time and beat well. Flavour with the vanilla.

Sift the flour and salt twice and fold into the mixture.

Have shallow trays heated and greased and drop teaspoonfuls of the mixture at even intervals on the tray, leaving a little room for each to spread.

Bake in a moderately hot oven, 375°F., for about 7 minutes. Lift onto a wire cooler. When quite cool join in pairs with a dab of jam and a spoonful of whipped and sweetened cream. Dust the tops with sifted icing sugar.

SPONGE PATTY CAKES

2 eggs, separated
a pinch of salt
¼ cup sugar
½ teaspoon vanilla essence
½ cup self-raising flour
½ teaspoon butter
1 dessertspoon water

For the filling and topping

½ pint cream whipped with 1
    teaspoon sugar and ½ teaspoon
    vanilla essence
sifted icing sugar or grated
    chocolate

Place the whites in a bowl with the salt and beat until stiff. Gradually add the sugar and continue beating until thick and glossy. Add the egg yolks one at a time, beating well after each addition. Flavour with the vanilla.

Sift the flour and fold lightly into the egg and sugar mixture. Heat the butter and water until the butter melts, then fold into the sponge mixture.

Carefully spoon into greased patty tins or paper cases and bake in a moderate oven, 375°F., for about 12 minutes. Turn out and allow to cool. Whip the cream, flavouring it with the sugar and vanilla. Cut a piece from the centre of each cake, pipe in a swirl of cream and top with the piece of cake cut from the centre.

Sprinkle with sifted icing sugar or finely grated chocolate before serving.

Sponge Patty Cakes

½ pound flaky pastry
4 rounded tablespoons cornflour
3 level tablespoons sugar
2 egg yolks
1½ pints milk
1 teaspoon vanilla essence
1 packet lemon jelly crystals
2 cups boiling water

For the icing and decoration

4 ounces vanilla glacé icing
coconut or chopped walnuts

VANILLA SLICES

Divide the pastry in half and roll each piece into a 9-inch square. Place on a shallow baking tray and prick the surface well with a fork. Mark into squares. Bake in a hot oven, 450°F., for 10 to 15 minutes or until golden. Remove to a wire cooler and allow to become quite cold.

Make the filling by combining the cornflour, sugar and egg yolks in a bowl and blending until smooth with a little of the cold milk. Heat the remainder of the milk, and when almost boiling pour onto the blended mixture. Return to the saucepan and cook, stirring constantly until the custard boils and thickens. Cook for 5 minutes, stirring well. Remove from the heat and add the vanilla. Let it become lukewarm.

Make the jelly by dissolving the crystals in the boiling water. Allow to become lukewarm, then combine with the cooled custard, mixing well.

Pour into a 9-inch square tin and allow to set overnight. Turn the set filling onto one piece of pastry and cover with the other piece of pastry, pressing firmly. Ice with vanilla-flavoured glacé icing (page 142) and sprinkle with coconut or chopped walnuts. When set cut into squares to serve.

CAKE FILLINGS AND FROSTINGS

ALMOND ICING

1 pound sifted icing sugar
½ pound ground almonds
2 egg yolks
½ teaspoon lemon juice
2 tablespoons sherry

Sift the icing sugar into a bowl and add the ground almonds, mixing well.

Beat the egg yolks and add the lemon juice and the sherry. Stir into the icing sugar and almond mixture to make rather a dry dough.

Turn onto a board which has been lightly dusted with sifted icing sugar. Knead only until the paste is smooth on the outside. Roll to the shape and size required. This is sufficient to cover a half-pound fruit cake made in an 8-inch tin.

BOILED ICING FOR LAMINGTONS

2 cups brown or white sugar
½ cup milk or water
1 heaped tablespoon cocoa

Place the ingredients in a saucepan and stir until the mixture comes to the boil. Boil for 2 or 3 minutes, or until it drips from the spoon like a hair.

If the icing becomes too thick when you are coating the lamingtons, add a little more milk.

CHOCOLATE ALMOND BUTTER CREAM

2 ounces butter
1 ounce ground almonds
1 cup icing sugar
1 level tablespoon cocoa

Soften the butter by beating, then add the ground almonds. Sift the icing sugar and cocoa together and stir into the butter and almond mixture, beating until well blended.

A little almond essence may be added to give a more distinct almond flavour.

CHOCOLATE CREAM-CHEESE ICING

2 ounces butter
4 ounces cream cheese
3 cups sifted icing sugar
2 level dessertspoons cocoa
a pinch of salt
1 teaspoon vanilla essence
⅓ cup thick cream

Beat the butter until soft, then add the cream cheese which has first been allowed to soften to room temperature. Beat until well blended. Sift the icing sugar with the cocoa and salt and add to the butter and cream-cheese mixture alternately with the vanilla-flavoured cream. Beat until thick and smooth.

Chocolate Glacé Icing

CHOCOLATE GLACÉ ICING

1 cup sifted icing
a slightly rounded tablespoon
   cocoa
1 teaspoon vanilla essence
1 tablespoon water

Sift the icing sugar and cocoa together and combine with the vanilla and water. Heat briefly over low heat, stirring until smooth.

CHOCOLATE MOCHA

2 ounces butter
1 cup icing sugar
1 level tablespoon cocoa
1 dessertspoon coffee essence
   mixed with 1 tablespoon boiling water
1 teaspoon vanilla essence or rum

Beat the butter to a soft cream. Sift the icing sugar and cocoa together and gradually beat into the butter alternately with the combined coffee essence and water. Flavour with the vanilla. For a piping consistency it may be necessary to add a little more sifted icing sugar.

CHOCOLATE TOPPING

2 ounces semi-sweet chocolate
3 dessertspoons milk
1 cup icing sugar
1 teaspoon vanilla essence
1 egg
3 dessertspoons butter

Melt the chocolate in the top of a double saucepan over hot water. Stir in the milk, icing sugar, vanilla, beaten egg and softened butter. Chill for about 10 minutes, then stand the pan on some ice cubes and beat until the topping is fluffy and of an even spreading consistency.

   This is sufficient to ice a 9-inch square cake. Mark the icing into sections when almost set.

CHOCOLATE VIENNA ICING

2 ounces butter or margarine
1 cup sifted icing sugar
¼ teaspoon vanilla essence
2 ounces chocolate, melted

Beat the butter or margarine to a soft cream, then gradually beat in the sifted icing sugar. Add the vanilla and the melted chocolate and beat until smooth.

Cocoa may be used in place of the chocolate: use 1 level tablespoonful and sift it with the icing sugar.

CREAMY LEMON FILLING

2 ounces butter
1 egg
a pinch of salt
¼ cup liquid glucose
1½ tablespoons lemon juice
3 cups sifted icing sugar

Beat the butter to a soft cream, then beat in the egg, salt, liquid glucose and lemon juice. Gradually add the icing sugar, continuing to beat until fluffy.

DATE FILLING

⅓ cup boiling water
1 teaspoon grated orange rind
1 dessertspoon honey
4 ounces chopped dates

Combine the boiling water, grated rind and honey. Soak the chopped dates in the mixture and let it get cold, then beat to a pulp.

ECONOMICAL LEMON CHEESE

1 cup sugar
1 cup water
juice of 1 large lemon or of 2 small lemons
2 rounded tablespoons custard powder
¼ cup milk
grated rind of 1 lemon

Place the sugar, water and lemon juice in a saucepan to boil. Blend the custard powder with the milk and when the lemon syrup is boiling pour it onto the blended mixture and stir until smooth. Return the mixture to the saucepan and stir until it boils and thickens. Cook for 1 minute, then add the grated lemon rind.

Use to fill small patty cakes and tarts. This lemon cheese will not last for more than two or three days.

FONDANT ICING

1 pound icing sugar
2 ounces liquid glucose
1 egg white
flavouring
liquid vegetable colour

Sift the icing sugar into a bowl, make a bay in the centre and add the softened glucose, egg white and flavouring. Beat, drawing the icing sugar into the centre until the mixture becomes a stiff paste. Turn onto a board which has been dusted with sifted icing sugar, and knead.

To colour the fondant. If only one colour is required, a few drops of colouring may be added to the egg-white mixture. If more than one colour is required from the same mixture, make it up in white, then divide the fondant as required. Add a dab of the required colour to each portion and knead it in until evenly tinted.

141

GLACÉ ICING

1 cup icing sugar
1 tablespoon water, milk or
    fruit juice
colouring and flavouring

Sift the icing sugar into a bowl or small saucepan and add the liquid, making a thick consistency. Colour and flavour as required.

Heat briefly over low heat for about 30 seconds. Do not overheat or the sugar will crystallize and the icing become too thin. Pour quickly over the cake, or use as required.

Lemon icing. Use lemon juice as half the liquid.
Orange icing. Use orange juice as the liquid.
Chocolate icing. Sift 1 level tablespoon cocoa with the icing sugar. Flavour with sherry if liked.
Coffee icing. Add ½ teaspoon instant coffee to the icing sugar before it is sifted.
Passionfruit icing. Use the pulp of 2 small or 1 large passionfruit instead of the liquid in the recipe.

LEMON CHEESE OR LEMON BUTTER

2 whole eggs or 4 egg yolks
1 cup sugar
4 ounces butter or margarine
juice of 3 lemons
grated rind of 2 lemons

Beat the whole eggs or the egg yolks with the sugar. Place in a saucepan with the butter and lemon juice and stir over low heat until the mixture is the consistency of honey. Add the grated lemon rind. Cool, and use for tarts, cakes, pavlovas or sandwiches.

LEMON FILLING

1 rounded tablespoon cornflour
¾ cup sugar
a pinch of salt
1 slightly beaten egg yolk
¾ cup water
1½ tablespoons lemon juice
1 teaspoon grated lemon rind
1 dessertspoon butter

Combine the cornflour, sugar and salt, then stir in the egg yolk, water and lemon juice. Cook over medium heat, stirring constantly until the mixture boils and thickens. Cook for a further 2 minutes, then remove from the heat and stir in the lemon rind and butter. Cool before spreading on the cake.

MOCHA BUTTER ICING

4 ounces butter
1 egg yolk
3 tablespoons cocoa
2¼ cups icing sugar
hot strong coffee

Cream the butter well and blend in the egg yolk. Sift the cocoa and icing sugar together and add to the creamed mixture with enough hot strong coffee to make the icing smooth and easy to spread. This makes enough icing to fill and cover an 8-inch sandwich cake.

MOCHA CREAM

2 ounces butter
1 cup sifted icing sugar
1 level tablespoon cocoa
1 dessertspoon coffee essence or
    1 level teaspoon instant coffee
rum or sherry, or vanilla essence

Beat the butter until soft. Sift the icing sugar with the cocoa and instant coffee, if used, and gradually work into the butter mixture. Flavour with rum, sherry or vanilla essence.

MOCHA CREAM FILLING

2 dessertspoons icing sugar
1 rounded teaspoon instant coffee
  powder
½ teaspoon vanilla essence or rum
½ pint cream

Combine the icing sugar, instant coffee and vanilla or rum with the cream. Beat until stiff.

MOCK CREAM OR BUTTER CREAM

1 rounded tablespoon butter
1 rounded tablespoon sugar
2 level tablespoons cornflour
1 cup milk
vanilla essence

Beat the butter and sugar to a soft cream.

Blend the cornflour with a little of the cold milk, heat the remainder of the milk and, when nearly boiling, pour it onto the blended mixture. Return it to the saucepan and cook over medium heat, stirring well, until the mixture boils and thickens.

Cool, then beat into the creamed butter and sugar. Flavour with the vanilla and chill well before using.

ORANGE BUTTER ICING

1 dessertspoon butter
1 cup sifted icing sugar
1 tablespoon orange juice
grated rind of ½ orange

Melt the butter in the top of a double saucepan and stir in the sifted icing sugar. Leave over hot water for about 10 minutes. Remove from the heat and beat in the orange juice and the grated orange rind. Beat until smooth.

This makes enough icing to cover the top of a 7-inch sponge sandwich cake.

ORANGE FILLING 1

2 rounded dessertspoons
  cornflour
½ cup sugar
⅓ cup water
1 teaspoon butter
1 teaspoon grated orange rind
2 tablespoons orange juice

Combine the cornflour and sugar in a bowl and blend with a little of the cold water, then add the remaining water.

Place in a saucepan and bring to the boil, stirring well. Cook for a further 2 minutes. Remove from the heat and add the butter, then cool slightly and add the orange rind and juice.

Allow to become completely cold before using. This is enough to join two 7-inch layer cakes.

ORANGE FILLING 2

1½ level tablespoons cornflour
¾ cup sugar
a pinch of salt
¾ cup orange juice
1 dessertspoon lemon juice
1 dessertspoon butter
2 egg yolks
1½ teaspoons grated orange rind

Combine the cornflour, sugar and salt. Add the orange and lemon juices, mixing until smooth, then add the butter and cook over medium heat, stirring constantly until the mixture is thick. Add a small amount of this hot liquid to the beaten egg yolks, then stir them into the main mixture. Cook for a further 3 minutes.

Remove from the heat and stir in the grated orange rind. Cool before using.

143

PASSIONFRUIT BUTTER

2 whole eggs or 4 egg yolks
1 cup sugar
2 tablespoons lemon juice
4 ounces butter
pulp of 6 or 8 passionfruit

Beat the whole eggs or egg yolks and the sugar. Add the lemon juice, butter and passionfruit pulp and place in the top of a double saucepan. If no double saucepan is available use a bowl standing in a saucepan with enough water to reach half-way up the sides of the bowl.

Cook, stirring frequently, until the mixture is the consistency of honey. This may take up to 1 hour, depending on the size of the bowl and the temperature of the water.

Cool and store in screw-topped jars in the refrigerator. The passionfruit butter will thicken a little more as it cools.

PASSIONFRUIT CREAM

2 ounces butter or margarine
1 cup sifted icing sugar
pulp of 2 passionfruit

Beat the butter to a cream, gradually add the sifted icing sugar and beat in the passionfruit pulp.

PINEAPPLE TOPPER

2 ounces butter
1 cup brown sugar
1½ cups flaked coconut
½ cup chopped walnuts
1 cup drained crushed pineapple

Melt the butter and blend in the remaining ingredients. Spread over the surface of a hot or cold 13-inch by 9-inch cake. Grill about 3 inches from the heat for about 2 minutes or until the frosting is brown and bubbly.

RICH CREAM FILLING

3 egg yolks
2½ tablespoons sugar
1 level teaspoon cornflour
½ teaspoon vanilla essence
¼ pint cream
1 teaspoon brandy

Combine the egg yolks, sugar, cornflour and vanilla in a bowl and whisk over hot water until thick and fluffy. Remove from the heat and continue beating until cool.

Whip the cream until stiff, fold into the custard and flavour with the brandy. Chill well before using to fill a sponge sandwich cake.

ROYAL ICING

1 egg white
1 to 1½ cups sifted pure icing
   sugar
1 teaspoon liquid glucose
a squeeze of lemon juice
colouring

Beat the egg white slightly, then gradually beat in the sifted icing sugar. Add the liquid glucose which has been softened over hot water, and the lemon juice.

Beat until the mixture forms peaks when the beater is lifted.

Colour as required. Keep covered with a damp cloth when not in use.

Use only pure icing sugar for this icing. Icing sugar mixture contains a small quantity of cornflour which prevents icing from keeping its shape when piped.

SNOW FROSTING

2 cups sugar
½ cup water
2 dessertspoons liquid glucose
2 egg whites
1 teaspoon vanilla essence

Combine the sugar, water and glucose in a saucepan. Heat, stirring occasionally, until the sugar has dissolved. Boil to the medium or soft-ball stage (242°F.). Pour in a steady stream over the stiffly beaten egg whites, beating constantly.

Add the vanilla and continue beating at high speed until thick and glossy. The mixture should form peaks when the beater is lifted. Use at once.

SOUR CREAM VELVET FROSTING

1 cup semi-sweet chocolate
   pieces
2 ounces butter
½ cup sour cream
1 teaspoon vanilla essence
a pinch of salt
3 cups sifted icing sugar

Melt the chocolate pieces and the butter over hot, not boiling, water. Remove from the heat and add the sour cream, vanilla and salt. Gradually beat in the sifted icing sugar to make a spreading consistency.

This makes enough frosting for the top and sides of two 9-inch layer cakes. If liked, fresh cream may replace the sour cream.

SPONGE FILLINGS

CHOCOLATE CREAM CHEESE

2 ounces butter
4 ounces cream cheese
3 cups icing sugar
a pinch of salt
2 level dessertspoons cocoa
¼ cup cream
1 teaspoon vanilla essence

Beat the butter until soft, then add the cream cheese, beating until well blended. Sift the icing sugar, salt and cocoa together and add to the butter mixture alternately with the cream, beating well after each addition. Flavour with the vanilla.

LEMON FILLING

½ tin sweetened condensed milk
1 egg yolk
¼ cup lemon juice

Combine the condensed milk with the egg yolk and lemon juice. Beat until well mixed. Chill until set. Use as a filling for tarts or cakes.

PASSIONFRUIT FILLING

2 ounces butter
1 cup sifted icing sugar
pulp of 2 passionfruit

Beat the butter to a cream and gradually add the sifted icing sugar alternately with the passionfruit pulp.

VIENNA OR BUTTER ICING

2 ounces butter
1 cup sifted icing sugar
½ teaspoon vanilla essence

Beat the butter to a soft cream, gradually work in the sifted icing sugar, and flavour with the vanilla.

CHOCOLATE VIENNA ICING

Melt 2 ounces chocolate over hot water and beat into the creamed mixture. Rum or sherry may be used for flavouring in place of the vanilla.

COFFEE VIENNA ICING

Sift 1 teaspoon of instant coffee with the icing sugar.

MOCHA ICING

Use both the chocolate and the coffee as above.

LEMON VIENNA ICING

Add the grated rind of a medium-sized lemon and about 1 teaspoon of lemon juice to the icing. Omit the vanilla and, if necessary, add an extra dessertspoonful of sifted icing sugar.

ORANGE VIENNA ICING

As for Lemon Vienna Icing, using orange in place of lemon.

Vienna Icing: melted chocolate used as a final coating on Vienna Iced Slab Cake

146

CONFECTIONERY

ALMOND BUTTER CRUNCH

8 ounces butter
1⅓ cups sugar
½ tablespoon liquid glucose
1½ tablespoons water
1 cup coarsely chopped blanched
   almonds, toasted

Melt the butter in a large saucepan and add the sugar, glucose and water. Cook, stirring occasionally, until hard-crack stage (300°F.) has been reached. Watch the mixture carefully after the thermometer reaches 280°F.

Quickly stir in the chopped nuts and spread the mixture in a greased 14-inch by 9-inch pan. Cool thoroughly and allow to set before breaking into pieces.

If liked the almond crunch may be turned out of the tin in one piece when set, and the top coated with melted chocolate and sprinkled with toasted almonds. Allow the chocolate to set before breaking the almond crunch into pieces.

APPLES ON STICKS

6 to 8 apples
1 pound sugar
½ measuring-cup water
¼ level teaspoon cream of tartar
1 teaspoon vinegar
red colouring

Wash and dry the apples. Insert a wooden stick in each. Place the sugar, water, cream of tartar and vinegar in a saucepan and stir until the sugar has dissolved. Remove the spoon and cook without stirring until the syrup becomes a honey colour.

Colour if liked with red colouring. Allow to stand until the bubbles subside, then dip the apples in one at a time, tilting the saucepan for greater depth.

Place the coated apples on a greased tray and leave until the toffee is firm.

APRICOT COCONUT BALLS

1½ cups dried apricots
2 cups desiccated coconut
⅔ cup sweetened condensed milk
icing sugar or shredded coconut
   for rolling

Combine the finely chopped apricots with the coconut and add the condensed milk, blending well.

Shape into balls. Roll in icing sugar or shredded coconut. Place in the refrigerator until set.

BARCOM TOFFEE

1 cup sugar
¼ cup water
1 teaspoon butter
2 tablespoons golden syrup
1 dessertspoon vinegar
coconut or chopped nuts for
   topping

Place the first five ingredients in a saucepan and bring to the boil, stirring occasionally to make sure all the sugar crystals have dissolved.

Continue boiling at a moderate rate until the mixture reaches 280°F., or until a little of it cracks when dropped into cold water in a cup.

Pour into small greased tins or patty papers, sprinkle the tops with coconut or chopped nuts and allow the toffee to set.

a double quantity of cooked
    fondant
whole glacé cherries
blanched almonds
chopped dates and nuts

6-ounce can of unsweetened
    evaporated milk
6 ounces semi-sweet chocolate
    pieces or chocolate bits
2½ cups finely crushed sweet
    biscuits
½ cup sifted icing sugar
1¼ cups chopped walnuts
⅓ cup brandy

4 ounces liquid glucose
1 pound sugar
1 cup water
¼ teaspoon salt
4 ounces butter
¼ teaspoon lemon or vanilla
    essence

2 oranges
2 cups sugar for syrup
¼ cup sugar for coating
yellow food colouring

BON-BONS

Take pieces of the cooked fondant and mould it round cherries, blanched almonds, or pieces of date and nut mixed together.

Heat the remainder of the fondant over hot water until it melts, then dip each filled fondant ball in the liquid fondant to become completely covered. Place on waxed paper to set. Top each with a piece of nut, a cherry, or some silver cachous.

BRANDY BALLS

Combine the milk and the chocolate pieces in a heavy-based saucepan. Stir over medium heat until the chocolate melts and the mixture is smooth and thick. Remove from the heat.

Add the crushed biscuits, icing sugar, ½ cup of the chopped walnuts and the brandy. Mix well, then allow to stand at room temperature for about 30 minutes.

Take spoonfuls of the mixture and shape into balls about 1 inch in diameter. Roll them in the remaining chopped walnuts. Chill for 1 hour or until firm.

BUTTERSCOTCH

Combine all the ingredients except the flavouring in a saucepan and stir until the sugar has dissolved. Bring to boiling point, then remove the stirring spoon. Boil to 290°F., when the mixture should be a rich brown colour.

Remove from the heat and place the bottom of the saucepan in cold water for a minute or two. When the bubbles subside stir in the flavouring.

Pour into a well-greased 11-inch by 7-inch tin. Mark into squares while warm. When cold, break into pieces and store in airtight containers.

CANDIED ORANGE POMPONS

Using the point of a sharp knife, carefully remove the skin from the orange in quarters. Place this peel in a medium-sized saucepan and cover with cold water. Bring to the boil and simmer for 30 minutes or until the rind is tender.

Reserving 1 cup of the cooking water for use later, drain well. Put the orange peel through a mincer or chop it very finely. Place the 2 cups sugar with the reserved cup of cooking liquid in a saucepan and stir until the sugar has dissolved. Continue cooking until the syrup forms a soft ball when a little is dropped in cold water (238°F.). Add the minced orange peel and simmer for another 10 minutes or until most of the syrup has been absorbed.

Spread the mixture in a greased dish. When cool enough to handle, form into balls about ¾ inch in diameter. Tint the ¼ cup a light yellow and roll each ball in some of this coloured sugar.

Place on trays and allow to dry for 24 hours. Store in covered containers in a cool place.

CARAMEL APPLES

6 medium-sized red apples
1 pound milk caramels
3 dessertspoons hot water
chopped walnuts

You will need 6 wooden skewers.

Wash and dry the apples, then remove the small stems. Insert a skewer into each apple.

In a double saucepan over boiling water, melt the caramels with the 3 dessertspoons of hot water to the consistency of a smooth sauce. It may be necessary to add a little more water, but don't make the mixture too thin or it will run off the apples.

Remove the saucepan containing the caramel from the heat. Twirl the apples one at a time in the caramel mixture, spreading it evenly. Quickly dip each apple into the chopped nuts and place on waxed paper to become set and dry.

Keep in the refrigerator until required.

CHOCOLATE APPLE NIBBLES

6 ounces semi-sweet chocolate pieces
4 medium-sized red apples

You will need a packet of cocktail picks. Put the chocolate on to melt over hot water. Wash and dry the apples, core them (leave the skins on), and cut each one into eight pieces. Insert a cocktail pick into each piece on the side where the skin is.

Remove the melted chocolate from the heat. Holding each section of apple by means of the cocktail pick, dip the pieces of apple into the chocolate, leaving the skin side uncoated.

Place on a buttered tray and store in the refrigerator until needed.

CHOCOLATE CLUSTERS

6 ounces semi-sweet chocolate pieces
$\frac{1}{4}$ cup liquid glucose
1 tablespoon water
1 cup raisins
1 cup salted peanuts

Place the chocolate pieces, glucose and water in the top of a double saucepan over hot, not boiling water and stir until the chocolate has melted.

Remove from the heat and divide the mixture in two. Stir the raisins into one half and the salted peanuts into the other.

Drop by teaspoonfuls onto a tray covered with waxed paper. Refrigerate until set—about 1 hour.

CHOCOLATE DIPPING SYRUP

4 ounces dark chocolate
2 ounces Copha or other white vegetable shortening

Place both ingredients in a saucepan over hot water and stir until blended. Cool slightly, then dip in squares of fudge or balls of fondant, completely covering them. Place the confections on waxed paper to set. Top each with an almond or a cherry.

CHOCOLATE FUDGE

2 level tablespoons butter
2 level tablespoons cocoa
3 cups sugar
1 cup milk
¼ cup honey
a pinch of salt
1 teaspoon vinegar
1 teaspoon vanilla essence
½ cup chopped nuts

Melt the butter in a saucepan and add the cocoa, sugar, milk, honey and salt. Stir gently until the sugar and honey have dissolved. Place the lid on the saucepan till the mixture comes to the boil—about 2 minutes.

Uncover and cook without stirring until a little dropped into cold water forms a soft ball (238° to 240°F.). Remove from the heat and add the vinegar. When lukewarm add the vanilla and beat until the mixture thickens and loses its gloss. Turn into a greased tin and sprinkle the chopped nuts over the surface, pressing in gently. Leave until cold before cutting into squares.

CHOCOLATE NUGGETS

1 cup chocolate bits
⅔ cup canned evaporated milk
2½ cups fine biscuit crumbs
½ cup icing sugar
1 teaspoon vanilla essence
2 teaspoons rum
½ cup finely chopped walnuts
finely chopped nuts for coating

Place the chocolate and the evaporated milk in a saucepan and stir over medium heat until the chocolate has dissolved.

Remove from the heat and add the biscuit crumbs, icing sugar, vanilla, rum and ½ cup chopped walnuts. Mix well. Chill for 30 minutes.

Shape into logs 1½ inches long and ½ inch thick. Roll the logs in finely chopped nuts and chill for at least 1 hour before serving.

CHOCOLATE ORANGE TREASURES

For the coating

1¼ cups sugar
⅔ cup evaporated milk
6 ounces chocolate pieces or 6 ounces grated chocolate

For the filling

2 cups icing sugar
2 dessertspoons cream or top milk
1½ dessertspoons butter
1 teaspoon grated orange rind
¼ cup icing sugar

To make the chocolate fudge coating combine the sugar and milk in a saucepan and bring to the boil, stirring occasionally. Boil for 3 minutes. Remove from the heat and stir in the chocolate. Divide the mixture in two, and form each half into a 12-inch by 4-inch strip on waxed paper. Chill.

To make the orange fondant filling blend the 2 cups of icing sugar with the cream or top milk, the softened butter and the grated orange rind. Knead in the extra ¼ cup of icing sugar. Divide in half and shape each piece into a roll 12 inches long.

Place a roll of filling in the centre of each of the chilled strips of chocolate coating. Roll up, sealing the edges. Wrap in waxed paper and chill.

Unwrap for serving and cut each roll into slices about ¼ inch thick.

CHOCOLATE MARASCHINO TREASURES

Omit the orange rind in the filling and add 2 dessertspoons of well-drained and finely chopped maraschino cherries and a little pink colouring.

Chocolate Treasures

CHOCOLATE PEPPERMINT TREASURES

CHOCOLATE PEPPERMINT TREASURES

Omit the orange rind in the filling and add ½ teaspoon of peppermint essence and a few drops of green colouring.

CHOCOLATE PINEAPPLE TREASURES

Omit the orange rind in the filling and substitute 2 dessert-spoons of pineapple juice for the cream.

CHOCOLATE ROUGHS

½ pound plain or cooking
  chocolate
1⅓ cups coconut
chopped almonds or hazelnuts

Dissolve the chocolate in the top of a double saucepan over hot, not boiling, water. Add the coconut and sufficient of the chopped nuts to form a stiff paste.

Lift out of the pan with a fork and pile in rough heaps on waxed paper. Allow to set.

CHOCOLATE RUM STICKS

12 ounces semi-sweet or dark
  chocolate
1 cup sweetened condensed milk
a dash of salt
2 teaspoons rum
1½ cups chopped walnuts

Melt the chocolate in a double saucepan over hot, not boiling, water. Stir in the condensed milk and salt.

Remove from the heat and beat until the mixture is smooth (an electric cake mixer is a help). Stir in the rum and walnuts. Pour into a waxed paper-lined 7-inch by 3-inch loaf tin and chill for 24 hours.

Cut into slices ½ inch thick, then cut each slice lengthwise in half. Store in airtight containers or, in hot weather, in the refrigerator.

151

CHOCOLATE RUM TRUFFLES

4 ounces butter
1 cup icing sugar
$\frac{1}{2}$ cup cocoa
2 tablespoons rum
2 cups coconut
2 cups mixed fruit (dates, raisins, cherries and ginger)
vanilla essence

Beat the butter and icing sugar to a cream. Add the cocoa and a little rum to moisten, blending well. Beat in the remainder of the rum, then fold in the coconut, chopped mixed fruit and vanilla essence.

Take spoonfuls, roll into balls and place on waxed paper. Chill well.

CHOCOLATE TORRONE

$\frac{1}{2}$ pound dark chocolate
2 tablespoons dark rum
$\frac{1}{2}$ pound softened unsalted butter
1 tablespoon castor sugar
2 eggs, separated
6 ounces ground almonds
a pinch of salt
12 shortbread biscuits, cut or broken into 1-inch pieces

Break the chocolate into small pieces and combine it with the rum in a heavy saucepan. Stir over moderate heat, but avoid boiling the rum: to do this, remove the saucepan from the heat before the chocolate has completely dissolved (the heat of the saucepan will then be sufficient to dissolve it completely). Let it cool.

Cream the softened butter with the sugar until smooth and satiny. Add the egg yolks one at a time, beating until thoroughly blended. Stir in the ground almonds, blending well.

Add the cooled chocolate (it must be cooled, or the butter will melt). Add the salt to the egg whites and beat until stiff but not dry. Using a rubber scraper, fold the egg whites into the chocolate mixture. Then carefully fold in the 1-inch pieces of biscuit, being careful not to break them.

Line an orange-cake tin with foil. Spoon in the chocolate torrone and cover with waxed paper. Refrigerate for at least 4 hours. Break gently into pieces before serving.

CHOCOLATE TRUFFLES

2 level tablespoons butter
1 egg yolk
$\frac{1}{4}$ pound semi-sweet chocolate, grated
1 level tablespoon cocoa
1 teaspoon rum
chocolate nonpariels

Cream the butter and slightly beaten egg yolk. Add the grated chocolate, cocoa and rum, mixing in thoroughly.

Form into balls and roll each in chocolate nonpariels or chocolate shot. Place on waxed paper and leave for several hours in the refrigerator to set.

COCONUT BON-BONS

3 ounces cream cheese
3 cups sifted icing sugar
$\frac{1}{4}$ teaspoon peppermint essence
a pinch of salt
a few drops of green colouring
about $\frac{1}{2}$ cup desiccated coconut

Beat the cream cheese with a wooden spoon until smooth. Gradually blend in the sifted icing sugar, mixing well. Flavour with the peppermint essence and add the salt, then just enough of the green colouring to tint the mixture a delicate green. Cover and refrigerate for 1 hour.

Take spoonfuls of the mixture, shape into balls and roll them in coconut. Flatten the top of each ball slightly with the fingertips. Place on a tray covered with waxed paper and chill until firm.

COCONUT ECLIPSES

2 tablespoons butter
2 tablespoons water
1 teaspoon vanilla essence
2 cups sifted icing sugar
¼ cup non-fat powdered milk
2 cups flaked coconut
¼ cup flaked coconut
melted chocolate for dipping

Place the butter and water in a saucepan and heat until the butter melts. Add the vanilla, then stir in the combined sifted icing sugar and powdered milk a little at a time. If too dry add a little more melted butter or water. Stir in the 2 cups of flaked coconut and mix well.

Take spoonfuls of the mixture and shape into balls about 1 inch in diameter. Dip one side in coconut, flattening the ball as you press into the coconut. Place on a tray which has been covered with waxed paper. Allow to set in the refrigerator.

Melt some chocolate in a saucepan, take each ball and dip the side without coconut in the chocolate, then place upside down on the waxed paper to set.

COCONUT ICE

4 cups sugar
1 cup milk
a good pinch of cream of tartar
1 teaspoon vanilla essence
1⅓ cups coconut
pink colouring

Place the sugar, milk and cream of tartar in a saucepan. Stir over medium heat until the sugar has dissolved and the mixture comes to the boil. Remove the stirring spoon and boil quickly for exactly 5 minutes (it must be timed from the moment when the mixture comes to a full rolling boil).

Remove from the heat and let the mixture cool slightly in the saucepan, then stand it in a bowl of cold water. Add the vanilla and coconut and beat until thick. Spread half in a greased tin and quickly colour the remainder a pale pink and spread over the white layer.

When set and cool, cut into blocks.

COFFEE FUDGE

3 cups sugar
1 cup milk
1 or 2 level dessertspoons instant coffee
2 teaspoons liquid glucose
a pinch of salt
3 dessertspoons butter
1 teaspoon vanilla essence
1½ cups broken walnuts

Butter the sides of a large saucepan. Place the sugar, milk, coffee, glucose and salt in the saucepan and cook over low heat, stirring constantly until the sugar has dissolved and the mixture comes to the boil.

Continue boiling until the mixture reaches the soft ball stage (238°F.), stirring only if necessary. Remove immediately from the heat and add the butter. Cool to lukewarm without stirring. Flavour with the vanilla.

Beat vigorously until the fudge begins to lose its gloss and becomes thick. Quickly stir in the nuts and spread in a greased shallow tray. Mark into squares while still warm, and separate the squares when cold.

COFFEE MARZIPAN BALLS

6 ounces ground almonds
8 ounces icing sugar
½ level teaspoon instant coffee
2 egg yolks
2 tablespoons brandy

Mix the ground almonds, icing sugar and instant coffee. Beat the egg yolks with the brandy and add, stirring until well blended. The mixture should be quite firm.

Take spoonfuls and roll into about 20 balls. Chill for about 1 hour.

153

For the coffee icing

8 ounces sifted icing sugar
½ level teaspoon instant coffee
1 teaspoon butter
1 to 2 tablespoons water
a squeeze of lemon juice

6 ounces dark chocolate, grated
6 ounces ground almonds
1 ounce mixed peel, chopped
6 ounces castor sugar
1 ounce blanched almonds cut
   into slivers
1 teaspoon rum- or coffee-
   flavoured liqueur
grated rind of ½ lemon
juice of ½ lemon
1 level teaspoon cinnamon
½ level teaspoon mixed spice
1 large egg

3 tablespoons cold water
½ pound sugar
1 teaspoon liquid glucose
vanilla essence

1 cup sugar
¾ cup liquid glucose
½ cup butter
1 cup cream
½ cup finely chopped nuts
½ teaspoon vanilla essence

To make the icing, first sift together the icing sugar and instant coffee. Melt the butter in the water and add the lemon juice, then stir into the dry ingredients, mixing until smooth. Warm slightly and use to coat the chilled balls. Allow to dry. If liked, a scroll of white or coffee icing may be piped on top of each.

CONTINENTAL CHOCOLATE SLICES

Place all the ingredients except the egg in the top of a double saucepan over boiling water. Stirring occasionally, heat until the chocolate has melted and the ingredients are well blended.

Remove the top saucepan from the heat and beat in the egg. Return to the heat and cook for about 1 minute, beating constantly.

Sprinkle a square of aluminium foil or greaseproof paper with sugar, place the mixture on it and shape into a roll about 6 inches long. Wrap tightly and store in the refrigerator until set.

To serve, cut the roll into thin slices.

COOKED FONDANT

Place the water, sugar and glucose in a saucepan and stir until the sugar has dissolved. Using a pastry brush, brush down the sides of the saucepan to remove any undissolved sugar. Skim well. When boiling, place the lid on the saucepan and boil for 2 minutes.

Remove the lid, put in a sugar thermometer and boil to 240°F. (or soft ball stage, when a little is dropped into cold water). Pour the mixture into a wetted bowl and beat with a wooden spoon until thick, flavouring with vanilla essence. Cover with a slightly damp cloth until required.

Colour and flavour as desired and use to make date or prune creams.

CREAMY NUT CARAMELS 1

Butter the sides of a heavy 2-quart saucepan and place the sugar, glucose, butter and half the cream in it. Bring to the boil, stirring over low heat constantly.

Slowly stir in the remaining cream. Cook over low heat to soft ball stage (240°F.), stirring constantly towards the end of the cooking period.

Remove from the heat and add the nuts and vanilla. Pour into a buttered 6-inch square sandwich tin and mark into squares as the caramel mixture cools.

When quite cold, cut into pieces, wrap in waxed papers and store in an airtight container.

CREAMY NUT CARAMELS 2

¼ pound butter
1 cup (firmly packed) brown
  sugar
2 tablespoons liquid glucose
1 can sweetened condensed milk
3 ounces chopped walnuts

Melt the butter in a saucepan and add the brown sugar, glucose and condensed milk. Stir over medium heat until the sugar has dissolved. Cook, stirring occasionally, until soft ball stage is reached (240°F.).

Stir in the chopped walnuts. Pour into a greased 6-inch square sandwich tin and allow to become partly set. Mark into squares.

When quite cold and set, break into pieces, wrap in grease-proof or waxed paper and store in an airtight container.

CRYSTALLIZED CUMQUATS

Pick the fruit free from stalks and place them in strong brine. Allow to stand for 2 or 3 days. Drain, rinse and boil in fresh water until the skins can be pierced easily with a fine knitting needle. If possible keep the fruit whole.

Drain, and when cold enough to handle prick each cumquat several times with a straw or a fine knitting needle.

Make a strong syrup of sugar and water (about 3 cups of water and 6 cups of sugar should be enough for 12 dozen cumquats).

Place the cumquats in the syrup, bring to the boil and boil for 5 minutes. Remove from the heat and place in a deep bowl. Allow to stand for 2 days. Drain off the syrup, add to it 2 more cups of sugar and stir until boiling. Pour over the cumquats in the bowl.

Let stand again for 2 days, then repeat the process of pouring over the syrup, strengthening it each time. Do this four or five times, allowing 2 days to elapse between processing.

Now remove the fruit from the syrup and drain it on a fine sieve for 2 or 3 days. When all the syrup has drained off, roll the cumquats in sugar and store in airtight jars.

EASY MARSHMALLOW

2 cups sugar
2 tablespoons liquid glucose
1½ cups boiling water
1 heaped tablespoon gelatine
vanilla essence
colouring if liked
toasted or plain coconut for
  rolling

Place the sugar, glucose and half the water in a saucepan and stir over medium heat until both the sugar and the glucose have melted.

Add the remaining water to the gelatine and stir until it has completely dissolved. If necessary, heat to dissolve the gelatine.

Combine the two mixtures in a large bowl and beat at high speed until thick and white. This will take about 20 minutes. Flavour with vanilla and add colouring if liked.

Pour into a 9-inch or 10-inch square tin which has been greased and dredged with sifted icing sugar or cornflour. Allow to set, then turn out onto a paper spread with the coconut. Cut into squares and roll each square in coconut to coat well.

155

EVERTON TOFFEE

1 pound sugar
¼ pint water
1 teaspoon lemon juice
a good pinch of cream of tartar
3 ounces butter

Place the sugar, water and lemon juice in a saucepan and stir over gentle heat until the sugar has dissolved. Bring to the boil and add the cream of tartar. Boil to 290°F. (hard-crack stage).

Remove from the heat and gradually add the butter a small piece at a time.

Return the toffee to the heat again and bring back to 290°F. Do not stir the mixture at this stage.

Pour into a greased sandwich tin and when nearly set mark into squares.

When the toffee has set, separate the pieces and wrap each one in waxed paper.

FRENCH CHOCOLATE

8 ounces bitter chocolate
15-ounce can of sweetened condensed milk

Melt the chocolate in the top of a double saucepan over hot water, add the milk and stir until thick. Cool. Roll into small balls, enclosing a cherry in the centre of each; or roll in balls and then in chopped nuts or chocolate nonpariels.

Alternatively, make a mixture of finely chopped cherries and walnuts, and flavour with a little rum. Allow to stand overnight. Use as a centre for the above chocolate.

FRENCH CHOCOLATE CANDY

8 ounces unsweetened chocolate
4 ounces semi-sweet chocolate
1 can sweetened condensed milk
chopped nuts, chocolate sprinkles
or coconut

Combine both types of chocolate and heat over hot, not boiling, water until melted. Add the condensed milk and mix until smooth and well blended. Cool until the mixture begins to thicken.

Shape into small balls, using about a teaspoonful of the mixture for each ball. Roll in the chopped nuts or in the chocolate sprinkles or the coconut.

Allow to set before storing in a covered container.

FRENCH JELLIES

6 level dessertspoons gelatine
1¼ pints cold water
2 pounds sugar
1 level teaspoon tartaric acid
colouring and flavouring

Place the gelatine, water and sugar in a saucepan and stir over gentle heat until the sugar has dissolved. Continue cooking for 20 minutes, stirring gently all the time. Take off the heat and add the tartaric acid.

Divide the mixture evenly into three. Leave one portion white, or tint it with a little lemon colouring and flavour with either lemon or pineapple essence. Colour the second portion pink and flavour with cherry or strawberry. Add a few drops of green colouring to the third portion and flavour with lime.

Pour each of the jellies into individual flat trays. When set, turn each one out onto a piece of paper which has been dusted with sifted icing sugar, piling one layer on top of the other. Cut into squares with scissors and roll in icing sugar or crystal sugar.

Candied Orange Pompons
Frosty Grapefruit Peel

2 grapefruit
3 cups sugar
2¼ cups water for syrup
a good pinch of salt
3 teaspoons gelatine
3 tablespoons water
¼ cup sugar for coating

FROSTY GRAPEFRUIT PEEL

Remove the peel from the grapefruit in quarters with the point of a sharp knife. Using scissors, cut the peel into ¼-inch-wide strips, place in a medium-sized saucepan, cover with water and bring to the boil. Boil for 15 or 20 minutes, then drain. Repeat the boiling process with fresh water twice more.

After the third boiling drain the grapefruit and return it to the saucepan. Add the sugar, the 2¼ cups of water for the syrup, and the salt. Cook, stirring occasionally, for 1 hour or until the syrup is thick and the grapefruit peel clear. Remove from the heat. Be careful not to overcook, or the mixture will caramelize and turn a deep brown.

Soften the gelatine in the 3 tablespoons of cold water and add to the hot peel mixture. Stir until the gelatine has dissolved. Let the peel stand in the syrup until it is quite cold. Drain well.

Roll each piece of peel in sugar and spread on a tray. Leave for 24 hours to dry, then store in covered jars in a cool place.

157

HONEYCOMB

2 tablespoons golden syrup
1 dessertspoon water
4 slightly rounded tablespoons sugar
1 slightly rounded teaspoon bi-carbonate of soda

Place the golden syrup, water and sugar in a large saucepan and stir until the sugar has dissolved. Bring to the boil and boil for 7 minutes or to 312°F., when a little of the syrup will crackle when dropped into some cold water in a cup.

Remove from the heat and stir in the soda. The mixture will foam up (this is why you need to make the honeycomb in a large saucepan). Pour into a greased dish and leave until firm.

MARSHMALLOWS

2 cups sugar
2 tablespoons liquid glucose
$\frac{3}{4}$ cup boiling water
1 heaped tablespoon gelatine
$\frac{1}{4}$ cup cold water
$\frac{1}{2}$ cup boiling water
vanilla essence
colouring (optional)
cornflour, sifted icing sugar or coconut for covering

Dissolve the sugar and the glucose in the $\frac{3}{4}$ cup of boiling water. Soften the gelatine in the cold water, then dissolve in the $\frac{1}{2}$ cup of boiling water.

Combine both mixtures and flavour with vanilla. Cool slightly, then beat until thick. Colour if liked. Turn into a greased Swiss roll tin and leave until set.

Turn out onto paper covered with either cornflour, sifted icing sugar or plain or toasted coconut, and cut into squares, tossing each square to cover it completely.

MOCK RUM TRUFFLES

1 cup cake crumbs
1 cup coconut or ground almonds
$\frac{1}{2}$ cup castor sugar
rum
chocolate glacé icing
chocolate nonpariels
crystallized cherries (optional)

Combine the cake crumbs, coconut and sugar with enough rum to bind the mixture together. Take small portions and roll into balls. Place on greaseproof paper and allow to set.

Coat each ball with chocolate glacé icing (page 142) and sprinkle with chocolate nonpariels. A cherry may be placed on top of each.

NO-BAKE ALMOND BALLS

6 ounces chocolate pieces
6 ounces milk caramels
$\frac{3}{4}$ cup sifted icing sugar
$\frac{1}{2}$ cup sour cream
1 teaspoon grated lemon rind
a pinch of salt
$1\frac{3}{4}$ cups plain sweet biscuits
about $\frac{3}{4}$ cup ground almonds

Melt the chocolate and the caramels together over hot water. Remove from the heat and add the icing sugar, sour cream, lemon rind and salt. Mix well and stir in the biscuit crumbs. Chill for about 1 hour.

Take teaspoonfuls of the mixture and form into 1-inch balls. Roll each ball in ground almonds. Store in a tightly covered container in the refrigerator.

PEANUT TOFFEE

1 pound sugar
½ measuring cup water
¼ level teaspoon cream of tartar
1 teaspoon vinegar
½ teaspoon vanilla essence
peanuts

Grease a shallow tin about 6 inches in diameter. Place the sugar, water, cream of tartar and vinegar in a saucepan and stir over medium heat until the sugar has dissolved and the mixture comes to the boil.

Remove the stirring spoon and boil without stirring until the mixture is a honey colour.

Remove from the heat and add the vanilla. Sprinkle the peanuts in the bottom of the prepared tin and pour the toffee over them. Allow to become cold and set, then break into pieces.

Blanched or unblanched almonds may be used in place of the peanuts.

RAISIN COCONUT CANDY

3 cups sifted icing sugar
1 cup seeded raisins
1 cup coconut
1 teaspoon grated orange rind
5 ounces Copha or other white
  vegetable shortening
3 ounces chocolate

Place the icing sugar, raisins, coconut and orange rind in a bowl. Melt the Copha and allow it to cool slightly, then pour it onto the dry ingredients. Blend thoroughly.

Press the mixture into a foil-lined tin measuring about 8 inches by 11 inches, making the candy about ¼ inch thick. Allow to set. Melt the chocolate over hot water and spread over the top. Mark into squares before the chocolate has set.

RIBBON NUT FONDANT

1 pound icing sugar
2 ounces ground almonds
2 ounces liquid glucose
1 egg white
2 ounces blanched and chopped
  almonds

Sift the icing sugar into a bowl and add the ground almonds. Soften the glucose over boiling water, cool slightly, then add the beaten egg white. Make a bay in the centre of the icing sugar and pour in the liquid. Using a wooden spoon gradually draw in the icing sugar, making the mixture into a stiff paste.

Divide the paste into three equal portions. Colour one portion pink and flavour with raspberry; leave one portion white and flavour with vanilla; flavour and colour the third portion with coffee.

Toast the blanched and chopped almonds.

Roll pieces of paste into oblong shapes of equal size, about ¼ inch thick. Now place one layer on top of the other, beginning with the white portion and brushing each layer with a little egg white and sprinkling with the chopped almonds before covering with the next layer.

Allow to stand for several hours to set. Cut into strips about ¼ inch thick and 2 inches long. Store in an airtight container.

ROCKY ROAD

1 quantity marshmallow mixture
⅓ cup chopped almonds
¼ cup chopped glacé cherries
4 ounces chocolate
2 ounces Copha or other white vegetable shortening

Make the marshmallow to the stage where the mixture has been beaten until thick and white (see page 155). Divide into three equal portions. Colour one part pink, one green and leave the remainder white. Set these mixtures in separate tins which have been greased.

When the marshmallow has set, cut it into square and pile it into one tin which has been lined with waxed paper. Alternate the colours and sprinkle the almonds and cherries between the squares of marshmallow.

Place the chocolate and shortening in the top of a double saucepan over boiling water. Heat until both have melted and become thoroughly combined. Allow to cool slightly, then pour it over the marshmallow, nut and cherry mixture in the tin. When it has set cut into squares.

RUM BALLS

½ cup raisins
¼ cup glacé cherries
½ cup blanched almonds
¾ pound orange cake
2 slightly rounded tablespoons coconut
2 slightly rounded tablespoons cocoa
½ cup castor sugar
½ cup sultanas
1 tablespoon chopped crystal-lized ginger
1 teaspoon almond essence
3 tablespoons rum
¼ cup melted Copha
chocolate shot or chocolate non-pariels

Finely chop the raisins, cherries and almonds and crumble the cake. Combine the cake crumbs with the coconut, cocoa and castor sugar and add the sultanas, raisins, ginger, cherries and almonds. Mix the almond essence, rum and melted Copha together and stir into the dry mixture, blending well.

Form into balls about 1 inch in diameter and roll in the chocolate shot or in the nonpariels. Chill overnight in the refrigerator.

RUSSIAN TOFFEE

¼ pound butter
½ pound sugar
1 can of sweetened condensed milk
4 dessertspoons golden syrup
3 ounces chopped nuts (optional)

Place the butter and sugar in a saucepan and stir over low heat until both have melted.

Add the condensed milk and the golden syrup. Bring to the boil over gentle heat, stirring lightly to prevent sticking. Boil to 240°F. or when a little dropped into cold water forms a soft ball. Watch the mixture carefully because it burns easily.

Remove from the heat and add the chopped nuts. Pour into a greased tin and chill until set, marking into squares as the mixture cools.

SNOWBALLS

3 level dessertspoons gelatine
2 cups sugar
2 cups boiling water
vanilla essence

For the icing and coating

½ pound icing sugar
1 tablespoon cocoa
about 2 tablespoons cold water
coconut

Soften the gelatine in a little cold water. Place the sugar, softened gelatine and boiling water in a saucepan and stir until the sugar has dissolved. Remove the spoon and cook for 20 minutes, stirring occasionally. Cool slightly and pour into a large bowl.

Flavour with vanilla, colour if desired, and beat until thick. Spoon the mixture into wet or greased gem irons and allow to set.

Make a chocolate icing by sifting the icing sugar and cocoa together then placing it in a saucepan and adding the cold water. Stir briefly over low heat. Unmould the snowballs and coat with chocolate icing. Roll each one in coconut and leave on waxed paper to set.

TOFFEE ALMONDS

blanched almonds
1 pound sugar
½ measuring cup of water
¼ level teaspoon cream of tartar
1 teaspoon vinegar

Arrange the almonds on a well-greased oven tray, allowing about 2 inches of space between each almond.

Place the sugar, water, cream of tartar and vinegar in a saucepan and stir until the sugar has dissolved. Remove the spoon and boil without stirring until the mixture is a honey colour.

Let stand until the bubbles subside and the toffee becomes slightly cool. Now pour about 1 teaspoonful of the toffee over each almond on the tray. Allow to become cold and set.

When quite cold, remove from the tray and store in airtight jars.

UNCOOKED FONDANT

⅓ cup soft butter
⅓ cup liquid glucose
¼ teaspoon salt
1 teaspoon vanilla essence
1 pound icing sugar, sifted
prunes or apricots

Place the butter, glucose, salt and vanilla in a large bowl. Blend well, then add the sifted icing sugar all at once. Mix with a wooden spoon until stiff. Turn onto a board and knead until well blended and smooth.

Use to fill stoned prunes or dates, or to join dried apricots together in pairs, using about 1 teaspoon of the fondant for each.

VANILLA CARAMELS

1 cup white sugar
1⅓ cups (firmly packed) brown sugar
¼ pint milk
¼ pint cream
2 tablespoons liquid glucose
4 ounces butter
1 teaspoon vanilla essence

Place both sugars in a saucepan with the milk, cream and glucose and stir gently over low heat until dissolved. Add the cut-up butter and stir over moderate heat until the mixture reaches a temperature of 250°F. Flavour with the vanilla.

Pour into a greased tin and as soon as the caramel begins to set mark it into squares. Allow to become quite cold, then break the squares apart and wrap each piece in waxed paper.

Snowballs

2 cups fine biscuit crumbs
1 cup icing sugar
1 cup chopped walnuts
¼ cup cocoa
3 tablespoons liquid glucose
6 dessertspoons whisky

2 cups fine biscuit crumbs
1 cup finely chopped walnuts
1 cup icing sugar, sifted
2 tablespoons cocoa
a pinch of salt
2 tablespoons golden syrup
4 tablespoons whisky
coconut, sugar or chocolate non-
    pariels (for covering)

½ pound Copha
1 cup rice bubbles
1 cup powdered milk
1 cup coconut
1 cup sifted icing sugar
1 cup mixed fruits, including
    cherries and nuts

WHISKY BALLS 1
Mix all the ingredients thoroughly together. Roll into balls, using about 2 teaspoonfuls for each ball. Store in covered containers for several days. Before serving roll the balls in sifted icing sugar or cocoa.

WHISKY BALLS 2
Place the dry ingredients in a bowl and add the golden syrup and whisky. Mix thoroughly.

Take rounded teaspoonfuls of the mixture and shape into balls. Roll each ball in the coconut, sugar or chocolate non-pariels.

Store in covered containers and keep for several days before using.

WHITE CHRISTMAS
Melt the Copha and pour it onto the other ingredients, which have been combined in a bowl.

Press the mixture into a flat tin that has been lined with greaseproof or waxed paper. Chill until firm, then cut into squares.

DESSERTS

Cold Deserts

ALMOND MOCHA TORTE

1 cup sugar
4 eggs, separated
½ teaspoon vanilla essence
1 tablespoon melted butter
½ cup plain flour
1 level teaspoon baking powder
a pinch of salt
1 cup ground almonds

For the filling and topping

1 tablespoon castor sugar
½ pint cream
1 level tablespoon powdered
  coffee
toasted almonds

Add the sugar to the egg yolks and beat until creamy. Add the vanilla, then beat in the melted butter. Sift the flour with the baking powder and salt and stir in. Beat the egg whites stiffly in a separate bowl, add the ground almonds and fold into the first mixture.

Divide evenly between two well-greased 7-inch sandwich tins and bake in a moderate oven, 350°F., for 25 minutes. Cool.

To make the filling, add the sugar to the cream and beat until thick, then add the powdered coffee. Join the two layers with some of this whipped cream, spread the remainder on top and decorate with toasted almonds.

ALMOND PEACH RUSSE

1 sponge layer made in an
  8-inch tin
1 packet strawberry jelly
2 cups boiling water
16 sponge fingers
3 level teaspoons gelatine
¼ cup water
½ pint cream
½ ounce castor sugar
¼ pint milk
1 teaspoon lemon juice
1 teaspoon almond essence
1 large can of peach halves
extra cream, whipped and
  sweetened for garnishing

Line the base and sides of a deep-sided 8-inch spring-form pan with foil. Place the sponge layer in the bottom of the pan. Make up the jelly with the boiling water and allow it to cool to the stage where it is beginning to set. Spoon half the jelly over the cake layer and chill until firm. Keep the remainder of the jelly at room temperature.

Cut the sponge fingers in halves and stand them up round the edge of the pan with the ends touching the jelly. Trim the top level with the pan.

Soften the gelatine in the ¼ cup water and dissolve it over hot water. Whip the cream, add the sugar, milk, lemon juice and almond essence, then stir in the gelatine a little at a time. Chill until the mixture is beginning to set, then spoon half over the jelly layer in the pan. Allow to set.

Chop half the peaches, place them on top of the set gelatine mixture in the pan and cover with the remaining jelly. Allow to set, then add the remainder of the cream mixture. Chill.

Just before serving, unmould and peel off the foil, then top with the remaining peaches and decorate with the whipped and sweetened cream.

163

APPLE SNOW

4 cooking apples
4 tablespoons sugar
2 cloves
2 small pieces lemon rind
$\frac{1}{4}$ pint water
1 or 2 egg whites
cochineal or red colouring

Peel and core the apples and cut into quarters. Place in a saucepan with the sugar, cloves, lemon rind and water and simmer gently until quite tender. Transfer to a mixing bowl and beat to a pulp, then set aside to cool.

Beat the egg whites to a stiff froth and whisk into the cold apple pulp. Place half this purée in another bowl and colour it a pale pink. Place alternate spoonfuls of the white and pink mixtures in a serving dish. Chill.

Serve with custard made from the egg yolks.

APPLE PARFAITS

1 cup boiling water
1 packet raspberry jelly crystals
2 dessertspoons lemon juice
$1\frac{3}{4}$ cups apple purée
2 egg whites
a pinch of salt
$\frac{1}{3}$ cup sugar
whipped cream and strawberries
   to garnish

Add the boiling water to the jelly crystals and stir until dissolved. Add to this the apple purée and the lemon juice. Cool, then chill until partly set.

Beat the egg whites with the salt until stiff, then gradually add the sugar, beating until thick and glossy. Fold into the partly set jelly mixture and spoon into individual glasses. Chill until set.

When ready to serve, top each with a swirl of whipped cream and a whole strawberry. If preferred, the apple mixture may be set in a bowl, then spooned into parfait glasses with alternate layers of vanilla ice cream and topped with cream and strawberries.

APPLES CAPRICE

4 firm apples
2 cups sugar
3 cups water
$\frac{1}{2}$ teaspoon vanilla essence

For the sauce

$\frac{1}{3}$ cup plain flour
$\frac{3}{4}$ cup sugar
a pinch of salt
2 eggs
1 cup milk
1 cup cream
1 teaspoon vanilla essence
$\frac{1}{2}$ cup chopped toasted almonds

Peel and core the apples and cut them in halves. Put the sugar, water and vanilla into a frying pan and bring to the boil, stirring to dissolve the sugar. Place the apple halves in a single layer in the hot syrup and simmer uncovered for about 10 minutes, or until just tender. Lift out with an egg slice and place side by side in an ovenproof dish.

For the sauce, mix the flour with the sugar and salt, beat the eggs well and mix with the milk and cream, then gradually add to the dry ingredients, beating until smooth. Cook over boiling water, stirring constantly with a wooden spoon. When the sauce is thick and smooth, remove from the heat and let it get cool. Add the vanilla, then pour over the apples and sprinkle with the chopped almonds. Bake in a moderate oven, 350°F., for 20 minutes.

Apricot Gateau

4 ounces butter
$\frac{1}{2}$ cup sugar
$\frac{1}{2}$ teaspoon vanilla essence
2 eggs
1 cup self-raising flour
$\frac{1}{2}$ cup plain flour
$\frac{1}{3}$ cup milk

For the filling and decoration

1 large can of apricot halves
6 ounces butter
$3\frac{3}{4}$ cups icing sugar
1 tablespoon rum
browned flaked almonds
2 tablespoons apricot jam

$\frac{1}{2}$ pint cream
$\frac{1}{4}$ teaspoon vanilla essence
1 teaspoon castor sugar
1 family-sized brick of ice cream
6 small bananas
some grated chocolate
6 walnut halves

APRICOT GATEAU
Beat the butter and sugar until creamy. Flavour with the vanilla. Gradually add the well-beaten eggs. Sift the flours and add to the creamed mixture alternately with the milk. Divide evenly between two well-greased 8-inch sandwich tins and bake in a moderate oven, 350°F., for about 20 minutes. Remove from the tins and allow to cool.

To make the filling, first drain the apricots well, reserving a tablespoonful of the syrup. Beat the butter until smooth, gradually add the sifted icing sugar and flavour with the rum. Reserve one-third of this butter cream mixture. Keep enough apricot halves to cover the top of the gateau. Chop the remainder of the apricots, add to the larger proportion of butter cream, and use to fill the cake. Chill until firm.

Spread the sides of the cake with the reserved one-third of butter cream. Press the browned flaked almonds into the sides, then chill the cake again. Arrange drained apricot halves on top, rounded sides up. Sieve the apricot jam, heat with the reserved tablespoonful of apricot syrup and spoon over the apricot topping. Allow to set.

BANANA SPLIT
Whip the cream with the vanilla and sugar until thick.

Cut the ice cream brick into 6 slices and place in individual serving dishes. Peel the bananas and slice each one in half lengthwise.

Place a piece of banana on either side of the ice cream in each dish and spoon some whipped cream over the ice cream. Sprinkle with grated chocolate and top with a walnut half. Serve immediately.

BISCUIT TORTINI

3 egg whites
¾ cup sugar
¼ cup water
a pinch of salt
1½ cups cream
¾ teaspoon vanilla essence
1½ teaspoons almond essence
⅓ cup ground almonds

Allow the egg whites to stand in a bowl at room temperature for about 1 hour.

Place the sugar and water in a saucepan and stir over medium heat until the sugar has dissolved. Bring to the boil, and boil uncovered until the syrup spins a fine thread when dropped from a spoon (or 236°F. on a candy thermometer).

Beat the egg whites with a pinch of salt until stiff peaks form, then pour the hot syrup in a thin stream over them, beating constantly until the mixture forms very thick peaks when the beaters are raised. Refrigerate, covered, for 30 minutes.

Combine the almond essence and the ground almonds, mixing well.

Whip the cream, flavour with the vanilla and fold into the egg-white mixture, blending evenly. Spoon into paper-lined patty tins and sprinkle the top of each with a little ground almond. Freeze until firm, or overnight.

BRANDIED ORANGE SLICES

6 ripe navel oranges
6 slightly rounded tablespoons sugar
4 tablespoons brandy
2 slightly rounded teaspoons cornflour
1 cup water

Grate enough rind from the oranges to make 1 tablespoonful, then peel them, being careful to remove all the white pith and the centre cores. Slice neatly, sprinkle with 1 tablespoon of sugar, then add the brandy. Allow to stand for about 30 minutes.

Combine the cornflour with the remainder of the sugar, blend with a little of the cold water, then stir in the remainder of the water. Drain the juice and brandy from the cut-up oranges and stir this in too. Cook, stirring well, until the syrup boils and thickens slightly. Cook for 1 minute, then add the grated orange rind.

Pour this syrup over the oranges, lifting the slices so that it runs through them. Chill well and serve as a dessert, garnishing each serving with a maraschino cherry.

BURNT ALMOND MOUSSE

½ cup white sugar
½ cup boiling water
1 teaspoon gelatine
1 dessertspoon cold water
1½ cups chilled undiluted evaporated milk
1 teaspoon vanilla essence
¼ cup blanched almonds

Place the sugar in a heavy saucepan and cook over gentle heat, stirring only until it has dissolved. Continue cooking without stirring until the sugar is golden in colour or caramelized. Pour in the boiling water and stir over medium heat until the caramelized sugar has dissolved.

To this mixture add the gelatine which has been softened in the cold water. Stir until the gelatine has dissolved, then add half a cup of chilled evaporated milk. Cool until the mixture begins to thicken.

166

In a separate bowl whip the remaining cup of evaporated milk until stiff. Flavour it with the vanilla and fold into the partly set caramel mixture. Freeze in the refrigerator trays until mushy, then turn into a bowl, add the almonds and beat for 2 minutes. Return the mixture to the trays and freeze for 3 to 4 hours.

BUTTERSCOTCH ALMOND ICE CREAM

¾ cup sugar
1 tablespoon cold water
2½ cups fresh milk
2 level tablespoons cornflour or custard powder
2 tablespoons golden syrup
1½ level teaspoons gelatine
1 tablespoon hot water
1 cup cream or chilled unsweetened canned milk
2 teaspoons vanilla essence
2 ounces almonds, blanched, shredded and toasted

Place ¼ cup of the sugar and the tablespoon of water in a small heavy saucepan. Stir over low heat until the sugar has dissolved, then cook without stirring until it turns a caramel colour. Add 1 cup of the milk and stir over low heat until the caramel has dissolved into the milk.

Mix the cornflour or custard powder with the remaining ½ cup of sugar and blend with 3 tablespoons of milk. Add to the caramel milk, and cook until the mixture boils and thickens, stirring constantly. Continue cooking for 2 minutes, then remove from the heat and add the golden syrup.

Soften the gelatine with the hot water, add to the caramel mixture and stir until the gelatine has dissolved. Add the remainder of the milk and flavour with the vanilla. Pour into the refrigerator trays and freeze until mushy.

Turn into a chilled bowl and beat for 3 or 4 minutes. Whip the cream or the chilled canned milk and fold into the ice cream together with the toasted almonds. Return the ice cream to the trays and freeze until firm, stirring once during freezing.

When the ice cream is firm turn the control of the refrigerator back to normal.

BUTTERSCOTCH CREAM PIE

2 egg yolks
1 cup (firmly packed) brown sugar
¼ cup cornflour
a pinch of salt
2½ cups milk
3 ounces butter or margarine
½ cup sliced dates
½ teaspoon vanilla essence
1 baked pastry case (of biscuit pastry)
½ cup whipped cream
¼ cup chopped walnuts

Combine the egg yolks with the brown sugar, cornflour and salt in a bowl and blend in half a cup of the cold milk. Heat the remainder of the milk with the butter and, when almost boiling, pour onto the blended mixture, stirring until smooth.

Pour into the saucepan and cook over medium heat, stirring constantly until the mixture boils and thickens. Cook for 2 minutes, then remove from the heat and add the dates and vanilla.

Cool this filling slightly, then spread it in the cooked pastry case. When cold spread with the whipped cream and sprinkle the chopped walnuts round the edge.

167

CANTALOUP WHIP

⅔ cup chilled canned
    unsweetened milk
1 medium-sized cantaloup
⅓ cup sugar
¼ cup lemon juice
2 teaspoons grated lemon rind
cantaloup balls and sprigs of fresh
    mint for garnishing

The canned milk should be well chilled before use. Cut the melon in half and remove the seeds. Make half a cup of melon balls, using a melon baller or a teaspoon, and set aside to use as a garnish.

Mash the remainder of the melon (you should have about ¾ cup) and add the sugar. Turn the chilled milk into a bowl and beat until thick and more than doubled in bulk, then beat in the lemon juice and lemon rind and fold in the mashed cantaloup.

Pour into refrigerator trays and freeze until firm. Serve garnished with the cantaloup balls and fresh mint sprigs.

CARAMEL ICE CREAM

1½ cups chilled canned
    unsweetened milk
½ cup sugar
½ cup boiling water
1 teaspoon gelatine
1 dessertspoon cold water
1 teaspoon vanilla essence

The canned milk should be well chilled before use.

Dissolve the sugar in a heavy-base saucepan over gentle heat, then cook without stirring till it is a honey colour. Take off the heat, add the boiling water and stir until blended, if necessary returning the pan to the heat to dissolve the caramel.

Soften the gelatine in the cold water and stand it over hot water to dissolve. Add to the caramel mixture together with half a cup of the chilled canned milk. Chill until the mixture begins to thicken.

Beat the remaining cup of canned milk until thick, then fold in the caramel mixture. Flavour with the vanilla.

Place in refrigerator trays and freeze until mushy. Turn out into a chilled bowl and beat, scraping down the mixture from the sides of the bowl. Return the ice cream to the refrigerator trays and freeze until set.

CARAMEL RICE CUSTARD

1 ounce rice
1 cup water
a pinch of salt
1 level tablespoon sugar
¾ cup cream
¾ cup milk
4 egg yolks
½ teaspoon vanilla essence
apricot halves
caramelized sugar

Wash the rice and place it in a saucepan with the water and salt. Simmer gently until the water has been absorbed and the rice is tender. Remove from the heat and add the sugar, cream and milk.

Beat the egg yolks and stir them into the rice mixture. Add the vanilla. Return the mixture to the heat and cook, stirring constantly, for about 5 minutes or until the custard thickens slightly.

Pour into a greased pie-dish or individual moulds and place in a shallow pan containing about an inch of cold water. Bake in a moderate oven, 350°F., for 25 to 30 minutes or until the custard has set. Allow to cool.

Drain a small can of apricot halves and arrange on top of the custard, then drizzle over some caramel made by heating about 3 tablespoons of sugar in a small saucepan until it turns a honey colour. If the caramel is too stiff to pour add a little warm water and stir over gentle heat.

CASSATA

1½ pints vanilla ice cream
¾ pint chocolate ice cream
¾ pint strawberry ice cream
½ cup cream
1 dessertspoon rum or
   maraschino liqueur
1 egg white
2 level dessertspoons sugar
1 tablespoon chopped cherries
1 tablespoon chopped angelica
1 tablespoon chopped mixed peel
extra cream for decorating if
   liked

You will need a bowl measuring 6½ inches in diameter and 3 inches deep. Line the base with vanilla ice cream, freeze, then line the sides in two sections. Freeze well. Repeat with a layer of chocolate ice cream, freeze, well and repeat with a layer of strawberry ice cream. Freeze again.

Beat the cream until stiff and add the rum or liqueur. Beat the egg white until stiff and gradually beat in the sugar. Continue to beat until thick and glossy, then fold into the whipped cream together with the cherries, angelica and peel. Spoon this mixture into the centre of the ice-cream-lined bowl. Cover and freeze until firm.

To serve, unmould and decorate with whipped cream. Keep frozen until serving time. Cut into wedges to serve.

CHARLOTTE RUSSE

1 packet of strawberry jelly
   crystals
¾ pint boiling water
1½ dozen sponge fingers
brandy or sherry
4 teaspoons gelatine
¼ cup cold water
2 tablespoons sugar
2 eggs, separated
1 pint milk
1 cup cream, whipped
chopped jelly for decoration

Dissolve the jelly crystals in the boiling water. Allow to become cool, then pour into the bottom of an oiled or wetted 6-inch round cake tin or a charlotte russe mould. Chill until set.

Split the sponge fingers, trim them and use to line the dish containing the jelly. They may be sprinkled with brandy or sherry. Chill while you make the creamy custard filling.

Soften the gelatine in the cold water, then dissolve it over boiling water.

Add the sugar to the egg yolks and beat until well mixed, then add about ½ cup of the milk. Heat the remainder of the milk and, when almost boiling, pour it onto the egg, mixing well. Return the mixture to the saucepan and stir over low heat until the custard is almost boiling. Remove from the heat and cool slightly before adding the dissolved gelatine (if the custard is too hot the gelatine will curdle it). Chill until about the consistency of unbeaten egg white.

Flavour the custard with brandy or sherry (or vanilla essence if preferred). Add the stiffly beaten egg whites and half the whipped cream, blending well. Pour into the lined tin and chill until firm.

Unmould for serving, and decorate with the remainder of the cream and some chopped jelly.

CHEESECAKE PIE

1½ cups plain or coconut biscuit
   crumbs
¼ cup butter, melted
8 ounces cream cheese
½ cup sugar

Combine the biscuit crumbs and butter and press into an 8-inch spring-form pan, building the crumbs about halfway up the sides. Chill well.

Beat the cream cheese in a bowl until fluffy, then beat in the ½ cup of sugar and the lemon juice, vanilla and salt. Add the

Cheesecake Pie
Banana Nog
Pineapple Cream Squares

1 dessertspoon lemon juice
½ teaspoon vanilla essence
a dash of salt
2 eggs
½ pint sour cream
2 dessertspoons sugar and ½ tea-
　spoon vanilla essence for cream

1 dessertspoon gelatine
¼ cup cold water
¾ cup boiling water
3 ounces semi-sweet chocolate
8 ounces cream cheese
1 cup sugar
1 teaspoon vanilla essence
¾ teaspoon peppermint essence
1½ tablespoons lemon juice
¼ cup melted butter
1⅓ cups chocolate ripple biscuit
　crumbs
1 large can of unsweetened
　evaporated milk, well chilled
whipped cream and shaved
　chocolate for decoration

eggs one at a time, beating well. Pour into the prepared pan
and bake at 325°F. for about 40 minutes or until set.

Combine the sour cream with the 2 dessertspoons of sugar
and ½ teaspoon of vanilla and spoon over the top of the pie.
Bake for a further 10 minutes. Cool, then chill for several
hours. Decorate with strawberries before serving.

CHEESECAKE ROYALE

Soak the gelatine in the cold water for 5 minutes. Add the
boiling water, stirring till dissolved. Cool.

Melt the chocolate over hot water and put aside to cool.

Place the cream cheese, sugar, vanilla, peppermint essence
and lemon juice in a large bowl. Beat well, then blend in the
melted chocolate and the dissolved gelatine. Chill until the
mixture is the consistency of unbeaten egg white.

Grease an 8-inch spring-form pan and line the sides with a
double thickness of aluminium foil. Add the melted butter to
the biscuit crumbs, mixing well. Press two-thirds of this
mixture into the bottom of the pan and place in the refrigerator
to chill while you complete the filling.

Whip the chilled, slightly thickened gelatine mixture at slow
speed, at the same time gradually adding the chilled evaporated
milk. Now beat at high speed until the mixture doubles in
volume. Turn into the prepared tin and sprinkle the remaining
crumb mixture on top. Chill for several hours or overnight.

Remove from the pan onto a serving dish and garnish with
swirls of whipped cream and shaved chocolate.

For the crust

1¼ cups shredded-wheat biscuit crumbs

¼ teaspoon cinnamon

2 dessertspoons sugar

¼ cup soft butter

For the filling

1 pound cream cheese

1 cup cream

1 cup sugar

2 level dessertspoons plain flour

¼ level teaspoon salt

3 eggs, separated

1 teaspoon vanilla essence

¾ teaspoon grated lemon rind

For the topping

1-pound can of cherries

2 level dessertspoons cornflour

⅓ cup sugar

¼ teaspoon grated lemon rind

1 level teaspoon gelatine

6 dessertspoons sugar

½ cup Marsala wine or dry sherry

6 egg yolks

1 dessertspoon brandy

1 teaspoon vanilla essence

½ pint cream

3 egg whites

a pinch of cream of tartar

a pinch of salt

1 ounce chocolate for topping

2 level teaspoons gelatine

2 tablespoons cold water

1 ounce butter

3 tablespoons sugar

4 ounces semi-sweet chocolate

1 large can of unsweetened evaporated milk, well chilled

a pinch of salt

½ cup toasted slivered almonds

CHERRY CHEESECAKE

Combine the ingredients for the crust and press into the bottom and sides of a well-greased 10-inch spring-form pan. Chill.

Soften the cream cheese at room temperature and stir in the cream. Add the sugar, flour and salt. Beat the egg yolks until light and creamy and fold carefully into the cream mixture. Flavour with the vanilla and lemon rind.

Beat the egg whites until soft peaks form, then fold them into the cream mixture. Pour into the chilled crust. Bake at 325°F. for 1 hour, then leave in the oven for another hour with the heat off. Cool thoroughly.

For the topping, drain the cherries, reserving the syrup (there should be ¾ cup). Mix the cornflour with the syrup, add the sugar and lemon rind and cook, stirring well, until the mixture boils and thickens. Cool and add the cherries. Pour the cooled cherry topping over the cooled cheesecake. Chill thoroughly before serving.

CHILLED ZABAGLIONE CREAM

Place the gelatine and 4 dessertspoons of the sugar in a saucepan with the wine. Beat the egg yolks until light and lemon-coloured and stir in the sugar mixture. Stirring constantly over low heat, cook until the mixture thickens. Remove from the heat and stir in the brandy and the vanilla. Cool.

Whip the cream until almost stiff and fold into the cooled custard.

Beat the egg whites in a warm dry bowl with the cream of tartar and salt until soft peaks form. Sprinkle with the remaining sugar and beat to a stiff meringue. Fold this into the custard mixture. Spoon into tall glasses and chill for an hour or so.

Just before serving top with grated chocolate or chocolate curls.

CHOCOLATE ALMOND VELVET

Soak the gelatine in the cold water, then dissolve it over hot water. Place in a saucepan with the butter, sugar and chocolate and heat gently until the chocolate has melted. Mix well, then allow to cool.

Place the chilled evaporated milk in a large bowl, add the salt and whip until thick. Beat in the cooled chocolate mixture, then fold in the almonds. Pour into two refrigerator trays and freeze until firm (if the almonds sink to the bottom, stir the mixture as soon as it has set lightly).

CHOCOLATE CHARLOTTE RUSSE

½ pint milk
2 tablespoons sugar
3 ounces semi-sweet chocolate
4 eggs, separated
1 teaspoon vanilla essence
2 slightly rounded teaspoons
  gelatine
2 tablespoons cold water
18 sponge fingers
¼ teaspoon cream of tartar
½ pint cream
whipped and sweetened cream
  for decorating

Place the milk, sugar and chocolate in a saucepan and heat gently until the chocolate has melted. Carefully pour onto the beaten egg yolks, blending well. Return the mixture to the saucepan and cook, stirring constantly, over low heat until the custard thickens slightly. Remove from the heat and add the vanilla.

Soak the gelatine in the cold water, then dissolve over hot water. Cool slightly and stir into the chocolate custard. Chill until the mixture is the consistency of unbeaten egg white.

Line an orange-cake tin with foil, then lightly grease the foil. Now line the bottom and sides with sponge fingers cut to fit the shape of the tin.

Beat the egg whites stiffly, adding the cream of tartar. Whip the cream until stiff and fold into the chocolate custard, then lightly but thoroughly fold in the egg whites.

Pour half the chocolate mixture into the lined tin, cover with a layer of the remaining sponge fingers then top with the rest of the mixture. Chill for several hours or overnight.

Unmould onto a serving plate and decorate with whipped cream and, if liked, some strawberry halves or grated chocolate.

CHOCOLATE CHIFFON PIE

1 rounded dessertspoon gelatine
3 tablespoons cold water
2 level tablespoons cocoa
¾ cup sugar
1 cup milk
3 eggs, separated
1 teaspoon vanilla essence
a pinch of salt
1 baked pastry case (biscuit or
  sweet shortcrust pastry)
whipped cream and chopped
  walnuts for topping

Soak the gelatine in the cold water, then dissolve it over boiling water. Combine the cocoa with ½ cup of the sugar and blend with a little of the milk. Add the remainder of the milk and heat until almost boiling.

Beat the egg yolks lightly and add to the milk mixture. Using a wooden spoon stir over low heat until the mixture coats the back of the spoon. Cool slightly, then add the vanilla, salt and gelatine. Chill until the mixture begins to thicken.

Beat the egg whites in a separate bowl until stiff, add the remainder of the sugar and beat until thick and glossy. Fold into the lightly set chocolate mixture. Pour into the prepared pastry case and chill until set.

Spread with whipped cream and sprinkle with chopped walnuts.

CHOCOLATE CRACKLE PIE

For the crackle crust
2 cups rice bubbles
½ cup coconut
4 rounded tablespoons icing
  sugar

Place the rice bubbles, coconut, icing sugar and cocoa in a bowl. Melt the Copha over gentle heat till just warm, then pour it over the ingredients in the bowl. Mix thoroughly, then press evenly into an 8-inch or 9-inch tart plate and place in the refrigerator to set.

1½ rounded tablespoons cocoa
¼ pound Copha

For the filling

2 egg yolks
1 can of sweetened condensed
    milk
½ cup lemon juice

For the topping

1 cup cream, sweetened and
    whipped

2 ounces butter
½ cup sugar
½ teaspoon vanilla essence
1 egg, separated
¾ cup self-raising flour
1½ level tablespoons cocoa
¼ cup milk
½ pint cream

For the ice cream

1 tablespoon water
¼ level teaspoon gelatine
1 small can of unsweetened
    evaporated milk, well chilled
3 rounded dessertspoons castor
    sugar
¼ teaspoon vanilla essence or rum

2 level tablespoons sugar
3 level dessertspoons cornflour
1 level tablespoon cocoa
½ pint milk
2 egg yolks
1 dessertspoon butter
½ teaspoon vanilla essence
2 dozen pastry cases made from
    biscuit pastry

Beat the egg yolks with the milk and a good ½ cup of lemon juice until well mixed, then pour into the chocolate crackle crust (it is important to have a good measure of lemon juice, otherwise the filling will not set). Chill until set.

Decorate with the whipped sweetened cream.

CHOCOLATE ICE-CREAM CAKE

Beat the butter to a cream, add the sugar and continue beating until soft and fluffy. Flavour with the vanilla and add the egg yolk.

Sift the flour with the cocoa and stir into the mixture alternately with the milk. Lastly fold in the stiffly beaten egg white.

Place in a well-greased 7-inch sandwich tin and bake in a moderate oven, 350°F., for about 20 minutes. Cool, then split into two layers.

To make the ice cream, combine the water and gelatine and allow to stand for about 5 minutes, then dissolve it over boiling water. Beat the chilled evaporated milk until it has almost trebled in volume, then gradually beat in the sugar. Add the gelatine and the vanilla or rum. Pour into a greased and foil-lined 7-inch sandwich tin and freeze until firm.

Remove the ice cream from the tin and peel off the foil. Place it on one layer of the chocolate cake and top with the other chocolate layer.

Whip the cream with a little sugar and vanilla and completely cover the cake (pipe the cream through a star tube if liked). Replace in the freezer until serving time.

CHOCOLATE MERINGUE TARTS

Place the sugar, cornflour and cocoa in a bowl and blend with a little of the cold milk until smooth. Heat the remainder of the milk and when almost boiling gradually pour it onto the blended mixture, stirring until smooth. Return the mixture to the saucepan and cook, stirring well, until it boils and thickens, then cook for a further minute. Remove from the heat and add the egg yolks, butter and vanilla. Cool slightly and use to fill the cooked and cooled patty pastry cases.

To make the meringue, beat the egg whites with the salt

For the Meringue

2 egg whites
a pinch of salt
4 level tablespoons sugar

6 ounces semi-sweet chocolate
1 teaspoon instant coffee
½ cup sugar
2 tablespoons water
½ teaspoon vanilla essence
3 eggs, separated
a pinch of salt
whipped cream for decoration

until stiff, then gradually beat in the sugar. Pile or pipe onto the chocolate filled cases. Place in a slow oven to lightly brown and set the meringue.

FRANGIPANI TARTS

Follow the recipe for chocolate meringue tarts but omit the cocoa from the ingredients and add ½ cup well-drained crushed canned pineapple and ½ cup coconut.

BANANA CREAM TARTS

Follow the recipe for chocolate meringue tarts but omit the cocoa from the ingredients, then place a little mashed banana in the bottom of the tart shell, fill with the custard and top with a piece of banana which has been dipped in lemon juice.

CHOCOLATE MOUSSE

Place the chocolate, instant coffee, ¼ cup of the sugar and the water in a saucepan and stir over low heat until the chocolate and sugar have dissolved.

Remove from the heat and beat with a wooden spoon until smooth. Allow to cool, then flavour with the vanilla.

Beat in the egg yolks one at a time, beating well after each addition.

Add the salt to the egg whites and beat until stiff. Gradually beat in the remaining ¼ cup of sugar. The mixture should be thick. Fold gently into the chocolate mixture.

Spoon into 6 individual serving dishes and chill for an hour or more. Decorate with whipped cream before serving.

Chocolate Mousse Cake

CHOCOLATE MOUSSE CAKE

18 to 20 sponge fingers
18 ounces chocolate
3 dessertspoons water
4 dessertspoons icing sugar
7 egg yolks
1½ teaspoons vanilla essence
5 egg whites
½ cup cream, whipped and
    sweetened
1 ounce grated or shaved
    chocolate for decoration

Line a 9-inch by 5-inch loaf tin with waxed paper. Split the sponge fingers and arrange a layer on the bottom of the tin, trimming them where necessary to completely cover the area.

Heat the chocolate with the 3 dessertspoons of water in the top of a double saucepan over hot water until the chocolate has melted. Remove from the heat.

Mix the sifted icing sugar with the egg yolks and vanilla, then stir in the melted chocolate. Beat until smooth, then allow to cool.

Beat the 5 egg whites until stiff but not dry, and fold into the chocolate mixture. Spread half this mixture over the layer of sponge fingers. Add another layer of sponge fingers, then top with the remainder of the chocolate mixture and arrange the remaining sponge fingers on top. Cover lightly with aluminium foil and freeze until firm.

To serve, soften slightly in the refrigerator by removing the dish from the freezing compartment to one of the lower shelves. Turn out onto a serving plate and frost the top and sides with the sweetened whipped cream and grated or shaved chocolate.

CHOCOLATE ROYALE TORTE

For the meringue

4 egg whites
1½ cups sugar
1 teaspoon vinegar
1 teaspoon cinnamon

For the filling

4 ounces semi-sweet chocolate
4 egg yolks
¼ cup water
2 level tablespoons cocoa
1 cup cream
¼ cup sugar for cream
½ level teaspoon cinnamon
    for filling

Cover a baking tray with paper, draw an 8-inch circle in the centre and grease the paper well on both sides.

Add a pinch of salt to the egg whites and beat until stiff. Beat in half the sugar a dessertspoonful at a time. Fold in the remaining sugar and add the vinegar and cinnamon.

Spread the meringue mixture within the circle on the prepared tray, making the bottom layer ¾ inch thick and moulding the remaining mixture around the edges to form a shell with sides about 2 inches high. Lightly press the back of a teaspoon round the sides at regular intervals, making a ridged pattern. Bake at 275°F. for about 1¼ hours or until the meringue is set.

Melt the chocolate for the filling over hot water, cool slightly and spread 2 tablespoonfuls in the bottom of the cooled meringue shell.

Add the egg yolks, water and cocoa to the remaining chocolate, blending well, and cook over hot water until thickened. Chill.

Combine the cream, sugar and cinnamon and whip until thick, then spread half over the chocolate in the shell. Fold the other half into the chilled chocolate custard and spread this on top of the filled shell. Chill for several hours or overnight.

Decorate with whipped cream, sprinkled if liked with chopped nuts.

175

CITRUS CHIFFON PIE

For the crumb crust

22 wholemeal biscuits, or 1½
   cups biscuit crumbs
¼ cup sugar
¼ teaspoon cinnamon
a pinch of nutmeg
a pinch of allspice
2 ounces soft butter or margarine

For the filling and topping

1 dessertspoon gelatine
¼ cup cold water
4 eggs, separated
1 cup sugar
1 cup orange juice
1 dessertspoon lemon juice
a good pinch of salt
1 teaspoon grated orange rind
1 teaspoon grated lemon rind
whipped cream and orange slices
   for serving

Preheat the oven to 375°F. and grease an 8-inch tart plate. Combine the ingredients for the crumb crust, mixing well. Using the back of a wooden spoon, press firmly into the sides and bottom of the plate. Bake for 8 minutes. Cool.

To make the chiffon filling first soften the gelatine in the cold water and dissolve it over boiling water. Beat the egg yolks in another bowl with half the sugar and the fruit juices and salt, then cook in the top of a double saucepan until slightly thickened, stirring well—this will take 10 to 12 minutes. Cool slightly, then add the cooled gelatine and the grated fruit rinds. Refrigerate until the mixture is the consistency of unbeaten egg white, then beat until smooth.

Beat the egg whites in a large dry bowl until soft peaks form when the beater is lifted, then gradually beat in the remaining ½ cup sugar, and continue to beat until glossy. Fold the citrus mixture lightly and evenly into this meringue mixture and pour into the pie shell. Chill until firm.

Before serving decorate the top with swirls of whipped and sweetened cream and thin slices of fresh orange.

Do not use navel oranges for this recipe or the flavour will be bitter.

CITRUS CREAM TART

For the crumb crust

½ pound plain sweet biscuits
½ cup castor sugar
4 ounces butter
1 teaspoon cinnamon

For the filling and topping

1 can of sweetened condensed
   milk, chilled
grated rind of 1½ oranges
grated rind of 1 lemon
juice of 1 orange
juice of 1 lemon
2 eggs, separated
2 tablespoons of sugar
   for meringue
orange slices for decorating

Crush the biscuits finely and mix with the sugar. Melt the butter and stir into the crumbs together with the cinnamon. Mix well and press into the base and sides of a greased 8-inch or 9-inch tart plate. Chill while preparing the filling.

Beat the condensed milk slightly and add the grated orange and lemon rind and the orange and lemon juice. Blend well, then stir in the beaten egg yolks. Pour into the prepared tart case and chill until the filling has set.

Beat the egg whites stiffly, then gradually beat in the sugar, making a thick meringue. Pipe or pile on top of the pie and place it in a moderate oven for about 10 minutes to lightly brown and set the meringue.

Chill again before serving decorated with orange slices.

COCONUT PINEAPPLE SLICES

4 ounces soft butter
¾ cup sugar
1¼ cups plain flour
1 cup well-drained crushed
  pineapple
1 egg
1 dessertspoon melted butter
1½ cups shredded coconut
whipped and sweetened cream
  for serving

Mix the soft butter with ¼ cup of the sugar, using a fork. Add the flour and mix until crumbs form. Now mix with the hand to form a dough.

Press the dough evenly into the bottom of an 8-inch square tin, extending the mixture up the sides. Prick the surface with a fork. Bake in a moderate oven, 350°F., for 15 minutes or until the crust begins to brown, then remove from the oven and spread with the well-drained pineapple.

Beat the egg well, add the remaining ½ cup of sugar, then fold in the melted butter and the coconut. Spread evenly over the layer of pineapple. Bake for a further 30 minutes or until the top is brown. Cool.

Cut into slices and serve with whipped and sweetened cream.

COFFEE CHIFFON

1½ cups milk
1 cup cream
2 dessertspoons instant coffee
5 eggs, separated
½ cup sugar
2 dessertspoons gelatine
a little cold water
⅔ cup sugar for egg whites
grated chocolate for topping
whipped cream for serving

Place the milk, cream and instant coffee in a saucepan and heat till tiny bubbles form.

Beat the egg yolks until thick, then gradually add ½ cup sugar, beating well after each addition. Add gradually to the hot coffee and cook until the mixture coats the back of a wooden stirring-spoon—it should be the consistency of custard.

Remove from the heat and stir in the gelatine which has been soaked in a little cold water and dissolved over boiling water. Chill until about the consistency of unbeaten egg white.

Place the egg whites in a clean dry bowl, add a pinch of salt and beat until stiff. Gradually beat in the ⅔ cup of sugar. Fold into the coffee custard, pour into a 2-quart mould and chill in the refrigerator until set.

Unmould, sprinkle with grated chocolate and serve with canned pears and whipped cream.

CONTINENTAL CHEESECAKE

6 ounces biscuit pastry
2 tablespoons plain flour
a pinch of salt
⅓ cup sugar
8 ounces cream cheese
½ cup milk
2 eggs, separated
½ teaspoon vanilla essence
1 dessertspoon grated lemon rind

Roll the pastry to line an 8-inch tart plate or sandwich tin. Pinch the edges and chill while you make the filling.

Sift the flour with the salt and the ⅓ cup of sugar. Cut in or sieve in the cream cheese. Add the milk, egg yolks, vanilla and lemon rind, mixing well. Fold in the stiffly beaten egg whites. Pour into the uncooked pastry case and bake in a moderate oven, 325°F., for 45 minutes or until the filling has set. Allow to cool before removing from the pan.

French Strawberry Tart

CUSTARD TART

For the pastry

3 rounded tablespoons plain
　flour
1 rounded tablespoon
　self-raising flour
a pinch of salt
2 ounces butter
1 level tablespoon sugar
1 egg yolk
1 dessertspoon water

For the custard

2 eggs
1 cup milk
1 dessertspoon sugar
½ teaspoon vanilla essence
ground nutmeg

Sift the flours with the salt, rub in the butter and add the sugar. Mix the egg yolk with the water and stir into the dry ingredients, making a fairly dry dough. Turn onto a floured board and knead only until smooth on the outside. Roll to line a 7-inch sandwich tin which has been greased with butter or margarine.

Trim the edges of the pastry and, if liked, glaze the bottom of the uncooked pastry case with a little egg white.

For the custard combine all the ingredients except the nutmeg, beat until blended, and pour into the uncooked pastry shell. Sprinkle with the nutmeg.

Bake in a hot oven, 425°F., for 10 minutes, then reduce the temperature to 325°F. and bake for a further 20 minutes or until the custard has set.

FRENCH STRAWBERRY TART

6 ounces short or biscuit pastry
1 level teaspoon gelatine
1 tablespoon cold water
6 ounces cream cheese
¼ cup sugar
grated rind of 1 lemon

Line a 7-inch tart plate or flan tin with the pastry and bake in a moderate oven, 350°F., until light brown.

Soften the gelatine in the cold water and dissolve it over boiling water. Beat the cream cheese until fluffy, then gradually beat in the sugar, grated rind and 2 tablespoons of the lemon juice. Beat in the dissolved gelatine.

178

3 tablespoons lemon juice
a box of strawberries
1 slightly rounded tablespoon
  cornflour
¼ cup cold water
½ cup strawberry jam
whipped and sweetened cream

Spread this mixture in the bottom of the cooked and cooled pastry case. Wash the strawberries, cut half of them into halves or slices, and arrange over the layer of cream cheese in the tart case. Chill.

Blend the cornflour with the ¼ cup of water, the strawberry jam and the remaining tablespoon of lemon juice. Place in a saucepan and stir over low heat until the mixture boils and thickens.

Reserve a few whole strawberries for garnishing. Fold the remaining whole strawberries into the cornflour mixture and pour into the pie case. Chill for several hours.

When ready to serve, decorate the top of the tart with swirls of whipped cream and the reserved whole strawberries.

FRESH BERRY TART

For the shortcake base

4 ounces butter or margarine
½ cup sugar
1 egg
1 dessertspoon grated orange
  rind
1 cup plain flour
½ level teaspoon baking powder
a pinch of salt

For the topping

2 dessertspoons gelatine
¾ cup boiling water
2 cups sliced fresh strawberries
  or whole raspberries
1 cup cream, sweetened and
  whipped

Beat the butter and sugar and add the well-beaten egg. Flavour with the grated orange rind. Sift the flour with the baking powder and salt and add to the creamed mixture, making a smooth dough.

Line a 9-inch square baking pan with greased paper or foil and spread the shortcake dough evenly over it. Bake in a moderate oven, 375°F., for 15 to 20 minutes or until lightly browned. Cool thoroughly.

To make the topping first dissolve the gelatine in the boiling water and chill until it is syrupy. Spread about one-third of this over the cooled shortcake mixture and arrange the berries on top (if they are tart in flavour sprinkle them with a little sugar). Brush or spoon the remaining gelatine over the fruit and chill until set.

To serve, cut into 12 even-sized pieces and spoon or pipe the whipped cream on top.

FRUIT FLUMMERY

1 cup sugar
1 rounded tablespoon gelatine
1½ level tablespoons plain flour
2 cups water
1 level teaspoon grated lemon
  rind
juice of 1 medium-sized lemon
juice of 1 medium-sized orange
3 passionfruit
2 or 3 bananas

Combine the sugar, gelatine and flour and blend with the cold water. Pour into a saucepan and cook, stirring well, over medium heat until the mixture comes to the boil. Remove the spoon and simmer for 10 minutes, then add the lemon rind and allow the mixture to cool.

Add the lemon and orange juice and whisk well. Chill until the mixture begins to thicken. Now beat until it has doubled in bulk, and fold in the passionfruit and the sliced bananas.

Chill until set. Serve with boiled custard or whipped cream.

179

FRUIT GATEAU

For the cake base

8 ounces butter
1 cup sugar
3 eggs
½ teaspoon vanilla essence
2 cups self-raising flour
1 cup plain flour
¾ cup milk

For the filling

1 small can of pineapple pieces
1 small can of apricot halves
1 small can of peach slices
½ pint fruit syrup
4 tablespoons Cointreau
1 slightly rounded dessertspoon
    gelatine
2 tablespoons strawberry jam or
    jelly
2 ounces blanched, chopped and
    toasted almonds

The cake is best made the day before the dessert is required.

Cream the butter and sugar until light and fluffy. Gradually add the well-beaten eggs and flavour with the vanilla. Sift the flours together and add to the creamed mixture alternately with the milk.

Grease well and line the base of a 9-inch square cake tin. Spoon the mixture evenly into the tin and bake in a moderate oven, 350°F., for about 50 minutes. Cool.

Trim the cake to an oval shape and mark a one-inch rim round the top with a knife. Scoop out the centre neatly inside the rim to make an oval shell. Place on a serving dish.

Drain the canned fruits well, then mix 2 tablespoons of the fruit syrup with half the Cointreau. Sprinkle this over the cake shell. Arrange the well-drained fruits attractively in the shell.

Soak the gelatine in 4 tablespoons of the fruit syrup, and heat until dissolved. Mix in the remaining syrup and Cointreau and allow to cool until almost set. Meanwhile brush the sides and rim of the filled shell with the sieved and warmed jam and coat with the almonds. Spoon the partly set gelatine mixture evenly over the fruits. Allow to set.

FRUIT MINCE CHEESE PIE

6 ounces biscuit pastry
8 ounces soft cream cheese
2 eggs
⅓ cup sugar
¼ teaspoon vanilla essence
1 cup prepared fruit mince
1 cup cream, whipped

Roll the pastry to line an 8-inch or 9-inch tart plate. Pinch a frill round the edge. Bake at 375°F. for 10 to 12 minutes. Remove from the oven to cool. Meanwhile reduce the temperature of the oven to 350°F.

Beat the cream cheese in a bowl until light and fluffy. Add the slightly beaten eggs and the sugar and vanilla and beat until well blended. Spread the fruit mince in the bottom of the cooked and cooled pastry case and top with the cream cheese mixture. Bake for 25 to 30 minutes or until the top is lightly brown.

Cool. Serve plain or with whipped cream.

FRUIT MINCE TARTS

3 ounces suet
4 ounces sultanas
6 ounces seeded raisins
2 ounces currants
2 ounces mixed peel
4 ounces sugar
1 large cooking apple, peeled and
    grated

This fruit mince must be made several weeks before it is needed. Grate the suet finely, removing any skin. Chop the dried fruit and mixed peel into uniform-sized pieces. Combine all the filling ingredients and mix thoroughly. Let stand several hours, stirring occasionally. Pack into jars, cover and seal. Store for several weeks.

To make the tarts, knead the pastry lightly, roll thinly and cut into rounds with a fluted cutter. Use to line greased patty

180

grated rind of ½ lemon
grated rind of ½ orange
strained juice of ½ lemon
½ teaspoon mixed spice
a pinch of salt
2 tablespoons brandy
12 ounces biscuit pastry
sifted icing sugar for topping

For the rich pastry

2 cups plain flour
¼ teaspoon salt
4 ounces butter
2 ounces margarine
1½ tablespoons sugar
1 teaspoon grated lemon rind
2 egg yolks

For the pastry cream

5 egg yolks
⅔ cup sugar
¼ cup plain flour
2 cups hot milk
1 teaspoon vanilla essence or a
   liqueur to flavour

For the filling and glaze

1 can of preserved apricots
1 dessertspoon gelatine
1 tablespoon brandy or cognac

1 can of rice cream
1 teaspoon gelatine
1 tablespoon cold water
1 packet of strawberry jelly
½ cup boiling water
1½ cups ice-cold water
1 small can of tropical fruit salad
1 cup whipped cream
strawberries or candied cherries
   for garnishing

tins. Place a spoonful of mince in each pastry case, and decorate the top with a pastry cut-out if liked. Bake in a moderate oven, 350°F., for 15 to 20 minutes or until the pastry is a light golden colour. Cool. Dust with sifted icing sugar before serving.

FRUIT TART WITH PASTRY CREAM

Sift the flour and salt into a bowl and rub in the butter and margarine. Add the sugar and the lemon rind and mix to a firm dough with the beaten egg yolks. Roll the dough between two sheets of waxed paper large enough to line the bottom of a 9-inch tart plate. This is a rich dough and there is a tendency for it to break: if this happens, simply patch it up with pieces of dough. Chill the uncooked pastry shell before baking in a hot oven, 450°F., for 10 minutes. Reduce the heat to 400°F. and bake for a further 8 to 10 minutes or until the pastry is cooked.

Beat the egg yolks and sugar for the pastry cream until the mixture forms a ribbon when you lift the beater. Stir, then blend in the plain flour. Add the hot milk in a steady stream, beating constantly. Cook in the top of a double saucepan with the water simmering underneath, until the cream is thick and smooth—about 15 minutes. Remove from the heat and add the vanilla or any flavouring you wish. Cool, then spread in the bottom of the cooked and cooled pastry case.

Arrange the well-drained apricots, rounded side up, on top of the cream. Place the drained syrup in a saucepan and bring to the boil. Add the gelatine which has been softened with a little cold water, and stir until it has dissolved, then add the brandy and chill until the syrup is just at the point of setting. Spoon over the apricots and chill until serving time.

HAWAIIAN PARFAITS

Chill the rice cream. Soften the gelatine in the cold water, dissolve it over boiling water, and add to the rice cream. Place in the refrigerator to set lightly.

Make up the jelly by dissolving the crystals in the boiling water and then adding the ice-cold water. This method gives a quicker setting jelly.

Drain the syrup from the canned fruit salad and place a spoonful of the fruit in the bottom of each of 4 parfait glasses. Over the fruit place a spoonful of the rice cream, then one of jelly. Continue in this order until the glass is full.

Top each parfait with a swirl of whipped cream and a fresh strawberry or a candied cherry.

181

ITALIAN ICE CREAM

½ cup sugar
3 ounces water
3 egg yolks
½ pint cream
1 dessertspoon rum
1 teaspoon vanilla essence
½ cup ground praline (recipe
  follows)
extra whipped cream and ground
  praline

Place the sugar and water in a saucepan and stir over low heat until the sugar has dissolved. Bring gently to the boil, and boil without stirring until the temperature reaches 220°F. on a candy thermometer. Remove from the heat.

Beat the egg yolks in the top of a double saucepan, add the hot syrup and continue cooking over simmering water, beating well until stiff peaks form—this takes about 7 minutes. Remove from the heat, place over cold water and continue beating the mixture until it is cold.

Whip the cream until thick and add the rum and vanilla. Fold into the egg mixture and add the praline. Turn into a wetted mould and freeze overnight.

To serve, unmould and garnish with whipped cream, and sprinkle with ground praline.

PRALINE

Heat ½ a cup of sugar in a saucepan over medium heat until it liquefies and turns an amber colour. Add ¾ of a cup of mixed chopped walnuts and almonds and stir until the nuts are coated. Turn into a greased tin. Cool, then grind in a blender or break up with a foil-covered hammer.

JAFFA CHIFFON PIE

For the rice-bubble crust

2 cups rice bubbles
½ cup coconut
1 cup icing sugar
1½ rounded tablespoons cocoa
4 ounces Copha

For the filling

½ cup sugar
a pinch of salt
1 level tablespoon gelatine
1 cup orange juice
3 eggs, separated
½ teaspoon grated lemon rind
1 teaspoon grated orange rind
⅓ cup sugar for egg whites
1 cup diced orange segments
⅓ cup coconut
1 cup whipped cream

Place the rice bubbles, coconut, icing sugar and cocoa in a bowl. Melt the Copha over gentle heat till warm, not hot and pour it over the ingredients in the bowl. Blend thoroughly, then press evenly into a 9-inch tart plate.

For the filling, place the ½ cup of sugar and the salt, gelatine, orange juice and slightly beaten egg yolks in the top of a double saucepan and cook over simmering water, stirring all the time, until the gelatine has dissolved and the mixture has thickened slightly. Remove from the heat and add the grated lemon and orange rind. Chill until partly set.

Beat the egg whites stiffly, then gradually beat in the ⅓ cup of sugar, making a meringue. Fold lightly but thoroughly into the partly set gelatine mixture, then fold in the orange segments and coconut. Pour into the rice bubble crust, piling high in the centre. Chill until firm.

Just before serving decorate with the whipped cream and some orange slices.

JELLIED FRUIT SLICE

8 ounces butter
1 cup sugar
2 eggs
1 dessertspoon grated orange
   rind
2 cups plain flour
1 level teaspoon baking powder
1 small can of peach slices
1 small can of apricot halves
bananas and fresh strawberries
1 packet of lemon jelly crystals

Beat the butter and sugar to a light cream and gradually add the beaten eggs. Stir in the grated orange rind. Sift the flour with the baking powder and add to the creamed mixture, making into a smooth dough.

Line a 12-inch by 10-inch Swiss roll tin with greased foil or paper and spread the dough in the bottom. Bake at 375°F. for about 20 minutes. Leave in the tin to cool.

Arrange drained peach slices, drained apricot halves, sliced bananas and halved strawberries in rows across the shortcake base.

Make the jelly according to the directions on the packet and chill until it is just beginning to set. Carefully spoon it over the fruit, then chill the slice in the refrigerator until the jelly is firm. Cut into squares to serve.

LEMON CAKE PIE

1 level dessertspoon gelatine
2 tablespoons cold water
1 can of condensed milk
¼ cup lemon juice
1 teaspoon grated lemon rind
2 eggs, separated
18 sponge fingers
whipped sweetened cream and
   fresh raspberries for decoration

Soak the gelatine in the cold water for 5 minutes, then dissolve it over boiling water.

Blend the condensed milk, lemon juice and grated rind with the egg yolks, stir until thick, then gradually add the slightly cooled gelatine mixture. Stir in the stiffly beaten egg whites.

Split the sponge fingers and use some to line a mould or serving dish. Now fill the dish with alternate layers of lemon mixture and split sponge fingers until all have been used. Chill for at least 6 hours.

Unmould and decorate with whipped and sweetened cream and fresh raspberries.

LEMON CAKE PUDDING

1 ounce butter
½ cup sugar
1 teaspoon grated lemon rind
¼ cup lemon juice
3 eggs, separated
¼ cup plain flour
¼ cup flaked coconut
1 cup milk
a pinch of salt
whipped cream and grated
   lemon rind for serving

Beat the butter and sugar until well combined, then blend in the lemon rind and juice. Add the egg yolks one at a time, beating well after each addition.

Mix the flour well with the coconut and add to the creamed mixture alternately with the milk, beginning and ending with flour mixture.

Whip the egg whites with the salt until soft peaks form. Fold gently into the batter until blended.

Pour into a greased 1½-quart dish and place this dish in another dish containing about an inch of water. Bake at 325°F. for 45 to 50 minutes or until the top is a golden brown.

Serve warm with whipped cream topped with a little grated lemon rind.

LEMON CHIFFON RING

4 teaspoons gelatine
½ cup cold water
⅔ cup lemon juice
1 cup sugar
6 eggs, separated
a pinch of salt
1 teaspoon grated lemon rind
whipped and sweetened cream
frosted grapes
orange slices

Sprinkle the gelatine over the cold water, allow to stand for about 5 minutes then dissolve it over boiling water.

Combine the lemon juice and ¾ cup of the sugar.

Add a pinch of salt to the egg yolks and beat until light and lemon-coloured. Add the lemon juice and sugar and cook in the top of a double saucepan over simmering water until the mixture coats the back of a wooden stirring spoon. Remove from the heat, cool slightly and add the dissolved gelatine. Flavour with the grated lemon rind and chill until the mixture begins to thicken.

Beat the egg whites in a warm, dry bowl until stiff, then slowly beat in the remaining ¼ cup of sugar. Fold into the lemon mixture. Pour into a 3-pint mould and chill until set. Just before serving unmould the dessert and decorate with whipped and sweetend cream, frosted grapes and orange slices.

To frost grapes, beat 1 tablespoon of water with 1 egg white. Wash and dry the grapes, then lightly brush them with the egg-white mixture. Sprinkle with caster sugar and place on a wire rack until the sugar dries.

LEMON FANCHONETTES

8 ounces biscuit pastry
4 ounces semi-sweet chocolate
1 level teaspoon gelatine
¼ cup cold water
⅓ cup sugar
⅓ cup lemon juice
3 eggs, separated
1 teaspoon grated lemon rind
¼ cup sugar for egg whites
whipped cream and fresh straw-
    berries for topping

Roll the pastry thinly and use to line small patty tins (for larger, dessert-sized tarts, turn the individual tart tins upside down and mould the thinly rolled pastry over them). Bake in a moderate oven, 350°F., for about 10 or 15 minutes. Cool.

Melt the chocolate over hot water and spread a layer over the inside of each cooled pastry case. Allow to set.

Soften the gelatine in the cold water and dissolve it over boiling water.

Mix the ⅓ cup of sugar with the lemon juice and egg yolks, place in the top of a double saucepan and using a wooden spoon stir over simmering water until the mixture coats the back of the spoon. Add the dissolved gelatine and the grated lemon rind, mixing well. Pour into a bowl and chill until the mixture begins to thicken.

Beat the egg whites in a warm, dry bowl until stiff. Gradually beat in the sugar. Fold into the cooled and slightly set custard, then spoon the custard into the chocolate-lined pastry cases. Chill until firm.

Just before serving. top each with a swirl of whipped and sweetened cream and a whole strawberry.

184

LEMON MERINGUE PIE

1 cup sugar
3 level dessertspoons plain flour
a pinch of salt
3 level dessertspoons cornflour
1½ cups water
3 eggs, separated
¼ teaspoon grated lemon rind
1 tablespoon butter
⅓ cup lemon juice
1 baked 8-inch pastry case of short or biscuit pastry
1 teaspoon lemon juice and 6 level tablespoons sugar for meringue

Blend the sugar, flour, salt, cornflour and water in a bowl. Place in a saucepan and cook, stirring constantly over medium heat until the mixture boils and thickens—about 5 minutes. Remove from the heat, add the slightly beaten egg yolks and stir well. Return to the heat and cook for a further 3 minutes.

Remove again from the heat and add the grated lemon rind and the butter and lemon juice, blending well. Cool slightly, then pour into the cooked and cooled pie-shell. Allow to cool to room temperature.

Beat the egg whites in a warm dry bowl until stiff peaks form, adding the teaspoon of lemon juice. Gradually add the 6 tablespoons of sugar, beating until glossy peaks form. Spread over the lemon filling, making sure the meringue touches the pastry at the edges. Bake in a moderate oven, 325°F., for 12 or 15 minutes or until the tips of the meringue are lightly tinged with brown. Cool thoroughly before serving.

LEMON PUFF

14-ounce can of unsweetened evaporated milk
1 packet of lemon-flavoured jelly crystals
1¾ cups boiling water
¼ cup lemon juice
1 teaspoon grated lemon rind
½ cup sugar
½ cup fine white bread crumbs
½ cup fine cake crumbs
cherries or walnuts for decorating (optional)

Chill the unopened can of milk, preferably overnight. Dissolve the jelly crystals in the boiling water and leave until the jelly begins to set. Now whip it until light and fluffy and add the lemon juice and grated rind and the sugar.

Whip the chilled milk until it has more than doubled in bulk. Combine with the lemon jelly mixture.

Toss the breadcrumbs and cake crumbs together. Lightly grease the bottom and sides of a shallow serving dish and sprinkle with half the crumbs. Pour in the lemon mixture and top with the remaining crumbs. Chill until set.

Cut into squares to serve. If liked, top each serve with a walnut half or a cherry.

LEMON SNOW

3 teaspoons gelatine
¼ cup sugar
a pinch of salt
1¼ cups boiling water
¼ cup fresh lemon juice
2 egg whites
grated rind of 1 lemon

Place the gelatine, sugar and salt in the large bowl of an electric mixer. Stir well, then add the boiling water and stir until the sugar and gelatine have dissolved. Add the lemon juice, blending well. Chill in the bowl until the mixture is the consistency of unbeaten egg white—about 45 minutes.

Add the egg whites and the grated lemon rind and beat at high speed until the mixture forms stiff peaks when the beaters are raised slowly. This may take up to 20 minutes.

Turn into a wetted mould and allow to set. Unmould and serve with a custard made with the egg yolks.

LEMON SNOWFLAKE PIE

4 eggs, separated
a pinch of salt
$\frac{1}{4}$ level teaspoon cream of tartar
1$\frac{1}{2}$ cups sugar
$\frac{1}{2}$ cup sugar for filling
2 lemons
2 cups cream

Beat the egg whites with the salt until soft peaks form, then add the cream of tartar and beat until stiff. Gradually add the 1$\frac{1}{2}$ cups sugar, beating after each addition. The mixture should be thick and glossy.

Spread two-thirds of this meringue evenly in a well-greased 8-inch tart plate, carrying the mixture well out to the edges of the plate. Bake at 275°F. for 50 to 60 minutes or until the meringue is set and faintly tinged with brown. Remove from the oven and cool.

Take the remainder of the meringue mixture and, using a plain éclair tube and a cream bag, pipe about 24 tiny meringues onto a greased slide. Bake these for about 30 minutes.

For the filling, beat the 4 egg yolks until thick, adding the $\frac{1}{2}$ cup sugar, $\frac{1}{4}$ cup lemon juice and the finely grated rind of 1 lemon. Place in the top of a double saucepan and cook over simmering water, stirring well with a wooden spoon until the mixture thickens. Remove from the heat. Cool.

Whip 1 cup of the cream and fold into the cooled lemon filling. Turn this mixture into the cooled meringue case. Use the remainder of the cream, also whipped, to decorate the top of the pie together with the miniature meringues.

LEMON SOUFFLÉ

$\frac{3}{4}$ pint milk
6 eggs, separated
3 tablespoons sugar
1$\frac{1}{2}$ teaspoons grated lemon rind
3 rounded teaspoons gelatine
6 tablespoons lemon juice
$\frac{1}{4}$ teaspoon cream of tartar
$\frac{3}{4}$ pint cream, whipped
3 tablespoons finely chopped
  nuts
whipped cream and fresh strawberries for topping (optional)

Lightly grease eight individual soufflé moulds or a 2-pint mould. Pin a paper collar round the outside to stand an inch or more above each mould. Grease this paper lightly.

Heat the milk slightly. Beat the egg yolks and sugar well until light in colour. Gradually pour on the heated milk, stirring constantly. Place in the top of a double saucepan over simmering water and stir with a wooden spoon until the custard coats the back of the spoon. Remove from the heat, add the grated lemon rind and allow the mixture to cool.

Sprinkle the gelatine on top of the lemon juice, allow to stand for 5 minutes, then set in a pan of hot water and stir until the gelatine has dissolved. When it has cooled slightly, add to the lemon custard and chill until the consistency of unbeaten egg white.

Beat the egg whites until stiff, adding the cream of tartar. Gently fold the whipped cream into the gelatine mixture, and then lightly and thoroughly fold in the stiffly beaten egg whites.

Place in the prepared soufflé dishes and chill until firm. To serve, gently remove the paper collar and press the chopped nuts round the sides. Decorate with extra cream and straw-berries if liked.

186

Almond Peach Russe, Pineapple Boats, Hawaiian Parfaits

Marshmallow Puffs

1 large can of unsweetened
    evaporated milk
4 level teaspoons gelatine
½ cup boiling water
¾ cup castor sugar
1 teaspoon vanilla essence
strawberries and cream for
    decorating

For the crust
1 cup crushed shredded wheat
    biscuits
¼ cup desiccated coconut
¼ cup melted butter

For the filling
½ cup sugar
1 dessertspoon cornflour
2 teaspoons instant coffee
2 cups scalded milk
4 eggs, separated
1 teaspoon vanilla essence
4 to 5 ounces semi-sweet
    chocolate
1 dessertspoon gelatine
¼ cup cold water
½ cup sugar for egg whites
½ cup cream, whipped

MARSHMALLOW PUFFS

Chill the unopened can of milk. Dissolve the gelatine in the boiling water and allow to cool. Turn the milk into a chilled bowl and add the gelatine, sugar and vanilla. Beat until thick. Pour into six individual moulds which have been brushed with unbeaten egg white. Chill until set.

Unmould and serve decorated with strawberries and whipped cream.

MOCHA MARBLE PIE

Mix the biscuit crumbs with the coconut and melted butter and press into the bottom and sides of an 8-inch pie plate. Place in a moderate oven, 350°F., and bake for 15 minutes.

Combine the ½ cup of sugar with the cornflour. Add the powdered coffee to the scalded milk and gradually add to the beaten egg yolks, then stir this into the sugar mixture. Cook over medium heat, stirring well until the mixture boils and thickens. Remove from the heat and add the vanilla and chocolate, and the gelatine which has been softened in the cold water. Stir until the chocolate and gelatine have dissolved, then chill until the mixture begins to thicken.

Beat the egg whites until soft peaks form, gradually beat in ½ cup sugar and beat again until thick and glossy. Fold lightly into the custard mixture. Pour into the cooled biscuit crumb case, spread the whipped cream over the top and swirl through the filling to make a marble effect. Chill until set—about 2 hours.

Royal Plum Pudding and Orange Sauce

MOCHA MOUSSE CUPS

For the chocolate cups

½ pound semi-sweet chocolate
1½ tablespoons grated Copha

For the filling

2 egg yolks
¼ cup castor sugar
3 tablespoons hot milk
3 tablespoons hot black coffee
a few drops of coffee essence
1½ level teaspoons gelatine
1 tablespoon cold water
½ pint cream

Chop the chocolate, place it with the Copha in a small saucepan, set the pan over hot water and leave until melted, stirring occasionally. Cool slightly, then spread evenly to line some small paper patty cases. Place these cases in metal patty tins to keep them a good shape. Chill to set the chocolate.

Beat the egg yolks with the sugar and add the hot milk and coffee and the coffee essence. Stir over gentle heat until the mixture thickens. Remove from the heat, cool slightly and add the gelatine which has been softened in the cold water and then dissolved over hot water. Allow to cool.

Whip the cream and fold half into the coffee mixture as it begins to set.

Remove the paper cases from the chocolate shapes. Spoon in the mousse mixture and chill until set, then pipe a swirl of whipped cream on top of each.

MOCHA REFRIGERATOR CAKE

2 rounded dessertspoons cocoa
1 teaspoon coffee essence
¼ cup sugar
3 tablespoons water
2 eggs, separated
½ teaspoon vanilla essence
2 ounces butter
½ cup icing sugar
½ cup chopped walnuts
1 layer of day-old sponge
½ pint sweetened and whipped cream

Blend the cocoa, coffee essence, sugar and water until smooth. Add the well-beaten egg yolks and place in the top of a double saucepan. Cook over simmering water until thick and smooth, stirring constantly. Remove from the heat, add the vanilla and allow to cool.

Cream the butter with the icing sugar until smooth. Add half the walnuts, then the chocolate mixture and lastly fold in the stiffly beaten egg whites.

Line a sandwich tin the same size as the sponge cake with greaseproof paper. Cut the sponge into four thin layers. Place one layer in the paper-lined tin and add one-third of the chocolate mixture.

Continue in layers with sponge and chocolate, ending with a layer of sponge. Chill overnight.

To serve, turn onto a platter and remove the paper. Frost the outside with the whipped cream and sprinkle with the remaining nuts.

NO-BAKE CHOCO-MINT CHEESECAKE

1 large can of unsweetened evaporated milk
1 slightly rounded dessertspoon gelatine
¼ cup cold water
¾ cup boiling water
3 ounces semi-sweet chocolate
8 ounces cream cheese
1 cup sugar
1 teaspoon vanilla essence

Have the evaporated milk well chilled in the can, preferably overnight. Soak the gelatine in the cold water for about 5 minutes. Add the boiling water and stir until the gelatine has dissolved. Cool. Melt the chocolate over hot water.

Beat the cream cheese, sugar, essences and lemon juice in a large bowl. Blend in the melted chocolate and the cooled gelatine. Chill until the mixture is the consistency of unbeaten egg white.

Grease an 8-inch spring-form pan, then line the sides with a double thickness of foil.

No-bake Choco-mint Cheesecake

¾ teaspoon peppermint essence
1½ tablespoons lemon juice
1⅓ cups chocolate ripple biscuit
   crumbs
2 ounces butter, melted
whipped cream and grated
   chocolate for decoration

For the crumb crust

½ pound plain sweet biscuits
1½ teaspoons grated orange rind
3 ounces butter

For the filling

2 ounces butter
4½ ounces castor sugar
10 ounces cottage cheese
2 ounces ground almonds
2 ounces ground rice
1 ounce sultanas
2 eggs, separated

Measure 1⅓ cups of biscuit crumbs and mix in the melted butter. Press two-thirds of this into the bottom of the pan and leave to chill while you make the remainder of the filling.

When the gelatine mixture has thickened slightly, whip at low speed while adding the chilled evaporated milk. Now beat at high speed until the mixture has doubled in volume and is thick. Turn into the prepared tin and top with the remaining biscuit crumbs. Chill for several hours or overnight.

Unmould onto a serving dish, carefully remove the foil, and garnish the top with swirls of whipped cream and a sprinkling of shaved or grated chocolate. For special occasions add fresh strawberries.

ORANGE CHEESECAKE

Crush the biscuits and mix with the orange rind. Melt the butter and stir into the crumbs. Mix well and use to line the bottom and sides of a 6-inch spring-form pan. Refrigerate for 1 hour.

Cream the butter and sugar for the filling, stir in the cottage cheese and beat well. Add the ground almonds, ground rice, sultanas and beaten egg yolks, mixing well. Whip the egg whites until stiff and fold in. Spoon into the prepared biscuit case and bake in a slow oven, 300°F., for 1 hour. Chill well before serving.

1 rounded teaspoon gelatine
¼ cup cold water
⅓ cup sugar
⅓ cup orange juice
3 eggs, separated
1 teaspoon grated orange rind
¼ cup sugar for egg whites
1 tart case of biscuit or shortcrust
  pastry cooked in an 8-inch tin
whipped cream for topping

3 oranges
2 tablespoons sugar
1 rounded tablespoon cornflour
1 egg, separated
½ pint milk
vanilla essence
a pinch of salt
1 tablespoon sugar for the egg
  white

For the crust
1½ cups crushed ginger biscuits
¼ cup icing sugar
½ cup melted butter or margarine

For the filling
1 level tablespoon gelatine
¼ cup cold water
½ cup sugar
1½ cups orange juice
1 tablespoon lemon juice
1 cup cream, whipped

ORANGE CHIFFON

Soak the gelatine for a few minutes in the cold water, then dissolve it over boiling water.

Blend the ⅓ cup sugar with the orange juice and egg yolks, place in a saucepan and cook over gentle heat, stirring well with a wooden spoon until the mixture coats the back of the spoon. Add the grated orange rind, remove from the heat, cool slightly and add the dissolved gelatine. Pour into a bowl and chill until the mixture begins to thicken.

Beat the egg whites in a warm dry bowl until stiff, then gradually beat in the ¼ cup sugar. Fold this into the partly set orange custard. Turn into the cooked pastry shell and chill until set. Top with whipped and sweetened cream before serving.

ORANGE DELIGHT

Peel the oranges, removing the white pith, slice them thinly, then cut again into small pieces. Place in a serving dish and sprinkle with the 2 tablespoons of sugar (more may be added if the oranges are a little sour).

Blend the cornflour with the egg yolk and a little of the cold milk. Place the remainder of the milk on to heat, and when almost boiling take off the heat and pour a little onto the blended mixture. Stir until smooth, then add the remainder of the milk. Return the mixture to the saucepan and cook, stirring well, until it boils and thickens. Cook for 3 minutes. (Don't add sugar to this custard or the dessert will be too sweet.)

Cool the custard slightly and flavour with vanilla. Pour over the oranges.

Beat the egg white with a pinch of salt until stiff, then gradually beat in the sugar. Beat until thick and glossy, then pile or pipe on top of the custard. Place in a moderately hot oven to lightly brown and set the meringue. Serve cold.

Sliced bananas and passionfruit may be added to the oranges if liked.

ORANGE DREAM TARTS

Combine the biscuit crumbs with the sugar and the melted butter and press into greased patty tins. Chill until set, or bake in a moderate oven, 350°F., for about 10 minutes then cool and chill.

Soften the gelatine in the cold water and dissolve it over boiling water. Stir in the sugar and the fruit juices. Chill until the mixture begins to set, then beat until fluffy. Chill again until almost set, then fold in half the whipped cream and pile into the ginger patty cases. Top each with a swirl of whipped cream.

190

ORANGE MERINGUE TRIFLE

¼ cup sugar
2 slightly rounded dessertspoons
   cornflour
3 eggs, separated
½ pint orange juice
2 teaspoons grated orange rind
12 sponge fingers
whipped cream
sliced oranges and mint sprigs
   for decoration

Navel oranges can produce a bitter custard when cooked, so use oranges other than navels for this dish.

Combine ¼ cup of the sugar with the cornflour and beat in the egg yolks, beating until smooth. Gradually stir in the orange juice, then cook for about 2 minutes over medium heat, stirring constantly until the mixture boils and thickens. Remove from the heat and stir in 1 teaspoon of the grated orange rind.

Use the sponge fingers to line the bottom and sides of a shallow ovenproof dish. Pour over the orange custard and allow to stand in the refrigerator overnight or at least for several hours.

Next day make the meringue by beating the egg whites until stiff, then gradually beating in the remainder of the sugar until the mixture is thick and glossy. Fold in the remaining teaspoonful of grated orange rind.

Spread the meringue over the custard in the dish. Bake in a moderate oven until the meringue is lightly browned and set. Cool. Garnish with fresh orange slices and mint sprigs and serve with cream.

ORANGE RICE RING

1 cup raw rice
¾ cup sugar
2 teaspoons grated orange rind
1 cup orange juice
3 eggs
½ cup cream
1 teaspoon vanilla essence
orange sections
sweetened and whipped cream

Cook the rice in boiling salted water for 12 minutes. Drain well. Return it to the saucepan and add the sugar, orange rind and juice. Cook, stirring occasionally until the mixture boils, then simmer for a further 15 minutes or until almost all of the liquid has been absorbed and the rice is tender.

Beat the eggs, spoon a little of the hot rice into them, then stir in the remaining rice. Return the mixture to the saucepan and cook for a further 2 minutes. Cool.

Whip the ½ cup of cream until thick, flavouring it with the vanilla. Fold it into the cooled rice mixture, then spoon into a moistened ring tin. Chill for several hours. Unmould for serving, and decorate with peeled orange sections and whipped cream.

ORANGES CAPRICE

5 level teaspoons gelatine
1 cup cold water
1½ cups sugar
a pinch of salt
1½ cups boiling water
2 teaspoons grated lemon rind
¼ cup lemon juice
6 egg whites

Sprinkle the gelatine on the cold water and allow to stand until it has softened. Add the sugar, salt and boiling water and stir until the gelatine has dissolved. Add the grated lemon rind and the lemon juice and stir until blended. Chill, stirring occasionally, until the mixture is beginning to set (about the consistency of unbeaten egg white).

Add the unbeaten egg whites to the partly set lemon mixture. Using an electric mixer at medium speed, beat until

191

custard sauce (made from egg yolks)

fresh orange slices and whipped cream for decoration

the mixture will hold its shape and becomes very frothy—about 20 minutes.

Spoon into a mould which has been brushed with egg white (you could use a little of the whites measured for the recipe) and chill until set. Unmould onto a serving dish and garnish with slices or segments of orange and whipped and sweetened cream. Serve with custard sauce (recipe follows).

CUSTARD SAUCE

2 cups milk
6 egg yolks
2 tablespoons sugar
$\frac{1}{4}$ teaspoon vanilla essence

Place the milk in the top of a double saucepan and heat until tiny bubbles appear round the edges.

Place the egg yolks in a bowl with the sugar and vanilla essence. Beat well, then slowly pour on the hot milk. Return the mixture to the top of the double saucepan and cook over hot, not boiling, water, stirring well with a wooden spoon until the custard is thick enough to coat the back of the spoon. Pour at once into a bowl and allow to cool. A little more vanilla essence may be added at this stage.

PARADISE TART

4 ounces short or biscuit pastry
2 eggs
$\frac{1}{3}$ cup sugar
$\frac{1}{2}$ pint milk
$\frac{1}{2}$ cup coconut
pulp of 2 passionfruit
whipped cream and passionfruit pulp for serving

Line a greased sandwich tin with the pastry. Pinch a frill round the edges. Break the eggs and use a little of the white to brush the inside of the uncooked pastry case.

Add the sugar to the eggs and beat until mixed, then stir in the milk, coconut and passionfruit pulp. Pour into the pastry case. Bake in a hot oven, 425°F., for 10 minutes, then reduce the heat to 350°F. and cook for a further 20 to 30 minutes or until the custard has set.

Cool and serve with swirls of whipped and sweetened cream topped with passionfruit pulp.

PAVLOVA

4 egg whites
a pinch of salt
$\frac{1}{8}$ teaspoon cream of tartar
$1\frac{1}{2}$ cups sugar
1 slightly rounded dessertspoon cornflour
1 teaspoon vinegar
1 teaspoon vanilla essence
whipped cream and fruit or chocolate for topping

Grease a tart plate well and sprinkle with equal quantities of icing sugar and cornflour sifted together. (Or cover the bottom of a shallow tray with foil, draw an 8-inch circle, grease it and sprinkle with a mixture of icing sugar and cornflour, then prepare a band of the same foil about 2 inches wide, secure with a paper clip or pin, and stand it up round the edge of the greased circle.)

Beat the egg whites with the salt in a warm dry bowl until stiff, then add the cream of tartar and beat until well mixed. Gradually add half the sugar (about a dessertspoonful at a time), beating well between each addition.

Fold in the remainder of the sugar, then quickly add the sifted cornflour and the vinegar and vanilla. Spoon carefully into the prepared tart plate or shallow tray and bake in a slow oven, 300°F., for $1\frac{1}{4}$ hours.

192

Cool thoroughly, out of draughts, before topping with whipped cream and one of the following: strawberries; passionfruit; drained fruit salad; grated chocolate with rum-flavoured whipped cream; lemon cheese made from the left-over egg yolks.

PEACH CHEESECAKE

For the crust

1 cup plain sweet biscuit crumbs
1 tablespoon sugar
$\frac{1}{4}$ teaspoon nutmeg
$\frac{1}{4}$ teaspoon cinnamon
3 ounces melted butter

For the filling

1 packet of lemon jelly crystals
6-ounce can of peach nectar
$\frac{1}{2}$ pound creamed cottage cheese
1 cup sugar
$\frac{1}{2}$ teaspoon almond essence
1 large can of chilled
   unsweetened evaporated milk
3 tablespoons lemon juice
1 large can of peach halves
Strawberries

Place the biscuit crumbs, sugar, nutmeg and cinnamon in a bowl and blend well with the melted butter. Press into the base of a greased and lined 9-inch spring-form pan. Chill while preparing the filling.

Dissolve the jelly crystals in the peach nectar (which has been brought to the boil). Cool. Beat the cottage cheese with the sugar and almond essence until light and fluffy, then add the cooled jelly mixture and set aside to become partly set.

Whip the icy cold evaporated milk in a chilled bowl until soft peaks form, adding the lemon juice as the milk is beaten. Whip in the jelly and cream cheese mixture. Drain the peaches well, chop enough to make 1 cup, and fold into the mixture. Pour into the prepared tin and chill several hours or overnight.

Unmould and decorate with the remaining peach halves which have been sliced and sliced strawberries if liked.

Syrup drained from the canned peaches may be used in place of the peach nectar.

Peach Cheesecake

193

PEACH CREAM-CHEESE PIE

2 level dessertspoons cornflour
½ cup sugar
½ cup peach purée
½ cup water
1 tablespoon lemon juice
4-ounce packet of cream cheese
¼ cup icing sugar
1 baked pie-shell of biscuit or
    short pastry
1 small can of sliced peaches
whipped cream for decoration

Combine the cornflour and sugar and blend in the peach purée, water and lemon juice. Place in a saucepan and stir over medium heat until the mixture boils and thickens. Cook for 1 minute, then remove from the heat and allow to cool.

Blend the cream cheese well with the icing sugar and spread evenly over the bottom of the baked and cooled pastry shell. Chill until set.

Drain the peaches well and arrange the slices in the pie-shell on top of the cream cheese mixture. Pour over the cooled peach purée mixture. Chill until serving time.

Decorate with whipped and sweetened cream.

PEACH MARSHMALLOW CREAM

3 level teaspoons gelatine
½ cup boiling water
1 large can of chilled
    unsweetened evaporated milk
¾ cup castor sugar
1 teaspoon vanilla essence or ½
    teaspoon almond essence
1 small can of sliced peaches
½ pint cream whipped with 1
    dessertspoon sugar
pulp of 1 or 2 passionfruit

Dissolve the gelatine in the boiling water and place it in a bowl with the well-chilled milk and the sugar. Beat until thick, using an electric or a rotary beater. Flavour with the vanilla or almond essence. Pour into a greased 8-inch recess tin and chill until firm.

When ready to serve, unmould onto a plate and top with the drained peaches. Pipe the whipped and sweetened cream round the edge and fill the centre with the passionfruit pulp.

PEACH MELBA

½ pound fresh raspberries
¼ cup sugar
1 tablespoon water
4 peaches
a family-size brick or tray of
    vanilla ice cream
wafers

Place the washed raspberries in a saucepan with the sugar and water. Cook slowly until the raspberries are soft. Sieve them and put aside to become cold.

Place the whole fresh peaches in a bowl and pour over enough boiling water to cover. Leave for 2 or 3 minutes, then drain. Peel the peaches, cut into quarters, and remove the stones. (Some peaches are easily peeled without the boiling water.)

Place four quarters of peach in each of four serving dishes. Spoon ice cream into the centre, cover with some of the raspberry sauce, add a wafer to each dish and serve at once.

Canned peaches may be used instead of fresh, in which case they should be drained of their syrup.

194

1½ cups self-raising flour
½ cup plain flour
¼ teaspoon salt
4 ounces butter or margarine
1 tablespoon sugar
1 egg
½ cup milk or cream
butter for spreading
canned or freshly stewed peaches
    and whipped cream for top-
    ping

2 cups finely chopped fresh
    peaches
sugar
1⅓ cups sweetened condensed
    milk
1 cup cream, whipped
¼ cup slivered blanched almonds

2 cups milk
3 cups soft white breadcrumbs
2 eggs, separated
¼ cup sugar
a pinch of salt
grated rind and juice of 1 lemon
¼ teaspoon grated nutmeg
2 dessertspoons butter, melted
1 large can of peach halves or
    slices, drained
2 tablespoons strawberry jam
¼ cup sugar for meringue

1 sponge layer 8 inches in
    diameter
2 tablespoons apricot jam
about 4 tablespoons sherry or
    Madeira
about 4 tablespoons pear juice
1 large can of pear halves
1 pint cooled egg custard
½ pint whipped and sweetened
    cream
cherries and almonds for
    decorating

PEACH SHORTCAKES

Sift the flours with the salt, rub in the butter and add the sugar. Beat the egg and mix with the milk or cream, then stir in to the flour, making a light dough. Turn onto a floured board, knead lightly, and pat or roll into a dough ½ inch thick.

Cut into six rounds, using a 2½-inch cutter. Place the short-cake circles on a shallow greased tray and bake in a hot oven, 425°F., for 12 minutes. Split the shortcakes, spread some butter on the bottom layer, join them together and serve topped with drained peaches and whipped cream.

PEACH-TREE ICE CREAM

Stew the peaches with a little sugar. Drain, reserving the syrup. Add enough water to the syrup to make up to ¾ cup. Combine the peaches and juice with the sweetened condensed milk and pour into refrigerator trays. Freeze until lightly set.

Turn into a chilled bowl and beat until fluffy. Fold in the whipped cream and slivered almonds and freeze.

PEACHES PRINCESSE

Combine the milk and the breadcrumbs. Beat the egg yolks with the sugar, salt, lemon rind, lemon juice and nutmeg and stir into the milk mixture. Add the melted butter.

Turn into a well-greased 9-inch ovenproof dish about 2 inches deep, and set it in a dish containing about an inch of water. Bake in a moderate oven, 350°F., for 45 minutes or until the pudding has set. Remove from the oven and spread the top with the strawberry jam.

Beat the egg whites until stiff, then gradually beat in the ¼ cup sugar. Place the drained peach halves over the pudding and swirl the meringue on top. Return the pudding to a slow oven, 300°F., for a further 15 minutes to lightly brown and set the meringue. Serve warm.

PEAR TRIFLE

Split the sponge layer through the centre and spread with the apricot jam. Rejoin the layers and cut into eight wedges. Place these in a shallow serving dish and sprinkle with the sherry and pear juice. Cover and allow to stand for about 30 minutes.

Pour over the cooled custard. Arrange the pears, rounded side up, on top of the custard. Decorate with the whipped and sweetened cream, the glacé cherries and the blanched almonds. Chill well before serving.

195

PEAR VELVET TORTE

For the torte

4 egg whites
½ teaspoon salt
1½ cups sugar
½ teaspoon cinnamon
1 teaspoon vinegar

For the filling

4 ounces dark chocolate
4 egg yolks
¼ cup water
1 cup cream
¼ cup sugar
¼ teaspoon cinnamon
1 medium-sized can of pear
   halves

Cover a baking tray with a sheet of foil, draw an 8-inch circle on it and grease well. Beat the egg whites until stiff, adding the salt, then gradually add half the sugar, beating until the meringue is thick and glossy. Mix the cinnamon with the remaining sugar and fold into the meringue before adding the vinegar.

Spread this meringue within the circle drawn on the foil, first spreading it about ½ inch thick on the bottom then building up the sides about 3 inches high. Using the back of a teaspoon swirl a pretty trim round the meringue shape. Bake at 300°F. for about 1¼ hours.

Allow to cool, then lift onto a serving dish, removing the foil.

Now make the filling. Melt 3 ounces of the chocolate over hot water, then add the beaten egg yolks and the water. Return to the heat just long enough to blend the two mixtures together. Chill until thick.

Place the cream, sugar and cinnamon in a bowl and whip until thick, then spread half in the bottom of the cooled meringue shell. Fold the remainder into the chilled chocolate custard and spread this over the cream layer. Chill for several hours.

Just before serving, arrange the well-drained pear halves on top and sprinkle with the grated or shaved left-over ounce of chocolate.

PINEAPPLE BOATS

1 large pineapple
2 bananas, peeled and sliced
2 oranges, peeled and sliced
1 cup strawberries
sugar and lemon juice
ice cream or whipped cream for
   serving

Cut the pineapple in halves lengthwise, leaving the green top attached to each half. Using a sharp knife, cut out the flesh. Discard the core and cut the flesh into pieces. Combine with the banana slices, orange slices and sliced strawberries. Add lemon juice and sugar to sweeten if liked.

Replace the fruit mixture in the pineapple shells and serve accompanied with either whipped cream or ice cream.

PINEAPPLE CHEESECAKE

For the crust

1¼ cups plain sweet biscuit
   crumbs
2 ounces butter, melted
1 dessertspoon sugar

For the filling

½ cup drained crushed pineapple
1 level tablespoon gelatine

Combine the biscuit crumbs with the melted butter and sugar for the crust. Place in a greased 7-inch flan tin, pressing well into the sides and bottom. Bake in a moderate oven, 350°F., for 10 minutes. Chill.

Soak the gelatine in 2 tablespoons of the drained pineapple syrup. Combine the egg yolks, sugar, lemon rind, salt and the remaining tablespoonful of pineapple syrup in the top of a double saucepan. Cook over hot, not boiling, water, stirring well until the mixture is smooth. Add the softened gelatine and stir until it has dissolved.

196

3 tablespoons pineapple syrup
2 eggs, separated
$\frac{1}{2}$ cup sugar
1 teaspoon grated lemon rind
a pinch of salt
$\frac{1}{2}$ pound cottage cheese
1 teaspoon vanilla essence
1 cup whipped cream
slices of drained pineapple and
   glacé cherries for decorating

Remove from the heat and pour into a large bowl. Add the drained pineapple, cottage cheese, vanilla, stiffly beaten egg whites and half the whipped cream. Stir until smooth.

Pour into the well-chilled pie-case and chill for about 5 hours. Turn out onto a serving plate and decorate with the remainder of the whipped cream and the drained pineapple slices and glacé cherries.

PINEAPPLE CREAM SQUARES

2 cups fine biscuit crumbs
3 tablespoons melted butter
6 ounces butter
2 cups soft icing sugar
2 eggs, separated
15-ounce can of crushed
   pineapple
1 teaspoon vanilla essence
$\frac{1}{2}$ cup chopped walnuts
whipped cream and cherries or
   strawberries for serving

Combine the biscuit crumbs with the melted butter and press into the bottom of two 6-inch sandwich tins.

Cream the 6 ounces of butter in a bowl and gradually beat in the sifted icing sugar. Add the egg yolks one at a time, beating well after each addition. Flavour with the vanilla and beat again. Fold in the stiffly beaten egg whites.

The mixture at this point may appear to curdle, but beating for a few more minutes at medium speed should make it smooth. Fold in the well-drained pineapple and the nuts and spread evenly in the prepared tins. Top with the remaining biscuit crumbs and chill for several hours or overnight.

Cut into squares for serving and garnish each square with a swirl of whipped cream and a cherry or a strawberry.

PINEAPPLE LEMON CHEESECAKE

For the crust

2 cups crushed Marie biscuit
   crumbs
$\frac{1}{4}$ cup sugar
1 level teaspoon powdered
   ginger
$\frac{1}{2}$ to $\frac{3}{4}$ cup melted butter

For the filling

1$\frac{1}{2}$ level tablespoons gelatine
$\frac{1}{2}$ cup pineapple juice (drained
   from crushed pineapple)
$\frac{1}{2}$ pound creamed cottage cheese

Combine the biscuit crumbs, sugar and ginger for the crust and add enough of the melted butter to bind the mixture together. Press into the bottom and sides of a well-greased 8-inch or 9-inch spring-form pan. Bake at 350°F. for 10 minutes, or chill (uncooked) for several hours.

Soften the gelatine in the pineapple juice, then dissolve it over hot water. Cool. Beat the cottage cheese with the sugar and add the cooled gelatine and the lemon rind and juice. Chill until partly set.

Beat the well-chilled evaporated milk in a large chilled bowl until soft peaks form, then beat in the gelatine mixture. Flavour with the vanilla and fold in the well-drained crushed pineapple. Pour into the cooled or chilled crumb crust and chill for several hours, or overnight.

197

1 cup sugar
1 level tablespoon grated lemon
    rind
¼ cup lemon juice
14½-ounce can of evaporated
    milk, well chilled
1 teaspoon vanilla essence
15-ounce can of crushed
    pineapple

For the glaze and topping

1 level dessertspoon cornflour
2 level tablespoons sugar
¼ cup lemon juice
½ cup pineapple juice
    (drained from the can)
pineapple slices and glacé
    cherries (optional)

4 cups sweetened cooked rice
4 tablespoons sugar
½ pint cream
1 or 2 drops red colouring
½ teaspoon almond essence
1 punnet strawberries
extra whipped cream for
    garnishing

To make the glaze, blend the cornflour and sugar with the lemon and pineapple juices. Cook, stirring over medium heat, until the mixture boils and thickens slightly. Spread this glaze over the cake and arrange the drained pineapple slices and cherries, if used, on top. Chill again before serving.

PINK PARFAITS

To sweeten the rice add 2 tablespoons of the sugar to the cooking water. Drain and chill.

Just before serving, whip the cream, add the food colouring, the almond essence and the remainder of the sugar and fold into the rice.

Wash and hull the strawberries. Reserve 6 whole strawberries for garnishing and crush the remainder. Fill parfait glasses with alternate layers of rice and crushed strawberries. Swirl whipped cream on top of each and add a whole strawberry for a garnish.

Pink Parfaits

QUICK FRUIT MINCE

½ cup sultanas
½ cup currants
¼ cup chopped peel
¼ teaspoon mixed spice
¼ teaspoon nutmeg
⅓ cup brown sugar
grated rind and juice of 1 lemon
2 cooking apples

Wash and pick over the sultanas and currants, then combine them with the peel, spices, sugar and lemon rind and juice.

Wash and dry the apples, then grate them—they need not be peeled. Add to the fruit mixture and stir until evenly mixed. Cover and let stand for about 30 minutes. This mixture is sufficient for a 7-inch tart plate or sandwich tin.

Make 6 ounces of your favourite pastry and use a little more than half of it to line the bottom and sides of the greased tin. Add the fruit mince, and roll the remainder of the pastry to cover the top (a little water brushed on the edges of the pastry will make it stick). Pinch the edges together, glaze the top with water and sprinkle with sugar. Bake at 375°F. for 10 minutes, then reduce the heat to 325°F. and cook for a further 20 to 30 minutes.

Serve cold with cream, custard or ice cream.

RICE ROYALE

1 cup uncooked rice
1¼ pints milk
pink colouring
1 small can of unsweetened
    evaporated milk, well chilled
¼ cup sugar
1 teaspoon vanilla essence
1 level dessertspoon gelatine
¼ cup cold water
15-ounce can of sliced pineapple
cherries and angelica or straw-
    berries for decorating

Place the rice and milk in a saucepan with a few drops of pink colouring. Cover and simmer gently, stirring occasionally until the rice is tender. Cool.

Put the well-chilled evaporated milk into a chilled bowl and add the sugar, vanilla and a few drops of pink colouring. Beat until thick.

Soak the gelatine in the cold water, then dissolve it over hot water. Stir into the rice, then fold in the whipped evaporated milk. Spoon into a well-greased mould and chill until set.

Unmould onto a serving platter and decorate with pineapple slices, and with cherries and angelica or strawberries.

RUM MACAROON TRIFLE

1 cup cream
3 egg yolks
3 dessertspoons sugar
1 dessertspoon flour
a pinch of salt
1 teaspoon vanilla essence
6 coconut macaroons
¼ cup rum
1 box strawberries
2 egg whites
2 dessertspoons sugar for
    meringues

Heat the cream in the top of a double saucepan until tiny bubbles appear round the edges. Beat the egg yolks slightly in a bowl and add the sugar, flour and salt, stirring until smooth. Slowly add to the cream in the double saucepan, stirring well. Cook, stirring constantly with a wooden spoon, over hot, not boiling water, until the custard coats the back of the spoon. Allow to cool, add the vanilla, then chill.

Crumble the macaroons and divide the crumbs evenly into four. Place one quantity in the bottom of each of four individual serving dishes and sprinkle each with about 1½ teaspoons of rum. Allow to stand for a few minutes, then add the washed, hulled and sliced strawberries.

Beat the egg whites in a warm dry bowl until stiff, then gradually add the 2 dessertspoons of sugar and beat until stiff. Fold half this meringue mixture into the cooled custard. Spoon ½ a cup of custard into each serving dish.

Rum Macaroon Trifle

Beat an extra tablespoon of sugar to the remaining meringue and pipe in small rosettes, or place in small spoonfuls, on a greased oven tray. Bake in a slow oven, 300°F., for 30 to 40 minutes. When they are cold use these tiny button meringues to decorate the top of each macaroon trifle.

SHERRY PUMPKIN PIE

2 eggs, separated
½ cup (firmly packed) brown sugar
½ teaspoon salt
1 level teaspoon cinnamon
½ level teaspoon ground cloves
½ level teaspoon ground ginger
½ level teaspoon ground nutmeg
1 cup mashed pumpkin
¾ cup milk
¼ cup sweet sherry
1 unbaked shell of short or biscuit pastry
whipped cream and walnuts for topping

Mix the egg yolks with the brown sugar, salt, cinnamon, cloves, ginger and nutmeg, then stir in the mashed pumpkin. Beat with a rotary beater until smooth.

Add the milk and sherry. In a separate bowl beat the egg whites until stiff and fold into the pumpkin mixture. Pour into the uncooked pastry case and bake in a hot oven (425°F.) for 10 minutes, then reduce the heat to moderate (350°F.) and cook for a further 20 minutes or until the filling has set.

Serve warm or cold with whipped cream and walnuts. If liked the cream may be flavoured with a little ground ginger.

SOUFFLÉ SURPRISE

1 layer of sponge cake
1½ tablespoons sweet sherry
1 quantity ice cream (recipe follows)
½ pound fresh raspberries or 2 cups well-drained canned peaches or apricots
3 egg whites
a pinch of salt
½ cup icing sugar

Line a shallow oblong dish with the sponge cake and sprinkle with sherry. Place the ice cream in the centre of the dish and surround it with the raspberries or the drained canned fruit. Place in the freezer while you make the meringue.

Beat the egg whites with a pinch of salt until they stand in stiff peaks. Gradually beat in the sifted icing sugar and continue beating until thick and glossy. Completely cover the ice cream and the fruit with this meringue.

Place in a hot oven for 3 to 5 minutes, or until the meringue is set on the outside and lightly tinged with brown. Serve immediately.

200

1 pint fresh milk
4 slightly rounded tablespoons
 powdered milk
½ cup condensed milk
½ teaspoon gelatine
1 tablespoon hot water
1 teaspoon vanilla essence

Warm the fresh milk and add the powdered milk. Beat well together, add the condensed milk and beat again. Dissolve the gelatine in the hot water and add gradually to the mixture, beating well. Freeze for about 1 hour, or until the ice cream begins to set round the edges. Turn out into a chilled bowl and beat the mixture again until thick, flavouring with the vanilla.

Place in the refrigerator trays or in a loaf tin and freeze until firm.

SPANISH CREAM

1 level tablespoon gelatine
2 tablespoons cold water
2 cups milk
2 eggs, separated
2 tablespoons sugar
1 teaspoon vanilla essence

Soften the gelatine in the cold water and dissolve it over boiling water. Heat the milk and when almost boiling pour onto the beaten egg yolks and sugar. Stir until smooth, then return the mixture to the saucepan and cook, stirring well with a wooden spoon, until the custard coats the back of the spoon. Cool slightly, then add the dissolved gelatine and the vanilla.

Beat the egg whites in a clean dry bowl until stiff, then fold them into the custard. Turn into a wetted mould and chill until set.

Unmould and serve with fresh or stewed fruit.

SPUMONI

½ cup sugar
3 ounces water
3 egg yolks
½ pint cream
3 teaspoons rum or liqueur
1 teaspoon vanilla essence
½ cup toasted and chopped
 blanched almonds

Place the sugar and water in a saucepan and stir over low heat until the sugar has dissolved. Remove the spoon and boil the syrup until the temperature reaches 220°F. on a candy thermometer. Remove from the heat.

Beat the egg yolks in the top of a double saucepan until thick, then gradually beat in the hot syrup. Place over hot water and continue beating until stiff peaks form—about 7 minutes. Remove from the heat, place over cold water and beat until cold.

Whip the cream until thick, then fold in the rum and the vanilla. Fold into the egg yolk mixture with the toasted almonds. Turn into a wetted mould, cover and freeze until firm or overnight.

Unmould and serve with strawberries if liked.

STRAWBERRIES ROMANOFF

Place equal quantities of washed and hulled whole strawberries and chunky pieces of fresh or canned pineapple in individual serving dishes.

Sprinkle with sugar and add rum or brandy to flavour.

Chill for at least 30 minutes, then serve with sweetened and lightly whipped cream.

201

Spanish Cream

For the Swiss roll
3 eggs, separated
½ cup sugar
¼ teaspoon vanilla essence
1 cup plain flour
1 level teaspoon cream of tartar
a pinch of salt
½ level teaspoon bicarbonate of
   soda
1½ tablespoons hot water

For the filling
strawberry jam

For the custard
1 tablespoon cornflour
1 tablespoon sugar
1 pint milk
2 eggs, separated
1 teaspoon vanilla essence

For the topping
½ pint whipped cream
sugar and vanilla essence for the
   cream
sherry
½ box strawberries
slivered almonds

STRAWBERRY CHANTILLY

Line the bottom of a greased Swiss roll tin with greased paper. Grease the sides well. Add a pinch of salt to the egg whites and beat until stiff. Gradually add the sugar and continue beating until the mixture stands in stiff, glossy peaks. Beat in the egg yolks one at a time. Add the vanilla.

Sift the flour with the cream of tartar and salt and add to the mixture, then stir in the soda which has been dissolved in the hot water.

Spread evenly in the prepared tin and bake in a moderate oven, 375°F., for 12 to 15 minutes.

Turn the sponge out onto a damp cloth and peel off the paper. Cut off the side crusts and roll up. Lift onto a paper dusted with sifted icing sugar, unroll and spread with strawberry jam. Re-roll and allow to cool.

Meanwhile make a boiled custard. Combine the cornflour and sugar and mix to a smooth paste with some of the cold milk. Add the beaten egg yolks. Place the remainder of the milk on to heat and, when almost boiling, pour onto the blended mixture and stir until smooth. Return the custard to the saucepan and cook, stirring until it boils and thickens. Flavour with the vanilla. Beat the egg whites until stiff, then pour the hot custard into them, stirring lightly but thoroughly.

Add sugar and vanilla to the cream and whip until thick. Sprinkle the Swiss roll with sherry and spread the cream over, completely covering the roll. Top with fresh strawberries and slivered almonds. When the custard has cooled completely, pour it round the roll in the dish, then chill until serving time.

STRAWBERRY SHORTCAKE

6 ounces butter
½ cup castor sugar
½ teaspoon vanilla essence
2 eggs
2 cups plain flour
2 rounded teaspoons baking powder
a good pinch of salt
½ cup cornflour
1 box strawberries
½ pint cream
1 tablespoon icing sugar and a little vanilla for the cream
1 tablespoon melted butter

Cream the butter and sugar and flavour with the vanilla. Stir in the beaten eggs. Sift the flour with the baking powder, salt and cornflour and stir into the mixture, making a firm dough. Spread evenly in two well-greased 7-inch sandwich tins. Bake in a moderate oven, 350°F., for about 40 minutes.

While the shortcakes are baking, wash and hull the strawberries and sweeten with sugar. Add the icing sugar and a little vanilla to the cream and whip until thick.

As soon as the shortcakes come from the oven, pour the melted butter over the surface of one. Cool, then join the two layers together, using half the cream and the strawberries. Decorate the top with the remainder of the cream and, if liked, a few whole berries.

For a softer shortcake, make half the mixture, split while hot and pour the butter over, then join the layer together when cold with the strawberries and cream as above.

STRAWBERRY SATIN TORTE

For the torte mixture

3 ounces butter
1 cup sugar
2 eggs
1½ cups plain flour
1½ level teaspoons baking powder
¼ level teaspoon salt
½ cup milk
¼ teaspoon grated lemon rind

For the topping

⅔ cup sugar
juice of 1 lemon

For the topping and glaze

3 cups strawberries
1 level tablespoon cornflour
¼ cup cold water
½ cup strawberry jam
1 tablespoon lemon juice

Beat the butter and sugar for the torte mixture to a cream and add beaten eggs, beating until light. Sift the flour with the baking powder and salt and add to the creamed mixture alternately with the milk and grated lemon rind.

Pour the batter into a well-greased fluted flan tin and bake in a moderate oven, 350°F., for 25 minutes.

While the torte is baking mix the sugar and lemon juice for the topping. Carefully spoon it over the torte after it has been cooking for 25 minutes. Bake for a further 5 minutes. Remove from the tin and allow to cool.

Wash and hull the strawberries and cut them in halves. Arrange on top of the torte. Blend the cornflour with the cold water, add the strawberry jam and the lemon juice and stir over low heat until the mixture boils and thickens. Cool slightly and spoon over the berries. (If liked, a strawberry jelly could be used for the glaze in place of the jam and cornflour mixture.) Chill well and serve with whipped cream.

SUPER DELUXE TRIFLE

1½ cups unsweetened evaporated milk
½ cup water
4 egg yolks
½ cup brown sugar

Combine the evaporated milk and the water in the top of a double saucepan and heat over hot, not boiling water. Beat the egg yolks in a bowl and add the brown sugar, flour and salt. Stir in the hot milk, blending well, then return the mixture to the top of the double saucepan.

1 level tablespoon plain flour
a pinch of salt
¼ teaspoon vanilla essence
a few drops of almond essence
1 dozen sponge fingers
¼ cup sherry
⅓ cup seedless raspberry jam
¼ cup slivered almonds
whipped cream and slivered
    almonds for topping

Cook, stirring well, until the custard thickens. Remove from the heat, add the vanilla and almond essences and chill well.

Arrange the sponge fingers (or thin slices of sponge cake) on the bottom and sides of a one-quart mould and sprinkle with the sherry. Spread with the jam and sprinkle with the slivered almonds. Pour the chilled custard into the centre and chill for at least 12 hours.

Before serving, top with whipped cream and sprinkle with a few slivered almonds.

TRIFLE

¼ cup sugar
1 level teaspoon cornflour
2 eggs
2 cups milk
½ teaspoon vanilla essence
1 Swiss roll
¼ cup sweet sherry
½ cup strawberry jam
2 cups whipped cream
fresh strawberries or other fruit
    for decorating

Mix the sugar with the cornflour and add the slightly beaten eggs, blending with a little of the cold milk. Heat the remainder of the milk and, when almost boiling, pour onto the blended mixture. Stir until smooth. Place in the top of a double saucepan over simmering water and cook, stirring well with a wooden spoon until the custard coats the back of the spoon. Remove from the heat, cool and add the vanilla.

Arrange a layer of Swiss roll slices in the bottom of a serving dish, sprinkle with sherry and top with jam and half the whipped cream.

Add a second layer of cake. Pour the boiled custard over and chill. Decorate with the remaining whipped cream and the strawberries or other fruit.

TROPICAL CHEESECAKE

For the crust

1¼ cups coconut biscuit crumbs
1 teaspoon grated lemon rind
¼ cup soft butter

For the filling and topping

1 level dessertspoon gelatine
¼ cup cold water
¼ cup boiling water
½ pound cream cheese
1 cup sugar
1½ teaspoons grated lemon rind
1 teaspoon vanilla essence
½ cup lemon juice
14–ounce can of chilled
    evaporated milk
4 passionfruit
whipped and sweetened cream

Line the sides of an 8-inch spring-form pan with a double thickness of foil. Lightly grease the inside of the foil. Combine the ingredients for the crumb crust and press two-thirds of it into the base of the pan. Chill well.

Soften the gelatine in the cold water for about 5 minutes, then add the boiling water and stir until the gelatine has dissolved. Cool.

Beat together the cream cheese, sugar, grated lemon rind and vanilla until creamy, then blend in the gelatine and the lemon juice. Chill until the mixture is the consistency of unbeaten egg white, then place in a large bowl and whip at low speed while gradually adding the well-chilled evaporated milk. Now beat at high speed until the mixture doubles in bulk. Fold in the passionfruit pulp. Pour into the prepared spring-form pan and sprinkle the remainder of the crumbs on top. Chill for 5 or 6 hours.

To serve, unmould onto a serving plate and decorate with whipped and sweetened cream and, if liked, more passionfruit.

Hot Desserts

APPLE AND APRICOT PIE

¾ pound dried apricots
1½ pounds cooking apples
¾ cup sugar
juice and grated rind of 1 lemon
8 ounces short or biscuit pastry
castor sugar for topping

Place the apricots in a bowl, cover with cold water and leave to soak overnight. Drain well. Peel, core and slice the apples thinly and place in a saucepan with the sugar and lemon juice. Cover and simmer until tender. Add the lemon rind. Cool, then mix with the drained apricots.

Take a little more than half the pastry and roll to line an 8-inch tart plate. Fill with the apple and apricot mixture, piling it high in the centre. Roll the remainder of the pastry to cover the top. Glaze with water or egg white and sprinkle with sugar.

Bake in a hot oven, 400°F., for 10 minutes, reduce the heat to 325°F. and cook for a further 20 or 30 minutes.

Serve with custard or cream or, if liked, make a sauce with the liquid drained from the apricots by thickening with blended arrowroot or cornflour, sweetening with sugar and flavouring with a little lemon juice.

APPLE AND RICE MERINGUE

4 level tablespoons sugar
¼ pint water
4 cloves
4 apples
1 pint water
a pinch of salt
2 ounces rice
1 egg yolk
2 level tablespoons sugar
¼ pint milk

For the topping

1 egg white
a pinch of salt
1 level tablespoon sugar
a little pink sugar if liked

Bring the sugar, ¼ pint water and the cloves to the boil in a saucepan. Add peeled and sliced apples and cook with the lid on until tender. Turn into an ovenproof dish.

Put the pint of water into a saucepan with the salt and bring to the boil. Sprinkle in the rice and boil for about 15 minutes or until it is tender. Strain through a colander, then return the rice to the saucepan and add the egg yolk, sugar and milk. Cook for 3 minutes. Pour over the apples in the dish.

To make the meringue topping beat the egg white with a pinch of salt until peaks form. Gradually add the sugar and continue beating until stiff. Heap this meringue on the rice. Place in a slow oven and cook until the meringue is set and lightly tipped with brown. Sprinkle pink sugar over the top and serve warm or cold.

APPLE CHARLOTTE

4 to 6 slices day-old bread
¼ cup butter or margarine
½ teaspoon grated lemon rind
2½ cups stewed apple

Cut the crusts from the bread, then cut the slices into fingers. Brush with the melted butter.

Use a little more than half the bread strips to line the bottom and sides of a pie-dish, placing the bread buttered side down.

1 teaspoon sugar and ½ teaspoon
    cinnamon for topping

1 level tablespoon plain flour
½ level teaspoon cinnamon
¼ level teaspoon nutmeg
2½ cups cold stewed apple
1 dessertspoon lemon juice
1 unbaked pastry case of short
    or biscuit pastry
2 dessertspoons butter

For the topping
1 beaten egg
1¼ cups flaked coconut
¼ cup sugar
2 tablespoons milk

4 ounces biscuit or sweet
    shortcrust pastry
1 cup stewed and drained apple
2 eggs
1 dessertspoon sugar
½ pint milk
½ teaspoon vanilla essence
nutmeg

1 cup plain flour
½ level teaspoon salt
¼ level teaspoon bicarbonate of
    soda
½ level teaspoon cinnamon
¼ level teaspoon nutmeg
4 ounces butter
⅔ cup sugar
1 egg
1 tablespoon milk
1½ cups coarsely chopped peeled
    apples
½ cup chopped dates
½ cup raisins

Add the grated lemon rind to the stewed apple and turn
into the dish. Top with the remaining bread strips, this time
with the buttered side up.

Bake in a moderate to hot oven, 400°F., for 30 or 40 minutes
or until the bread on top is crisp and lightly browned.

While the charlotte is still hot, sprinkle the sugar and
cinnamon over the top. Serve hot with either whipped cream
or ice cream.

APPLE COCONUT TART

Combine the plain flour with the spices and mix with the cold
stewed apple and lemon juice. Spread in the uncooked pastry
case and dot with pieces of butter.

Bake in a moderate oven, 350°F., for 20 minutes. Combine
the ingredients for the topping and spread over the apples,
then bake for a further 20 minutes or until the topping is
brown. Serve with custard or cream.

APPLE CUSTARD TART

Roll the pastry to line a well-greased 7-inch sandwich tin.
Spread the cooled apple on the bottom of the pastry case.

Beat the eggs with the sugar, add the milk and flavour with
the vanilla. Pour carefully over the apples. Sprinkle the top
with a little nutmeg.

Bake in a hot oven, 425°F., for about 10 minutes, then reduce
the heat to 325°F. and continue cooking until the custard has
set and is a light brown on top. Serve warm or cold with ice
cream.

APPLE DATE TORTE

Grease the bottom and sides of an 8-inch sandwich tin. Sift the
flour with the salt, soda, cinnamon and nutmeg.

Place the softened butter in a bowl and gradually beat in the
sugar. Continue beating until light and fluffy, then blend in the
beaten egg and the milk. Add the dry ingredients a little at a
time, mixing thoroughly. Stir in the apples, dates and raisins.

Spoon the mixture into the prepared tin and bake in a
moderate oven, 350°F., for about 55 minutes. Serve warm with
ice cream, whipped cream or brandy sauce.

APPLE FRITTERS

1 cup self-raising flour
a good pinch of salt
1 egg, separated
about ¾ cup tepid milk
1 dessertspoon melted butter
peeled and cored apples cut into
    rings

Sift the flour and salt into a bowl, make a well in the centre and add the egg yolk which has been beaten with the milk.

Using a wooden spoon, gradually beat the flour into the mixture and continue beating until the batter is smooth. Add the melted butter. Beat the egg white stiffly and fold it in.

Dip the apple rings one at a time in the batter, drain briefly, then drop into deep hot fat in a saucepan. When brown on one side, turn and cook on the other.

Drain the fritters on paper and serve them with sugar and lemon or with whipped cream.

Pineapple slices or bananas may be used in place of the apple.

APPLE PANCAKES

2 cups sifted self-raising flour
1 teaspoon salt
1 tablespoon sugar
2 eggs, separated
2 cups milk
1 tablespoon melted butter
1 cup finely chopped apple
butter, sugar and lemon juice for
    serving

Sift the flour and salt into a bowl and add the sugar. Beat the egg yolks, mix with the milk and stir into the flour, making a smooth batter. Add the melted butter, then the chopped apple. Fold in the stiffly beaten egg whites and allow the batter to stand for a few minutes.

Grease a hot griddle or a heavy-base frying pan and add the batter by tablespoonfuls. When the top of each pancake is bubbly, and some bubbles have broken, turn and cook on the other side.

Just before serving dot each with butter and sprinkle with sugar and lemon juice.

APPLE SHORTCAKE 1

3 ounces butter or margarine
3 ounces sugar
¼ teaspoon vanilla essence
2 eggs
6 ounces self-raising flour
a pinch of salt
2 tablespoons milk
1 cup stewed apple
cinnamon

Beat the butter and sugar to a soft cream. Add the vanilla, then the well-beaten eggs.

Sift the flour with the salt and add to the mixture alternately with the milk. Spread half in a well-greased 7-inch sandwich tin.

Flavour the apple with cinnamon and place on the uncooked cake mixture. Cover with the remainder of the cake mixture. Bake in a moderate oven, 350°F., for 30 to 35 minutes. Serve with custard, cream or ice cream.

APPLE SHORTCAKE 2

2 cups of plain flour and 2 level
    teaspoons baking powder (or
    1 cup plain flour and 1 cup
    self-raising flour)
a good pinch of salt
4 ounces butter or margarine

Sift the flour with the baking powder and salt (or the two flours and salt). Rub in the butter and add the sugar. Beat the egg, add to it about 1 tablespoon of milk and stir into the dry ingredients, making a medium dough.

Turn onto a floured board and knead only until smooth on the outside. Divide in two, making one piece slightly larger

207

1 rounded tablespoon sugar
1 egg
a little milk or water

For the filling

4 good-sized cooking apples
2 rounded tablespoons sugar
1 teaspoon butter
a little nutmeg

For the glaze

egg or a little milk

For the filling

4 medium-sized Granny Smith
    apples
4 tablespoons sugar
4 tablespoons water
a little lemon rind or 2 or 3
    cloves

For the pastry

3 ounces butter
2 rounded tablespoons sugar
1 egg
½ teaspoon vanilla essence·
1½ cups plain flour
½ level teaspoon baking powder
a pinch of salt

For the pastry

3 ounces butter
3 slightly rounded tablespoons
    sugar
1 egg
½ teaspoon vanilla essence
1½ cups plain flour
½ level teaspoon baking powder
a pinch of salt

than the other. Roll the larger piece to line a well-greased 7-inch sandwich tin.

Peel, core and thinly slice the apples and place in the uncooked pastry case. Sprinkle with the 2 tablespoons sugar, dot with butter and sprinkle with nutmeg. Cover with the remainder of the pastry rolled to fit the top. Glaze with egg or milk and bake in a moderate oven, 350°F., for about 40 minutes.

If liked the apples may be stewed with a little water, then allowed to cool before being placed in the uncooked pie-case.

APPLE SLICE

Peel and slice the apples. Place them in a saucepan with the sugar, water and lemon rind or cloves, cover and simmer until tender. Allow to become quite cold. Remove the rind or cloves.

Cream the butter and sugar for the pastry and add the egg and vanilla. Sift the flour with the baking powder and salt and add to the mixture, making a firm dough. (The consistency will depend on the softness of the butter and the size of the egg. A little more flour may have to be kneaded into the pastry to make it easy to handle.)

Turn onto a floured board and knead only until smooth on the outside. Divide in two. Use a little more than half to roll and line the bottom and sides of a well-greased 7-inch sandwich tin. Add the cooled apple, then cover with the remainder of the pastry rolled to fit the top. Pinch a frill round the edges and make three or four vents in the top to prevent the filling boiling out of the pie.

Bake in a moderate oven, 350°F., for 50 to 60 minutes. Serve warm or cold with cream or ice cream.

APRICOT SLICE

Soak the dried apricots in the 2 cups of cold water overnight.

Next day, cream the butter and sugar for the pastry and add the egg and vanilla. Sift the flour with the baking powder and salt and stir into the mixture, making a rather firm dough. Turn onto a floured board and knead only until smooth on the outside. Chill the pastry while you make the filling.

Cook the apricots until tender, using the water in which they were soaked and sweetening them with the sugar. Stir the blended cornflour into the apricots, then cook for 2 or 3 minutes. Turn into a bowl and allow to become quite cold.

For the filling

½ pound dried apricots
2 cups cold water
1 rounded tablespoon sugar
1 dessertspoon cornflour blended
  with a little cold water

For the glaze

water and sugar

For the syrup

1 cup sugar
1 cup water
a pinch of nutmeg
a pinch of cinnamon
red colouring
2 ounces butter or margarine

For the pastry

2 cups plain flour
1 level teaspoon baking powder
½ level teaspoon salt
5 ounces butter or margarine
⅓ cup cold water
a squeeze of lemon juice

For the filling

6 whole apples
sugar, spices and butter

6 bananas
1 orange, peeled and cut into
  chunks
1 tablespoon orange juice
1 tablespoon lemon juice
⅓ cup sugar
a dash each of cinnamon and
  nutmeg

Divide the pastry in two and use a little more than half to line a greased 7-inch sandwich tin. Spread with the cooled apricot mixture, then cover with the remainder of the pastry, rolled to fit the top. Pinch the edges together, glaze the top with water and sprinkle with sugar.

Bake in a moderate oven, 350°F., for about 50 minutes or until the top is golden and the pastry cooked through. Serve with ice cream, cream or custard.

BAKED APPLE DUMPLINGS

Place the sugar, water, spices and red colouring in a saucepan and stir until boiling. Add the butter.

Sift the flour, baking powder and salt for the pastry and rub in the butter. Mix to a firm dough with the water and lemon juice. Turn onto a lightly floured board and knead only until smooth on the outside. Roll to a little less than ¼ inch thick and, using a large knife or a pastry wheel, cut into 6-inch squares.

Place a peeled and cored apple on each square of pastry, sprinkle it with sugar and spices and dot with butter. Moisten the edges of the pastry with a little water, then bring the four corners together at the top of the apple and pinch together.

Place the dumplings 1 inch apart in a greased dish, pour over the syrup and sprinkle each apple with a little more sugar. Bake in a hot oven, 425°F., for 10 minutes, then reduce the heat to 325°F. and bake for a further 20 minutes or until the apples are soft. Serve plain or with cream or ice cream.

BAKED BANANAS

Preheat the oven to 325°F. Peel the bananas (it is best if they are slightly underripe, their skins green tipped with yellow). Arrange the whole bananas in a shallow baking dish and add the remaining ingredients.

Bake for 25 to 30 minutes or until the bananas are golden and tender. Serve hot.

209

Baked Fruit Roll

BAKED FRUIT ROLL

For the pastry

2 ounces butter
¼ cup sugar
1 egg
¼ teaspoon vanilla essence
1½ cups self-raising flour

For the filling

1 apple, grated
½ cup sultanas
½ cup raisins
½ cup chopped dates
2 dessertspoons mixed peel,
    chopped
1 dessertspoon golden syrup
1 teaspoon cinnamon

For the glaze

about 1 tablespoon apricot jam
    thinned with a little water

Cream the butter and sugar for the pastry, add the slightly beaten egg and flavour with the vanilla. Stir in the sifted flour, making a light dough. Chill for about 1 hour if time permits, then roll to a rectangular shape about ¼ inch thick.

Combine the fruits, golden syrup and cinnamon for the filling. Place in a roll along the centre of the pastry and wrap the pastry rounded the filling, sealing the edges with water. Glaze the top with the thinned apricot jam.

Bake in a hot oven, 400°F., for 10 minutes, then reduce the heat to moderate, 350°F., and continue baking for about 15 minutes or until the roll is nicely browned and the pastry cooked. Serve warm with cream or ice cream.

Biscuit crust or a sweet shortcrust may replace the cake-like pastry in this recipe if preferred.

BANANA FRITTERS

3 firm bananas
2 dessertspoons orange juice
1 dessertspoon castor sugar

Peel the bananas, cut in halves crosswise, then cut again lengthwise. Let them stand in the combined orange juice and sugar while you make the batter.

1 cup self-raising flour
a pinch of salt
1 egg, separated
$\frac{1}{2}$ cup milk
2 dessertspoons butter, melted
$\frac{1}{4}$ teaspoon vanilla essence
1 teaspoon grated lemon rind
oil for frying
orange lemon sauce and whipped
    cream for serving

$\frac{1}{2}$ cup sugar
1 level tablespoon cornflour
a pinch of salt
$\frac{3}{4}$ cup water
2 dessertspoons butter
$\frac{1}{4}$ cup orange juice
1 dessertspoon lemon juice

1$\frac{1}{2}$ tablespoons cornflour
$\frac{2}{3}$ cup sugar
a pinch of salt
2 cups fresh raspberries
1 teaspoon lemon juice
1 dessertspoon butter
4 cups pitted cherries
6 ounces short or biscuit pastry
egg white for glazing
sugar for topping

2 cups blackberries
sugar to taste
2 ounces butter
$\frac{1}{4}$ cup sugar
1 egg
$\frac{1}{2}$ teaspoon vanilla essence
1 cup self-raising flour
a pinch of salt
3 tablespoons milk

Sift the flour and salt into a bowl. Beat the egg yolk with the milk, melted butter, vanilla and grated lemon rind, and add to the dry ingredients, stirring with a wooden spoon until smooth. Add the stiffly beaten egg white.

Drain the banana pieces and dip them into the batter. Deep-fry in hot oil or fat until a golden brown. Drain and serve with orange lemon sauce and whipped cream.

ORANGE LEMON SAUCE

Place the sugar, cornflour and salt in a bowl and blend in the water. Turn into a saucepan and cook, stirring constantly, over medium heat until the mixture boils and thickens. Simmer for 3 minutes. Add the butter, orange juice and lemon juice, mixing well. Serve warm with the banana fritters.

BERRY CHERRY PIE

Place the cornflour, sugar, salt, raspberries and lemon juice in a saucepan and stir gently over medium heat until the mixture comes to the boil. Reduce the heat and simmer for another 5 minutes, stirring occasionally.

Add the butter and stir until melted, then add the cherries. Turn into a 1$\frac{1}{2}$-quart pie-dish.

Roll the pastry to fit the top of the pie-dish. Place it carefully over the fruit. Flute the edges, then make a few slits in the top to allow the steam to escape and to prevent the filling from boiling out of the pie. Brush the top with egg white and sprinkle with sugar. Bake in a moderate oven, 350°F., for 15 or 20 minutes.

BLACKBERRY SPONGE PUDDING

Place the blackberries in a saucepan with enough sugar to sweeten them. Bring to the boil.

Cream the butter and sugar and add well-beaten egg and the vanilla. Sift the flour with the salt and add to the mixture alternately with the milk.

Have the blackberries at boiling point. Pour them into a pie-dish and immediately top them with the cake mixture. Bake in a moderate oven, 350°F., for about 30 minutes. Serve with custard, cream or ice cream.

Any type of fruit, either freshly cooked or canned, may be used for this dessert, but the fruit must be boiling when the cake mixture is placed on top, otherwise the underneath of the cake mixture will not cook.

211

2 cups plain flour

a pinch of salt

1 level teaspoon mixed spice

1 rounded teaspoon baking
    powder

4 ounces suet

3 slightly rounded tablespoons
    sugar

1½ cups sultanas

¼ cup diced mixed peel

1 egg

6 tablespoons milk

⅓ cup finely chopped walnuts

½ pound short or biscuit pastry

2 cups fruit mince

½ cup orange marmalade

1 cup peeled and diced apple

1 tablespoon brandy

1 tablespoon plain flour

For the pastry

1 cup plain flour

½ teaspoon salt

⅓ cup butter

⅓ cup ground almonds

2 dessertspoons iced water

BOILED SULTANA PUDDING

Sift the flour with the salt, spice and baking powder. Skin the suet, then flake and finely chop it. Rub it into the flour mixture and add the sugar, sultanas and mixed peel.

Beat the egg and mix with the milk. Pour into the dry ingredients, making a medium dough.

Have ready a pudding cloth which has been wrung out of boiling water and rubbed with flour where it will come in contact with the pudding mixture. Gather up the cloth round the pudding and, leaving very little space for the mixture to swell, tie securely with string.

Plunge the pudding into a large saucepan of rapidly boiling water, cover, and boil for 1½ to 2 hours. The water must not be allowed to go off the boil during the cooking period. If it is necessary to add more water, see that it is boiling.

Lift the pudding into a colander to drain well, then remove the string and open up the cloth. Turn the pudding onto a hot plate and serve immediately.

Raisins or chopped dates may replace the sultanas and peel, and if you have no baking powder you may use half plain and half self-raising flour.

BRANDIED MINCE PIE

Blend the walnuts into the prepared pastry. Roll a little more than half the dough to line an 8-inch tart plate.

Mix the fruit mince with the marmalade, apple and brandy. Sprinkle the flour over the mixture and stir, blending it in. Spoon into the uncooked pie-shell.

Roll out the remainder of the pastry to a piece large enough to cover the top of the tart plate, or cut the rolled pastry into shapes, using small decorative biscuit cutters.

If using the large piece of pastry, place it on the top of the filled pie-shell, pinch the edges together and slit the top here and there to allow the steam to escape. If using the biscuit shapes, arrange them in an attractive design on the filled pie-shell. Brush the top of the pastry or the cut-outs with beaten egg.

Bake in a moderate oven, 350°F., for 35 to 40 minutes or until the pastry is golden and the filling is quietly bubbling. Serve warm with cream or ice cream or fluffy hard sauce.

BRANDIED PUMPKIN PIE

Sift the flour and salt into a bowl and rub in the butter. Add the ground almonds. Sprinkle in the iced water and blend lightly with a fork. Turn onto a board, knead lightly, then roll between two sheets of waxed or greaseproof paper into an 11-inch circle. Chill for 15 minutes, then use to line a tart plate. Trim the edges.

For the filling

1 cup mashed cooked pumpkin
1 cup canned unsweetened milk
1 cup (firmly packed) light
    brown sugar
3 eggs
¼ cup brandy
1 teaspoon cinnamon
½ teaspoon ginger
½ teaspoon nutmeg
¼ teaspoon mace
¾ teaspoon salt

2 cups plain flour
a pinch of salt
1 teaspoon nutmeg or cinnamon
3 ounces butter or margarine
2 dessertspoons sugar
2 dessertspoons golden syrup
1 cup milk
1 level teaspoon bicarbonate of
    soda
golden syrup for serving

½ pound sweet shortcrust pastry
3 medium-sized apples
¼ cup chopped dates
lemon juice
¼ level teaspoon mixed spice
1 egg

For the caramel

2 level tablespoons white sugar
¾ cup water
⅓ cup brown sugar
2 dessertspoons butter

Place the pumpkin, milk and sugar in a large bowl, blend well, then add beaten eggs, brandy, spices and salt. Pour into the prepared pie-shell. Bake for 10 minutes at 450°F., then reduce the heat to 325°F. and cook until the filling has set. Serve warm with whipped cream.

BUDGET PUDDING

Sift the flour with the salt and spice. Rub in the butter until the mixture resembles breadcrumbs, then add the sugar and the golden syrup.

Heat the milk, stir in the soda, and pour into the dry ingredients. Mix well (the consistency will be rather soft).

Place in a well-greased pudding basin lined on the bottom with a round of greased paper. Cover with greased foil or paper and steam over boiling water for 2 hours. Serve with slightly warmed golden syrup.

CARAMEL APPLE DUMPLINGS

Roll the pastry ⅛ inch thick. Cut three 7-inch squares, then re-roll the remaining pastry and cut out three small rounds 1 inch in diameter.

Wash, peel and core the apples and place one on each square of pastry. Mix the dates with the lemon juice and the spice. Use to stuff the apples.

Turn all four points of the pastry up to the top of the apple, forming four "ears", and press the edges gently together. Place a circle of pastry on top of each. Brush the dumplings with beaten egg and place in a shallow baking tray.

To make the caramel, first place the white sugar in a saucepan, cook without stirring until it is honey coloured, then remove from the heat and add the water. Stir over low heat until the caramel has dissolved into the water. Add the brown sugar and the butter and stir until both have dissolved. Bring to the boil. Pour over the apples.

Bake at 400°F. for about 40 minutes or until the apples are tender. Spoon the caramel over the apples occasionally while they are cooking.

Just before serving time, the dumplings may be sprinkled with some slivered blanched almonds, or simply dusted with icing sugar.

213

For the caramel

3 rounded tablespoons sugar for
   caramel
1 tablespoon cold water
1 cup milk

For the pudding

6 ounces butter
$\frac{3}{4}$ cup sugar
3 eggs, separated
1$\frac{1}{2}$ cups plain flour
1$\frac{1}{2}$ cups self-raising flour
1 level teaspoon cinnamon
a pinch of salt
4 ounces dates, chopped

$\frac{1}{2}$ cup chopped dates
1 tablespoon orange juice
1 tablespoon butter
1 tablespoon plain flour
1 cup milk
2 tablespoons sugar
1 egg white

6 ounces biscuit pastry
1$\frac{3}{4}$ cups prepared fruit mince
8 ounces cream cheese
2 eggs
1 cup cream
$\frac{1}{2}$ teaspoon grated lemon rind
1 teaspoon rum
$\frac{1}{2}$ cup sugar
1 level dessertspoon plain flour
sifted icing sugar for topping

2 ounces butter
$\frac{3}{4}$ cup sugar
grated rind of 1 orange
2 rounded tablespoons sifted
   self-raising flour
1 level tablespoon cocoa
2 eggs, separated
1 cup milk
3 tablespoons orange juice

CARAMEL DATE PUDDING

Place the sugar for the caramel in a saucepan and heat gently. Shake the saucepan at intervals until the sugar has melted, then cook until it is a light honey colour. Remove the saucepan from the heat and add the cold water, then return to the heat and stir until the caramel has dissolved. Stir in the milk, and heat again if necessary until both are thoroughly combined.

Cream the butter and sugar for the pudding and add the egg yolks, beating well. Sift the flours with the cinnamon and salt and add to the creamed mixture alternately with the cooled caramel milk. Fold in the stiffly beaten egg whites and the chopped dates.

Place in a greased pudding basin, cover the top with greased paper and steam for 2 hours. Serve hot with date sauce.

DATE SAUCE

Soak the dates in the orange juice for several hours. Melt the butter in a small saucepan and add the flour. Stir until smooth, then cook without browning for 1 minute. Add the milk and stir until the sauce boils and thickens. Add the sugar and the soaked dates. Remove from the heat and stir in the stiffly beaten egg white.

If liked, sherry may replace the orange juice.

CHEESECAKE MINCE TARTS

Roll the pastry and use to line small greased patty tins. Reserving half the quantity, spoon some fruit mince into each pastry-lined tin.

Soften the cream cheese at room temperature and beat until smooth. Add well-beaten eggs, mixing well. Stir in the cream, lemon rind and rum.

Mix the sugar with the flour and stir into the cream mixture. Spoon some of this over the fruit mince in the patty tins. Bake at 375°F. for 30 minutes or until the crust is lightly browned and the cream-cheese mixture set.

To serve, top each tart with a spoonful of the reserved fruit mince and sprinkle with sifted icing sugar.

CHOCOLATE DELICIOUS PUDDING

Beat the butter and sugar to a cream and add the grated orange rind. Sift the flour with the cocoa and stir in half at a time, mixing well between each addition.

Mix the egg yolks with the milk and add in small amounts alternately with the orange juice. Beat the egg whites stiffly and fold in lightly.

Pour into a greased pie-dish, set in another dish containing about an inch of water, and bake in a moderate oven, 350°F., for about 40 minutes. Serve warm with ice cream.

214

CHOCOLATE MERINGUE PIES

6 ounces biscuit pastry
2 tablespoons sugar
3 level dessertspoons cornflour
1 tablespoon cocoa
½ pint milk
2 egg yolks
1 dessertspoon butter
½ teaspoon vanilla essence

For the meringue

2 egg whites
a pinch of salt
4 level tablespoons sugar

Roll the pastry thinly, cut into rounds and line small patty tins. Bake in a moderate oven, 365°F., for about 10 minutes. Remove from the oven and allow to cool.

Blend the sugar, cornflour and cocoa with a little of the cold milk to make a smooth paste. Place the remainder of the milk on to heat and when almost boiling pour it onto the blended mixture, stirring until smooth. Return the mixture to the saucepan and cook, stirring constantly, until it boils and thickens. Cook for a further minute. Remove from the heat and add the egg yolks, butter and vanilla. Cool slightly, then use to fill the cooked pastry cases.

Make a meringue by beating the egg whites with the salt until stiff and gradually beating in the sugar. Pile or pipe on top of the chocolate filling. Place in a slow oven to lightly brown and set the meringue.

CHOCOLATE SOUFFLÉ

1 ounce butter
1 rounded tablespoon plain flour
1 rounded tablespoon cocoa
¼ pint milk
1 ounce sugar
½ teaspoon vanilla essence
3 egg yolks
4 egg whites

Melt the butter in a saucepan and add the sifted flour and cocoa. Stir with a wooden spoon until blended, then cook for 1 minute. Add the milk and stir until the mixture boils and thickens. Remove from the heat, cool slightly, then add the sugar and vanilla. Stir in the egg yolks one at a time, beating well after each addition.

Beat the egg whites in a separate bowl to a stiff froth. Fold them as lightly as possible into the chocolate mixture.

Pour into a well-greased soufflé dish which has a band of greased paper tied round the outside and extending about 1 inch above the rim of the dish. Bake in a moderate oven, 350°F., for approximately 50 minutes or until a knife, inserted in the centre, comes out clean. Serve immediately.

CINNAMON DESSERT CAKE

2 ounces butter or margarine
2 slightly rounded tablespoons
   sugar
½ teaspoon vanilla essence
1 egg
½ cup self-raising flour
2 level tablespoons cornflour
1 level teaspoon cinnamon
a pinch of salt
1 tablespoon milk
about ¼ pound soaked and
   well-drained dried apricots

Cream the butter and sugar until light, add the vanilla, then the well beaten egg, mixing well.

Sift the flour with the cornflour, cinnamon and salt and add to the creamed mixture alternately with the milk.

Place half the cake mixture in a well-greased 7-inch sandwich tin and cover with a layer of well-drained apricots which have been soaked overnight. Top with the remaining cake mixture, spreading it to the sides of the tin.

Bake at 350°F. for about 40 minutes. Sprinkle the top with a little cinnamon and sugar. Serve warm, cut into wedges, with ice cream, whipped cream or custard.

COLLEGE PUDDING

2 ounces butter or margarine
¼ cup sugar
1 egg
½ teaspoon vanilla essence
1 cup self-raising flour
a pinch of salt
3 tablespoons milk
2 tablespoons jam

Cream the butter and sugar and gradually add the well-beaten egg. Flavour with the vanilla.

Sift the flour with the salt and add to the creamed mixture alternately with the milk.

Place a teaspoonful of jam in each of four well-greased individual pudding moulds or cups, cover with greased paper and steam for 30 to 40 minutes. Serve with custard.

CONTINENTAL APPLE CAKE

For the pastry

1¼ cups plain flour
4 ounces butter
1 egg yolk
1 teaspoon rum
1 tablespoon sour milk or cream
milk for glazing

For the filling

2 ounces ground almonds
2 rounded tablespoons sugar
2 tablespoons strawberry jam
1 pound apples
1 egg white

Sift the flour into a bowl and rub in the butter. Beat the egg yolk with the rum and sour milk and add enough to the flour mixture to make into a fairly firm dough. Divide in two, having one piece slightly larger than the other, and chill for about 30 minutes.

Grease an 8-inch sandwich tin and sprinkle with a little flour. Line the tin with the larger piece of pastry, rolled to fit. Bake in a hot oven, 450°F., for about 10 or 12 minutes or until a pale straw colour.

Mix the ground almonds with the sugar. Spread the strawberry jam over the baked pastry shell and sprinkle with half the almond and sugar mixture.

Peel, core and thinly slice the apples. Beat the egg white until stiff and mix with the apple slices. Arrange evenly in the tin and cover with the remaining almond and sugar mixture.

Roll the remainder of the pastry and use to cover the top. Brush with milk and prick with a fork. Bake in a hot oven, 400°F., for about 35 minutes.

DATE AND CHOCOLATE PUDDING

4 ounces butter
½ cup sugar
2 eggs
½ teaspoon vanilla essence
2 cups self-raising flour
a good pinch of salt
½ level teaspoon nutmeg
¼ level teaspoon allspice
½ cup milk
½ pound chopped dates
2 ounces grated chocolate

Beat the butter and sugar to a cream and gradually add the well-beaten eggs. Flavour with the vanilla. Sift the flour with the salt, nutmeg and allspice and add to the creamed mixture alternately with the milk. Add the chopped dates and the chocolate.

Place in a well-greased pudding basin, cover the top with greased paper, and stand the basin in a saucepan with enough water to come halfway up the sides. Cover with a tightly fitting lid. Steam for 1½ hours. Unmould and serve with custard, sauce or ice cream.

DATE AND ORANGE PUDDING

4 ounces butter or margarine
½ cup sugar
grated rind of 1 orange
2 eggs
2 cups self-raising flour
a pinch of salt
⅓ cup orange juice
⅓ cup milk
¾ cup dates

Beat the butter and sugar to a soft cream. Add the grated orange rind then gradually add the well-beaten eggs. Sift the flour with the salt and add to the creamed mixture alternately with the combined orange juice and milk.

Grease a pudding basin. Arrange some of the dates on the bottom and fold the remainder into the pudding mixture. Spoon the mixture into the basin and cover the top with greased paper. Place in a saucepan holding enough boiling water to come halfway up the sides of the basin. Cover with a tightly fitting lid. Steam for about 2 hours. Unmould and serve with custard or a sauce.

DATE AND WALNUT FRITTERS

¾ cup plain flour
2 level teaspoons baking powder
¼ cup sifted icing sugar
a pinch of nutmeg
1 egg
1 dessertspoon salad oil
⅓ cup orange juice
1 dessertspoon lemon juice
½ cup chopped dates
⅓ cup chopped walnuts

Sift the flour, baking powder, icing sugar and nutmeg into a bowl. In a smaller bowl beat the egg with the salad oil and fruit juice, and stir into the flour mixture, beating until smooth. Add the dates and nuts.

Drop spoonfuls of the batter into hot fat or oil, turning once to brown on both sides. Drain on paper and serve with brandy sauce.

DOUGHNUTS

1 egg
½ cup sugar
1 tablespoon melted butter or
    margarine
2 cups self-raising flour
¼ level teaspoon cinnamon
¼ level teaspoon nutmeg
½ level teaspoon salt
⅓ cup milk
sifted sugar for topping

Beat the egg with the sugar, and add the melted butter. Sift the flour with the cinnamon, nutmeg and salt and stir into the egg, sugar and butter mixture alternately with the milk, making into a medium dough.

Turn onto a floured board and knead lightly. Roll ¼ inch thick and cut into rings, using a doughnut cutter or two plain cutters.

Lower the doughnut rings into hot fat and cook until brown on one side. Turn and cook on the other.

Drain on paper and serve dusted with sifted icing sugar or with crystal sugar. If liked, serve with whipped cream and jam.

DUTCH APPLE CAKE

1½ cups plain flour
2 level teaspoons baking powder
½ level teaspoon salt
2 ounces butter
⅓ cup milk
1 egg, beaten
3 large apples

Sift the flour with the baking powder and salt. Rub in the butter until the mixture resembles coarse breadcrumbs. Add the milk to the beaten egg and stir into the flour mixture. The dough will be quite stiff. Pat evenly into the bottom of a well-greased shallow baking tray measuring about 11 inches by 7 inches or an 8 inch-sandwich tin.

Peel and core the apples and slice them thinly. Arrange the

Dutch Apple Cake

For the topping

2 ounces butter
½ cup sugar
¼ teaspoon nutmeg
¼ teaspoon cinnamon

slices in neat rows on top of the dough. Bake in a hot oven, 425°F., for 25 minutes.

Make the topping by creaming the butter and sugar and adding the spices. Remove the apple cake from the oven and spread with the creamed mixture. Reduce the heat to 350°F., return the apple cake to the oven and bake for a further 20 minutes. Serve warm with cream, ice cream or custard.

ECONOMICAL PLUM PUDDING

3 ounces margarine
3 rounded tablespoons sugar
1 egg
1½ cups plain flour
1 level teaspoon mixed spice
a pinch of salt
½ cup milk
8 ounces raisins, chopped
8 ounces sultanas
2 ounces mixed peel, chopped
1 level teaspoon bicarbonate of
  soda
1 dessertspoon cold water

Cream the margarine and sugar until light and fluffy, then blend in beaten egg. Sift the flour with the mixed spice and salt and add to the creamed mixture alternately with the milk. Stir in the raisins, sultanas and peel. Dissolve the soda in the cold water and add, mixing well.

Have ready a greased pudding basin, place the mixture in and cover with a layer of greased paper, then a layer of foil. Tie down securely with string. Place in a saucepan with enough boiling water to come halfway up the sides of the basin. Cover and cook for 2 hours, adding more boiling water as required. Turn out and serve with cream, custard or ice cream.

218

Date and Orange Pudding, Orange Rice Ring,
Lemon Chiffon Ring with frosted grape garnish

ENGLISH PLUM PUDDING

$\frac{3}{4}$ cup raisins, chopped
$\frac{3}{4}$ cup currants
8 ounces sultanas
4 ounces mixed peel, chopped
1 teaspoon grated lemon rind
6 ounces finely shredded suet
$\frac{1}{2}$ cup plain flour
$\frac{1}{4}$ level teaspoon bicarbonate of
   soda
$\frac{3}{4}$ teaspoon cinnamon
$\frac{3}{4}$ teaspoon powdered ginger
$\frac{3}{4}$ teaspoon powdered mace
$\frac{3}{4}$ teaspoon ground nutmeg
a pinch of allspice and of cloves
4 cups soft white breadcrumbs
3 eggs
$\frac{3}{4}$ cup (firmly packed) light
   brown sugar
$\frac{1}{2}$ cup milk
1 tablespoon lemon juice
3 tablespoons brandy

Combine the raisins, currants and sultanas with the peel, the grated lemon rind and the shredded suet. Sift the flour with the soda and spices and combine with the fruit mixture, then add the breadcrumbs and mix well.

Beat the eggs, gradually add the brown sugar, then beat in the milk, lemon juice and brandy. Add to the dry ingredients, blending thoroughly.

Grease a 2$\frac{1}{2}$-pint pudding basin or mould well and line the bottom with paper. Spoon the pudding mixture in and cover with a double layer of greased paper and two thicknesses of foil. Tie down securely.

Place in a saucepan of boiling water with enough water to reach halfway up the side of the basin. Cover. Boil steadily for 4 hours, replacing the water with more boiling water as it boils away.

Store until required for use. Reboil for a further 2 hours on the day the pudding is to be served. Serve with brandy sauce, hard sauce or cream.

Fresh Plum Dessert Cake

219

Baked Apple Dumplings, Steamed Fruit Pudding,
Peach Berry Cobbler

FRESH PLUM DESSERT CAKE

1½ pounds fresh tart plums
¼ cup sugar
3 ounces butter
3 ounces sugar
1 teaspoon grated lemon rind
2 eggs
1½ cups self-raising flour
2 tablespoons milk
1 tablespoon of sugar and 1 teaspoon of cinnamon for topping

Halve and stone the plums and place them in a lightly greased casserole with the ¼ cup sugar.

Cream the butter and the 3 ounces of sugar until light and fluffy, then add the grated lemon rind. Beat the eggs and add them gradually. Sift the flour and add to the creamed mixture alternately with the milk.

Spoon this cake batter over the plums and sprinkle the top with a mixture of cinnamon and sugar.

Bake in a moderate oven, 350°F., for about 1 hour or until the cake is cooked. Serve with cream.

FRESH RHUBARB PIE WITH ORANGE CRUST

For the pastry

1 cup self-raising flour
1 cup plain flour
¼ teaspoon salt
3 ounces lard
3 ounces butter or margarine
1 tablespoon grated orange rind
a squeeze of lemon juice
½ cup iced water
1 egg yolk (optional)

For the filling

1 bunch rhubarb
1 cup sugar
⅓ cup plain flour
1 tablespoon butter
extra sugar for topping

Sift both flours with the salt. Blend the lard with the butter and divide into four equal portions. Take one portion of the mixed shortening and rub it into the flour.

Add the grated orange rind and the lemon juice to the iced water and stir in the egg yolk if used. Add this liquid to the flour mixture to make a soft dough. Turn onto a lightly floured board, knead lightly and roll into an oblong shape. It should be three times as long as it is wide.

Spread a second portion of shortening over two-thirds of the rolled dough, sprinkle lightly with flour and fold into three. Give the dough a half turn, then roll again into an oblong shape.

Repeat with the remaining two portions of shortening, then roll and fold again without the fat or extra flour. Now roll the dough out to fit a 9-inch tart plate (reserve the scraps for latticing). Chill the lined pastry case while you prepare the filling.

Wash the rhubarb and cut it into 1-inch pieces. Mix the sugar and flour well together, then add the chopped rhubarb. Turn into the prepared pastry shell, piling high in the middle. Dot with butter and cover with strips of pastry in the form of a lattice. Brush the pastry with water and sprinkle with sugar.

Bake in a hot oven, 400°F., for 10 minutes, then reduce the heat to 350°F. and bake for a further 45 minutes or until the rhubarb is soft and the pastry golden. Serve warm with whipped cream or ice cream.

FRUIT MINCE CUSTARD TART

6 ounces biscuit pastry
1½ cups prepared fruit mince
2 eggs
1 dessertspoon sugar
½ teaspoon vanilla essence

Roll the pastry thinly and use to line an 8-inch tart plate or sandwich tin. Roll scraps of pastry, cut out the shapes with small biscuit cutters and use to decorate the edges.

Spread the fruit mince on the bottom of the uncooked pastry case.

220

½ pint milk
nutmeg for topping

Beat the eggs with the sugar, flavour with the vanilla, stir in the milk and beat again. Pour over the fruit mince. Sprinkle the top with nutmeg.

Place in a hot oven, 425°F., and bake for 10 minutes. Reduce the heat to 325°F. and bake for a further 30 minutes or until the custard has set and the pastry is lightly browned. Serve warm or cold.

FRUITED FLAMBÉ

⅓ cup water
¼ cup sugar
2 dessertspoons orange juice
¼ teaspoon grated orange rind
¼ teaspoon grated lemon rind
1 teaspoon butter
4 firm bananas
3 dessertspoons rum
whipped cream for serving

Place the water and sugar in a shallow pan and stir until the sugar has dissolved and the mixture comes to the boil. Boil until slightly thick—about 4 minutes.

Add the orange juice and grated orange and lemon rinds and bring to the boil. Add the butter and stir until melted.

Peel the bananas and, if liked, cut in halves lengthwise. Arrange them in the pan and cook for 3 or 4 minutes, basting frequently.

Heat the rum slightly, pour over the bananas, ignite, and serve immediately with whipped cream.

GLAZED APPLE ROLY

For the pastry

2 cups self-raising flour
1 level teaspoon salt
3 ounces butter
1 slightly rounded tablespoon
   sugar
5 tablespoons water

For the filling

3 medium-sized cooking apples
1 cup sultanas
½ cup brown sugar
1 level teaspoon cinnamon
½ level teaspoon grated lemon
   rind

For the glaze

2 ounces butter
4 ounces brown sugar
½ cup water

To make the pastry, sift the flour with the salt, rub in the butter, add the sugar and mix to a medium dough with the water. Turn onto a lightly floured board and knead only until smooth on the outside. Roll thinly into a rectangle.

Peel the apples and grate them into a bowl. Add the sultanas, brown sugar, cinnamon and grated lemon rind, mixing well. Spread this mixture on the rolled pastry to within ½ inch of the edges. Roll up as a roly-poly.

Place the apple roly in a shallow ovenproof dish and bake at 400°F. for 10 minutes. Reduce the heat to 350°F. and bake for a further 20 or 25 minutes.

To make the glaze combine the 2 ounces of butter with the brown sugar and water in a saucepan, and stir until the mixture boils. Remove the spoon and boil for 1 more minute. Pour over the apple roly during the last 15 minutes' baking. Serve warm with custard, ice cream or cream.

GOLD COAST PIE

2 tablespoons cornflour
2 tablespoons sugar
1½ cup milk
2 eggs, separated
½ teaspoon vanilla essence
3 tablespoons coconut
1 baked pastry case of short or
   biscuit pastry
15-ounce can of crushed
   pineapple
4 tablespoons sugar
   for meringue

Blend the cornflour and the sugar with a little of the cold milk. Place the remainder of the milk in a saucepan and heat until almost boiling, then pour onto the blended mixture, stirring until smooth. Return the mixture to the saucepan and cook, stirring well, over medium heat until it boils and thickens. Add the egg yolks, vanilla and coconut.

Pour half the coconut custard into the cooked and cooled pastry case, top with the drained pineapple, then with the remainder of the custard.

Beat the egg whites until stiff and gradually add the extra sugar, beating until the meringue is stiff and glossy. Pipe or pile on top of the pie. Place in a moderate oven, 350°F., to lightly brown and set the meringue.

If the pie is served cold it may be decorated with whipped cream and cherries.

GOLDEN SYRUP DUMPLINGS

1 cup self-raising flour
a pinch of salt
1 level tablespoon butter
1 egg beaten with 1 tablespoon
   milk or a little more

For the syrup

1 cup water
½ cup sugar
1 tablespoon butter
1 tablespoon golden syrup

Sift the flour with the salt and rub in the butter. Mix with the beaten egg and milk to make a reasonably dry dough.

Take small pieces of dough about the size of a walnut and roll in balls between the palms of the hands.

Combine the ingredients for the syrup and heat until boiling. Add the dumplings, cover and cook gently for 15 minutes.

Serve the dumplings hot with the syrup, accompanied by cream if liked.

GRANDMA'S CHRISTMAS PUDDING

1 pound currants
1 pound sultanas
1 pound raisins
6 ounces candied peel
1 cup blanched almonds
5 ounces minced apple
2 cups plain flour
1 teaspoon salt
½ teaspoon ground cloves
1 teaspoon cinnamon
1 teaspoon mixed spice
1 pound beef suet
1 pound breadcrumbs

Grease two 2½-pint pudding basins and line the base of each with greaseproof paper. Cut two rounds of greaseproof paper and two of aluminium foil to cover the top of each basin.

Chop the fruit, peel and nuts into uniform sized pieces and combine with the minced apple.

Sift the flour with the salt and spices into a large bowl.

Prepare the suet by grating it finely. Rub it well into the flour, then add the combined breadcrumbs, brown sugar and grated orange rind. Stir in the fruit and nuts.

Beat the eggs well, and gradually add the brandy and rum. Add to the pudding mixture with the beer, stirring well.

Divide evenly between the two basins and cover with the greaseproof paper and foil. Tie down securely with string.

222

1 cup brown sugar
grated rind of 1 large orange
5 eggs
2 tablespoons brandy
4 tablespoons rum
¾ pint beer

Place each basin in a large saucepan of boiling water. The water should come halfway up the side of each basin. Boil for 6 hours. The saucepan should be tightly lidded.

Keep the water boiling all the time the puddings are cooking, and add only boiling water to the saucepan to keep the level up.

Steam for a further 2 hours on the day the pudding is to be served.

LEMON CAKE PUDDING

1½ dessertspoons butter
½ cup sugar
1 teaspoon grated lemon rind
¼ cup lemon juice
3 eggs, separated
¼ cup plain flour
¼ cup coconut
1 cup milk
a pinch of salt

Preheat the oven to 325°F. Lightly grease a 1½-quart casserole. Cream the butter and sugar and add the grated lemon rind and the lemon juice. Add the egg yolks one at a time, beating well after each addition.

Combine the flour and the coconut and add to the creamed mixture alternately with the milk, beginning and ending with the flour mixture.

Beat the egg whites with the salt in a warm dry bowl until soft peaks form. Gently fold into the batter until just combined. Pour into the prepared casserole.

Set the dish containing the pudding in another dish containing an inch of water. Bake for 40 to 45 minutes or until the pudding is set and the top lightly browned.

Serve warm or cold with whipped cream sprinkled with grated lemon rind.

LEMON CUPS

1 cup sugar
¼ cup sifted plain flour
a dash of salt
1½ cups scalded milk
3 eggs, separated
1 tablespoon melted butter
1 tablespoon grated lemon rind
⅓ cup lemon juice

Combine the sugar with the sifted flour and salt in a bowl. Mix the milk with the egg yolks and pour onto the sugar mixture. Allow to cool.

Add the melted butter, then the grated lemon rind and the lemon juice. Fold in the stiffly beaten egg whites lightly but thoroughly.

Divide the mixture evenly between six 6-ounce custard cups or dariole moulds. Set them in a pan containing about an inch of cold water and bake at 325°F. for 40 minutes or until the cake part of the dessert is cooked and lightly browned.

Turn each mould out onto individual serving plates or dishes and serve at once. The dessert makes its own sauce.

LEMON SAUCE PUDDING

1 rounded tablespoon butter
$\frac{3}{4}$ cup sugar
1 teaspoon grated lemon rind
2 rounded tablespoons
   self-raising flour
2 eggs, separated
1 cup milk
3 tablespoons lemon juice

Beat the butter and sugar to a cream and add the grated lemon rind. Add the sifted flour half at a time, mixing well between each addition.

Combine beaten egg yolks with the milk and add gradually to the mixture alternately with the lemon juice. Fold in stiffly beaten egg whites.

Pour the mixture into a greased pie-dish and stand the dish in another one containing about an inch of water. Bake in a moderate oven, 350°F., for about 40 minutes. Serve warm or cold.

CHOCOLATE SAUCE PUDDING

Substitute orange rind and juice for the lemon and sift 1 level tablespoon of cocoa with the flour.

PASSIONFRUIT SAUCE PUDDING

Add the pulp of 3 or 4 passionfruit with the lemon juice.

MOCK PLUM PUDDING

5 ounces soft white breadcrumbs
$1\frac{1}{2}$ cups hot stewed apple
1 cup (firmly packed) brown
   sugar
2 ounces currants
2 ounces sultanas
5 ounces plain flour
1 level teaspoon mixed spice
$1\frac{1}{2}$ level teaspoons bicarbonate of
   soda
$\frac{1}{2}$ cup melted butter or
   margarine

Stir the breadcrumbs into the hot stewed apple and allow to stand for 30 minutes. Add the brown sugar and stir until it has dissolved. Add the currants and sultanas.

Sift the flour, spice and soda and add to the apple mixture, blending well. Add the melted butter or margarine, mixing till thoroughly combined.

Turn into a well-greased pudding basin and cover with a layer of greased paper, then a layer of oil. Tie down securely. Steam for 3 hours. Serve with spicy custard sauce (page 417).

ORANGE COCONUT PUDDING

4 ounces butter
$\frac{1}{2}$ cup sugar
1 teaspoon grated orange rind
1 teaspoon grated lemon rind
2 eggs
$\frac{3}{4}$ cup coconut
2 cups self-raising flour
a pinch of salt
4 tablespoons orange juice
$\frac{1}{2}$ cup milk
dates (optional)

Cream the butter and sugar until light and fluffy, then add the grated fruit rinds. Gradually add the well-beaten eggs, then stir in the coconut. Add the sifted flour and salt to the creamed mixture alternately with the combined orange juice and milk. The dough should be soft and smooth.

Grease a $2\frac{1}{2}$-pint pudding basin and, if liked, place a few stoned dates in a pattern on the bottom of the basin. Spoon in the pudding mixture and cover the top with a double thickness of greased paper, then a layer of aluminium foil. Tie down securely. Place in a large saucepan containing enough boiling water to come halfway up the side of the basin. Steam for $1\frac{1}{2}$ hours. Serve hot with orange sauce, custard or cream.

1 cup dates
1 cup orange juice
1 tablespoon lemon juice
2 ounces butter
3 slightly rounded tablespoons
    sugar
1 teaspoon grated orange rind
1 egg
1 cup self-raising flour
a pinch of salt
sugared cornflakes, crushed

2 bananas
1 dessertspoon butter, melted
$\frac{1}{2}$ cup brown sugar
1 dessertspoon grated orange
    rind
$\frac{1}{4}$ cup orange juice
2 teaspoons chopped candied
    ginger

3 ounces butter
3 slightly rounded tablespoons
    sugar
grated rind of 1 orange
2 eggs
$\frac{1}{2}$ cup raisins, chopped
$1\frac{1}{2}$ cups self-raising flour
a pinch of salt
4 tablespoons milk
1 tablespoon orange juice
a few extra raisins

1 tablespoon chopped walnuts
$1\frac{1}{4}$ cups sweet fruit mince
1 uncooked pastry case of short
    biscuit pastry
1 tablespoon butter
1 tablespoon plain flour
$\frac{1}{3}$ cup sugar
2 eggs, separated
$\frac{1}{2}$ cup milk
1 teaspoon grated orange rind
1 tablespoon orange juice

ORANGE CRUMBLE

Chop the dates and place them in a saucepan with the orange and lemon juices. Cook, stirring well, until the mixture becomes thick and smooth. Cool.

Cream the butter with the sugar and add the grated orange rind. Add the well-beaten egg and then the sifted flour and salt. Spread in the bottom of a greased 7-inch sandwich tin and cover with the cooled date mixture. Top with the crushed cornflakes.

Bake in a moderate oven, 350°F., for about 20 minutes. Serve warm with custard, whipped cream or ice cream.

ORANGE GLAZED BANANAS

Cut each peeled banana in halves lengthwise and then crosswise. Arrange the pieces in a single layer in a lightly greased baking dish.
Melt the butter and mix with the brown sugar, orange rind and juice and the chopped ginger. Pour over the bananas.

Place in a moderate oven, 350°F., and bake for about 10 minutes, basting occasionally.

Serve in hot dessert dishes, allowing two pieces of banana to each person. Top each with a spoonful of ice cream and spoon a little of the cooking glaze over it.

ORANGE RAISIN PUDDING

Grease a pudding basin and cut a piece of paper to cover the top. Beat the butter and sugar to a soft cream, adding the grated orange rind.

Beat the eggs well and add them gradually to the creamed mixture. Stir in the raisins. Sift the flour and salt and add to the mixture alternately with the combined milk and orange juice.

Place a few raisins in the bottom of the greased pudding basin and add the pudding mixture. Cover with the paper and steam for $1\frac{1}{2}$ hours. Serve hot with custard sauce.

ORANGE-TOPPED MINCE PIE

Stir the walnuts into the fruit mince and spread evenly in the bottom of the uncooked pastry case.

Rub the butter into the flour and add the sugar. Blend in the egg yolks, milk, orange rind and juice. Beat the egg whites until soft peaks form, then fold in. Spoon this mixture over the mince in the pie-shell.

Bake in a hot oven, 425°F., for 10 minutes, then reduce the heat to 325°F. and bake for a further 35 to 40 minutes or until the topping is set. Serve with whipped cream.

PEACH BERRY COBBLER

1 dessertspoon cornflour
1 packet frozen raspberries
a pinch of salt
2½ cups sweetened peach slices

For the topping

1 cup self-raising flour
a pinch of salt
1 dessertspoon butter
1 rounded teaspoon sugar
1 egg
5 tablespoons milk
sugar for topping

Combine the cornflour in a saucepan with a little of the syrup drained from the thawed raspberries. Add the remaining syrup and the salt. Cook over medium heat, stirring constantly, until the mixture is thick and clear. Add drained peaches and raspberries. Reheat, and keep hot while you make the topping.

Sift the flour with the salt, rub in the butter, and add the sugar. Beat the egg, mix with the milk, and stir into the flour mixture, making a soft batter.

Turn the hot fruit mixture into a 1½-quart casserole or a 10-inch by 6-inch ovenproof dish. Drop the batter by dessertspoonfuls onto the hot fruit. Sprinkle with sugar.

Bake in a hot oven, 400°F., for 20 minutes, or until the topping is cooked. Serve warm with cream.

PEACH CRUMB DESSERT

Stew some halves of peeled and stoned peaches gently until they are tender but have not lost their shape. Cool, then place in individual serving dishes.

Melt 1 dessertspoon of butter or margarine in a saucepan and stir in ½ teaspoon of cinnamon and 1 cup of soft white breadcrumbs. Toss over medium heat until the crumbs are a golden colour. Add 2 teaspoons of brown sugar and toss again.

Spoon this hot mixture over the peaches and serve immediately with whipped cream or ice cream.

PINEAPPLE BUTTER PIE

6 ounces short or biscuit pastry
2 ounces butter or margarine
½ cup sugar
2 eggs
juice of 1 lemon
15-ounce can of pineapple
  pieces

Roll the pastry out and line a 7-inch sandwich tin or tart plate with it (the scraps will make the lattice top). Cream the butter and sugar and add the eggs one at a time, beating well after each addition. Mix in the lemon juice.

Drain the pineapple and add the pieces to the creamed mixture. Pour into the prepared pie-case. With the left-over pieces of pastry make lattice strips to cover the top.

Bake in a moderate oven, 350°F., for 30 to 40 minutes. Serve warm or cold with whipped cream or ice cream.

PINEAPPLE DESSERT CAKE

2½ ounces butter
⅓ cup sugar
1 teaspoon vanilla essence
1 egg
½ cup coconut
1¼ cups plain flour

Cream the butter and sugar, add the vanilla, then the beaten egg, mixing well. Stir in the coconut.

Sift the flour with the baking powder and salt and add to the creamed mixture alternately with the pineapple syrup.

Spread half the cake mixture in the bottom of a well-greased 7-inch sandwich tin and spoon the well-drained pineapple on

1½ level teaspoons baking
  powder
a good pinch of salt
½ cup pineapple syrup
1 medium-sized can of crushed
  pineapple
¼ cup brown sugar
¼ cup chopped walnuts
2 ounces butter, melted

top, spreading it evenly. Top with the remainder of the cake mixture.

Combine the brown sugar and nuts and sprinkle over the cake, drizzle over the melted butter, then bake in a moderate oven, 350°F., for about 45 minutes. Serve warm with whipped cream and, if liked, extra pineapple.

QUEEN PUDDING

1 pint milk
2 eggs, separated
½ teaspoon vanilla essence
2 ounces cake crumbs
about 2 tablespoons berry jam or
  other soft jam
2 tablespoons sugar for the
  meringue

Warm the milk and pour it over the beaten egg yolks and vanilla. Stir in the cake crumbs.

Pour into a lightly greased dish and bake in a slow oven, 300°F., for about 40 minutes or until set. Remove from the oven and spread the top with jam.

Beat the egg whites until stiff and gradually beat in the sugar. Pile on top of the jam layer. Replace the pudding in the oven and bake at 300°F. for about 20 minutes to set and lightly brown the meringue. Serve warm.

Pineapple Butter Pie

QUICK CHOCOLATE PUDDING

1½ ounces cooking chocolate
3 dessertspoons butter
½ cup sugar
1 egg
1 cup plain flour
1½ level teaspoons baking
   powder
a pinch of salt
½ cup milk
½ teaspoon vanilla essence

Melt the chocolate and the butter in a saucepan over gentle heat. Stir in the sugar and the beaten egg. Sift the flour with the baking powder and salt and add to the chocolate mixture alternately with the combined milk and vanilla.

Place in a greased pudding basin and cover with greased paper, then stand the basin in a saucepan containing enough boiling water to come halfway up the side of the basin. Cover and cook for 1½ hours. Serve with custard, sauce or ice cream.

RAISIN MERINGUE BREAD PUDDING

2 cups milk
2 cups one-inch cubes day-old
   bread
¼ cup brown sugar
a pinch of salt
2 dessertspoons melted butter
2 egg yolks
1 teaspoon vanilla essence
2 cups seeded raisins

For the topping

2 egg whites
3 dessertspoons sugar
¾ teaspoon grated orange rind

Pour the milk over the bread cubes. Add the brown sugar, salt, melted butter, beaten egg yolks, vanilla and raisins. Toss lightly to blend.

Pour into an 8-inch ovenproof dish which has been greased with butter, and set the dish in a shallow pan containing hot water to a depth of about an inch. Bake in a moderate oven, 350°F., for about 50 minutes. Remove from the oven and spread with the orange meringue topping (method follows), then return the pudding to the oven and bake for a further 10 minutes or until the meringue is set and lightly browned.

To make the meringue topping, beat the egg whites until stiff, gradually beat in the sugar and flavour with the grated orange rind.

RHUBARB CREAM PIE

6 ounces sweet shortcrust or
   biscuit pastry
1½ cups sugar
3 tablespoons plain flour
½ teaspoon nutmeg
1 dessertspoon butter
2 eggs
3 cups diced rhubarb

Line a tart plate with the pastry. Re-roll the scraps and cut into fancy shapes.

Blend the sugar and the flour with the nutmeg and chopped butter. Add well-beaten eggs, stirring until smooth. Stir in the diced rhubarb.

Turn the mixture into the lined tart plate and top with the pastry shapes. Bake in a hot oven, 425°F., for 10 minutes, then reduce the heat to 350°F. and bake for a further 30 minutes. Serve warm with cream or ice cream.

ROYAL PLUM PUDDING

¼ pound whole or ground
   almonds
1½ pounds seeded raisins
½ pound sultanas
½ pound currants
½ pound mixed peel
½ pound plain flour

Grease a large pudding basin 9 inches in diameter and cut two thicknesses of greaseproof paper and two of foil to cover and tie down over the top of the basin.

Blanch and chop the almonds if not using ground almonds. Chop the fruit and peel into pieces of uniform size.

Sift the flour with the salt and spices. Rub in the butter. Add the fruit, nuts, breadcrumbs and sugar.

a good pinch of salt
1 level teaspoon mixed spice
1 level teaspoon ground nutmeg
10 ounces butter or margarine
½ pound soft white breadcrumbs
½ pound sugar
6 eggs
6 tablespoons brandy, rum or
    whisky
½ pint milk

Beat the eggs, add the brandy and milk and pour into the dry ingredients, blending to make a soft mixture. Place in the prepared basin, cover with the greaseproof paper and then the foil, and tie down securely with string.

Place in a saucepan containing enough boiling water to reach halfway up the side of the basin. Cover tightly with a lid and boil steadily for 6 hours. As the water boils away, replace with more boiling water.

The day the pudding is to be served, boil for a further 2 hours.

SAGO PLUM PUDDING

1 cup soft white breadcrumbs
2 scant tablespoons sago
2 ounces butter
¾ cup milk
½ cup sugar
1 cup sultanas or raisins
    (or mixed fruits)
1 tablespoon chopped mixed
    peel
¼ teaspoon nutmeg
½ level teaspoon bicarbonate of
    soda
1 teaspoon cold water
1 small egg

Place the breadcrumbs, sago and butter in a bowl. Heat the milk and stir it in, mixing till the butter has melted. Allow to stand for 30 minutes, then add the sugar, fruit, peel and nutmeg.

Dissolve the soda in the cold water and add to the mixture, then lightly but thoroughly stir in the beaten egg.

Pour into a greased mould, cover with greased paper and place in a saucepan containing enough boiling water to reach halfway up the side. Steam for 2½ hours. Serve with cream or custard.

This mixture may be cooked in six individual moulds. They will take 1¼ hours to cook.

SIMPLE STEAMED PUDDING

1 egg
2 tablespoons sugar
a pinch of salt
1 cup self-raising flour
3 tablespoons milk
1 teaspoon vanilla essence
1 tablespoon melted butter
jam, fruit or syrup

Place the egg, sugar and salt in a bowl and beat well. Stir in the sifted flour, then add the combined milk and vanilla, blending well. Add the melted butter and beat the mixture well.

Grease a small pudding basin, place 1 or 2 dessertspoons of jam, fruit or syrup in the bottom and pour in the batter. Do not cover the basin itself but put it in a saucepan containing an inch of water and put the saucepan lid on. Cook for exactly 30 minutes.

STEAMED CHOCOLATE PUDDING

3 ounces butter
3 rounded tablespoons sugar
2 eggs
½ teaspoon vanilla essence
1½ cups self-raising flour
2 level tablespoons cocoa
a pinch of salt
3 tablespoons milk

Grease a 6-inch pudding basin. Cut a round of paper about an inch larger than the top, then grease the paper.

Beat the butter and sugar to a soft cream and gradually add the well-beaten eggs. Flavour with the vanilla. Sift the dry ingredients and add them to the creamed mixture alternately with the milk.

Place the mixture in the prepared basin, cover with paper and steam over boiling water (or place the basin in a large saucepan containing sufficient boiling water to come halfway up the side of the basin). Cook for 1½ hours. Serve with custard sauce.

229

4 ounces butter
½ cup sugar
¼ teaspoon vanilla essence
2 eggs
2 cups self-raising flour
1 level teaspoon mixed spice
a pinch of salt
¾ cup milk
4 ounces mixed dried fruit

3 ounces butter
3 rounded tablespoons sugar
1 large egg
2 ounces preserved ginger
¼ teaspoon grated lemon rind
1½ cups self-raising flour
¼ level teaspoon cinnamon
1 level teaspoon ground ginger
½ cup milk

4 ounces butter
¾ cup castor sugar
2 well-beaten eggs
1½ cups self-raising flour
a pinch of salt
3 heaped tablespoons well-drained canned pineapple pieces
2 tablespoons pineapple syrup
1 teaspoon lemon juice
2 tablespoons milk

1 cup sugar
a pinch of salt
2 dessertspoons quick-cooking tapioca
¼ teaspoon nutmeg
¼ cup orange juice
3 cups washed and chopped rhubarb
6 ounces orange-flavoured short or biscuit pastry
1 cup washed and sliced strawberries
1 dessertspoon butter

STEAMED FRUIT PUDDING

Prepare a medium-size pudding basin by greasing it well. Cut a round of paper to cover the top and grease it well also.

Beat the butter and sugar to a soft cream, flavour with the vanilla and add the well-beaten eggs.

Sift the flour with the spice and salt and add to the creamed mixture alternately with the milk and fruit.

Place the mixture in the prepared basin and cover with the round of paper. Stand the basin in a saucepan containing enough boiling water to reach halfway up the side of the basin, cover with a tight-fitting lid and steam for 2 hours. Serve with custard, sweet white sauce or cream.

STEAMED GINGER PUDDING

Cream the butter and sugar, gradually add the well-beaten egg, and stir in chopped ginger and grated lemon rind.

Sift the flour with the cinnamon and ginger and add to the creamed mixture alternately with the milk.

Place in a greased pudding basin and cover with greased paper or foil. Stand the basin in a saucepan containing enough boiling water to come halfway up the side of the basin. Cover and steam for 1½ hours. Serve with custard, cream, ice cream or a sweet white sauce.

STEAMED PINEAPPLE PUDDING

Cream the butter and sugar and gradually add the well-beaten eggs. Sift the flour with the salt and add to the creamed mixture alternately with the pineapple pieces and the combined syrup, lemon juice and milk.

Place the mixture in a greased pudding basin, cover with greased paper, and stand it in a saucepan containing enough boiling water to come halfway up the side of the basin. Steam for 2 hours. Serve with German wine sauce (page 416).

STRAWBERRY RHUBARB PIE

Place the sugar, salt, tapioca, nutmeg, orange juice and rhubarb in a bowl.

Roll out the pastry and line a greased tart plate with it. Trim and decorate the edges. Add the rhubarb mixture, cover with the strawberry slices, and dot with butter.

Re-roll the left-over pastry, cut into fancy shapes and place on top of the fruit.

Bake in a hot oven, 400°F., for 10 minutes. Reduce the heat to moderate, 350°F., and continue baking for a further 30 minutes. Serve warm with cream, custard or ice cream.

Sugar-crusted Apples

SUGAR-CRUSTED APPLES

6 cooking apples
⅓ cup plain flour
2½ ounces butter or margarine
⅔ cup sugar
½ teaspoon cinnamon
¾ cup orange juice

Peel and core the apples and place them in a pie-dish.

Sift the flour, rub in the butter, then add the sugar and cinnamon, mixing well. Fill the cored apples with half this mixture and sprinkle the remainder on top, pressing so that it coats the top of the apples. Now pour the orange juice round the apples (not over them).

Bake uncovered in a moderate oven, 350°F., for about 1 hour, or until the apples are tender. Serve warm with the thick orange sauce which forms at the base of the apples, and accompany, if liked, with plain or whipped cream.

SWEDISH APPLE CAKE

6 good-sized cooking apples
½ cup sugar
1 level tablespoon butter
1⅓ cups soft white breadcrumbs
a little cinnamon or nutmeg (optional)
3 tablespoons grated chocolate for topping

Peel, core and slice the apples and place them in a saucepan with half the sugar. Cover and simmer until cooked (without water they must be cooked very slowly). If the apples look too dry add a few tablespoons of water.

Heat the butter in a saucepan and add the breadcrumbs and the remainder of the sugar. Toss over the heat until the crumbs are crisp.

Grease a pie-dish and add a layer of the crisp crumbs. Arrange the cooked apple slices on these and, if liked, add some cinnamon or nutmeg. Cover with the remaining crumbs.

Bake in a moderate oven, 350°F., for 30 minutes. Cool slightly and top with grated chocolate before serving with cream, ice cream or boiled custard.

SWISS APPLE CAKE

5 ounces butter
¾ cup sugar
3 eggs

Heat the oven to 350°F. Beat the butter and sugar to a soft cream, then add the eggs one at a time, beating well after each addition.

231

1¾ cups plain flour
2 level teaspoons baking powder
½ level teaspoon salt
1 level teaspoon grated lemon rind
2 medium-sized apples
2 dessertspoons sugar (for the apples)
a little thinned apricot jam for topping

Sift the flour, baking powder and salt and add to the creamed mixture, then stir in the grated lemon rind. Place in a well-greased 8-inch cake tin.

Peel and core the apples and cut each apple into five wedges. Cut into each wedge on the rounded side halfway through, making another five slices in each wedge. Fan these wedges out and arrange them evenly on top of the cake. Sprinkle with the 2 dessertspoons of sugar. Bake for 1 hour.

As soon as the cake comes from the oven, brush it over with the thinned jam. Serve warm with custard or cream.

TWO-CRUST PINEAPPLE PIE

6 ounces short or biscuit pastry
2 level tablespoons cornflour
¼ cup lemon juice, orange juice or water
15-ounce can of crushed pine-apple
grated rind of 1 orange or 1 lemon
1 tablespoon butter

Cut the pastry into two pieces, one larger than the other. Roll out the larger piece to line the bottom and sides of a 7-inch sandwich tin.

Blend the cornflour with the juice or water and add the crushed pineapple. Place in a saucepan and stir over medium heat until the mixture boils and thickens. Continue cooking for 1 or 2 minutes. Remove from the heat and add the grated fruit rind and the butter. Allow to cool.

Spoon the filling into the uncooked pastry shell and cover with the remainder of the pastry, rolled to fit the top. Pinch the edges together. Bake in a hot oven, 425°F., for 10 minutes. Reduce the heat to moderate, 350°F., and continue baking for a further 20 minutes. Serve with ice cream, cream or custard.

WAFFLES

2 cups self-raising flour
a good pinch of salt
1 level tablespoon sugar
2 eggs, separated
1½ cups milk
1 tablespoon melted butter
1 teaspoon vanilla essence

Sift the flour with the salt into a bowl and add the sugar.

Mix the egg yolks with the milk.

Make a well in the centre of the flour and sugar mixture, pour the liquid in and beat with a wooden spoon, gradually drawing the flour mixture in from the sides until you have a smooth batter. Add the stiffly beaten egg whites, then the melted butter and vanilla.

Heat and grease the waffle iron, pour in some of the batter, close the lid and cook until steam ceases to escape. Remove the waffle and keep hot.

Grease the waffle iron again for each waffle.

ZABAGLIONE

8 egg yolks
3 to 4 dessertspoons sugar
½ cup Marsala or sweet sherry

Beat the egg yolks, sugar and wine in the top of a double boiler or in a round-bottomed bowl over a saucepan of simmering water. Whip the mixture with a wire whisk continually until it is thick enough to hold a slight peak briefly when the whisk is withdrawn. This will take about 5 minutes. Make sure that the water in the bottom saucepan is only simmering gently and that the top of the double saucepan does not touch the water, for too much heat will curdle the custard.

Pour into glasses and serve immediately, accompanied by a crisp cookie or a macaroon.

ZABAGLIONE WITH CREAM

Spoon a little icy-cold whipped cream into the bottom of each serving glass. Top with the hot zabaglione.

ZABAGLIONE WITH GRENADINE

Add $\frac{1}{2}$ teaspoon of vanilla essence to zabaglione made with dry sauterne. Pour $\frac{1}{2}$ inch of chilled grenadine into the bottom of a serving dish, fill with the hot custard and top with grated nutmeg.

ZABAGLIONE IN MOULDS

This dessert can be converted into a cold moulded sweet with the addition of softened gelatine, brandy and whipped cream. To make this sweet, prepare the custard as above and cook to the stage where it thickens.

Remove from the heat. Dissolve 1 dessertspoon of gelatine in 2 tablespoons of water and stir into the custard.

Have ready a bowl of cracked ice. Place the bowl containing the zabaglione on the ice and stir until it begins to thicken. Fold in $1\frac{1}{2}$ tablespoons of brandy and 1 cup of whipped cream. Pour into individual moulds which have been oiled or rinsed out with egg white. Chill until set, then unmould and serve with a rosette of cream and a finger biscuit.

233

ENTREES

ASPARAGUS AND CHICKEN PIE

6 ounces shortcrust pastry
1 small can of asparagus spears
1¼ cups diced cooked chicken
3 slices bacon, fried and
  crumbled
½ cup shredded cheese
1 tablespoon Parmesan cheese
2 eggs
1 dessertspoon plain flour
1 cup milk
½ teaspoon salt
¼ teaspoon nutmeg
¼ teaspoon cayenne pepper

Roll the pastry and cut to fit a 9-inch tart plate. Drain the liquid from the asparagus spears. Mix the chopped chicken, bacon and cheese and spread in the bottom of the uncooked pastry case.

Beat the eggs slightly, then beat in the flour, milk, salt, nutmeg and cayenne. Pour carefully over the mixture in the pastry shell. Arrange the well-drained asparagus spears on top in a spoke design.

Bake in a hot oven, 400°F., for 10 minutes, then reduce the heat to 350°F. and bake for another 40 to 45 minutes or until the custard has set.

ASPARAGUS CASSEROLE

16-ounce can of asparagus spears
1 medium-sized green pepper
3 eggs
1 teaspoon salt
¼ teaspoon pepper
¾ cup soft white breadcrumbs
1 cup Cheddar cheese cut into
  ¼-inch cubes
1 cup milk
1½ tablespoons butter or
  margarine
tomato slices and parsley sprigs
  to garnish

Drain the asparagus and cut the spears into pieces about 2 inches in length. Remove the seeds from the green pepper and cut it into small pieces.

Beat the eggs well and add the salt, pepper, breadcrumbs, green pepper, cheese and milk. Add the asparagus. Pour into a 1½-quart casserole or a 9-inch tart plate. Melt the butter and pour over the top.

Bake uncovered in a moderate oven, 350°F., until the custard has set—about 30 to 40 minutes. Serve warm garnished with fresh tomato slices and sprigs of parsley.

This casserole may be made in advance and reheated. It is substantial enough to serve as a main luncheon dish.

Asparagus and Chicken Pie

ASPARAGUS CHEESE BAKE

14-ounce can of asparagus spears
8 slices ham
1 ounce butter
1 dessertspoon chopped onion
2 dessertspoons chopped green
    pepper
2 level tablespoons plain flour
½ teaspoon salt
a pinch of cayenne pepper
¼ teaspoon mustard
½ pint milk
¼ teaspoon Worcester sauce
3 ounces grated cheese
extra tablespoonful of grated
    cheese for topping

Drain the asparagus well, place 2 spears on each piece of ham and roll up. Arrange in a greased casserole dish.

Melt the butter in a saucepan and sauté the onion and green pepper until soft but not brown. Stir in the flour and cook for a few more minutes, then season with the salt, cayenne and mustard. Add the milk and stir until the sauce boils and thickens.

Cook for 2 minutes, then add the Worcester sauce and the grated cheese. Stir until the cheese melts.

Pour the sauce over the rolls and sprinkle with the extra cheese. Bake in a moderate oven, 350°F., for about 20 minutes or until the cheese on top melts and browns and the sauce bubbles.

ASPARAGUS CREAM RAMEKINS

3 dessertspoons butter
3 level tablespoons plain flour
½ teaspoon salt
a pinch of pepper
1 teaspoon mustard
1½ cups milk
1 large can of asparagus spears
2 tablespoons cream
3 hard-boiled eggs
½ cup chopped ham
½ cup grated cheese
1 cup fried bread cubes

Melt the butter and add the flour, salt, pepper and mustard. Stir over medium heat until smooth, then cook for 1 minute. Add the milk and stir until the sauce boils and thickens. Drain the liquid from the asparagus and add about ¼ cup to the sauce, then add the cream (if preferred, omit the cream and increase the quantity of asparagus liquid by 2 tablespoonfuls). Fold in chopped hard-boiled eggs, chopped ham, and the asparagus which has been cut into 1-inch pieces.

Spoon the mixture into lightly greased ramekins, sprinkle the tops with grated cheese, then add the fried bread cubes. Bake in a hot oven, 425°F., until the sauce is bubbly.

ASPARAGUS HAM AU GRATIN

2 ounces butter or margarine
¼ cup plain flour
¼ teaspoon dry mustard
¼ teaspoon salt
a pinch of cayenne pepper
2 cups milk
1 cup chopped cooked ham
2 cups soft white breadcrumbs
1 medium-sized can of asparagus
1 cup shredded cheese

Melt the butter in a saucepan and add the flour, mustard, salt and pepper. Stir until smooth, then cook for 1 minute without browning. Add the milk and stir until the sauce boils and thickens. Remove from the heat and add the ham.

Spread 1 cup of the breadcrumbs in the bottom of a greased casserole dish. Add half the drained asparagus, half the cheese, then the remainder of the asparagus. Cover with the creamed ham, top with the rest of the breadcrumbs then with the remaining cheese.

Bake in a moderate oven, 350°F., for about 30 minutes or until the sauce bubbles and the top is lightly browned.

235

ASPARAGUS SAVOURY

14½-ounce can of asparagus
    spears
4 hard-boiled eggs
2 cups sliced cooked potatoes
2 rashers bacon
1 dessertspoon butter
2 rounded dessertspoons plain
    flour
¼ teaspoon salt
a pinch of pepper
1½ cups milk
¼ cup grated cheese
2 tablespoons buttered
    breadcrumbs
parsley to garnish

Cut the well-drained asparagus spears into 2-inch lengths and place in a lightly greased casserole. Cover with a layer of sliced hard-boiled egg, then with a layer of sliced cooked potato. Sprinkle with the cooked and crumbled bacon.

Make a white sauce by melting the butter and adding the plain flour, salt and pepper. Stir until smooth, then cook without browning for 1 minute. Add the milk and cook while stirring well until the sauce boils and thickens. Simmer for 3 minutes. Pour over the ingredients in the casserole and sprinkle with the grated cheese and buttered breadcrumbs.

Bake at 350°F. for about 20 minutes or until the top is browned and the mixture bubbles. Serve garnished with parsley.

ASPARAGUS SOUFFLÉ

1 small can of asparagus spears
1 dessertspoon butter

For the sauce

1 cup milk (or half milk and
    half asparagus liquid)
4 thin slices onion
1 bayleaf
1 clove
1½ tablespoons butter
1½ slightly rounded tablespoons
    plain flour
salt and pepper
nutmeg and paprika
3 eggs, separated

Drain the liquid from the asparagus spears, place them in a saucepan with the dessertspoon of butter and sauté over medium heat until hot. Keep hot while you make the soufflé sauce.

Place the milk in a saucepan with the onion, bayleaf and clove and bring to the boil. Strain and cool.

Melt the 1½ tablespoons butter and add the flour. Stir until smooth, then cook for 1 minute without browning. Add the strained milk, season with salt, pepper, nutmeg and paprika to taste and stir until the sauce boils and thickens. Cook for 2 minutes. Add the egg yolks, and cook for another minute. Beat the egg whites until soft peaks form, then fold into the sauce.

Place the hot asparagus spears in a greased soufflé dish and pour over the soufflé sauce. Bake at 350°F. for 35 to 40 minutes. Serve immediately.

BACON AND TOMATO PIZZA

For the pizza crust

2 ounces plain flour
2 ounces self-raising flour
¼ teaspoon salt
¼ level teaspoon dry mustard
a pinch of cayenne pepper
1 ounce butter or margarine
1 egg
about 2 tablespoons milk

Sift the flours into a bowl with the salt, mustard and cayenne. Rub in the butter or margarine.

Beat the egg with the milk and use to mix the dry ingredients into a rather firm dough. Turn onto a floured board and knead only until smooth on the outside. Roll out ⅛ inch thick and use to line a pizza plate, pressing the dough neatly into the form of the plate.

Sauté the bacon lightly in a pan and drain it, reserving about 2 tablespoons of the bacon fat. In this fat sauté the onion slices until tender.

For the filling

½ pound bacon rashers
2 cups sliced onion
3 tomatoes
1 teaspoon oregano
½ teaspoon salt
¼ teaspoon pepper
8 ounces Mozzarello cheese
¼ cup stuffed olives

Peel the tomatoes and cut into ¼-inch-thick slices. Arrange these in a single layer in the uncooked pizza shell, spread over them the sautéed onion and sprinkle with the oregano, salt and pepper. Cover with the bacon rashers and arrange slices of cheese and stuffed olive over all.

Bake at 375°F. for 20 to 25 minutes or until the crust is cooked and the cheese melted and lightly browned. Serve piping hot cut into wedges.

BEEF CHARLOTTE

4 rounded tablespoons bacon fat
   or margarine
about 10 slices bread
1 dessertspoon margarine or
   butter for filling
1 medium-sized onion
1 pound finely minced steak
½ teaspoon salt
a dash of pepper
¾ cup tomato soup
2 tablespoons chopped parsley
2 tablespoons grated cheese

Melt the bacon fat or margarine in a saucepan. Remove the crusts and cut the bread into finger lengths. Brush each finger of bread on both sides with the melted fat or margarine. Use some of these fingers to line the bottom and sides of an 8-inch tart plate. Keep the remainder for the top.

Melt the dessertspoon of margarine or butter in a pan, add the finely chopped onion and cook until soft but not brown. Add the minced steak and cook, stirring well until it changes colour. Add the salt, pepper, tomato soup and chopped parsley. When boiling, reduce the heat, cover and simmer for 10 minutes.

Pour into the lined tart plate, top with the remaining fingers of bread and sprinkle with the grated cheese. Bake in a hot oven, 425°F., for 20 minutes or until a golden brown. Serve immediately.

BEEF CROQUETTES

2 rashers of bacon
½ pound finely minced steak
1½ to 2 cups mashed potato
2 tablespoons finely chopped
   onion
1 tablespoon finely chopped
   parsley
salt and pepper
seasoned flour
beaten egg and about
   1 tablespoon milk
breadcrumbs
fat or oil for frying

Sauté the bacon until crisp. Drain and dice. Add the meat to the fat left in the pan, and cook, stirring well until it changes colour. Combine with the mashed potato, onion, bacon and parsley and season to taste with salt and pepper. Chill well to make the mixture easier to handle.

Take spoonfuls of the mixture and shape into croquettes or cork shapes in the seasoned flour. Beat the egg with the milk and use to coat each croquette before covering with the breadcrumbs. Deep-fry the croquettes until they are golden in colour, and drain on paper. Serve garnished with wedges of fresh tomato, accompanied by vegetables in season.

BRAIN AND WALNUT PIES

3 sets cooked brains
1½ cups medium thick white
   sauce

Cut the brains into small pieces and mix with the sauce. Add chopped ham and walnuts.

Roll the pastry thinly and cut some into rounds to line small

237

2 ounces cooked ham
½ cup chopped walnuts
½ pound flaky pastry

patty cases. Cut an equal number of rounds a little smaller to cover the pies.

Place a spoonful of the brain mixture in each lined patty case, glaze the edges with water and cover with a smaller round of pastry. Make a hole in the top of each to allow the steam to escape. Bake in a hot oven, 450°F., for about 20 minutes.

BRAIN CAKES

2 sets cooked brains
1½ dessertspoons butter
3 level tablespoons plain flour
½ teaspoon salt
a pinch of cayenne pepper
a pinch of nutmeg
1 cup milk
1 hard-boiled egg
seasoned flour
1 egg beaten with 1 tablespoon
   milk
breadcrumbs
fat or oil for frying
grilled bacon or tomato wedges
   for serving
parsley sprigs

Cut the well-chilled cooked brains into ½-inch pieces. Melt the butter in a saucepan, add the flour and stir until smooth, then cook for 1 minute without browning. Flavour with the salt, cayenne and nutmeg. Add the milk and stir until the sauce boils and thickens—it will be very thick.

Fold in the chopped brains and chopped egg and turn onto a plate to become quite cold. Take spoonfuls of the mixture and shape into round flat cakes in seasoned flour. Dip each cake in the egg and milk mixture, then cover with breadcrumbs. Deep-fry in hot fat until a golden brown, then drain on paper.

Serve with grilled bacon rolls or wedges of fresh tomato. Add a garnish of parsley sprigs.

BRAINS ITALIAN STYLE

4 sets cooked brains
2 slightly beaten eggs
2 teaspoons cold water
½ teaspoon grated Parmesan
   cheese
½ teaspoon chopped parsley
¼ teaspoon salt
a pinch of pepper
breadcrumbs
oil for frying

For the sauce

2 dessertspoons butter
3 cups sliced tomatoes
2 stalks celery, chopped
1 slice of onion
1 bayleaf
2 dessertspoons cornflour
½ teaspoon salt
a pinch of pepper
½ teaspoon sugar
a little water or stock

Cut the brains into quarters. Blend the beaten eggs, water, cheese, parsley, salt and pepper.

Dip the pieces of brain in this mixture, then roll them in breadcrumbs. Fry in hot oil until a golden brown on all sides, then drain on paper. Serve with the tomato sauce.

To make the sauce melt the butter in a saucepan and fry the tomato slices, chopped celery, slice of onion and bayleaf until soft. Cover and simmer for 15 minutes, then press through a sieve. Blend the cornflour with the salt, pepper, sugar and a little water or stock, add to the tomato purée and stir over medium heat until the sauce boils and thickens. Simmer for 2 minutes before serving.

BURGER PIZZA

1 unbaked pizza crust (see bacon and tomato pizza, page 236)
1 tablespoon butter
1 tablespoon oil
½ pound finely minced steak
1 large onion
1 clove of garlic
1 tablespoon chopped celery
1 tablespoon chopped parsley
3 medium tomatoes
2 ounces salami
¼ pound sharp cheese

Prepare the pizza crust and dot with pieces of butter.

Heat the oil in a pan and lightly sauté the minced steak until it changes colour. Turn onto a plate and allow to cool.

Combine chopped onion, crushed garlic, and chopped celery and parsley. Spread the minced steak over the uncooked pastry and sprinkle the onion mixture over it. Arrange over-lapping tomato slices and thinly sliced salami on top, then add thin slices of cheese.

Bake at 375°F. for about 25 minutes or until the filling is cooked and the pastry nicely browned.

CAULIFLOWER AND BACON FLAN

6 ounces cheese pastry
1 medium-sized cauliflower
2 tablespoons grated cheese
½ teaspoon mustard
a pinch of cayenne pepper
1½ cups white sauce
3 rashers of bacon

Roll the pastry to fit an 8-inch tart plate. Bake at 450°F. for 15 minutes. Place the cooked and well-drained cauliflower in the pastry case. Add the grated cheese, mustard and cayenne to the white sauce and when the cheese has melted, pour the sauce over the cauliflower.

Chop the bacon and toss in a pan over medium heat until the fat is clear. Sprinkle this over the sauce. Place in a moderate oven, 350°F., to reheat before serving.

CAULIFLOWER AND OYSTER FLAN

6 ounces good shortcrust or cheese pastry
1 medium-sized cauliflower
¾ pint white sauce
a squeeze of lemon juice
1 egg yolk
1 dozen oysters
2 tablespoons grated cheese
1 tablespoon breadcrumbs
6 small bacon rolls

Roll the pastry to fit an 8-inch tart plate. Bake at 450°F. for 15 minutes. Meanwhile prepare the filling. First cook the cauli-flower in boiling salted water until tender, drain thoroughly and place in the cooked pastry case. Make the white sauce, adding the lemon juice and egg yolk. Stir until boiling. Beard the oysters, add to the hot sauce and pour over the cauliflower in the pie-case.

Sprinkle the top with the grated cheese and breadcrumbs and add the bacon rolls. Place in a moderate oven, 350°F., to lightly brown and melt the cheese and cook the bacon. Serve as a luncheon dish.

CHEESE AND BACON SOUFFLÉ

3 dessertspoons butter
½ cup chopped bacon
4 dessertspoons plain flour
¼ teaspoon dry mustard
¼ teaspoon salt
a pinch of cayenne pepper
1 cup milk
1 cup grated tasty cheese
3 eggs, separated
¼ teaspoon cream of tartar

Melt the butter in a medium-sized saucepan, add the bacon, and fry lightly until the bacon fat is clear. Add the plain flour, stir until smooth then cook without browning for 3 minutes. Season with the mustard, salt and cayenne and add the milk. Stir until the sauce boils and thickens, then add the cheese and stir until it has melted. Let the sauce cool, then stir in the egg yolk.

Place the egg whites in a clean dry bowl with the cream of tartar and beat until stiff. Fold into the cheese and bacon mixture.

Pour into a well-greased soufflé dish and bake in a moderate oven, 325°F., for about 60 minutes. Serve immediately.

CHEESE AND KIDNEY CHARLOTTE

6 sheep's kidneys or 1 ox kidney
1 good-sized onion
1½ cups cold water
½ teaspoon salt
a good pinch of pepper
1 teaspoon lemon juice
3 bacon rashers
2 tablespoons plain flour
2 eggs
¾ cup milk
8 slices bread
1 cup grated tasty cheese

Soak the kidneys for about 15 minutes in tepid water. Drain and dry, then remove the fine skin and white core. Chop finely and place in a saucepan with the peeled and sliced onion, the cold water, salt, pepper and lemon juice, and the bacon rashers which have the rind removed.

Cover and simmer until the kidney is tender. Take off the heat. Blend the flour with a little cold water and stir into the mixture, return the saucepan to the heat and cook, stirring well until the mixture boils. Cook for a further minute. Set aside.

Beat the eggs lightly and add the milk. Remove the crusts and cut each slice of bread in half then dip the pieces lightly into the egg and milk mixture, then into the grated cheese.

Line a buttered dish with some of the bread slices and spoon in the kidney mixture. Cover with the remaining bread slices and add any left-over cheese.

Bake in a moderate oven, 350°F., for about 20 minutes or until the cheese on top has melted and cooked to a golden brown. Garnish with parsley and serve hot.

CHICKEN CRUNCH

¾ cup uncooked rice
1 medium-sized onion
1 tablespoon butter
1 medium-sized green pepper
3 cups diced celery
1¼ cups chicken stock
1 dessertspoon soy sauce
2 cups diced cooked chicken
1 small can of buttered
　　mushrooms
salt and pepper
1 tablespoon cornflour
½ cup slivered almonds
freshly boiled rice

Cook the rice in plenty of boiling salted water. Sauté chopped onion in the butter until tender. Stir in chopped green pepper, diced celery, chicken stock and soy sauce.

Simmer for 10 minutes, then add the chicken and mushrooms. Season to taste with salt and pepper.

Blend the cornflour with a little cold water and stir into the chicken mixture. Cook, stirring well until the mixture returns to the boil. Add the nuts. Serve over freshly cooked rice.

CHICKEN LIVER SAUTÉ

½ pound bacon rashers
¾ pound chicken livers
seasoned flour
1 cup stock, or water and a soup
　　cube
1 small can of buttered
　　mushrooms
1 tablespoon soy sauce
2 tablespoons sherry
salt and pepper
hot buttered toast
parsley sprigs to garnish

Remove the rind from the bacon, cut each rasher into 2 or 3 pieces and make into small rolls, securing each with a cocktail pick. Place the rolls in a dry pan and cook until the bacon fat is clear. Lift out and keep hot.

Roll the chicken livers in seasoned flour and cook in the pan with the bacon fat for about 10 minutes. Lift out. Add about 1 tablespoon of seasoned flour to the pan and stir until brown, then pour in the stock or water and stir until boiling. Add the mushrooms, soy sauce, and sherry with salt and pepper to taste. Replace the cooked livers in the hot gravy and cook for a few more minutes. Pile onto hot buttered toast, top with the bacon rolls and garnish with parsley sprigs.

CURRIED LAMB PIES

1 dessertspoon fat
1 teaspoon finely chopped onion
1 rounded dessertspoon plain
    flour
1 rounded teaspoon curry
    powder
salt and pepper
1 soup cube
1 cup stock or water
1 cup chopped cooked lamb
½ an apple
2 tablespoons coconut
a squeeze of lemon juice
½ pound flaky pastry
egg glazing (1 egg beaten with a
    little milk)

Melt the fat in a saucepan, add the onion and cook until soft and brown. Add the flour and curry powder, and salt and pepper to taste. Cook for 1 minute. Dissolve the soup cube in the stock or water and add, stirring until the mixture boils and thickens. Add the lamb, peeled and diced apple, the coconut and the lemon juice. Allow to cool.

Roll the pastry and cut some into rounds to line small patty tins, with smaller rounds to cover. Place one of the larger rounds in each patty tin and add a spoonful of the curried mixture to each. Glaze the edges and cover with a small round of pastry.

Make a small hole in the centre of each pie. Brush the tops with egg glazing. Bake in a hot oven, 450°F., for 15 or 20 minutes.

FRESH CORN SOUFFLÉ

2 tablespoons butter
1 tablespoon finely chopped
    onion
2½ tablespoons plain flour
1 teaspoon salt
a dash of pepper
¾ cup milk
2 cups freshly cooked corn,
    scraped from the cob
5 eggs, separated

Melt the butter in a saucepan and sauté the onion until soft but not brown. Stir in the flour, salt and pepper. Cook, stirring well, for 1 minute (do not allow to brown). Remove from the heat, add the milk, and return the saucepan to the heat. Stir until the sauce boils and thickens, then add the corn and cook for a further minute.

Remove from the heat, add the egg yolks, return the pan to the heat and cook for a few seconds.

Place the egg whites in a warm, dry bowl, add a pinch of salt and beat until stiff. Fold half into the sauce, then lightly stir in the remainder.

Turn the mixture into a greased soufflé dish and bake in a moderate oven, 350°F., for 40 to 45 minutes. Serve immediately.

FRIED RICE BAMBOO

1½ cups raw rice
½ pound pork fillets
1 slightly rounded teaspoon
    cornflour
a pinch of salt
a pinch of pepper
1 teaspoon sugar
1 dessertspoon soy sauce
½ bunch spring onions
1 egg beaten with ¼ cup milk
2 tablespoons lard or peanut oil
½ pound firm cooked peas

The day before the dish of fried rice is to be made, wash the rice thoroughly and cook in plenty of boiling salted water. Drain, rinse and spread to dry.

Slice the pork into very thin strips and place in a bowl with the cornflour, salt, pepper, sugar and soy sauce, mixing to make sure each piece of pork is coated. Trim and wash the spring onions then chop into small dice. Beat the egg, mix with the milk, and season lightly with salt and pepper.

Heat the oil in a pan until it is smoking. Add the pork pieces and sauté over high heat, turning the meat frequently until it is browned on all sides. Remove from the pan and chop into small pieces.

241

Return the frying pan to the heat, add a little more oil and lightly fry the onions and the peas. Add the minced pork and the cooked rice, mixing well together. Heat thoroughly over low heat.

In a separate pan fry the egg and milk mixture, making a thin, flat omelette. Chop and add to the rice in the pan. Reheat thoroughly, adjusting the seasonings and using a little more soy sauce if liked, or serve with soy sauce.

ITALIAN CHEESE PIE

6 ounces shortcrust pastry
4 good-sized tomatoes
two 4-ounce cans of sardines
2 cups grated cheese
2 dessertspoons chopped onion
salt and pepper
1 dessertspoon finely chopped parsley
8 stuffed olives
2 teaspoons Worcester sauce
1 rounded tablespoon plain flour

Roll the pastry to line an 8-inch tart plate. Prick the bottom to prevent rising, and pinch a frill round the edge. Bake in a hot oven, 400°F., for 10 to 12 minutes.

While the pastry shell is cooking, cut two of the tomatoes into thin slices and the other two into slices about $\frac{1}{4}$ inch thick. Reserve the thin slices for topping the pie.

Drain the oil from the sardines and arrange them in the cooked pastry shell. Cover with a layer of grated cheese, add the onion, some salt and pepper, the parsley, the sliced olives and the thick slices of tomato. Sprinkle with the Worcester sauce, add another layer of grated cheese, then dust lightly with the plain flour.

Arrange the thin slices of tomato in the form of petals on top of the pie. Place in a slow oven for about 20 minutes to heat and cook the filling.

ITALIAN RISOTTO WITH HAM

4 ounces butter
1 onion
$1\frac{1}{2}$ cups raw rice
$2\frac{1}{2}$ cups consommé or chicken stock
1 cup water
2 teaspoons salt
a pinch of pepper
1 cup diced ham
grated Parmesan cheese

Heat the butter in a pan, add chopped onion and sauté until soft. Add the rice and cook to a straw colour, stirring constantly. Add enough hot consommé and water to just cover the rice, stir well and continue to cook, adding more water or stock as needed and stirring to prevent sticking and burning.

When the rice is a little more than half done, add the salt, pepper and ham. Continue cooking, adding more liquid as required and continuing to stir.

When the rice is soft and most of the liquid has been absorbed, take off the heat and turn the rice into a dish. Sprinkle with the cheese just before serving.

KIDNEY D'AMOUR

6 rashers of bacon
9 sheep's kidneys or $1\frac{1}{2}$ ox kidneys
seasoned flour
1 tablespoon chopped onion
$1\frac{1}{2}$ cups stock, or $1\frac{1}{2}$ cups water and a soup cube

Remove the rind from the bacon and cut the rashers into small pieces. Roll each piece up and secure with cocktail picks. Fry lightly in a pan until the fat is clear.

Soak the kidneys in tepid water for 30 minutes. Drain and dry them and remove the white tubes, then slice and roll in seasoned flour.

Remove the bacon from the pan, add the kidney slices and

242

salt and pepper
½ teaspoon mixed mustard
1 teaspoon lemon juice
1 teaspoon sugar
2 tablespoons sherry or port
3 eggs
¼ teaspoon salt and a dash of
    pepper for eggs
4 tablespoons milk
1 tablespoon chopped parsley
parsley sprigs to garnish

fry lightly. Add the chopped onion and fry for a further 3 minutes, then add the stock, salt and pepper to taste, mustard, lemon juice and sugar. Stir until boiling. Cover and simmer for about 40 minutes (the time will depend on the thickness of the kidney slices).

Add the sherry or port, and thicken if necessary with a little blended flour.

Scramble the eggs with the salt, pepper, milk and chopped parsley. Place the cooked kidney on a hot serving dish and surround with the scrambled egg. Garnish with the bacon rolls and some parsley sprigs.

LITTLE CHICKEN RAMEKINS

2 medium-sized carrots
2 medium-sized potatoes
1 pint white sauce
1 teaspoon chopped parsley
3 cups chopped cooked chicken
¼ cup chopped celery
2 tablespoons minced onion
2 tablespoons chopped cooked
    bacon or ham
1 small can of buttered
    mushrooms
4 ounces shortcrust pastry or 1
    pound fluffy mashed potato

Cook the carrots and potatoes until almost tender. Drain and cut into ½-inch pieces. Divide evenly between six greased ramekins.

Make the white sauce and add the parsley, chicken, celery, onion, bacon and mushrooms. Spoon this over the vegetables in the ramekins.

Roll the pastry thinly and cut into six rounds large enough to cover the top of each ramekin. Tuck the pastry inside the rim of the ramekin, make a slit or two in the top to allow the steam to escape, and bake in a hot oven, 425°F., for about 20 minutes.

Instead of the pastry, fluffy mashed potato could be spread or piped on top—in this case bake in a moderate oven, 350°F., until the sauce mixture bubbles and the potato topping is a light brown.

MACARONI CHEESE

1 rounded tablespoon butter
2 rounded tablespoons plain
    flour
¼ teaspoon salt
a dash of cayenne pepper
½ level teaspoon mustard
2 cups milk
1 cup cooked macaroni
¾ cup grated cheese
1 tablespoon soft white
    breadcrumbs

Melt the butter in a saucepan and add the flour, salt, cayenne and mustard. Stir until smooth, then cook for 1 minute over medium heat. Do not allow to brown.

Add the milk and stir until the sauce boils and thickens. Stir in the cooked macaroni and half the grated cheese.

Place in a greased casserole and sprinkle the remainder of the cheese and the breadcrumbs on top. Bake in a moderate oven until the sauce bubbles and the cheese melts and lightly browns.

243

MACARONI SUPPER RAMEKINS

½ pound macaroni
1 tablespoon butter
1 tablespoon finely minced
   onion
2 tablespoons plain flour
½ teaspoon salt
a pinch of pepper
1 teaspoon mustard
2 cups milk
1 cup grated cheese
1 cup cooked peas
½ teaspoon Worcester sauce
2 hard-boiled eggs
2 tomatoes

Cook the macaroni in plenty of boiling salted water for 15 minutes, then drain. Melt the butter in a saucepan and sauté the onion until soft but not brown. Add the plain flour, salt, pepper and mustard. Cook for 1 minute. Add the milk and continue to cook, stirring well, until the sauce boils and thickens.

Remove the sauce from the heat and add the macaroni and half the grated cheese. If peas are used, add them at this stage. Flavour with the Worcester sauce. Shell and quarter the eggs and add to the mixture.

Divide evenly between six well-greased ramekins and top each with a thick slice of tomato and a sprinkling of the remaining cheese. Bake in a moderate oven, 350°F., until the cheese melts and browns and the tomato softens.

MEATBALL AND MOZZARELLO PIZZA

1 pound finely minced steak
¼ cup dry breadcrumbs
2 tablespoons minced onion
1 egg
1 teaspoon salt
¼ teaspoon pepper
½ teaspoon oregano
3 dessertspoons olive oil
1½ cups tomato sauce
   (recipe follows)
8 ounces grated Mozzarello
   cheese
1 unbaked pizza case (see bacon
   and tomato pizza, page 236).

Combine the minced steak with the breadcrumbs, onion, beaten egg, salt, pepper and oregano, mixing until well blended. Shape portions into 1-inch balls, then flatten each with the palm of the hand.

Heat the oil in a pan and brown the meatballs on all sides. This will take about 10 minutes. Drain well.

Spread the tomato sauce over the unbaked pizza case, cover with the meatballs and sprinkle with the cheese.

Bake at 375°F. for 20 to 25 minutes or until the pizza case is cooked and the cheese melted and lightly browned. Cut into wedges and serve piping hot.

TOMATO SAUCE FOR PIZZA

3 dessertspoons oil
1 cup sliced onion
1 clove of garlic
15-ounce can of undrained
   tomatoes
1 dessertspoon chopped parsley
1½ teaspoons salt
1 teaspoon oregano
½ teaspoon sugar
¼ teaspoon basil
¼ teaspoon black pepper

Heat the oil in a medium-sized saucepan and sauté the sliced onion and crushed garlic until the onion is golden.

Add the tomatoes, parsley, salt, oregano, sugar, basil and pepper. Bring to the boil. Reduce the heat, then simmer uncovered for 45 minutes, stirring occasionally. Remove from the heat and allow to cool before using in the pizza fillings.

MOCK CHICKEN FRICASSEE

1½ pounds tripe
1 dessertspoon salt
2 large white onions
1 packet of chicken noodle soup
½ cup milk
2 tablespoons plain flour blended
   with a little cold milk
1 dessertspoon butter
a pinch of cayenne pepper
1 tablespoon chopped parsley

Wash the tripe and cut it into ½-inch squares. Place in a saucepan, cover with cold water and bring to the boil. Drain. Add the salt and onions, cover with fresh cold water, and simmer for 2 hours or until the tripe is tender.

Remove all but 1½ cups of the cooking liquid. Lift out the onion, chop it finely then replace in the saucepan with the tripe. Add the chicken noodle soup and the milk and simmer for 10 minutes.

Add the blended flour to the contents of the saucepan and stir until the mixture comes to the boil, then cook for 3 minutes. Add the butter, cayenne and chopped parsley. Serve with triangles of dry toast.

MUSHROOM AND ONION QUICHE

4 ounces shortcrust pastry
2 medium-sized onions
2 ounces butter
1 small can of buttered
   mushrooms
2 eggs
¾ cup grated cheese
a pinch of dry mustard
a squeeze of lemon juice
salt
1 cup milk

Roll the pastry to line an 8-inch tart plate or sandwich tin.

Slice the onions, melt the butter in a pan and lightly fry the onion until soft but not brown. Cool, then spread in the bottom of the uncooked pastry case. Cover with the mushrooms.

Beat the eggs, add the cheese, mustard, lemon juice, salt to taste, and the milk. Pour carefully over the mushroom mixture in the uncooked pastry case. Bake in a hot oven, 425°F., for 10 minutes, then reduce the heat to moderate, 350°F., and continue baking for a further 20 minutes or until the custard has set and the pastry is lightly browned.

PIZZA MILANO

1 unbaked pizza crust (see bacon
   and tomato pizza, page 236)
1 dessertspoon butter
1 tablespoon olive oil
½ pound finely minced steak
3 medium-sized tomatoes
4 tablespoons finely chopped
   anchovies (optional)
1 large onion
1 clove of garlic
1 tablespoon chopped celery
1 tablespoon chopped parsley
¼ pound good sharp cheese

Prepare the pizza crust and dot with pieces of butter.

Heat the oil in a pan and lightly sauté the minced steak until it changes colour. Turn out onto a plate and allow to cool.

Peel and coarsely chop the tomatoes and combine with the anchovies, finely chopped onion, crushed garlic, chopped celery and parsley, grated cheese and cooked meat. Spread this mixture over the unbaked pizza crust and bake in a moderate oven, 375°F., for 20 to 25 minutes or until the filling is cooked and the crust brown.

245

POTATO ROLL WITH MUSHROOM FILLING

1 medium-sized potato
2½ tablespoons butter
3 eggs, separated
3 to 4 tablespoons sour cream
3 level tablespoons self-raising
    flour
a pinch of salt
dry breadcrumbs

For the filling

1 medium-sized onion
2 tablespoons melted butter or
    oil
½ pound fresh mushrooms
salt and pepper
2 eggs

Boil the potato and grate it. Cream the butter and add the egg yolks one at a time, creaming well with each addition, then add the sour cream, the sifted flour and salt and the grated boiled potato. Beat the egg whites stiffly and fold into the mixture.

Grease a Swiss roll tin well with butter and sprinkle with breadcrumbs. Spread the potato mixture evenly in the tin. Bake at 350°F. for 30 minutes. Turn out and, while still hot, roll up like a Swiss roll. Unroll, fill with the mushroom filling and serve sliced.

To make the filling, chop the onion and fry it in the heated butter until soft but not brown; add sliced mushrooms and cook until soft, seasoning with salt and pepper. Beat the eggs, add to the mixture and cook, stirring with a wooden spoon until the mixture resembles scrambled eggs.

QUICHE LORRAINE

2 or 3 rashers of bacon
4 ounces shortcrust pastry
2 eggs
1 to 1½ cups grated cheese
½ pint milk (for half milk and
    half cream)
salt
a dash of cayenne pepper and of
    dry mustard
1 tomato for garnishing

Chop the bacon (after removing the rind) and fry lightly. Lift out and drain.

Roll the pastry thinly and line a greased 8-inch tart plate or sandwich tin. Sprinkle with the cooked bacon.

Beat the eggs with the cheese, milk, salt to taste, cayenne and mustard. Pour over the bacon in the flan.

Bake in a hot oven, 450°F., for 10 minutes. Reduce the heat to moderate, 350°F., and bake for a further 20 minutes or until the cheese custard filling has set.

Garnish the top with thin slices of peeled tomato before serving.

BACON QUICHE

Use the same method as given for Quiche Lorraine but omit the fried bacon. Instead, take rashers of bacon, remove the rind, and when the quiche has been baking for about 20 minutes, lattice the top with bacon strips and allow them to cook with the quiche.

You may prefer to garnish the baked quiche, just before serving, with strips of hot cooked bacon and slices of stuffed olives.

RISOTTO PROVENCAL

For the risotto
2 tablespoons olive oil
1 large onion
½ pound raw rice

Heat the oil for the risotto in a pan and sauté the chopped onion until golden. Add the rice and cook, stirring constantly, until it is golden. Moisten with ½ pint of hot water and simmer gently, stirring occasionally and adding more hot water as

246

hot water
salt and pepper

For the sauce

2 tablespoons finely chopped
   onion
1 tablespoon olive oil
¼ pint dry white wine
4 tomatoes
salt and pepper
1 clove of garlic
2 tablespoons chopped parsley
¼ teaspoon saffron powder
½ green pepper

½ cup raw rice
1 tablespoon butter
2 cups chicken broth, or water
   and a chicken soup cube
¼ cup grated cheese
a dash each of cayenne pepper
   and paprika
a pinch of saffron
1 teaspoon salt
1 small clove of garlic (optional)

1 pound finely minced steak
¼ pound Italian sausage
1 egg
1 cup soft white breadcrumbs
½ cup milk
1 clove of garlic
1 small onion
1 teaspoon salt
1 tablespoon butter
1 tablespoon oil

1½ cups tomato sauce (page 244)
1 unbaked pizza crust (see bacon
   and tomato pizza, page 236)
¼ pound salami
½ cup onion rings
½ cup green pepper rings
8 ounces Mozzarello cheese

required and as the liquid is absorbed by the rice. Continue cooking until the rice is soft but not mushy. Season to taste with salt and pepper.

To make the sauce, sauté the 2 tablespoons onion in the oil until tender, then stir in the wine. Add peeled and coarsely chopped tomatoes. Season with salt and pepper, then add crushed garlic, chopped parsley and saffron. Simmer gently for 20 minutes, then add finely chopped green pepper and simmer for a further 15 minutes.

RISOTTO WITH SAUSAGEBURGERS

Sauté the raw rice in the butter until a straw colour. Pour the heated broth over it, then add the cheese, cayenne, paprika, saffron, salt and the garlic if used. Steam in the top of a double saucepan for about 30 minutes or until the rice is tender but not mushy, stirring occasionally to prevent sticking. Serve topped with sausageburgers.

SAUSAGEBURGERS

Mix the minced steak, finely chopped or minced sausage and slightly beaten egg. Soak the breadcrumbs in the milk, squeeze dry and combine with the meat. Sauté crushed garlic, chopped onion in the butter with the salt. Add this to the meat mixture, then form into tiny balls and brown quickly in hot oil. Cover and cook for about 5 minutes.

SALAMI AND GREEN PEPPER PIZZA

Spread the tomato sauce over the unbaked pizza crust and arrange salami slices, onion rings and green pepper rings on top. Cover with sliced cheese.

Bake at 375°F. for 20 to 25 minutes or until the crust is cooked and the cheese melted and lightly browned. Serve piping hot.

247

SAUSAGE AND EGG CASSEROLE

1 pound pork sausage mince
4 hard-boiled eggs
2 tablespoons butter
¼ cup plain flour
½ teaspoon salt
a dash of pepper
2 cups milk
1-pound can of whole kernel
  corn
2 tablespoons chopped parsley
1 cup buttered breadcrumbs
parsley

Brown the pork sausage mince and drain it of any fat.

Remove the shells from the eggs, slice 2 of them and place in a well-greased 3-pint casserole.

Melt the butter in a saucepan, add the flour and stir until smooth, then cook for 1 minute without browning. Season with the salt and pepper, then add the milk and stir until the sauce boils and thickens. Stir in the well-drained corn and parsley, and simmer for 3 minutes.

Pour half the sauce over the sliced eggs in the casserole and arrange the browned and drained pork mince on top. Cover with the rest of the sauce. Slice the remaining eggs and place on top, then sprinkle with buttered breadcrumbs.

Bake at 375°F. for 20 to 25 minutes or until the crumbs are brown and the filling heated through. Garnish with parsley.

SALMON AND ASPARAGUS CHANTILLY

1-pound can of salmon
milk
2 tablespoons butter
2 teaspoons grated or finely
  chopped onion or shallot
2 slightly rounded tablespoons
  plain flour
1 dessertspoon chopped parsley
1 teaspoon mixed mustard
1 tablespoon mayonnaise
1 level teaspoon salt
a little pepper
3 hard-boiled eggs
1 small can of asparagus spears
2 tablespoons soft white
  breadcrumbs
2 tablespoons grated cheese
lemon and parsley to garnish

Drain the liquid from the salmon, remove the skin and bones and flake the flesh lightly. Measure the salmon liquid and make up to 2 cups with milk.

Melt the butter in a saucepan, add the onion and sauté until soft but not brown. Stir in the flour and cook for 1 minute, then add the milk. Cook, stirring constantly until the sauce boils and thickens, then remove from the heat and add the parsley, mustard, mayonnaise, salt and pepper.

Place a layer of the sauce in a lightly greased casserole, then add alternate layers of salmon, sliced egg and asparagus. Cover with the remainder of the sauce, and sprinkle the top with the combined breadcrumbs and cheese.

Bake in a moderate oven, 350°F., for about 30 minutes or until the top is lightly browned. Serve garnished with lemon and parsley.

SAUSAGE AND TOMATO PIE

1 small onion
1 teaspoon butter or margarine
1 pound pork sausages
2 large tomatoes
¼ pint stock or water
1 pound mashed potatoes
milk
butter

Peel and slice the onion and fry it in the teaspoon of butter until it is quite soft. Place the sausages in tepid water, bring to the boil, simmer for 5 minutes, then drain. Take off the skin, slice the sausages and place half of them in a shallow dish. Skin and slice the tomatoes and place half the slices on top of the sausage, then add the onion. Season with salt and pepper and add the stock or water, then the remaining slices of sausage and the rest of the sliced tomato.

Spread a thick layer of mashed potato over the top, brush with milk and dot with small pieces of butter. Score the surface with the back of a knife.

Bake in a hot oven, 400°F., until the potato topping is a golden brown.

248

Salmon and Asparagus Chantilly

SEAFOOD QUICHE

4 to 6 ounces shortcrust pastry
a little egg white
¼ pound shredded cooked or canned crabmeat, prawns or crayfish
2 tablespoons chopped spring onions
½ cup coarsely grated Swiss or Cheddar cheese
2 eggs
⅔ cup milk
1 tablespoon tomato paste
½ teaspoon salt
¼ teaspoon pepper

Line an 8-inch flan tin or pie plate with the pastry. Brush the surface with egg white. Spread the seafood over the pastry, then sprinkle with the spring onion and half the cheese.

Beat together the eggs, milk, tomato paste, salt and pepper. Pour over the seafood and onions and sprinkle with the remaining cheese.

Bake in a hot oven, 425°F., for 10 minutes. Reduce the heat to 350°F. and bake for a further 30 to 35 minutes or until the custard has set and the top is a golden colour.

SPAGHETTI BOLOGNESE

3 ounces butter
1 onion
2 rashers of streaky bacon
1 carrot
1 stalk of celery
4 ounces finely minced steak
2 ounces chicken livers
1 dessertspoon tomato paste

Melt 1 ounce of the butter, slice the onion and sauté until soft but not brown. Add chopped bacon, diced carrot, and chopped celery, and cook and stir until lightly browned. Add the minced meat and stir over the heat until all of it is moistened, then add the chicken livers, stirring and cooking till moistened also. Add the tomato paste, wine and stock, season with salt and pepper, then add crushed garlic. Cover and simmer gently for 40 minutes or until the sauce is thick and the meat very tender.

¼ pint white wine
½ pint stock, or water and a soup
   cube
salt and pepper
1 clove of garlic
12 ounces spaghetti
4 ounces grated cheese for
   topping

1 medium-sized can of kernel-
   style sweet corn
1 cup white sauce
1 cup cooked and drained green
   peas
1 tablespoon chopped red or
   green pepper
1 teaspoon chopped shallot
2 rashers of bacon

6 slices bacon
6 ounces shortcrust pastry
1 medium-sized firm tomato
3 eggs
1¼ cups milk
½ teaspoon salt
¼ teaspoon pepper
¼ cup finely chopped parsley
4 ounces grated Cheddar cheese

1 bayleaf
4 thin slices of onion
1 clove
¾ cup milk
1 tablespoon butter
2 tablespoons plain flour
½ cup tomato purée or soup
¼ teaspoon salt
a dash of pepper
1¼ cups grated cheese
4 eggs, separated
a pinch of salt for egg whites
¼ teaspoon dry mustard or curry
   powder

Cook the spaghetti in the usual way. Drain, then stir in one-third of the meat sauce and the remaining 2 ounces of butter. Place in a hot serving dish, pour over the remainder of the sauce and sprinkle liberally with grated cheese.

SWEET CORN AND GREEN PEA RAMEKINS

Drain the liquid from the sweet corn. Mix the corn with the white sauce and add the peas and the chopped pepper and shallot.

Remove the rind from the bacon, and cut each rasher in half, then roll and secure each piece with a skewer or a cocktail pick.

Divide the sweet corn mixture between four lightly greased ramekins. Top each with a bacon roll. Bake in a moderate oven, 350°F., for about 15 minutes or until the sauce bubbles and the bacon is cooked.

TOMATO CHEESE PIE

Fry the bacon crisply, drain, then crumble it.

Roll the pastry thinly and use to line an 8-inch tart plate. Flute or pinch the edges. Cut the tomato into eight wedges and arrange on the bottom of the uncooked pastry case.

Beat the eggs with the milk, salt, pepper and chopped parsley, and sprinkle in the grated cheese and crumbled bacon. Pour this over the tomato wedges.

Bake in a hot oven, 450°F., for 10 minutes. Reduce the temperature to 325°F. and bake for another 30 to 35 minutes or until the custard has set and is lightly browned. Let stand for 10 minutes, then cut into wedges to serve.

TOMATO CHEESE SOUFFLE

Place the milk in a saucepan, add the bayleaf, onion and clove and bring to the boil. Strain and cool.

Melt the butter in another saucepan, add the flour and stir until smooth, then cook for another minute without browning. Add the strained milk and stir and cook until the sauce boils and thickens. Add the tomato purée, the salt, pepper and grated cheese. Remove from the heat and add the egg yolks, beating well.

Add a pinch of salt to the egg whites and beat until peaks form, then add the dry mustard or curry powder. Fold into the tomato and cheese mixture, then place in a greased soufflé dish and bake in a moderate oven, 350°F., for 35 to 40 minutes or until puffed and brown.

250

Lobster Thermidor with Curried Rice,
Curried Prawns, Seafood Cocktail

TRIPE AND TOMATO PIE

3 tablespoons butter or
   margarine
3 level tablespoons plain flour
½ teaspoon salt
a good pinch of pepper
2 cups milk
4 ounces bacon
3 tomatoes
2 pounds cooked tripe cut into
   1-inch squares
1 egg
2 cups mashed potato
2 tablespoons grated cheese for
   topping

Melt the butter in a saucepan, add the flour, salt and pepper, and stir until smooth. Cook for another minute without browning, then add the milk and stir and cook until the sauce boils and thickens.

Lightly fry or grill the bacon, then cut it into small pieces. Skin and thinly slice the tomatoes.

Stir the cooked tripe squares into the sauce and pour half into a lightly greased casserole. Add half the bacon and tomatoes, then the remainder of the tripe, sauce, bacon and tomatoes.

Add the beaten egg to the mashed potato and spread over the top of the mixture in the casserole. Score the surface with a fork and sprinkle with grated cheese. Bake in a hot oven, 425°F., for about 15 minutes.

VOL-AU-VENT ST GEORGE

1 pound puff pastry
2 level tablespoons butter
2 level tablespoons plain flour
½ level teaspoon salt
a dash of pepper
½ pint milk
2 cups chopped cold cooked
   rabbit, chicken or veal
1 set cooked brains cut into
   1-inch cubes
2 ounces chopped cooked ham
2 ounces chopped cooked
   tongue
1 small can of mushrooms
3 hard-boiled eggs
   (one for decoration)
1 teaspoon chopped parsley

Roll the pastry into an oblong shape about ½ an inch thick. Using a large oval cutter dipped in boiling water, cut out an oval shape, then with a smaller cutter cut halfway through the pastry (as you would when making small patties that are to be filled). Glaze the top lightly with egg yolk and place on a shallow oven tray. Bake in a hot oven, 450°F., for 10 to 15 minutes. Reduce the temperature to 375°F. and bake for a further 10 minutes. Lift the centre piece of pastry and set it aside.

Split the large piece of pastry through the centre and add the filling (method follows), piling it a little higher in the centre. Decorate the centre with slices of hard-boiled egg and top with the small piece of pastry that was set aside.

To make the filling, melt the butter in a saucepan, add the flour, stir until smooth, cook for 1 to 2 minutes without browning, then add the salt, pepper and milk. Stir over medium heat until the mixture boils and thickens, then stir in the chopped meats, the mushrooms, 2 sliced hard-boiled eggs and the chopped parsley. Stir gently over the heat, and when piping hot pile the filling into the hot cooked pastry.

Sweet and Sour Scallops, Fish in Tomato Cases,
Baked Fish with Grapes

FISH

BAKED AND STUFFED BARRAMUNDI

2 or 3 fish steaks
lemon juice
2 cups soft white breadcrumbs
salt and pepper
1 tablespoon butter
a pinch of mixed herbs
1 tablespoon chopped parsley
½ onion or 2 tablespoons
  chopped shallots
1 egg

Rub both sides of each fish steak with lemon juice. Grease a piece of foil, place it in a shallow baking dish and arrange the fish steaks in the dish.

Mix the breadcrumbs with salt and pepper to taste. Rub in the butter. Add the herbs, parsley and chopped onion, and enough beaten egg to bind the mixture together. Place a thick layer of this stuffing on each fish steak. Bake in a moderate oven, 350°F., for about 20 minutes.

BAKED FILLETS AU GRATIN

1½ pounds fish fillets
1 tablespoon chopped onion
1 tablespoon chopped celery
salt and pepper
1 tablespoon lemon juice
2 tablespoons water or white
  wine
1 tablespoon butter
1 tablespoon plain flour
1 cup milk, or milk and fish
  stock
½ cup grated cheese
a good pinch of mustard

Place the fillets in a greased shallow baking dish, sprinkle with the onion and celery, and season with salt and pepper. Add the lemon juice and the 2 tablespoons of water or white wine. Cover and bake in a hot oven, 400°F., for about 10 minutes.

If wine has been used instead of water you may like to include some of the cooking liquid in the sauce. If so, strain and measure the liquid from the fish after cooking it, and make up to 1 cup with milk. Melt the butter in a saucepan, add the flour and stir until smooth. Cook for 1 minute, then add the cup of milk (or milk and fish stock) and stir until the sauce boils and thickens. Add all but 1½ tablespoons of the cheese and season the sauce with mustard, salt and pepper. Stir over the heat until the cheese melts. If a little too thick, add some milk.

Pour the sauce over the fish in the baking dish, and top with the remainder of the cheese. Bake in a moderate oven, 350°F., for about 15 minutes or until the cheese melts and has slightly browned.

BAKED FISH WITH GRAPES

8 thin strips of carrot about 2
  inches long
¼ cup melted butter or salad oil
¼ teaspoon salt
a pinch of pepper
a squeeze of lemon juice
8 fillets of white-fleshed fish
1 tablespoon chopped parsley

Parboil the carrot sticks until almost tender. Drain well, then brush them with melted butter or oil and season with the salt, pepper and lemon juice.

Sprinkle each fish fillet with a little parsley, place a carrot strip on each and roll up. Secure with cocktail picks and place in a shallow greased dish. Add the chopped shallot, the water and the wine and cover with foil. Bake in a moderate oven, 350°F., for about 25 minutes or until the fish is tender.

1 shallot
1 tablespoon water
1 tablespoon white wine

For the sauce
1 level tablespoon butter
1 slightly rounded tablespoon
   plain flour
½ teaspoon mustard
¼ teaspoon salt
a dash of pepper
1 cup milk
1 dessertspoon mayonnaise
peeled grapes and parsley sprigs
   to garnish
paprika (optional)

2 pounds fish fillets
lemon juice
¼ cup melted butter or oil
salt and pepper
monosodium glutamate
parsley and lemon wedges to
   garnish

For the lemon sauce
½ cup mayonnaise
⅓ cup milk
1 teaspoon lemon juice
1 teaspoon capers
a pinch of salt
a dash of pepper
½ pound frozen, cooked or
   canned shrimps

1 medium-sized whiting, bream
   or flathead
lemon juice
2 level tablespoons butter
salt and pepper
lemon and parsley to garnish

For the stuffing
1 rounded tablespoon butter
2 level tablespoons chopped
   onion
2 medium-sized tomatoes
½ level teaspoon mixed herbs
1 cup cooked rice
1 egg

Melt the butter for the sauce in a saucepan, add the flour, stir until smooth and cook for 2 minutes without browning. Add the mustard, salt and pepper, then the milk, and stir over medium heat until the sauce boils and thickens. Cook for 2 minutes, then add the mayonnaise.

Lift the cooked fish rolls onto a hot serving dish and cover with the sauce. Serve garnished with peeled grapes and parsley sprigs and, if liked, sprinkle with paprika.

BAKED FISH WITH LEMON SAUCE

Cut the fish fillets into serving sized pieces and sprinkle lightly with lemon juice. Brush each piece with melted butter or oil and season with salt, pepper and monosodium glutamate.

Arrange the fish in an ovenproof dish and bake uncovered at 450°F. for about 20 minutes or until the flesh is easily flaked with a fork. Do not turn the fish during cooking.

Spoon the lemon sauce over the fish and serve directly from the dish, adding a lemon and parsley garnish.

To make the lemon sauce blend the mayonnaise, milk and lemon juice thoroughly, then add the capers, salt and pepper. Place over a saucepan of boiling water on low heat for about 5 minutes to cook the sauce, then add the shrimps, either chopped or left whole. Heat this sauce again before spooning over the fish.

BAKED FISH WITH RICE STUFFING

Sprinkle the fish inside and out with lemon juice. Melt the 2 tablespoons of butter and brush it over the fish. Season the inside with salt and pepper.

Melt the butter for the stuffing in a pan, add the chopped onion and fry until a golden brown. Chop the tomatoes, add to the pan with the herbs, and cook until soft. Stir in the rice and the beaten egg and cook until the egg has set.

Place half the mixture inside the fish and the remainder down the centre of the back. Cover with greased paper and bake in a moderate oven, 350°F., allowing 8 minutes for every pound weight of fish and 8 minutes over for whole. Serve garnished with lemon and parsley.

BAKED SCALLOPS

Remove the beards from the scallops. Cover with boiling water and allow to stand for 5 minutes. Drain well.

Flavour some melted butter or some top milk or cream with sherry or Worcester sauce. Dip the scallops into this mixture, then roll them in breadcrumbs or crushed cereal flakes. Let the crumbed scallops stand for about 15 minutes. This allows the covering to dry slightly and helps to keep it on during the cooking process.

Grease a shallow dish well with butter and arrange the scallops in a single layer in it. Bake uncovered in a moderate oven, 375°F., for 10 to 15 minutes. Serve with lemon wedges.

BAKED STUFFED FISH

1 whole white-fleshed fish, about 2 pounds
salad oil
1 teaspoon salt
¼ teaspoon pepper
flour and about 1 tablespoon butter for topping

For the stuffing
2 slices bacon
1 cup dried breadcrumbs
1 hard-boiled egg
1 small onion
1 dessertspoon melted butter
1 teaspoon chopped parsley
¼ teaspoon thyme
1 teaspoon Worcester sauce
3 dessertspoons chicken broth
salt and pepper

Wash the fish, wipe it dry, then brush it inside and out with salad oil. Season with the salt and pepper.

Chop the bacon finely and add the breadcrumbs, chopped egg, chopped onion, melted butter, parsley, thyme, Worcester sauce and chicken broth. Season if necessary with salt and pepper. Stuff the fish with this mixture and sew or skewer the opening. Place the fish in a well-greased baking dish, dredge lightly with flour and dot with butter. Bake in a hot oven, 400°F., for 30 minutes. Serve if liked with lemon sauce.

BARRAMUNDI BONNE FEMME

2 fish steaks
2 tablespoons sherry
2 shallots
2 thin slices of lemon
6 peppercorns
4-ounce can of mushrooms
½ pint white sauce
2 tablespoons grated cheese
lemon slices and parsley sprigs for garnishing

Put the fish steaks into a greased shallow baking dish and sprinkle with the sherry. On top of each steak place some chopped shallot, 1 lemon slice and 3 peppercorns. Cover with greased paper or foil and bake in a moderate oven, 350°F., for about 20 minutes or until the flesh of the fish is white and soft. Drain off the liquid and add it to the white sauce.

Spread the mushrooms over the cooked fish (if fresh mushrooms are available, chop and sauté about ½ pound and use in place of the canned mushroom). Pour over the white sauce, sprinkle with the grated cheese and bake in a moderate oven, 350°F., long enough to bubble the sauce and melt and lightly brown the cheese. Garnish with lemon slices and sprigs of parsley.

Barramundi Bonne Femme

CODFISH PATTIES

2 cups cooked and flaked codfish
2 cups cold mashed potato
2 tablespoons finely chopped
  onion
2 tablespoons finely chopped
  parsley
1 dessertspoon lemon juice
$\frac{1}{4}$ level teaspoon dry mustard
a pinch of pepper
1 egg
seasoned flour
egg glazing (1 egg beaten with
  a little milk)
soft white breadcrumbs
fat for frying
lemon slices and parsley sprigs
  for garnishing

Combine the flaked codfish with the mashed potato, onion, parsley, lemon juice, mustard and pepper. Bind with a little beaten egg. Shape into 9 round patties in seasoned flour. Dip into the egg glazing, covering each patty completely, then coat well with the breadcrumbs. Chill for several hours.

Deep-fry the patties in hot fat or oil until a golden brown, adding a few at a time and allowing the fat or oil to reheat after each batch has been cooked. Drain on paper and serve garnished with parsley sprigs and lemon slices. Accompany with parsley sauce or egg sauce if liked.

255

COQUILLES ST JACQUES

butter
6 shallots
1 bouquet garni (parsley, celery
   leaves, bayleaf and thyme)
1½ cups dry white wine
1½ pounds scallops
12 mushrooms
⅓ cup water
juice of 1 lemon
½ teaspoon salt
¼ teaspoon pepper
3 level tablespoons plain flour
½ cup cream or top milk
breadcrumbs and grated cheese
   for topping

Heat 1 tablespoon of butter in a saucepan and sauté the chopped shallots. Add the bouquet garni and the white wine and bring to the boil. Simmer gently for a few minutes.

Clean the scallops and place them in a bowl. Pour over them the hot wine mixture, cover and allow to stand for 10 minutes. Drain, reserving the liquid. Slice the scallops if they are large.

Chop the mushrooms and sauté them for a few minutes in another tablespoon of butter. Add the water, lemon juice, salt and pepper. Simmer gently for a few minutes or until the mushrooms are tender. Drain and reserve the liquid.

Melt another 2 tablespoons of butter in a saucepan and add the flour. Stir until smooth, then cook for 1 minute without browning. Combine the liquid from the mushrooms and the scallops and add to the saucepan. Stir until the sauce boils and thickens. Add the scallops and reheat. Fold in the mushrooms and cream and adjust the seasoning.

Spoon into scallop shells or individual ramekins. Sprinkle with the bread crumbs and cheese and place under the griller until the cheese melts and lightly browns.

CREAMED COD PIE

1½ pounds potatoes
2 ounces butter
salt and pepper
1 rounded tablespoon plain flour
½ teaspoon dry mustard
½ pint milk
2 teaspoons chopped parsley
2 hard-boiled eggs
1½ pounds cooked and flaked
   cod
milk for glazing

Boil the potatoes and mash them with half the butter, seasoning with salt and pepper. Melt the remaining ounce of butter in a saucepan, add the flour and mustard and stir until smooth. Cook for 1 minute, then add the milk and stir over the heat until the sauce boils and thickens. Continue cooking for 2 minutes.

Stir in the chopped parsley, chopped eggs and flaked cod. Line a greased pie-dish with a little more than half the potato, add the creamed cod and spread the remainder of the potato smoothly over the top. Score with a fork and glaze with milk.

Bake in a moderate oven, 350°F., long enough to heat the pie through and lightly brown the top.

CURRIED FISH

4 fish fillets
4 teaspoons chutney
6 tablespoons water
6 peppercorns
a pinch of herbs
1 slice lemon

For the sauce
1 level tablespoon butter

Spread each fish fillet with chutney, roll up and secure with a cocktail pick. Place in a saucepan with the water, peppercorns, herbs, and lemon slice. Cover and simmer for about 15 minutes or until the fish is tender.

To make the sauce, melt the butter in a smaller saucepan, add the flour, salt, pepper and curry powder and stir until smooth. Cook for 2 minutes without browning, then add the milk and stir until the sauce boils and thickens.

Drain the liquid in which the fish was cooked, add a little to

1 slightly rounded tablespoon
   plain flour
½ level teaspoon salt
a pinch of pepper
1½ level teaspoons curry powder
1 cup milk
a squeeze of lemon juice

For serving

1 cup freshly cooked rice
lemon slices and parsley sprigs to
   garnish

1 teaspoon butter
1 teaspoon finely chopped onion
   or shallot
1 teaspoon curry powder
1 cup cooked and flaked fish, or
   an 8-ounce can of salmon
   (drained)
grated rind of 1 lemon
1 dessertspoon chopped parsley
1 teaspoon lemon juice
2 cups mashed freshly cooked
   potato
salt and pepper
1 egg
seasoned flour
breadcrumbs
lemon slices and parsley sprigs to
   garnish

3 pounds prawns
2 ounces butter
¼ cup diced apple
1 medium-sized onion
½ cup diced celery
¼ cup water
2 level tablespoons plain flour
2 level dessertspoons curry
   powder
½ teaspoon salt
a good pinch of pepper
¼ teaspoon turmeric
1¼ cups milk
¾ cup cream
freshly cooked rice for serving

the sauce, and adjust the seasonings. Add a squeeze of lemon juice.

Place the fish rolls in a hot serving dish and cover with the sauce. Serve with a border of freshly cooked rice and a lemon and parsley garnish.

CURRIED FISH CAKES

Melt the butter in a saucepan and add the chopped onion. Cook until soft but not brown. Add the curry powder and cook for a few minutes longer.

Add the flaked fish, lemon rind, parsley, lemon juice and mashed potato. Season with salt and pepper and bind with a little beaten egg (mix the rest of the egg with milk to make egg glazing). Turn onto a plate and allow to cool.

Take spoonfuls of the mixture and shape into round flat cakes in the seasoned flour. Dip in the egg glazing then cover with breadcrumbs. Deep-fry in hot fat until a golden brown. Drain on paper and serve hot with a lemon and parsley garnish.

CURRIED PRAWNS

Shell the prawns. Place the butter in a pan and add diced apple, minced onion and diced celery. Sauté for about 3 minutes or until soft. Add the water, cover and simmer for about 10 minutes or until almost all the liquid has evaporated and the vegetables are quite soft.

Stir in the flour, curry powder, salt, pepper and turmeric, blend until smooth, then cook for 2 minutes. Add the milk and cream and stir over medium heat until the sauce boils and thickens, then simmer for 2 minutes. Add the prepared prawns and continue cooking for a further 3 minutes. Serve on a bed of freshly cooked rice.

CURRIED SCALLOPS

1 pound scallops
3 level tablespoons butter
2 tablespoons chopped apple
2 tablespoons chopped onion
3 level tablespoons plain flour
salt
cayenne pepper
1 dessertspoon curry powder
¾ pint milk
1 teaspoon lemon juice

Place the scallops in a bowl and pour boiling water over them. Cover and let stand for 5 minutes. Drain.

Melt the butter in a saucepan and add the apple and onion. Cook until soft but not brown. Remove from the heat and add the flour, salt, cayenne pepper and curry powder. Stir until smooth, then cook for 1 minute. Add the milk and stir over medium heat until the sauce boils and thickens. Flavour with lemon juice and simmer for 5 minutes.

Add the prepared scallops and cook for a few minutes, or just long enough to heat the scallops through.

FILLETS OF SOLE BONNE FEMME

2 sole about 1 pound each (or fillets of whiting, flathead or bream)
salt
freshly ground black pepper
1 tablespoon finely chopped shallot
1 to 2 tablespoons finely chopped mushrooms
¼ pint white wine
fish stock
  (made from fish trimmings)
1 bouquet garni (a bayleaf, some thyme and 4 sprigs parsley)
12 button mushrooms
1 tablespoon butter
1 dessertspoon lemon juice
1 level tablespoon butter for sauce
1 level tablespoon plain flour
1 tablespoon cream
grated cheese for topping

If you buy the whole fish, after filleting use the bones and head to make the stock. Season the fillets generously with salt and freshly ground black pepper and place them in a greased baking dish. Sprinkle with the chopped shallot and mushroom and add half the wine and just enough fish stock to cover. Add the bouquet garni, cover with buttered paper and bake at 375°F. for 10 minutes. Lift the fillets into a hot serving dish.

Meanwhile, sauté the whole mushrooms in a pan in 1 tablespoon butter and 1 dessertspoon lemon juice until tender.

Strain the fish stock or liquid from the baking dish into a saucepan, add the remaining wine, and cook until reduced to half the quantity.

Melt the butter in another saucepan, blend in the flour and cook for 1 minute without browning. Add the fish liquid and stir till the sauce boils and thickens. Stir in the cream. Season with salt and pepper to taste.

Place two or three mushrooms caps on each fish fillet and pour over the cream sauce. Sprinkle with grated cheese and bake in a moderate oven to lightly brown the top and melt the cheese.

FILLETS OF WHITING FLORENTINE

6 whiting fillets
1 small onion
½ cup white wine
¼ teaspoon salt
a dash of pepper
a good squeeze of lemon juice
1 cup milk
1 level tablespoon butter
2 level tablespoons plain flour

Roll the fish fillets, secure them with cocktail picks, and place in a buttered casserole dish. Sprinkle with chopped onion, white wine, salt, pepper and lemon juice. Cover and bake in a moderate oven, 350°F., for about 10 minutes. Lift the fillets from the dish.

Strain the liquid in the casserole dish and, when cold, mix it with the milk. Melt the butter in a saucepan, add the flour and stir until smooth. Cook for 1 minute. Add the liquid and stir until the sauce boils and thickens. Simmer for 2 minutes.

2 egg yolks

1 cup well-drained cooked
　　spinach

grated cheese

lemon slices and parsley sprigs to
　　garnish

8 fillets of whiting or other
　　white-fleshed fish

lemon juice

cayenne pepper

salt

pieces of potato cut into cork
　　shapes

1 wine-glass sherry

¼ pint fish stock or water

1 ounce butter

1 ounce flour

1 tablespoon cream

1 egg yolk

1 cup peeled prawns or lobster
　　meat

seasoned flour

egg glazing (beaten egg mixed
　　with a little milk)

breadcrumbs

fat for deep-frying

lemon slices and parsley sprigs
　　to garnish

1 pound potatoes

1 teaspoon butter

1 tablespoon chopped shallot

8-ounce can of salmon or tuna

salt and pepper

1 dessertspoon chopped parsley

a squeeze of lemon juice

2 or 3 tablespoons seasoned flour

1 egg

about 3 tablespoons milk

1 cup breadcrumbs

fat for deep-frying

lemon slices and parsley sprigs to
　　garnish

cucumber sauce for serving

Beat the egg yolks and add to the sauce, mixing well. Adjust the flavourings if necessary. Place a layer of cooked spinach in an ovenproof dish and top with the fish rolls, (first removing the cocktail picks).

Spoon the sauce over the fish and sprinkle with grated cheese. Bake at 400°F. for about 15 minutes or until the sauce bubbles and the cheese melts and lightly browns. Serve with a lemon and parsley garnish.

FISH A LA CHESTERFIELD

Remove any skin from the fillets and flatten them on a board. Season with lemon juice, cayenne and salt. Roll each fillet round a piece of potato and secure with a cocktail pick. Place in a large saucepan with the sherry, fish stock and a pinch of salt. Poach gently for 3 or 4 minutes, then lift out carefully and drain well. Strain and reserve the cooking liquid.

Melt the butter in a saucepan and add the flour. Stir until smooth, then cook without browning for 1 minute. Add the liquid in which the fish was cooked and stir until the sauce boils and thickens. Cook for 2 minutes, then stir in the cream, egg yolk and prawns. Season with salt and cayenne.

When the fish rolls are quite cold, remove the potato pieces and fill the rolls with the rich prawn sauce mixture. Coat with seasoned flour, dip in egg glazing, then coat well with breadcrumbs. Chill for about 1 hour.

Deep fry in hot fat or oil until a golden brown. Serve with a lemon and parsley garnish.

FISH CAKES

Peel, boil, drain and mash the potatoes (do not add any milk or butter at this stage). Heat the butter in a saucepan and add the chopped shallot. Toss until it is soft but not brown, then mix with the mashed potato. Drain the liquid from the canned salmon. Flake the salmon and add it to the potato. Season with salt and pepper and add the parsley and lemon juice. Turn onto a plate and allow to cool. If the mixture is inclined to crumble, add a little of the liquid drained from the can, or a little of the beaten egg.

Take spoonfuls of the mixture and shape into round flat cakes in the seasoned flour. Beat the egg with the milk and dip each cake in this mixture before covering with breadcrumbs. Firm the crumbs on with a broad knife and, if convenient, chill well before frying.

Have ready a large saucepan with enough fat to completely

cover the cakes when cooking. Place the fish cakes in a basket, lower them gently into the hot fat and cook until they are a golden brown—this will take only a few minutes.

Lift out and drain on paper before serving with a lemon and parsley garnish. A cucumber sauce is a nice accompaniment to this dish.

FISH IN TOMATO CASES

6 fillets of whiting or small flathead
1 teaspoon butter
1 tablespoon white wine
1 tablespoon water
1 tablespoon chopped shallot
½ teaspoon salt
a pinch of pepper
3 large or 6 medium-sized tomatoes
1 level tablespoon butter
1 rounded tablespoon plain flour
milk
¼ teaspoon salt (for sauce)
a pinch of pepper (for sauce)
a squeeze of lemon juice
3 tablespoons grated cheese
6 rounds fried bread
lemon slices and parsley sprigs to garnish

Remove the skin from the fish and roll the fillets up firmly. Secure with cocktail picks and place in a greased casserole dish. Combine the butter, wine, water, shallot, salt and pepper and pour over the fish. Cover and bake in a moderate oven for about 15 to 20 minutes. Lift out gently. Pour the liquid off and make up to 1 cup with milk.

If using large tomatoes, cut them in halves and scoop out the pulp (with medium-sized tomatoes, cut a slice from the top of each and scoop out the pulp). Season with salt and pepper, and, if liked, a little sugar. Place a fish roll in each tomato case. Place the filled cases on a greased oven slide.

To make the cheese sauce melt the tablespoon of butter in a small saucepan, add the flour and stir over the heat until smooth. Cook for 1 minute, then add the combined fish liquid and milk and stir until the sauce boils and thickens. Flavour with salt, pepper and lemon juice and cook for 2 minutes. Add the grated cheese and stir until melted.

Pour the cheese sauce over the filled tomato cases, and bake in a moderate oven for about 15 minutes or until the sauce bubbles and lightly browns. Serve on fried bread rounds with a lemon and parsley garnish.

FISH MORNAY IN ORANGE CUPS

4 oranges
1 teaspoon chopped parsley
¼ teaspoon mustard
a pinch of cayenne pepper
a squeeze of lemon juice
½ pint white sauce
1 pound fish fillets
2 tablespoons water or white wine
1 dessertspoon chopped shallot
a few peppercorns
1 tablespoon grated cheese

Wash and dry the oranges, cut the top from each and remove the flesh (reserve this for a fruit salad or a fruit cocktail).

Add the parsley, mustard, cayenne and lemon juice to the white sauce.

Place the fish fillets in a baking dish and add the water or wine, the chopped shallot and a few peppercorns. Cover and bake in a moderate oven, 350°F., for about 20 minutes.

Drain the liquid from the fish. Flake the flesh lightly and fold it into the flavoured white sauce, adding, if liked, a little of the fish liquid. Fill the orange cases with this mixture and sprinkle the tops with grated cheese. Bake in a moderate oven until the cheese melts and lightly browns.

The same mixture may be made in ramekin dishes instead of in orange cups.

Fish Parmesan

FISH PARMESAN WITH WHITE WINE SAUCE

6 fillets of whiting
¾ cup packaged dry
   breadcrumbs
¼ cup grated Parmesan cheese
salt and pepper
3 tablespoons plain flour
1 egg beaten with 2 tablespoons
   milk
fat for deep-frying
lemon wedges and parsley sprigs
   to garnish

For the sauce

2 ounces butter or margarine
1½ level tablespoons plain flour
1 cup milk
½ teaspoon salt
a pinch of pepper
1 cup grated cheese
1 to 2 tablespoons white wine
1 tablespoon finely chopped
   shallot
2 hard-boiled eggs

Wash and dry the fillets. Combine the breadcrumbs and Parmesan cheese with salt and pepper to taste. Dip each fillet in flour, brush with the beaten egg and milk and coat with the breadcrumb mixture. Cover and chill if time permits.

Deep-fry in hot oil or fat until a golden brown. Drain well on white paper, arrange on a hot serving platter and serve garnished with lemon wedges and parsley sprigs. Accompany with the white wine sauce.

To make the sauce melt the butter in a small saucepan, add the flour and stir until smooth, cook without browning for 1 minute, then add the milk and stir until the sauce boils and thickens. Simmer for 3 minutes. Add the salt, pepper, grated cheese, wine, shallot and diced hard-boiled eggs. Stir over low heat until the cheese has melted.

261

FRIDAY PIE

2 eggs
¼ cup milk
1 tablespoon butter
¼ cup chopped onion
1 tablespoon chopped parsley
salt and pepper
2 cups salmon or tuna
4 ounces shortcrust pastry

Combine beaten eggs with the milk, melted butter, chopped onion, parsley, and salt and pepper to taste. Drain the salmon and break into chunky pieces, removing the skin and the bones. Stir into the egg mixture together with the liquid drained from the fish. Pour into an 8-inch tart plate.

Make the pastry, roll it into an 8-inch circle, then cut into six wedges. Arrange the wedges on top of the tart or pie filling. Bake in a hot oven, 425°F., for 25 minutes. Serve immediately, accompanied by cucumber or tartare sauce.

FRIED SCALLOPS

1 pound fresh scallops
1 tablespoon salad oil
a good squeeze of lemon juice
2 tablespoons seasoned flour
1 egg beaten with ¼ cup milk
breadcrumbs
hot oil or fat for deep-frying
lemon wedges and parsley sprigs
    to garnish

Wash the scallops and cut away the black part or "beard", but do not remove the orange-coloured roe that clings to the flesh. Place the scallops in a bowl and blanch them by pouring boiling water over them. Cover and leave for about 2 minutes, then drain well.

Toss the blanched scallops in the oil and lemon juice and let stand for about 10 minutes.

Roll each scallop lightly in the seasoned flour, dip in the egg glazing, then cover with breadcrumbs. Chill for 30 minutes if time permits. Place in a wire basket and deep-fry in hot fat or oil until the covering is a golden brown. Drain on paper and serve with a lemon and parsley garnish. Accompany if liked with tartare sauce.

GOLDEN FISH FILLETS WITH ONION

1 tablespoon butter or
    margarine
1 large onion
¼ cup plain flour
1 level teaspoon salt
¼ level teaspoon pepper
¼ level teaspoon paprika
6 fillets of whiting, flounder or
    sole
2 ounces butter
¼ cup lemon juice
½ teaspoon Worcester sauce
lemon slices and parsley sprigs to
    garnish

Heat the tablespoon of butter in a small saucepan, add thinly sliced onion and sauté until tender. Remove from the heat and keep warm.

Mix the flour with the salt, pepper and paprika and use to coat the fish fillets. Heat the 2 ounces of butter in a pan and sauté the fish until a golden brown, turning once. Drain well and keep warm.

To any butter left in the pan add the lemon juice and Worcester sauce. Bring to the boil.

Arrange the fish fillets on a hot serving dish, pour over the lemon mixture and top with the sautéed onion. Garnish with lemon and parsley and serve with boiled potatoes.

262

GOLDEN FISH PIE

1¼ pound smoked cod fillets
1 tablespoon butter
1 tablespoon plain flour
½ pint milk
salt and pepper
½ level teaspoon dry mustard
1 dessertspoon chopped parsley
2 hard-boiled eggs
½ pound flaky pastry
a little beaten egg or milk for
  glazing

Place the fish in a large pan, cover with cold water and bring slowly to the boil. Reduce the heat and simmer for 10 or 15 minutes or until the flesh is easily flaked with a fork. Drain, remove the skin and bones and place the fish in a pie-dish.

Melt the butter in a small saucepan, add the flour, stir until smooth, and cook for 1 minute without allowing it to brown. Add the milk and cook until the sauce boils and thickens, stirring constantly. Simmer for 2 minutes longer. Remove from the heat and add salt and pepper to taste, and the mustard, parsley and chopped hard-boiled eggs. Pour over the fish in the pie-dish.

Roll the pastry to fit the top. Trim the edges, decorate the top with small pieces of pastry, then glaze with a little egg or milk. Bake in a hot oven, 425°F., for about 20 minutes.

GRILLED FISH WITH ORANGE

1 pound fish fillets
3 level tablespoons butter
2 tablespoons orange juice
½ level teaspoon salt
a dash of pepper
1 teaspoon grated orange rind

Wash and dry the fillets and place them in a buttered shallow baking dish.

Melt the butter and add the orange juice, salt, pepper and grated rind. Pour half over the fish fillets and cook for 3 or 4 minutes. Turn the fillets, add the remainder of the orange mixture and cook for a further 3 or 4 minutes (the time will depend on the thickness of the fillets).

Serve with the sauce from the dish spooned over the fillets.

GRILLED FISH WITH TARTARE SAUCE

2 medium-sized snapper or
  bream
lemon, salt and pepper
1 tablespoon finely minced
  shallot
melted butter
lemon juice and Worcester sauce
1 dessertspoon chooped parsley

Season the fish by rubbing inside and out with lemon and sprinkling with salt and pepper. Make 3 cuts across the flesh of each fish and fill with the minced shallot. Brush with melted butter. Place under a glowing griller and cook for 10 minutes or longer, according to the thickness of the fish and the heat of the griller. Turn the fish frequently while cooking and brush again with butter. Place on a hot serving platter.

Add lemon juice and Worcester sauce to the drippings in the pan and sprinkle in the chopped parsley, then pour over the fish. Serve with tartare sauce (page 413).

GRILLED SALMON STEAKS

4 large salmon steaks
salt
freshly ground black pepper
4 tablespoons melted butter
lemon and parsley butter
  (recipe on next page)
lemon wedges to garnish

Season both sides of each salmon steak with salt and freshly ground black pepper. Allow to stand for about 15 minutes.

Place the steaks on a greased shallow tray and brush them with melted butter. Grill about 3 inches from the heat for about 5 minutes. Turn the fish, brush with more butter, and grill for a further 5 minutes or until the flesh will flake when tested with a fork.

Serve with lemon and parsley butter on each steak and accompany with a wedge of lemon. To make the lemon and parsley butter cream 1 tablespoon of butter until soft, then add 1 teaspoon finely chopped parsley and a squeeze of lemon juice.

HAWAIIAN-STYLE PRAWNS

3 rashers of bacon
½ pound hamburger steak
1 cup finely chopped onion
1 clove of garlic
2 cups shelled prawns
3 cups cooked rice
⅓ cup finely chopped celery, including a little celery leaf
1 level teaspoon salt
a pinch of pepper
¼ level teaspoon dry mustard
2 tablespoons soy sauce
3 bananas
1 tablespoon butter

Dice the bacon and fry it in its own fat until almost crisp. Add the hamburger steak, onion and finely minced garlic and cook until the onion is tender but not brown. Stir constantly to separate the meat. Add the prawns, rice, celery, salt, pepper, mustard and soy sauce. Stir gently, and allow to heat through.

Meanwhile peel and slice the bananas and brown them lightly in the butter in a pan. Arrange the bananas on top of the rice and garnish with extra prawns if liked.

Hawaiian-style Prawns

KEDGEREE

8-ounce can of salmon
2 hard-boiled eggs
4 to 6 ounces rice, cooked
2 ounces butter
salt and pepper
a squeeze of lemon juice
1 rounded teaspoon curry
   powder
1 teaspoon chopped parsley
lemon wedges and parsley sprigs
   to garnish

Flake the salmon with a fork, removing the bones. Remove the yolks from the hard-boiled eggs and chop the whites. Press the yolks through a sieve and set aside for topping.

Melt the butter in a saucepan, add the cooked rice, season with salt, pepper and lemon juice and add the curry powder, flaked salmon, chopped egg white and chopped parsley. Heat well.

Serve very hot with the sieved egg yolk sprinkled on the top, and with a lemon and parsley garnish.

LEMON-STUFFED FILLETS

1 cup cooked rice
$\frac{1}{4}$ cup melted butter
1 egg yolk
1 dessertspoon chopped onion
juice of $\frac{1}{2}$ lemon
1 teaspoon salt
a dash of pepper
2 pounds fish fillets such as
   flounder, sole or bream

Toss together the rice, 3 teaspoons of the melted butter, the slightly beaten egg yolk, and the onion which has been sautéed in a little butter. Season with half the lemon juice and half the salt and pepper.

Place half the fish fillets in the bottom of a greased ovenproof dish. Spoon some of the stuffing on each fillet, then cover with another fillet. Secure the top fillets in place with cocktail picks and season with the rest of the salt and pepper. Pour over the remaining melted butter and lemon juice.

Bake in a moderate oven, 375°F., for 25 to 30 minutes, basting frequently with the melted butter and lemon juice from the dish.

LOBSTER CROQUETTES

2 tablespoons butter
3 tablespoons plain flour
$\frac{1}{2}$ level teaspoon mustard
$\frac{1}{2}$ level teaspoon salt
a pinch of cayenne pepper
1 cup milk
2 cups diced cooked lobster
2 hard-boiled eggs
1 tablespoon chopped parsley
a squeeze of lemon juice
seasoned flour
1 egg and $\frac{1}{4}$ cup milk for glazing
breadcrumbs
hot oil or fat for frying
lemon wedges and parsley sprigs
   to garnish

Melt the butter in a medium-sized saucepan, add the plain flour and stir until smooth. Cook without browning for 1 minute. Add the mustard, salt and cayenne, then the milk, and stir over medium heat until the mixture boils. It will be very thick. Add the lobster and chopped hard-boiled eggs, chopped parsley and the lemon juice. Turn onto a plate and allow to cool.

Take spoonfuls of the mixture and make into cork shapes in the seasoned flour. Dip into egg glazing and then into breadcrumbs. Chill if time permits.

Deep-fry the croquettes in hot fat or oil until they are golden brown. Drain on paper. Serve with a lemon and parsley garnish.

265

LOBSTER THERMIDOR WITH CURRIED RICE

2 ounces butter
2 ounces plain flour
1 level teaspoon salt
a pinch of pepper
¼ level teaspoon dry mustard
¾ pint milk
¼ cup cream
1 tablespoon sherry
1 teaspoon lemon juice
1 pound cooked lobster meat
¼ cup grated cheese

For the curried rice

1 ounce butter
1 cup uncooked rice
1 level teaspoon curry powder
1 small onion
1 pint boiling water

Melt the butter in a saucepan and blend in the flour until smooth. Add the salt, pepper and mustard and cook for 1 minute, then add the milk. Cook for 2 or 3 minutes, stirring until the sauce boils and thickens.

Remove from the heat and add the cream, sherry and lemon juice. Dice the lobster meat, fold it in and adjust the seasonings if necessary. Place in lightly greased individual remekins or a casserole and top with the grated cheese. Place under a heated griller or in a moderate oven to heat through and lightly brown.

To make the curried rice melt the butter in a pan, add the uncooked rice and stir over high heat to brown slightly. Transfer to a greased casserole and stir in the curry powder and the finely chopped onion. Add the boiling water. Bake uncovered at 400°F. for 30 to 35 minutes or till the rice is tender. Fluff with a fork before serving.

OVEN-FRIED FISH

1 egg
1 tablespoon water
14-ounce packet of frozen fish
  fillets, or 6 fresh fillets of fish
salt and pepper
1 cup instant potato flakes
1 dessertspoon lemon juice
1 ounce butter

Beat the egg slightly and beat again with the water. Dip the thawed fish fillets in the mixture, then season each fillet well with salt and pepper and roll it in dry potato flakes.

Combine the lemon juice and melted butter in a shallow ovenproof dish and arrange the fish fillets in a single layer in the dish. Bake uncovered in a moderate oven, 350°F., for about 25 minutes, turning the fillets after 15 minutes.

PORTUGUESE FISH CUTLETS

2 cups freshly cooked rice
2 pounds fish cutlets
½ cup seasoned flour
2 tablespoons butter
¾ cup finely chopped onion
1 clove of garlic
1 teaspoon salt
a pinch of pepper
½ cup sauterne
3 medium-sized tomatoes
chopped parsley and lemon to
  garnish

Spread the cooked rice in the bottom of a greased casserole. Coat the fish cutlets in the seasoned flour and fry them lightly on both sides in melted butter. Drain well and place on top of the rice.

In the butter left in the pan (or add a little more), fry the onion and crushed garlic until soft but not brown. Add the salt, pepper and wine and heat to boiling point. Pour over the fish.

Peel the tomatoes and cut into thick slices. Arrange on top of the fish in the casserole. Cover and bake in a moderate oven, 350°F., for about 30 minutes.

Sprinkle with chopped parsley and serve with a lemon garnish.

266

PRAWN AND PINEAPPLE FRITTERS

½ pound cooked and peeled
   prawns
1½ cups plain flour
3 level teaspoons baking powder
1 teaspoon salt
¼ teaspoon curry powder
2 eggs
1 tablespoon salad oil
1 tablespoon lemon juice
1 small can of crushed pineapple
curry sauce to serve

Chop the prawns into small pieces.

Sift the flour, baking powder, salt and curry powder into a bowl.

Beat the eggs, oil and lemon juice together in another bowl and add the undrained pineapple. Stir into the dry ingredients, beating with the back of a wooden spoon to make a smooth batter. Add the chopped prawns and mix well.

Drop spoonfuls of the mixture into hot fat or oil in a deep saucepan. When brown, turn and cook each fritter on the other side. Drain on paper and serve with curry sauce (page 407).

SALMON AND CORN CASSEROLE

4 tablespoons butter
1 cup chopped celery
¼ cup chopped onion
¼ cup chopped green pepper
1 cup sliced mushrooms
8-ounce can of whole kernel
   corn
16-ounce can of salmon
milk
2 rounded tablespoons plain
   flour
½ teaspoon salt
a dash of white pepper
¼ teaspoon curry powder
buttered breadcrumbs or crushed
   potato crisps
lemon slices and parsley sprigs to
   garnish

Melt 2 tablespoons of the butter in a saucepan and add the celery, onion, green pepper and mushrooms. Sauté until tender. Set aside.

Drain the corn and set aside. Drain the salmon, flake the flesh and to the salmon liquid add enough milk to make up to 2 cups.

Arrange the sautéed vegetables, drained corn and flaked salmon in layers in a lightly greased casserole.

Melt the remaining 2 tablespoons of butter in a saucepan and stir in the flour, salt, pepper and curry powder. Add the salmon liquid and milk and stir over medium heat until the sauce boils and thickens. Pour over the ingredients in the casserole.

Top with buttered breadcrumbs or crushed potato crisps and bake in a moderate oven, 350°F., for about 25 minutes or until the sauce bubbles and the topping browns. Serve with a lemon and parsley garnish.

SALMON BALLS

16-ounce can of salmon
1 level tablespoon butter
1 level tablespoon plain flour
1 cup milk
¼ teaspoon salt
a dash of pepper
1 level teaspoon mustard
1 teaspoon lemon juice
1 teaspoon chopped parsley
½ cup chopped celery
seasoned flour

Drain and flake the salmon. Melt the butter in a saucepan, add the flour, stir until smooth, then cook for 1 minute. Add the milk and stir until the sauce boils and thickens. Flavour with the salt, pepper, mustard and lemon juice. Cook for 2 minutes, then add the flaked salmon, the chopped parsley and the celery. The mixture must be firm enough to shape into balls when cold, but if it is very thick at this stage add a little of the salmon liquid.

Take spoonfuls of the cold mixture and shape into balls in seasoned flour. Dip each ball in egg glazing, then coat with breadcrumbs. Chill for about 30 minutes.

egg glazing (1 egg and a little
   milk)
breadcrumbs
pineapple rings sautéed in butter
lemon slices and parsley sprigs
   to garnish

Deep-fry until a golden brown, then drain on paper. Serve on pineapple rings which have been sautéed in butter. Garnish with lemon and parsley and, if liked, accompany with tartare sauce.

SALMON LOAF SUPREME WITH CREAMY SAUCE

3 cups soft white breadcrumbs
½ cup milk
2 eggs
¾ teaspoon salt
¼ teaspoon Tabasco
¼ teaspoon monosodium
   glutamate
1 teaspoon lemon juice
2 tablespoons finely chopped
   shallot
1 tablespoon finely chopped
   parsley
½ teaspoon mixed herbs
1½ pounds canned salmon

For the sauce

1 ounce butter
1 rounded tablespoon plain flour
½ pint milk
½ teaspoon salt
a pinch of pepper
1 teaspoon mixed mustard
1 cup cooked peas
⅓ cup chopped chives

Combine the breadcrumbs, milk, well-beaten eggs, salt, Tabasco, monosodium glutamate, lemon juice, shallot, parsley and mixed herbs in a large bowl. Toss lightly with a fork.

Drain and flake the salmon, removing the bones, and mix it lightly with the other ingredients.

Line an orange-cake tin with foil and brush with melted butter or oil. Place the salmon mixture in the lined tin, smoothing the top. Bake at 375°F. for about 45 minutes or until the loaf is firm to the touch. Turn out onto a heated platter and serve with creamy sauce.

To make the sauce melt the butter in a small saucepan, stir in the four and cook for 1 minute, then add the milk and stir until the sauce boils and thickens. Cook for 2 minutes, then flavour with the salt, pepper and mustard. Add the peas and chives and cook for a further 3 minutes.

SALMON MORNAY

16-ounce can of salmon
2 ounces butter or margarine
2 or 3 spring onions
2 rounded tablespoons plain
   flour
2 cups milk
salt and pepper
1 teaspoon dry mustard
4 tablespoons grated cheese
a squeeze of lemon juice
2 tablespoons soft white
   breadcrumbs for topping

Drain and reserve the liquid from the salmon. Melt the butter in a saucepan, add the spring onions and sauté until soft. Add the flour, stir until smooth then cook for 1 minute without browning. Add the milk and the salmon liquid and cook, stirring well, until the sauce boils and thickens. Season to taste with salt and pepper and add the mustard, 2 tablespoons of the grated cheese and the lemon juice.

Fold in the flaked salmon and turn the mixture into a lightly greased casserole. Top with the remaining grated cheese and with the breadcrumbs. Bake in a moderate oven, 350°F., for about 20 minutes or until the cheese and breadcrumbs brown and the sauce bubbles.

Use the same proportions as for the salmon mornay, but this dish is improved if it has 1 or 2 tablespoons of sherry and 2 chopped hard-boiled eggs mixed in before adding the lobster.

OYSTER MORNAY

The basic proportions are the same as for the salmon mornay, using 1 cup of oysters to 2 cups of sauce.

FISH MORNAY

The proportions are the same as for the salmon mornay, but if a cheaper type of fish is preferred the flavour will be improved if 2 egg yolks are added to the sauce at the same time as the cheese.

For a richer mornay, substitute ½ a cup of cream for ½ a cup of the milk used in the sauce.

SALMON POTATO BAKE

8-ounce can of salmon
1 rounded dessertspoon butter
1½ rounded tablespoons plain
   flour
¼ teaspoon salt
1 level teaspoon dry mustard
a pinch of cayenne pepper
1 cup milk
a squeeze of lemon juice
1 teaspoon chopped parsley
2 tablespoons chopped celery
1 pound cooked potatoes
butter and milk for mashing
pepper for potatoes
milk for brushing
lemon slices and parsley sprigs to
   garnish

Drain and reserve the liquid from the salmon. Remove the bones and skin and flake the flesh.

Melt the butter in a small saucepan and add the flour, salt, mustard and cayenne. Stir until smooth, then cook for 1 minute. Add the milk and the liquid drained from the salmon and stir until the sauce boils and thickens. Flavour with the lemon juice and add the parsley and celery. Stir in the flaked salmon and turn the mixture into a greased pie-dish.

Have the potatoes freshly cooked and mash them with a little butter and milk. Season with pepper, spread over the salmon mixture, glaze the top with a little milk and score the surface with a fork.

Place in a hot oven, 450°F., and bake for about 15 minutes or until the potatoes are lightly browned. Garnish with lemon and parsley.

SALMON PUFF

1½ cups grated cheese
8-ounce can of salmon
6 slices bread without crusts
2 eggs
1 cup milk
½ cup sherry
salt and pepper
¼ teaspoon Worcester sauce
lemon slices and parsley sprigs to
   garnish

Arrange alternate layers of grated cheese, drained and flaked salmon and cubed bread in a lightly greased casserole. The top layer should be of bread cubes.

Beat the eggs and add the milk and sherry, season with salt and pepper and add the Worcester sauce. Pour carefully over the ingredients in the casserole. Bake in a slow oven, 300°F., for 45 minutes or until the custard has set and the top is lightly browned. Serve immediately, garnished with lemon and parsley.

1 tablespoon butter
1 rounded tablespoon plain flour
1 cup milk
2 egg yolks
¼ cup grated cheese
1 cup cooked rice
8-ounce can of salmon
1 teaspoon chopped parsley
1 dessertspoon chopped onion
a squeeze of lemon juice
salt and pepper
8 rings of canned pineapple
lemon juice
brown sugar
a little melted butter
seasoned flour
2 egg whites
soft white breadcrumbs
fat for deep-frying

16-ounce can of salmon
3 tablespoons melted butter
2 tablespoons chopped shallots
  or spring onions
2 cups cooked rice
2 tablespoons chopped parsley
1 tablespoon lemon juice
1 teaspoon salt
a dash of cayenne pepper
½ teaspoon celery salt
2 eggs
½ cup milk

SALMON RICE CONES

Melt the butter in a saucepan and stir in the flour. Cook for 1 minute without browning. Add the milk and stir until the sauce boils and thickens. Simmer for 2 minutes. Remove from the heat and stir in the egg yolks, cheese and rice, then drained and flaked salmon, chopped parsley and onion, lemon juice, and salt and pepper to taste. Mix thoroughly and spread on a plate to cool. Chill for several hours if time permits.

Meanwhile, drain the pineapple rings, place them on a foil-covered tray, sprinkle with lemon juice and brown sugar and drizzle over a little melted butter. Set aside.

Take spoonfuls of the salmon and rice mixture, make into cone shapes in the seasoned flour, dip into lightly beaten egg whites and coat with breadcrumbs. Chill for 1 hour.

Place the pineapple in the oven to heat. Deep-fry the salmon cones in hot fat until they are a golden brown. Drain, and serve each one on top of a pineapple slice. Accompany with tartare sauce if liked.

SALMON RICE LOAF

Drain and flake the salmon. Place the melted butter in a saucepan and sauté the shallot until soft.

Into the salmon mix the rice, parsley, lemon juice, salt, pepper and celery salt, then add the beaten eggs and milk and the sautéed shallot.

Place in a loaf tin which has been lined with greased foil. Bake in a moderate oven, 350°F., for 45 minutes. Turn out and serve hot.

Salmon Rice Loaf

270

Scallop Ramekins

1 pound fresh scallops
a slice of lemon
2 cups water
6 ounces macaroni
2 tablespoons butter
1 cup soft white breadcrumbs
2 tablespoons plain flour
1 teaspoon dry mustard
½ teaspoon salt
¼ teaspoon pepper
2 cups milk
1 teaspoon chilli sauce
4 ounces grated Cheddar cheese
  for topping
3 small tomatoes for serving

SCALLOP RAMEKINS

Wash the scallops and if large cut into pieces. Place the lemon slice and the water in a saucepan and heat until boiling, then pour over the scallops, cover and allow to stand for 5 minutes. Drain.

Cook the macaroni in plenty of boiling salted water until tender. Drain. Melt the butter in a saucepan and add 1 dessertspoon of it to the breadcrumbs.

Add the flour, mustard, salt and pepper to the remaining butter and stir until smooth. Cook without browning for 1 minute, add the milk and stir over medium heat until the sauce boils and thickens. Simmer for 2 minutes, then remove from the heat and stir in the chilli sauce. Fold in the scallops and the macaroni.

Spoon the mixture into greased ramekins (or into a large casserole if preferred), sprinkle the top of each with grated cheese and the edges with buttered breadcrumbs.

If in ramekins, bake in a moderate oven, 350°F., for about 15 minutes (if in a casserole, it will take about 30 minutes). Top with pieces of fresh tomato before serving.

2 cups cooked flaked fish
  (or use salmon or tuna)
1 teaspoon curry powder
grated rind of 1 lemon
1 teaspoon lemon juice
2 cups well-seasoned white
  sauce
2 cups freshly cooked rice
1 cup grated cheese
½ cup crushed cornflakes

SCALLOPED FISH AND RICE

Combine the fish with the curry powder, lemon rind and juice and mix with the white sauce. Arrange the cooked rice in a greased casserole dish and top with the fish mixture.

Sprinkle the top with the cheese and cornflakes. Bake in a moderate oven, 350°F., for about 15 or 20 minutes or until the cheese melts and the cornflake crumbs turn brown.

271

SCALLOPS HAWAIIAN

bacon rashers
scallops
pineapple wedges

Cut the bacon into pieces about 4 inches long. Place the scallops in a bowl, pour over enough boiling water to cover them, and leave for 5 minutes. Drain.

On one end of each piece of bacon place a drained scallop, and on the other end a piece of pineapple. Roll both ends to the centre so that both the scallop and the pineapple are wrapped in the bacon.

Thread two or three of these rolls on a skewer and grill until the bacon fat is clear, the bacon crisp and the scallops tender. This should take about 10 minutes. Turn at least once during cooking.

STUFFED CRAYFISH

3 medium-sized crayfish
1 large onion
1 green pepper
2 stalks celery
2 level tablespoons butter
3 level tablespoons flour
$\frac{3}{4}$ pint milk
1 teaspoon Worcester sauce
salt and pepper
$\frac{1}{4}$ teaspoon paprika
1 tablespoon dry sherry
$\frac{1}{2}$ pound fresh mushrooms
1 tablespoon butter for
    mushrooms
grated cheese
lemon slices and parsley sprigs to
    garnish

Cut the crayfish in half lengthwise and remove the meat. Cut the meat into bite-sized pieces. Clean the shells thoroughly by washing and draining.

Dice the onion, green pepper and celery and sauté in 2 tablespoons of butter until tender but not brown. Stir in the flour, blending smoothly, then cook for 2 minutes. Add the milk and stir over medium heat until the sauce boils and thickens. Flavour with the Worcester sauce, salt, pepper, paprika and sherry. Add the crayfish meat, mixing well.

While the crayfish mixture is heating through, sauté the mushrooms in 1 tablespoon of butter. Season them with salt and pepper, place some in each crayfish shell, top with the crayfish mixture, and sprinkle a little grated cheese over each. Bake in a hot oven to melt and brown the cheese. Serve garnished with lemon and parsley.

SWEET AND SOUR SCALLOPS

$1\frac{1}{2}$ pounds scallops
4 ounces self-raising flour
a good pinch of salt
1 teaspoon melted butter
1 egg, separated
1 cup milk

For the sauce
$\frac{1}{2}$ cup shredded carrot
3 spring onions, with some green
    tops left on
$\frac{1}{2}$ a medium-sized green pepper
1 cup water
2 level tablespoons sugar

Wash the scallops well and place in a bowl. Pour boiling water over them, cover and let stand for 5 minutes. Drain off the water.

To make a batter, sift the flour and salt into a bowl, make a well in the centre, add the melted butter and egg yolk, pour in the milk and beat with the back of a wooden spoon until smooth. Fold in the stiffly beaten egg white.

To make the sweet and sour sauce shred the vegetables and place them in a saucepan with the water, sugar, salt, pineapple juice, vinegar and soy sauce, then bring to the boil and cook for a few minutes. Blend the cornflour with a little cold water, stir into the hot liquid and keep stirring until smooth. Chop the pineapple, add it to the sauce and keep hot while you fry the scallops.

½ teaspoon salt
¼ cup pineapple juice
3 tablespoons vinegar
1 dessertspoon soy sauce
1 rounded dessertspoon
   cornflour
1 slice canned pineapple

For the salmon loaf
2 level dessertspoons gelatine
½ cup cold water
1 cup chicken stock
1-pound can of salmon
1 cup diced celery
¼ cup chopped gherkin
1 dessertspoon minced onion
2 dessertspoons lemon juice
¼ teaspoon salt
¼ teaspoon paprika
½ cup mayonnaise
½ cup cream

For the aspic glaze
1 level teaspoon gelatine
1 tablespoon cold water
¼ cup mayonnaise
2 tablespoons tomato sauce

For the garnish
shredded lettuce, celery curls,
   tomato wedges and devilled
   eggs

1 pound fish fillets
1 teaspoon salt
¼ teaspoon pepper
¼ cup butter or margarine
4 teaspoons prepared or French
   mustard
1 tablespoon chopped parsley
lemon juice
lemon slices and parsley sprigs to
   garnish

Coat the well-drained scallops in seasoned flour, dip them in the batter, then fry in hot oil or fat until a golden brown, turning them as they become brown underneath. Drain on paper. Serve with the sweet and sour sauce, accompanied with freshly boiled rice if liked.

TANGY COLD SALMON LOAF

Soften the gelatine for the salmon loaf in the cold water, then dissolve it over boiling water. Add to the chicken stock and allow to become cold but not set.

Combine the drained and flaked salmon with the celery, gherkin, onion, lemon juice, salt and paprika. Add the stock and then the mayonnaise and cream. Toss lightly to blend the ingredients thoroughly.

Place the mixture in an orange-cake tin which has been either oiled or wetted. Chill until firm. Unmould onto a serving platter and cover the top and sides with the aspic glaze. Chill until the glaze has set. Serve with the suggested garnishes.

To make the aspic glaze, soak the gelatine in the cold water and dissolve over hot water. Cool slightly, then add the combined mayonnaise and tomato sauce. Mix well before using.

TANGY FISH BAKE

Season the fish fillets on both sides with salt and pepper. Beat the butter to a cream and work in the mustard, parsley and a good squeeze of lemon juice. Spread this mixture lightly over all surfaces of the fillets.

Have ready a piece of greased aluminium foil for each fish fillet. Wrap each fillet loosely in foil, fastening securely by bringing the foil up over the fish, folding it tightly and turning in the ends.

Place the foil-wrapped fillets in a shallow oven tray and bake in a hot oven, 425°F., for 12 to 15 minutes.

Serve each fish fillet in its foil wrapping, but open it first and add a garnish of lemon and parsley.

273

JAMS AND JELLIES

Jam-making

The fruit used for making jam should be fresh and, if anything, slightly underripe, but not immature. In some cases a mixture of whole ripe but firm fruit gives a good result, the ripe fruit providing the colour and flavour and the firmer fruit the pectin and the acid. Do not have all the fruit overripe: the jam would not set well, nor would it keep.

In fruit such as strawberries, cherries and melons there is a deficiency of acids. This can be remedied by the addition of fresh lemon juice: use 2 tablespoonfuls to 2 pounds of fruit. Or you may add citric or tartaric acid in the proportion of 1 level teaspoonful to each 2 pounds of fruit.

The preserving pan used for boiling the jam should be clean and bright. Rub it with a little butter before placing the fruit in to cook: this lessens the risk of the fruit catching and burning. With the exception of some of the berry jams, most fruit is cooked until soft before the sugar is added. The sugar should be added slowly to extract the pectin.

Only the best quality sugar should be used. Poor quality sugar is wasteful because it requires so much skimming.

Warm the sugar before adding it, for it will dissolve more quickly and more perfectly. Always see that the sugar has completely dissolved before the jam comes to the boil.

Occasional stirring is necessary after the addition of the sugar, for the jam must boil quickly if it is to have a good colour and flavour and for the evaporation of all surplus moisture.

PREPARATION OF JARS

All jars used for home-made jam should be sterilized before use. This is most important when making diabetic jams, for there isn't any preserving sugar in this type of jam.

Wash and dry each jar, then stand them on several thicknesses of wet cloth on a tray and place the tray in a cool oven. Increase the heat, and leave for 30 minutes.

BOTTLING

Berry fruit jams such as strawberry jam, also melon jam and marmalades, are best if left to stand for about 5 minutes before they are poured into the jars. This prevents the fruit rising to the top of the jar.

SEALING JAMS

The safest way to seal jam is to cover with a layer of melted paraffin wax and then with a paper seal or a screw top. When the jam has cooled in the jar pour the wax over it, tilting the jars to fill the crevices.

Label and date the jam and store it in a cool, dry, well-ventilated cupboard.

APRICOT AND PINEAPPLE JAM

1 large pineapple
6 pounds apricots
6 pounds sugar
½ pint water
3 tablespoons lemon juice

Peel and grate the pineapple. Wash, halve and stone the apricots. Place both fruits in a large bowl, cover with half the sugar and put aside overnight.

Next day place the fruit with the water and lemon juice in a preserving pan and bring to the boil. Simmer until soft. Add the remainder of the sugar (which should be warm) and stir until it has dissolved. Boil until the mixture reaches a good consistency—about 40 minutes. Pour into heated jars. Seal when cold.

If canned pineapple is used in place of fresh, reduce the sugar to 5 pounds and in place of the water use the liquid drained from the can.

APRICOT JAM

6 pounds apricots
5 pounds sugar
½ pint water
3 tablespoons lemon juice

Wash the apricots, cut them in halves and remove the stones. Place in a preserving pan with the water and simmer until very soft—about 40 minutes.

Meanwhile remove the kernels from about a quarter of the stones, blanch them, slip off the skins, and cut each kernel in half or chop it up.

When the apricots are very soft add the warmed sugar and the lemon juice and stir until the sugar has dissolved. Now cook at a brisk pace for about 30 minutes, stirring occasionally, adding the kernels just before taking the pan off the heat. If a deep saucepan is used instead of a preserving pan, allow a little longer cooking time after the sugar has dissolved.) Pour into heated jars. Seal when cold.

Sealing marmalade jars with melted paraffin wax

ARNA'S SEVILLE MARMALADE

3 Seville oranges
1 lemon
6 pints water
6 pounds sugar

Wash the oranges and the lemon and slice very thinly. Place in a bowl and cover with cold water. Allow to stand overnight.

Next day, place in a preserving pan, bring to the boil, and simmer until the fruit is quite tender—about 45 minutes.

Add the warmed sugar and stir until it has dissolved. Bring to the boil and cook rapidly until the jam will jell when tested—about 30 or 40 minutes. Pour into jars. When cold, seal with paraffin wax.

BLACKBERRY AND APPLE JAM

2 pounds apples
6 pounds blackberries
8 pounds sugar
juice of 2 lemons

Peel and core the apples, then slice them and place in a saucepan with only a very little water. Cook until they are very soft.

Place in a preserving pan with the washed blackberries, the sugar and the lemon juice. Stir until the sugar has dissolved, then boil at a steady pace until the jam will jell when a little is tested on a cold saucer. Pour into clean hot jars. Seal when cold.

BLACKBERRY AND APPLE JELLY

3 pounds sour apples
6 pounds firm blackberries
water
sugar

Wash the apples, cut them up roughly and place in a preserving pan. Cover with water and simmer until very soft.

Strain the liquid from the apples into the preserving pan with the blackberries. Cook slowly until the berries are very soft. Strain, allowing the liquid to drip through muslin.

Measure the strained liquid into the preserving pan and add a cup of sugar for each cup of liquid. Return the pan to the heat and boil rapidly until a little of the mixture jells when tested on a cold saucer. Pour into heated jars. Seal when cold.

BLACKBERRY JAM

6 pounds good firm blackberries
$\frac{1}{2}$ cup cold water
4 tablespoons lemon juice
6 pounds sugar

Pick over the blackberries, place in a colander and run cold water through them. Drain well and place in a preserving pan with the $\frac{1}{2}$ cup cold water and the lemon juice.

Press the fruit lightly with the back of a wooden spoon to draw the juices, then bring slowly to the boil.

Cook gently until the berries are soft—about 30 minutes. Add the warmed sugar, stir until the sugar has dissolved, then boil rapidly until setting point is reached. Pour into warm jars. Seal when cold.

BRANDIED PEACHES

Scald, skin and stone some firm, ripe yellow peaches and allow 1 pound of sugar and 1 cup of water for each pound of prepared peaches.

Combine the sugar and water in a saucepan and stir over medium heat until the sugar has dissolved. Bring to the boil and simmer for 5 minutes. Cooking a few at a time, poach the peaches until they can be easily pierced with a straw. As they are cooked, lift them out with a slotted spoon and place into sterilized jars.

When all the peaches have been cooked, boil the syrup until it reaches 220°F. on a candy thermometer. Cool.

To each pint of syrup add ¼ pint of brandy. Mix well and pour over the peaches, completely covering them. Seal down, making airtight.

The peaches may be bottled in screw-topped jars with metal inserts and rubber rings. After these have been positioned, dip the lids in melted paraffin wax to obtain a perfect seal.

Keep for at least 3 months before using.

CARROT MARMALADE

4 large carrots
4 lemons
4 pounds sugar
11 cups water

Grate the washed carrots, slice the lemons thinly, combine, and pour over half the water. Allow to stand overnight.

On the following day, add the remainder of the water and bring to the boil. Cook gently for about 45 minutes or until the lemon is very soft. Add the sugar, stir until dissolved, then bring to the boil.

Boil until a little of the jam jells when cooled on a saucer— about 30 minutes. Pour into heated jars. Seal when cold.

CHERRY JAM

6 pounds cherries
1½ pints water or fruit juice
6 pounds sugar

Choose sound cherries a little on the underripe side. Sweet cherries make rather tasteless jam.

Wash and dry the cherries and remove the stones. Place the fruit in a preserving pan, add the fruit juice or water and cook until the cherries are tender.

Add the warmed sugar and stir until it has dissolved, then cook until a little of the jam jells when cooled on a saucer. Pour into heated jars. Seal when cold.

Apple juice in place of water improves the flavour of this jam.

CUMQUAT MARMALADE

2 pounds cumquats
4 pints water
4 pounds sugar

Wash the cumquats and slice them thinly. Tie the seeds in a piece of muslin. Place the fruit, water and seeds in a bowl and soak overnight.

Next day, place in a preserving pan and simmer gently for 1 hour or until the fruit rind is quite soft. Remove the bag of seeds.

Add the warmed sugar and stir until dissolved. Bring to the boil and cook rapidly until a little will jell when cooled on a saucer. Pour into warm, dry jars. Seal when cold.

277

DIABETIC JAM

1 pound fruit
water (¼ cup to each pound of fruit)
3 ounces glycerine

If using peaches, apricots or plums, remove the stones and cut the fruit up roughly, then weigh.

Wash and prepare the fruit and cook it gently in the water until tender—the time should not be less than 20 minutes. Add the glycerine and simmer for 15 minutes, or until it has a good consistency. Pour into heated jars immediately. Seal when cold.

Saccharine may be added, but should not be necessary, since the glycerine will sweeten the jam. In any case, do not add saccharine to plum jam, for it changes the colour and makes it very unattractive in appearance. Sweetex or Sucaryl may be used successfully if you want to add a sweetener as well as the glycerine.

DIABETIC MARMALADE

1½ lemons
1 orange
¾ pint water
2 ounces glycerine
(fluid measure)

Wash the fruit and peel it finely, leaving on the white pith. Cut the pith finely and soak it overnight in water. Strain off the water before using.

Slice the flesh of the fruit thinly and place in a saucepan with the water, the peel and soaked pith. Simmer for 20 minutes, or until tender.

Add the glycerine and simmer for another 15 minutes, or until the correct consistency. Pour immediately into hot sterilized jars. Seal with paraffin wax when cold.

DRIED APRICOT JAM

1 pound dried apricots
3 pints cold water
3 pounds sugar

Wash the apricots in several changes of cold water, then soak overnight in the 3 pints of cold water.

Next day, take out the apricots and strain the liquid through muslin into a preserving pan. Add the apricots and bring to the boil. Warm the sugar, add to the contents of the pan and stir until it has dissolved. Boil for 30 minutes or until the jam is thick. Pour into heated jars. Seal when cold.

DRIED APRICOT AND PASSIONFRUIT JAM

Add the pulp of 6 passionfruit to the apricots at the same time as the sugar.

DRIED APRICOT AND PINEAPPLE JAM

2 pounds apricots
water
1 large pineapple
7 pounds sugar

Soak the apricots overnight in just enough water to cover them.

Next day, grate or finely slice the pineapple and add to the apricots. A little more water may be required if the apricots look too dry or have absorbed all the soaking water. Cook until the fruit is tender, then add the warmed sugar and boil until the jam is a good consistency. Pour into heated jars. Seal when cold.

FEIJOA JAM

4 pounds peeled and sliced feijoas
½ pint water
grated rind and juice of 2 lemons
4 pounds sugar

Place the prepared fruit in a preserving pan and add the water. Bring slowly to the boil, then simmer until the fruit is tender. Add the lemon juice and rind and then the sugar, preferably warmed. Make sure the sugar has dissolved before the jam comes back to the boil.

Boil hard for 10 minutes, then test. It should only take about 15 minutes after the sugar has been added, if cooked in a preserving pan. Pour into heated jars. Seal when cold.

Feijoas can also be combined with rhubarb or apple. Use half feijoas and half rhubarb, or half apple, and the same amount of sugar as fruit.

FIG JAM

6 pounds ripe figs
3 ounces green root ginger
4½ pounds sugar
juice of 3 lemons

The figs should all be barely ripe. Top and tail them, then slice them a little less than ¼ inch thick. Place in a bowl.

Wash, dry, scrape and bruise the ginger and add, measure the sugar and add half to the contents of the bowl. Allow to stand for several hours, turning the figs over in the sugar occasionally.

Place in a preserving pan and heat slowly, stirring until the sugar has dissolved. Simmer gently until the fruit is tender— about 20 minutes.

Warm the remainder of the sugar and add with the lemon juice to the figs. Stir until the sugar has dissolved, then boil at a steady pace until the jam is a good consistency. It will take approximately 30 to 40 minutes for this quantity of figs. Pour into heated jars. Seal when cold.

FRUIT SALAD MARMALADE

2 pounds fresh pineapple
sugar
4 medium oranges
1 lemon
3 or 4 small bananas, slightly
  underripe
3 or 4 passionfruit

The day before the marmalade is to be cooked, cut the skin from the pineapple, shred the flesh coarsely and weigh 2 pounds. Sprinkle with ½ pound sugar. In another bowl place the finely sliced oranges and lemon and cover them with 8 cups of water.

Next day, simmer the oranges and the lemon until the rind is quite tender, then add the pineapple and simmer again until the pineapple is tender. When it has been cooking for about 30 minutes, add the sliced bananas and the passionfruit pulp.

Measure the cooked mixture, return it to the pan and for each cup allow a cup of sugar. Stir until the sugar has dissolved, then bring to the boil and cook at a steady pace until a little of it jells when tested on a cold saucer. Pour into heated jars. Seal when cold.

GINGER MARMALADE

3 Seville oranges
2½ pints water
¼ pint water
4 ounces green root ginger
1½ pounds apples
3¼ pounds sugar

Wash the oranges and slice them very thinly. Place them in a bowl with the 2½ pints water and the root ginger which has been scraped and bruised. Allow to stand overnight.

Next day, place in a preserving pan and bring to the boil. Simmer until the fruit rind is tender—about 45 minutes.

Peel, core and thinly slice the apples and cook them in the ¼ pint of water until they are mushy and soft. Add to the orange mixture in the preserving pan. Add the sugar and stir until dissolved. Bring to the boil and cook rapidly until the jam will jell when tested on a saucer. Pour into heated jars. Seal when cold.

GOLDEN SHRED MARMALADE

grapefruit
water
lemon juice
sugar

Wash the fruit and weigh it. Thinly slice off the yellow peel, shred it finely, place in a bowl, cover with cold water and allow to stand overnight.

Next day, cut up the pulp of the grapefruit and add 2 tablespoons of lemon juice to each pound of fruit. Place the pulp, peel and lemon juice in a preserving pan and add a quart of water to each pound of fruit. If liked the pips may be tied in a piece of muslin and cooked with the fruit. Bring to the boil, then simmer until the rind is quite tender. Remove the pips.

Measure, and for every cup of cooked mixture, add 1 cup of sugar. Stir over the heat until the sugar has dissolved, then boil steadily until the marmalade flakes from the wooden stirring spoon, or jells when cooled on a saucer. The time for cooking after adding the sugar should be between 40 and 60 minutes. Cool slightly before pouring into heated jars. Seal securely.

GOOSEBERRY AND STRAWBERRY JAM

1 pound strawberries
1 pound gooseberries
½ cup water
2 pounds sugar
1 tablespoon lemon juice

Wash and hull the strawberries and top and tail the gooseberries.

Place the gooseberries in a saucepan with the water, bring to the boil, and cook for 5 minutes or until the berries are soft. Add the strawberries and cook for a further 5 minutes.

Add the warmed sugar and lemon juice and stir until the sugar has dissolved. Continue boiling for 15 to 20 minutes or until the jam flakes from the wooden stirring spoon or jells when tested on a saucer. Pour into heated jars. Seal when cold.

GOOSEBERRY JAM

4 pounds gooseberries
4 pounds sugar
½ pint cold water

Choose fresh young gooseberries (the skins should not be tough). Top, tail, wash and drain them well. Place the sugar and water in a preserving pan and stir over low heat until the sugar has dissolved. Skim if necessary. Add the gooseberries and cook until the jam jells when tested on a cold saucer. This will take about 30 minutes. Pour into heated jars. Seal when cold.

Firm, slightly underripe but not immature fruit is best for berry jams

GRAPE JAM

6 pounds grapes
½ pint water
4½ pounds sugar
2 level teaspoons citric acid

Wash and seed the grapes. Tie the seeds in a piece of muslin and add to the grapes and water in the preserving pan. Cook for 30 minutes.

Remove the bag containing the seeds and add the warmed sugar. Bring to the boil and add the citric acid. Cook for 20 minutes before testing for setting. Pour into heated jars. Seal when cold.

GRAPEFRUIT AND PINEAPPLE MARMALADE

2 medium-sized grapefruit
2 medium-sized smooth yellow
   lemons
1 medium-sized pineapple
6 cups water
sugar

Remove the outer rind from the grapefruit and lemons and shred very finely. Squeeze the juice from the fruits and strain through a fine strainer. Cut up the white pith and tie it in a piece of muslin with the pips.

Place the fruit rind and juice in a bowl and add the water. Allow to stand overnight.

Next day, place in a preserving pan with the pineapple which has been peeled and shredded, and the bag of pips and pith. Simmer gently until the fruit rind is quite soft—this may take 40 to 60 minutes.

Measure the fruit and liquid (first removing the muslin bag) and to each cupful add 1 cup of sugar. Stir over the heat until the sugar has dissolved, then bring to the boil. Boil steadily for about 40 minutes, or until a little will jell when tested on a cold saucer. Cool slightly before pouring into heated jars. Seal when cold.

GRAPEFRUIT MARMALADE 1

Wash and weigh the fruit—it is not advisable to have more than 3 pounds of fruit for the one boiling. Note the weight, so that you use the correct amount of water and lemon juice.

Remove the rind from the fruit, slice it very thinly, and place in a bowl, then cover with water and allow to stand overnight.

Next day place the rind in a preserving pan with the finely sliced pulp of the fruit, and to each pound of fruit add 1 quart of water (part of which has been drained from the soaked rind) and 2 tablespoons of lemon juice for each pound of fruit.

Cook slowly until the rind is quite soft. Measure again and for each cupful add 1 cup of sugar. Stir over the heat until the sugar has dissolved, then boil fairly steadily until the mixture flakes from the wooden stirring spoon or jells when tested on a cold saucer.

During the final stages of cooking, the marmalade will tend to foam up in the pan. This is a good indication that cooking is completed. After the sugar has been added the marmalade will need about 40 minutes cooking. Allow to stand for a couple of minutes, then remove any scum. Pour into heated jars. Seal when cold.

GRAPEFRUIT MARMALADE 2

2 large grapefruit
1 lemon
6 pints water
6 pounds sugar

Wash and dry the grapefruit and lemon and shred the rind finely. Thinly slice the pulp of both, discarding the white membrane. Cover rind and pulp with water and allow to stand overnight.

Next day, bring to the boil and simmer until the rind is quite tender. Add the warmed sugar and stir until it has completely dissolved. Bring to the boil and cook at a steady pace until a little of it jells when tested on a cold saucer: this should take 35 to 45 minutes if the marmalade is being made in a preserving pan. Allow extra time if cooking in a saucepan. Cool slightly, then pour into heated jars. Seal when cold.

GREEN TOMATO JAM

6 pounds green tomatoes
2 ounces green ginger
4½ pounds sugar
rind and juice of 2 lemons

Wash the tomatoes, scald them and remove the skins. Chop them up and place in a preserving pan.

Scrape and bruise the ginger, tie it in a piece of muslin, and add to the tomatoes in the preserving pan. Sprinkle over half the sugar. Leave overnight.

Next day, bring to the boil and cook for a few minutes or until the tomatoes begin to soften. Remove the ginger. Add the sugar and stir until it has dissolved, then bring to the boil and boil for 5 minutes. Stir in the lemon rind and juice and cook until a little will jell when tested on a cold saucer. Pour into heated jars. Seal when cold.

282

LEMON MARMALADE

1½ pounds lemons
3 pints water
sugar

Wash and dry the lemons, then peel off the yellow rind very thinly and slice it finely into a bowl. Remove the white pith, chop it up and tie in a piece of musline with the lemon pips. Slice the lemons thinly and place in the bowl with the rind.

Cover the fruit with the water and add the bag of pith and seeds. Allow to stand overnight.

Next day, place in a preserving pan and bring to the boil. Simmer gently until the fruit is quite tender—about 45 minutes. Lift out the bag.

Measure the cooked mixture and return it to the preserving pan, adding 1 cup of sugar to each cupful. Stir over the heat until the sugar has dissolved, then bring to the boil. Boil rapidly until a little of the marmalade will jell when tested on a saucer.

Allow the marmalade to stand for about 4 or 5 minutes, then pour into clean, warm, dry jars. Seal when cold.

MANDARIN MARMALADE 1

3 pounds mandarins
4½ pints water
juice of 2 lemons
1 ounce Jamsetta
sugar

Wash the mandarins and slice them thinly, discarding any pips. Cover with the water and allow to stand overnight.

Next day, bring slowly to the boil and simmer until the fruit rind is tender—about 1 hour. Cool slightly, then measure the fruit and liquid, using a cup. Measure out an equal quantity of sugar.

Return the measured fruit and liquid to the preserving pan and add the lemon juice and the Jamsetta. Bring to the boil and boil for 1 minute, stirring constantly, then add the warmed sugar and stir until it has dissolved.

Boil rapidly for 10 minutes, then test for setting. If necessary boil until a little cooled on a saucer will jell. Allow to stand for about 5 minutes before pouring into heated jars. Seal when cold.

MANDARIN MARMALADE 2

7 tight-skinned (known as thorny) mandarins
1 lemon
4 cups water
2 pounds sugar

Wash the mandarins and the lemon and slice very finely. Tie the pips in a piece of muslin, place in a bowl with the sliced fruit, add the water and allow to stand overnight.

Next day, place in a preserving pan and bring slowly to the boil. Simmer until the fruit is very soft. Remove the muslin bag. Add the warmed sugar and stir until it has completely dissolved. Bring to the boil and cook steadily until a little will jell when tested on a cold saucer. Cool slightly before pouring into heated jars. Seal when cold.

283

MELON JAM

melon
sugar
lemon juice

Peel the melon, slice it thickly and remove the seeds, then cut the slices into small cubes.

To every pound of prepared melon allow ¾ of a pound of sugar. Melon has little or no pectin, so lemon juice is needed: add the juice of a medium-sized lemon for every 2 pounds of prepared fruit.

Sprinkle the melon with half the sugar and allow to stand overnight.

Next day, add the lemon juice, bring slowly to the boil in a preserving pan and simmer until the fruit is soft and clear. This will take about 40 minutes. Add the remainder of the sugar (first warm it) and stir until it has dissolved. Boil at a steady rate until a little of the jam will jell when tested on a cold saucer. This second boiling will take 30 to 40 minutes. Pour into heated jars. Seal when cold.

Flavouring fruits may be prepared and combined with the melon and allowed to stand overnight with it (the only exception being passionfruit—see below). Try these combinations:

MELON AND ORANGE
Add the grated rind and the juice of 4 medium-sized oranges to 6 pounds of prepared melon.

MELON AND PINEAPPLE
Add 1 medium-sized pineapple, peeled and grated, to 6 pounds of prepared melon.

MELON AND GINGER
The quantity of ginger will vary according to taste. For a strong ginger flavour add 1 ounce of green root ginger to every 2 pounds of melon (scrape and bruise the ginger before adding to the prepared melon).

MELON AND PASSIONFRUIT
This is the only flavouring that should not be soaked overnight with the melon. After the melon has been cooked with the first lot of sugar, add the passionfruit pulp (use 6 passionfruit to 6 pounds of melon).

MOCK RASPBERRY JAM

2 pounds quinces
3 pounds tomatoes
2 cups water
juice of 2 lemons
5 pounds sugar

Peel and core the quinces, then dice the fruit finely or put it through a mincer. Tie the cores and the peelings in a piece of muslin. Place the tomatoes in a bowl and pour boiling water over them. Drain, then remove the skins and chop the tomatoes up roughly.

284

Place the quinces, tomatoes, water and lemon juice in a preserving pan and simmer until the fruit is quite soft. Add the warmed sugar and stir until it has dissolved. Bring to the boil and boil rapidly until the jam will set when a little is tested on a cold saucer. Remove any scum, then pour the jam into heated jars. Seal when cold.

NECTARINE JAM

6 pounds nectarines
1 pint water
5 pounds sugar
3 tablespoons lemon juice

Prepare and stone the fruit before weighing. Place in a preserving pan with the water and simmer until the fruit is soft. Add the warmed sugar and the lemon juice and stir until the sugar has dissolved. Bring to the boil, then cook at a steady pace until the jam is a good consistency. Pour into heated jars. Seal when cold.

ORANGE AND APPLE MARMALADE

6 Granny Smith cooking apples
2 sweet oranges
1 lemon
5 pounds sugar

Peel, core and quarter the apples. Place the peel and the cores in a saucepan, barely cover with water and simmer for 30 minutes. Place the apples in the preserving pan and strain onto them the liquid in which the peelings were cooked. Simmer until soft.

Wash and dry the oranges and the lemon. Grate the rind of both fruits and add to the apples together with the juice. Add the warmed sugar and stir over medium heat until the sugar has dissolved. Bring to the boil and boil at a steady rolling pace until the marmalade jells when tested on a saucer. Pour into heated jars. Seal when cold.

ORANGE AND APRICOT MARMALADE

3 large oranges
1 pound dried apricots
5 pints water
4 pounds sugar

Wash the oranges and slice them very thinly. Place in a bowl with the apricots and cover with the water. Allow to stand overnight.

Next day, place in a preserving pan and bring to the boil. Simmer until the rind is tender—about 45 minutes. Add the warmed sugar and stir until dissolved. Bring to the boil and boil steadily until the jam will jell when tested on a cold saucer. Pour into heated jars. Seal when cold.

PASSIONFRUIT JAM

Cut $4\frac{1}{2}$ dozen passionfruit in halves and scoop out the pulp. Place the shells in a saucepan, add enough water to cover them, and bring to the boil. Boil for 30 minutes. Strain, but do not discard the water.

Scoop out any soft pulp from inside the cooked shells.

Measure half the water in which the passionfruit shells were cooked, place it in a clean saucepan, add the passionfruit pulp and cook for 10 minutes.

Now add 4 pounds warmed sugar and stir until it has dissolved. Bring to the boil and boil for 45 to 60 minutes, stirring well during the boiling period. Pour into heated jars. Seal when cold. Store in a cool, dark cupboard.

PEACH AND ORANGE MARMALADE

6 medium-sized freestone
  peaches
3 medium-sized oranges
1 medium-sized lemon
sugar

Wash and peel the peaches, cut in halves and remove the stones. Wash the oranges, discard the ends and the pips and cut into chunky pieces (do not peel the oranges). Peel the lemon, removing all the white pith, discard any pips, and cut the flesh into chunky pieces.

Put the peach halves and the lemon and orange pieces through a mincer, using the medium blade (place a bowl under the mincer to catch the juices). Measure the pulp and the juices of the combined fruits, and for each cupful add 1 cup of sugar. Place in a preserving pan and bring slowly to the boil, stirring until the sugar has dissolved.

Reduce the heat and boil gently for about 40 minutes, stirring occasionally. The marmalade will be cooked when the mixture will sheet or flake from the wooden stirring spoon or when a little will jell when tested on a saucer. Pour into heated jars. Seal when cold.

PEACH AND PASSIONFRUIT JAM

5 pounds peaches
4 pounds sugar
4 tablespoons lemon juice
2 dozen passionfruit

Peel the peaches and cut the flesh into thin slices. Cover with half the sugar and the lemon juice and allow to stand overnight.

Next day, simmer until the fruit is quite tender. Add the remainder of the sugar (warmed), and the passionfruit (if liked, with some of the seeds strained out). Stir until the sugar has dissolved, then boil until a good consistency. Pour into heated jars. Seal when cold.

PEACH AND PINEAPPLE JAM

4 pounds peaches
1 medium-sized pineapple
$\frac{3}{4}$ pint water
$4\frac{1}{2}$ pounds sugar
juice of 2 lemons, or 2 teaspoons
  citric acid

Peel and dice the peaches. Peel and grate the pineapple. Place the peach stones and the pineapple peel and cores in a saucepan with the water, bring to the boil and simmer for 30 minutes. Strain and reserve the liquid.

Add this liquid to the chopped and grated fruits and simmer until the fruit is soft. Add the warmed sugar and the lemon juice and stir until the sugar has dissolved. Bring to the boil and boil rapidly until the mixture will jell when a little is tested on a cold saucer. Pour into heated jars. Seal when cold.

PEACH JAM

6 pounds peaches
1½ pints water
1 rounded teaspoon citric acid
4½ pounds sugar

Wash, peel and stone the fruit. Place the peelings and the stones in a saucepan, add enough water to barely cover and simmer for 20 minutes. Strain. Use this liquid as part of the 1½ pints required for the jam.

Slice the peaches and place in a preserving pan. Add the strained liquid and the acid and bring to the boil. Simmer until the peaches are quite tender—about 40 minutes.

Add the warmed sugar, stir until the sugar has dissolved, then boil until the jam is thick—about 30 minutes. Pour into heated jars. Seal when cold.

PEAR GINGER

6 pounds hard pears
3½ pounds sugar
1½ pints cold water
½ to 1 pound preserved ginger
3 lemons

Use Packham, Bosse or other very hard pears for this conserve. William pears are unsuitable.

Peel and dice the pears and sprinkle with the sugar. Allow to stand overnight.

Next day, add the water and bring the pears slowly to the boil. The mixture should not reach boiling point until all the sugar has dissolved.

Add the chopped ginger and lemon juice and boil until a good consistency. This will take at least 40 minutes. Pour into heated jars. Seal when cold.

PINEAPPLE JELLY

This is made from the core and the skin of a large pineapple. Place the skin and core in a saucepan or preserving pan and cover with water. Allow to stand for about 2 hours.

Bring to the boil very slowly, then simmer gently for 1 hour or until the rind is very tender. Pour through fine muslin, catching the juice in a basin. Measure the juice.

For every cup of pineapple juice add 1 cup of sugar and 2 tablespoons of lemon juice. Return the mixture to the saucepan and stir until the sugar has dissolved. Bring to the boil.

Boil rapidly until the mixture will jell when a little is placed on a cold saucer. Pour into heated jars. Seal when cold.

PLUM JAM

6 pounds plums
6 pounds sugar
1 pint water

Wash and, if possible, remove the stones from the plums. Slice if very large. Place in a preserving pan with the water, bring to the boil and simmer until quite soft—about 30 minutes. Add the warmed sugar and stir until it has dissolved. Increase the heat and bring to the boil. Cook at a steady rolling boil until a little tested on a cold saucer will jell. This could take from 20 to

287

40 minutes, according to the size and quality of the plums. Pour into heated jars. Seal when cold.

For a well flavoured plum jam a small wineglass of sherry may be added a few minutes before the jam is taken from the stove. Use a wineglassful to every 4 pounds of plums.

Another suggestion for flavouring plum jam is to add a tin of raspberry jam to 4 pounds of plums (add to the jam just before taking from the stove to place in the jars).

PLUM AND GOOSEBERRY JAM

3 pounds plums
2 pounds gooseberries
5 pounds sugar
$\frac{3}{4}$ pint water

Follow the same method as for plum jam, adding the gooseberries to the plums.

PLUM AND PEACH JAM

Equal quantities of plums and peaches, pound for pound of sugar and $\frac{1}{2}$ pint of water to 6 pounds of combined fruit.

PLUM AND PINEAPPLE JAM

6 pounds plums
1 medium-sized pineapple
6 pounds sugar
$\frac{1}{2}$ pint water

Follow the same method as for plum jam, adding the grated flesh of the pineapple to the plums.

PLUM AND RASPBERRY OR LOGANBERRY JAM

2 pounds berries
4 pounds plums
6 pounds sugar

No water is used. Crush the berries in a saucepan over low heat, then add the plums.

POORMAN'S ORANGE MARMALADE

1 pound poorman's oranges
4 ounces lemons
a good pinch of salt
$3\frac{1}{2}$ pints water
sugar

Cut the oranges in halves and remove the pips. Slice the unpeeled fruit (including the lemon) as thinly as possible. Tie the pips from both fruits in a piece of muslin. Place both fruits in a preserving pan and add the salt, pips, and water.

Bring very slowly to the boil, then simmer until the peel of both fruits is quite tender. This will take about 40 minutes. Take off the stove and leave the mixture for 24 hours. Remove the bag of pips.

Measure, and for every cupful of cooked mixture allow 1 cup of sugar. Stir over the heat until the sugar has dissolved, then bring to the boil. Boil steadily until the jell stage is reached: this will take between 50 and 60 minutes, but begin testing after about 45 minutes cooking. Allow to stand for a few minutes before pouring into heated jars. Seal when cold.

PRESERVED FIGS

6 pounds figs, firm, not too ripe
6 measuring cups sugar
2 measuring cups water
3 tablespoons vinegar

Wash the figs, then drain and dry them. Discard any with blemishes. Prick them all over with a skewer or a fine-tined fork.

Combine the sugar and water in a large saucepan and stir over gentle heat until the sugar has dissolved. Add the vinegar and bring to the boil.

Add the figs, lower the heat and simmer very gently without the lid for 1 hour. Turn the figs and syrup into a bowl and allow to stand overnight.

Next day, bring to the boil and simmer for a further hour. Turn into a bowl and let stand again overnight.

Next day, make a third boiling of 1 hour, by which time the figs should be heavily saturated with syrup. At this stage they may be bottled in the syrup and sealed, or placed on a wire tray and dried in the sun: if the figs are dried, roll them in sugar before storing in jars.

QUINCE AND PASSIONFRUIT JAM

4 pounds peeled and cored
  quinces
4 pints water
2 tablespoons lemon juice
3 pounds sugar
pulp of 8 passionfruit

Wash, peel and core the quinces, then weigh them. Place the cores and peelings in a saucepan with 1 pint of the water and simmer for 1 hour, covered, then strain, reserving the liquid.

Put the quinces through a mincer, or chop finely. Place in a preserving pan with the water and simmer until the fruit is quite tender. Add the strained liquid from the peelings, and the lemon juice and the warmed sugar. Stir until the sugar has dissolved, then bring to the boil. Boil rapidly for 20 minutes. Add the passionfruit pulp and continue boiling for a further 20 to 25 minutes, or until the jam will jell when tested. Pour into heated jars. Seal when cold.

QUINCE AND PINEAPPLE JAM

4 pounds peeled and cored
  quinces
4 pints water
2 tablespoons lemon juice
3 pounds sugar
15-ounce can crushed pineapple

Wash, dry, peel and core the quinces. Weigh them. Place the cores, seeds and peelings in a saucepan with 1 pint of the water. Cover and simmer for 1 hour. Strain and reserve this liquid.

Put the quinces through a mincer or chop them very finely. Place in a lightly greased preserving pan with the remainder of the water, the liquid strained from the cooked peelings, and the lemon juice. Boil until the fruit is quite tender.

Add the warmed sugar and the drained pineapple, stirring until the sugar has dissolved. Boil rapidly until the jam is a good colour and a little will set when cooled on a saucer. This will take about 40 minutes. Pour into heated jars. Seal when hot.

QUINCE JAM

4 pounds peeled and cored
  quinces
4 pints water
3 pounds sugar
2 tablespoons lemon juice

Wash, peel and core the quinces, then weigh them. Place the cores and peelings in a saucepan with 1 pint of water, cover, and simmer for 1 hour. Strain and reserve the liquid.

Put the quinces through a mincer or chop them very finely, place in a preserving pan with the water and simmer until tender. Add the strained juice from the cores, and the lemon juice.

Add the warmed sugar and stir until it has dissolved. Bring to the boil, then boil rapidly until the jam is a good colour and will jell when a little is cooled on a saucer. This should take about 40 minutes when cooked in a preserving pan, but allow longer if a deep saucepan is used. Pour into heated jars. Seal when cold.

QUINCE JELLY

Before making quince jelly make sure you have the right kind of quince. The old style quinces with the rough shape and appearance are far better for jelly making than the smooth, better looking fruit, which do not contain enough pectin to make the jelly set.

When you cut the quince, there should be a clear looking ring around the seeds. If this is not there, don't attempt to make jelly. Instead, use the quinces to make jam, adding lemon juice to ensure setting.

Wash, dry and cut up the quinces. Place them in a preserving pan, cover with water and bring very slowly to the boil. Cover and simmer until the fruit is very soft. This may take a couple of hours. Allow to cool slightly, then strain the quinces through a piece of muslin.

Measure the juice, and to every cupful add 1 cup of sugar and a teaspoon of lemon juice. Return the mixture to the preserving pan and stir until the sugar has dissolved. Remove the spoon and boil at a steady pace until a little, when tested on a cold saucer, will jell. This may take 40 minutes or more. Pour into heated jars. Seal while hot.

Do not attempt to make jelly from quinces which have been attacked by codlin moth.

RASPBERRY JAM

6 pounds raspberries
3 tablespoons lemon juice
6 pounds sugar

Pick over the raspberries and place them in a colander. Wash under running water for a few minutes, then allow to drain well.

Place the berries in a preserving pan and crush them lightly with the back of a wooden stirring spoon to free some of the juices. Cook over medium heat until the berries are quite tender—this will take about 20 minutes.

Add the lemon juice and the warmed sugar, stir until the sugar has dissolved, then bring to the boil. Boil rapidly until a little of the jam, tested on a cold saucer, will jell. This will take about another 20 minutes, but it will depend on the size of the vessel in which the jam is being made and the speed of cooking. The times above are based on jam cooked in a preserving pan, not a deep saucepan.

Pour into heated jars. Seal when cold.

SEVILLE ORANGE MARMALADE

5 Seville oranges
3 lemons
9 pounds sugar
9 pints water

Wash and dry the fruit, then slice both very finely. Place in a preserving pan and cover with the water. Allow to soak for 48 hours.

Bring to the boil and simmer for 45 minutes or until the rind of both fruits is tender. Add the sugar and stir until dissolved. Bring to the boil and boil briskly for about 1 hour, or until the marmalade will jell when a little is placed on a cold saucer. Pour into heated jars. Seal when cold.

SHADDOCK MARMALADE

Take 2 or 3 shaddocks, or enough to weigh 2 pounds. Make a brine, using 1 level tablespoon of salt to 1 quart of water. Soak the shaddocks in the brine for 24 hours.

Wash thoroughly in several changes of fresh cold water. Wipe, then cut into quarters and remove the thick skin, the white core and the seeds. Slice the quarters as thinly as possible, cover with 16 cups of water and allow to soak overnight.

Next day, pour off 8 cups of the water in which the shaddocks were standing, and replace with 8 cups of fresh water. Place in a preserving pan and bring to the boil. Simmer until the rind is tender. Now add 16 cups of warmed sugar and stir until the sugar has dissolved. Boil rapidly until a little of the jam jells when tested on a cold saucer. Allow to cool slightly, then pour carefully into warmed jars. Seal when cold.

STRAWBERRY JAM

3 pounds strawberries
3 dessertspoons lemon juice
3 pounds sugar

Wash and hull the strawberries, drain them and place in a preserving pan with the lemon juice. Heat gently, crushing the fruit lightly with the back of a spoon, until the strawberries are cooked—about 20 minutes.

Add the warmed sugar and stir over the heat until dissolved. Bring to the boil and boil at a steady pace until the jam will jell when tested on a cold saucer. For this small quantity it should not take more than about 15 or 20 minutes. Pour into warmed jars while it is hot. Seal when cold.

SWEET ORANGE MARMALADE

Wash some sweet oranges, dry them, then slice them very thinly. Place the pips in a bowl and just cover with water. Place the sliced oranges in another bowl and add 2 cups of water to each cupful of fruit. Allow to stand overnight.

Pour the water drained from the pips into a preserving pan then add the soaked fruit. Bring to the boil, then simmer until the rind is quite soft. This will take at least one hour.

Measure the fruit and liquid, return it to the pan and add 1 cup of sugar to each cupful of the mixture. Stir over the heat until the sugar has dissolved, then boil steadily until a little will jell when tested on a cold saucer. Pour into clean, warm, dry jars while hot. When cold, seal securely.

THREE-FRUIT MARMALADE

1 grapefruit
1 orange
1 lemon
sugar
water

Peel the grapefruit and discard half the rind. Thinly slice the remainder of the grapefruit rind. Cut the peeled grapefruit into slices. Thinly slice the orange and the lemon.

Measure the cut-up fruit and place in a preserving pan: to every cup of fruit add 3 cups of water. This may be soaked overnight or cooked straight away.

Bring to the boil, then simmer until the fruit rind is quite soft—about 45 minutes. Measure again, and to every cup of the softened fruit add 1 cup of sugar. Stir over medium heat until the sugar has dissolved, then cook fairly rapidly until a little of the jam jells when cooled on a saucer—this takes about 35 minutes. Leave for 5 minutes or so before pouring into clean hot jars (if poured in immediately the fruit will rise to the top). Seal when cold.

Cooking time after the sugar is added depends on the quantity being made and on the type of pan. If using a deep saucepan allow a little longer to cook, and don't attempt more than the quantity given above.

TREE TOMATO JAM

3 pounds tree tomatoes
2 lemons
3 pounds sugar

Pour boiling water over the tomatoes and allow them to stand for a few minutes. Drain, then remove the skins.

Slice the tomatoes, place in a preserving pan and add enough water to cover. Grate the outer rind from the lemons and add to the tomatoes. Remove the pith and the pips. Cut the lemon pulp into small pieces and add to the tomatoes. Bring to the boil and simmer until tender—about 30 minutes.

Add the warmed sugar, stir until dissolved, then boil fairly rapidly until setting point is reached. Skim the jam as the scum rises to the surface. While still hot, pour into warm jars. Seal when cold.

292

MEATS

AUSTRALIAN GOOSE

1 boned leg of lamb or mutton,
  3 to 3½ pounds
1 sheep's kidney
½ cup mashed cooked green peas
1 teaspoon butter
1 teaspoon chopped mint, parsley
  or herbs
1 onion
2 rashers of bacon
potatoes
2 extra bacon rashers (optional)

Have the butcher bone the leg of mutton or lamb. Skin the kidney, chop it and combine in a bowl with the peas, butter, mint, grated or finely chopped onion, and chopped bacon. Stuff the leg with this mixture, securing the opening with fine skewers.

Bake for about 2½ hours in a moderate oven, 350°F., placing some potatoes in a little fat in the same baking dish. When the meat is half cooked it may be covered with a couple of bacon rashers.

AUTUMN CURRY

1 large onion
½ green pepper
2 dessertspoons butter
¼ teaspoon monosodium
  glutamate
1 teaspoon salt
1 dessertspoon curry powder
1 pound minced steak
1 cup seeded raisins
1 bayleaf
1 cup water
½ cup salted peanuts
6 ounce packet frozen peas
1 level dessertspoon cornflour
  blended with a little water

Peel and slice the onion. Seed and slice the green pepper. Melt the butter in a pan and sauté the onion and green pepper for 5 minutes. Sprinkle the monosodium glutamate, salt and curry powder over the meat and place it in the pan. Cook, stirring well, until it changes colour.

Add the raisins, bayleaf and water. Stir until boiling, then cover and simmer for about 30 minutes. Add the peanuts and peas and cook for a further 5 minutes. Stir in the blended cornflour and cook, stirring well, until the curry boils and thickens. Cook for another 2 minutes, then serve over freshly cooked rice.

BAKED CUTLETS SUPREME

1 small onion
2 cups soft white breadcrumbs
1 tablespoon lemon juice
¼ teaspoon grated lemon rind
1 tablespoon finely chopped
  parsley
1 teaspoon mixed herbs
salt and pepper
1 tablespoon butter

Peel and chop the onion and place it in a saucepan with a little water to cook until tender. Drain. Combine the breadcrumbs, lemon juice, lemon rind, onion, parsley, herbs, salt, pepper and butter. Take about 1 tablespoonful of this seasoning, squeeze flat between the hands and mould over the meaty part on both sides of each cutlet. Hold the seasoning in place with a rasher of bacon secured with a cocktail pick.

Dip each cutlet in seasoned flour, then in the glaze, and finally in breadcrumbs. Chill for about 30 minutes.

293

6 lamb cutlets
6 thin rashers of bacon
seasoned flour
egg and milk glaze
soft white breadcrumbs for
    covering
oil or butter for baking
brown vegetable gravy for
    serving

Heat a little oil or butter in a shallow oven dish, place the cutlets in it and bake at 350°F. for 30 to 35 minutes or until tender. Serve with a brown vegetable gravy.

BAKED DEVILLED PORK CHOPS

3 dessertspoons chopped onion
1 ounce butter
2 cups soft white breadcrumbs
1 dessertspoon grated orange
    rind
1 tablespoon orange juice
2 teaspoons chilli powder
6 thick pork chops
a little oil for frying

For the orange sauce

$\frac{1}{3}$ cup vinegar
1$\frac{1}{2}$ cups orange juice
3 dessertspoons chopped onion
3 dessertspoons green pepper
1 clove of garlic
1 dessertspoon salt
1 dessertspoon chilli powder
1 teaspoon oregano
1 teaspoon sugar
a pinch of pepper

Sauté the chopped onion in the butter. Add to the breadcrumbs together with the orange rind and juice and the chilli powder, mixing well.

Cut a pocket in each of the pork chops and add enough of the stuffing to fill. Secure the opening with cocktail picks. Fry the chops in a little oil until brown on both sides, then lift out and place in a casserole.

To make the sauce, combine the vinegar, orange juice, onion, green pepper and crushed garlic and heat until boiling, then add the salt, chilli powder, oregano, sugar and pepper. Pour half the sauce over the chops, cover, and bake at 350°F. for 1 hour or until the chops are tender, turning them once during cooking.

Thicken the remainder of the orange sauce with a little blended flour. Skim the fat off the juices in the casserole and add these to the sauce. Heat thoroughly and serve in a gravy boat.

BAKED STUFFED CUTLETS

6 lamb cutlets
3 tablespoons soft white
    breadcrumbs
1 dessertspoon chopped onion
1 teaspoon chopped parsley
1 tomato
salt and pepper
1 egg mixed with a little milk
seasoned flour
breadcrumbs for covering

Mix the soft white breadcrumbs with the onion, parsley, chopped tomato, salt and pepper. Bind with a little of the egg and milk (use the remainder as a glaze to coat the cutlets).

Cut a pocket in each cutlet and fill with some of the prepared seasoning. Dip each cutlet in flour, then glaze with the beaten egg and milk mixture and cover with breadcrumbs.

Place on a greased shallow oven tray, cover with greased paper and bake in a moderate oven, 350°F., for 30 minutes.

Instead of the tomato, try mushrooms or sautéed chicken liver in the seasoning mixture.

Barbecued Pot Roast

BARBECUED POT ROAST

2 teaspoons salt
¼ teaspoon pepper
¼ cup plain flour
½ teaspoon paprika
4-pound sirloin beef
1 tablespoon fat
1 cup tomato juice
1 teaspoon chilli sauce
1 tablespoon lemon juice or
   vinegar
1 teaspoon Worcester sauce
½ teaspoon dry mustard
1 dessertspoon brown sugar
½ teaspoon celery seed
1 large onion

Mix the salt, pepper, flour and paprika and rub it into the meat. Heat the fat in a heavy saucepan and brown the meat well on all sides. Combine the tomato juice, chilli sauce, lemon juice, Worcester sauce, mustard, brown sugar and celery seed and pour over the meat. Turn the meat until it is well coated, then place sliced onion on top, cover the pan tightly, and simmer gently for about 2½ hours or until the meat is tender.

The liquid remaining in the saucepan may be thickened with a little blended flour or cornflour and served as a gravy with the meat.

BEEF AND TOMATO HOTPOT

1 pound topside steak
1 tablespoon fat
1 or 2 onions
1 tablespoon plain flour
¼ teaspoon salt
⅛ teaspoon pepper
¾ pound fresh tomatoes
4 potatoes
¾ cup hot water

Slice the beef paper thin in narrow strips. Melt the fat in a saucepan, add the beef and sliced onions and cook until both have slightly browned. Sprinkle in the flour, salt and pepper. Cook until the flour is brown.

Wash the tomatoes and slice them lengthwise. Place on top of the meat, then add peeled and quartered potatoes. Pour in the hot water. Bring gently to the boil, then cover and simmer for about 1 hour or until the meat and potatoes are tender.

295

BEEF CHOP SUEY

1½ pounds beef
¼ cup oil
2 dessertspoons soy sauce
a good pinch of pepper
1 teaspoon salt
3 cups celery pieces
2 small onions (or ½ cup
    chopped shallots)
1 teaspoon sugar
2 cups beef stock
2 cups bean shoots
3 dessertspoons cornflour
¼ cup cold water

Cut the beef into slivers and fry in the heated oil at a high temperature for about 3 minutes, stirring constantly. Stir in the soy sauce, pepper and salt. Remove from the pan and keep hot.

Add the celery pieces, chopped onion, sugar and stock to the hot oil remaining in the pan and cook for 10 minutes, stirring frequently.

Add the bean shoots and cook for 3 minutes, then add the beef. Blend the cornflour with the cold water and add to the mixture. Cook, stirring frequently until thickened. Continue cooking for 3 minutes after the mixture comes to the boil. Serve over hot boiled rice.

BEEF CURRY

1½ pounds steak
seasoned flour
1 ounce butter
2 medium-sized onions
1 clove of garlic
1 dessertspoon curry powder
1 tablespoon plain flour
1 tablespoon chutney
1 large tomato
1 large peeled apple
1 large banana
½ teaspoon salt
a pinch of allspice
½ pint stock
1 teaspoon lemon juice

Cut the steak into cubes, discarding any fat, and toss in the seasoned flour. Melt the butter in a large saucepan and brown the meat on all sides. Lift out. To the butter left in the pan (if necessary add a little more), add chopped onion and minced garlic and cook until the onion is brown. Stir in the curry powder and flour and cook for 2 minutes.

Add the chutney, sliced tomato, chopped apple and sliced banana. Season with the salt and allspice. Stir in the stock and lemon juice and bring to the boil. Return the browned meat to the saucepan.

Cover and simmer very gently for about 2 hours or until the meat is tender. Serve with freshly boiled rice and curry accompaniments.

BEEF ESTERHAZY

1½ pounds good steak, 1 inch
    thick
2 tablespoons plain flour
1 teaspoon salt
¼ teaspoon pepper
2 dessertspoons fat
2 carrots
1 onion
2 stalks celery
¼ cup snipped parsley
½ pound fresh mushrooms
1 dessertspoon paprika
2 soup cubes
1½ cups water
½ cup sour cream

Rub the steak with the combined flour, salt and pepper. Heat the fat in a saucepan and brown the steak on both sides. Remove the meat, leaving any fat in the saucepan.

Peel and slice the carrots and onion and chop the celery. Place in the pan with the parsley and mushrooms and sauté for a few minutes, then add 1 tablespoon of seasoned flour and the paprika.

Dissolve the soup cubes in the water, add to the mixture and stir until boiling.

Return the meat to the pan, cover, and simmer for about 1 hour or until fork-tender.

Beat the sour cream in a bowl with a little of the liquid from the pan. Stir into the meat until almost boiling. Serve with freshly boiled noodles or rice.

BEEF GOULASH

1½ cups lima or navy beans
3 level tablespoons plain flour
1 level teaspoon salt
¼ level teaspoon pepper
1 medium onion
3 level tablespoons dripping
1½ pounds round or chuck steak
warm water
1 tablespoon vinegar
2 or 3 tomatoes

Soak the beans in warm water for at least 12 hours. Strain, cover with hot water and cook for 20 minutes or until tender, adding a little salt to the water.

Cut the steak into 1-inch cubes and roll in the combined flour, salt and pepper. Slice the onion.

Heat the dripping in a saucepan and fry the meat, stirring occasionally until it has browned on all sides. Add the onion slices and fry until brown, then stir in any remaining flour. Add the drained beans, barely cover with warm water, add the vinegar and stir until the mixture boils. Skin the tomatoes, cut into quarters and add to the goulash. Cover and simmer for about 2 hours, or transfer to a casserole and bake in a moderate oven, 350°F., for about the same time.

VARIATIONS

1. Use claret or Burgundy wine in place of half the water.
2. Add a dozen oysters a few minutes before serving.
3. Add ½ pound field or cultivated mushrooms (or a small can of mushrooms).
4. Omit the beans and substitute 1½ cups chopped celery.
5. Omit the beans and tomatoes and substitute 2 cups of mixed diced carrots, parsnips and celery.
6. Add 2 level teaspoons of curry powder, an extra onion, 1 diced apple and 1 sliced banana just before adding the water and a squeeze of lemon juice.

BEEF NAPOLI

1½ pounds good stewing steak
½ teaspoon salt
⅛ teaspoon pepper
1 tablespoon oil or melted butter
6-ounce can of tomato paste
¾ cup water
1 dessertspoon lemon juice
¼ teaspoon sugar
½ teaspoon marjoram
1 small carrot
½ clove of garlic
½ pound elbow macaroni
2 tablespoons grated cheese
1 dessertspoon chopped chives or
  parsley

Cut the meat into 1-inch pieces and sprinkle with the salt and pepper. Heat the oil in a pan and fry the meat to lightly brown it.

Mix the tomato paste with the water, lemon juice, sugar, marjoram, thinly sliced carrot and crushed garlic. Pour over the meat. Cover the pan (or transfer to a saucepan and cover) and cook for about 2 hours or until the meat is tender.

Cook the macaroni in boiling salted water, drain, and toss with the cheese and chives. Place in a serving dish and spoon the cooked meat on top.

297

BEEF OLIVES

1½ pounds good stewing steak
3 tablespoons soft white
   breadcrumbs
about 1 teaspoon chopped suet
1 teaspoon salt
¼ teaspoon pepper
½ teaspoon thyme
½ teaspoon marjoram
a few drops of lemon juice or a
   little rind
1 dessertspoon chopped parsley
1 egg or a little milk
2 cups water
1 slightly rounded dessertspoon
   plain flour blended with a little
   cold water

Cut the steak into pieces about 4 inches square. Mix the breadcrumbs with the suet, salt, pepper, thyme, marjoram, lemon, and parsley, and bind with a little egg or milk.

Place a portion of the stuffing on each piece of steak, roll up, and tie firmly with fine white string. Heat a little fat in a saucepan and brown the rolls on all sides. Pour away the fat and add the water. Cover and simmer for about 2 hours or until the meat is tender.

Add the blended flour to the saucepan to provide a thickening for the gravy, stir until boiling, then cook for about 5 minutes. Lift out the beef olives, remove the string and return them to the gravy to reheat before serving.

BEEF RAGOUT

1½ pounds stewing steak
2 medium-sized onions
2 medium-sized carrots
1 bayleaf
½ cup red wine
1 dessertspoon oil
1 rounded tablespoon plain flour
salt and pepper
1 cup stock, or water and a beef
   soup cube
2 tomatoes
1 small clove of garlic
a pinch of mixed herbs

Trim the steak and cut into ¾-inch cubes. Place in a bowl with 1 sliced onion, the sliced carrots and the bayleaf. Add the wine, cover, and allow to stand overnight.

Next day drain off and reserve the liquid. Fry the meat on all sides in the heated oil until brown. Lift it out, add the remaining sliced onion and cook until brown. Stir in the flour, about 1 teaspoon of salt and a dash of pepper and cook until the flour has browned.

Add the stock and the liquid drained from the meat and stir until it boils and thickens. Return the meat to the saucepan and add peeled and sliced tomatoes, crushed garlic and the herbs. Cover. Simmer gently for about 2 hours or until the steak is tender.

BEEF ROLLS WITH WINE

1½ pounds topside steak
1 clove of garlic
½ pound sausage meat
¾ cup finely chopped onion
1 tablespoon chopped parsley
salt and pepper
about 2 tablespoons seasoned
   plain flour
1 tablespoon melted fat or heated
   oil
½ cup claret
½ cup stock, or water and a beef
   soup cube

Trim the fat from the steak. Cut the steak into pieces about 2 by 3 inches and flatten with a meat mallet or a rolling-pin.

Crush the garlic and mix with the sausage meat, onion, parsley and a little salt and pepper. Spread some of this mixture on each piece of steak. Roll up and secure with cocktail picks before covering with seasoned flour.

Heat the fat or oil in a saucepan and brown the meat rolls on all sides. Pour away any surplus fat and add the wine and stock. Cover and simmer gently for about 1 hour or until the meat is tender.

The gravy may be thickened with a little blended flour. Serve with fluffy mashed potatoes and buttered carrots.

BEEF STEW WITH ORANGE DUMPLINGS

1 small onion
½ turnip or carrot
1½ pounds good stewing steak
1 tablespoon seasoned plain flour
1 dessertspoon fat
1 cup stock, or water and a soup
    cube
6 pickled walnuts
chopped parsley

For the orange dumplings

3 rounded tablespoons
    self-raising flour
a good pinch of salt
1 dessertspoon grated orange
    rind
1½ ounces shredded suet
water and orange juice to mix

Peel and dice the onion and turnip. Cut the meat into cubes and roll in the seasoned flour. Melt the fat in a saucepan, fry the vegetables lightly, then add the steak and cook until it changes colour. Pour on the stock.

Cover and simmer gently for 1½ hours or until the steak is almost tender, then add the sliced or halved walnuts. Drop the dumplings on top (see below) and cook for a further 30 minutes. Serve sprinkled with parsley.

To make the dumplings sift the flour with the salt, add the orange rind, rub in the suet, and mix to a soft dough with the combined water and orange juice. Divide into small portions, each about 1 inch in diameter, and roll into balls. Drop on top of the meat when adding the walnuts.

BEEF STROGANOFF

2 pounds buttock steak
4 tablespoons butter
4 level tablespoons plain flour
1 level teaspoon salt
1½ cups thinly sliced mushrooms
1 cup finely chopped onion or
    shallot
2 cloves of garlic
2 dessertspoons tomato paste
2 cups stock, or 2 cups water and
    a beef soup cube
3 tablespoons sherry
¼ to ½ cup cream

Cut the meat into ¼-inch slivers. Melt 2 tablespoons of the butter in a pan. Combine 1 tablespoon of the flour with the salt, and dredge the meat with this mixture, then lightly fry until brown. Add the mushrooms, onion and crushed garlic and cook for 3 or 4 minutes or until the onion is barely tender. Remove the meat mixture from the pan. Add the remaining butter to the pan and, when melted, stir in the rest of the flour, add the tomato paste and gradually stir in the stock. Cook, stirring constantly until the sauce boils and thickens.

Add the meat and mushrooms to the sauce, cover and cook over low heat until the meat is tender—about 1 hour.

Just before serving, stir in the cream and sherry and heat thoroughly without boiling. Serve with freshly cooked rice which has finely chopped parsley tossed through it.

BEEF-STUFFED PEPPERS

6 good-sized green peppers
1 dessertspoon butter or
    margarine
¼ cup finely chopped onion
1 pound finely minced steak
½ cup chopped celery
1½ cups cooked rice
½ teaspoon salt

Cut the tops from the peppers and remove the membrane and seeds. Cover the peppers with boiling salted water and simmer for 10 minutes. Drain.

Melt the butter in a pan and brown the onion, then add the meat and celery. Cook, stirring well until the meat changes colour. Add the rice and the salt. Spoon into the parboiled peppers and place them in an upright position in a deep casserole.

For the creole sauce

16-ounce can of tomatoes
¼ cup chopped onion
½ teaspoon salt
1 teaspoon sugar
1 teaspoon crushed sweet basil
1 dessertspoon plain flour
¼ cup water

2 pounds stewing steak
1 tablespoon butter
½ cup sliced onion
1 dessertspoon curry powder
1 teaspoon salt
⅛ teaspoon pepper
⅛ teaspoon powdered cloves
1 tablespoon slivered crystallized
    ginger
1 dessertspoon chopped mint
1 tablespoon plain flour
½ pint stock, or water and a soup
    cube
¼ cup flaked or desiccated coco-
    nut
1 tablespoon lemon juice
½ cup cream
1 tablespoon slivered almonds
pineapple rice (recipe follows)
cashew nuts, chutney, raisins and
    tomato slices

1¼ cups raw long-grain rice
¼ cup water
2 dessertspoons butter
1 small can crushed pineapple
    drained

6 lamb shanks
1 tablespoon plain flour
½ teaspoon salt

Make the sauce by simmering the tomatoes, onion, salt, sugar and sweet basil in a saucepan for 10 minutes, then thickening with the flour blended with the cold water. Pour over the peppers, cover, and bake in a moderate oven, 350°F., for about 45 minutes. Uncover and bake for a further 15 minutes.

BENGAL CURRY

Make the curry the day before it is required. Cut the steak into 1-inch cubes and sauté in the hot butter until brown on all sides — about 20 minutes. In the fat left in the pan, sauté the onion, curry powder, salt, pepper, cloves, ginger and mint. Cook, stirring well, until the onion is tender. It may be necessary to add a little more butter.

Remove from the heat, add the flour and stir until smooth. Cook for 1 minute, then add the stock and bring to the boil, stirring constantly. Reduce the heat, add the sautéed beef, cover, and simmer for at least 1½ hours or until the meat is tender. Refrigerate overnight.

Next day, allow to stand at room temperature for 30 minutes, then place over low heat and heat gently until just simmering, stirring occasionally. Don't overcook at this stage, or the meat will be ragged.

Stir in the coconut, lemon juice, cream and almonds, and heat for 5 minutes. Serve with rice and the curry accompaniments.

PINEAPPLE RICE

The day before the rice is needed, cook it in a pint of water with 2 teaspoons of salt until just tender. Drain if necessary. Refrigerate, covered, overnight.

About an hour before the rice is to be served, place it in a large baking dish with ¼ cup water. Cover with foil, place in a 300°F. oven and cook, stirring occasionally for about 30 minutes. Add the butter and the crushed pineapple, toss well, re-cover and leave in the oven until thoroughly heated through.

BRAISED LAMB SHANKS WITH ORANGE

Roll the shanks in the seasoned flour, then brown them in a pan in the hot oil. Add the remaining ingredients (except the orange sections). Cover and bring to the boil, then lower the

1 tablespoon oil or shortening
1 dessertspoon light brown sugar
a pinch of ground ginger
1 dessertspoon grated orange rind
1 cup orange juice
1 cup orange sections

heat and simmer until the shanks are tender. This will take from 1¾ to 2 hours. Serve garnished with the fresh orange sections.

BRAISED STEAK AND TOMATOES

¼ pound bacon
2 pounds oyster blade steak
seasoned flour
1 clove of garlic
3 or 4 tomatoes
1 cup chopped onion
1 cup chopped celery
2 tablespoons sherry
1 teaspoon Worcester sauce
2 teaspoons brown sugar
1 tablespoon soy sauce
½ cup stock or water
salt and pepper

Remove the rind and cut the bacon into 1-inch pieces. Place in a pan and fry until crisp, then lift out and drain leaving the fat in the pan. Cut the steak into cubes, roll in seasoned flour, and fry lightly in the bacon fat. Lift out and place in a casserole, cover with the cooked bacon, then add crushed garlic, sliced tomatoes and the chopped onion and celery.

Combine the sherry with the Worcester sauce, brown sugar, soy sauce and stock. Pour over the meat, and season to taste with salt and pepper. Cover and simmer for 2 hours or until the meat is tender. Adjust the seasoning, adding more salt and pepper if necessary.

BRAISED VEAL

5 level dessertspoons butter or margarine
2 pounds veal steak
salt and pepper
½ pound mushrooms
1 medium-sized onion
1 clove of garlic
½ bayleaf
1 dessertspoon tomato sauce
¼ teaspoon oregano
¼ teaspoon thyme
¼ teaspoon pepper
1 tablespoon plain flour
¾ cup chicken stock, or water and a chicken soup cube
2 dessertspoons red wine
2 teaspoons finely chopped parsley

Melt 3 dessertspoons of the butter in a pan and lightly brown the thinly sliced veal. Sprinkle with salt and pepper while frying. Place in a casserole dish.

Melt the remaining 2 dessertspoons of butter in the pan and sauté the sliced mushrooms and chopped onion. Cook until the onion is soft and lightly browned. Season with the crushed garlic, bayleaf, tomato sauce, oregano, thyme and pepper. Blend in the flour and cook for 2 minutes, then add the stock and wine and stir until the mixture boils and thickens. Simmer for 5 minutes, then pour over the veal in the casserole. Sprinkle with parsley, cover, and bake in a moderate oven, 350°F., for 1 hour or until the veal is tender.

301

6 ounces shortcrust pastry

3 dessertspoons butter or
    margarine

1 cup very thinly sliced onion

1 pound hamburger steak

1 teaspoon salt

$\frac{1}{4}$ teaspoon monosodium
    glutamate

$\frac{1}{4}$ teaspoon pepper

1 tablespoon plain flour

1 cup sour cream or milk

2 eggs

1 teaspoon salt for the topping

paprika

2 dessertspoons oil

2 pounds lean beef

2 dessertspoons plain flour

1 teaspoon salt

$\frac{1}{4}$ teaspoon pepper

1 cup Burgundy

1 cup water

1 clove of garlic

$\frac{1}{2}$ teaspoon thyme

1 bayleaf

3 sprigs of parsley

6 small onions

6 small potatoes

3 small carrots

3 small parsnips

1 pound cooked peas

2 medium onions

$\frac{1}{2}$ cup melted butter

1$\frac{1}{2}$ pounds round or buttock
    steak

2 tablespoons seasoned flour

2 dessertspoons curry powder

$\frac{1}{2}$ teaspoon chilli powder

1 clove of garlic

1 sprig of parsley

1 peeled green apple

$\frac{1}{4}$ cup coconut

$\frac{1}{2}$ teaspoon salt

1 cup sliced tomatoes

$\frac{1}{2}$ cup stock or water

BURGER ONION PIE

Roll the pastry thinly and use to line an 8-inch tart plate or sandwich tin. Melt the butter in a heavy based pan and cook the onion until it is soft and transparent.

Add the hamburger steak to the onion and cook, stirring well, until it changes colour. Stir in 1 teaspoon of salt and the monosodium glutamate, pepper and flour. Stir for a few minutes longer, then spread evenly over the pastry in the tart plate.

Beat the sour cream with the slightly beaten eggs and a teaspoon of salt. Spoon gently over the meat mixture and sprinkle generously with paprika. Bake in a hot oven, 400°F., for 10 minutes, then reduce the heat to 325°F. and bake for a further 25 minutes or until a knife, inserted in the centre, comes out clean.

BURGUNDY BEEF RAGOUT

Heat the oil in a pan. Cut the beef into 1-inch cubes and brown on all sides. Sprinkle in the flour, salt and pepper and cook until the flour browns. Add the wine, water, crushed or chopped garlic, thyme, bayleaf, and parsley sprigs. Stir until boiling, then transfer to a casserole, cover, and bake in a moderate oven for about 1$\frac{1}{2}$ hours or until the meat is almost tender.

Peel the onions and potatoes and scrape the carrots and parsnips. If any are too large cut into uniform-sized pieces. Add to the casserole, cover, and bake for another 45 minutes. Add the peas and return the casserole to the oven till they are heated through.

CALCUTTA CURRY

Peel and chop the onions and brown in the melted butter in a heavy pan. Remove the onions from the pan.

Toss the meat in the seasoned flour and brown it in the same pan, then lower the heat and add the curry powder, chilli powder, crushed garlic, parsley, sliced apple, coconut and salt. Stir well, then add the tomatoes, onion, stock and browned meat.

Cover with a tight-fitting lid and simmer for about 2 hours or until the meat is tender. Serve with freshly boiled rice and curry accompaniments.

CARIBBEAN LAMB

6 best end neck or barbecue chops
seasoned flour
2 tablespoons butter
1 tablespoon olive oil
1 dessertspoon curry powder
½ teaspoon turmeric
a good pinch of powdered
  ginger
¼ teaspoon cayenne pepper
salt and pepper
1 tablespoon lemon juice
½ pint stock

Trim the excess fat from the chops. Coat them well with seasoned flour and sauté in the heated butter and oil until lightly browned on the outside.

Combine the curry powder, turmeric, ginger, cayenne, salt and pepper and stir into the meat. Sprinkle with the lemon juice and stir again.

Add the well-flavoured stock and, if necessary, enough water to barely cover the meat. Cover and simmer until the lamb is tender and the liquid reduced to a good consistency. Serve with hot boiled rice, fried bananas and chutney.

CASSEROLE OF PORK CHOPS

4 pork chops about ½ inch thick
1 tablespoon plain flour
½ teaspoon salt
¼ teaspoon pepper
⅓ cup grated cheese
4 medium-sized potatoes
2 medium-sized onions
3 beef soup cubes
¾ cup hot water
1 dessertspoon lemon juice

Trim the excess fat from the chops and heat these trimmings in a frying pan until you have about a tablespoon of liquid fat. Remove the trimmings. Coat the chops with flour, brown on both sides in the fat, drain on paper, then place in a casserole.

Mix the salt and pepper with the grated cheese and sprinkle about 2 dessertspoons of this over the chops. Cut the peeled potatoes into thin slices and arrange a layer over the cheese. Sprinkle on the remaining cheese, then add the sliced onion.

Dissolve the soup cubes in the hot water, add the lemon juice, and pour over the meat and vegetables. Cover and bake in a moderate oven, 350°F., for about 1½ hours or until the meat and vegetables are tender.

CASSEROLE SUPREME

5 lamb shoulder chops
2 level tablespoons seasoned
  flour
1 tablespoon hot fat
2 or 3 small onions
1 cup kernel-style corn
½ cup diced celery
salt and pepper
½ cup tomato purée
1 teaspoon meat extract, or a
  soup cube
½ pint stock or water
5 small potatoes
1 dessertspoon chopped parsley

Trim the excess fat from the chops and dust them with the seasoned flour. Fry on both sides in the hot fat until lightly browned. Place in a casserole and sprinkle with the remainder of the seasoned flour.

Slice the peeled onions and add to the casserole, then add a layer of corn and one of chopped celery, seasoning each layer with salt and pepper as you fill the casserole.

Mix the tomato purée and the meat extract or soup cube with the water and pour into the casserole. Slice the peeled potatoes and arrange on top. Cover and bake in a moderate oven, 350°F., for 2 to 2½ hours or until the meat is tender (remove the lid during the last half-hour of cooking to brown the potatoes). Sprinkle with the parsley before serving.

CHILLI CON CARNE

2 cups brown kidney beans
cold water and ½ teaspoon salt
2 tablespoons oil or lard
2 medium-sized onions
1½ pounds stewing steak
about 1½ tablespoons seasoned
    flour
3 fresh tomatoes
1 green pepper
½ cup boiling water
1 clove of garlic
2 or more dessertspoons chilli
    powder
½ teaspoon dry mustard
1 dessertspoon vinegar or wine
1 teaspoon brown sugar

Soak the kidney beans overnight. Next morning drain them, place in a saucepan, cover with the cold water and salt and bring to the boil. Cook for 40 minutes or until tender. Drain well.

Heat the oil in a pan, stir in thinly sliced onions and cook until a golden brown. Remove from the pan. Cut the meat into ½-inch cubes, roll in the seasoned flour and fry in the same oil until brown on all sides.

Pour the oil from the pan into a large saucepan and add the onions, peeled and quartered tomatoes, chopped green pepper and boiling water. As the mixture comes to the boil, add crushed garlic, then the beef, chilli powder and mustard. Cover and simmer gently for 30 minutes.

Add the cooked kidney beans and simmer for a further 30 minutes. Add the vinegar and brown sugar, and some salt if necessary, cover, and simmer again until the meat is tender but not ragged. Serve with freshly cooked beans and a tossed green salad.

CHINESE SWEET AND SOUR PORK

2 pounds boned pork
1 tablespoon soy sauce
1 tablespoon dry sherry
lard or oil for frying
1 clove of garlic
1 onion
1 green pepper
2 small carrots
1 teaspoon root ginger
1 tablespoon brown sugar
3 tablespoons vinegar
6 tablespoons water
1 level tablespoon cornflour
salt

Cut the pork into one-inch cubes. Combine the soy sauce and sherry in a large bowl and add the pork. Mix well and let stand for at least 10 minutes. Fry the pork cubes in the hot oil until they are browned on all sides and almost cooked through. Remove from the pan.

Heat 2 tablespoons of oil in the same pan and sauté the minced garlic, finely sliced onion, green pepper (seeded and cut into strips), finely sliced carrot and ginger for about 2 minutes.

Mix the brown sugar, vinegar, water and cornflour to a smooth paste and season with salt. Stir into the vegetables and continue stirring until the mixture boils. Add the pork, cover, and simmer for about 10 minutes. Serve with freshly boiled rice.

CITY CHICKEN

2 pounds boneless veal
½ cup fine cracker crumbs
½ cup cornflake crumbs
1 teaspoon salt

You will need 6 skewers. Cut the veal into 1½-inch cubes and push several cubes onto each skewer.

Combine the cracker crumbs with the cornflake crumbs and the seasonings. Dip the meat cubes into the egg and milk glaze,

304

1 teaspoon paprika
¾ teaspoon poultry seasoning or
   thyme
½ teaspoon monosodium
   glutamate
a dash of pepper
1 egg beaten with 2 tablespoons
   milk
2 or 3 tablespoons fat or butter
¾ cup hot water and a chicken
   soup cube

then into the crumb mixture. Brown the cubes slowly on all sides in the hot fat or butter. Place in a casserole.

Dissolve the soup cube in the hot water and pour into the casserole. Cover and bake in a moderate oven, 375°F., for 1 hour or until the meat is tender.

CORDON BLEU VEAL

1½ pounds veal steak cut into 6
   pieces
¼ pound ham
½ pound sharp Cheddar cheese
2 tablespoons seasoned flour
1 egg beaten with 2 tablespoons
   milk
breadcrumbs
2 tablespoons oil
1 large or 2 small cloves of garlic
1 level tablespoon flour
1½ cups water or stock, or ¾ cup
   stock and ¾ cup sherry
lemon slices to garnish

Flatten the veal cutlets with a meat mallet or a rolling-pin, making them as thin as possible. Place a small piece of ham on each piece of veal and add a thick slice of cheese, then another piece of ham. Fold the veal over the filling and secure with a cocktail pick. Dip in seasoned flour, then in the egg and milk glazing. Toss in the breadcrumbs until completely covered, then chill for about 30 minutes.

Heat the oil in a frying pan. Peel and chop the garlic and add to the pan. Add the stuffed veal, cook until brown on both sides, drain, and place in a single layer in a large, shallow casserole.

Mix the tablespoonful of flour with the oil left in the pan, stir until smooth, cook for 1 minute, then add the water or stock and stir until boiling. Pour round the meat in the casserole. Cover and bake in a moderate oven, 350°F., for about 30 minutes. The time will depend on the thickness of the meat. Serve garnished with lemon slices.

CORNED BEEF

3 to 4 pounds corned brisket
1 large onion, quartered
1 clove of garlic, quartered
1 stick (about 3 inches) of
   cinnamon
1 orange, sliced
2 stalks of celery, cut in halves
6 whole cloves
1 bayleaf

Corned beef should be placed in tepid water to which flavourings have been added, then simmered gently. The time will depend on the size of the joint: allow 30 minutes to each pound weight, and 30 minutes over. Here is a very pleasant mixture of flavourings you might like to try next time you are cooking corned beef.

Place the corned beef in a large boiler and just cover with tepid water. Add the remaining ingredients and simmer until tender. If the meat is to be served cold, allow it to cool in the water in which it was cooked.

CORNISH PASTIES

½ pound shortcrust pastry
½ pound round steak
½ carrot
1 potato
½ turnip
1 teaspoon chopped parsley
1 tablespoon chopped onion
salt and pepper
egg glazing (egg beaten with a
   little milk)

Make the pastry and knead it lightly. Divide into six or eight equal portions, knead each into a round, then roll to about the size of a saucer.

Cut the steak into small dice. Scrape or peel the carrot, potato and turnip, grate, then mix with the parsley, onion, salt, pepper and diced meat. Divide into six or eight equal portions.

Place one portion of the meat and vegetable mixture on each round of pastry. Glaze the edges and fold the pastry over the filling, joining it at the top and pinching a frill around the edge of each. Twist into a crescent shape and glaze the tops with egg and milk.

Place on a shallow tray and bake in a hot oven, 450°F., for 10 minutes, then reduce the heat to 325°F. and bake for a further 20 to 25 minutes. Serve with a brown vegetable gravy.

COTTAGE PIE

4 potatoes
a little milk
1 egg
¾ teaspoon salt
a dash of pepper
1 dessertspoon margarine
1 medium-sized onion
1 pound finely minced steak
½ pound cooked peas or carrots
1 small can of tomato soup
1 tablespoon grated cheese

Cook the potatoes and mash while still hot, adding the milk and beaten egg. Season to taste with salt and pepper.

Melt the margarine in a saucepan and cook the chopped onion until a light golden colour. Add the meat and seasonings and stir over medium heat until it changes colour. Add the peas or cubed carrots and the soup and bring to the boil. Turn into a casserole, then drop spoonfuls of the potato mixture on top and sprinkle with grated cheese. Bake in a moderate oven, 350°F., for 20 to 30 minutes.

CURRIED SAUSAGES

1 pound sausages
1 tablespoon raisins or sultanas
1 medium-sized onion
1 cooking apple
1 medium-sized tomato
2 tablespoons margarine or fat
1 rounded tablespoon plain flour
½ level teaspoon salt
1 dessertspoon curry powder
¼ pint water and a beef soup
   cube
a squeeze of lemon juice
4 ounces rice

Place the sausages in a saucepan of tepid water, bring slowly to the boil, and simmer for about 15 minutes. Drain, then remove the skins and cut the sausages in halves.

Wash the raisins or sultanas and remove any stems.

Peel and chop the onion, and peel core and dice the apple. Cook these in the melted margarine in a large pan until soft, then add chopped tomato. Cook for a few more minutes, stirring well. Add the flour, salt and curry powder and stir until smooth, then cook for another 2 or 3 minutes.

Add the water and soup cube, raisins and lemon juice and stir until the sauce boils and thickens. Add the sausages, cover, and simmer for about 20 minutes.

Cook the rice in the usual way, drain, and serve with the curried sausages.

306

CURRY PUFFS

1 apple
1 small onion
1 banana
1 tomato
½ pound finely minced steak
1 dessertspoon fat
1 teaspoon flour
1 teaspoon curry powder
½ pint stock or water
½ teaspoon salt
¼ teaspoon pepper
1 dessertspoon raisins or sultanas
1 dessertspoon chutney
¾ pound rough puff pastry
egg glazing (beaten egg and milk)

Peel and dice the apple and onion. Peel and slice the banana and tomato. Fry the meat in the fat until brown, then remove it from the pan. Add the apple, onion, tomato and banana and cook for a few minutes, then add the flour and curry powder and stir until brown. Pour in the stock and stir until boiling, then add the salt and pepper and the raisins and chutney. Return the meat to the pan. Cover and simmer for 1 hour.

Roll the pastry thinly and cut into rounds. Place a tablespoonful of the cooled mixture on each round of pastry, glaze the edges and fold over. Brush the tops with egg glazing and bake in a hot oven, 450°F., for about 10 minutes. Serve hot.

DANISH VEAL WITH PINEAPPLE

½ pound fresh button mushrooms
1 tablespoon butter
1 pound thinly sliced veal steak
seasoned flour
¼ cup butter
½ cup water
2 level dessertspoons flour
¼ cup cream
4 well-drained pineapple slices
a little butter

Slice the mushrooms thinly and sauté in the tablespoon of butter until tender—about 5 minutes. Lift out. Coat the veal with seasoned flour, heat the ¼ cup of butter in the same pan and brown the veal on both sides. Add the mushrooms, reduce the heat and add the water.

Cover and simmer for about 1 hour or until the veal is very tender. Thicken with the 2 dessertspoons flour which have been blended with a little water. Stir until boiling, then add the cream and bring just to boiling point. Serve topped with the pineapple slices which have been sautéed in a little butter, and with freshly boiled rice.

DEVILLED LAMB CHOPS

6 shoulder chops
mixed mustard
¼ cup plain flour
1 teaspoon salt
a dash of pepper
½ teaspoon onion salt, or garlic
   or celery salt
1 dessertspoon fat
2 medium-sized onions
1 green pepper
¼ cup water
grated rind of 1 lemon

Spread one side of each chop with a little mustard which has been mixed with water. Mix the flour with the salt, pepper and flavoured salt and use to cover each chop on both sides. Melt the fat in a pan and brown the chops all over.

Slice the peeled onions, and cut the peppers into rings after removing the seeds, then arrange on top of the chops and add the water and the lemon rind. Cover and cook over low heat (adding a little more water if necessary) for about 1 hour or until the chops are tender. Serve with vegetables.

DEVILLED PORK CHOPS

4 lean pork chops
seasoned flour
about 1 tablespoon lard (or melt
   the fat trimmed from the
   chops)
4 slices of lemon
½ cup tomato sauce
½ cup water
1 dessertspoon brown sugar

Remove the rind and any surplus fat from the chops and coat them lightly with seasoned flour. Heat the lard in a pan and lightly fry the chops until brown on both sides. Drain on paper and place in an ovenware dish. Top each chop with a slice of lemon.

Mix the tomato sauce with the water and add the brown sugar. Pour over the chops. Bake uncovered in a moderate oven, 350°F., for 1 hour or until the chops are tender.

DINNER IN A DISH

4 shoulder chops
1 tablespoon seasoned flour
2 tablespoons oil
1 clove of garlic
½ cup sherry
½ cup boiling water
1 soup cube
4 small white onions
4 small carrots
4 small potatoes
salt and pepper

Trim any excess fat from the chops and roll them lightly in seasoned flour. Heat the oil in a pan, add the garlic and the chops, and cook until the chops are brown on both sides. Remove the garlic.

Add the sherry, boiling water and soup cube, and stir until the liquid boils. Cover and simmer for about 30 minutes or until the chops are almost tender. Peel the onions, scrape and slice the carrots and peel and halve the potatoes. Arrange these round the chops and sprinkle with salt and pepper. Cover, then simmer for a further 20 or 30 minutes or until the meat and vegetables are tender.

FILLETS OF BEEF GOURMET

1 fillet of beef, about 2 pounds
about 11 thin slices of cooked
   ham
brandy
½ pound mushrooms
1 onion
2 tablespoons butter
salt and freshly ground black
   pepper
½ pound flaky pastry
1 egg yolk

Brush the fillet of beef with brandy, trim it neatly and slice into 12 equal parts. Trim the ham slices to the same size and shape as the beef slices. Sauté the chopped mushrooms and finely sliced onion in the butter until soft, then flavour lightly with salt and black pepper.

Spread each slice of ham with mushroom mixture. Sandwich the ham slices between the slices of beef, then re-form the fillet. (There should be a little mushroom mixture left over.) Skewer through the centre to hold the meat and filling together, wrap in foil and bake in a moderate oven, 375°F., for about 15 minutes. Allow the fillet to cool slightly, then remove the foil. Season the meat with salt and pepper and spread the left-over mushroom mixture on the top.

Roll the flaky pastry thinly, making a piece that is large enough to completely cover the meat. Place on a shallow oven tray, brush with cold water, and bake in a hot oven, 450°F., for 15 minutes. Brush with beaten egg yolk, return the pastry to the oven and bake for another 15 minutes or until the crust is brown. Serve with Bearnaise sauce (page 405).

GOLDEN BEEF CASSEROLE

1½ pounds chuck steak
seasoned flour
2 tablespoons fat
2 onions
1 large tomato
1 teaspoon salt
¼ teaspoon pepper
½ cup water and a beef soup
    cube
1 green pepper
2 medium-sized parsnips
16-ounce can of whole-kernel
    corn

Cut the meat into cubes and toss in about 1½ tablespoons of seasoned flour. Heat the fat in a pan and brown the meat on all sides. Remove and place in a casserole.

Thinly slice the onions and sauté in the pan until soft, then add to the casserole. Cover with peeled and sliced tomato, add the salt and pepper, and pour over stock made from the soup cube and water.

Cover and bake in a moderate oven, 350°F., for about 1 hour. Add rings of green pepper and prepared sliced parsnips and bake for another 40 minutes or until the meat and vegetables are tender. Add the drained canned corn and bake for a further 20 minutes.

GOURMET CASSEROLE

2 pounds round or oyster blade
    steak
1 level teaspoon brown sugar
1 teaspoon salt
¼ teaspoon pepper
1 level tablespoon plain flour
a sprinkle of nutmeg
1 onion
1 tablespoon vinegar
1 teaspoon Worcester sauce
1 tablespoon tomato sauce
1 tablespoon fat
1 rounded tablespoon plain flour
¾ cup water
¾ cup red wine, claret or
    Burgundy

Cut the meat into 1-inch pieces and place in a shallow dish.

Mix the sugar, salt, pepper, flour, nutmeg, onion, vinegar, Worcester sauce, and tomato sauce and spoon over the meat. Cover and marinate for about 1 hour, stirring occasionally.

Heat the fat in a pan and fry the meat until brown on all sides. Lift out and place in a casserole.

Add the rounded tablespoon of flour to the pan and cook until it is a golden brown. Add the water and the wine and stir until the mixture boils, scraping any browned pieces from the bottom of the pan. Pour this gravy over the meat in the casserole. Cover and bake in a moderate oven, 350°F., for about 1½ hours or until the meat is tender.

GOURMET PORK CHOPS

4 thick pork chops
1 tablespoon flour
1 teaspoon salt
a dash of pepper
1 medium-sized onion
10-ounce can of cream of
    mushroom soup
¾ cup water
½ teaspoon ginger
¼ teaspoon rosemary
½ cup sour cream
French fried onion rings

Trim the excess fat from the chops, place it in a pan and heat until a tablespoon of liquid fat has collected. Remove the pieces of fat from the pan.

Roll the chops in the combined flour, salt and pepper. Brown them in the hot fat, then remove to a shallow baking dish or a casserole dish.

Slice the onion and cook until brown in the fat that is left in the pan. Combine the soup with the water, ginger and rosemary and add to the onion. Stir over the heat until boiling, then pour over the chops.

Bake with the lid on in a moderate oven, 350°F., for 1 hour or until the chops are tender. Remove them to a heated dish.

Add the sour cream to the gravy and bring to the boil. Pour some over the chops. Garnish with **French-fried** onion rings (page **421**) and serve with the remaining gravy in a gravy boat or jug

GREEN PEPPER STEAK

1½ pounds buttock steak
½ cup soy sauce
1 clove of garlic
½ cup cold water
a little oil
2 medium-sized green peppers
1 medium-sized onion
5 stalks celery
1 dessertspoon cornflour
extra ½ cup water

Cut the steak into thin strips. Combine the soy sauce, crushed garlic and water, and marinate the meat in this mixture for 15 minutes. Drain, reserving the liquid.

Heat enough oil in a heavy-base frying pan to cover the surface of the pan. Add the meat and brown it quickly all over. Push it to one side of the pan. Slice the peppers and onion thinly, and cut the celery into pieces diagonally. Cook in the pan for 2 minutes or until the vegetables are tender-crisp.

Mix the reserved marinade with the cornflour, blending until smooth, add the extra water and pour into the pan. Cook, stirring well until the mixture boils and thickens.

If the meat has been cut thinly enough it will now be cooked sufficiently. If not, cover and simmer for about 10 or 15 minutes. Arrange on hot rice and serve with tomato wedges.

HAM

With modern methods of curing, so the distributors say, it is no longer necessary to soak ham before cooking. However, if you have any doubts about the saltiness, and the ham you have bought has a strong salt odour, cover it with tepid water and allow to stand overnight. Next day trim and scrape before cooking. Ham may be either boiled or baked.

BAKED HAM

For this you will need a covering, which may be heavy duty foil or a plain dough. The amount of dough will depend on the size of the ham: as a guide it will take about 4 pounds of plain flour and 1½ pints of water to make a dough to cover a 10-pound ham. The covering must be thick. For a recipe for ham-covering dough see **opposite page**.

Heat the oven to moderate, 350°F., and whether the ham is covered with foil or dough place it fat side up on a shallow dish. Do not add any water or fat.

The baking time will depend on the size and thickness of the ham. It is usual to allow 25 to 30 minutes to the pound for a ham weighing up to 12 pounds. Over this weight allow 20 minutes to each pound. Consider, too, the shape of the ham. A long thin ham, even though it may weigh the same, will take less time to cook than a short thick one.

About 30 to 45 minutes before the calculated baking time is up, lift the ham from the oven and remove the foil or dough. Now lift off the skin and make a series of shallow cuts across the fat, cutting into squares or diamonds. Spread with a glaze (recipes follow), insert some cloves if liked, and return the ham to the oven for the remainder of the time or until tender.

Place the ham in a large vessel with enough tepid water to cover it completely. Add a bunch of fresh herbs (parsley, thyme and marjoram) about ½ teaspoon of whole peppercorns, and one or two bayleaves. Cover, then bring the water very slowly to the boil: this should take about 2 hours. Simmer gently for another hour (or longer if the ham is very large), turn off the heat, pack the top of the lid with thick wads of newspaper, put more paper round the outside of the cooking vessel, and allow the ham to cool in the water. Next day peel off the skin after draining, and either sprinkle with breadcrumbs or use a glaze as for baked ham.

HAM GLAZES

1. Heat 1 cup of brown sugar with the rind and juice of 1 orange. Pour over the ham, basting occasionally during the cooking.
2. Combine ¾ cup of pineapple juice, ¾ cup of honey and 1 teaspoon of mustard in a saucepan. Cook, stirring well until thick. Pour over the ham and baste occasionally during the cooking.
3. Blend 1 cup of brown sugar with 1 tablespoon of dry mustard, 2 tablespoons of sherry and enough syrup drained from a can of apricots to moisten. Spread over the ham before baking. When serving the ham decorate with the drained apricot halves speared with a whole clove.

COVERING DOUGH FOR HAM

4 pounds plain flour
2 rounded teaspoons dry mustard
2 level teaspoons mixed spice
½ cup vinegar
1½ pints water

Sift the flour, mustard and spice into a bowl. Mix the vinegar with the water and stir into the flour to make a medium dough. Turn onto a floured board and knead into a smooth shape. Roll out thickly and use to cover the ham to be baked.

HARICOT PIE

For the filling
¼ cup bacon fat or dripping
½ cup finely chopped onion
1½ pounds finely minced steak
¼ level teaspoon salt
¼ teaspoon pepper
2 level tablespoons plain flour
¾ cup water
½ cup cooked green peas
½ cup sliced cooked carrot
½ cup sliced cooked parsnip

Melt the bacon fat for the filling in a saucepan and add the onion. Cook until golden, then take out 1 tablespoonful and put it aside for the topping.

Place the steak into the pan in which the onion was cooked. Add the salt, pepper and plain flour. Cook, stirring well over medium heat until the meat changes colour. Add the water and stir until the mixture comes to the boil. Lower the heat, cover and simmer for about 30 minutes. Stir in the peas, carrot and parsnip and allow the mixture to cool.

Sift the dry ingredients together for the topping, rub in the shortening and add the reserved tablespoonful of chopped

311

1 cup plain flour
1 level teaspoon baking powder
a good pinch of salt
2 ounces good shortening
1 egg yolk
1 tablespoon water
2 tablespoons grated cheese

onion. Beat the egg yolk with the water and stir into the mixture, making a firm dough. Knead on a floured board until smooth.

Place the cold cooked meat and vegetable mixture in a pie-dish. Roll the pastry to fit the top. Trim the edges and glaze the top of the pie with milk, then sprinkle with the grated cheese. Make a few slits in the crust to allow the steam to escape.

Bake in a hot oven, 425°F., for about 20 minutes.

HAWAIIAN SAUSAGE PLATTER

1 pound sausages
2 tablespoons cold water
8 rings of canned pineapple
½ teaspoon curry powder
1 dessertspoon cornflour
syrup from the pineapple, made up to 1 cup with water
salt and pepper
2 cups freshly cooked rice

Place the sausages in a saucepan with the water and cook over gentle heat for about 5 minutes. Drain. Add a little butter to the pan and lightly brown the pineapple pieces and the sausages. Lift out.

Combine the curry powder with the cornflour and blend until smooth with the pineapple syrup and water. Add to the pan and stir over medium heat until the liquid boils and thickens. Season with salt and pepper.

Arrange the hot rice on a serving dish, top with the pineapple slices and then with the sausages. Spoon over the hot sauce.

HERBED LEG OF LAMB

2 cloves of garlic
1 boned leg of lamb, 3 to 4 pounds
1 dessertspoon dry mustard
2 teaspoons salt
a pinch of pepper
½ teaspoon thyme
¼ teaspoon crushed rosemary
1 dessertspoon lemon juice
2 dessertspoons plain flour
water
salt and pepper

Peel and halve one clove of garlic and use to rub the surface of the boned leg. Peel the other clove of garlic and cut into slivers.

Slit the skin of the lamb at intervals and insert the garlic slivers. Blend the mustard, salt, pepper, thyme and crushed rosemary with the lemon juice and spread over the lamb. Place in an uncovered roasting dish and bake at 325°F. for 2 to 2½ hours. Remove to a hot platter.

Drain the drippings from the baking dish, leaving 1 dessertspoonful. Add the flour, stir until smooth, then cook for 1 minute. Add enough cold water to make 1½ cups of gravy and stir until boiling. Season with salt and pepper.

HOT BEEF CURRY

2 tablespoons curry powder
½ teaspoon turmeric
2 onions, peeled and chopped

Heat a heavy-base saucepan and place in it the curry powder and turmeric. Shake over the heat for about 3 minutes, then add the remaining ingredients in the order listed. Place over

2 green apples, peeled, cored and
  chopped
2 cloves of garlic, peeled and
  crushed or minced
1 tablespoon tart jam, such as
  plum
1 teaspoon salt
½ teaspoon pepper
½ teaspoon paprika
1 green pepper, seeded and
  chopped
1 dessertspoon soy sauce
1 dessertspoon tomato sauce
1 dessertspoon chutney
1 teaspoon dry mustard
¼ cup desiccated coconut
2 bayleaves
¼ cup sultanas or seeded raisins
2 pounds buttock or round steak
  cubed and floured (use ½ cup
  seasoned flour)
1 cup stock, or water and a soup
  cube
½ teaspoon lemon juice

medium heat, stirring occasionally, until the curry comes to
the boil. Reduce the heat, cover and simmer for 1½ to 2 hours
or until the meat is tender.

Serve with freshly boiled rice, and curry accompaniments.

2 pounds round or chuck steak
1 level tablespoon curry powder
1 teaspoon salt
2 small onions
1 clove of garlic
1 level tablespoon margarine
¼ cup salad oil
1½ cups water
1 soup cube
1 teaspoon sugar
1 cooking apple
1 banana
1 tomato
½ cup sultanas
juice of ½ lemon
2½ cups hot cooked rice
1 egg
2 tablespoons melted butter

INDIAN RICE PIE

Remove any fat or gristle from the meat. Cut into cubes and
place in a bowl with the curry powder and salt, then rub the
mixture into the meat cubes. Chop the onion and crush the
garlic.

Melt the margarine in a saucepan and fry the onion and
garlic for about 10 minutes, but do not allow to become too
brown. Push to one side, add the oil and when it is hot add the
meat and stir until it changes colour. Now add the water and
soup cube and the sugar, and stir until the mixture boils. Cover
and simmer for 30 minutes.

Peel, core and chop the apple, peel and chop the banana and
tomato, and add these with the onion, garlic, sultanas and
lemon juice to the curry. Cover and simmer for 2 hours or
until the meat is tender.

Turn the well-drained rice into a bowl and stir in beaten egg
and melted butter (a few chopped salted peanuts may be
added at this stage if liked). Use three-quarters of this mixture
to line a casserole dish. Spoon in the hot curry and cover it
with the remaining rice. Dot lightly with butter and place in
a moderate oven, 350°F., to heat. Serve immediately.

313

INDIVIDUAL HAMBURGER PIES

12 ounces shortcrust pastry
1 small onion
1 medium green pepper
1 dessertspoon fat
1 pound finely minced steak
1 level dessertspoon plain flour
3 dessertspoons chopped parsley
1 teaspoon salt
¼ teaspoon pepper
¼ teaspoon dried thyme, sage or marjoram
1 tablespoon Worcester sauce
1 teaspoon chilli sauce
¼ cup tomato sauce
1 tablespoon finely chopped fresh or canned mushrooms (optional)

Roll the pastry thinly and cut into rounds to line and cover the tops of six 4½-inch pie-tins.

Peel and mince the onion and seed and chop the green pepper, then cook both in the fat for a few minutes. Add the meat and cook, stirring lightly with a fork, until it changes colour. Sprinkle the flour and blend in smoothly. Add the parsley, salt, pepper, herbs, Worcester sauce, chilli sauce, tomato sauce and mushrooms. Stir until boiling, then cover and simmer for about 30 minutes. Cool.

Place a spoonful of the cooled meat mixture in each pastry-lined pie-tin, and top with the second piece of pastry. Press the edges lightly together and make a few slits in the top to allow the steam to escape. Bake at 400°F. for about 25 minutes or until the pastry is lightly browned.

KEBABS

For the marinade
1 dessertspoon soy sauce
½ teaspoon salt
½ teaspoon pepper
¼ cup salad oil
⅓ cup lemon juice
1 dessertspoon grated lemon rind
1 clove of garlic, crushed

For the kebabs
2 pounds rump steak
2 medium-sized green peppers
1 pound small round tomatoes
some small onions (or larger ones cut into wedges or eighths)
bacon rashers

Combine all the ingredients for the marinade in a saucepan and heat without boiling.

Cut the steak into 2-inch cubes, place in a flat dish, and pour the warm marinade over the steak. Allow to stand for about 2 hours at room temperature, turning the meat once or twice.

Meanwhile cut the peppers into 2-inch squares, wash the tomatoes, peel and cut the onions if necessary, and cut the bacon into 2-inch squares. Drain the meat cubes well and arrange on skewers alternately with the green peppers, tomatoes, onion and bacon.

Have a glowing hot griller and cook the kebabs as long as necessary, basting occasionally with the marinading liquid. Serve on a bed of buttered rice.

KAI-SEE-MEIN

1 dessertspoon shortening
1 pound finely minced steak
2 onions
1 cup raw rice
1 tablespoon curry powder
1 packet of frozen French beans
½ cup shredded cabbage
1 packet of chicken noodle soup
4 cups boiling water

Preheat an electric fry-pan to 380°F. Add the shortening and when hot add the meat and chopped onions. Cook, stirring well, until the meat browns and the onion is soft.

Reduce the heat of the fry pan to 220°F. Add the rice, curry powder, beans, cabbage, soup and boiling water. Simmer for 15 or 20 minutes or until the rice is tender.

Lamb Chop Bake

LAMB AND MUSHROOM CASSEROLE

4 lamb leg chops
2 tablespoons seasoned flour
1 tablespoon butter or margarine
¼ pound fresh mushrooms
4 small white onions
1 bayleaf
¾ cup green peas
1 tablespoon sherry
1 tablespoon lemon juice
½ cup stock, or water and a soup
    cube
salt and pepper

Trim the excess fat from the chops and coat them well with seasoned flour. Melt the butter in a pan and brown the chops on both sides. Drain, then place in a lightly greased casserole, sprinkling over any left-over seasoned flour. Add sliced mushrooms, peeled whole onions, bayleaf, peas and the combined sherry, lemon juice and stock. Season with salt and pepper.

Cover and bake in a moderate oven, 350°F., for about 1½ hours or until the chops are tender.

LAMB CHOP BAKE

6 lamb chops
2 dessertspoons well-seasoned
    flour
1 tablespoon fat or oil
6 green pepper rings
6 thin slices of onion
6 thin slices of lemon
1 cup tomato soup
½ cup water

Coat the chops lightly with the seasoned flour. Melt the fat in a pan and brown the chops on both sides. Pour away the excess fat.

Place the chops in a single layer in a casserole. Cover each one with a green pepper ring, a slice of onion and a slice of lemon.

Blend the tomato soup with the water and pour over the chops. Cover and bake in a moderate oven, 350°F., for about 1½ hours or until the chops are tender.

315

6 shoulder or barbecue chops
2 tablespoons seasoned flour
about 2 tablespoons fat
1 or 2 onions
1 green pepper
10-ounce can of tomato-rice
   soup
½ soup-can of water
a good pinch of dried thyme

1½ pounds shoulder chops
2 tablespoons butter or
   margarine
2 onions
1 small apple
1 banana
1 tablespoon curry powder
2 tablespoons plain flour
2 tomatoes
1 cup water and a beef soup cube
salt and pepper
1 tablespoon chutney
1 cup canned pineapple pieces
1 dessertspoon lemon juice

3 dessertspoons fat
2 pounds lamb chops
3 medium-sized onions, sliced
1 dessertspoon paprika
1 dessertspoon vinegar
10-ounce can of condensed beef
   soup
½ cup sour cream

1 tablespoon fat
4 lamb shanks
1 tablespoon seasoned flour
1 medium-sized onion
½ cup tomato sauce
½ cup water
1 teaspoon brown sugar
1 dessertspoon vinegar
1 dessertspoon Worcester sauce
1 teaspoon salt
1 teaspoon dry mustard

LAMB CHOPS CREOLE

Rub the chops well with the seasoned flour. Melt the fat in a pan and fry the chops until brown on both sides. Lift out and place in a casserole.

Place sliced onion and green pepper rings on top of the chops.

Mix the soup, water and thyme together, and pour over the chops. Cover and bake in a moderate oven, 350°F., for about 1 hour or until tender.

LAMB CURRY

Trim the chops, melt the butter in a pan and brown them on both sides. Remove from the pan.

In the remaining butter in the pan, fry chopped onions, peeled and chopped apple and sliced banana for 5 minutes. Add the curry powder and flour, stir until smooth and cook for a further 5 minutes. Peel and slice the tomatoes and add with the water and soup cube, stirring until the sauce boils and thickens.

Return the meat to the pan, adding salt and pepper to taste. Cover and simmer for about 1¼ hours or until the chops are tender. Add the chutney, the well-drained pineapple and the lemon juice and continue cooking for about 3 minutes.

Serve with freshly boiled rice. If liked, the pineapple may be omitted from the curry and served as an accompaniment.

LAMB PAPRIKA

Heat the fat in a heavy based saucepan, add the chops and brown them on both sides. Lift out and drain on paper while you fry the onions. Add the paprika and the vinegar, stir in the beef soup and bring to the boil. Return the chops to the pan, cover, and simmer for about 1½ hours or until they are tender.

Beat the sour cream in a bowl with a little of the liquid in which the meat is cooking, pour into the meat and heat to almost boiling, stirring well. Serve with boiled potatoes.

LAMB SHANKS CREOLE

Place the fat in a frying pan and heat until a light haze rises. Toss the shanks in the seasoned flour, then fry them in the fat until browned on all sides. Lift out and place in a casserole.

Chop the onions and brown them in the same pan. Add the remaining ingredients, stir until boiling, then pour over the shanks in the casserole. Cover and bake in a moderate oven, 350°F., for about 2 hours or until the meat is tender.

Serve over hot cooked rice or mashed potato. If preferred the shanks may be cooked over low heat in a saucepan on top of the stove.

316

LEG OF LAMB OLYMPIA

1 leg of lamb, 5 to 6 pounds
½ cup lemon juice
2 teaspoons salt
¼ teaspoon pepper
1 teaspoon oregano
2 cloves of garlic
egg and lemon sauce (recipe
　follows)

The day before the lamb is to be roasted, wipe it over with a damp cloth and place in a baking dish. Pour over half the lemon juice and sprinkle with 1 teaspoon of salt, ¼ teaspoon of pepper and ½ a teaspoon of oregano. Turn the meat fat side up. Peel the garlic and cut into thin pieces or slivers (you will need between 20 and 25 for a leg of lamb of this size). Make small slits in the surface of the lamb and insert a piece of garlic in each. Pour over the remaining lemon juice and add the rest of the salt, pepper and oregano. Cover and refrigerate overnight.

Remove the lamb from the refrigerator about 30 minutes before it is to be roasted. Preheat the oven to 325°F. Insert a meat thermometer into the fleshy part of the meat and roast the joint (without adding any fat to the dish) for about 2 hours.

Skim off any fat from the liquid in the dish. Baste the lamb with the remaining liquid, then return the meat to the oven and continue baking for a further 30 minutes or until the meat thermometer registers 165°F. (medium) or higher if you like the lamb well done. Remove from the oven and let stand for about 20 minutes in a warm place before carving.

Serve with egg and lemon sauce. As the meat is baked without fat, potatoes to be served with the lamb will have to be roasted in a separate dish.

EGG AND LEMON SAUCE

2 dessertspoons butter
3 dessertspoons plain flour
¾ teaspoon salt
1½ cups water and 2 chicken soup
　cubes
3 dessertspoons lemon juice
2 egg yolks
1 dessertspoon chopped parsley

Melt the butter and stir in the flour and salt. Cook until smooth but not brown. Dissolve the soup cubes in the water and add together with the lemon juice. Cook, stirring well, until the sauce boils and thickens.

Beat the egg yolks well and mix a little of the sauce with them. Add to the rest of the sauce and stir to blend well. Cook, stirring until the sauce comes to the boil again. Cook for 2 minutes, then stir in the chopped parsley.

LEMON PORK CHOPS

4 loin pork chops
½ teaspoon paprika
a dash of pepper
½ teaspoon salt
¼ cup uncooked rice
1 medium-sized onion
4 thin slices lemon
1 large green pepper
2 cups tomato juice
1 teaspoon salt
2 teaspoons sugar
¼ teaspoon chilli powder
1 bayleaf

Trim the excess fat from the chops, then slash the edges of the fat remaining on each chop (to prevent them curling up during cooking).

Rub each chop with a mixture of the paprika, pepper and salt. Heat a large pan and rub the surface with some of the fat cut from the chops. Brown the chops slowly on each side. While they cook, boil the rice in salted water for about 5 or 10 minutes, then drain and reserve for the pepper filling.

Cut one slice from the centre of the onion, separate it into rings and reserve these for garnishing the chops. Chop the remaining part of the onion and combine it with the parboiled rice.

Put the chops in a pan with the lemon slices and onion rings.

Cut the green pepper into 4 thick rings and arrange them around the chops, then fill them with the rice and onion mixture. Season the tomato juice with 1 teaspoon salt and the sugar, chilli powder and bayleaf, and pour some into the pan (to a depth of $\frac{1}{4}$ inch). Cover and simmer for 1 hour or until the chops are fork-tender and the rice cooked (during the cooking time add the remaining tomato juice as needed to keep the liquid $\frac{1}{4}$ inch deep).

Arrange the chops on a platter, arrange the rice-stuffed pepper rings round them, top the chops with a ring of onion, and pour over the tomato gravy.

LIVER AND BACON BURGERS

1 pound lamb's fry
$\frac{1}{2}$ pound bacon rashers
2 medium-sized onions
$\frac{1}{2}$ cup soft white breadcrumbs
1 egg
salt and pepper
a dash of Worcester or chilli
    sauce
seasoned flour
tomatoes for serving

Remove the fine skin and the white tubes from the lamb's fry. Place it in boiling water and cook for 2 minutes. Drain, cool and put through a mincer.

Remove the rind from the bacon rashers and chop them. Cook the bacon in a pan until the fat is clear, add chopped onions and sauté until the onion is soft and the bacon crisp. Add to the minced liver, then mix in the breadcrumbs, egg, salt, pepper and sauce.

Using a little seasoned flour, shape the mixture into round flat patties. Grill or dry-fry for 3 or 4 minutes on each side.

Cut the tomatoes into thick slices and alternate them with the liver and bacon burgers on a hot serving dish.

MONDAY MEAT PIE

1 tablespoon fat
$\frac{1}{2}$ cup diced celery
$\frac{1}{2}$ cup diced onion
$\frac{1}{2}$ cup chopped green pepper
2 cups cubed cold cooked beef
1 cup cubed cooked potato
1 cup sliced cooked carrots
1 cup cooked green peas
1 cup gravy
salt and pepper
4 slices stale bread
butter

Melt about a tablespoonful of fat in a saucepan and add the celery, onion and green pepper. Cook until the onion is lightly browned. Add the meat, potato, carrot and peas.

Place in a casserole dish, pour over the gravy and season with some salt and pepper.

Cut the bread into small cubes, toss them in enough butter or margarine to coat, then sprinkle them on top of the pie.

Bake in a moderate oven, 350°F., for 30 minutes.

MUSHROOM POT ROAST

3 to 4 pounds beef
2 tablespoons seasoned flour
1 tablespoon fat
salt and pepper
2 onions
½ cup water
¼ cup dry sherry
1 clove of garlic, crushed
¼ teaspoon each of mustard,
    marjoram and thyme
1 bayleaf
1 carrot, peeled and sliced
1 small can of buttered
    mushrooms

Trim any excess fat from the joint of beef and dust it with seasoned flour. Heat the fat in a saucepan and brown the meat on all sides. Season generously with salt and pepper. Slice the onions and add them.

Mix the remaining ingredients (except the mushrooms) and add them to the contents of the saucepan. Cover and cook slowly for about 2½ hours or until the meat is done. Lift the meat from the saucepan.

Skim off any surplus fat, blend 1 dessertspoon of plain flour with ¼ cup cold water and add to the sauce together with the mushrooms. Stir until the mixture boils and thickens. Serve as a gravy with the pot roast.

NASI GORENG

2 ounces butter or lard
¼ pound lean pork fillets
1 onion
1 clove of garlic
1 large tomato
4 cups cooked rice
¼ teaspoon dry chilli powder
1 tablespoon soy sauce
salt and pepper
fried bananas or fried egg for
    serving

Melt the butter in a saucepan. Cut the pork into small pieces and add with sliced onion and crushed garlic. Cook, stirring well, until the meat is brown and tender. Peel and slice the tomato, add to the mixture and cook for another 5 minutes.

Gently stir in the rice, mixing thoroughly, then add the chilli powder and the soy sauce. Season with salt and pepper.

Serve with fried egg or fried bananas.

ORANGE LAMB CHOPS

6 loin lamb chops
a little oil or butter
1 small onion
1 dessertspoon brown sugar
¼ cup orange juice
1 teaspoon lemon juice
1 tablespoon grated orange rind
1 teaspoon mustard
½ cup diced celery
salt and pepper
1 teaspoon flour blended with a
    little water

Brown the chops on both sides in the heated oil. Push them to one side of the pan, add finely chopped onion and cook until it is lightly browned.

Combine the sugar, fruit juices and orange rind with the mustard, celery, salt and pepper. Place the browned chops in a baking dish and pour over the orange and celery mixture. Cover and bake in a moderate oven, 350°F., for about 35 minutes or until the chops are tender. Remove them to a heated platter.

Thicken the gravy with about a teaspoon of blended flour. Cook for 1 or 2 minutes, then pour over the chops and send to the table accompanied by mashed potatoes and green peas, with a parsley garnish.

319

ORANGE-GLAZED PORK CHOPS

6 thick pork chops
1 tablespoon oil or shortening
1 tablespoon plain flour
1 dessertspoon light brown sugar
a good pinch of ground ginger
1 dessertspoon grated orange
   rind
1 cup orange juice
½ teaspoon salt
1 cup orange sections

Trim the excess fat from the chops. Heat the oil in a pan and brown the chops on both sides.

Combine the remaining ingredients with the exception the orange sections, and pour over the chops. Cover, reduce the heat, and simmer for about 45 minutes or until the chops are tender.

Add the orange sections just before serving.

ORANGE-TOPPED BEEF CASSEROLE

1½ pounds topside steak
1 tablespoon seasoned flour
1 dessertspoon fat
¾ cup diced onion
½ cup peeled and diced turnip
½ pint stock, or water and a beef
   soup cube
1 level teaspoon salt
1 level teaspoon pepper
4 pickled walnuts (optional)

For the orange dumplings

¼ cup finely chopped onion
1 dessertspoon fat
1½ cups self-raising flour
½ teaspoon salt
1 tablespoon butter or margarine
1 teaspoon finely chopped
   parsley
2 teaspoons grated orange rind
1 slightly beaten egg
1 tablespoon milk
1 tablespoon orange juice

Cut the meat into cubes and toss it in the seasoned flour. Melt the fat in a pan, fry the onion and turnip lightly, then lift them out. Add the meat (and a little more fat if necessary) and cook, stirring until the meat is lightly browned. Add the stock, salt and pepper and stir until the mixture boils. Transfer to a casserole with the onion and turnip. Cover and bake in a moderate oven for about 1½ hours or until the meat is tender. Add the walnuts if used.

To make the dumplings first cook the onion in the fat until soft but not brown, then sift the flour with the salt, rub in the butter and add the cooked onion, parsley and orange rind. Beat the egg with the milk and orange juice and stir into the dry ingredients to make a soft dough. Knead lightly and roll ½ inch thick. Cut into rounds and place on top of the hot cooked casserole.

Return the casserole to the oven and bake at 450°F. for 10 to 15 minutes.

ORIENTAL BEEF WITH VEGETABLES

1½ pounds round steak
2 small onions
3 medium-sized tomatoes
1 green pepper
1 teaspoon grated fresh ginger,
   or ¼ teaspoon powdered
   ginger
½ teaspoon sugar
1 dessertspoon soy sauce

Cut the steak into thin slivers, slicing diagonally across the grain. Cut the onions into rings. Remove the stem ends from the tomatoes. Halve the peppers and remove the seeds. Cut the tomatoes and peppers into bite-sized triangular pieces.

Combine the ginger, sugar, soy sauce, curry powder, water and soup cube. Set aside.

Heat the oil in a large frying pan and sauté the meat quickly, shaking the pan to turn it. Cook until brown on all sides, then push it to one side of the pan to make room for the onions,

Orange-topped Beef Casserole

1 dessertspoon curry powder
½ cup water and a beef soup cube
1 tablespoon salad oil
1 tablespoon cornflour
1 tablespoon water

tomatoes and green pepper. Sauté these for 1 minute, then mix with the meat. Pour over the stock mixture. Stir until boiling, cover, and simmer for about 45 minutes or until the meat is tender.

Blend the cornflour with the water, add to the mixture, and stir until it comes to the boil and thickens. Taste and adjust the seasonings.

Serve over freshly cooked rice, with some drained, crushed pineapple if liked.

ORIENTAL POT ROAST

1 tablespoon oil or dripping
3 pounds topside steak in one
   piece
2 medium-sized onions
5-ounce can of bamboo shoots
1 tablespoon soy sauce
1 teaspoon brown sugar
1 beef soup cube
1 cup sliced celery
¼ cup sliced canned pimento
1 tablespoon plain flour blended
   with 1 tablespoon cold water

Heat the oil in a heavy-base saucepan. Add the meat and brown on all sides. Lift out. Slice the onions and sauté in the same pan until golden brown. Replace the meat. Drain the bamboo shoots, mix enough water with the drained liquid to make ½ cup, and add to the contents of the saucepan together with the soy sauce, brown sugar and soup cube. Stir until the soup cube has dissolved. Cover and simmer until the meat is almost tender—about 1½ hours.

Add the celery and bamboo shoots and continue cooking until the celery is tender yet crisp—about 25 minutes. Lift out the meat and vegetables. Add the pimento to the liquid in the saucepan, then stir in the blended flour. Cook, stirring well, until the gravy boils and thickens.

321

1½ pounds good stewing steak
2 dessertspoons plain flour
1½ teaspoons salt
¼ teaspoon pepper
2 dessertspoons fat
2 or 3 carrots
2 or 3 onions
2 tablespoons tomato sauce
1 bayleaf
a pinch of dried thyme
1 clove of garlic
1½ cups water
1 dessertspoon vinegar
1 packet frozen peas

6 medium-sized mushrooms
2 dessertspoons butter
6 thick pieces of fillet steak
royal mushroom sauce
    (recipe follows)
piquant carrots (see page 421)
green peas and sautéed onions

¼ cup finely chopped spring
    onions
½ cup chopped fresh mushrooms
    (including the stems)
1 level tablespoon cornflour
1 cup Burgundy
½ cup water
2 dessertspoons chopped parsley
1 teaspoon salt
a dash of pepper

OVEN BEEF STEW

Cut the steak into cubes. Combine the flour with the salt and pepper and toss the meat in it. Heat the fat in a frying pan and brown the meat on all sides.

Place the browned meat in a 2-quart casserole, add sliced carrots and onions and the tomato sauce, bayleaf, thyme, crushed garlic, water and vinegar. Cover and bake in a moderate oven, 350°F., for about 1½ hours or until the meat is tender.

Add the frozen peas, return the casserole to the oven, and bake for another 30 minutes.

PAMPERED BEEF FILLETS

First prepare the mushroom crowns. Remove the stems but do not peel the mushrooms. (Keep the stems for the sauce.) Holding a small, sharp vegetable knife on a slant, cut from the top of each mushroom, in the centre, a V-shaped piece, not too deep, then cut out a second piece at right angles to the first. The result is a shallow cut-out in the form of a cross. (The pieces are used for the sauce together with the stems.)

Heat the butter in a heavy-base pan, add the steaks and brown quickly on both sides over moderately high heat.

Place each browned piece of steak on a square of foil, spoon about 2 dessertspoons of royal mushroom sauce over each, and top with a prepared mushroom crown. Bring the corners of the foil up over the steaks and twist gently, leaving the top slightly open. Place on a baking tray and bake at 500°F. for 12 minutes for a rare steak; 15 minutes for medium; and 19 to 20 minutes for a well done steak.

Remove the steaks from the foil and place on a hot dish. Serve with piquant carrots and green peas, with chopped onions that have been sautéed in a little butter. Accompany with the remainder of the royal mushroom sauce.

ROYAL MUSHROOM SAUCE

Add the chopped onions and mushrooms to the fat in the pan after browning the steaks. Cook until tender but not brown, then blend in the cornflour, Burgundy, water, parsley, salt and pepper. Cook, stirring well, until the sauce boils and thickens. This makes about 1½ cups of sauce.

322

PIQUANT ROAST LAMB

1 teaspoon mustard
1 teaspoon salt
¼ teaspoon pepper
2 tablespoons plain flour
1 leg of lamb, 3 or 4 pounds
2 tablespoons fat
½ cup tomato sauce
2 tablespoons Worcester sauce
1½ cups water
1 soup cube
1 medium-sized onion
1 clove of garlic
1 tablespoon flour for gravy

Combine the mustard, salt and pepper with the flour. Trim any excess fat from the lamb and rub the flour mixture well in.

Melt the fat in a baking dish, place the lamb in the dish and brown it quickly on all sides (either in the oven or on top of the stove).

Bake the lamb in a moderate oven, 350°F., for about 30 minutes, then pour away all the fat. Mix the sauces with the water, soup cube, sliced onion and crushed garlic and pour over the meat. Continue baking in a moderate oven for 1½ hours or until the lamb is cooked, basting with the piquant liquid at frequent intervals and adding a little more water if necessary.

Lift the meat onto a hot dish and keep it hot while you make the gravy. Strain the liquid in the baking dish, return it to the heat and take off any excess fat. Blend about a tablespoon of plain flour with a little water, add to the liquid, and stir until boiling, then cook for 2 minutes.

PLATTER PIE

For the filling

¼ cup bacon fat or dripping
¼ cup finely chopped onion
1½ pounds finely minced steak
1½ level teaspoons salt
¼ level teaspoon pepper
2 level tablespoons plain flour
¾ cup water
¼ cup cooked peas (optional)
¼ cup sliced cooked carrot
¼ cup sliced cooked parsnip

For the onion pastry

2 cups plain flour
2 level teaspoons baking powder
½ level teaspoon salt
4 ounces butter or margarine
1 tablespoon sautéed onion
1 egg
1 tablespoon water
1 tablespoon milk
2 tablespoons grated cheese

Melt the fat in a saucepan, add the onion and sauté to a golden brown. Take out 1 tablespoonful of onion and set it aside for the pastry.

Add the steak, salt, pepper and plain flour to the onion in the saucepan and cook over medium heat, stirring well, until the meat changes colour. Add the water and stir until the mixture comes to the boil. Lower the heat, cover, and simmer for about 30 minutes. Add the peas, carrot and parsnip. Cool.

Sift the flour, baking powder and salt for the pastry, rub in the butter and add the reserved onion. Beat the egg with the water and add to the dry ingredients, making a firm dough. Knead until smooth on a floured board.

Roll a little more than half the dough to line the bottom and sides of a greased 11-inch by 7-inch shallow tray. Fill with the cooled meat mixture, then top with the remaining pastry rolled to fit. Pinch the edges together, glaze with milk, then sprinkle with the grated cheese. Make a few slits in the top to allow the steam to escape.

Bake in a hot oven, 450°F., for 15 minutes, then reduce the temperature to 350°F. and bake for a further 40 minutes or until cooked. Cut into squares to serve.

POLISH POT-ROAST

⅓ cup margarine or butter
a boned and rolled joint of beef,
  5 to 6 pounds
1 cup water and a beef soup cube
1 large and 3 medium-sized
  onions
2 level teaspoons salt
2 cups soft white breadcrumbs
2 level teaspoons salt for the
  stuffing
¼ teaspoon pepper
¼ cup melted butter or
  margarine
a pinch of dried herbs
plain flour
parboiled potatoes

Melt the ⅓ cup margarine in a heavy-base saucepan and brown the meat well on all sides (over medium heat, or the outside of the meat will be hard).

Pour in the water and soup cube, add the whole large onion and the 2 teaspoons of salt. Cover and simmer for 2 to 2½ hours or until the meat is tender, turning the joint once or twice while it is cooking.

Combine the breadcrumbs in a bowl with the medium-sized chopped onions, 2 teaspoons salt, the pepper and the melted butter and dried herbs.

Remove the roast from the saucepan. Cut into ¼-inch-thick slices from the top of the joint to 1½ inches from the bottom, then place some of the breadcrumb stuffing between the slices of meat. Insert two skewers into each end of the stuffed roast to hold the stuffing and meat slices together.

Skim all the fat from the drippings in the saucepan, replace the meat and sprinkle with some plain flour. Cover and cook for another 30 minutes.

This dish was originally served with the drippings just as they came from the saucepan, but they may be thickened with blended flour to make a gravy.

If potatoes are to be served with the joint, add them, parboiled, to the pan when the pot-roast is replaced after it has been cut and stuffed.

POLYNESIAN PORK CHOPS

1 ounce butter
6 pork chops
salt and pepper
3 oranges
½ cup chopped onion
1 tablespoon soy sauce
½ cup thin bias-cut celery
1 rounded teaspoon cornflour
¾ cup uncooked rice
lightly fried bananas (optional)

Heat the butter in a pan and brown the pork chops on both sides. Season with salt and pepper. Squeeze the juice from one of the oranges and make up to 1 cup with water or stock.

Remove the chops from the pan, add the onion and fry until lightly browned, then add the liquid and the soy sauce. Stir until boiling.

Return the chops to the pan, cover, and simmer until they are tender. Add the celery pieces and cook for a further 5 minutes.

Blend the cornflour with a little water and use to thicken the liquid in the pan.

Serve with the freshly boiled rice which has been topped with the remaining 2 oranges (peeled and broken into segments) or with lightly fried bananas.

PORK BON FEMME

1 loin of pork (about 7 chops)
2 ounces softened butter
1 crumbled bayleaf
a pinch of thyme

Remove the rind from the pork. Mix the softened butter, bayleaf and thyme to a soft paste and rub it into the fat on the surface of the loin. Allow to stand for several hours before baking.

324

salt
freshly ground black pepper
2 tablespoons olive oil
8 small new potatoes
8 tiny onions
8 sautéed mushrooms
1 bouquet garni
chopped parsley for serving

Sprinkle with salt and pepper, then place the pork, fat side up, in a casserole. Add the olive oil. Bake in a moderate oven, 350°F., for 1 hour or until the pork is half cooked.

Place the peeled new potatoes, onions and sautéed mushrooms around the pork. Add the bouquet garni. Continue baking, basting from time to time, until the pork is tender.

Sprinkle with chopped parsley before serving.

PORK CHOP AND CORN SCALLOP

6 pork chops
1 teaspoon salt
½ teaspoon pepper
⅓ cup water
scalloped potatoes
  (recipe follows)
10-ounce can of whole kernel
  corn
½ cup chopped onion
½ green pepper
a good pinch of chilli powder

Trim the chops, removing the surplus fat. Place a little of the trimmed fat in a pan and when it has melted add the chops and brown them lightly on both sides. Sprinkle them with the salt and pepper and add the water. Cover the pan and simmer the chops for 30 minutes. Meanwhile make the scalloped potatoes, and when they are cooked arrange the chops on top of them, cover, and bake for 30 minutes. Drain the corn, toss it with the onion, finely chopped green pepper and chilli powder, and spoon it between the chops. Cover and bake for another 15 minutes or until the corn is heated through.

SCALLOPED POTATOES

1½ pounds potatoes
2 tablespoons plain flour
½ level teaspoon salt
a good pinch of pepper
½ cup chopped shallot
a good pinch of dried thyme
½ pint milk

Peel the potatoes and cut them into ¼-inch slices. Arrange in layers in a lightly greased casserole, sprinkling each layer with flour, salt, pepper, shallot and thyme. Pour over the milk, cover, and bake at 400°F. for about 1 hour.

PORK CHOP LOAF

6 pork chops
1 ounce butter
¾ cup chopped onion
¾ cup chopped celery
3 cups soft white breadcrumbs
¾ teaspoon salt
½ teaspoon pepper
3 tablespoons chopped parsley
fried apple rings and parsley
  sprigs to garnish

Remove the rind from the chops. If they are very fat, trim some of the fat off. Heat the butter in a pan and cook the chops until a light brown on each side, then lift out and brown the onion and celery in the same pan.

Combine the breadcrumbs with the salt, pepper and chopped parsley, then add the onion and celery.

Place a chop at one end of a loaf pan, fat side up, then place some stuffing alongside it in the tin. Alternately place chops and stuffing in this way in the tin, then run a skewer through the chops to keep them together with the stuffing. Bake in a moderate oven, 350°F., for about 1½ hours or until the chops are tender: the time will depend on the thickness of the chops.

To serve, garnish the dish with rings of fried apple and sprigs of parsley.

PORK CHOP RISOTTO

6 thick pork chops
salt and pepper
a little peanut or olive oil
1 cup uncooked rice
2 tablespoons chopped onion
1 large green pepper
2½ cups water and a soup cube
a good pinch of monosodium
  glutamate
chilli sauce
6 slices lemon and some parsley
  sprigs to garnish

Trim the surplus fat from the chops and season them with salt and pepper. Heat a little oil in a heavy pan and brown the chops on both sides, then lift out. Fry the rice in the same pan until it is straw coloured, then place it in a casserole dish.

Add a little more oil to the pan and lightly sauté the onion and half the chopped green pepper. Add the water, soup cube and monosodium glutamate, and stir until boiling. Pour this over the rice in the casserole, top with the chops and sprinkle each chop with a little chilli sauce. Cover and bake in a moderate oven, 350°F., for about 1 hour or until the chops are tender.

About 15 minutes before taking from the oven, place a little of the remaining chopped green pepper and a slice of lemon on each chop. Serve with a parsley garnish.

PORK CHOPS BAKED IN CREAM

4 thick pork chops
¼ pound mushrooms
2 ounces butter
1 tablespoon lemon juice
1 tablespoon plain flour
freshly ground black pepper
a pinch of thyme or oregano
4 tablespoons cream
finely chopped parsley

Trim the excess fat from the chops and sauté them in a heavy pan until brown on both sides. Remove from the pan and pour away the fat.

Chop the mushrooms finely and sauté them in the melted butter in the same pan until soft. Add the lemon juice and the flour and stir until boiling. Cook for 1 minute, then season with salt and freshly ground black pepper.

Place each chop on a square of foil and sprinkle with the salt, pepper and thyme. Top with the mushroom mixture, then spoon 1 tablespoon of cream over each chop. Sprinkle with chopped parsley.

Fold the foil over the chops and crimp the edges to seal them. Place on a baking tray and cook in a moderate oven, 325°F., for 50 to 60 minutes or until the chops are tender.

PORK CHOPS IN WINE

4 thick pork chops
2 tablespoons soft butter
1 teaspoon salt
¼ teaspoon pepper
½ teaspoon mustard
1 medium-sized onion
¼ pint white wine
2 tablespoons chopped parsley to
  garnish

Trim the excess fat from the chops. Pound the butter, salt, pepper and mustard into a smooth paste and spread it on both sides of the chops.

Brown the chops on both sides in a heavy-base pan. Add finely chopped onion and cook until the onion is transparent. Add the wine and heat until boiling.

Transfer to a casserole, cover, and bake in a moderate oven, 350°F., for 45 to 50 minutes or until the chops are tender. Sprinkle with finely chopped parsley before serving.

1 piece of pork fillet, 2 pounds
1 ounce butter
½ cup chopped onion
⅔ cup orange juice
1 teaspoon grated orange rind
⅓ cup dry sherry
1 tablespoon sugar
2 teaspoons salt
a dash of pepper
1 medium-sized bayleaf
1¼ dessertspoons cornflour
1 dessertspoon cold water

1½ pounds pork sausage mince
1 pound finely minced steak
1 teaspoon salt
½ teaspoon pepper
1 tablespoon chopped parsley
3 tablespoons chopped shallots
2-ounce can of buttered mushrooms
gherkins or stuffed olives

For the pastry

2 cups plain flour
1 level teaspoon salt
5 ounces butter or margarine
about 5 dessertspoons water

Pork Pie
Roast Pork with Oranges
Pork Fillet with Orange Sauce

PORK FILLETS WITH ORANGE SAUCE

Brown the piece of pork fillet on all sides in the butter. Remove from the pan. Using the same pan cook the onion until tender, then add the orange juice, rind, sherry, sugar, salt, pepper and bayleaf.

Return the meat to the pan, cover, and simmer for about 1 hour or until tender. Remove to a hot platter and cut into slices.

Combine the cornflour and water, blending until smooth, then add it to the orange gravy in the pan, stirring until the mixture boils and thickens. Cook for 1 or 2 minutes. Pour some of this gravy over the slices of pork and serve the remainder in a gravy boat.

PORK PIE

Combine the sausage mince, minced steak, salt, pepper, parsley, shallots and mushrooms in a large bowl and mix until well blended.

327

Sift the flour with the salt and rub in the butter. Add enough cold water to make a dry dough, turn onto a floured board and knead only until smooth on the outside.

Take two-thirds of the dough and roll to line a greased orange-loaf tin which has first been lined with foil. Place one-third of the meat mixture in the lined tin and add a row of stuffed olives or gherkins. Add another layer of meat, then another layer of olives or gherkins and top with the remainder of the meat.

Roll the remaining dough to fit the top, glaze the edges of the pastry and place this top piece on, pinching the edges together. Brush the top with beaten egg and milk and make a few slits to allow the steam to escape.

Bake in a hot oven, 450°F., for 10 minutes, then reduce the temperature to 325°F. and bake for a further $1\frac{1}{4}$ hours or until the pastry is golden and the filling cooked. Cut into slices to serve. The pie may be served hot with a brown vegetable gravy, or cold with a salad.

PORK SAUSAGES IN BARBECUE SAUCE

8 pork sausages
2 tablespoons fat
1 medium-sized onion
2 tablespoons flour
3 tablespoons vinegar
1 tablespoon brown sugar
1 tablespoon sweet chutney
$\frac{3}{4}$ cup diced celery
1 tablespoon Worcester sauce
$\frac{1}{2}$ teaspoon mixed mustard
$1\frac{1}{4}$ cups water
salt and pepper
chopped parsley
pineapple rings

Brown the sausages lightly in the hot fat. Remove them from the pan. Add sliced onion, cook until soft, then add the flour and cook, stirring well, until it browns. Now add the vinegar, brown sugar, chutney, celery, sauce, mustard and water. Stir until the mixture boils. Season with salt and pepper.

Return the sausages to the pan, cover, and cook over low heat for about 30 minutes.

Serve hot, sprinkled with chopped parsley and garnished if liked with well-drained canned pineapple rings which have been sautéed in a little butter or grilled until lightly browned.

RABBIT CASSEROLE

$1\frac{1}{2}$ pounds rabbit fillets (or a 2-pound rabbit)
seasoned flour
3 bacon rashers
1 medium-sized onion
1 cup sliced carrot
1 cup sliced parsnip
2 tablespoons plain flour
2 cups chicken stock, or water and a chicken soup cube
salt and pepper
parsley sprigs to garnish

If using the whole rabbit, soak for 30 minutes in warm water, then drain, dry, and cut into joints.

Coat the rabbit pieces or fillets with the seasoned flour and set aside. Cut the bacon rashers into 2-inch pieces and fry until the fat is clear, then remove from the pan. Fry the rabbit pieces in the same pan until brown on all sides, then transfer to a casserole.

Chop the onion and place it in the bacon drippings left in the pan (or add a little butter or margarine), together with the sliced carrot and parsnip. Cook until lightly browned, then stir in the flour and cook until it is pale brown. Add the stock, stirring until the mixture boils and thickens. Season to taste with salt and pepper. Pour this gravy over the rabbit in the casserole and top with the bacon pieces.

Cover the casserole and place it in a moderate oven, 350°F. to bake for 1½ to 2 hours or until the rabbit is tender.

Serve garnished with parsley, and accompany with fluffy mashed potatoes and green peas.

RICH BEEF CASSEROLE

2 pounds round or bladebone
  steak
¼ pound bacon
2 or 3 onions
1 level teaspoon salt
⅛ teaspoon pepper
1 clove of garlic
a good pinch of marjoram
¾ cup white wine
1 pound potatoes
3 carrots
2 parsnips
1½ cups stock or water
1 level tablespoon plain flour

Cut the steak into 1-inch cubes. Cut up the bacon and fry it in a saucepan until the fat is clear, then lift out. Peel and chop the onions and fry until brown in the bacon fat. Add the meat, salt, pepper, crushed garlic, marjoram and wine. Cover and bring slowly to simmering point, then simmer for 45 minutes.

Meanwhile prepare the potatoes, carrots and parsnips, by scraping or peeling and cutting into slices. Add the stock or water to the meat and thicken it with the blended flour, pour into a casserole, add the vegetables, cover, and bake in a moderate oven, 350°F., for about 1½ hours or until both the meat and vegetables are tender.

ROAST PORK WITH ORANGES

1 piece of loin of pork, 3½ to 4
  pounds
1 teaspoon sage
salt and pepper
grated rind of 1 orange
juice of 1 orange
½ cup sherry
3 to 6 peeled oranges
parsley sprigs to garnish

Rub the pork with the sage, salt and pepper, place in a baking dish without any fat and bake at 400°F. for 15 minutes. Reduce the temperature to 325°F. and bake until the meat is tender, or until a meat thermometer, inserted to the bone, registers 170°F. This will take about 2 hours, but about 45 minutes before the meat has finished cooking, remove it from the oven, pour away any fat, and sprinkle the pork with the grated orange rind, then pour the orange juice and sherry around the meat. Finish roasting.

Five minutes before serving, add half the peeled and partly sectioned oranges. Place the cooked meat on a platter and surround with the remaining whole oranges and a garnish of parsley. Serve with freshly boiled new potatoes.

ROAST VEAL

4 ounces soft white breadcrumbs
1 or 2 ounces chopped ham
2 teaspoons chopped parsley
¼ teaspoon mixed dry herbs
1 teaspoon salt
¼ teaspoon pepper
grated rind of half a lemon

Combine the breadcrumbs, ham, parsley, herbs, salt, pepper, lemon rind, shallot, celery and apricots. Toss lightly. Melt the ounce of butter and add to the mixture, then add enough egg to moisten.

Cut a pocket in the veal and stuff with the apricot seasoning. Secure the opening with a skewer and place the veal in a baking dish. Brush the surface with the melted butter and roast

329

1 dessertspoon chopped shallot
½ cup chopped celery
¾ cup well-drained and chopped
    canned apricots
1 ounce butter
beaten egg to bind
4-pound fillet of veal
¼ cup melted butter

without fat in a moderate oven, 350°F., allowing 35 minutes cooking time for each pound of veal.

Serve with gravy made from the pan drippings and a macedoine of vegetables.

ROUND STEAK WITH GHERKINS

2 pounds round steak
1 tablespoon butter
1 medium-sized onion
10-ounce can of consommé (or
    ½ pint stock, or water and a
    soup cube)
½ bayleaf
1 teaspoon salt
a dash each of pepper and
    cinnamon
¼ teaspoon ground ginger
4-ounce can of mushrooms
3 medium-sized gherkins
1 tablespoon flour blended with
    1 dessertspoon of gherkin
    liquid

Cut the steak into serving sized pieces and brown all over in the melted butter in a heavy-base frying pan. Add sliced onion and cook until lightly browned. Add consommé or stock, ½ bay-leaf, salt, pepper, cinnamon, ginger and mushrooms. Stir until boiling, then cover and simmer until the meat is tender—about 2 hours.

Cut the gherkins into 1-inch pieces and cook, then thicken the liquid with the blended flour and cook it for 2 minutes.

SAUSAGE AND TOMATO PIE

1 pound potatoes
1 pound sausages
1 dessertspoon fat
1 medium-sized onion
2 tomatoes
salt and pepper
milk and butter for potatoes
4 ounces grated cheese

Peel the potatoes and put on to boil. Cover the sausages with warm water, bring slowly to the boil, simmer for 6 minutes, then drain, skin and slice lengthwise.

Chop the onion and fry in a pan in the melted fat until soft, then push to one side of the pan, add the skinned and sliced tomatoes and cook these until soft. Season with salt and pepper.

Drain the potatoes and mash them with milk and a piece of butter. Add half the grated cheese.

Place the sliced sausages in a casserole or pie-dish and cover with the tomatoes and onion. If the tomatoes are firm, add a little water. Spread the mashed potato over the top and sprinkle with the remainder of the grated cheese.

Bake in a hot oven, 450°F., for about 15 minutes or until the cheese on top has melted and become lightly browned.

SAUSAGE STRATA

6 slices stale bread
1 pound sausage meat
1 teaspoon mustard

Remove the crusts from the bread and place it in the bottom of a greased casserole. Cook the sausage mince in a saucepan until it changes colour, stirring constantly. Drain off any fat.

1 cup shredded processed cheese
3 eggs, lightly beaten
2 cups milk
$\frac{1}{2}$ teaspoon salt
a dash each of pepper and nutmeg
1 teaspoon Worcester sauce

Add the mustard, stir until mixed and spread over the bread in the casserole. Sprinkle with the shredded cheese.

Combine the remaining ingredients and pour over the cheese. Bake in a moderate oven, 350°F., for 25 to 30 minutes or until puffed and set. Serve immediately.

SAUSAGES IN BARBECUE SAUCE

8 sausages
fat for frying
1 medium-sized onion
2 tablespoons plain flour
salt and pepper
3 tablespoons vinegar
1$\frac{1}{4}$ cups water
1 tablespoon sweet chutney
$\frac{1}{2}$ teaspoon mixed mustard
1 teaspoon brown sugar
$\frac{3}{4}$ cup diced celery
chopped parsley

Place the sausages in tepid water, bring slowly to the boil and simmer for 5 minutes. Drain. Place in a pan and fry in the hot fat until brown on all sides. Remove from the pan.

Add sliced onion to the fat left in the pan and cook until brown. Add the flour, stirring until it becomes brown, then season with salt and pepper.

Add the vinegar and water and stir until the sauce boils and thickens. Add the chutney, mustard, brown sugar and celery. Return the sausages to the pan, cover, and simmer for about 20 minutes. Serve sprinkled with chopped parsley.

SHEEP'S TONGUES GOURMET

12 sheep's tongues
3 teaspoons vinegar
2 tablespoons butter
$\frac{1}{4}$ cup finely chopped onion
3 level tablespoons plain flour
2 cups tomato purée
1 tablespoon chopped green pepper or 2 tablespoons chopped green olives
3 teaspoons brown sugar
1 teaspoon meat extract
1 teaspoon Worcester sauce
salt and pepper

Prepare the tongues by placing in a saucepan, covering with cold water and adding the vinegar. Place the lid on the saucepan and simmer for 4 hours or until the skin can be easily removed. Drain and skin, then remove the small bones from the root of each tongue. Place them in a casserole.

Heat the butter in a pan, add the chopped onion and cook until soft but not brown. Add the flour and cook for 1 minute, then the tomato purée, stirring until well blended. Add the green pepper, brown sugar, meat extract, Worcester sauce, and salt and pepper to taste. Pour over the tongues in the casserole.

Cover and bake in a slow oven for about 1 hour. Serve with fluffy mashed potatoes and green peas.

SPANISH PORK CHOPS

4 pork chops
1 clove of garlic
2 tablespoons plain flour
salt and pepper
2 tablespoons oil
$\frac{3}{4}$ cup tomato purée
$\frac{1}{4}$ cup white wine or sherry

Remove the surplus fat from the chops. Rub the surface of the meat with the cut clove of garlic. Season the flour with some salt and pepper and use to coat the chops.

Heat the oil in a heavy pan and brown the chops on both sides. Add the tomato purée and the wine and, if liked, the piece of garlic. Cover and simmer for 35 to 45 minutes or until the chops are tender. Serve with boiled rice.

331

STEAK AND KIDNEY PIE

1½ pounds bladebone or buttock
   steak
2 sheep's kidneys
2 tablespoons seasoned flour
1 dessertspoon chopped parsley
1 cup stock or water
salt and pepper
½ pound flaky pastry

Cut the steak into 1-inch cubes. Remove the skin and core from the kidneys and chop into small pieces, then add to the cubed meat. Combine the seasoned flour with the parsley and roll the meat in it, then place in a saucepan and add the stock or water and a little salt and pepper. Stir until boiling, cover, and simmer gently for about 1 hour or until the meat is tender. Cool, then place in a pie-dish.

Roll the pastry to cover the top of the pie-dish and place over the filling. Trim the edges, then glaze the top with milk, or with a mixture of beaten egg and milk. Decorate with any left-over scraps of pastry and bake in a hot oven, 450°F., for 10 minutes. Reduce the heat to moderate, 350°F., and bake for a further 15 minutes or until the pastry is crisp and golden.

STEAK AND KIDNEY PUDDING

12 ounces suet pastry
2 pounds round steak
1 onion
2 sheeps' kidneys
3 level tablespoons flour
1 level teaspoon salt
¼ level teaspoon pepper
2 to 3 tablespoons water

Line a 2-pint pudding basin with two-thirds of the pastry. Cut the meat into cubes and chop the onion. Scald the kidneys in boiling water, remove the core, and chop them finely.

Combine the steak, onion, kidney, flour, salt and pepper and place in the basin. Add the water. Roll the remaining pastry to cover the top. Pinch the edges together. Tie a scalded and floured cloth securely over the top and boil the pudding for 2½ hours.

As a change, a dozen oysters or a quarter of a pound of mushrooms may replace the kidneys.

STEAK AND MUSHROOM PIE

2 pounds good stewing steak
1 medium-sized onion
1½ teaspoons salt
¼ teaspoon pepper
2 cups water
½ pound mushrooms
¼ pound bacon rashers
2 tablespoons plain flour blended
   with a little cold water
8 ounces flaky pastry

Cut the meat into 1-inch pieces and chop the onion. Place in a saucepan with the salt, pepper and water. Cover and bring very slowly to boiling point. Reduce the heat and cook very slowly for about 1½ hours or until the meat is tender.

Wash and slice the mushrooms. Remove the rind from the bacon rashers and chop finely, then fry in a hot pan, lift out, place the mushrooms in the pan and cook them until tender.

Add the blended flour to the meat together with the mushrooms and bacon. Stir until boiling, then cool.

Place the cooked meat in a pie-dish and cover with the pastry rolled to fit the top. Brush with milk, or an egg and milk glaze. Bake in a hot oven, 450°F., for 20 to 25 minutes.

STEAK DIANE

fillet steak
butter
finely chopped parsley
crushed garlic
Worcester sauce

Pound the meat about $\frac{1}{4}$ inch thick. Melt 2 ounces of butter in a pan and when it is sizzling add the steaks. Cook for about 40 seconds on one side, then turn the steak over, sprinkle with the chopped parsley and garlic, and add more butter if necessary. Cook for 40 seconds on the second side, and add another sprinkling of parsley and garlic as well as a dash of Worcester sauce.

Move the steak quickly around in the pan to distribute the sauce evenly, then lift onto a hot serving dish and pour over any juices left in the pan.

STEAK ORIENTAL

1 pound round steak
$\frac{3}{4}$ cup sliced green pepper
$\frac{3}{4}$ cup diagonally sliced celery
$\frac{1}{2}$ cup water
6-ounce packet of frozen beans
2 dessertspoons cornflour
1 dessertspoon brown sugar
$\frac{1}{2}$ teaspoon salt
$\frac{1}{4}$ teaspoon pepper
1 dessertspoon soy sauce
2 dessertspoons water
1 dessertspoon butter
4-ounce can of buttered
  mushrooms
$\frac{1}{2}$ cup blanched and chopped
  almonds
2 cups freshly cooked rice
1 tablespoon finely chopped
  parsley

Slice the steak into thin slivers about $\frac{1}{8}$ inch thick. Place the green pepper, celery and water in a small saucepan, cover, and cook for 5 minutes, then add the frozen beans and cook for another 5 minutes.

Combine the cornflour, brown sugar, salt and pepper, soy sauce and 2 dessertspoons water. Set aside.

Melt the butter in a pan, add the meat and cook until it changes colour. Add the mushrooms and undrained vegetables, then the almonds and the soy sauce mixture. Cook, stirring until the mixture boils and thickens. Lower the heat, cover, and simmer until the meat is tender.

Serve over freshly cooked rice which has had the chopped parsley tossed through it.

STUFFED LAMB PROVENÇAL

1 boned leg of lamb, 3 to 4
  pounds
olive oil

For the stuffing
$\frac{1}{2}$ pound pork sausage mince
1 clove of garlic
$\frac{1}{2}$ cup finely chopped onion
$\frac{1}{4}$ cup stuffed olives
$\frac{1}{4}$ teaspoon salt
$\frac{1}{4}$ teaspoon thyme
a dash of pepper
1 slightly beaten egg
3 slices brown bread
2 dessertspoons milk

Lightly mix all the ingredients for the stuffing and fill the cavity where the bone was removed from the leg. Sew the edges together with thin string or thick cotton.

Rub olive oil over the surface of the meat and place in a roasting dish. Bake at 325°F. for about 2$\frac{1}{2}$ hours or until a thermometer, inserted in the centre, registers 170°F.

Remove the string and place the meat on a platter. Skim the fat from the drippings in the pan and thicken them to make a gravy, seasoning to taste with salt and pepper.

STUFFED MEAT ROLLS

1 pound finely minced steak
½ cup mashed potato
2 dessertspoons dry breadcrumbs
1 egg
1 teaspoon salt
¼ teaspoon ground allspice
1 tablespoon milk
4 bacon rashers

For the stuffing

⅓ cup minced onion
⅓ cup minced celery
⅓ cup minced parsley
¼ teaspoon salt
a pinch of pepper

Combine the meat with the potato, breadcrumbs, egg, salt and allspice. Mix well, adding enough milk to make a consistency that can be rolled. Spread the mixture on sheet of dampened greaseproof paper. Place another sheet of dampened paper over the top and roll the meat mixture into a rectangle about 8 inches by 12 inches.

Combine the ingredients for the stuffing and pat or spread on the rolled meat. Roll up like a jelly roll, then cut the roll into eight equal portions. Wrap a piece of bacon round each and secure it with a cocktail pick. Arrange the rolls in a shallow dish, leaving enough space between each roll to allow the bacon to become crisp.

Bake at 375°F. for about 30 minutes or until the bacon is crisp and the meat cooked.

STUFFED PORK CHOPS

6 thick pork loin chops
1 small onion
1 stick celery
2 dessertspoons butter
½ teaspoon dried mixed herbs
salt and pepper
1 cup soft white breadcrumbs
seasoned flour
a little oil
1 tablespoon plain flour
1 cup water
1 chicken soup cube
6 small carrots, scraped and
   halved
½ pound green beans, cut into
   chunky pieces

Make a 1-inch slit in the fat side of each chop to form a pocket. Chop the onion and celery and sauté in the butter until golden, then add the mixed herbs, ½ teaspoon salt, ¼ teaspoon pepper and the breadcrumbs, and a little water if necessary. Use this seasoning to stuff the chops, then coat them with seasoned flour. Heat a little oil in a pan, brown the chops well on both sides, then remove and place in a greased casserole.

Pour away all but 1 tablespoonful of fat from the pan, add the tablespoonful of plain flour, and cook, stirring well until brown, then add the water and soup cube and keep stirring over the heat until the gravy boils and thickens.

Season the chops with salt and pepper, place the vegetables round them in the casserole and pour over the gravy. Cover the casserole and bake in a moderate oven, 325°F., for 1½ hours or until the chops are tender.

STUFFED STEAK DINNER

2 tablespoons fat
½ cup chopped onion
¾ cup chopped celery
3 cups cubed day-old bread
2 dessertspoons chopped parsley
2 dessertspoons water
2 teaspoons salt
1½ pounds round or skirt steak
2 dessertspoons melted butter or
   fat

Melt the fat in a pan and cook the chopped onion and celery slowly for about 5 minutes. Remove from the heat and add the bread cubes, parsley, water, and about ½ teaspoon of the salt. Mix well.

Wipe the steak with a damp cloth. Using a sharp knife, make light gashes on both sides diagonally across the grain (cutting the fibres makes the meat more tender). Spread the filling made with the breadcrumbs to within an inch of the edges, roll up (beginning at the narrow end of the steak), and fasten with skewers or tie with string in three or four places.

334

1 cup hot water
about 8 small white onions
6 small carrots

For the gravy

1½ cups liquid
   (see method at right)
3 level dessertspoons plain flour
½ cup cold water

1 pound rump steak
1 stick celery
3 leaves spinach
¼ cup chopped shallot
¼ cup parsnip straws
¼ cup carrot straws
½ cup sliced beans
1 tablespoon oil
1 small can of mushrooms
⅓ cup stock
1 dessertspoon soy sauce
salt and pepper
1 teaspoon cornflour
1 tablespoon sherry (optional)
½ cup bamboo shoots (optional)

2 pounds round steak
seasoned flour
1 dessertspoon butter, margarine
   or oil
1 teaspoon salt
½ cup chopped onion
¾ cup water
1 clove of garlic
½ cup tomato purée
⅓ cup vinegar
⅓ cup brown sugar
1 dessertspoon mixed mustard
2 cups mixed cubed vegetables
   (carrots, parsnip, potato, green
   pepper)
1 cup drained pineapple pieces
freshly boiled rice for serving
1 dessertspoon chopped parsley

Heat the melted butter in a heavy-base pan and add the rolled steak. Brown on all sides, using medium heat. Add the hot water and the remaining salt. Bake, covered, in a moderate oven for about 1½ hours. After the first 30 minutes add the onions, and half an hour later add the carrots (sliced in halves lengthwise). Bake until the vegetables and meat are tender.

To make the gravy, skim off any excess fat, measure the liquid and add water to make 1½ cups. Blend the plain flour with the cold water and add to the stock mixture. Stir until boiling, then cook for about 3 minutes.

SUKIYAKI

Cut the meat into thin slivers about 3 inches long. Dice the celery and shred the spinach. Prepare the other vegetables.

Heat the oil in a heavy-base frying pan and brown the meat on all sides. Add the shallot, carrot, parsnip, celery and beans. Fry for about 5 minutes, stirring gently, then add the spinach, mushrooms and stock.

Simmer until the vegetables are cooked, but be careful not to overcook them. Stir in the soy sauce and season to taste with salt and pepper. If necessary thicken with cornflour blended with a little stock or water. Add the sherry and bamboo shoots if liked. Serve with freshly boiled rice.

SWEET AND SOUR BEEF STEW

Cut the steak into 1-inch cubes and toss in seasoned flour. Brown it in the heated butter in a heavy pan, season with the salt and add the chopped onion. Cook until the onion is lightly browned, then add the water. Cover and simmer for 1 hour.

Add crushed garlic, tomato purée, vinegar, brown sugar and mustard, and bring to the boil. Now add the vegetables and cook, covered, until the meat and vegetables are tender. Add the pineapple pieces and adjust the seasonings. Reheat.

Serve with freshly boiled rice which has been sprinkled with the chopped parsley.

SWEET AND SOUR PORK 1

1 pound pork fillets
1 tablespoon oil
⅓ cup water
1 tablespoon cornflour
½ cup pineapple juice
3 tablespoons vinegar
1 tablespoon soy sauce
1 dessertspoon brown sugar
1 teaspoon salt
¾ cup pineapple pieces
¼ cup sliced green pepper
¼ cup chopped shallots
chopped Chinese ginger
(optional)

Cut the pork into slices or cubes. Heat the oil in a pan and fry the pork until brown all over, then add the water and lower the heat.

Blend the cornflour with a little of the pineapple juice, add the remainder of the juice together with the vinegar, soy sauce, sugar and salt, and add to the pork. Cover. Simmer until the pork is tender: if it has been cut into very thin slices this will only take about 10 minutes, but longer if the pork has been cubed.

Add the pineapple pieces, green pepper, shallot and ginger, then cover and simmer for another 10 minutes. Serve over freshly cooked rice or noodles.

SWEET AND SOUR PORK 2

1 pound pork fillets
1 dessertspoon sherry
1 tablespoon soy sauce

For the batter

4 ounces self-raising flour
a pinch of salt
1 egg
about ¾ cup milk

For the sauce

1 green pepper
1 cooked carrot
1 dessertspoon oil
½ cup chopped shallot
2 dessertspoons sugar
½ cup pineapple syrup
1 dessertspoon soy sauce
½ cup chicken stock, or water and
   a chicken soup cube
1 tablespoon cornflour
⅓ cup vinegar
¾ cup drained pineapple pieces

Remove all the fat from the pork and cut the meat into thin slivers. Sprinkle with the sherry and soy sauce and allow to stand for about 1 hour.

Sift the flour and salt for the batter into a bowl and add beaten egg and enough milk to make into a light, smooth batter.

Cut the green pepper for the sauce into thin strips and slice the carrot. Heat the oil in a saucepan, add the pepper, carrot and shallot and sauté until almost soft, then add the sugar, pineapple syrup, soy sauce and chicken stock and heat until boiling.

Blend the cornflour and vinegar and add to the mixture, stirring until boiling. Add the pineapple pieces and allow to stand over low heat while preparing the pork.

Dip the drained pork pieces in a little seasoned flour and then into the batter. Drain lightly, then deep-fry in heated oil until a golden brown.

Reheat the oil, then fry the pork pieces again for a few minutes (unless the pork has been very thinly sliced it will not have been sufficiently cooked).

Adjust the seasoning in the sauce and serve over the fried pork.

SWEET AND SOUR PORK CHOPS

4 thick pork chops
1½ teaspoons salt
¼ cup water
1 chicken soup cube

Trim the excess fat from the chops. Brown them in a little heated fat in a pan, then add the salt and ¼ cup water. Cover. Simmer for 30 minutes, then remove the chops and pour away any fat left in the pan.

1 cup hot water
½ teaspoon Worcester sauce
1 dessertspoon soy sauce
⅓ cup pineapple juice
1 dessertspoon vinegar
¼ teaspoon prepared mustard
3 dessertspoons cornflour
2 dessertspoons water
1 cup drained pineapple pieces
½ green pepper
1 tomato
½ cup chopped celery
4 cups cooked rice

Dissolve the soup cube in the cup of hot water and add the Worcester sauce, soy sauce, pineapple juice, vinegar and mustard. Blend the cornflour with the 2 dessertspoons water and stir in, then cook until this sauce boils and thickens.

Return the chops to the pan with the pineapple, thinly sliced green pepper, peeled and sliced tomato and chopped celery. Bring to the boil, cover, then simmer for about 25 minutes or until the chops are tender. Serve over the hot cooked rice.

SWEET AND SOUR VEAL WITH RICE

1 small can of pineapple pieces
1½ pounds veal steak
2 dessertspoons hot fat
1 cup celery slices
½ cup chopped onion
¾ teaspoon salt
a dash of pepper
1 soup cube dissolved in ½ cup
    hot water
2 cups bean sprouts
3 dessertspoons cornflour
3 dessertspoons soy sauce
3 cups cooked rice

Drain the pineapple and reserve the syrup. Brown the veal in the hot fat and add the celery, onion, salt, pepper, the stock made from the soup cube, and the reserved pineapple syrup. Cover and simmer for about 1 hour or until the veal is tender.

Add the pineapple pieces and the bean sprouts. Blend the cornflour with the soy sauce and stir into the hot mixture. Cook, stirring constantly, until thickened and boiling. Serve with the boiled rice.

This dish will be improved in flavour if ½ teaspoon of mono-sodium glutamate is added with the soy sauce.

SWISS SAUSAGES

¼ cup plain flour
1½ level teaspoons salt
a good pinch of pepper
1 level teaspoon dry mustard
½ level teaspoon brown sugar
2 pounds thick sausages
3 level tablespoons margarine
1 medium-sized onion
1 cup water
1 dessertspoon Worcester sauce
1 dessertspoon tomato sauce
1 bayleaf

Combine the flour, salt, pepper, mustard and brown sugar.

Place the sausages in a saucepan of cold water and bring to the boil. Drain well, then coat the sausages with the flour mixture.

Heat the margarine in a heavy-base pan and brown the coated sausages on all sides. Remove from the pan and keep hot. Fry the chopped onion until brown.

Add any remaining flour mixture to the pan and stir over medium heat until brown. Add the water, Worcester sauce, tomato sauce and bayleaf. Stir until boiling. Return the sausages to the pan, or transfer both the gravy and the sausages to a casserole.

Cover and simmer gently for about 45 minutes, or bake in a moderate oven, 350°F., for the same length of time. Serve with sautéed carrots and a parsley garnish.

SWISS STEAK

¼ cup plain flour
1½ teaspoons salt
¼ teaspoon pepper
1 teaspoon dry mustard
½ teaspoon brown sugar
1½ pounds round or buttock
    steak
2 tablespoons fat
1 cup water
2 teaspoons Worcester sauce
1 bayleaf
1 onion

Combine the flour, salt, pepper and mustard with the brown sugar. Sprinkle over the steak, then pound well in, using the edge of a saucer.

Heat the fat in a pan and fry the meat on both sides (do this rather slowly to avoid drying or hardening the outside of the meat). Remove from the pan.

Add the water, sauce, bayleaf and finely chopped onion to the pan and stir until boiling. Add the meat and either leave in the pan or transfer to a casserole. Cover and cook for 1½ to 2 hours or until the meat is tender.

SWISS VEAL BALLS WITH POULETTE SAUCE

1½ pounds veal steak
½ pound bacon rashers
1 large egg
1 tablespoon chopped parsley
1 tablespoon chopped onion or
    chives
⅛ teaspoon each salt, pepper and
    marjoram
a pinch each of nutmeg and
    cayenne pepper
about 1 cup cooked rice
1 cup stock, or water and a soup
    cube

For the sauce

2 tablespoons butter
2 tablespoons flour
1 cup milk
1 cup stock, or the liquid in
    which the meatballs were
    cooked
2 egg yolks
2 dessertspoons lemon juice
salt and pepper
2 teaspoons chopped parsley

Put the veal and bacon through a mincer. Add the egg, parsley, onion, salt, pepper, marjoram, nutmeg and cayenne, then add sufficient cooked rice to make the mixture firm enough to mould into balls about the size of a walnut.

Bring the stock to the boil, add the meatballs and simmer, covered, for 15 minutes.

To make the sauce, melt the butter, add the flour and stir until smooth, cook for 1 minute without browning, then add the milk and stock and stir until the sauce boils and thickens. Add the egg yolks and lemon juice and season with salt and pepper. Stir in the parsley.

Combine the meatballs with the sauce and cook until they are thoroughly reheated.

TRIPE AND ASPARAGUS PIE

3 tablespoons butter
3 level tablespoons plain flour
1½ cups milk
½ cup liquid drained from the can
    of asparagus

Melt the butter in a medium-sized saucepan and add the flour. Stir until smooth, then cook for 1 minute without browning. Add the milk and asparagus liquid and stir until the sauce boils and thickens. Season with salt and pepper.

Reserve about 1 tablespoon of the drained asparagus to mix

salt and pepper
10-ounce can of asparagus cuts
2 pounds cooked tripe
1 dessertspoon chopped parsley
2 cups mashed potatoes
1 egg
a little butter
2 tablespoons grated cheese

For the pastry

2 cups plain flour
1 level teaspoon salt
5 ounces butter or margarine
about 3 dessertspoons water

For the filling

2 pounds veal
1 small onion
2 teaspoon salt
$\frac{1}{2}$ teaspoon marjoram
$\frac{1}{4}$ teaspoon pepper
$\frac{1}{2}$ cup cold water
1 soup cube
1 tablespoon gelatine and 2
    tablespoons cold water
$\frac{1}{4}$ pound diced cooked ham
1 dessertspoon chopped parsley
2 or 3 hard-boiled eggs
egg for glazing the top

$1\frac{1}{2}$ pounds thinly sliced veal steak
5 thin sausages
$\frac{1}{4}$ pound bacon rashers
2 tablespoons flour
1 teaspoon salt

with the potatoes. Add the remainder together with the tripe and parsley to the white sauce. Turn into a buttered casserole.

Mash the potatoes, adding the reserved asparagus pieces, the beaten egg, salt and pepper if required, and a little butter. Spread on top of the tripe mixture, score the surface and sprinkle with the cheese. Bake in a hot oven for about 15 minutes or until the top is a golden brown.

VEAL AND HAM LOAF

This loaf should be made the day before it is required.

Sift the flour and salt into a bowl and rub in the butter. Sprinkle with the cold water and toss lightly with a fork until combined. Knead very lightly, then chill until required.

Cut the veal into $\frac{1}{2}$-inch cubes and place in a saucepan with chopped onion, salt, marjoram, pepper, $\frac{1}{2}$ cup water and the soup cube. Cover and simmer for at least 30 minutes or until the veal is tender. Meanwhile, soak the gelatine in a bowl in the 2 tablespoons cold water.

When the meat is done drain the liquid from it into the gelatine and stir until the gelatine has dissolved. Chill until partly set, then add about 6 tablespoonfuls to the veal. Fold in the ham and the parsley and adjust the seasonings if necessary. Reserve the remainder of the jellied liquid.

Roll about two-thirds of the pastry to line a 9-inch by 5-inch loaf tin. Spread half the cooked meat mixture in this uncooked pastry case and place the shelled whole boiled eggs down the centre. Top with the remaining meat mixture.

Roll the remainder of the pastry to fit the top, place in position and pinch the edges together. Make a few slits in the top to allow the steam to escape. Brush with a little egg glazing and bake at 350°F. for about $1\frac{1}{4}$ hours or until the pastry is golden and cooked through.

Melt the remainder of the jellied liquid and pour into the loaf through the slits in the pastry. When cold, place in the refrigerator and chill overnight. Serve sliced with salad.

VEAL BIRDS WITH SAUSAGE

Pound the veal and cut into pieces, each measuring about 3 by 5 inches.

Parboil the sausages for 5 minutes. Drain well. Roll half a sausage in each piece of veal, then roll a piece of bacon round each, securing with cocktail picks. Roll each bundle in the

½ teaspoon pepper
about 1 tablespoon fat or oil
2 small onions
2 cups hot water and 1 soup cube
tomato slices and lemon wedges
    to garnish

flour (which has been seasoned with the salt and pepper), then brown in the hot fat in a pan. Transfer to a casserole.

Add the finely chopped onions to the fat left in the pan and cook until a light brown. Stir in any remaining flour and brown it. Dissolve the soup cube in the water and add. Stir until boiling, then pour over the veal birds in the casserole. Cover and bake in a moderate oven for about 45 minutes or until the veal is tender.

Remove the cocktail picks from the rolls, arrange on a heated platter, and pour the gravy over. Garnish with tomato slices and lemon wedges.

VEAL CHOPS AND MUSHROOM SAUCE

¼ cup plain flour
1 teaspoon salt
¼ teaspoon pepper
6 veal chops
¼ cup butter
1 clove of garlic
½ pound mushrooms
1 level tablespoon flour for sauce
½ pint hot water and a soup cube
1 teaspoon tomato paste
1 teaspoon paprika
¾ teaspoon salt for sauce
a pinch of marjoram
½ teaspoon monosodium
    glutamate

Combine the ¼ cup flour with the salt and pepper and use to coat the chops. Melt the butter, add crushed garlic, and brown the chops well on both sides. Remove from the pan.

Chop the mushrooms and add them to the same pan. Sauté until tender, then remove from the pan and pour away any excess fat. Stir in 1 level tablespoon flour, mix until smooth, and cook for 1 minute. Dissolve the soup cube in the hot water and add together with the tomato paste, paprika, salt, marjoram and monosodium glutamate. Heat until boiling, stirring well.

Return the chops to the pan and cover with a lid. Simmer until tender, then add the sautéed mushrooms, cover again and cook for a further 5 minutes. Serve hot with suitable vegetables.

VEAL CLEMENTINE

1 pound veal steak
juice of ½ lemon
salt and pepper
¼ pound bacon rashers
seasoned flour
fat for frying
1 large onion
1 tablespoon plain flour
½ cup stock, or water and a soup
    cube
½ cup white wine
4 ounces mushrooms
a sprig of thyme
a pinch of dried marjoram
1 clove of garlic

Cut the veal into serving pieces and flatten with a rolling-pin or a meat mallet. Rub with lemon juice and season with salt and pepper. Remove the rind from the bacon, place a piece of bacon on each piece of veal, roll the two together and fasten with a cocktail pick. Toss the rolls in seasoned flour.

Melt enough fat to barely cover the bottom of the frying pan, add the veal and bacon rolls and cook until brown all over. Lift out and place in a casserole.

There should be about 1 tablespoonful of fat in the pan but if not add some. Chop the onion and cook in the pan until brown. Add 1 tablespoon of plain flour and some salt and pepper. Cook, stirring well until the flour is brown. Add the stock and wine and stir until boiling.

Wash and chop the mushrooms and sprinkle over the veal rolls. Pour over the gravy and add the thyme and marjoram, and the clove of garlic speared with a cocktail pick. Cover and bake in a moderate oven, 350°F., for about 1 hour or until the meat is tender. Remove the garlic before serving.

VEAL CURRY HAWAIIAN

2 tablespoons butter
2 cloves of garlic
3 pounds lean veal
2 tablespoons seasoned flour
10-ounce can of cream of mushroom soup
½ soup-can of milk
¼ teaspoon pepper
a squeeze of lemon juice
1 to 1½ tablespoons curry powder
about 10 shallots
1 small can of pineapple pieces

Melt the butter in a saucepan and sauté peeled and chopped garlic until tender. Cut the veal into 1½-inch cubes and roll in the seasoned flour. Add to the hot butter in the pan and cook until brown on all sides.

Add the soup, milk, pepper, lemon juice, curry powder and chopped shallots. Bring to the boil, reduce the heat, cover, and simmer gently for about 1 hour or until the veal is tender.

Add the well-drained pineapple pieces and reheat gently, stirring as little as possible to avoid breaking up the meat cubes.

Serve with freshly boiled rice and curry accompaniments.

VEAL IN WINE SAUCE

1 pound veal steak
¼ cup grated cheese
¼ cup plain flour
a dash of garlic salt (optional)
1½ tablespoons butter or margarine
1 cup water
3 beef soup cubes
½ cup sherry

Cut the veal into 2-inch or 3-inch squares. Mix the cheese with the flour and the garlic salt and use to coat the meat.

Melt the butter in a large pan and sauté the veal until brown on all sides. Lift out and drain.

Add the water and the soup cubes to the pan. Stir well to dissolve, scraping the brown portions from the bottom of the pan. Cook for about 3 minutes, then add the sherry and simmer for another 2 or 3 minutes.

Add the veal, cover, and simmer until tender. Season to taste. If the sauce needs thickening, blend about a dessertspoonful of flour with a little water or wine and add to the pan. Cook, stirring well until boiling. Cover and simmer for another 3 or 4 minutes.

Veal Milano

341

VEAL MILANO

2 pounds veal steak cut into 8
   pieces
4 ounces mushrooms
2 ounces ham
1 tablespoon finely chopped
   onion
$\frac{1}{4}$ cup chopped celery
$\frac{1}{4}$ teaspoon dried thyme
$\frac{1}{2}$ teaspoon salt
$\frac{1}{4}$ teaspoon pepper
seasoned flour
1 egg beaten with 2 tablespoons
   milk
soft white breadcrumbs
butter for frying
tomatoes and parsley to garnish

For the sauce

1 tablespoon flour
$\frac{1}{2}$ cup dry white wine
$\frac{3}{4}$ cup stock, or water and a soup
   cube
1 teaspoon tomato paste
$\frac{1}{2}$ teaspoon salt
a pinch of pepper
1 teaspoon Worcester sauce
1 clove of garlic

Pound the veal pieces very thinly. Sauté the mushrooms in a little hot butter and chop them finely. Mix with the finely chopped ham and onion, chopped celery, dried thyme, salt and pepper. Roll each veal piece around some of this filling and secure with a cocktail pick. Cover with seasoned flour, dip into the egg glazing and coat with soft white breadcrumbs. Chill well.

Melt some butter in a pan and fry the veal until golden on all sides. Drain and place in a single layer in a lightly greased, shallow casserole.

To make the sauce stir the tablespoon of flour into the butter in the pan and cook for 1 minute, then add the wine, stock, tomato paste, salt, pepper, Worcester sauce and crushed garlic. Stir until the sauce boils and thickens, then pour it around the veal rolls in the casserole.

Cover the casserole and bake in a moderate oven, 350°F., for about 1 hour or until the veal is tender. Serve garnished with fresh tomato slices and parsley and, if liked, green peas.

VEAL PARMESAN

1 tablespoon butter or margarine
1 pound veal steak
$\frac{1}{3}$ cup evaporated milk
1 tablespoon grated Parmesan
   cheese
$\frac{1}{4}$ cup plain flour
$\frac{1}{2}$ teaspoon salt
a pinch of pepper
$\frac{1}{3}$ cup evaporated milk for sauce
$\frac{1}{2}$ cup grated Parmesan cheese for
   sauce
1 cup undiluted tomato soup
1 tablespoon chopped shallot

Melt the butter in an ovenproof dish. Cut the veal into serving pieces and pound thinly. Dip into the evaporated milk. Mix the tablespoon of cheese with the flour, salt and pepper and use to coat the veal. Place in the oven dish and bake uncovered for 30 minutes at 350°F.

Mix the other $\frac{1}{3}$ cup of evaporated milk with the $\frac{1}{2}$ cup of grated cheese. Remove the veal from the oven, pour the tomato soup and chopped shallot around it, spoon the cheese mixture on top, place the lid on and return to the oven to bake for a further 20 to 25 minutes or until the veal is tender.

VEAL PICCATA

1 tablespoon plain flour
½ teaspoon salt
¼ teaspoon pepper
1 pound thinly sliced veal
¼ cup butter or margarine
¼ cup dry white wine
1 lemon
¼ cup chopped parsley
parsley sprigs to garnish

For the sauce
1 dessertspoon butter or
   margarine
1 egg yolk
¼ cup dry white wine

Season the flour with the salt and pepper and use to coat the veal pieces. Heat the butter in a pan and sauté the veal until brown all over. Add the wine, thinly sliced lemon and chopped parsley, then cover and simmer for 10 minutes. Remove to a serving plate and keep hot, discarding the lemon slices.

To make the sauce, slowly heat the dessertspoonful of butter in the pan that was used for the veal. Beat the egg yolk with the wine and add, stirring constantly. Still stirring, cook over low heat until the sauce is thick and hot. Pour over the veal.

Serve garnished with parsley sprigs, and additional lemon slices if desired.

VEAL SCALLOPINI

2 pounds thinly sliced veal
2½ dessertspoons plain flour
salt and pepper
1 clove of garlic
¼ cup butter
1 tablespoon salad oil
½ pound thinly sliced
   mushrooms
½ cup water
½ cup Marsala wine or sherry

Pound the veal very thinly. Sprinkle lightly with a mixture of the plain flour, ¼ teaspoon salt and ¼ teaspoon pepper. Crush or chop the garlic and brown it in 1 tablespoon of the butter and 1 tablespoon of salad oil. Remove the garlic from the pan.

Add the veal to the hot fat in the pan, brown on both sides, then transfer to a casserole. Melt the remaining butter in the pan and sauté the mushrooms until they are golden. Add the water, 1 teaspoon salt, and the wine, and cook, scraping the bottom of the pan to collect any browned pieces. When the liquid boils, simmer for about 2 minutes to blend the flavours.

Pour this mushroom sauce over the veal, then cover and bake in a moderate oven, 350°F., for 30 minutes or until the veal is tender. Baste once or twice during cooking. Serve with boiled rice and a tossed green salad.

VEAL WITH PINEAPPLE

1 pound veal steak cut into 4
   pieces
seasoned flour
3 ounces butter
2 slices canned pineapple
¼ pound mushrooms
5 ounces cream or canned milk

Pound the veal cutlets with a meat mallet or a rolling-pin until very thin. Sprinkle on both sides with seasoned flour.

Heat 1½ ounces of the butter in a frying pan and cook the veal gently on both sides until lightly browned. Remove the meat from the pan and keep it warm in the oven.

Drain the pineapple slices, cut them in half and sauté lightly in the butter left in the pan. Remove and put aside with the veal.

Slice the mushrooms and cook in the remaining 1½ ounces of butter until tender. Lift out.

Stir the cream or milk into the drippings in the pan and cook, stirring gently until well heated.

Arrange the veal on a flat serving platter, top each piece with a half pineapple slice, cover with the sautéed mushrooms, and pour over the sauce. Serve with potato chips and green peas.

WIENER SCHNITZEL

thin slices of veal steak
seasoned flour
1 egg beaten with 1 tablespoon
   milk
soft white breadcrumbs
2 ounces butter
a squeeze of lemon juice
thin slices of lemon, hard-boiled
   egg and anchovies
chopped parsley

Pound the veal with a meat mallet or a rolling-pin until very thin (be careful not to break the slices). Toss in seasoned flour, dip in the egg and milk glaze, then cover with breadcrumbs. Press each piece of meat with the blade of a knife to flatten the meat and firm on the egg and breadcrumbs. Chill well.

Heat the butter in a pan and fry the veal for 10 minutes, turning once.

Add a squeeze of lemon juice to the butter remaining in the pan and pour this over the veal. Serve garnished with slices of lemon, hard-boiled egg and anchovy and a sprinkle of chopped parsley.

WINE MERCHANT'S STEAK

Choose a good thick T-bone or porterhouse steak. Melt some butter in a heavy-base pan (enough to cover the bottom of the pan when melted). When the butter is sizzling, add the steak and fry for 3 minutes on each side. Lift out and place on a hot dish.

In the butter left in the pan, fry some chopped shallot (allow 1 shallot for each serve). When cooked, add about ½ cup of red wine (Burgundy is the favourite for this dish). Cook until the liquid has reduced by half, then add a few drops of vinegar, 1 tablespoon of cream, and some salt and pepper. Pour over the steak and sprinkle with chopped parsley before serving.

Wine Merchant's Steak

344

Meatballs and Loaves

ABERDEEN SAUSAGE

4 to 6 ounces bacon
1 pound finely minced steak
salt and pepper
6 ounces soft white breadcrumbs
1 egg
½ cup browned breadcrumbs

Remove the bacon rind. Mince the bacon and mix it with the meat, salt and pepper, breadcrumbs and lightly beaten egg. Make into an oblong shape.

Rub some plain flour into the centre of a pudding cloth. Place the shaped meat on the cloth and roll up. Tie each end with a piece of string. There should not be too much "slack" in the cloth, otherwise the water may enter while cooking. Use a safety pin to secure the centre of the cloth.

Plunge the sausage into rapidly boiling water and boil gently for 2 hours.

Remove from the cloth and roll in browned breadcrumbs. Chill before slicing, and serve with a salad.

SAUSAGE LUNCHEON ROLL

2 pounds sausage meat
1 small onion
4 bacon rashers
4 rounded tablespoons soft white
  breadcrumbs
1 teaspoon curry powder
1 egg

Combine the meat with finely chopped onion and bacon and the other ingredients, mixing well with two forks.

With floured hands, shape into a thick roll. Flour a pudding cloth and place the sausage mixture in the centre. Roll up and tie the ends firmly (a safety pin may be used in the centre at the open edge).

Plunge the roll into a large saucepan of boiling water, cover, and boil for 2 hours.

Remove from the cloth and allow to become cold. Serve sliced with salad.

BEEF LAYER LOAF

1½ pounds minced steak
1 rasher of bacon
2 tablespoons finely chopped
  onion
salt and pepper
rosemary
1 egg
¼ cup dried browned
  breadcrumbs
1 cup soft white breadcrumbs
1 tablespoon melted butter
1 cup peeled and diced tomatoes
2 or 3 spring onions
salt and pepper

Combine the minced steak, diced bacon and chopped onion with salt, pepper and rosemary to taste. Bind with a little beaten egg. Line a loaf tin with greased foil, then sprinkle the inside with the ¼ cup of dried browned breadcrumbs. Press half the meat mixture into this tin.

Mix the soft white breadcrumbs, melted butter, diced tomatoes and finely chopped spring onions, seasoning with salt and pepper. Spoon this mixture over the meat layer in the tin, cover with the remainder of the meat mixture, then cover the tin with foil.

Bake at 350°F. for 1¼ hours. Leave in the tin for about 10 minutes before turning out.

Serve hot with vegetables in season, or cold with salad.

BEEFBALL STROGANOFF

1½ pounds finely minced steak
⅓ cup dry breadcrumbs
¼ cup chopped onion
1 teaspoon salt
¼ teaspoon pepper
1 egg
1 teaspoon Worcester sauce
2 tablespoons butter or
   margarine

For the sauce

¼ cup finely chopped onion
10-ounce can cream of mushroom soup
5 ounces water (½ soup can)
1 or 2 tablespoons sour cream
freshly boiled rice
chopped parsley

Combine the meat, breadcrumbs, onion, salt, and pepper in a large bowl. Beat the egg, and the Worcester sauce and use enough to bind the meat mixture together. Take spoonfuls and shape into 18 balls, each about 2 inches in diameter. A little seasoned flour may be used for shaping.

Heat the butter in a pan and brown the meatballs well. Cover, reduce the heat and cook for 8 minutes. Remove the meatballs from the pan.

In the same pan cook the chopped onion for the sauce until soft but not brown. Add the soup and water and stir until boiling.

Return the meatballs to the pan, placing them in the sauce. Cover and cook gently for another 5 minutes or until heated through. Stir in the cream and cook for a further 3 minutes. Serve on hot rice lightly sprinkled with finely chopped parsley.

BRAWN

1 knuckle of veal, or 2 pounds
   shin of beef
6 sheep's tongues
1 pound pickled pork or a pig's
   cheek
a good pinch of mixed herbs
1 bayleaf
water

Wash the meats and place them in a large saucepan with the herbs and bayleaf. Cover with water. Place a lid on the saucepan, bring to the boil and simmer for about 4 hours or until the meat is easily removed from the bones.

Lift the meat from the liquid, remove the flesh and cut it into pieces. Before slicing the tongues remove the skin, the root bones and gristle. Pack the meats into a wetted mould or a meat press.

Reduce the liquid in which the meat was cooked and pour a little of it over the meat. Leave until cold, then place in the refrigerator and chill well. Serve sliced with salad vegetables.

BURGUNDY BEEFBURGERS

2 pounds finely minced steak
1 cup soft white breadcrumbs
1 teaspoon salt
a dash of pepper
1 egg
¼ cup dry red wine
   (Burgundy for preference)
4 ounces butter or margarine
1 tablespoon chopped onion
1 tablespoon chopped green
   pepper
8 slices French bread

Toss the meat in a large bowl with the breadcrumbs and seasonings. Mix in the beaten egg and the wine. Take spoonfuls and shape into round flat cakes about 1 inch thick.

Heat the butter in a saucepan and cook the onion and green pepper in it until the onion is tender. Brush the burgers with this mixture, place them in a flat dish and pour over the remaining butter, onion and green pepper mixture.

Bake in a moderate oven, 350°F., for about 20 minutes, basting at intervals with the liquid in the dish. Serve the burgers on slices of French bread.

346

Creole Meat Loaf, Caribbean Lamb, Beef Curry

CHIP PUFF STROGANOFF

1 tablespoon butter
½ cup chopped onion
1½ pounds minced steak
2 level tablespoons plain flour
¾ cup water
1 beef soup cube
½ teaspoon salt
a dash of pepper
10-ounce can of cream of
  mushroom soup
1 cup sour cream

For the chip puffs

¾ cup water
½ teaspoon salt
1 tablespoon butter
¾ cup milk
1 packet instant mashed potato
8 one-inch cubes cheddar cheese
1½ cups crumbled potato chips

Melt the butter in a saucepan, add the onion and cook until soft. Add the meat and cook until it changes colour. Stir in the flour and mix well, then add the water, soup cube, salt and pepper and cook until thickened. Stir in the soup and sour cream and bring to boiling point before pouring into a casserole.

Place the water, salt and butter for the puffs in a saucepan and bring to the boil. Remove from the heat and add the milk. Stir in the instant potato flakes and whip with a fork.

Shape into eight balls while the potato is still warm. Insert a cube of cheese in the centre of each ball and roll them in the crushed potato chips.

Place the balls on top of the meat in the casserole and bake at 425°F. for about 25 minutes or until the chip puffs are a golden brown and heated through.

CHOP SUEY

1 onion
2 stalks celery
¼ of a cabbage
4 ounces butter or margarine
1 cup peas or beans
½ cup diced carrot
salt and pepper
1 teaspoon curry powder
1 pound finely minced steak
1 packet chicken noodle soup
4 cups water
1 cup uncooked rice
soy sauce

Finely dice the peeled onion and the celery and shred the cabbage finely. Melt the butter in a large saucepan and add the onion, celery, cabbage, peas and diced carrot.

Cook over medium heat for about 10 minutes or until the vegetables are tender yet still crisp. Season to taste with salt and pepper, then add the curry powder and the minced steak, mixing well. Stir in the chicken noodle soup, the water and the uncooked rice. Cook, stirring well until the mixture comes to the boil. Reduce the heat and cook for about 45 minutes or until all the moisture has been absorbed.

Before serving, stir in 1 or 2 dessertspoons of soy sauce, according to taste.

CONTINENTAL LOAF

1 pound finely minced steak
1 pound minced veal
2 eggs
1 small onion
1 dessertspoon plain flour
2 teaspoons salt
½ teaspoon marjoram
¼ teaspoon pepper

Combine the minced steak and veal in a bowl. Beat the eggs, slightly, then measure 1 tablespoonful into a cup and set aside. Add the remainder of the beaten egg to the meat with the finely chopped onion and the flour, salt, marjoram, pepper and beef broth.

Make the pastry (see p. 348). Roll two-thirds into a rectangle measuring 15 by 10 inches and use to line 9-inch by 5-inch loaf tin.

Roast Veal, Roast Pork with Oranges, Roast Chicken

½ cup beef broth
10 small gherkins
pastry (recipe follows)

Spread one third of the meat mixture in the bottom of the lined tin. Quarter the gherkins lengthwise and place half of them in a layer over the meat. Repeat with another layer of meat and gherkins, then top with the remaining meat.

Roll the remaining one-third of pastry to fit the top of the tin. Glaze the edges of the lining pastry, place the top on and pinch a frill round the edges to seal them. Make a few slits in the top to allow the steam to escape. Brush with the reserved egg. Bake at 350°F. for 1 hour 45 minutes or until golden.

PASTRY

2 cups plain flour
1 teaspoon salt
5 ounces butter or margarine
about 5 dessertspoons cold water
a squeeze of lemon juice

Sift the flour and salt into a bowl and rub in the butter. Mix the cold water with the lemon juice and blend in with a fork until the pastry holds together. Turn onto a floured board and knead only until smooth on the outside.

1 pound finely minced steak
½ pound finely minced pork
½ pound finely minced veal
¼ cup chopped onion
½ cup chopped green pepper
1 dessertspoon chopped parsley
1½ cups fine breadcrumbs, toasted
1 egg
¼ cup tomato sauce
1 dessertspoon Worcester sauce
2 level teaspoons salt
2 teaspoons prepared mustard
a good pinch of flavouring herbs
¼ level teaspoon pepper
chilli or tomato sauce
pineapple rings

CREOLE MEAT LOAF

Combine all the ingredients (except the chilli or tomato sauce and pineapple rings) in a bowl, mixing well. Pack into a greased 9-inch by 5-inch loaf tin and bake in a moderate oven, 350°F., for 1½ hours.

Drain away any liquid which has accumulated in the tin. Turn the loaf onto a shallow baking tray and pour over it half a cup of chilli or tomato sauce. Return the loaf to the oven for another 5 minutes. Serve with well-drained pineapple rings which have been tossed in butter.

For the filling
½ pound pork sausage mince
¼ cup finely chopped green pepper
¼ cup finely chopped onion
¼ cup plain flour
1 level teaspoon salt
a dash of pepper
1 cup diced peeled tomatoes
⅓ cup stock, or water and a soup cube
2 cups diced cooked mixed vegetables

CREOLE PIE

Brown the pork sausage mince in a large pan, add the green pepper and onion and cook until soft. Stir in the flour, salt and pepper, mixing well, then add the tomatoes and stock. Cook, stirring constantly until thick and smooth. Add the cooked mixed vegetables and simmer, covered, for about 15 minutes.

To make the pastry sift the flour, baking powder and salt into a bowl, rub in the butter and mix to a medium dough with the combined egg and milk. Turn onto a floured board and knead until smooth on the outside.

Roll the pastry to fit a greased 9-inch tart plate. Flute the edges and prick the bottom of the pastry case. Bake at 425°F. for about 15 minutes. Remove from the oven and fill with the meat and vegetable mixture. Return to the oven and bake at 350°F. for a further 10 or 15 minutes, or until cooked.

348

For the pastry
2 cups plain flour
2 level teaspoons baking powder
1 level teaspoon salt
3 ounces butter or margarine
1 egg beaten with about $\frac{1}{4}$ cup milk

1½ pounds finely minced steak
1 teaspoon salt
$\frac{1}{4}$ teaspoon pepper
1 dessertspoon oil
$\frac{3}{4}$ cup finely chopped onion
1 cup diced celery
2 tablespoons butter
3 teaspoons curry powder (or more to taste)
1 tablespoon dry sherry
2 teaspoons sugar
1 dessertspoon chopped parsley
1 soup cube
1 cup hot water
1 level tablespoon cornflour
freshly cooked rice

For the meat mixture
1 pound minced beef or veal
1 bread roll, soaked in cold water then squeezed almost dry
2 tablespoons grated onion
1 clove garlic, crushed
1 tablespoon olive oil or melted butter
a dash of pepper
$\frac{1}{2}$ level teaspoon salt
$\frac{1}{4}$ level teaspoon grated lemon rind
1 to 2 tablespoons lemon juice
1 large or 2 small eggs
$\frac{1}{4}$ level teaspoon marjoram (optional)

For the filling
2 eggs
1 tablespoon water
2 tablespoons chopped parsley
a pinch of salt
1 level teaspoon self-raising flour

For the covering
egg white and dry breadcrumbs

Serve cut into wedges and garnished with extra tomato slices and parsley sprigs.

CURRY MEATBALLS
Season the meat with salt and pepper and form into walnut-sized balls. Brown in the oil in a frying pan, cover, lower the heat and cook for about 15 minutes, turning occasionally with a fork to prevent sticking. Remove from the pan.

In the same pan sauté the onion and celery in the butter until soft. Stir in the curry powder, sherry, sugar, parsley, soup cube and water. Stir until boiling, then simmer for 7 minutes, stirring occasionally.

Blend the cornflour with a little cold water and gradually stir into the sauce. Cook, stirring well until the sauce boils and thickens. Add the meatballs, reheat over gentle heat and serve with freshly cooked rice.

CZECH MEAT LOAF
Combine the ingredients for the meat mixture in a bowl, then press into an oblong shape on greased paper.

Beat the eggs for the filling with the water and parsley and add the salt and the self-raising flour. Pour into a greased omelette pan and cook until just set, but still soft. Place this on the meat and roll up as for a jelly or Swiss roll. Brush the top with egg white and roll in dry breadcrumbs. Place in a baking dish and bake in a moderate oven, 350°F., for about 30 to 45 minutes. Serve hot or cold, cut into slices.

DANISH MEATBALLS

1 pound finely minced steak
½ pound finely minced lean pork
5 dessertspoons cornflour
½ level teaspoon each of ground
   nutmeg and ground ginger
½ level teaspoon pepper
2 level teaspoons salt
1 egg
2 tablespoons milk
1½ cups peeled and chopped
   onion
2 dessertspoons bacon fat
½ cup chopped green pepper
10-ounce can of condensed
   vegetable soup
¾ cup water
2 tablespoons tomato paste

Thoroughly combine the minced steak and pork. Stir in the cornflour, seasonings, egg and milk, mixing lightly. Form into balls about 1½ inches in diameter.

Sauté the onion in the bacon fat until tender, then remove from the pan. Fry the meatballs in the pan until brown on all sides. Drain well on paper.

Remove all but about 1 dessertspoon of fat from the pan and add the sautéed onion, green pepper, soup, water and tomato paste. Blend well.

Add the meatballs to the contents of the pan and simmer for about 15 minutes, stirring occasionally. Lift the meatballs out, arrange on a hot serving dish. Pour some of the sauce over them and serve the remainder in a sauce boat.

FAVOURITE MEAT LOAF

1 pound finely minced steak
1 pound sausage meat
¼ pound chopped bacon
½ cup soft white breadcrumbs
1 medium onion
1 dessertspoon chopped parsley
1 clove of garlic
1 egg
2 tablespoons tomato sauce
1 teaspoon Worcester sauce
salt and pepper

Combine the minced steak in a large bowl with the sausage meat, bacon, breadcrumbs, finely chopped onion, parsley and crushed garlic.

Beat the egg and mix with the tomato and Worcester sauce. Stir into the meat mixture, flavouring to taste with salt and pepper.

Form into a loaf and pack into a well-greased loaf tin. Cover with greased paper or greased foil and bake in a moderate oven, 350°F., for 1¼ to 1½ hours.

Remove the greased paper or foil and bake the loaf for a further 15 minutes. Drain away any surplus fat and turn the meat out onto a serving dish.

Serve hot with gravy or cold with salads.

FRICADELLES

1 tablespoon butter
2 shallots
3 cups soft white breadcrumbs
1 egg
½ cup milk
3 tablespoons white wine
¾ teaspoon salt
a pinch of pepper

Melt 1 tablespoon of butter in a pan and sauté the finely chopped shallots. Combine the breadcrumbs, beaten egg, milk and 3 tablespoons white wine. Add sautéed shallots, salt, pepper, nutmeg and minced pork. Mix well. Shape into about 24 balls, using a little seasoned flour to prevent sticking.

Add the second tablespoon of butter to the pan in which the shallots were cooked. Brown the meatballs on all sides, then add the cocktail onions, the broth and the extra tablespoonful

¼ teaspoon ground nutmeg
1 pound finely minced pork
seasoned flour
1 extra tablespoon butter
1 rounded tablespoon white
    cocktail onions
¾ cup beef broth
1 extra tablespoon white wine
¼ teaspoon salt
a pinch each of pepper, nutmeg
    and herbs
chopped parsley

of white wine. Season with the extra salt and pepper, and with the nutmeg and herbs.

Cover and simmer for 30 minutes. Arrange the meatballs on a hot dish, pour over the gravy and sprinkle with the chopped parsley. Serve with boiled new potatoes.

FROSTED MEAT LOAF

2 onions
1 clove garlic
a little oil
1 cup soft white breadcrumbs
1½ pound finely minced steak
1 teaspoon salt
½ teaspoon mixed herbs
1 dessertspoon chopped parsley
½ cup tomato purée
2 tablespoons red wine
1 egg
1½ pounds potatoes
milk and butter for mashing
    potatoes

Sauté chopped onion and garlic in a little oil and mix in the breadcrumbs, meat, salt, herbs and parsley. Bind with the combined tomato purée, wine and lightly beaten egg.

Pack into a greased loaf tin and bake in a moderate oven, 350°F., for 40 to 50 minutes.

Boil the potatoes in the usual way, drain them and mash with milk and butter. Turn the meat loaf out on a shallow oven tray and frost the top and sides with the mashed potato.

Return the loaf to a hot oven and bake for a further 12 to 15 minutes or until the potato topping is lightly browned. Serve with tomato sauce.

GIPSY CUTLETS

1 pound finely minced steak
1 cup soft white breadcrumbs
1 tablespoon finely minced onion
1 dessertspoon chutney
1 teaspoon chopped parsley
½ teaspoon mixed herbs
salt and cayenne pepper
1 egg
seasoned flour
a soup cube and ¾ cup hot water
a few drops Parisian essence
1 or 2 rashers of bacon

Combine the steak with the breadcrumbs, onion, chutney, parsley and herbs. Season with salt and cayenne pepper and bind with beaten egg.

Shape into round flat cakes in seasoned flour and place in a lightly greased casserole dish. Mix the soup cube with the hot water and add a few drops of Parisian essence to colour it. Pour over the meatballs.

Remove the rind from the bacon and place on top. Bake uncovered in a moderate oven, 350°F., for about 30 minutes or until the meatballs are cooked.

351

GLAZED MEAT ROLL

2 pounds minced steak
1 teaspoon salt
¼ teaspoon pepper
¼ cup tomato sauce
1 dessertspoon Worcester sauce
a few drops chilli sauce
1 dessertspoon vinegar
2 cups grated carrot
1 cup soft white breadcrumbs
½ cup chopped parsley
1 teaspoon salt
2 eggs
1 cup hot water
1 tablespoon plain flour

Place the beef with the salt and pepper in a large bowl and toss lightly with a fork. Form into a rectangle about 12 by 14 inches on dampened greaseproof paper.

Mix the tomato sauce, Worcester sauce and chilli sauce with the vinegar. Brush some of this mixture over the meat.

Mix the carrot, breadcrumbs, parsley, salt and beaten eggs in a bowl, blending well. Spread evenly over the meat and roll up as for a jelly or Swiss roll. Lift onto a large, greased baking dish and brush the sides of the roll with some of the remaining sauce mixture. Bake at 350°F. for about 1 hour, brushing with the sauce during cooking. When ready, remove from the baking dish and keep hot while you make the gravy.

Blend the flour with the drippings in the pan, scraping any browned pieces from the bottom. Cook until well browned, then add the water. Cook, stirring well, until the gravy boils and thickens. Season to taste with salt and pepper and serve with the meat roll.

HAMBURGER LOAF

¾ cup finely minced onion
½ cup finely minced green pepper
½ cup finely minced celery
1 pound finely minced steak
1½ cups soft white breadcrumbs
1 level dessertspoon dry mustard
1 teaspoon salt
1 egg beaten with ⅓ cup milk

Combine the onion, green pepper, celery, steak and breadcrumbs in a large bowl and season with mustard and salt. Bind with the egg and milk, mixing lightly but thoroughly. Turn into a well-greased loaf tin and bake at 350°F. for about one hour.

Serve hot with grilled tomatoes and a brown gravy, or cold with salad vegetables.

Hamburger Loaf

HAMBURGER STEAK AND BANANAS

1 onion
1 pound finely minced steak
1 egg
1 cup soft white breadcrumbs
1 tablespoon tomato sauce
1 teaspoon salt
¼ teaspoon pepper
1 dessertspoon Worcester sauce
1 teaspoon gravy powder
1 beef soup cube
1 dessertspoon plain flour
1 cup water
3 bananas
¼ pound bacon rashers

Mince the onion finely and mix with the steak, egg and breadcrumbs. Flavour with the tomato sauce and season with the salt and pepper. Shape tablespoonfuls of the mixture into rounds and place in a lightly greased casserole.

Mix the Worcester sauce with the gravy powder, soup cube and plain flour and blend with the water. Pour this mixture over the hamburgers in the casserole. Cover, then bake in a moderate oven, 350°F., for 1 hour.

Meanwhile, peel the bananas, cut in halves and roll each half in a bacon rasher, securing with a cocktail pick.

Just before serving time, top the hamburgers in the casserole with the prepared bacon rolls and bake without the lid on until the fat on the bacon is clear.

LIVER LOAF

1 pound liver
1 medium onion, peeled and
   finely chopped
½ pound pork sausage meat
1 cup soft white breadcrumbs
1 teaspoon Worcester sauce
1 teaspoon lemon juice
1 teaspoon salt
1 teaspoon celery salt
a dash of pepper
1 beaten egg
½ cup stock
4 slices bacon

Cover the liver with hot water and simmer for 5 minutes. Drain, reserving some of the liquid to use as stock.

Put the liver through a mincer and add the remaining ingredients except the bacon. Form into a loaf and pack into a greased 9-inch by 5-inch loaf tin. Remove the bacon rinds and place the bacon on top of the loaf. Bake uncovered in a moderate oven, 350°F., for about 45 minutes.

MEATBALLS AND VEGETABLE MEDLEY

¼ cup chopped onion
1 dessertspoon butter
¾ pound finely minced steak
½ pound finely minced veal
4 dessertspoons plain flour
1 teaspoon salt
a dash of pepper
1 egg
2 extra dessertspoons butter
1⅓ cups beef broth
½ cup water
6 medium potatoes
6 medium carrots
5 or 6 spring onions
extra salt and pepper
10-ounce packet of frozen peas
parsley sprigs to garnish

Cook the onion in 1 dessertspoon butter until soft but not brown. Combine the steak, veal, 2 dessertspoons of the flour, the salt, pepper, egg and cooked onion and form into 1-inch balls. Heat the 2 dessertspoons of butter in the pan, add the meatballs and brown them on all sides. Push them to one side and add the remaining flour, blending well and browning slightly. Add the broth and water. Cook, stirring constantly until thickened and boiling.

Add the halved potatoes and carrots and the spring onions to the pan, sprinkling lightly with salt and pepper. Cover and simmer until the vegetables are tender—40 to 45 minutes.

Pour boiling water over the peas to separate them, then drain. Add to the pan, cover and simmer for a further 5 minutes.

Serve garnished with parsley sprigs.

¾ pound boneless pork
¼ pound streaky bacon
1 slice bread, 1 inch thick
1 egg
1 level teaspoon salt
¼ level teaspoon pepper
2 tablespoons minced parsley
seasoned flour
1 ounce butter or oil

For the sauce
1 onion
2 stalks celery
1 ounce butter
1 rounded dessertspoon flour
1 large can tomatoes (1 pound
   15 ounces), or use 1 pound
   fresh tomatoes and ¼ pint
   water
1 level teaspoon salt
¼ teaspoon pepper
1 teaspoon sugar

For the spaghetti
½ pound spaghetti
boiling salted water
a small piece of butter
parsley to garnish

For the meatballs
1½ pounds finely minced steak
¾ cup soft white breadcrumbs
1 cup milk or tomato juice
1 egg
½ cup chopped onion
2 level teaspoons salt
a pinch of pepper
seasoned flour
¼ cup margarine or fat

For the curry sauce
⅓ cup chopped onion
⅓ cup chopped celery
1½ level tablespoons plain flour
1 level teaspoon curry powder
1 level teaspoon salt
2 whole cloves
2 cups milk
1 dessertspoon lemon juice
1 cup frozen peas

MEATBALLS MILANESE

Cut the pork, bacon and bread into small pieces. Mince together finely, then add beaten egg, salt, pepper and parsley, mixing well. Take pieces and shape into balls, using a little seasoned flour (you should have about 15 meatballs). Heat the butter or oil in a heavy pan and brown the meatballs on all sides.

For the sauce, mince the onion and dice the celery and sauté both in the melted butter until the onion is tender, then add the flour and stir until smooth; cook for 1 minute, then add the canned tomatoes or the chopped fresh tomatoes and water, salt, pepper and sugar. Stir until the sauce boils and thickens, then simmer uncovered for about 30 minutes.

Add the browned meatballs and the pan drippings and simmer with a lid on for a further 20 minutes, stirring occasionally.

Cook the spaghetti in boiling salted water until tender. Drain well, add a few small pieces of butter, return the saucepan to the heat and shake the spaghetti over low heat to coat lightly with the butter.

Turn the spaghetti onto a heated serving plate and top with the meatballs and sauce. Accompany with a tossed salad if liked.

MEATBALLS WITH CURRY SAUCE

Combine the ingredients for the meatballs with the exception of the seasoned flour and margarine. Toss lightly to mix, then form into about 20 balls, using the seasoned flour.

Melt the margarine in a saucepan and brown the meatballs on all sides. Lift out, place in a casserole and keep warm while you make the sauce.

Drain away all but 1 tablespoon of the margarine in which the meatballs were fried, add the onion and celery and sauté until tender but not brown. Blend in the flour, curry powder, salt and cloves and cook for 2 minutes. Add the milk and stir until the sauce boils and thickens. Stir in the lemon juice and add the peas, then pour this sauce over the meatballs in the casserole. Cover, then bake in a moderate oven, 350°F., for about 20 minutes or until the peas are tender.

If liked, the meatballs may be cooked in a covered pan on the top of the stove.

354

MEATBALLS WITH FRENCH CREAM SAUCE

1 pound finely minced steak
1 cup soft white breadcrumbs
2 tablespoons crisply cooked and
    crumbled bacon
$\frac{1}{4}$ cup chopped shallot
salt and pepper
1 egg or enough to bind
seasoned flour
4 tablespoons butter or
    margarine
2 cups hot buttered rice

For the sauce

1 dessertspoon Worcester sauce
2 teaspoons finely chopped
    shallot or onion
$\frac{1}{2}$ teaspoon dried herbs
1 cup unsweetened canned milk
    (or $\frac{1}{2}$ cup milk and $\frac{1}{2}$ cup
    cream)
$\frac{1}{2}$ teaspoon lemon juice

Combine the meat with the breadcrumbs, bacon and shallot, season to taste with salt and pepper, and bind with beaten egg. Take dessertspoonfuls and shape into balls in some seasoned flour. Melt about 2 tablespoons of the butter in a pan and brown the meatballs on all sides. Reduce the heat, cover and cook for a further 12 minutes. Stir frequently during this cooking period. Keep hot.

Boil the rice in the usual way and drain well. Heat the remaining 2 tablespoons of butter in a frying pan and toss the rice until all the grains are coated with butter. Place on a hot dish and top with the meatballs.

Pour away any excess fat from the pan in which the meatballs were cooked. Add the Worcester sauce, onion and herbs to the browned pieces in the pan and cook for 1 minute. Add the milk, or the milk and cream, and cook over low heat, stirring well until thoroughly hot and thickened. Flavour with the lemon juice and pour over the meatballs.

MEATBALLS WITH MUSHROOMS

$\frac{1}{2}$ pound lean beef
$\frac{1}{4}$ pound veal
$\frac{1}{4}$ pound pork
1 small onion, peeled
1 bacon rasher
1 cup soft white breadcrumbs
1 teaspoon salt
$\frac{1}{4}$ teaspoon pepper
1 small egg
1 tablespoon fat
1 rounded tablespoon plain flour
1 cup milk
$\frac{1}{2}$ cup sherry
$\frac{1}{4}$ pint cream or undiluted canned
    milk
$\frac{1}{4}$ pound mushrooms
freshly cooked rice

Put the meats, onion and bacon through a fine mincer then combine with the breadcrumbs, salt and pepper and bind with beaten egg. Take spoonfuls and roll into balls about $1\frac{1}{2}$ inches in diameter.

Heat the fat in a pan and brown the meatballs. Lift them from the pan and place in a casserole.

Remove all but 1 tablespoon of fat from the pan, add the flour and stir over medium heat until the flour browns. Add the milk, stir until the sauce boils and thickens, then add the sherry, cream and the finely sliced mushrooms. Pour this sauce over the meatballs in the casserole, cover, and bake in a moderate oven, 350°F., for about 45 minutes. Serve over freshly cooked rice.

MOCK CHICKEN LOAF

2 rabbits
1 stalk celery

Soak the rabbits for 1 hour in warm water, place in a large saucepan with chopped celery, carrot and onion, and the

1 carrot
1 small white onion
1 bayleaf
1 packet of chicken noodle soup
1 level teaspoon salt
6 cups boiling water
2 level teaspoons gelatine
1 teaspoon lemon juice
1 tablespoon chopped parsley
$\frac{1}{2}$ cup blanched and chopped
   almonds
1 teaspoon curry powder
1 cup medium thick white sauce
1 tablespoon mayonnaise
lettuce and salad greens for
   serving

bayleaf, chicken noodle soup, salt and boiling water. Simmer for 1 hour or until the meat can easily be removed from the bones. Cool the stock, skim well, then strain it.

Dissolve the gelatine in 3 cups of the stock, add the lemon juice and chill until just beginning to set.

Chop the rabbit meat—there should be about $3\frac{1}{2}$ cups—and add the parsley, almonds and curry powder. Add to the stock (which is beginning to set) together with the white sauce and mayonnaise. Taste, and adjust the flavour if liked. Pour into a mould and chill until set.

Serve the loaf on a lettuce-lined platter with a garnish of salad greens.

ORANGE-GLAZED MEAT LOAVES

6 teaspoons brown sugar
$\frac{1}{2}$ teaspoon mustard
6 thin slices of unpeeled orange
$1\frac{1}{2}$ pounds finely minced steak
$\frac{1}{4}$ teaspoon pepper
1 teaspoon salt
1 medium-sized onion
1 medium green pepper
2 cups soft white breadcrumbs
1 egg
$\frac{1}{2}$ cup orange juice
juice of 1 lemon

Place teaspoon of brown sugar in the bottom of each of six small greased moulds or ramekins. Sprinkle with a little of the mustard and add a slice of orange.

Place the meat in a bowl and add the seasonings, minced onion, seeded and minced green pepper, breadcrumbs, egg and fruit juices. Blend lightly and thoroughly and divide the mixture between the six ramekins. Press the meat mixture down lightly.

Bake in a moderate oven, 350°F., for about 1 hour. Allow to stand a few minutes before turning out.

ORIENTAL MEATBALLS

$1\frac{1}{2}$ pound minced steak
$\frac{1}{2}$ teaspoon salt
$\frac{1}{4}$ teaspoon pepper
$\frac{1}{4}$ cup minced onion
1 cup soft white breadcrumbs
1 egg
hot oil or lard
1 cup diced celery
1 small cucumber
1 medium-sized onion
1 large tomato

Season the minced steak with the salt and pepper and mix in the onion and breadcrumbs. Bind with a little beaten egg, into about 30 balls and brown them in the heated oil or lard. Remove from the pan. Dice the celery, peel and slice the cucumber, cut the tomato into wedges, and seed and slice the green pepper. Lightly fry these vegetables, then remove them from the pan.

Combine the sugar, vinegar, pineapple juice, soy sauce, ginger and monosodium glutamate in the pan and heat until boiling. Return the meatballs and vegetables to the pan, add the pineapple pieces, cover, and simmer for about 30 minutes.

356

Oriental Meatballs

1 large green pepper
1 teaspoon sugar
½ cup vinegar
½ cup pineapple juice
2 teaspoons soy sauce
½ teaspoon ground ginger
¼ teaspoon monosodium
  glutamate
15-ounce can of pineapple pieces
1 slightly rounded dessertspoon
  cornflour
freshly boiled rice

Blend the cornflour with a little water and stir into the gravy. Cook, stirring constantly until thickened. Add more flavouring sauce if necessary, and serve with freshly boiled rice.

1 red or green pepper
1 egg
½ cup tomato sauce
¼ cup water
1½ cups soft white breadcrumbs
2 pounds finely minced steak
½ cup chopped onion
1 clove of garlic
1 level teaspoon salt
½ level teaspoon dried thyme
¼ level teaspoon pepper
¼ level teaspoon nutmeg
a dash of ground cloves

PEPPERSTEAK LOAF

Lightly grease a 9-inch by 5-inch loaf tin. Cut the pepper into rings, remove the ribs and seeds and place the pepper rings in a large saucepan containing about one inch of boiling water. Cover. Cook for 5 minutes, then drain.

Beat the egg with the tomato sauce and water, add the breadcrumbs and stir until the crumbs are moistened. Add the minced steak, onion, crushed garlic, salt, thyme, pepper, nutmeg and cloves. Stir with a fork until lightly but thoroughly blended.

Line the bottom of the prepared tin with the peppers. Lightly pack in the meat mixture, then invert the tin onto a shallow tray. Leave the tin in place and bake for 1½ hours in a moderate oven, 350°F.

Remove the tin, place the loaf on a serving dish and serve hot with mushrooms or brown gravy, or cold with salad.

SWEDISH MEATBALLS IN BURGUNDY

¾ pound minced chuck steak or
    hamburger steak
¾ cup packaged dry breadcrumbs
1 teaspoon cornflour
1 small onion
a pinch of allspice
1 egg
¾ cup cream
1 teaspoon salt
butter or oil for frying
3 dessertspoons plain flour
1½ cups water
1 cup Burgundy
1 soup cube
a dash of pepper
1 teaspoon sugar
a little Worcester sauce

Combine the meat, breadcrumbs, cornflour, minced onion, allspice, beaten egg, cream and ½ teaspoon of the salt. Shape into 24 balls. Heat the butter or oil in a large frying pan and brown the meatballs on all sides (fry them a few at a time). Drain on paper.

Stir the flour into the butter or oil remaining in the pan and add the water, Burgundy, soup cube, the remaining ½ teaspoon of salt, the pepper, sugar and enough Worcester sauce to colour the gravy. Cook, stirring well until smooth.

Arrange the meatballs in the sauce, cover, and simmer for 30 minutes. Serve with freshly boiled rice or with mashed potato.

SWEET AND SOUR BEEF BALLS

1½ pounds finely minced steak
1 teaspoon salt
¼ teaspoon pepper
1 tablespoon finely chopped
    onion
1 egg
about 2 tablespoons of seasoned
    flour
1 dessertspoon heated oil or
    butter
½ cup chopped onion
¾ cup water
1 teaspoon salt
1 clove of garlic
½ cup tomato purée
⅓ cup vinegar
⅓ cup brown sugar
1 dessertspoon mixed mustard
2 cups mixed sliced vegetables
    (carrot, parsnip, green pepper)
1 cup drained pineapple pieces

Combine the minced steak with the salt, pepper and 1 tablespoon of chopped onion. Beat the egg and add to the mixture, blending well. Form into balls in seasoned flour and brown them all over in the oil or butter. Remove from the pan.

Add the ½ cup of onion to the pan and cook until lightly browned. Add the water, salt, crushed garlic, tomato purée, vinegar, brown sugar and mustard. Bring to the boil, then add the prepared vegetables, cover, and cook for about 15 minutes.

Return the meatballs to the pan, cover, and cook for a further 15 minutes or until the vegetables are tender and the meatballs are cooked. Add the drained pineapple pieces and adjust the seasonings if necessary.

Reheat and serve with freshly cooked rice, and sprinkled with finely chopped parsley.

PASTRY

ALMOND PASTRY

4 ounces butter
3 slightly rounded tablespoons castor sugar
1½ cups plain flour
½ cup ground almonds
1 egg yolk
½ teaspoon vanilla essence or grated lemon rind

Beat the butter and sugar to a light cream. Blend in the remaining ingredients to form a firm dough. Turn onto a floured board, knead lightly and wrap in waxed paper. Chill for several hours, or until required.

BISCUIT CRUMB CRUST

1¼ cups biscuit crumbs
1 tablespoon sugar
¼ cup melted butter

Combine the biscuit crumbs with the sugar, then stir in the melted butter. Press into the bottom and sides of an 8-inch tart plate and chill until required.

This crust is easier to handle when serving if it is baked in a moderate oven for about 10 minutes. Chill well before adding any filling.

BISCUIT PASTRY

4 ounces butter or margarine
3 slightly rounded tablespoons sugar
1 egg yolk
1 tablespoon water
½ teaspoon vanilla essence
2 cups plain flour
1 level teaspoon baking powder
a pinch of salt

Beat the butter with the sugar until light and fluffy. Add the egg yolk, water and vanilla and beat well. Sift the flour, baking powder and salt and add to the mixture, making a medium dough. Knead until smooth on a lightly floured board. Use as required.

CHAMPAGNE PASTRY

3 ounces butter or margarine
2 slightly rounded tablespoons sugar
1 egg yolk
1 dessertspoon water
½ teaspoon vanilla essence
¾ cup plain flour
½ cup self-raising flour
¼ cup cornflour
a pinch of salt

Beat the butter and sugar to a light cream. Beat the egg yolk with the water and add to the creamed mixture with the vanilla. Sift the flours with the salt, then add to the mixture, blending to a firm dough. Turn onto a lightly floured board and knead only until smooth on the outside. Use as required.

359

CHEESE PASTRY

1½ cups plain flour
½ level teaspoon baking powder
¼ level teaspoon salt
¼ level teaspoon mustard
a pinch of cayenne pepper
3 ounces butter or margarine
2 ounces finely grated cheese
1 egg yolk
2 tablespoons water
a squeeze of lemon juice

Sift the flour, baking powder, salt, mustard and cayenne. Rub in the butter and add the grated cheese. Beat the egg yolk and add to the water and lemon juice, then stir into the dry ingredients, making a rather dry dough. Turn onto a lightly floured board and knead into a smooth shape. Use as required.

CHOUX PASTRY 1

2 ounces butter
½ pint water
a pinch of salt
1 cup plain flour
3 eggs

Place the butter, water and salt in a saucepan and bring to the boil. Stir in the sifted flour. Cook, stirring constantly until the mixture leaves the sides of the saucepan. Remove from the heat and cool slightly.

Add well-beaten eggs a little at a time, beating after each addition. The mixture should be smooth and shiny.

Use for éclairs or cream puffs as required. For éclairs pipe the mixture through a half-inch plain tube onto a greased oven tray. For puffs spoon small portions onto a greased oven tray. Bake in a hot oven, 425°F., for 15 minutes, then reduce the heat to moderate, 350°F., and bake for a further 20 minutes.

CHOUX PASTRY 2

½ cup water
2 ounces butter
½ cup plain flour
a pinch of salt
2 eggs

Bring the water to the boil in a saucepan and add the butter. When melted, take the pan off the heat, add the flour and salt and stir vigorously until smooth. Return the saucepan to the heat and cook, stirring well, until the mixture leaves the sides of the saucepan and forms a ball. Remove from the heat and cool slightly.

Add the well-beaten eggs a little at a time, beating after each addition until the mixture is smooth. Drop in spoonfuls on a greased tray with the puffs about three inches apart. This quantity will make 8 large or 24 medium-sized puffs. Bake at 450°F. for 15 minutes, then reduce the temperature to 325°F. and bake for another 25 minutes. Remove the puffs from the oven, split each one and return them to the oven with the heat turned off for about another 20 minutes.

SAVOURY PUFFS

Add 2 teaspoons of caraway seed to the mixture before spooning onto the cooking tray, and serve hot with a creamed chicken or ham and egg filling.

Puffs made with choux pastry

SWEET PUFFS

Allow the puffs to become quite cold, then fill with ice cream and serve with a chocolate or a caramel sauce.

APPETIZER PUFFS

Make up half the mixture and add ¼ cup of shredded cheese before spooning onto the baking tray (use a teaspoon to spoon the mixture on). Bake at 400°F. for about 20 minutes, split the puffs, remove any uncooked centre and return to the oven for about 10 minutes to dry. Fill with savoury filling.

CONTINENTAL PASTRY

1¼ cups plain flour
¼ pound butter
1 egg yolk
1 teaspoon rum
1 tablespoon sour milk or cream

Sift the flour into a bowl and rub in the butter. Beat the egg yolk with the rum and sour milk and stir into the flour mixture to make a rather dry dough. Chill for several hours before using.

CREAM-CHEESE PASTRY

2 cups plain flour
4 ounces butter
4 ounces cream cheese
1 egg

Sift the flour into a bowl and either cut in or rub in the butter and the cream cheese until the mixture resembles coarse breadcrumbs. Beat the egg and stir in, making a firm dough.

Turn onto a floured board and knead lightly until smooth on the outside. Roll to the size and shape required.

This pastry should be a little thicker than regular short or biscuit pastry. Use it for vegetable pies, or for small pastry shapes for savouries.

361

FLAKY PASTRY

4 ounces self-raising flour
4 ounces plain flour
¼ level teaspoon salt
3 ounces lard
3 ounces margarine
½ teaspoon lemon juice
½ cup water

Sift the flours and salt into a bowl. Blend the lard and margarine on a plate and divide in four. Take one part and rub into the flour. Add lemon juice to the water and stir into the dry ingredients, making a firm dough.

Knead the dough lightly on a floured board and roll to an oblong shape, three times as long as it is wide. Spread another portion of the shortening over two-thirds of the dough. Sprinkle lightly with flour and fold into three. Give the pastry a half turn and roll again into an oblong shape.

Repeat the rolling and folding process until all the shortening has been used, then roll once again without shortening or flour. Wrap and chill for about an hour before using as required.

GOOD SHORTCRUST

1½ cups plain flour
a good pinch of salt
4 ounces butter or margarine
1 egg yolk
2 tablespoons water
1 teaspoon lemon juice

Sift the flour and salt into a bowl and rub in the butter. Beat the egg yolk with the water and lemon juice. Add to the flour mixture, making a fairly firm dough. Turn onto a floured board and knead only until smooth on the outside. Roll to the size and shape required. Bake in a hot oven.

ORANGE PASTRY

3 ounces butter or margarine
2 slightly rounded tablespoons
    sugar
1 teaspoon grated orange rind
1 tablespoon orange juice
1 egg yolk
1½ cups plain flour
½ level teaspoon baking powder
a pinch of salt

Beat the butter and sugar to a cream and add the orange rind. Mix the orange juice with the egg yolk and stir into the creamed mixture.

Sift the dry ingredients together and add to the mixture, making rather a firm dough. Turn onto a lightly floured board and knead only until smooth on the outside. Roll to the size and shape required.

Instead of the plain flour and baking powder you may use ¾ cup plain flour and ¾ cup self-raising flour.

POTATO PASTRY

1 cup plain flour
1 level teaspoon baking powder
a good pinch of salt
2 ounces butter
1½ cups dry mashed potato
1 egg

Sift the flour, baking powder and salt into a bowl and rub in the butter. Add the mashed potato and mix to a smooth dough with the beaten egg. Cover and chill thoroughly for about 30 minutes. Knead on a lightly floured board. Use as required.

362

Filling puff pastry shells for oyster patties

PUFF PASTRY

2 cups plain flour
¼ level teaspoon salt
1 egg yolk
½ cup water
1 teaspoon lemon juice
½ pound butter

Sift the flour and salt into a bowl. Combine the egg yolk, water and lemon juice in a measuring cup and add to the flour, mixing to a soft dough. Knead lightly, then cover and place in the refrigerator to chill while you prepare the butter.

Using a large broad-bladed knife, blend the butter until smooth and of an even consistency, about the same as the dough.

Roll the pastry into a rectangle twice as long as it is wide. Make the butter into a shape not quite as big as half the pastry rectangle. Place it on the pastry, moisten the edges with water and fold the pastry over the butter, joining the edges. Turn the pastry so that the folded edge is on the left-hand side. Press lightly with the rolling-pin, then (rolling the one way) roll the pastry into a long thin sheet. Fold it in three, give it a half-turn and roll again. This folding and rolling should be repeated six times, chilling the dough for at least 15 minutes between rollings.

When ready to use, roll evenly ¼ inch thick. Cut with a hot knife or cutter, and place on a wetted baking tray. Use a very hot oven, 450°F. to 500°F., for the first 10 minutes baking.

Use for pastry cases or for a pie.

363

ROUGH PUFF PASTRY

2 cups plain flour
1 level teaspoon baking powder
$\frac{1}{4}$ level teaspoon salt
a squeeze of lemon juice
1 egg yolk
$\frac{1}{4}$ cup cold water
3 ounces butter or margarine
3 ounces lard

Sift the flour, baking powder and salt into a bowl.

Beat the lemon juice, egg yolk and water together.

Blend the butter and the lard on a plate until soft and easily spread, then take pieces the size of a walnut and add to the flour (do not rub in). Add the liquid and mix to a soft dough, turn onto a lightly floured board, knead until smooth on the outside, then roll into a rectangle.

Fold into three by placing the lower third over the centre third and the top third over the lower third. Now give the pastry a half-turn, so that the folded edge is to the left.

Repeat rolling and folding the pastry twice more. Chill, then roll as required. Bake in a hot oven.

SHORTCRUST

2 cups plain flour
1 level teaspoon baking powder
$\frac{1}{4}$ level teaspoon salt
4 ounces butter, margarine or good beef dripping
4 tablespoons cold water
a squeeze of lemon juice

Sift the flour, baking powder and salt into a bowl. Rub in the butter and mix to a fairly firm dough with the combined water and lemon juice. Turn onto a lightly floured board and knead only until smooth on the outside. Roll to the size and shape required. Bake in a hot oven.

For a sweet shortcrust, add 2 level tablespoons of sugar to the flour after rubbing in the butter.

Platter Pie (with shortcrust pastry)

364

Suet Pudding (with suet crust)

SUET PASTRY

2 cups self-raising flour
1 cup plain flour
¼ level teaspoon salt
6 ounces finely chopped suet
6 tablespoons cold water

Sift the flours and salt into a bowl. Rub the chopped suet into the flour until well mixed. Mix to a firm dough with cold water. Turn onto a lightly floured board and knead only until smooth on the outside. Use as required.

POULTRY

BROWN CHICKEN CASSEROLE

1 chicken, 2½ to 3 pounds
seasoned flour
butter
1 large onion
1 ounce butter for gravy
1 rounded tablespoon plain flour
1½ cups stock, or water and a
   chicken soup cube
1 level dessertspoon tomato
   paste
salt and pepper
1 teaspoon Worcester sauce
½ cup diced celery
1 cup sliced carrots
¾ cup sliced mushrooms
1 cup cooked green peas
parsley sprigs for garnishing

Cut the chicken into neat serving pieces and coat well with seasoned flour. Heat enough butter to cover the bottom of a large frying pan and sauté the chicken pieces on all sides until brown. Drain well and place in a casserole.

Slice the onion and fry it in the butter remaining in the pan. Add to the chicken in the casserole.

Melt the ounce of butter for the gravy in the same pan and stir in the rounded tablespoon of plain flour. Cook, stirring well until brown. Add the stock and the tomato paste and stir until boiling (be sure to scrape up all the browning from the bottom of the pan). Flavour with salt and pepper and the Worcester sauce.

Add the celery, carrot and mushrooms to the sauce and pour over the chicken and onion in the casserole. Cover and bake in a moderate oven, 350°F., for about 1½ hours or until the chicken is tender.

About 15 minutes before removing the dish from the oven, add the cooked green peas. Serve with a parsley garnish.

BROWN CHICKEN STEW

1 chicken, 3 to 3½ pounds
seasoned flour
¼ cup melted butter
1 medium-sized onion
½ pound mushrooms
¼ cup white wine
½ cup stock, or water and a soup
   cube
1 clove of garlic
½ teaspoon curry powder
1 tablespoon diced celery
salt and pepper

Cut the chicken into neat serving pieces and coat in the seasoned flour. Heat the butter in a large saucepan and sauté the chicken until golden on all sides. Lift out and drain on paper.

Place sliced onion in the saucepan and cook until golden. Add the mushrooms, wine, stock, crushed garlic, curry powder and celery, with salt and pepper to taste. Stir until boiling.

Replace the chicken in the saucepan, cover and simmer it gently for about 1 hour or until tender. Serve with a French salad and with boiled new potatoes which have been tossed in chopped parsley.

CHICKEN A LA KING

½ pound flaky pastry
2 ounces butter
3 level dessertspoons plain flour
¼ level teaspoon salt
a pinch of pepper

To make the pastry cases, first roll the flaky pastry ¼ inch thick, cut into rounds with a 3-inch cutter, and remove the centres from half the rounds with a 2-inch cutter. Now slightly moisten the edges of the 3-inch round with water, place a ring of pastry on each and press lightly. Place on a shallow baking

Chicken Tetrazzini

1 cup chicken stock, or ½ cup
    cream and ½ cup chicken stock
1 cup milk
2 cups chopped cooked chicken
1 small can of mushrooms
parsley

tray and chill well. Glace the tops with a little beaten egg and milk.

Bake in a hot oven, 450°F., for 10 minutes, reduce the heat to moderate and continue baking for about 20 minutes longer or until the cases are puffed, and a golden brown.

For the filling, melt the butter in a saucepan and add the flour, salt and pepper. Stir until smooth, then cook for 1 minute. Add the stock and the milk and stir until the sauce boils and thickens. Fold in the chicken and mushrooms and reheat, stirring until smooth.

Spoon the mixture into the hot pastry shells and serve with a parsley garnish. If the pastry cases are made ahead, reheat before filling and using.

CHICKEN ALOHA

1 roasting chicken, about 3
    pounds
1 tablespoon seasoned flour
1 tablespoon butter
¼ pound bacon
15-ounce can of pineapple rings
1 tablespoon plain flour
1 cup stock (or water and a soup
    cube)
1 tablespoon soy sauce
salt and pepper

Truss the chicken into a neat shape and rub lightly with seasoned flour. Melt the butter in a frying pan and fry the chicken, turning it until brown all over. Lift out.

Cut the bacon into 2-inch pieces, roll and secure with cocktail picks. Using the same pan, fry with the well-drained pineapple rings, then lift out. Replace the chicken, cover and cook for about 1½ hours or until tender, turning it occasionally. Remove from the pan.

Sprinkle in the plain flour and stir and cook, scraping up any browned pieces. Add the stock and stir over the heat until the gravy boils and thickens. Flavour with the soy sauce, add salt and pepper to taste, and simmer for about 3 minutes, then return the chicken, pineapple and bacon to the pan and reheat thoroughly in the gravy.

Serve with freshly boiled rice or potato crisps, and your favourite vegetables.

CHICKEN AND ALMOND FRITTERS

1½ cups plain flour
3 level teaspoons baking powder
½ teaspoon salt
2 eggs
10-ounce can of cream of mushroom soup
¼ cup milk
1 tablespoon salad oil or melted butter
⅓ cup chopped almonds
1½ cups chopped cooked chicken
almond sauce

Sift the flour with the baking powder and salt. Beat together in a large bowl the eggs, soup, milk and oil. Using a wooden spoon, gradually stir the liquid into the flour mixture, making a smooth batter. Add the almonds and the chicken, mixing well.

Have ready a deep saucepan with about 2½ to 3 inches depth of fat. Heat till a light blue haze rises from the fat, then drop in the mixture a tablespoonful at a time. Turn the fritters as they brown, then drain on paper and serve immediately with almond sauce (recipe follows).

ALMOND SAUCE

1 tablespoon butter
1 dessertspoon finely chopped onion
¼ cup finely chopped almonds
1½ tablespoons flour
¼ teaspoon salt
a dash each of nutmeg and pepper
5 ounces water
5 ounces undiluted cream of chicken soup
1 dessertspoon lemon juice

Melt the butter and sauté the onion and the almonds until the onion is soft. Remove from the heat and stir in the flour, salt, nutmeg and pepper. Stir until smooth, return to the heat and cook for 1 minute. Add the water and soup. Cook, stirring constantly until the sauce boils and thickens. Add the lemon juice.

CHICKEN AND ASPARAGUS

2 ounces butter
1 slightly rounded tablespoon plain flour
1 teaspoon salt
a pinch of cayenne pepper
2 cups milk, or 1½ cups milk and ½ cup cream
1 egg
2 cups diced cooked chicken
1 tablespoon chopped pimento
1 medium-sized can of asparagus spears
2 tablespoons white breadcrumbs

Melt 1 ounce of butter in a saucepan and add the flour, salt and pepper. Stir until smooth, then cook for 2 minutes without browning. Add the milk and stir until the sauce boils and thickens. Pour onto the beaten egg and blend thoroughly, then return the sauce to the pan.

Add the chicken and pimento to the sauce and stir until boiling. Drain the asparagus, cut the spears into 2-inch lengths, and fold in.

Turn the mixture into a lightly greased casserole and sprinkle the top with the breadcrumbs. Dot with the remaining butter. Bake in a moderate oven, 350°F., until the sauce bubbles and the crumbs brown.

368

CHICKEN BUFFET MOULDS

1 tablespoon gelatine
½ cup cold water
1 cup mayonnaise or salad
    dressing
1½ cups diced cooked chicken
⅓ cup chopped celery
3 dessertspoons chopped green
    olives
1 tablespoon lemon juice
¼ teaspoon paprika
½ cup chopped cucumber
3 dessertspoons minced onion
1 dessertspoon minced pimento
½ teaspoon salt
1 cup cream, whipped

Soften the gelatine in the cold water. Dissolve over boiling water, then stir into the mayonnaise. Add the remaining ingredients with the exception of the whipped cream. Stir thoroughly, then mix in the whipped cream.

Divide the mixture between eight individual moulds and chill until firm. Unmould to serve. Decorate with olive slices and pieces of pimento or sprigs of parsley.

CHICKEN CACCIATORE

1 roasting chicken, 2½ to 3
    pounds
2 tablespoons seasoned flour
3 dessertspoons cooking oil
¼ cup minced onion
¼ cup minced green pepper
1 clove of garlic
1¾ cups quartered tomatoes
¼ cup dry white wine
¼ cup chicken stock
1½ teaspoons salt
¼ teaspoon pepper
¼ teaspoon allspice
1 bayleaf
¼ teaspoon thyme
a dash of cayenne pepper

Cut the chicken into serving sized pieces and coat with the seasoned flour. Heat the oil in a pan and fry the chicken until lightly browned on all sides. Lift out and keep hot.

Place the onion, green pepper and crushed garlic in the pan and cook until lightly browned. Add the tomatoes, wine, stock, salt, pepper, allspice, bayleaf, thyme and cayenne and stir until boiling.

Return the chicken pieces to the pan or transfer the whole to a casserole. Cover and cook in a moderate oven, 350°F., or over low heat for about 1 hour or until the chicken is tender.

CHICKEN CHASSEUR

1 roasting chicken
2 tablespoons seasoned flour
2 shallots or a little onion
1 bayleaf
a little celery, carrot or parsnip
salt and pepper
3 tablespoons butter or
    margarine
½ pound fresh mushrooms
1 dessertspoon chopped shallot
½ cup chicken stock

Cut the chicken into neat serving pieces and coat lightly with the seasoned flour.

Make up a stock with the carcass, 2 chopped shallots or a little chopped onion, a bayleaf and scraps of celery, carrot or parsnip. Cover with water and simmer for about 1 hour. Strain before using.

Heat half the butter in a pan and fry the chicken pieces until brown all over. Lift out and drain on white paper.

Add a little more butter to the pan and sauté the mushrooms (sliced if they are large) and the dessertspoon of chopped shallot. Lift out and place with the chicken.

⅓ cup dry white wine
bacon rolls
chopped parsley to garnish

To the butter left in the pan (about 1 tablespoonful is needed) add the remaining seasoned flour (or 1 tablespoonful) and cook, stirring well until brown. Add the stock and wine and stir until the mixture boils and thickens.

Place the chicken and mushrooms in a casserole, pour the gravy over, cover and bake in a moderate oven for about 1 hour or until tender.

Adjust the seasonings and serve the chicken accompanied with rolls of grilled bacon and sprinkled with chopped parsley.

CHICKEN CREOLE

2 roasting chickens, each about 2 pounds
salt and pepper
⅓ cup butter
freshly boiled rice

For the sauce

⅓ cup butter
1 cup thinly sliced onion
2 thinly sliced green peppers
1 large can of peeled tomatoes
12 stoned and sliced green olives
1 cup sliced fresh mushrooms
a bouquet garni (1 bayleaf, 4 sprigs parsley, 1 sprig thyme)
2 whole cloves
1 clove of garlic
1 cup dry white wine

First make the sauce. Melt the butter and sauté the onion and green pepper for about 5 minutes, stirring gently. Cover and cook for another 5 minutes, stirring occasionally, then add the tomatoes, olives, mushrooms and the bouquet garni, cloves and garlic. Cover again and simmer for about 30 minutes, stirring now and then. Discard the bouquet garni, cloves and garlic. Add the white wine and simmer while the chicken is being prepared.

Cut each chicken into four pieces. Season each piece well with salt and pepper and sauté in the hot butter until golden all over. Drain and arrange in a casserole dish, pour the sauce over, cover, and bake in a moderate oven, 350°F., for 1 hour or until the chicken is tender.

Arrange the chicken pieces on a hot platter. Reduce the sauce by simmering uncovered for about 15 minutes. Serve with freshly boiled rice.

CHICKEN CURRY

1 boiling fowl, about 5 pounds
1 medium-sized onion
4 whole cloves
2 stalks of celery (include some leaves)
1 level dessertspoon salt
1 medium-sized bayleaf
6 cups water
freshly boiled rice
parsley sprigs
curry accompaniments, such as pineapple pieces, quartered tomatoes, spring onions

Place the fowl in a large saucepan with the clove-studded onion, the celery and leaves, and the salt, bayleaf and water. Cover, bring slowly to the boil, and simmer gently for about 2 hours or until the fowl is tender. Remove from the liquid and allow to cool.

Strain the liquid and reserve 2 cups to use in the sauce. When the fowl is cold, remove all the flesh from the bones and cut into bite-sized pieces.

To make the sauce, first pour the hot milk over the coconut and allow to stand for about 45 minutes. Melt 2 ounces of the butter in a saucepan and add crushed garlic, chopped onion and powdered ginger. Cook over medium heat until the onion is tender—about 5 minutes. Add the curry powder, reserved

For the curry sauce

2½ cups hot milk
2 cups packaged coconut
4 ounces butter
2 cloves of garlic
1½ cups chopped onion
¼ teaspoon powdered ginger
1½ to 2 dessertspoons curry
   powder
2 cups reserved stock
4 level tablespoons plain flour
1 teaspoon salt
1 dessertspoon lemon juice
1 cup cream, or ½ cup milk and
   ½ cup cream

1 large boiling fowl, about 4
   pounds
1 bunch spinach or broccoli
1 teaspoon salt
¼ teaspoon pepper
2 cups medium thick white sauce
½ to 1 cup grated Parmesan
   cheese

⅓ cup plain flour
¼ teaspoon salt
¼ teaspoon paprika
¼ teaspoon garlic salt
3½-pound chicken, jointed
3 tablespoons salad oil
6-ounce can of champignons
¼ teaspoon ground nutmeg
2 teaspoons sugar
10-ounce can of cream of
   mushroom soup
½ cup water
1 chicken soup cube
1 cup orange juice
2½ cups diagonally sliced peeled
   carrot

stock and soaked coconut, bring slowly to the boil, stirring constantly, then reduce the heat, cover and simmer gently for about 1 hour. Strain, pressing out as much liquid as possible (it should amount to 3 cups). Discard the coconut, onion and garlic.

In another saucepan melt the remaining 2 ounces butter and add the flour. Stir until smooth, then cook for 1 minute without browning. Add the strained liquid, and stir over medium heat until the sauce boils and thickens. Add the salt, lemon juice, cream and chicken pieces. Heat gently until almost boiling.

Serve with freshly boiled rice and a garnish of parsley, accompanied with pineapple pieces, quartered tomatoes and spring onions.

CHICKEN DIVAN

Steam or boil the fowl until quite tender. Remove the flesh from the bones, cutting as much of it as possible into slices.

Wash and trim the spinach or broccoli, cutting away any tough parts. Cook until barely tender in the usual way. If spinach is used, chop it finely after cooking and draining; if using broccoli slice lengthwise. Arrange in the bottom of a greased casserole dish, and season with salt and pepper.

Prepare the sauce, using half cream and half milk (or half milk and half the liquid in which the chicken was cooked). Add half the grated cheese and cook until it melts.

Cover the spinach or broccoli with the slices of chicken and pour over the sauce. Sprinkle the remainder of the cheese over the top and bake in a moderate oven until the sauce bubbles and the cheese on top melts and lightly browns.

CHICKEN IN ORANGE GRAVY

Combine the flour with the salt, paprika and garlic salt, and use to coat the chicken pieces. Heat the oil in a heavy based pan and brown the chicken on all sides. Remove to a greased casserole. Drain the champignons, reserving the liquid, and add them to the casserole. Sprinkle with the nutmeg and sugar.

Drain away any oil remaining in the pan. Blend until smooth the mushroom liquid, mushroom soup, water, soup cube and orange juice. Pour into the pan in which the chicken was browned and heat until boiling, at the same time scraping any brown pieces from the bottom of the pan.

Pour the gravy over the chicken, cover, and bake in a moderate oven, 350°F., for 25 minutes. Add the carrots, cover and bake for a further 30 minutes or until the chicken and carrots are tender. Remove any fat from the gravy. Serve with freshly boiled rice.

2½ ounces butter
1 clove of garlic
1 tablespoon minced onion
1½ tablespoons plain flour
1 cup beef stock, or water and a
    beef soup cube
¼ cup plain flour
½ teaspoon salt
a dash of pepper
1 pound chicken livers
1 ounce butter
1½ tablespoons Madeira or
    Marsala wine (optional)
boiled rice for serving
parsley sprigs

1 tender fowl
1 ounce butter
2 tablespoons oil
1 teaspoon salt
¼ teaspoon pepper
1 tablespoon plain flour
3 shallots
1 glass sherry of Marsala
3 tablespoons tomato purée
a bouquet garni
stock or water
½ pound button mushrooms
a squeeze of lemon juice
cayenne pepper
croutons of fried bread and 2
    hard-boiled eggs to garnish

1½ ounces butter
1 cup chopped celery
¾ cup sliced green pepper
¾ cup drained pineapple pieces
2 dessertspoons plain flour
1 cup chicken stock
½ cup pineapple juice
2 teaspoons soy sauce
½ teaspoon salt
a pinch of cayenne pepper
2 cups sliced cooked chicken
1 tablespoon lemon juice
2 tablespoons vinegar
3 cups cooked rice

CHICKEN LIVERS CONTINENTAL

Melt 1½ ounces of the butter in a pan and add the crushed garlic and onion. Cook over medium heat until the onion is tender but not brown. Blend in the flour and cook for 1 minute without browning, then stir in the beef stock. Cook, stirring constantly, until the mixture comes to the boil and thickens. Simmer for 3 minutes.

Combine the ¼ cup of plain flour with the salt and pepper and use to coat the sliced livers. Melt the remaining ounce of butter in a medium-sized frying pan and quickly fry the coated livers until brown on all sides. Quickly stir in the wine if used.

Combine the livers with the sauce and heat thoroughly. Serve with freshly boiled rice and a garnish of parsley.

CHICKEN MARENGO

Cut the fowl into neat joints, removing as much of the skin as possible. Heat the butter and oil in a deep saucepan, add the pieces of fowl, and season with salt and pepper. Cook until the pieces are brown, sprinkling with the flour and chopped shallots as they cook.

Add the wine, tomato purée, bouquet garni and sufficient stock or water to cover. Stir well, then add the mushrooms, cover, and simmer gently until the fowl is tender (the time will depend on the size and age of the bird). When cooked, arrange the chicken pieces on a heated platter.

Remove any fat from the liquid in the saucepan. Blend some flour with a little water and use to thicken the liquid. Flavour with lemon juice and cayenne, and add more salt if required.

Strain the gravy over the fowl, arrange the mushrooms in the centre and garnish with croutons of fried bread and quarters of hard-boiled egg.

CHICKEN ORIENTAL

Melt the butter in a saucepan and add the celery, green pepper and pineapple. Sauté over medium heat for about 5 minutes, then stir in the flour. Add the chicken stock, pineapple juice, soy sauce, salt and pepper. Cook, stirring constantly until the mixture boils and is slightly thickened.

Add the chicken, lemon juice and vinegar, and cook for another 5 minutes to thoroughly heat the chicken.

Arrange the rice on a hot serving dish and spoon the hot chicken over it.

CHICKEN PAPRIKA

1 roasting chicken, about 3
   pounds
2 tablespoons oil
2 onions
1 clove of garlic
2 teaspoons paprika
1 tablespoon chopped carrot
1 tablespoon chopped parsnip
salt
½ pint stock
1 large tomato
1 small green pepper
2 tablespoons plain flour
½ pint sour or fresh cream
boiled potatoes or rice, spaghetti
   or noodles for serving

Cut the chicken into neat serving pieces. Heat the oil in a heavy based frying pan and fry chopped onion and crushed garlic until lightly browned. Add the paprika, carrot and parsnip and cook for 2 minutes.

Add the chicken pieces and cook until they are brown on all sides. Season with salt, then add the stock, peeled and sliced tomato, and diced green pepper. Stir until boiling. Cover and simmer until the chicken pieces are tender—about 1 hour.

Blend the flour with a little water, add to the mixture and stir until it boils and thickens. Stir in the cream and allow to heat through but not to boil. Serve with either boiled potatoes, rice, spaghetti or noodles.

CHICKEN RICE CROQUETTES

2 ounces butter
4 level tablespoons plain flour
½ pint milk
½ teaspoon salt
¼ teaspoon pepper
1 cup cooked rice
2 cups chopped cooked chicken
1 tablespoon finely chopped
   onion
1 tablespoon finely chopped
   parsley
1 egg
3 tablespoons seasoned flour
egg glazing (1 egg beaten with
   about 2 tablespoons milk)
breadcrumbs
fat or oil for frying
parsley sprigs to garnish

Melt the butter in a saucepan and add the flour. Stir until smooth, then cook for 1 minute without browning. Add the milk and stir over medium heat until the sauce boils and thickens. Season with salt and pepper.

Stir in the rice, cnicken, onion and parsley, then add beaten egg. Mix thoroughly. Turn onto a plate and allow to cool (chill for several hours if time allows).

Take spoonfuls of the mixture and make into cork shapes, using a little seasoned flour. Dip them into the egg glazing, then cover with breadcrumbs.

Deep-fry the croquettes in hot fat or oil until a golden brown. Drain on paper and serve garnished with parsley.

CHICKEN RIVIERA

3½ pounds chicken breasts
seasoned flour
4 ounces butter
1 clove of garlic
2 tablespoons lemon juice
1 teaspoon Worcester or soy
   sauce
¾ cup water
1 chicken soup cube

Dust the chicken breasts lightly with seasoned flour. Melt 2 ounces of the butter in a pan and fry the chicken pieces until brown on all sides. Drain and place in a casserole. Mix the crushed garlic with the lemon juice and sauce and pour over the chicken.

Pour any butter left in the pan into a container (you will need it to make the sauce). Add the cold water and the soup cube to the pan and stir, scraping up any brown pieces. Stir until boiling. This stock will be used to make the sauce.

Chicken Riviera

½ pound potato balls
2 rounded teaspoons plain flour
salt and pepper
¼ cup cream
chopped parsley

In another pan melt the remaining 2 ounces of butter and fry the potato balls until golden brown. Place these (with the butter in which they were cooked) beside the chicken in the casserole. Cover and bake in a moderate oven for about 30 minutes or until the chicken is tender.

To make the sauce heat 1 dessertspoon of the butter left from frying the chicken, blend in the flour, season with salt and pepper, stir until smooth, cook for 1 minute, then add the stock. (If a wine flavour is preferred, reduce the amount of stock by 1 or 2 tablespoons and replace with white wine.) Stir the sauce over medium heat until the mixture boils and thickens, then add the cream.

Lift the chicken pieces onto a hot serving dish. Surround with the potato balls and sprinkle these with chopped parsley. Spoon the hot sauce over the chicken.

CHICKEN TETRAZZINI

1 chicken, 3 pounds
3 cups water
1 cup dry white wine
2 carrots
1 medium-sized onion
2 sprigs parsley
¼ teaspoon thyme
1½ teaspoons salt
4 tablespoons butter

Place the chicken in a large saucepan with the cold water and add the wine, sliced carrot, chopped onion, parsley sprigs, thyme and salt. Cover and simmer for 1½ hours or until the flesh is tender. Lift the chicken into a bowl, strain the liquid over it, cover and allow to cool. When cold, lift out the chicken and remove the meat from the bones. Chop coarsely. Reserve the stock.

Melt 3 tablespoons of the butter in a saucepan, add the flour and stir until smooth. Cook for 1 minute, then add 3½ cups of

374

3 rounded tablespoons flour
½ cup milk or cream
¾ cup grated cheese
¾ pound fresh mushrooms, or 2 small cans
½ pound noodles

the chicken broth and the ½ cup milk or cream. Cook, stirring constantly until the sauce boils and thickens. Simmer for 2 minutes. Stir in ½ a cup of the cheese, then remove from the heat.

Measure 1 cup of this sauce and blend the remaining cheese into it.

Melt the remaining tablespoon of butter in a pan and sauté the peeled and sliced mushrooms. Cook the noodles in boiling salted water until tender. Drain.

Mix the noodles, chicken and mushrooms with the larger quantity of sauce and turn into a greased casserole. Spoon the reserved sauce over the top. Bake in a moderate oven for 20 to 30 minutes to thoroughly heat through and to lightly brown the top. Garnish with sliced mushrooms and parsley sprigs.

CHINESE CHICKEN WITH ALMONDS

½ pound bean sprouts
2 tablespoons melted butter or oil
½ cup chopped onion
1 cup chopped celery
1½ cups cooked chicken
1½ tablespoons butter for sauce
1½ rounded tablespoons plain flour
1¼ cups milk
1¼ cups chicken stock
½ teaspoon salt
½ teaspoon monosodium glutamate
2 teaspoons soy sauce
4-ounce can of mushrooms
4 cups hot cooked rice
chopped parsley
½ cup slivered almonds

Place the bean sprouts in a bowl, cover with boiling water, place a plate over the bowl and let them stand for 10 minutes. Drain.

Heat the butter in a pan and sauté the onion until soft but not brown. Add the celery, the drained bean sprouts and the cooked chicken.

In another saucepan melt the butter for the sauce, stir in the flour and cook without browning for 1 minute. Blend in the milk and stock and stir until the sauce boils and thickens. Add the chicken mixture and flavour with the salt, monosodium glutamate and soy sauce. Add the mushrooms and heat until boiling.

Make a border of hot cooked rice on a serving dish and fill the centre with the chicken mixture. Sprinkle the chopped parsley over the rice and the almonds over the chicken.

COQ AU VIN

1 roasting chicken
seasoned flour
2 tablespoons butter
2 tablespoon olive oil
4 slices bacon
4 tablespoons brandy
¼ pint red wine
1 bayleaf
2 cloves
a pinch of thyme

Cut the chicken into neat serving pieces or into four sections. Toss in a little seasoned flour, then fry in the butter and oil. Add chopped bacon and brown it lightly.

Heat the brandy, ignite it and pour over the chicken. Add the red wine, bayleaf, cloves, thyme and onions, with salt and pepper to taste. (If the onions are a little on the large side, use half the quantity.) Cover and simmer for 40 minutes or until tender.

Add the button mushrooms and the finely chopped parsley. Cover and cook for a further 5 or 10 minutes. Transfer the

Coq au Vin

12 tiny peeled white onions
salt
freshly ground black pepper
12 small button mushrooms
2 tablespoons finely chopped
  parsley

1½ dessertspoons butter
1½ dessertspoons plain flour
¾ cup chicken stock or chicken
  soup
¼ cup cream or top milk
¾ cup chopped cooked chicken
½ cup chopped cooked ham
¼ cup chopped celery or cooked
  green peas
1 teaspoon chopped parsley
1 egg
salt and paprika
toast cups or points, or waffles,
  or pastry cases

chicken to a hot serving dish and either reduce the sauce by boiling without the lid, or thicken it with a little blended flour. Adjust the seasonings, bring the sauce to the boil and pour over the chicken pieces.

CREAMED CHICKEN AND HAM

Melt the butter in a saucepan and add the flour. Stir until smooth, cook 1 minute then add the chicken stock and stir until the sauce boils and thickens. Add the cream.

Stir in the chicken, ham, celery and parsley. Pour a little of this mixture onto the lightly beaten egg, mix well, then stir it back into the chicken mixture. Lower the heat and cook without boiling for 2 or 3 minutes. Adjust the seasoning with salt and paprika. Serve over toast points, in toast cups or pastry cases, or over freshly cooked waffles.

TOAST CUPS

Cut some thin slices of fresh bread and remove the crusts. Brush the slices on both sides with melted butter or margarine and press into patty cases. Bake in a hot oven for about 10 minutes or until the bread is crisp and golden.

376

CROQUETTES MARYLAND

1 cold cooked chicken, about 2½
   pounds' weight before cooking
4 ounces ham or cooked bacon
1 tablespoon chopped parsley
1 teaspoon salt
½ teaspoon pepper
½ teaspoon dry mustard
2 hard-boiled eggs
1 tablespoon butter
2 slightly rounded tablespoons
   flour
1½ cups milk
seasoned flour
egg glaze (1 egg beaten with
   about 2 tablespoons milk)
breadcrumbs
oil or fat for frying

Remove the flesh from the chicken bones and chop it finely. Chop the ham and combine with the chicken, parsley, salt, pepper, mustard and chopped hard-boiled eggs.

Melt the butter in a saucepan and add the flour. Stir until smooth, then cook without browning for 1 minute. Add the milk and stir until the sauce boils and thickens. It should be very thick. Add the meat mixture and turn onto a plate to cool.

Take tablespoons of the cold mixture and shape into cork shapes in seasoned flour. Dip each in egg glazing and toss in breadcrumbs. Firm the crumbs on and, if time permits, chill for about 30 minutes.

Deep-fry the croquettes in hot fat until a golden brown. Drain on paper. Serve with fried bananas, cream corn in lettuce cups, potato crisps and green peas. Garnish with parsley. To fry bananas, peel some and sauté in a little butter in a shallow pan until lightly browned. Drain on paper before serving.

CURRIED CHICKEN WITH CREAM

1 boiling fowl, about 4 pounds
3 cups water
1 onion
2 carrots
2 or 3 stalks celery
2 bayleaves
4 peppercorns
2 teaspoons salt
2 ounces butter

Place the fowl in a large saucepan and add the water, onion, scraped and chopped carrots, and celery, bayleaves, pepper-corns and salt. Cover and bring to the boil, then simmer for about 1½ or 2 hours or until the bird is tender. Lift it into a bowl, strain the liquid over it, cover and allow to cool. Discard the vegetables.

Remove the fowl and cut the flesh into bite-sized pieces. Measure 1 cup of the chicken liquid and set aside to use in the sauce.

Curried Chicken with Cream

377

4 tablespoons plain flour
1½ teaspoons curry powder
1 cup canned milk or cream
½ teaspoon paprika
1 clove of garlic
salt and pepper
3 tablespoons coconut
3 cups cooked rice for serving
lemon and parsley garnish

1 boiling fowl
2 teaspoons salt
1 to 2 tablespoons plain flour
2 ounces butter
1 medium-sized onion
2 stalks of celery with leaves
1 pound tomatoes
1 level teaspoon sugar
¼ level teaspoon thyme
¼ teaspoon chilli sauce
1 chicken soup cube
1 bayleaf
about ½ cup water

two 4-pound ducklings, dressed
  and quartered
4 oranges
3 dessertspoons sugar
3 dessertspoons vinegar
2 cups chicken broth (or water
  and a soup cube)
2 cups orange juice
4 tablespoons brandy
1 teaspoon lemon juice
1 teaspoon grated orange rind
1 teaspoon salt
a good pinch of pepper
1 slightly rounded tablespoon
  cornflour
⅓ cup cold water
orange sections to garnish

Melt the butter in a saucepan, add the flour and stir until smooth, then cook for 1 minute without browning. Add the curry powder and cook for 2 or 3 minutes. Stir in the reserved cooking liquid and the milk. Cook, stirring well until the sauce boils and thickens. Flavour with the paprika and crushed garlic, and season to taste with salt and pepper.

Add the chicken pieces and the coconut and reheat to boiling point. Serve over the freshly boiled rice and garnish with lemon and parsley.

DIXIE CHICKEN
Cut the fowl into serving sized pieces. Peel and slice the onion. Peel and chop the tomatoes. Slice the celery and leaves.

Combine 1 teaspoon of the salt with the flour and use to coat the chicken pieces. Brown a few pieces at a time in heated butter in a frying pan, placing them as they are browned in a casserole or a heavy based saucepan (if using an electric fry pan, lift the chicken pieces out while you sauté the onions).

Sauté the onion until golden and add to the chicken together with the celery and leaves, tomato, sugar, thyme, chilli sauce, soup cube, bayleaf, water and the remaining teaspoon of salt. Cover and bring to the boil. Simmer for about 1½ hours or until the chicken is tender (or bake in a moderate oven, 350°F., for the same period of time). Serve with freshly cooked rice.

DUCKLING BIGARADE
Place the pieces of duck in an oven dish and bake at 350°F. for about 1½ hours (the time will depend on the weight and age of the birds). Turn while cooking, and prick the skin frequently to make sure all the fat runs out. After the first 30 minutes of roasting place partly squeezed orange halves on each piece of duckling (reserve the orange juice). Remove the orange halves 30 minutes before the end of the roasting time.

Place the sugar and vinegar in a saucepan, stir until the sugar has dissolved, and continue cooking until the mixture caramelizes. Do not allow to burn. Add the chicken stock, orange juice, brandy, lemon juice, orange rind, salt and pepper. Mix well and keep warm over low heat.

When the duckling meat is fork-tender remove from the oven and drain the pieces on white paper. Drain any fat from the baking dish, replace the duckling pieces in the baking dish skin side down, and pour the hot sauce over. Return to a moderate oven for 5 minutes, basting once.

Drain the sauce back into a saucepan. Keep the duckling pieces warm. Blend the cornflour with the cold water, add to the sauce and cook, stirring well until thick.

Arrange the duckling pieces on a large platter and spoon some of the sauce over each piece. Garnish with orange sections and serve the remainder of the sauce in a sauce boat.

DUCKLING WITH PINEAPPLE

1 duckling, about 4 pounds
2 teaspoons salt
¼ teaspoon pepper
1 onion
1 stalk of celery
1 peeled and cored apple
1 cup pineapple juice from a can
   of pineapple slices
2 level tablespoons plain flour
1 tablespoon butter
parsley sprigs to garnish

Rub the inside of the duckling with half the salt and pepper. Chop the onion, celery and apple and mix, then use to stuff the duckling. Skewer and truss it, and rub the outside with the remaining salt and pepper. Place in an open roasting dish and roast at 375°F., allowing 25 minutes per pound cooking time.

After the first 45 minutes baste with a little of the pineapple syrup. When the duckling is tender, place on a warm platter and keep hot while making the sauce.

Using a spoon, carefully lift the fat from the juices in the baking dish, place them in a cup and put back 2 tablespoons of the fat in the dish. Add the flour and stir until smooth. Cook for 2 minutes. To the pan juices in the cup add water and the remaining pineapple juice to make 1 cup altogether. Add this liquid to the dish and stir until the sauce boils and thickens. Flavour to taste with salt and pepper, then strain and place in a gravy boat.

Melt the butter in a pan and fry the well-drained pineapple slices on both sides. Serve with the duckling on a hot platter garnished with parsley.

FRENCH HERBED CHICKEN

1 chicken, about 3 pounds
⅓ cup plain flour
1½ teaspoons salt
¼ teaspoon pepper
2 ounces fat or butter
4 small onions
1 clove of garlic
½ cup roughly chopped carrots
1 bayleaf
¼ teaspoon dried thyme
2 or 3 sprigs of celery leaves
3 or 4 sprigs of parsley
1 cup sliced mushrooms, or a
   small can of buttered mushrooms
¾ cup chicken stock, or water
   and a soup cube
¾ cup Burgundy
chopped parsley

Cut the chicken into neat serving pieces. Mix the flour, salt and pepper and use to coat the chicken pieces. Heat the fat or butter in a saucepan and slowly fry the chicken until brown on all sides. Lift out. Add peeled onions, crushed garlic and carrot pieces. Cover and cook for 5 minutes.

Arrange in layers in a casserole the chicken, cooked vegetables, bayleaf, thyme, celery leaves, parsley sprigs, and mushrooms.

Place the chicken stock and wine in the saucepan in which the chicken was fried and stir until boiling, scraping all the browning from the bottom. Pour over the ingredients in the casserole, then cover and bake in a moderate oven, 350°F., for about 2 hours or until the chicken is tender. Take out the bayleaf and celery leaves. Serve sprinkled with chopped parsley.

The chicken may be cooked in the saucepan or in an electric frypan instead of in the oven.

FRIED CHICKEN PROVENÇAL

1 roasting chicken, 3 pounds
½ cup plain flour
1½ teaspoons salt
¼ teaspoon pepper

Cut the chicken into neat serving pieces. Mix the flour, salt and pepper and use to coat each piece of chicken.

Heat the butter and oil in a pan and fry the chicken until brown on all sides. Lift out and drain on paper.

379

¼ cup melted butter
¼ cup oil
¼ cup finely chopped onion
1 clove of garlic
1 cup chopped tomato
1 tablespoon finely chopped
 parsley

Sauté the onion in the same pan until golden, then add crushed garlic. Cover with the chopped tomato and arrange the chicken pieces on top. Cover tightly and cook gently until the chicken is tender—about 1 hour.

Remove the chicken to a heated serving dish and spoon over it the tomato gravy from the pan. Sprinkle with chopped parsley before serving.

This dish may be served with freshly boiled rice, or with boiled potatoes which have been tossed in butter just before serving.

GOURMET ROAST CHICKEN

3 tablespoons butter or
 margarine
2 roasting chickens
2 dessertspoons butter or
 margarine for mushrooms
about 2 dozen small button
 mushrooms
½ pound bacon
10 small white onions
2 chicken livers
1 teaspoon salt
¼ teaspoon pepper
¾ cup dry white wine

Heat the oven to 375°F. Heat the 3 tablespoons of butter in a frying pan until bubbly. Holding the chickens by their legs brown them one at a time until they are coloured all over. Place in a baking dish or a very large ovenproof dish with a lid.

Add the 2 dessertspoons of butter to the butter in the pan and sauté the whole mushrooms. Arrange them in the dish with the chicken along with the bacon which has been cut into inch lengths, the peeled onions and the chopped uncooked chicken livers. Sprinkle with salt and pepper, then pour in the wine. Cover tightly with a lid or with foil, and bake for about 1 hour or until the chickens are tender.

If gravy is required, drain the fat off the liquid in the dish, reduce it by boiling for a few minutes without a lid, then thicken with a little blended flour.

IMPERIAL CHICKEN

2 cups soft white breadcrumbs
¼ cup grated Parmesan cheese
1 clove of garlic
¼ cup chopped parsley
2 teaspoons salt
¼ teaspoon pepper
2 pounds chicken pieces
1 cup melted butter or margarine

Combine the breadcrumbs with the cheese, crushed garlic, parsley, salt and pepper. Dip each piece of chicken in the melted butter or margarine and then in the crumb mixture, coating completely.

Arrange the pieces in a single layer in a shallow baking dish. Pour the remaining butter over and bake in a moderate oven, 350°F., for about 1 hour or until the flesh of the chicken is fork-tender. Do not turn the chicken pieces during the cooking, simply baste them with the pan drippings.

NEW ENGLAND CHICKEN PIES

6 cups water
2 onions studded with cloves
6 stalks celery
1 dessertspoon salt
2 bayleaves
1 chicken, 2½ to 3 pounds
Supreme Sauce (recipe follows)
5 tiny white onions
10 medium-sized mushrooms
½ cup dry white wine
5 small cooked potatoes
½ cup cooked green peas
1 dessertspoon chopped chives
1 beaten egg
½ pound shortcrust pastry

Place the water, clove-studded onions, celery, salt, bayleaves and halved chicken in a large saucepan. Cover and simmer for about 1 hour or until the flesh comes away easily from the bones. Lift the chicken halves out of the saucepan, strain the cooking liquid and set it aside. Cool, then refrigerate both the chicken and the stock.

Cook the small white onions and the potatoes.

Quarter the mushrooms and simmer in the wine for 5 minutes. Drain. Arrange the chicken meat in 5 individual ramekins or in one medium-sized casserole or pie-dish. To each ramekin add 1 cooked onion, 8 simmered mushroom pieces, one cubed cooked potato, about 1 dessertspoon of cooked peas and a sprinkling of chopped chives. (If using the casserole instead of individual ramekins, add in layers in the same order.)

Divide the Supreme Sauce into 5 equal portions and pour over the mixture. Roll the pastry and cut to fit the top. Trim the edges and make slits in the centre to allow the steam to escape. Brush with beaten egg.

Bake at 425°F. for 20 minutes for the small pies. For the large pie, bake at 425°F. for 10 minutes, then reduce to 375°F. and bake for a further 20 minutes.

SUPREME SAUCE

2 ounces butter
2 ounces plain flour
3 cups chicken broth
½ cup dry white wine
1½ teaspoons celery salt
a pinch of pepper
1 clove of garlic
1 medium-sized onion
1 teaspoon salt
¼ pound mushrooms
¾ cup cream

Melt the butter in a saucepan over low heat, and add the flour. Stir until smooth, then cook for 2 minutes without browning. Add the broth and stir until the sauce boils and thickens.

Place the wine, celery salt, pepper, minced garlic, minced onion, salt and chopped mushrooms in a small saucepan and simmer for 5 minutes. Add to the sauce together with the cream. Bring to the boil, stirring constantly, then simmer uncovered for about 15 minutes.

OVEN-FRIED CHICKEN WITH LEMON SAUCE

For the sauce
1 dessertspoon soy sauce
¼ teaspoon salt

Make the sauce by combining all the ingredients and mixing well. Refrigerate for at least 1 hour before using. Prepare an oven at 400°F.

¼ teaspoon pepper
¼ cup salad oil
⅓ cup lemon juice
1 dessertspoon grated lemon
 rind
1 clove of garlic, crushed

For the chicken

½ cup flour
1 teaspoon salt
¼ teaspoon pepper
2 teaspoons paprika
1 roasting chicken, about 2½ to
 3 pounds
½ cup butter

Joint the chicken and coat each piece well with a mixture of flour, salt, pepper and paprika. Arrange the pieces in a fairly shallow ovenproof dish, skin side down and in a single layer. Brush each piece well with melted butter. Bake uncovered for 30 minutes.

Turn the chicken pieces over and pour on the sauce. Bake for 30 minutes longer or until the chicken pieces are tender and a golden colour.

PINEAPPLE GLAZED CHICKEN

1 roasting chicken, about 3
 pounds
15-ounce can of pineapple
 pieces
1 cup raw rice
1 tablespoon finely chopped
 green pepper
1 teaspoon butter
1 tablespoon minced onion
1 teaspoon salt
¼ teaspoon pepper
1 teaspoon ground ginger

Drain the pineapple, reserving the syrup. Take ½ cup of the syrup, add water to make it 1 cup, and place in a medium-sized saucepan with the rice, green pepper, butter, onion, salt, pepper and half the ginger. Bring to the boil. Cover, lower the heat and simmer for about 14 minutes or until the rice is barely tender. Add the pineapple pieces and fluff the rice with a fork. Use this mixture to stuff the prepared chicken.

After trussing the stuffed bird, place it in a baking dish, cover with foil and bake in a moderate oven, 350°F., for 1 hour. Remove the foil and bake for a further 30 minutes or until the chicken is tender, basting at intervals with the remaining pineapple juice which has been mixed with the remaining ½ teaspoon of ginger. Serve with the drippings in the pan.

ROAST CURRIED CHICKEN

1 roasting chicken, about 3
 pounds, with giblets
1 teaspoon salt
1 teaspoon each of curry powder
 and ginger
1 onion
1 stalk of celery with leaves
½ clove of garlic

Wipe the chicken inside and out with a damp cloth. Make some chicken stock by simmering the chicken giblets with the neck, salt and water.

Combine the salt, curry powder and ginger and rub the outside of the bird with this mixture. In the cavity of the bird place the whole onion, the chopped celery, the garlic and the peppercorns. Truss the bird into a good shape and close all cavities.

10 peppercorns
2 tablespoons butter mixed with $\frac{1}{2}$ teaspoon each of curry powder, salt and grated lemon rind
1 rounded teaspoon flour

For the gravy
$\frac{1}{4}$ cup chicken broth
$\frac{1}{2}$ cup cream
$\frac{1}{2}$ teaspoon each of salt and pepper
$\frac{1}{2}$ teaspoon each of curry powder and grated orange rind

Pour over the mixture of melted butter, curry powder, salt and grated lemon rind. Wrap in foil and bake in a moderate oven for 1 hour or until the bird is tender.

Remove all but 2 tablespoons of fat from the dish after the chicken has been unwrapped and removed. Add the flour and blend until smooth. Cook without browning for 1 minute, then add the chicken broth, cream, salt, pepper, curry powder and grated orange rind. Stir until boiling. Serve this gravy with the roast chicken and accompany with saffron rice.

ROAST TURKEY

Prepare the bird by cutting off the neck close to the body, but leave on the neck skin. Wash the bird inside and out with a little warm water to which has been added a good pinch of bicarbonate of soda. Dry with a cloth, then rub the inside with salt.

Fill the body cavity with a bread or sausage stuffing, and, if liked, fill the crop with another type of stuffing such as oyster or celery. Tie back the flap of the neck skin. Truss the bird so that the wings are bent behind the back and the legs are close to the body and tied together.

Place breast side up in a baking dish and brush with melted butter or bacon fat. To protect the breast meat during cooking cover with a piece of greased paper.

Bake the turkey in a slow oven, 325°F. or 300°F., until tender, basting it every half hour, and seasoning with salt and pepper when half cooked. To tell when the bird is cooked, protect your fingers with a piece of paper or cloth and press the fleshy part of the drumstick. The flesh should be soft. Now move the drumstick up and down. If the leg joint gives readily to pressure, the bird is cooked. A guide to cooking times for turkey is given below, but remember to add 5 minutes per pound if the bird is very cold when placed in the oven to cook, and to deduct 5 minutes per pound if the bird is not stuffed.

Weight (pounds)	Oven temperature	Cooking time per pound (minutes)	Total cooking time (hours)
8 to 10	325°F.	20 to 25	3 to $3\frac{1}{2}$
10 to 14	325°F.	18 to 20	$3\frac{1}{2}$ to 4
14 to 18	300°F.	15 to 18	4 to $4\frac{1}{2}$
18 to 20	300°F.	13 to 15	$4\frac{1}{2}$ to 5

NOTE: A frozen turkey will take two days to defrost in the general storage section of the refrigerator. It should be completely thawed out before it is placed in the oven to cook. On no account stuff a turkey the day before cooking, and do not stuff at all if the turkey is to be frozen after roasting.

SESAME BAKED CHICKEN

1 roasting chicken, about
   3 pounds
seasoned flour
egg glazing (1 egg beaten with 3
   tablespoons milk)
$\frac{1}{4}$ cup toasted sesame seeds
$\frac{1}{2}$ to $\frac{2}{3}$ cup cracker biscuit crumbs
$\frac{1}{4}$ cup melted butter

For the sauce

1 dessertspoon soy sauce
$\frac{1}{2}$ teaspoon salt
$\frac{1}{2}$ teaspoon pepper
$\frac{1}{4}$ cup salad oil
$\frac{1}{3}$ cup lemon juice
1 teaspoon grated lemon rind
1 clove of garlic, crushed

Make the sauce by combining all the ingredients in a bowl. Refrigerate for at least 1 hour before using.

Cut the chicken into neat serving pieces, coat them in seasoned flour, dip in the egg glazing and cover with the combined sesame seeds and cracker crumbs.

Arrange the chicken pieces in a shallow dish, skin side down and in a single layer. Brush them well with the melted butter. Bake uncovered at 400°F. for about 30 minutes. Turn each piece of chicken over and pour the sauce over. Bake for a further 30 minutes or until the chicken is tender. Remove to a hot serving dish and garnish with parsley.

To toast the sesame seeds, place them on a shallow tray and bake in a moderate oven, 350°F., for about 10 minutes, stirring once or twice.

STUFFED CHICKEN BREASTS

3 large breasts of chicken (boned,
   skinned and halved), or 6
   small breasts of chicken
salt
6 thin slices ham
3 small gherkins
$\frac{1}{4}$ cup seasoned flour
egg glazing (1 egg beaten with a
   little milk)
$1\frac{1}{2}$ cups soft white breadcrumbs
1 ounce butter
$\frac{1}{2}$ cup water
1 chicken soup cube
4-ounce can of buttered
   mushrooms
$\frac{1}{3}$ cup white wine
2 dessertspoons plain flour
salt and pepper
toasted slivered almonds

Place the chicken breasts boned side up on a board. Working from the centre, pound the chicken flesh lightly with a meat mallet to make a cutlet about $\frac{1}{4}$ inch thick. Sprinkle lightly with salt.

Place a slice of ham and half a gherkin on each piece of chicken. Tuck in the sides, roll up and secure with cocktail picks. Dip in seasoned flour, then in egg glazing, and coat well with breadcrumbs. Chill for about 30 minutes.

Melt the butter in a pan and brown the rolled chicken pieces on all sides. Transfer to a shallow oven dish and bake in a moderate oven for about 40 minutes or until cooked through.

Meanwhile make the gravy in the pan used for frying the chicken: add the water, soup cube, mushrooms and wine to the pan, then heat to boiling point, stirring in any browning from the bottom of the pan. Blend the 2 dessertspoons of plain flour with a little cold water or wine and add to the contents of the pan. Continue stirring until the gravy boils and thickens. Flavour with salt and pepper and cook gently for about 5 minutes.

Serve the chicken with a little of the gravy spooned over it, and sprinkle with almonds (the rest of the gravy can be placed in a gravy boat). Accompany the chicken with freshly cooked or sautéed canned asparagus, and buttered baby carrots. Follow with a tossed French salad.

TANGY OVEN-FRIED CHICKEN

1 chicken, 3 to 4 pounds
1 teaspoon salt
1 clove of garlic, minced
2 teaspoons curry powder
½ cup boiling water
1 chicken soup cube
½ teaspoon dry mustard
2 teaspoons Worcester sauce
½ teaspoon oregano
½ teaspoon paprika
2 or 3 dashes of hot pepper
   sauce

Cut the chicken into serving pieces, sprinkle with salt and place skin side down in a shallow baking tray.

Mix the remaining ingredients and brush both sides of the chicken with the mixture.

Bake at 350°F. for about 45 minutes, turning and basting often until the chicken is quite tender.

Just before serving, raise the temperature of the oven to 400°F. or put under the griller to crisp the outside.

STUFFINGS FOR POULTRY

As a guide to the quantity of stuffing needed for a chicken or any other type of poultry, it is usual to allow 1 cup of stuffing to each pound weight of bird. It is preferable to have too much stuffing ready than too little—the surplus may be baked in a separate dish. Remember that poultry stuffing swells as it cooks, so stuff the bird lightly.

The proportion of flavouring ingredients is a matter of individual taste, but no one flavour should predominate.

Chopped green peppers, shallots, sautéed fresh mushrooms, or fresh or canned oysters may be added to bread stuffing for poultry.

BREAD STUFFING
(for chicken, fish or veal)

3 cups soft white breadcrumbs
1 rounded teaspoon chopped
   fresh herbs
1 rounded teaspoon chopped
   parsley
a dash of nutmeg
grated rind of ½ lemon
1 rounded teaspoon salt
a good pinch of pepper
2 level tablespoons butter
1 egg (and a little milk if needed)

Combine the breadcrumbs, herbs, parsley, nutmeg, lemon rind, salt and pepper in a bowl. One tablespoon of chopped shallot may be added if liked. Rub in the butter. Beat the egg lightly and stir into the dry ingredients. The mixture should be moist but not sloppy—add a little milk only if required.

CELERY STUFFING
(for chicken)

1½ cups finely chopped celery
⅓ cup melted butter

Sauté the celery in the butter until tender. Allow to cool. Combine the breadcrumbs, onions and seasonings. Add the

385

4 cups soft white breadcrumbs
3 dessertspoons chopped onions
1 teaspoon salt
a little sage
¼ teaspoon pepper
¼ teaspoon mixed herbs
a little stock to moisten

celery and butter, tossing lightly and adding a little stock if necessary to moisten. This is sufficient to stuff a 4- or 5-pound chicken.

RICE STUFFING
(for duck or chicken)

2 dessertspoons butter
¼ cup chopped onion
¾ cup chopped celery
1 rasher bacon
2 dessertspoons chopped parsley
1 teaspoon salt
¼ teaspoon pepper
¾ teaspoon dried rosemary
1 small can of champignons
1½ cups cooked rice

Melt the butter in a saucepan and add the onion and celery. Sauté for about 5 minutes. Chop the bacon, add, and cook until the bacon fat is clear. Add the remaining ingredients, tossing lightly with a fork to mix. This is sufficient to stuff about a 4-pound duck or chicken.

SAGE AND ONION STUFFING
(for duck)

2 medium-sized onions
4 cups soft white breadcrumbs
1 teaspoon salt
¼ teaspoon pepper
2 ounces butter
1 teaspoon crushed sage leaves
a little beaten egg or milk to
  moisten

Place 2 peeled whole onions in a saucepan, add enough water to cover, and bring to the boil. Pour this water away and cover with fresh water. Cook until tender. Drain, then chop the onions finely.

Place the breadcrumbs in a bowl and add the chopped onion. Season with salt and pepper. Add the butter in small pieces, mix well, then stir in the crushed sage. If the seasoning is too dry add a little beaten egg or milk.

SAUSAGE STUFFING
(for Turkey)

1 pound sausage meat
1 cup chopped onion
2 cups chopped celery
10 cups soft white breadcrumbs
2 teaspoons salt
1 teaspoon mixed herbs
1 egg

Place the sausage meat in a saucepan and cook, stirring well, until lightly browned. Remove with a slotted spoon. Retain in the pan about 1 tablespoon of the fat extracted from the meat during cooking, and use to sauté the onion and celery for about 5 minutes or until tender.

Place the breadcrumbs, salt and herbs in a large bowl. Stir in the meat and the vegetables, toss lightly, then bind with slightly beaten egg. This is sufficient for a 10- or 12-pound turkey.

Duckling with Pineapple, Coquilles St Jacques,
Quiche Lorraine

SALADS

APPLE AND CELERY SALAD

2 tablespoons condensed milk
½ teaspoon salt
½ teaspoon sugar
½ teaspoon mustard
a pinch of cayenne pepper
3 dessertspoons vinegar
3 tablespoons cream or top milk
2 eating apples
1 small head of celery
lettuce
1 hard-boiled egg (yolk only)
celery curls

Combine the condensed milk with the salt, sugar, mustard and cayenne. Gradually add first the vinegar and then the cream, blending well.

Peel and dice the apples. Wash and chop enough celery to make about 2 cups. Combine the apple and celery with the dressing. Pile into lettuce cups and sprinkle the top of each with sieved egg yolk.

Make some of the left-over celery into curls, and use to decorate the top of the salad.

ASPARAGUS AND EGG SALAD

1 pound freshly cooked or
    canned asparagus
4 rashers of bacon
¼ cup white vinegar
2 teaspoons sugar
salt and pepper
2 shallots, finely chopped
shredded lettuce
2 hard-boiled eggs

Drain the asparagus. Cook the bacon in a frying pan until crisp, then lift out and drain, crumble and set aside. Pour most of the bacon fat from the pan and to the pan add the vinegar, sugar, a pinch of salt and pepper and the finely chopped shallot. Stir until simmering, then add the asparagus and heat it through.

Arrange the asparagus on a bed of shredded lettuce and pour over the dressing from the pan. Top with slices of hard-boiled egg and the crumbled bacon.

CAESAR SALAD

1 clove of garlic
½ cup salad oil
2 cups ¼-inch bread cubes
1½ tablespoons lemon juice
2 teaspoons Worcester sauce
¼ teaspoon salt
a pinch of pepper
4 anchovy fillets
1 lettuce
1 egg
1 dessertspoon grated Parmesan
    cheese
¼ cup crumbled blue cheese

Crush the garlic and place in a small bowl. Cover with the oil and refrigerate for 30 minutes. Place ¼ cup of the oil in a pan to heat, then add the bread cubes and fry until a golden brown. In another bowl combine the lemon juice, Worcester sauce, salt, pepper and chopped anchovies, mixing well.

Tear the washed and drained lettuce into bite-sized pieces and place in a large salad bowl. Drain the remaining oil from the garlic and pour over the lettuce. Toss to coat evenly.

Break the egg into the salad and toss well. Pour on the lemon and Worcester sauce mixture and toss again before adding the bread cubes and the cheese. Mix all well together and serve at once.

387

Tongue and Chicken Ring, Polish Potato Salad,
Orange Baskets

CALICO RICE SALAD

3 cups cooked rice
3 hard-boiled eggs, coarsely
  chopped
½ cup chopped onion
¼ cup chopped pimento
¼ cup chopped green pepper
¼ cup chopped celery
¼ cup chopped gherkin
1 teaspoon salt
a dash of pepper
¼ cup French dressing
⅓ cup mayonnaise or salad
  dressing
2 dessertspoons prepared mustard

Combine the first 9 ingredients in a large bowl. Blend the French dressing, mayonnaise and mustard, add to the bowl and toss to coat all ingredients. Chill well.

For individual servings, lightly pack the chilled rice salad into custard cups and immediately turn out onto crisp lettuce leaves and serve.

CHEF'S SALAD WITH ORANGE

1 medium-sized lettuce
1½ cups orange slices or wedges
1 cup peeled and diced apple
½ cup cubed Cheddar cheese
1 cup cubed cooked chicken
½ cup lemon French dressing
  (recipe follows)

Wash and dry the lettuce, tear it into bite-sized pieces, and place in a serving bowl. Add the orange, apple, cheese and chicken. Toss lightly.

Add the dressing and toss to coat the ingredients lightly. Add salt and pepper if necessary.

LEMON FRENCH DRESSING

½ cup lemon juice
½ cup salad oil
1 dessertspoon sugar
½ teaspoon salt
1 teaspoon paprika
¼ teaspoon pepper

Combine all the ingredients in a screw-topped jar and shake well together. Chill well before using.

CHICKEN SALAD SUPERB

1 boiling fowl, about 4 pounds
1 cup diagonally sliced celery
1 cup minced green pepper
2 teaspoons grated or finely
  chopped onion
⅔ cup mayonnaise
¼ cup cream
1 teaspoon salt
a good pinch of pepper
2 dessertspoons vinegar
lettuce cups

Simmer the fowl in a small amount of water with flavourings until tender. Remove the meat from the bones and cut it into chunky pieces (there should be about 4 or 5 cups). Strain the liquid in which the bird was cooked, pour it over the meat and chill well. This stock makes the cooked flesh soft and juicy.

Drain off the stock. Add the celery, green pepper and grated onion to the chicken meat, tossing well.

Combine the mayonnaise, cream, salt, pepper and vinegar and mix well. Pour over the chicken mixture and toss lightly and thoroughly. Chill for several hours.

Have ready well washed and chilled lettuce cups. Spoon the salad into the cups and serve.

Chunky Egg Salad

CHUNKY EGG SALAD

Cut the shelled eggs into chunky pieces or into wedges. Combine with the remaining ingredients, toss lightly and chill well.

Serve on lettuce leaves with tomato slices or wedges.

6 hard-boiled eggs
1 cup diagonally sliced celery
1 tablespoon minced green
  pepper
1 teaspoon minced onion
¼ cup mayonnaise or salad
  dressing
½ teaspoon Worcester sauce
a dash of Tabasco
1 dessertspoon vinegar
1 teaspoon salt
a good pinch of pepper
3 crisply cooked bacon slices,
  crumbled
2 stuffed olives, chopped
tomatoes and lettuce leaves for
  serving

389

COLESLAW 1

4 cups finely shredded cabbage
½ cup thinly sliced celery
¼ cup chopped cucumber
2 dessertspoons chopped green
   pepper
2 dessertspoons chopped shallot
1 dessertspoon chopped parsley
1 dessertspoon lemon juice
½ cup mayonnaise
¼ teaspoon salt
¼ teaspoon sugar
a dash each of pepper and paprika

Combine the cabbage with the celery, cucumber, green pepper, shallot and parsley. Cover and chill.

For the dressing, combine the lemon juice, mayonnaise, salt, sugar, pepper and paprika. Mix until smooth, then chill.

When ready to serve, add the dressing to the salad and toss lightly to mix.

COLESLAW 2

½ cup mayonnaise
¼ cup vinegar
1 teaspoon salt
2 teaspoons sugar
freshly ground black pepper
1 cup shredded carrot
about 1¼ pounds shredded
   cabbage

Combine the mayonnaise, vinegar, salt, sugar and pepper. Chill. Combine the carrot and cabbage and chill well. Just before serving pour the mayonnaise dressing over and toss, coating evenly.

CONFETTI SLAW

4 cups finely shredded cabbage
¼ cup finely minced onion
1 cup drained pineapple pieces
⅓ cup chopped red pepper
⅓ cup chopped green pepper
¼ cup sliced stuffed olives
½ cup grated carrot
1 cup grated Cheddar cheese
½ cup mayonnaise
1 tablespoon lemon juice
1 teaspoon salt
¼ teaspoon pepper
¼ cup cream

About 1½ hours before serving, toss together the cabbage, onion, pineapple, peppers, olives, carrot and cheese. Cover and place in the refrigerator.

Place the mayonnaise in a large bowl and stir in the lemon juice, salt and pepper. Mix until smooth.

Beat the cream in a medium-sized bowl until it just peaks. Gently fold in the mayonnaise mixture. Pour over the cabbage and pineapple mixture, then toss with a fork.

DEVILLED POTATO SALAD

6 medium-sized potatoes
6 hard-boiled eggs
3 dessertspoons vinegar
1 dessertspoon prepared mustard
½ cup mayonnaise

Boil the potatoes and cut them into cubes (they will make about 4½ cups).

Cut the eggs in halves. Remove the yolks and mash them, then blend with the vinegar and mustard. Add the mayonnaise, sour cream, celery salt and salt. Blend well.

½ cup sour cream
¼ teaspoon celery salt
1 teaspoon salt
2 tablespoons finely chopped onion
tomato wedges, cucumber slices and shredded lettuce for serving

Chop the egg whites and combine them with the potato and onion. Fold in the dressing and chill well.

Serve in a bowl garnished with tomato wedges and cucumber slices, and, if liked, some shredded lettuce.

EGG-SALAD STUFFED TOMATOES

5 medium-sized tomatoes
4 hard-boiled eggs
1 dessertspoon salad dressing
1 tablespoon devilled ham paste
salt and pepper
lettuce leaves
olives for garnishing

Cut a slice from the stem end of each unpeeled tomato. Scoop out the pulp and turn the tomato upside down to drain.

Chop the eggs, add the tomato pulp and moisten with the salad dressing. Add the devilled ham paste, and season to taste with salt and pepper. Spoon into the tomato cases.

Serve each filled tomato well chilled on a lettuce leaf with sliced olives to garnish.

Tangy Salmon Salad Loaf
Garden Platter Salad
Moulded Chicken Shape

391

GARDEN PLATTER SALAD

3 large onions
1 lemon
½ cup salad oil
¼ cup vinegar
1 tablespoon lemon juice
¼ teaspoon mixed herbs
½ teaspoon salt
lettuce leaves
2 or 3 large tomatoes
1 small cucumber
freshly ground black pepper
snipped parsley
radish roses or stuffed olives for
    garnishing

About 8 hours before serving peel the onions and cut into paper-thin slices. Cut the lemon in the same way. Arrange alternate layers of onion and lemon in a small bowl, ending with the lemon slices.

Thoroughly mix the salad oil, vinegar, lemon juice, herbs and salt, and pour over the onion and lemon slices. Chill for 8 hours or overnight. Drain, reserving the dressing.

At serving time, line a chilled platter with lettuce leaves. Arrange overlapping slices of tomato and cucumber around the edge of the platter and place the onion and lemon mixture in the centre.

Drizzle the reserved dressing over the tomato and cucumber slices and sprinkle with the black pepper and snipped parsley. Garnish with radish roses or stuffed olives.

GERMAN POTATO SALAD 1

6 medium-sized new potatoes
5 teaspoons salt
½ cup finely chopped onion or
    shallot
½ cup chopped green pepper
1 cup finely chopped celery
2 or 3 slices bacon
1 level tablespoon flour
¾ cup cold water
¼ cup vinegar
1 dessertspoon sugar
¼ level teaspoon white pepper
3 hard-boiled eggs
lettuce leaves
radish for garnishing

Scrub the potatoes thoroughly. Place in a saucepan with 3 teaspoons of the salt and enough cold water to cover. Cook with the lid on until tender. Drain and cool. Remove the skins and cut the potatoes into ½ to ¾ inch cubes. Return them to the saucepan and add the onion, green pepper and celery. Cover tightly with the lid.

Fry the bacon until crisp, then drain it well and crumble it. Blend the flour to a smooth paste with a little of the cold water. Add the vinegar, sugar and pepper, and the remaining salt and water. Cook, stirring well over medium heat until thickened. Cool slightly and pour onto the potato mixture.

Add the crumbled bacon and some of the sliced hard-boiled egg. Mix lightly, taste and adjust the seasonings.

Line a serving dish with lettuce leaves, add the salad and top with the remaining slices of egg. Garnish with sliced radish. This salad may be served at room temperature or well chilled.

GERMAN POTATO SALAD 2

2 pounds medium-sized potatoes
6 slices bacon
⅓ cup bacon fat
¼ cup cider vinegar
1 tablespoon chopped onion
½ teaspoon salt
½ teaspoon paprika

Peel the potatoes and put them on to cook in boiling salted water. While they are cooking, fry the bacon till crisp, then crumble it. Make the dressing by heating together the bacon fat, vinegar, onion, salt and paprika.

Drain the potatoes and cut into cubes or slices. Place in a serving bowl with the crumbled bacon. Pour on the dressing and toss lightly, being careful not to break up the potatoes. Serve at once.

1 tablespoon gelatine
¼ cup cold water
1 cup mayonnaise or salad
 dressing
1½ cups diced cooked tongue
½ cup diced cooked ham
½ cup chopped cucumber
⅓ cup diced celery
3 dessertspoons minced onion or
 shallot
3 dessertspoons diced green olives
 (optional)
1 dessertspoon diced pimento
2 dessertspoons lemon juice
¼ teaspoon salt
¼ teaspoon paprika
1 cup cream, whipped
mixed salad for serving

2 pounds small new potatoes
¼ cup diced bacon
¼ cup minced onion or shallot
1½ teaspoons plain flour
4 teaspoons sugar
1 teaspoon salt
¼ teaspoon pepper
⅓ cup vinegar
½ cup water
1 dessertspoon finely chopped
 parsley
1 teaspoon celery seed (optional)
½ cup sliced radish
celery leaves and radish roses for
 garnishing

1 tablespoon gelatine
¼ cup cold water
1½ cups boiling chicken stock
2 hard-boiled eggs
¼ cup grated carrot or chopped
 celery
parsley sprigs
salt and pepper
½ cup mayonnaise
1 tablespoon finely chopped
 onion or shallot
2 cups chopped cooked chicken
mixed salad for serving

HAM AND TONGUE MOULD

Soften the gelatine in the cold water, then dissolve it over boiling water. Stir in the mayonnaise, then add the remaining ingredients excepting the whipped cream. When well mixed, fold in the cream.

Brush the inside of a ring mould with a little egg white and pour in the mixture. Chill until set.

Unmould on a serving platter and serve with a mixed salad of lettuce, cucumber, tomato and radish or other salad ingredients.

HOT POTATO SALAD

Cook the potatoes in their jackets until just fork-tender. Drain, peel and cut into ¼-inch slices.

Fry the bacon in a small pan until crisp. Add the minced onion and sauté until tender but not brown. Mix the flour, sugar, salt and pepper in a bowl. Stir in the vinegar (the amount depends on the tartness desired) and the water and keep stirring until smooth. Add the bacon, then cook, stirring well until the mixture boils and thickens slightly.

Pour this hot dressing over the potato slices, then add the parsley, celery seed and sliced radish.

Serve lightly tossed and garnished with celery leaves and radish roses.

JELLIED CHICKEN RING

Soften the gelatine in the cold water, then dissolve it in the boiling chicken stock. Cool. Pour enough of this mixture into the bottom of a wetted ring tin to make a thin layer. When it begins to set, arrange slices of hard-boiled egg and either grated carrot or chopped celery to form a pattern. Add a few parsley sprigs if liked, and chill until set.

Add the rest of the ingredients to the remainder of the stock mixture. Pour into the ring tin and chill until set.

Unmould and serve with salad greens and your favourite mayonnaise.

LAMB AND ORANGE SALAD

1 medium-sized lettuce
1½ cups orange slices or wedges
1 cup peeled and diced apple
½ cup cubed Cheddar cheese
1 cup cubed cooked lamb
½ cup lemon French dressing
  (page 388)

Wash and lightly dry the lettuce, then tear it into bite-sized pieces and place in a salad bowl with the orange slices, apple, cheese and lamb. Toss lightly.

Add the dressing and toss again, just enough to coat the ingredients with the dressing. Add salt and pepper if necessary.

LAMB TONGUES VINAIGRETTE

8 lamb tongues
a bouquet garni
celery leaves
1 onion stuck with cloves
water
½ cup olive oil
1½ tablespoons vinegar
1 teaspoon salt
a dash of freshly ground black
  pepper
1 teaspoon each of chopped
  chives and chopped parsley
1 hard-boiled egg

Wash the tongues well and place in a saucepan with the bouquet garni, celery leaves, onion and enough water to cover. Place the lid on the saucepan and simmer until tender (this could take up to 2 hours). Drain, reserving the cooking liquid.

Remove the skin, gristle and small bones from the tongues and cut each tongue in half lengthwise. Place in a shallow serving dish.

Make a dressing by combining the oil, vinegar, salt, pepper, chives, parsley and chopped egg. Mix well and pour over the tongues. Refrigerate for 24 hours, turning the tongue several times during this period.

LIMA BEAN SALAD

½ pound lima beans
1 packet spaghetti sauce mix
2 cups sliced celery
½ cup sliced radish
½ cup chopped gherkins
2 hard-boiled eggs
¾ cup mayonnaise
¼ cup evaporated milk
1 dessertspoon vinegar
1 tablespoon prepared mustard
2 tablespoons chopped shallot
¼ teaspoon salt
lettuce leaves
2 tomatoes

Soak the lima beans overnight in cold water. Drain and place in a saucepan, cover them with cold salted water and simmer for about 1 hour or until tender. Drain well and, while still hot, sprinkle over the spaghetti sauce mix, tossing well.

Add the celery, radish, gherkin and some slices of hard-boiled egg (reserve a few slices of egg for garnishing). Toss lightly, then chill.

Blend the mayonnaise with the milk, vinegar, mustard, shallot and salt. Add to the lima bean mixture and toss to blend. Season to taste. Chill.

Serve in a lettuce-lined bowl and decorate with slices of hard-boiled egg and tomato wedges.

For the dressing
¼ cup vinegar
½ cup salad oil
½ teaspoon salt
¼ teaspoon pepper
¼ teaspoon dry mustard

MEATBALL SALAD

Combine all the ingredients for the dressing in a screw-topped jar and shake well together. Chill. Shake again before using.

For the salad, first peel and cook the potatoes. Drain them. Combine the meat with the herbs, marjoram, thyme, egg and breadcrumbs, mixing well, then shape into 32 small meatballs. Sauté the meatballs in the heated oil in a frying pan until they

a small clove of garlic, crushed
¼ teaspoon thyme

For the salad
1 pound small potatoes
1 pound finely minced steak
½ teaspoon mixed herbs
¼ teaspoon dried marjoram
¼ teaspoon dried thyme
1 egg
1 tablespoon dried breadcrumbs
1 tablespoon oil
15-ounce can of asparagus spears
lettuce, parsley and celery curls
   for garnishing
1 cup dressing for serving

1½ ounces butter
3 dessertspoons chopped shallot
3 level tablespoons flour
1 cup chicken stock
1 cup milk
1 teaspoon lemon juice
½ teaspoon mustard
½ teaspoon salt
¼ teaspoon pepper
2 level dessertspoons gelatine
¼ cup cold water
3 cups diced cooked chicken
¾ cup diced celery
2 tablespoons cream
2 tablespoons mayonnaise
grated carrot, hard-boiled egg
   slices and parsley sprigs for
   serving

1-pound can of salmon
2 dessertspoons gelatine
¼ cup cold water
1 cup mayonnaise
1 cup diced celery
1 tablespoon vinegar
1 dessertspoon prepared mustard
1 dessertspoon grated onion
½ teaspoon salt
¼ teaspoon garlic powder
a pinch of cayenne pepper
salad greens and cucumber sauce
   for serving

are brown on all sides and cooked through. Drain on paper and place on a shallow dish. Drain the asparagus and place it in a shallow dish. Place the cooked potatoes in another shallow dish. Divide the dressing evenly between the meatballs, asparagus and potatoes. Cover the dishes and refrigerate, turning the contents over occasionally during this period.

Wash the lettuce, drain well and use to line a serving platter. Arrange the meatballs, asparagus and potato on the lettuce. Garnish with parsley and celery curls.

If preferred the dressing may be strained and served separately.

MOULDED CHICKEN SALAD

Melt the butter in a saucepan and sauté the shallot until tender but not brown. Stir in the flour and cook for 1 minute. Add the stock and milk. Cook, stirring well until the sauce boils and thickens, then cook for another 2 minutes.

Flavour the sauce with the lemon juice, mustard, salt, and pepper. Soften the gelatine in the cold water, then dissolve it over boiling water. Add this to the slightly cooled sauce. Allow the sauce to cool but not set.

Fold the chicken and celery into the sauce, then add the cream and mayonnaise. Pour into an oiled or wetted 8-inch sandwich tin and chill until set.

Unmould onto a serving platter, surround with grated carrot and garnish with hard-boiled egg slices and parsley sprigs.

MOULDED SALMON SALAD

Drain the salmon, reserving the liquid. Remove the skin and bones and flake the flesh lightly. Soften the gelatine in the cold water.

Add enough water to the salmon liquid to make ½ cup. Heat until boiling. Add the softened gelatine and stir until dissolved. Cool the mixture until it begins to thicken.

Fold in the next 8 ingredients. Adjust the seasonings if necessary. Spoon into a wetted ring mould or into individual moulds. Chill until set.

Serve with salad greens and accompany with cucumber sauce.

MOULDED SHEEP'S TONGUES

12 sheep's tongues
1 bayleaf
1 onion
1 dessertspoon peppercorns
celery stalks
2 tablespoons gelatine and $\frac{1}{4}$ cup
    cold water
4 cups tongue stock (the strained
    liquid in which the tongues
    were cooked)
4 gherkins
6 stuffed olives
shredded lettuce and tomato
    slices for serving

To cook the tongues, wash them well and place in a large saucepan with the bayleaf, sliced onion, peppercorns, some stalks of celery and enough cold water to cover. Place the lid on and bring to the boil, then simmer very gently until the skin is easily removed. (They will take about 3 hours.) Strain the liquid off (keep it for the mould), then remove the skin, gristle and small bones from each tongue. Cut lengthwise into slices.

Soak the gelatine in the cold water, dissolve it over hot water and add to the tongue stock. Season if necessary. Pour a little of this mixture into the bottom of a wetted or oiled 6-inch square cake tin. Chill until set, then arrange a pattern on the bottom using sliced gherkins, sliced stuffed olives and some of the tongue slices. Spoon over a little more of the liquid and chill until set, then add the remainder of the tongue slices, pour over enough stock to cover, then chill until firm.

Unmould and serve with shredded lettuce and sliced tomatoes.

ORANGE BASKETS

For the dressing

1 orange
1 tablespoon vinegar
2 tablespoons salad oil
salt
paprika
chilli powder
freshly ground black pepper

For the salad

3 oranges
4 ounces cultivated mushrooms
4 ounces cooked rice
8 ounces chopped cooked
    chicken
8 ounces cooked prawns
orange slices

Cut the orange for the dressing in half. Squeeze the juice from one half (you should have 2 tablespoons) and reserve the other half for the salad garnish. Combine the orange juice, vinegar and oil in a screw-topped jar and shake until well mixed. Season to taste with salt, paprika, chilli powder and freshly ground black pepper.

Using a grapefruit knife, scoop out the flesh and the pith from the 3 oranges. Wash and slice the mushrooms and marinate them in the dressing. Mix the cooked rice with the chicken and half the prawns and add a little of the chopped orange flesh and the mushrooms.

Spoon this mixture back into the orange shells, topping with a few prawns and a twist or a triangle of orange.

ORANGE CHICKEN SALAD

4 cups diced cooked chicken
2 cups thinly sliced celery
1 cup chopped or broken
    walnuts
$\frac{1}{2}$ cup drained pineapple pieces

Combine all the salad ingredients except the salad greens and the dressing and chill well. Add about $\frac{3}{4}$ cup of the dressing and toss lightly to moisten. Serve on a bed of chilled salad greens.

To make the dressing, combine the ingredients in a bowl in the order given. Beat with a fork, not an egg-beater, for 3 or

1 cup orange sections
chilled salad greens for serving

For the dressing

¼ cup vinegar
2 tablespoons melted butter
1 whole egg, unbeaten
a pinch of salt
a pinch of cayenne pepper
2 level teaspoons mustard
1 can of sweetened condensed
  milk

4 minutes or until the mixture thickens. If necessary, thin down with a little milk.

Any remaining dressing may be stored in a screw-topped jar in the refrigerator for several weeks.

PARTY SALAD RING

12-ounce can of camp pie, luncheon meat or cooked corned beef
1 level tablespoon gelatine
¼ cup cold water
1½ cups tomato juice
2 teaspoons lemon juice
¼ teaspoon salt
½ cup chopped celery
½ cup chopped cucumber
1 cup salad dressing or mayonnaise
cucumber slices for garnishing
salad greens and radish roses for serving

Cut the canned meat into ½-inch cubes.

Soften the gelatine in the cold water, then dissolve it over boiling water. Stir in the tomato juice, lemon juice and salt.

Chill until partially set, then fold in the cubed meat and the remaining ingredients. Place in a wetted or oiled 8-inch ring mould and chill until set.

Unmould onto a serving place and garnish with cucumber slices. If liked, fill the centre with salad greens and radish roses.

PIQUANT SALAD PLATTER

⅔ cup cider vinegar
⅔ cup lemon juice
¼ cup olive oil
1 clove of garlic
1 teaspoon salt
½ teaspoon dill seed
½ teaspoon dried tarragon leaves
a good pinch of pepper
1 large green pepper
3 small white onions
2 medium-sized tomatoes
1 lettuce

Combine the vinegar, lemon juice and olive oil in a large bowl. Mix well, then add crushed garlic, salt, dill seed, tarragon and pepper. Mix again.

Add strips of green pepper, thinly sliced onion rings and peeled and sliced tomato. Toss lightly, then refrigerate for 1½ to 2 hours, stirring occasionally.

Using a slotted spoon, lift the vegetables carefully from the dressing and set aside. Wash the lettuce and separate the leaves. Dip them in the dressing and arrange on a platter. Place the green pepper strips in the centre, surround with the onion rings and arrange the tomato slices around the edge.

POLISH POTATO SALAD

6 large new potatoes
½ cup cooked peas
½ cup diced cooked carrot
1 apple
2 stalks celery
½ cup mayonnaise
½ cup sour cream
3 dessertspoons vinegar
1 teaspoon salt
¼ teaspoon pepper
lettuce leaves
1 dessertspoon chopped parsley
radishes and 2 gherkins for
   garnishing

Wash the potatoes and cook in boiling salted water until tender. Drain, peel and dice them. Combine with the peas, carrot, peeled and diced apple and chopped celery.

Mix the mayonnaise with the sour cream, vinegar, salt and pepper. Pour over the vegetables, tossing well to coat. Chill thoroughly.

Line a salad bowl with broken or shredded lettuce and add the potato salad. Top with the chopped parsley and garnish the edges with slices of gherkin and either radish roses or slices of radish.

POTATO SALAD 1

2 pounds cooked potatoes
½ teaspoon mixed herbs
¼ teaspoon marjoram
1 teaspoon salt
¼ teaspoon pepper
1 dessertspoon caraway seeds
   (optional)
¼ cup olive oil
¼ cup vinegar
½ cup mayonnaise
1 tablespoon prepared mustard
3 hard-boiled eggs
1 medium-sized onion, sliced
lettuce
tomato quarters for garnishing

Slice the cooked potatoes into a large bowl. Place the seasonings in a jar with the oil and vinegar and shake until well blended. Add the mayonnaise and mustard. Dice two of the hard-boiled eggs and add to the potato, then mix in sliced onion. Toss lightly to combine the ingredients thoroughly. Add the dressing, toss to blend, then chill well.

Line a large salad bowl with washed and drained lettuce leaves. Add the potato salad. Garnish with tomato quarters and the remaining egg which has been cut into slices.

POTATO SALAD 2

2½ cups sliced cooked potatoes
1 teaspoon sugar
1 teaspoon vinegar
½ cup chopped onions
1¼ teaspoons salt
1½ teaspoons celery seed
¾ cup mayonnaise or salad
   dressing
2 hard-boiled eggs

Sprinkle the potatoes with the sugar and vinegar. Add the onion, salt, celery seed and mayonnaise. Toss lightly without breaking the potato slices. Top with slices of hard-boiled egg. Chill well before serving.

RICE SALAD

1 cup rice
mustard dressing
1½ cups diced ham
1 red pepper, seeded and diced
1 cup cold cooked peas
lettuce leaves
chopped parsley and sliced
  tomato for garnishing

For the mustard dressing

1½ tablespoons dry mustard
a little cold water
1 tablespoon vinegar
1 dessertspoon salad oil
½ teaspoon salt
1 teaspoon sugar
¼ cup mayonnaise

Cook the rice in boiling salted water until tender. Drain well and, while still warm, mix with the mustard dressing. When the rice is cold, add the remaining ingredients, tossing well.

To serve, place in a lettuce-lined bowl and garnish with chopped parsley and tomato slices.

To make the dressing, combine the mustard with enough cold water to make a stiff paste (about 2 dessertspoonfuls). Add the vinegar, then the oil, and beat until creamy. Flavour with salt and sugar, then add the mayonnaise, blending well.

RUSSIAN POTATO SALAD

4 large new potatoes
1 medium-sized onion
½ teaspoon celery seed
1 teaspoon salt
2 teaspoons sugar
¼ teaspoon pepper
Russian dressing (recipe follows)
½ cup mayonnaise
1 dessertspoon vinegar
½ cup chopped radish
1½ cups diced celery
lettuce leaves

Boil the potatoes in their jackets. Drain and peel and while still warm add finely chopped onion and the seasonings, chilled Russian dressing and the combined mayonnaise and vinegar. Chill. Shortly before serving add the radish and celery. Toss together, adding more dressing if necessary. Serve in a lettuce-lined bowl.

RUSSIAN DRESSING

½ teaspoon mustard
a dash each of pepper and salt
¼ teaspoon sugar
¼ teaspoon curry powder
2 tablespoons vinegar
2 tablespoons olive oil
1 teaspoon Worcester sauce
2 teaspoons undiluted tomato
  soup
1 teaspoon chilli sauce

Combine the mustard, pepper, salt, sugar, curry powder and vinegar in a bowl. Mix well. Gradually stir in the oil, beating well, then add the Worcester sauce, tomato soup and chilli sauce. Chill before using.

Russian Salad

RUSSIAN SALAD

1 pound new potatoes, cooked
½ pound French beans, cooked
2 cups sliced cooked carrot
¼ pound dried beans, cooked (or
   1 small can of red kidney
   beans)
1 cup cooked peas
2 tablespoons vinegar
2 tablespoons olive oil
salt
freshly ground black pepper
1 tablespoon capers
1 tablespoon chopped gherkin
2 tablespoons finely chopped
   parsley
2 tablespoons finely chopped
   spring onions
2 or 3 hard-boiled eggs
about 1 cup mayonnaise
1 lettuce

Dice the cooked potatoes. Reserving some of each vegetable for decoration, combine the diced potatoes, French beans, sliced carrots, cooked dried beans and cooked peas. Add the vinegar and oil, season to taste with salt and black pepper, toss lightly. Chill.

When the salad is well chilled add the capers, chopped gherkin, parsley, and spring onions. Chop the egg whites and add, then mix in some of the mayonnaise and toss lightly. Heap the mixture into a lettuce-lined salad bowl. Decorate with the reserved vegetables. Sprinkle with sieved egg yolk. Serve with the remaining mayonnaise.

SALAD DRESSING

¼ cup water
¼ cup vinegar
1 egg
1 teaspoon sugar
¼ teaspoon salt
¼ teaspoon mustard
1 teaspoon butter
1 tablespoon cream or top milk
   (optional)

Place the water and vinegar in a saucepan and bring to the boil. Cool.

Beat the egg with the sugar, salt and mustard. Add the vinegar mixture and place in the saucepan. Stir with a wooden spoon over low heat until the mixture thickens and coats the back of the spoon. (Be careful not to allow the dressing to boil or it will curdle.) Add the butter while the dressing is still hot, then when cool add the cream.

Stored in a screw-topped jar in the refrigerator, this salad dressing will keep for weeks.

SALAD NICOISE

1 medium-sized onion
3 firm but ripe tomatoes
2 green peppers
4 centre stalks of celery
4 tablespoons olive oil
1 tablespoon vinegar
salt and pepper
2 medium-sized cans of salmon
   or tuna
1 small can of anchovies
4 hard-boiled eggs
8 green olives and 8 black olives
chopped parsley
lemon juice

Slice the onion tissue thin and separate into rings. Cut the tomatoes into eighths or quarters, not slices. Remove the seeds from the peppers and cut into strips no thicker than a matchstick. Place all these in a salad bowl.

Mix the oil, vinegar, salt and pepper to make a dressing, pour into the bowl and toss the ingredients.

Cover the mixed salad vegetables with the salmon or tuna and the anchovies. Cut the eggs into quarters and arrange on top, then decorate with green and black olives. Sprinkle with chopped parsley and a little lemon juice.

Toss lightly just before serving.

SAUSAGE SALAD ROLLS

18 thin slices of beef or ham
   sausage
about 2 cups potato salad
stuffed olives
leaves of lettuce or celery

Place a spoonful of the potato salad in the centre of each sausage slice, wrap the sausage slice round the salad filling and secure with cocktail picks. Press half a stuffed olive on the end of each pick. Arrange on a plate with lettuce or celery leaves.

TANGY SALMON SALAD LOAF

2 level dessertspoons gelatine
½ cup cold water
1 cup chicken stock
1-pound can of salmon
1 cup diced celery
¼ cup chopped gherkins
1 dessertspoon minced onion
2 dessertspoons lemon juice
¼ teaspoon salt
¼ teaspoon paprika

Soften the gelatine in the cold water, then dissolve it over boiling water. Add to the stock and cool, but do not allow to set.

Drain and flake the salmon and combine with the celery, gherkins, onion, lemon juice, salt and paprika. Add the stock and gelatine and then the mayonnaise and cream. Toss lightly to blend the ingredients thoroughly.

Place the mixture in a wetted or oiled orange-cake tin and chill until firm. Unmould onto a serving platter and cover the top and sides with aspic glaze. Chill until set.

½ cup mayonnaise
½ cup cream
aspic glaze (recipe follows)
shredded lettuce, celery curls,
   tomato wedges and devilled
   eggs for garnishing

To serve, garnish with shredded lettuce, celery curls, tomato wedges and devilled eggs.

ASPIC GLAZE

Soak 1 teaspoon of gelatine in 1 tablespoon of cold water. Dissolve it over hot water.

Cool slightly and add ½ cup mayonnaise which has been blended with 2 tablespoons tomato sauce.

Chill until the mixture begins to thicken, then spoon over the loaf. Chill until set.

THREE-BEAN SALAD

16-ounce can of green beans
two 10-ounce cans of red kidney
   beans
16-ounce can of baby lima beans
lettuce
1 medium-sized green pepper
1 medium-sliced onion

For the dressing

½ cup sugar
½ cup white wine vinegar
½ cup salad oil
1 teaspoon salt
½ teaspoon dry mustard
¼ teaspoon mixed herbs
1 tablespoon chopped parsley

Place the well-drained beans in a large lettuce-lined bowl. Add thinly sliced green pepper and onion (separate the sliced onion into rings). Thoroughly combine all the ingredients for the dressing and drizzle it over the surface of the salad vegetables.

Cover and let stand overnight. Just before serving, stir, then drain. The salad may be topped with sliced cucumber and radish roses.

Three-bean Salad

402

Papaw Cocktail, German Potato Salad,
Strawberry Satin Torte, Mock Chicken Loaf

Tomato Aspic Moulds
Potato Salad

1¾ cups tomato juice
1½ tablespoons chopped onion
1 tablespoon chopped celery
1 dessertspoon brown sugar
½ teaspoon salt
1 small bayleaf
2 whole cloves
1½ dessertspoons gelatine
¼ cup cold water
4 teaspoons lemon juice
potato salad and lettuce leaves
    for serving

1 small can of asparagus spears
5 teaspoons gelatine
¼ cup cold water
1½ cups sliced cooked tongue
½ pound cooked ham
pepper and salt
1 cup cream or canned
    evaporated milk
celery curls and lettuce
    for serving

TOMATO ASPIC MOULDS

Place the tomato juice, onion, celery, brown sugar, salt, bayleaf and cloves in a saucepan and simmer for 5 minutes. Strain. Soften the gelatine in the cold water and dissolve it in the hot tomato mixture, stirring well. Add the lemon juice.

Pour into individual moulds and chill for 2 hours or until firm.

At serving time pile potato salad in the centre of a lettuce-lined platter and unmould the tomato aspic moulds around the edge.

TONGUE AND ASPARAGUS SHAPE

Drain the asparagus, reserving half a cup of the liquid. Combine this liquid with 1½ cups of water and place in a saucepan to heat. Soak the gelatine in the ¼ cup water, add it to the hot liquid and stir until dissolved. Cool.

Swirl a little of the cooled asparagus and gelatine mixture around the base of 6 individual moulds and arrange the tips of the asparagus spears in a pattern on the bottom. Chill until set.

Mince together the tongue and ham, season lightly with pepper and salt if needed, add the gelatine mixture and the remaining asparagus which has been chopped. Add the cream and mix well.

Spoon the mixture carefully into the moulds and chill until set. Unmould onto serving plates and serve with celery curls and lettuce.

403

Bengal Curry, Fruit Gateau, Peach Cheesecake

TONGUE AND CHICKEN RING

1 chicken, about 4 pounds
1 onion
1 carrot
1 teaspoon salt
celery leaves
parsley
water
6 to 8 sheep's tongues
1 dessertspoon gelatine
1 or 2 hard-boiled eggs
   (optional)
lettuce, tomato and stuffed hard-
   boiled eggs for serving

Place the chicken in a large saucepan and add half the onion, half the carrot, the salt, some celery leaves and a few sprigs of parsley. Barely cover with water, put the lid on and simmer until the flesh of the chicken is easily removed from the bones. This could take about 2 hours.

Place the tongues in another saucepan, add the remaining carrot and onion, a few celery leaves and enough water to cover. Simmer with the lid on until the tongues are tender and the skin is easily removed (this could take from $2\frac{1}{2}$ to 3 hours). Drain, remove the small bones from the root of the tongue, peel off the skin, and slice the flesh.

Meanwhile drain the chicken, reserving the stock. Take the meat off the bones and cut it into neat pieces.

Cool the liquid in which the chicken was cooked, lift off any fat, strain the liquid, then boil in a saucepan without the lid until reduced to 2 cups.

Soften the gelatine in a little cold water, add to the 2 cups of stock and heat until thoroughly dissolved. Allow to cool to the consistency of unbeaten egg white.

Dip slices of the tongue in the partly set gelatine mixture and arrange them, overlapping, in the bottom of a wetted or oiled ring mould. Add a few slices of hard-boiled egg.

Cover with a quarter of the gelatine mixture and chill until firm. Mix the chicken with the remaining gelatine and add any remaining tongue slices. Spoon this mixture into the ring mould and chill until thoroughly set.

Unmould onto a serving plate and garnish with lettuce, tomato wedges and stuffed hard-boiled eggs.

TOSSED SALAD

For the dressing

$\frac{1}{2}$ teaspoon salt
a good pinch of freshly ground
   black pepper
$\frac{1}{2}$ teaspoon dry mustard
3 tablespoons olive oil
3 tablespoons vinegar
1 clove of garlic

For the salad

1 small lettuce
$\frac{1}{2}$ cup chopped celery
2 tomatoes, quartered
$\frac{1}{4}$ cup finely chopped parsley
$\frac{1}{3}$ cup grated carrot
3 dessertspoons chopped shallot

Combine the salt, pepper and mustard for the dressing and add the oil, vinegar and crushed garlic. Place in a screw-topped jar and shake well to combine the oil and vinegar and blend the flavours.

Meanwhile wash and drain the lettuce and chill well.

Just before serving combine all the vegetables in a serving bowl. Remove the crushed garlic clove from the dressing and pour the dressing over the salad. Toss well together and serve immediately.

SAUCES

Savoury Sauces

BARBECUE SAUCE

1 tablespoon butter
1 medium-sized onion, chopped
1 clove of garlic, crushed or
  minced
½ cup tomato sauce
¼ cup vinegar
1 teaspoon brown sugar
1 teaspoon salt
½ teaspoon dry mustard
¼ cup water

Combine all the ingredients in a saucepan and bring to the boil. Brush over meats when they are being barbecued.

BEARNAISE SAUCE

1 shallot
1 dessertspoon chopped tarragon
3 tablespoons white vinegar
4 ounces butter
4 egg yolks
a squeeze of lemon juice
cayenne pepper and salt

Chop the shallot and add with the tarragon to the vinegar. Bring to the boil. Strain.

Melt the butter. Beat the egg yolks and add with a little of the butter to the vinegar, beating well with a wire whisk. Gradually add the remaining butter, whisking well. (The mixture will curdle unless it is well whisked and the mixtures combined gradually.)

Flavour with the lemon juice, cayenne and salt.

BEEF OLIVE SAUCE

1 tablespoon oil
1½ pounds minced steak
1 large onion
¼ cup chopped green peppers
1 large clove of garlic
1 carrot
½ pound mushrooms
2 dessertspoons chopped parsley
16-ounce can of peeled tomatoes
1 cup tomato purée
6-ounce can of tomato paste
½ cup dry red wine
1 teaspoon basil
¼ teaspoon each of savoury, rosemary and marjoram
½ teaspoon each of sugar and salt
a dash of pepper
¼ cup sliced stuffed olives

Heat the oil in a large heavy-based saucepan and add the minced steak. Cook, stirring well until the meat has browned. Reduce the heat and add chopped onion, green pepper and peeled and minced garlic. Cook until soft but not brown, stirring occasionally.

Add grated carrot and the quartered mushrooms, chopped parsley, tomatoes, tomato purée, tomato paste, wine, herbs, sugar, salt and pepper. Cover and simmer for 1½ hours. Add the sliced olives and simmer uncovered for about 30 minutes or until the sauce is thick. Adjust the seasonings if necessary.

Serve with freshly cooked spaghetti sprinkled with Parmesan cheese.

1 shallot
1 clove of garlic
1 glass red wine
1 bayleaf
$\frac{1}{2}$ pint brown vegetable sauce
  (see below)
1 ounce bone marrow
1 teaspoon chopped parsley
1 teaspoon anchovy essence
a squeeze of lemon juice

1 rounded teaspoon butter
1 shallot
salt and pepper
a pinch of nutmeg
$\frac{1}{2}$ pint milk
1 heaped tablespoons soft white
  breadcrumbs

1 piece each of carrot, turnip,
  celery and onion
1 level tablespoon dripping
1 rounded tablespoon plain flour
a pinch of dried herbs
1 pint of water and a soup cube,
  or 1 pint vegetable water

2 tablespoons margarine or
  bacon fat
4 tablespoons finely chopped
  onion
4 level tablespoons plain flour
2 cups stock, or water and a soup
  cube
salt and pepper
1 ounce chopped ham
2 tablespoons sherry

1 cup white sauce
$\frac{1}{2}$ teaspoon made mustard
1 teaspoon sugar
a dash of cayenne pepper
$\frac{1}{4}$ teaspoon salt
1 cup grated tasty cheese
$\frac{1}{2}$ cup chopped cucumber

BORDELAISE SAUCE

Chop the shallot and garlic and place in a small saucepan with the wine and bayleaf. Simmer until reduced to half quantity. Add the brown sauce and simmer again for 15 minutes, removing any scum as it rises. Strain and return to the saucepan.

Cook the bone marrow in a little water for 5 minutes. Strain and add to the sauce with the parsley, anchovy essence and lemon juice. Taste and add salt and pepper if required.

BREAD SAUCE

Melt the butter in a saucepan. Add finely chopped shallot and toss over low heat until soft but not brown.

Add the salt, pepper and nutmeg. Heat the milk and pour over the breadcrumbs and shallots. Beat until well mixed.

Cover and stand the sauce on a warm part of the stove until serving time.

BROWN VEGETABLE SAUCE

Cut up the vegetables roughly. Melt the dripping in a saucepan, add the vegetables and cook them, stirring well until they are lightly browned.

Add the flour and herbs and stir until brown, then pour in the stock and stir until the sauce boils and thickens. Cover and simmer for 20 minutes.

Strain the vegetables from the sauce before using it.

CHASSEUR SAUCE

Melt the fat in a pan and add the onion. Cook for about 5 minutes or until soft, without browning. Add the flour, stir until smooth, then cook until brown.

Add the stock and season with salt and pepper. Stir over medium heat until the sauce comes to the boil and thickens, then simmer for 5 minutes.

Fold in the chopped ham and flavour with the sherry.

CHEESE AND CUCUMBER SAUCE

To the white sauce add the mustard, sugar, cayenne, salt and grated cheese. Stir in the cucumber, bring to the boil and simmer for 4 minutes.

1 cup finely chopped onion
1 clove of garlic
1 tablespoon oil
1 tablespoon melted butter
½ pound chicken livers
3 rashers of bacon
¼ cup finely chopped parsley
½ teaspoon salt
a dash of black pepper
1 medium-sized green pepper
1½ cups canned tomatoes
1 to 2 tablespoons red wine

¼ cup mayonnaise
½ cup undiluted tomato soup
¼ cup cream, semi-whipped
¼ level teaspoon curry powder
1 teaspoon Worcester sauce
1 teaspoon lemon juice
salt and pepper

1 small firm cucumber
½ cup cream
2 tablespoons vinegar
salt and pepper

⅔ of an average-sized cucumber
1 teaspoon grated onion
¼ cup mayonnaise or salad
   dressing
½ cup sour cream
2 teaspoons chopped parsley
a dash of pepper
salt to taste

3 dessertspoons butter
1 tablespoon finely chopped
   onion
3 dessertspoons plain flour
4 teaspoons curry powder
1 teaspoon sugar
1 teaspoon salt
a pinch of powdered ginger
a dash of pepper
1½ cups milk
1 dessertspoon lemon juice

CHICKEN LIVER SAUCE

Sauté the onion and minced garlic in the oil and butter for 10 minutes or until the onion is golden. Add finely chopped chicken livers and cook for 5 minutes. Add chopped bacon, parsley, salt, pepper and chopped seeded green pepper. Cover and simmer for 10 minutes.

Add the tomatoes and wine and bring to the boil. Cover and simmer for 20 minutes, stirring occasionally.

If a thicker sauce is required, simmer without the lid.

COCKTAIL SAUCE

Combine the mayonnaise and the undiluted soup. Fold in the semi-whipped cream, then add the curry powder, Worcester sauce and lemon juice, with salt and pepper to taste. Mix well.

CUCUMBER SAUCE

Chill all the ingredients. Peel the cucumber and grate or chop finely. Whip the cream till it is just beginning to thicken, gradually add the vinegar, and flavour to taste with salt and pepper. Add the grated cucumber.

CUCUMBER SAUCE

Grate the cucumber and press it and the onion through a strainer to remove the juice. Combine with the remaining ingredients. Chill well before serving.

CURRY SAUCE

Melt the butter in a saucepan and sauté the chopped onion until tender. Remove from the heat and add the flour, curry powder, sugar, salt, ginger and pepper. Stir until smooth, then cook for 1 minute.

Add the milk and stir over medium heat until the sauce boils and thickens. Reduce the heat and simmer the sauce for 5 minutes. Add the lemon juice just before serving.

EGG SAUCE

2 dessertspoons butter
3 level tablespoons plain flour
2 cups milk
½ teaspoon salt
a dash of pepper
1 teaspoon prepared mustard
1 teaspoon Worcester sauce
2 hard-boiled eggs
2 tablespoons finely chopped
   parsley

Melt the butter in a saucepan, add the flour and stir over medium heat until smooth. Cook without browning for 1 minute. Add the milk and cook until the sauce boils and thickens, stirring all the time.

Season with the salt, pepper, mustard and Worcester sauce. Fold in chopped eggs and parsley. Simmer for 2 or 3 minutes.

HOLLANDAISE SAUCE

4 ounces butter
¼ cup hot water
4 egg yolks
2 dessertspoons lemon juice
½ level teaspoon salt
a dash of cayenne pepper

Melt the butter in the top of a double saucepan over hot, not boiling, water. Stir in the ¼ cup of hot water. Remove from the heat. Add the unbeaten egg yolks and immediately beat with a whisk or rotary beater until the mixture almost doubles in bulk. Stir in the lemon juice, salt and cayenne.

Replace over the hot water and cook, stirring constantly, for about 5 minutes. At no time should the water boil, nor should it touch the bottom of the saucepan containing the sauce.

Remove from the heat immediately the sauce has thickened and let stand uncovered until ready to serve. Should it cool too much, place it over hot, not boiling, water and stir constantly until heated through.

HORSERADISH SAUCE

1 stick of horseradish
1 tablespoon vinegar
1 rounded teaspoon castor sugar
1 teaspoon made mustard
¼ pint cream, or 2 tablespoons of
   milk and 1 rounded tablespoon of soft white breadcrumbs

Wash and scrape the horseradish and soak in cold water for about 30 minutes. Drain, dry and grate down as much as possible.

Place in a bowl with the vinegar, sugar and mustard. Whip the cream and stir it lightly into the mixture.

Keep the sauce in the refrigerator until required (but use it the day it is made). Either sour or fresh cream may be used, and lemon juice could replace the vinegar.

LEMON SAUCE

½ cup melted butter
juice of 1 lemon
¼ teaspoon grated lemon rind
½ teaspoon salt
a pinch of pepper
¼ teaspoon grated onion or
   ½ teaspoon chopped chives

When you have melted the butter in a saucepan, add the other ingredients and cook over gentle heat until the sauce is foamy but not brown. Serve immediately.

MEAT SAUCE

1 dessertspoon butter or 1 tablespoon oil
2 medium-sized onions
2 cloves of garlic
1 pound finely minced steak
$\frac{1}{2}$ cup red wine
$\frac{1}{2}$ cup cold water
1 cup tomato soup
1 teaspoon fresh herbs or a pinch
  of dried herbs
salt and pepper

Melt the butter or heat the oil in a saucepan. Add finely chopped onion and crushed garlic and toss over medium heat until soft, but not brown. Add the meat and cook, stirring well until it changes colour.

Now add the wine, water, soup and herbs and stir until boiling. Season to taste with salt and pepper. Lower the heat, cover, and simmer for about 45 minutes.

Have ready some cooked spaghetti. Place a third of the sauce on the spaghetti and toss with two forks. Pour the remainder of the sauce over the top and sprinkle liberally with grated cheese.

MELTED BUTTER OR WHITE SAUCE

1 dessertspoon butter
2 tablespoons plain flour
$\frac{1}{4}$ teaspoon salt
a good pinch of white or cayenne
  pepper
$\frac{1}{2}$ pint liquid (milk, or milk and
  stock)

Melt the butter in a saucepan. Take it off the heat and add the flour, salt and pepper, stirring until smooth. Return the saucepan to the heat and cook for 1 minute but do not allow the mixture to brown. Add the liquid and stir until the sauce boils and thickens. Simmer for another minute or so.

ANCHOVY SAUCE

Add 2 teaspoons anchovy essence and 1 teaspoon lemon juice to the above quantity.

CAPER SAUCE

Add 1 tablespoon chopped capers.

CHEESE SAUCE

Add 3 or 4 tablespoons finely grated cheese, a pinch of cayenne and $\frac{1}{2}$ teaspoon mustard.

EGG SAUCE

Add 1 finely chopped hard-boiled egg.

ONION SAUCE

Add 2 tablespoons sautéed chopped onion.

PARSLEY SAUCE

Add 1 teaspoon finely chopped parsley.

OYSTER SAUCE

Add $\frac{1}{2}$ cup oysters and a squeeze of lemon juice.

MINT SAUCE

(for use in winter when mint is scarce)

Wash, dry and cut up finely 2 cups of fresh mint leaves. Place them in a jug.

Heat ½ pint of vinegar and 2 heaped tablespoons of sugar in a saucepan. When boiling, and the sugar has dissolved, pour over the mint leaves. Allow to cool, then bottle. Seal with an airtight sealer.

MUSHROOM SAUCE

¼ pound fresh mushrooms
1 clove of garlic
1 tablespoon butter
1 tablespoon oil
1¼ cups canned tomatoes
¼ teaspoon oregano
½ teaspoon salt
a dash of freshly ground black pepper

Peel and thinly slice the mushrooms. Peel and mince the garlic. Simmer in the heated oil and butter for 10 minutes, stirring frequently.

Add the tomatoes, oregano, salt and pepper and simmer uncovered for about 20 minutes.

MUSTARD SAUCE

1 egg
1 tablespoon mustard
3 dessertspoons sugar
½ cup vinegar
½ cup water from corned beef or other boiled meat

Mix the egg, mustard and sugar together, add the vinegar and the water in which corned beef or other boiled meat was cooked. Stir over gentle heat until thick, but not allow to boil.

ORANGE SAUCE

1¼ cups broth made from the giblets
1 bayleaf
2 whole cloves
1 level tablespoon butter or margarine
1 teaspoon very finely chopped onion
2 level tablespoons plain flour
¼ teaspoon salt
a dash of pepper
3 tablespoons orange juice
1 teaspoon sugar

Combine the broth, bayleaf and cloves in a saucepan, bring to the boil and simmer for 5 minutes. Remove the bayleaf and cloves.

Melt the butter in a saucepan, add the onion and cook until golden brown. Stir in the flour, salt and pepper and cook for 1 minute. Remove from the heat and add the broth. Return to the heat and cook, stirring well until the sauce boils and thickens.

Add the orange juice and sugar and serve with roast duck.

3 level tablespoons butter
1 teaspoon finely chopped onion
4 level tablespoons plain flour
1 pint stock or vegetable water
1 soup cube
1 bayleaf
3 sprigs parsley
1 level teaspoon mustard
salt and pepper
3 tablespoons Madeira wine or
    sherry

½ pint water and 1 packet brown
    onion gravy mix, or ½ pint
    brown vegetable sauce
2 dessertspoons tomato sauce
1 teaspoon prepared mustard
1 teaspoon Worcester sauce
½ cup cream
2 dessertspoons claret

1 tablespoon butter or margarine
1 medium-sized onion
1 pound finely minced steak
¾ cup tomato sauce or tomato
    soup
½ cup stock, or water and a soup
    cube
1 teaspoon soy sauce
1 teaspoon Worcester sauce
1 tablespoon saki or dry sherry
½ teaspoon monosodium
    glutamate
¼ teaspoon salt
¼ teaspoon pepper

2 medium-sized onions
1 clove of garlic
2 tablespoons oil
1 pound finely minced steak
5-ounce can of tomato paste
1 cup water
½ cup red wine
a good pinch of herbs
1 teaspoon salt
¼ teaspoon pepper

SAUCE MADERE

Melt the butter in a saucepan, add the chopped onion and sauté until golden brown. Add the flour and stir until the mixture colours a golden brown.

Add the stock, then cook, stirring constantly until the sauce boils and thickens.

Add the soup cube, bayleaf, parsley, mustard, salt and pepper. Cover and simmer for about 10 minutes. Remove the parsley and the bayleaf. Add the Madeira wine just before serving.

SAUCE PIQUANT

Add the water to the gravy mix and stir over medium heat until the mixture boils. Simmer for 10 minutes. Blend the tomato sauce, mustard and Worcester sauce and add to the brown gravy. Stir until it returns to the boil. Add the cream, stirring well.

Add the claret just before serving.

This sauce may be reheated, but not reboiled, after the cream and claret have been added.

SAUCE TOKYO

Melt the butter in a saucepan. Add the chopped onion and sauté until soft. Add the minced steak, then cook, stirring well until the meat is browned.

Stir in the tomato sauce or soup, the stock, soy and Worcester sauce, saki, monosodium glutamate, salt and pepper.

Simmer, uncovered, for about 30 minutes, stirring occasionally. Spoon over cooked spaghetti.

SIMPLE SPAGHETTI SAUCE

Peel and chop the onions. Peel and chop or crush the garlic. Heat the oil in a saucepan and fry the onion until a golden brown. Add the garlic and the meat, then cook, stirring well until the meat changes colour.

Mix in the tomato paste, water, red wine, herbs, salt and pepper. Stir over medium heat until the mixture comes to the boil. Cover and simmer gently for about 1 hour.

STEAK MARINADE

1 tablespoon brown sugar
2 tablespoons tomato sauce
2 tablespoons vinegar
2 teaspoons mustard
1 tablespoon Worcester sauce
salt and pepper

Combine all the ingredients and mix well. Pour into a shallow dish, place the meat in the mixture to marinate and allow to stand for at least 2 hours.

If the marinade does not cover the meat, turn it occasionally to make sure all the meat has been soaked.

This may be used as a basting liquid during cooking. If liked, red wine may replace the vinegar.

SUPREME SAUCE

⅓ cup butter
2 ounces plain flour
3 cups chicken broth, or water and 2 chicken soup cubes
½ cup dry white wine
1½ teaspoons celery salt
a good pinch of pepper
1 clove of garlic
1 medium-sized onion
1 teaspoon salt
¼ pound mushrooms
¾ cup cream

Melt the butter in a saucepan over low heat, then add the flour. Stir until smooth, then cook, stirring well for 2 minutes, without browning. Add the broth and stir until boiling.

Place the wine in a small saucepan and add celery salt, pepper, minced garlic, minced onion, salt and chopped mushrooms. Simmer for 5 minutes, then add the thickened sauce and the cream and bring to the boil. Simmer uncovered for 15 minutes.

TANGY APPLE SAUCE

1 cup apple purée
1½ tablespoons prepared horseradish

Combine both ingredients and blend well. Chill for 1 hour before serving. This sauce should be used on the day it is made.

Tomato Meat Sauce

412

TARTARE SAUCE

1 tablespoon whipped cream
¼ pint mayonnaise
1 teaspoon chopped parsley
1 tablespoon chopped gherkins
1 teaspoon chopped chives
a few capers

Blend the whipped cream into the mayonnaise and, just before the sauce is to be served, add the parsley, gherkins, chives and capers.

For a less rich sauce, omit the whipped cream.

TOMATO MEAT SAUCE

½ cup chopped onion
1 clove of garlic
1 tablespoon oil
1 tablespoon butter
½ pound minced steak
1 medium-sized tomato
2 cups tomato purée
1 bayleaf
1 teaspoon oregano
¼ teaspoon allspice
½ teaspoon salt
a pinch of black pepper
¼ cup chopped parsley
2 ounces salami (optional)

Sauté the chopped onion and minced garlic in the oil and butter for 10 minutes. Add the minced steak, then cook, stirring well until the meat changes colour.

Add peeled and diced tomato, tomato purée, crushed bay-leaf, oregano, allspice, salt and black pepper. Bring to the boil, reduce the heat, cover and simmer for about 1 hour. Remove the lid after 45 minutes and add the parsley, also finely chopped salami if used.

Sweet Sauces

BOILED CUSTARD

2 eggs
¼ cup sugar
a pinch of salt
1½ cups milk
½ teaspoon vanilla essence

Beat the eggs lightly with the sugar and salt.

Heat the milk and, when almost boiling, remove from the heat and pour a little onto the beaten eggs. Stir until smooth, then pour on the remaining hot milk.

Return the custard to the saucepan and cook over hot water, stirring with a wooden spoon until it thickens and lightly coats the back of the spoon. Cool slightly, then flavour with vanilla.

BRANDY SAUCE 1

1 rounded tablespoon sugar
1 rounded dessertspoon corn-flour
½ pint water
3 tablespoons brandy

Blend the sugar and cornflour with the water, stirring until smooth. Place in a saucepan and stir over medium heat until boiling. Cook for 3 minutes, stirring well. Add the brandy just before serving.

413

BRANDY SAUCE 2

2 ounces butter
½ cup sugar
1 tablespoon liquid glucose
⅓ cup cream
a pinch of salt
2 tablespoons brandy

Melt the butter and add the sugar, glucose, cream and salt. Bring to the boil, stirring constantly, then simmer for 2 minutes. Add the brandy and simmer for 2 minutes longer. Serve warm.

BUTTERSCOTCH RUM SAUCE

1 cup sugar
2 tablespoons liquid glucose
2 ounces butter
a pinch of salt
½ level teaspoon instant coffee
   powder
1 cup cream
2 teaspoons rum

Place the sugar, liquid glucose and butter in a saucepan and stir over medium heat until the sugar and glucose have dissolved and the butter has melted. Add the salt, instant coffee powder and cream. Continue cooking over medium heat, stirring well until the sauce boils. Reduce the heat and simmer for 15 to 20 minutes.

Add the rum and allow to cool. Pour into a container, cover and store in the refrigerator. This sauce will thicken as it cools.

BUTTERSCOTCH SAUCE

1 cup firmly packed brown sugar
½ cup liquid glucose
3 ounces butter
⅔ cup cream
1 teaspoon vanilla essence

Combine the brown sugar, glucose and butter in a saucepan and stir over the heat until the mixture comes to the boil. Cook for about 5 minutes, stirring occasionally. Remove from the heat and slowly add the cream and the vanilla.

CARAMEL SAUCE 1

2 ounces butter
1 cup brown sugar
1 tablespoon golden syrup
⅓ cup unsweetened evaporated
   milk
½ teaspoon vanilla essence

Combine all the ingredients in a saucepan and stir over medium heat until boiling. Simmer for about 1 minute.

This sauce thickens as it cools. It may be necessary to thin it down with top milk, cream or more evaporated milk before serving if the sauce is made ahead of time.

CARAMEL SAUCE 2

1 cup brown sugar
2 ounces butter
2 tablespoons cream or top milk
1 teaspoon vanilla essence

Combine the brown sugar with the butter and stir over low heat until most of the sugar has dissolved.

Remove from the heat and add the cream, then return to the heat and cook, stirring well until the sauce is smooth. Flavour with vanilla.

For a smoother sauce, add 1 tablespoon of liquid glucose to the brown sugar and butter.

CHOCOLATE RIPPLE WHIPPED CREAM SAUCE

4 ounces semi-sweet chocolate
3 dessertspoons milk
2 to 3 dessertspoons crême de menthe
½ pint cream
1 teaspoon vanilla essence
1 dessertspoon sugar

Place the chocolate and milk in the top of a double saucepan and heat over hot, not boiling, water until the chocolate has combined with the milk. Add the crême de menthe and stir until smooth. Cool.

Whip the cream with the vanilla and sugar, spoon it over the chocolate mixture, then use a fork to ripple the sauce lightly through the cream. Turn into a serving bowl and use at once.

CHOCOLATE SAUCE

2 ounces butter
1 level tablespoon cocoa, or 2 ounces dark eating chocolate
1 cup brown sugar
¼ pint cream or canned unsweetened milk
½ teaspoon vanilla essence

Combine the butter, cocoa or broken pieces of chocolate with the brown sugar in a saucepan. Stir over gentle heat until the butter has dissolved and the mixture is heated thoroughly. All the sugar crystals will not have dissolved at this stage.

Add the cream and stir until the mixture is smooth. Remove from the heat and add either vanilla· or peppermint essence. The sauce is improved if a tablespoonful of liquid glucose is added with the brown sugar.

Stored in a covered jar in the refrigerator, this sauce will keep for weeks.

CHOCOLATE VELVET SAUCE

1 cup semi-sweet chocolate pieces
⅔ cup liquid glucose
⅔ cup unsweetened evaporated milk

Combine the chocolate pieces and the glucose in a saucepan and stir over medium heat until the chocolate melts and combines with the glucose. Remove from the heat and allow to cool.

Stir in the milk, mixing thoroughly. Serve warm over ice cream.

If liked, the sauce may be flavoured with a few drops of peppermint essence.

This sauce may be placed in a screw-topped jar and stored in the refrigerator for several weeks.

CUSTARD SAUCE

2 eggs, separated
1 rounded tablespoon sugar
1 rounded dessertspoon cornflour
1 pint milk
½ teaspoon vanilla essence

Combine the egg yolks, sugar and cornflour in a bowl and blend to a smooth paste with a little of the cold milk.

Place the remainder of the milk on to heat and, when almost boiling, pour onto the blended mixture and stir until smooth.

Return the mixture to the saucepan. Cook, stirring well, over medium heat until the sauce boils and thickens. Cook for another minute, then pour onto the stiffly beaten egg whites. Stir until well mixed. Flavour with the vanilla.

415

FLUFFY BRANDY SAUCE

1 egg, separated
a good pinch of salt
¾ cup sifted icing sugar
½ cup cream, whipped
3 tablespoons brandy

Add a pinch of salt to the egg white and beat until stiff. Gradually beat in the sifted icing sugar, adding it to the egg white a tablespoonful at a time.

Beat in the egg yolk, then fold in the whipped cream. Flavour with brandy. Chill.

FLUFFY HARD SAUCE

4 ounces butter
1½ cups icing sugar
1 to 2 tablespoons brandy

Beat the butter until soft and fluffy, then gradually add the sifted icing sugar, beating well after each addition. Beat in the brandy. Place in the refrigerator.

For a soft sauce, leave in a bowl at room temperature.

GERMAN WINE SAUCE

6 tablespoons sherry
2 egg yolks
1 dessertspoon sugar

Place the sherry, egg yolks and sugar in the top of a double saucepan (or place in a bowl and stand it in a saucepan with enough water to reach halfway up the sides). Whisk over the hot water until the sauce becomes thick. Serve at once.

HARD SAUCE

2 ounces butter
1 cup sifted icing sugar
1 dessertspoon brandy

Beat the butter until creamy, then gradually beat in the sifted icing sugar. Flavour with the brandy.

Place in the trays of the refrigerator to harden, then cut into squares and serve with hot plum pudding. Or simply cream up the mixture, flavour with the brandy and chill before spooning onto the pudding.

LEMON CREAM SAUCE

1 dessertspoon plain flour
1 cup sugar
⅔ cup warm water
1 egg
1½ teaspoons grated lemon rind
⅓ cup lemon juice
1 dessertspoon butter
½ cup cream

Combine the flour and sugar in the top of a double saucepan. Using a wooden spoon, beat in the water, egg, lemon rind and lemon juice. Cook over boiling water, stirring until slightly thickened—about 10 minutes. Remove from the heat and add the butter.

Refrigerate until well chilled. Just before serving, beat the cream until thick and fold into the lemon mixture.

MARSHMALLOW OR SNOW SAUCE

1 cup sugar
½ cup water
16 marshmallows
2 egg whites
vanilla or almond essence

Boil the sugar and water together for about 5 minutes. Cut the marshmallows into small pieces and add to the hot syrup. Stir until dissolved.

Pour the mixture gradually over the stiffly beaten egg whites, beating well until the sauce is smooth and well blended.

Flavour to taste with vanilla or almond essence. If liked, about 4 marshmallows may be cut into small pieces and added to the sauce just before serving.

ORANGE CREAM SAUCE

3 egg yolks
½ cup sugar
1½ teaspoons grated orange rind
¼ cup orange juice
½ cup cream

Beat the egg yolks with the sugar, orange rind and orange juice. Place in the top of a double saucepan and cook over hot water, stirring constantly with a wooden spoon until the mixture coats the back of the spoon. Cool thoroughly.

Whip the cream until it is stiff, then fold into the cooled orange custard. Refrigerate in a covered container.

This sauce may be made the day before it is required.

PINEAPPLE NUT SAUCE

1 medium-sized pineapple
½ cup sugar
½ cup water
1 teaspoon grated lemon rind
2 tablespoons kirsch
1 cup coarsely chopped nuts

Cut the rind from the pineapple, then cut the flesh into ½-inch cubes, discarding the core. Place the fruit in a bowl.

Combine the sugar and water in a saucepan and bring to the boil. Simmer for 5 minutes, then remove from the heat and add the lemon rind and kirsch.

Pour this mixture over the pineapple cubes, cover and chill until serving time. Turn the fruit over in the syrup occasionally during refrigeration.

Spoon this pineapple sauce over ice cream and top with a sprinkling of chopped nuts.

RUM SAUCE

4 ounces butter
1 cup sugar
¼ cup cream
a dash of nutmeg
1 teaspoon vanilla essence
2 to 3 dessertspoons rum

Combine the butter, sugar and cream in the top of a double saucepan. Cook over hot water, stirring well, for 10 to 15 minutes or until the mixture is slightly thickened. Chill. About 15 minutes before serving, add the nutmeg, vanilla and rum, then reheat over hot water.

SPICY CUSTARD SAUCE

1 tablespoon butter
1 rounded tablespoon plain flour
½ pint milk
1 tablespoon sugar
1 level teaspoon mixed spice

Melt the butter, stir in the flour and cook until smooth. Add the milk. Cook, stirring well until the sauce boils and thickens. Add the sugar and mixed spice. Simmer for 3 minutes. Serve hot.

417

VEGETABLES

ASPARAGUS

Here are three methods of cooking asparagus:

PAN METHOD

Break off the tough ends of the asparagus stalks. Trim the scales and scrub the asparagus with a soft brush to remove the grit. Place in a large frying pan. Add 1½ teaspoons salt and about 1 inch of water. Cover and simmer very gently for 10 minutes or until the stalks are barely tender.

DOUBLE BOILER METHOD

Break off the tough ends of the asparagus stalks. Trim the scales and scrub the asparagus with a soft brush to remove the grit. Tie the asparagus in even-sized bundles and stand them upright in the bottom part of a double boiler. Add 1½ teaspoons salt and 2 inches of boiling water. Invert the top part of the boiler over the asparagus and bring it to the boil. Boil for 15 to 20 minutes.

SAUTÉ METHOD

Wash the asparagus, then snap off the tough ends of the stalks. Slice diagonally into pieces about 1 inch long. Melt 1 tablespoon of butter in a saucepan and add 1 tablespoon of oil. Add the asparagus and shake over gentle heat for 7 or 8 minutes. Add about 1 tablespoonful of water, cover and steam for 5 to 10 minutes. Season with salt and pepper before serving.

ASPARAGUS FRITTERS

1 large can of asparagus pieces
1½ cups plain flour
1 teaspoon salt
3 level teaspoons baking powder
2 teaspoons sugar
2 eggs
⅓ cup milk
1 tablespoon salad oil
1 tablespoon lemon juice

Drain the asparagus pieces and set aside. Sift the flour with the salt, baking powder and sugar. Beat the eggs, milk, salad oil and lemon juice together, then stir in the sifted flour and drained asparagus pieces.

Drop spoonfuls of the batter in hot fat and cook for about 5 minutes, turning once. Drain well on paper. Serve with Hollandaise sauce.

ASPARAGUS WITH CHIFFON SAUCE

1 large can of asparagus spears
2 egg yolks
2 ounces soft butter
1 dessertspoon lemon juice
a dash of salt
¼ teaspoon prepared mustard
¼ cup asparagus liquid drained
  from the can
2 egg whites

Drain the liquid from the asparagus and place the spears to heat in a large saucepan, being careful not to break the tips.

Beat the egg yolks in a small saucepan with the soft butter, lemon juice, salt and mustard. If the sauce appears curdled at this point do not worry. Heat the asparagus liquid and gradually stir it in, then cook, stirring until thickened. Remove from the heat.

Beat the egg whites stiffly and fold into the hot sauce. Heat the asparagus spears in the remaining liquid, then drain and arrange them on a hot dish. Pour the chiffon sauce over and, if liked, sprinkle the top with paprika.

BAKED STUFFED CUCUMBERS

3 medium-sized green
  cucumbers
1 dessertspoon butter
1½ dessertspoons plain flour
1 cup milk
½ cup chopped cooked meat
2 hard-boiled eggs
1 teaspoon finely chopped
  parsley
1 teaspoon chopped chives
1 teaspoon chopped onion
¼ cup tiny celery cubes
salt, pepper and nutmeg to taste
buttered breadcrumbs
parsley to garnish

Cut the unpeeled cucumbers in half lengthwise, remove the seeds and place in cold water for 15 minutes. Parboil for about 5 minutes in a small amount of water. Drain well and arrange on a shallow baking tray.

Melt the butter in a saucepan and stir in the flour. Cook for 1 minute, then add the milk and cook, stirring until the sauce boils and thickens slightly. Fold in the meat, chopped eggs, parsley, chives, onion, celery and seasonings to taste. Mix well.

Divide this mixture between the partly cooked cucumber shells and top with buttered breadcrumbs. Bake at 375°F. for 20 minutes or until tender. Serve immediately, garnished with parsley.

BAKED FRENCH-STYLE VEGETABLES

Place equal quantities of whole tender carrots, medium-sized onions (each stuck with a whole clove) and peeled medium-sized potatoes in a baking dish. Pour over melted butter, add a clove of garlic, and season to taste with salt and pepper. Bake for about 1 hour in a moderate oven or until brown, the potatoes should be crisp).

BEETS IN ORANGE AND LEMON SAUCE

2 pounds beetroot
½ cup orange juice
½ cup lemon juice
1 rounded dessertspoon cornflour
1 tablespoon sugar
1 teaspoon salt
1 tablespoon cider vinegar

Remove the leaves and all but about 1 inch of the stem from each beet. Cook in boiling water until the skin can be easily rubbed off. This will take about 45 minutes, but the time will depend on the quality of the vegetable. Drain, then remove the skins and cut each beet into ¼-inch slices.

Combine the orange and lemon juice in a saucepan. Mix the cornflour with the sugar and salt and blend to a smooth paste

1 tablespoon butter
1 teaspoon grated orange rind
1 teaspoon grated lemon rind

1 bunch baby carrots
1 teaspoon butter for carrots
boiling water
2 tablespoons butter for sauce
2 tablespoons chopped parsley
2 tablespoons chopped shallot
1 teaspoon salt
¼ teaspoon pepper
parsley to garnish

2 pounds carrots
1 dessertspoon salad oil
¼ teaspoon finely chopped garlic
½ teaspoon salt
a pinch of pepper
1 or 2 tablespoons water
2 ounces butter

with the vinegar, then add to the fruit juices in the saucepan and stir over medium heat until the mixture boils and thickens. Continue cooking for about 3 minutes, then add the sliced beets and simmer gently for about 10 minutes.

Add the butter and grated fruit rinds just before serving.

BUTTERED BABY CARROTS

Wash and scrape the carrots and place in a saucepan with the teaspoon of butter and enough boiling water to just cover. Cook until tender—approximately 20 minutes. Drain well.

Melt the 2 tablespoons of butter for the sauce in a saucepan and add the parsley, shallot, salt and pepper. Add the drained cooked carrots and sauté for about 5 minutes.

Serve garnished with parsley. If the carrots are a little large, cut into halves lengthwise.

BUTTERY GRATED CARROTS

Peel the carrots and grate them into a pan which has a tight-fitting lid. Toss with the oil, garlic, salt, pepper and 1 or 2 tablespoons of water.

Cover and cook over medium heat, stirring occasionally, for 10 to 12 minutes or until tender. Remove from the heat and toss in melted butter until well coated.

Carrots Vichy
Carrots in Cream
Buttery Grated Carrots

420

CARROTS IN CREAM

12 small young carrots
boiling salted water
about 2 dessertspoons butter
1 teaspoon sugar
¼ cup cream or top milk
chopped parsley to garnish

Scrape the carrots and trim the tops. Cook in boiling salted water until almost tender. Drain well. Cut them in halves lengthwise if they are thick at the top.

Heat the butter in a pan and sauté the carrots gently until they are tender. Season with the sugar and a little more salt if necessary. Add the cream or top milk and cook for a further 2 minutes. Serve sprinkled with chopped parsley.

CARROTS IN MUSTARD GLAZE

3 pounds carrots
boiling salted water
¼ cup butter
½ cup brown sugar
¼ cup prepared mustard
1 tablespoon chopped chives,
   parsley or mint

Wash and scrape the carrots and cut into slices. Cook in boiling salted water until tender—about 20 minutes.

Combine the butter, brown sugar and mustard in a small saucepan. Cook, stirring until the butter has melted and the sugar has dissolved. Cook for another 3 minutes.

Pour this mixture over the cooked and drained carrots, heat for several minutes, then add the chives, parsley or mint.

CARROTS PIQUANT

4 cups small whole carrots
1 level dessertspoon cornflour
1 dessertspoon orange juice
¼ teaspoon salt
a dash of nutmeg
2 dessertspoons butter
chopped parsley to garnish

Scrape the carrots and cook them whole in boiling salted water. Drain, reserving ¾ cup of the cooking water and allowing it to become cool.

Combine the cornflour, orange juice, salt, nutmeg and the reserved cooking liquid. Cook, stirring until the sauce boils and thickens, then add the butter and the cooked carrots.

Heat thoroughly over low heat, and serve sprinkled with chopped parsley.

DUCHESS POTATOES

1 pound potatoes
1 ounce butter
1 tablespoon cream or milk
1 beaten egg
salt and pepper

Cook the potatoes and rub them through a sieve. Melt the butter in a saucepan and add the potatoes. When warm, add the cream and the beaten egg (reserving a little egg for glazing). Season to taste with salt and pepper and beat thoroughly.

Put into a piping bag with a star nozzle and force in rosettes onto a greased baking tray. Glaze with the reserved beaten egg. Brown in a hot oven, 450°F.

FRENCH-FRIED ONION RINGS

3 white or brown onions
1 egg
½ cup milk
3 rounded tablespoons plain flour
salt and pepper

Peel the onions and cut into rings about ¼ inch thick. Beat the egg and add the milk, then place the onion rings in the egg mixture and stir until well coated. Lift out and drain.

Sift the flour with the salt and pepper and use to coat the onion rings a few at a time. Deep-fry (preferably in a basket) a few at a time until they are a golden brown. Drain on white paper, sprinkle with salt and serve hot.

*Carrots, Zucchini and Parsnips
with sauce*

1½ pounds small carrots
½ cup boiling water
1 teaspoon salt
½ teaspoon dried thyme
1½ pounds small zucchini
1 rounded tablespoon butter

2 pounds small potatoes
2 ounces butter or margarine
1½ dessertspoons lemon juice
1 dessertspoon chopped shallot
¼ teaspoon white pepper
¼ teaspoon nutmeg
grated rind of 1 lemon

½ pound fresh mushrooms
  (field or cultivated)
½ teaspoon salt
¼ teaspoon pepper
2 tablespoons finely chopped
  shallot
2 tablespoons finely chopped
  parsley
2 ounces grated tasty cheese
½ cup soft white breadcrumbs
1 tablespoon butter

HERBED BUTTERED ZUCCHINI AND CARROTS

Scrub the carrots well (scrape them if necessary). Cut into thin diagonal slices and add to the boiling water with the salt and thyme. Reduce the heat, cover tightly and simmer for 10 minutes or until the carrots are slightly underdone.

Scrub the zucchini well and cut into thin diagonal slices. Add to the carrots, mixing well. Bring to the boil, cover tightly and simmer for 5 minutes or until the vegetables are tender.

Add the butter, tossing gently to coat the vegetables.

LEMON POTATOES

Peel the potatoes and cook in boiling salted water until just fork-tender.

Heat the butter, lemon juice, shallot, pepper and nutmeg in a small saucepan. Toss the potatoes well in this butter mixture, and just before serving add the grated lemon rind.

MUSHROOMS AU GRATIN

Wash and drain the mushrooms. Remove the stalks and peel only if using the field mushrooms. Place them in a lightly greased shallow ovenproof dish. Sprinkle with the salt, pepper, shallot and parsley, then top with the cheese and breadcrumbs. Dot with the butter.

Bake, in a moderate oven, 350°F., for about 15 minutes or until the mushrooms are tender and the topping lightly browned.

ORANGE RICE

3 dessertspoons butter
1 tablespoon chopped onion
⅔ cup diced celery leaves
1 tablespoon grated orange rind
1 cup orange juice
1½ cups water
¾ teaspoon salt
1 cup uncooked rice

Melt the butter in a saucepan and add the onion and the celery leaves. Cook until tender but not brown. Add the water, orange rind, orange juice and salt. Bring to the boil and slowly add the rice. When boiling, cover, reduce the heat and cook at simmering point until the rice is tender and the liquid has been absorbed—about 25 minutes.

This orange rice makes an excellent accompaniment to roast duck or creamed chicken.

POTATO BALLS

4 cups warm mashed potato
2 ounces butter or margarine
salt and pepper
1 cup minced raw carrot
¾ cup chopped parsley
chutney

Mash the potato with the butter, adding salt and pepper to taste. Whip until light and fluffy. Stir in the carrot and parsley, mixing well.

Shape into round balls about 2 inches in diameter. Press a hole in the centre of each ball with the index finger, spoon a little chutney into the centre of each, close the opening and re-shape. Chill until needed.

Bake in a hot oven, 450°F., for about 20 minutes. When serving, garnish with more parsley if liked.

POTATOES PROVENÇAL

¼ pound bacon rashers
6 cups thinly sliced potatoes
¾ cup minced celery
¼ cup chopped shallot
3 dessertspoons minced parsley
1 clove of garlic
¼ pound Gruyère cheese, grated
salt and pepper
paprika
¼ cup melted butter
⅔ cup undiluted evaporated milk

Grease a shallow ovenproof dish. Fry the bacon till crisp, then crumble it. Using 2 cups of the potatoes, make a layer in the dish. Cover with half the crumbled bacon, then half each of the celery, shallot, parsley, crushed garlic and grated cheese. Season with salt, pepper and paprika and pour over half the melted butter.

Repeat the layers in the order given, then top with the remaining 2 cups of sliced potatoes. Pour over the milk.

Bake at 400°F. for 30 minutes, then reduce the heat to 350°F. and bake for a further 40 minutes or until the potatoes are tender and the top golden.

SAUTÉED CUCUMBERS WITH TOMATOES

¼ cup chopped spring onion
1 tablespoon butter
3 cups peeled and sliced
   cucumber
salt, sugar and pepper to taste
2 tomatoes
4 bacon rashers

Sauté the chopped onion in the butter until tender. Add the cucumber, with salt, sugar and pepper to taste. Cook, stirring gently over medium heat for 2 or 3 minutes.

Peel the tomatoes and cut them into wedges. Add to the pan and cook until thoroughly heated. Meanwhile fry the bacon till crisp, then crumble it.

Spoon the vegetables into a serving dish and sprinkle with the crumbled bacon.

SCALLOPED POTATOES

4 medium-sized potatoes
1 slightly rounded tablespoon
  plain flour
1 level teaspoon salt
a good pinch of pepper
¼ cup thinly sliced onion
1 rounded dessertspoon butter or
  margarine
1 cup milk
1 teaspoon chopped parsley to
  garnish

Peel and thinly slice the potatoes. Grease a casserole and place a layer of the potato slices in the bottom. Combine the flour, salt and pepper and sprinkle half over the potatoes.

Add half the onion slices to the casserole. Dot with the butter, then add another layer of potatoes, seasoned flour and onions. Pour the milk over the potatoes.

Cover and bake in a moderate oven, 350°F., for about 30 minutes. Remove the lid and continue baking for a further 45 minutes or until the potatoes are soft and lightly brown on top.

For a rich golden brown topping, sprinkle in some grated tasty cheese and return the casserole to the oven to melt and brown the cheese, or place under the griller. Serve sprinkled with chopped parsley.

SUNSHINE CARROTS

5 medium-sized carrots
1 dessertspoon sugar
1 teaspoon cornflour
¼ teaspoon salt
¼ teaspoon ground ginger
¼ cup orange juice
1 tablespoon butter or
  margarine

Peel or scrape the carrots and cut diagonally into 1-inch lengths. Cook in boiling salted water with the saucepan lid on until tender—about 20 minutes. Drain and keep hot.

Combine the sugar, cornflour, salt and ground ginger in a small saucepan. Add the orange juice, then cook, stirring well until the mixture boils and thickens. Boil for 1 minute, then add the butter. Pour over the hot, cooked carrots, tossing lightly to coat them evenly.

STUFFED CAULIFLOWER

1 large or 2 small cauliflowers
salted water
soft white breadcrumbs

For the stuffing

1 small onion
1½ ounces butter
1 tablespoon plain flour
salt to taste
½ cup milk or water
1 egg yolk
1 whole egg
7 ounces pickled brisket or
  smoked meat
2 tablespoons chopped parsley

Boil the cauliflower in salted water for 10 minutes. Drain and allow to cool. Prepare an aluminium bowl by greasing well and sprinkling with soft white breadcrumbs. Place the cooled cauliflower in this, upside down. Remove the centre stalk.

To make the filling, chop the onion, melt the butter in a pan and sauté the onion until soft. Stir in the flour and salt and cook for 1 minute, then add the milk. Cook, stirring constantly until the mixture boils and thickens, then cook for another 2 minutes. Beat the egg yolk with the whole egg and spoon a little of the sauce onto it, stirring well, then add to the contents of the saucepan and stir over the heat for a few moments. Chop the meat finely and add it together with the parsley.

Place the filling in the centre of the cauliflower with a few flowerlets. Cover the bowl with its own lid or use aluminium foil. Place in a saucepan of water (the water should reach almost to the top of the bowl) and cook for 1 hour.

Turn the mixture into a heatproof dish, cover if liked with grated cheese and knobs of butter and place for 15 to 20 minutes in a hot oven until the cheese melts and browns.

424

Serve with grilled tomatoes and sprinkle with parsley.

To serve as a cold dish, have ½ pint of stock ready (made if liked with a chicken soup cube). Soak 1 rounded tablespoon of gelatine in cold water, dissolve over boiling water, and add to the stock. Allow to cool, then add 4 tablespoons of thick mayonnaise. Let this become partly set, then spoon evenly over the cauliflower and allow to set.

STUFFED GREEN PEPPERS

5 ounces raw rice
1 pound finely minced steak, veal or pork
salt and pepper
1 egg
6 medium-sized green peppers
½ cup tomato purée, or tomato soup or sauce
½ cup water
2 tablespoons wine (optional)
1 teaspoon sugar

Cook the rice and drain it. To make the filling combine the rice with the minced meat and salt and pepper to taste, and bind with beaten egg.

Cut a slice from the top of each green pepper and remove the seeds. Pack each pepper tightly with meat filling. Stand the stuffed peppers in a saucepan.

Combine the tomato purée, water, wine and sugar. Pour over the peppers. Cover. Simmer the peppers in the sauce for about 30 minutes.

Serve on a heated dish with the sauce poured over them.

STUFFED VEGETABLE MARROW

1 small vegetable marrow
1 pound fine mincemeat
3 rounded tablespoons soft white breadcrumbs
1 teaspoon chopped parsley
1 dessertspoon chopped onion
a little grated lemon rind (optional)
1 tablespoon tomato sauce or 1 teaspoon Worcester sauce
salt and pepper
1 egg
mashed potato and ½ pint brown vegetable gravy for serving

Peel and wash the marrow. Cut a wedge-shaped piece from the top and scoop out the seeds and membrane.

For the stuffing combine the mincemeat, breadcrumbs, parsley, onion, lemon rind and tomato sauce, with salt and pepper to taste. Bind with beaten egg, pack into the marrow and replace the wedge. Wrap in well-greased paper or place in a greased paper bag. (If the marrow is large, bind with tape to prevent spreading.)

Place the prepared marrow in a greased baking dish, cover with another dish and bake in a moderate oven, 350°F., for about 1¼ hours.

Place the stuffed marrow on a heated serving platter and surround with mashed potato. Serve with brown gravy.

STUFFED ZUCCHINI

3 zucchini
1 tablespoon minced onion
about 1½ tablespoons soft butter
1 cup soft white breadcrumbs
1 medium-sized tomato, peeled and chopped
salt and pepper to taste

Wash the zucchini and cook in boiling salted water for 10 minutes. Drain well, then cut in halves lengthwise and scoop out some of the pulp from the centre. Mix this pulp well with the remaining ingredients. Fill the zucchini shells.

Place the stuffed zucchini in a shallow dish with a few tablespoons of water, cover with aluminium foil and bake for about 15 minutes at 350°F. The foil may be removed during the last 5 minutes of cooking.

SWEET POTATOES

There are two kinds of sweet potato available, one with a white skin and the other with a purple coloured skin. Don't peel these potatoes too far ahead of the time required, because they turn black when exposed to the air. If they have to stand any time before cooking, leave them in cold water.

Sweet potatoes can be baked in the usual way but will not take as long to cook as ordinary potatoes. Allow about the same cooking time as for pumpkin. They also can be boiled or made into chips.

BOILED SWEET POTATOES

Wash and brush the skins, being careful not to break them. Soak the potatoes in a bowl of cold water for a short time, then cook in boiling salted water until the skins can be pierced with a fork (there should only be sufficient water to cover the potatoes). Drain, then dry in a hot oven to make them mealy.

SWEET POTATO CRISP

Cook sweet potatoes by boiling as above until tender. Cut them into 2-inch pieces, wrap a piece of bacon round each, and place in the oven to cook until the bacon is crisp.

SWISS FRIED POTATOES

1¾ pound firm potatoes
3 ounces butter or margarine
salt
1 tablespoon milk or water
parsley sprigs

The day before they are required, boil the potatoes in their jackets until just tender. Drain well and allow to cool, then store in the refrigerator. Next day, peel the potatoes and cut them into thin slices.

Heat the butter in a large frying pan until very hot. Add the potatoes, sprinkling with salt to taste. Fry, turning them constantly until nearly all the butter has been soaked up.

Now push the potatoes towards the centre of the pan and flatten on top. Sprinkle with 1 tablespoon of milk or water, cover with a tight-fitting lid and leave over low heat for 15 to 20 minutes, shaking the pan occasionally to prevent burning.

The potatoes are ready when the bottom is lightly browned and adhering together. Invert onto a heated serving platter and serve with the browned side up. Garnish with parsley.

VARIATIONS

1. Sauté 1 tablespoon of chopped onion in a little fat in the pan before adding the potatoes. The onion should not be allowed to brown.

2. Sauté one or two rashers of diced bacon before adding the potatoes. Add a little less salt.

3. Sprinkle the cooked potatoes with grated cheese before serving.

426

VEGETABLE MORNAY

1½ ounces butter
2 tablespoons chopped onion or
   shallot
1½ ounces plain flour
¾ teaspoon salt
¼ teaspoon dry mustard
a pinch of cayenne pepper
¾ pint milk
1 cup diced cooked carrot
1 cup diced cooked parsnip
½ cup cooked peas
4 ounces grated cheese
1-2 tablespoons breadcrumbs

Melt the butter in a saucepan, add the onion or shallot and cook until soft but not brown. Add the flour, salt, mustard and cayenne and stir until smooth. Cook for 1 minute but do not brown. Add the milk and stir until the sauce boils and thickens. Cook for another 2 minutes.

Fold in the carrots, parsnips and peas and half the cheese. Pour into a greased pie-dish. Sprinkle the remainder of the cheese and the breadcrumbs on the top.

Bake in a moderate oven, 350°F., for about 15 minutes or until the sauce bubbles and the topping is browned.

VEGETABLE PIE

1½ pounds potatoes
a little butter
some milk
salt and pepper
1 pound green peas
6 to 8 small carrots
4 eggs
2 medium-sized tomatoes
4 ounces grated cheese

Cook and mash the potatoes, adding a little butter and milk, with salt and pepper to taste. Cook the peas until tender, and drain well. Scrape and wash the carrots and cook them until tender.

Boil the eggs for about 10 minutes and leave in cold water for a few minutes before shelling. Cut them in halves lengthwise. Cut each tomato into four even slices.

Place half the mashed potato in the bottom of a greased casserole. Sprinkle with half the grated cheese. Arrange tomato slices round the edge of the dish, and season with salt and pepper. Place the halved eggs in the centre and cover with peas. Arrange the drained whole carrots, points facing inwards, on top of the peas.

Spread with the remaining potato and sprinkle with the rest of the cheese. Bake at 400°F. for about 20 minutes or until the pie is heated through, with the top nicely browned.

INDEX

INDEX

431

435

439